# The BBC and Ultra-Modern Music, 1922–1936

This book examines the BBC's campaign to raise cultural awareness of British mass audiences in the early days of radio. As a specific case, it focuses on policies and plans behind transmissions of music by composers associated with Arnold Schoenberg's circle between 1922, when the BBC was founded, and spring 1936, when Edward Clark, a former Schoenberg pupil and central figure in BBC music, resigned from the Corporation. This reception study traces and analyses the BBC's attempts to manipulate critical and public responses to this repertory. The book investigates three interrelated aspects of early BBC history. Policy decisions relating to contemporary music transmissions are examined to determine why precious broadcast time was devoted to this repertory. Early personnel structures are reconstructed to investigate the responsibilities, attitudes and interests of those who influenced music broadcasting. Finally, broadcasts of Second Viennese School works are examined in detail.

Jennifer Doctor's extensive research in the BBC Written Archives has not only led to this book, but also contributed significantly to Humphrey Carpenter's *The Envy of the World: Fifty Years of the BBC Third Programme and Radio 3* (London, 1996). She was Senior Editor for 20th-Century Composers on *The New Grove Dictionary of Music and Musicians* (2nd ed., forthcoming), and is currently Librarian at the The Britten–Pears Library.

# Music in the Twentieth Century

GENERAL EDITOR Arnold Whittall

This series offers a wide perspective on music and musical life in the twentieth century. Books included will range from historical and biographical studies concentrating particularly on the context and circumstances in which composers were writing, to analytical and critical studies concerned with the nature of musical language and questions of compositional process. The importance given to context will also be reflected in studies dealing with, for example, the patronage, publishing, and promotion of new music, and in accounts of the musical life of particular countries.

*Recently published titles*

**Franz Schreker, 1878–1934: a cultural biography**
Christopher Hailey
0 521 39255 1

**The Music of John Cage**
James Pritchett
0 521 56544 8

**The Music of Ruth Crawford Seeger**
Joseph N. Straus
0 521 41646 9

**The Music of Conlon Nancarrow**
Kyle Gann
0 521 46534 6

**The Stravinsky Legacy**
Jonathan Cross
0 521 56365 8

**Experimental Music: Cage and Beyond**
Michael Nyman
0 521 65297 9 (hardback) 0 521 65383 5 (paperback)

**The BBC and Ultra-Modern Music, 1922–1936**
Jennifer Doctor
0 521 66117 X

# The BBC and Ultra-Modern Music, 1922–1936

## Shaping a Nation's Tastes

Jennifer Doctor

CAMBRIDGE
UNIVERSITY PRESS

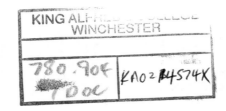
PUBLISHED BY THE PRESS SYNDICATE OF THE UNIVERSITY OF CAMBRIDGE
The Pitt Building, Trumpington Street, Cambridge CB2 1RP, United Kingdom

CAMBRIDGE UNIVERSITY PRESS
The Edinburgh Building, Cambridge CB2 2RU, UK    http://www.cup.cam.ac.uk
40 West 20th Street, New York, NY 10011–4211, USA   http://www.cup.org
10 Stamford Road, Oakleigh, Melbourne 3166, Australia

First published 1999

Printed in the United Kingdom at the University Press, Cambridge

Typeset in Adobe Minion 10.5/13.5 pt in QuarkXPress™   [SE]

*A catalogue record for this book is available from the British Library*

*Library of Congress cataloguing in publication data*

Doctor, Jennifer R. (Jennifer Ruth), 1958–
The BBC and ultra-modern music, 1922–1936 / Jennifer Doctor.
   p.    cm. – (Music in the twentieth century)
Includes bibliographic references and index.
ISBN 0 521 66117 X (hardback)
1. Radio and music – Great Britain.    2.  British Broadcasting
Corporation – History.    3.  Avant garde (Music) – Great Britain.
4.  Music – Great Britain – 20th century – History and criticism.
5.  Schoenberg, Arnold, 1874–1951 – Performances – Great Britain.
6.  Berg, Alban, 1885–1935 – Performances – Great Britain. 7. Webern,
Anton, 1883–1945 – Performances – Great Britain.    I. Title.
II. Series.
ML68.D63    1999
780′.9′04 – dc21    98–45824    CIP

ISBN 0 521 66117 X hardback

# Contents

# Tables

## Tables in Appendix B: BBC Concerts of Contemporary Music, 1926–1936

# Acknowledgements

Foremost on the long list of people to whom I feel indebted for assistance and encouragement over the years it has taken to finish this book is Professor Cyril Ehrlich, without whom it would simply never have been completed. I am extremely grateful for his interest, his practical advice and, most of all, for opening up to me an entirely new way of understanding social and cultural events that profoundly influenced music history in interwar Britain. I am also very grateful to Sophie Fuller and Paul Kildea for the countless stimulating conversations we've had about British music history and for giving me access to their research in related subjects.

I must pay special tribute to staff at the BBC Written Archives Centre in Caversham. My investigation of BBC archival materials would have been impossible without the extraordinary help, advice and encouragement that I have received from everyone who work at that unusual and wonderful place. Three people in particular assisted me unfailingly, giving much time and invaluable guidance: John Jordan, who helped acquaint me with the cataloguing system and prepared many files for my use; Gwyniver Jones, whose cordial help, practical advice and lateral thinking were fundamental to the completion of the project; and Jacquie Kavanagh, the Archivist, for her great interest, and her generosity in permitting me to reproduce the texts of the BBC WAC materials.

I would like to thank the members of my dissertation committee, Professor Alan Stout, Professor Judith Schwartz and Professor Richard Green, for their time and attention during the preparation of my thesis, the basis of this book. I am very grateful to the organizations that provided me with the financial means to complete my thesis: Northwestern University for the assistantships, the University Fellowship and the Northwestern University Alumnae Fellowship; Oberlin College for a Haskell Fund Grant; and most especially the Fulbright Commission for the Fulbright Scholarship that enabled me to study in the United Kingdom. I would also like to express appreciation to two institutions that provided affiliations that enabled me to continue my research in the United Kingdom: the Department of Music at King's College, London, and St Hilda's College, Oxford.

I thank James Clark for his assistance in providing biographical details about his father, Edward Clark. I also thank the following for permission to reproduce texts of previously unpublished letters and other documents: Frau Maria Halbich-Webern, Lawrence A. Schoenberg, Rachel Steuermann, Mary E. Parkin, Lady Bliss, Oxford University Press and the British Broadcasting Corporation. Thanks to the British Library for access to the Edward Clark Letters, Add.ms.52256–7, and to Northwestern University Music Library for access to the Edward Clark papers. Finally, I am very grateful to Nick Chadwick for permitting me to quote from his translations of letters published in his articles 'Alban Berg and the BBC' and 'The Berg Violin Concerto in London: Webern's Correspondence with the BBC, 1935–6'. Thanks also to Saskia Willaert for her advice about deciphering Berg's and Schoenberg's handwritings.

I have benefited greatly from the counsel of others who have worked with BBC materials in their own research and writings. I would especially like to thank Nicholas Kenyon for his interest and encouragement in this project and my work. Special thanks also to Stanley Sadie for his advice, support and his remarkable insights into the art of writing. I am grateful to the Trustees of the Britten–Pears Foundation for giving me time to complete the book, in particular Hugh Cobbe and Donald Mitchell.

I would like to thank Arnold Whittall for his encouragement over the years, and for recommending the book for the Music in the Twentieth Century series. I thank Cambridge University Press for publishing it, and Penny Souster for her patience during its slow preparation. I am especially grateful to Judith LeGrove for her invaluable help in preparing the indexes.

Finally, I would like to thank the many friends who have provided moral support throughout the years I have been working on this project, including Elizabeth Gibson, Dorothea Link, Suzie Wijsman, Anne Sheeran, Nicky Losseff, Joan Oberndorf, Margie Wood, Madeleine Ladell, Nicola LeFanu, Bruce Phillips and Michael Wood. I am very grateful to all the members of my family for their extensive support over the years, and most especially, I would like to thank Steve for putting up with it for so long!

# Abbreviations

| | |
|---|---|
| BBC | British Broadcasting Company (1922–6) or British Broadcasting Corporation (from 1927) |
| BBC WAC | BBC Written Archives Centre |
| ISCM | International Society for Contemporary Music |
| LCMC | London Contemporary Music Centre |
| MT | *The Musical Times* |
| RCM | Royal College of Music |
| RT | *Radio Times* |
| UE | Universal Edition |

# Introduction

This book began as a research project with an entirely different focus: to study the impact of the 12-tone method of composition on the British musical scene in the first post-war decade, before the technique came into widespread use by British composers, as internationally. While doing background work, I was surprised to find that standard historical accounts suggested that the influence of the Second Viennese School on British musicians was virtually nil before the mid-1950s. For instance, Peter J. Pirie, in his general history, *The English Musical Renaissance*, published in 1979, described Schoenberg's influence in England at the time of his death in 1951 as 'minimal, only Humphrey Searle and Elizabeth Lutyens among native composers acknowledging his example or his influence'.[1]

Searle and Lutyens were the first English composers to adopt the 12-tone technique, both having begun to experiment with it around 1939. In later writings, they were bitter about the compositional environment in which they had developed, stressing the sparsity of information and dearth of performances or published scores of 12-tone works in Britain at that time. The lack of acceptance, interest or support for their music and ideas had led to ostracization and isolation. In 1972, Searle described this period in bleak terms.

> There were relatively few performances of new works. Walter Goehr, a former pupil of Schoenberg, put on some concerts of new and unfamiliar works. Edward Clark, secretary of the ISCM's British section, was also able to give some concerts of contemporary music during the war. After the War, despite the fact that the BBC Third Programme was inaugurated in 1946, even modern classics were rarely heard. Stravinsky was usually represented only by his first three ballets; Bartók was seldom played and Schoenberg, Berg, Webern, the so-called second Viennese school, were hardly heard at all, either on radio or in concert halls.[2]

In her autobiography written the same year, Elisabeth Lutyens claimed to have discovered the 12-tone technique for herself around 1939, and attributed her initial failures as a professional composer to it.

> Apparently it is not un-English to study Palestrina and Bach at every musical institution; to be influenced by Brahms, Hindemith, or Bartók; but to adopt a technique, like the 12-tone, associated with a German, Schoenberg (albeit

1

that, earlier, I had thought I had 'discovered' it myself, from my study of Purcell), was '*mittel*-European', un-English and iconoclastic. I was soon made to feel like a Communist before the Committee for Un-American Activities. Performances in England grew fewer and fewer till for some twenty years they were almost non-existent.[3]

Lutyens also complained that she had access to few performances and fewer scores until after the war.

> [Lutyens] firmly maintained that in the beginning she came to serial methods by herself. In 1939, she claimed, she had never even encountered the expression 'twelve-tone'. She had heard only the *Gurrelieder* of Schoenberg, which she detested, and a limited amount of Webern – the String Trio Op. 20 and possibly the Five Movements for String Orchestra, and his cantata *Das Augenlicht*, performed at the ISCM Festival in London in 1938. This certainly had a devastating impact; her immediate reaction was that here was the 'guiding spirit to all future music'. But she insisted that she had had no opportunity to study a score, and had in fact seen no Webern score until 1948.[4]

Since Schoenberg's music had been performed and his ideas and activities widely written about in Europe and the United States before the war, I wondered why and how Britain had remained isolated from this controversial phenomenon. I began to investigate pre-war programming of avant-garde, or in the vocabulary of the day 'ultra-modern', music in Britain to assess the extent to which the music and ideas of Schoenberg and his associates had in fact been available at the time. It soon became apparent not only that Second Viennese School repertory and theories were known in Britain before 1939, but that they had been widely publicized, disseminated and discussed there in the years leading to World War II. This was due in large part to the high proportion of recently composed music that was made available to the public in BBC transmissions after British public broadcasting began in 1922.

Unlike secondary sources pertaining to British music history, sources relating to BBC history left no doubt that its new music policies and programmes were no less than extraordinary during the interwar years. This phenomenon was unanimously attributed to the presence on the BBC music staff from 1927 to 1936 of Edward Clark, a former pupil of Schoenberg. Clark was valued both for his remarkable ability to shape interesting and unusual music programmes and for his enthusiasm, knowledge and personal acquaintance with many British and continental composers of the day.

From there, I began to examine primary sources relating to interwar broadcasts of contemporary music at the BBC Written Archives Centre, the depository for the countless papers that were at one time written and received by Corporation staff in the course of their daily work. These materials provide invaluable evidence concerning BBC decisions, goals and activities. Although many early papers relating to music broadcasting are no longer extant, I discovered an amazing amount of exciting and previously unexplored material. In fact, I spent many months wading through hundreds of files at the archives, looking at those directly relevant to the dissemination of Second Viennese School repertory, and at the same time uncovering and exploring less obvious, but essential, related materials.

I eventually realized that the nature of my study had to change. Contrary to post-war historical accounts, the impact of Second Viennese School repertory and ideas on British society before World War II was far from negligible. In fact, the impact of this music affected not only musical circles, but, to a surprising extent, the British public at large. The music and compositional aesthetics espoused by Schoenberg and his colleagues were known, heard and discussed in Britain throughout the interwar years, and their impact took on special significance from 1927, when performances of Second Viennese School works began to be broadcast by the BBC on a regular basis. In this way, this book emerged in place of my original research project. I found that the complex interrelationships of BBC staff structure, working processes and policy decisions, and their impact on programme output was a fascinating and worthwhile topic in its own right, and one which would fill a significant lacuna in British music history of the twentieth century.

## Scope

It is necessary from the outset to define precisely what is referred to in this volume by 'the BBC'. Although the newly founded organization quickly developed regional branches from which music programmes were planned and transmitted, music by European contemporary composers was broadcast almost exclusively from the London studios during the interwar period, in the 1920s over the 2LO (5XX) and 5GB wavelengths and in the 1930s over the National and London Regional wavelengths. This study focuses on these London-based programmes and 'the BBC' refers to the organization and staff at the Head Office in London.

The period under discussion begins with the foundation of the British Broadcasting Company in November 1922 and concludes in spring 1936, when Edward Clark resigned from his position as music programme builder. Around the time of Clark's resignation, recommendations for changes to broadcasting policies and procedures were published in the

Ullswater Report in anticipation of the first renewal of the BBC's charter. In conjunction with Clark's resignation, this demarcates a discrete period in BBC music history, and serves here as a convenient ending point.

Finally, it is important to define specifically which composers and musicians fall within the scope of the Second Viennese circle for the purposes of this study. The composers were either *bona fide* associates of Schoenberg's circle at some time before he immigrated to the United States in 1933, or they were perceived to have belonged to this group by contemporary British writers and critics. Broadcasts involving works or performances by Arnold Schoenberg, Anton Webern and Alban Berg obviously come into the discussion, as do those by pupils of these composers, such as Egon Wellesz, Hanns Eisler, Paul Pisk, Roberto Gerhard, Viktor Ullmann, Norbert von Hannenheim, Adolph Weiss and Józef Koffler. Ernst Krenek considered himself to be an affiliate of the group in the early 1930s, and broadcasts of his music are noted. Although Josef Matthias Hauer was a rival of Schoenberg, his few BBC performances are discussed here, since they were associated idiomatically with the Schoenbergian school in BBC publicity and by the British press. In addition, certain performing artists associated with Schoenberg's circle were frequent guests of the BBC and also receive attention.

In its publicity and programme listings, the BBC did not necessarily use complete or accurate titles of musical works, and titles were invariably given in English to make them more accessible to the general public. Titles of works cited here in the text and tables are given in standardized, complete forms whenever possible, including opus number when appropriate; generic titles, such as symphony or sonata, are given in English, but in the case of distinctive titles, the original language is usually used. It is also worth noting here that idiosyncratic spellings in quoted material have been retained, but are not usually qualified by '*sic*'.

Reconstructed almost exclusively from the myriad of surviving written sources, the book takes the form of a documentary study, which closely explores and reflects contemporary evidence relating to BBC music activities. After initial chapters establish historical context in Part I, the discussion proceeds chronologically, with the span of years grouped into two periods. Part II explores the years between 1922 and spring 1930, the end of the final season of broadcasts influenced by Percy Pitt, the first BBC Music Director of significance. Part III covers the period between spring 1930 and spring 1936, when the Music Department was under the direction of Pitt's successor, Adrian Boult. Three appendices provide supplementary information. Appendix A is a list of Second Viennese School performances given in Britain, both in concert and as broadcasts, to the end of May 1936. This list is undoubtedly not comprehensive, but represents the span of works that were presented, as well as the frequency of their performance. Appendix B gives programme information for the series of contemporary music concerts that were sponsored by the BBC between 1926 and 1936. Finally, Appendix C provides short, biographical summaries of significant people who come into the discussion, primarily including BBC staff members, contemporary musicians and British critics.

## Sources

The fundamental source for this study is the vast body of documents and other materials held at the BBC Written Archives Centre (WAC) in Caversham, including many files of papers, microfilmed scripts, programme records, BBC periodicals, concert programmes and collections of contemporary press cuttings that survive at the WAC.[5] A brief description of the archives' complex arrangement clarifies the way in which these source materials were chosen for consultation.

As Jacqueline Kavanagh, the WAC Archivist, has explained, the materials available for research in the archive today are still organized according to the filing system that the BBC adopted in 1927.

> The BBC began as a commercial company: as it grew and expanded each new development is faithfully reflected in its papers . . . [After a few years, these] were increasing rapidly – too rapidly for the existing systems to cope [with] adequately – so a civil servant, Colonel Haldane, was invited to look at the Corporation's filing and make recommendations. The Haldane Report of 1927 . . . recommended the establishment of large centralised filing registries on Civil Service lines . . . The basic pattern imposed by these centralised systems survived into the 1970s, providing a firm but not inflexible framework, which adapted well to the many changes over that time.[6]

Within these central registries, the filing framework roughly matched the Corporation's organizational structure:

> The primary division of the files . . . mirrors the organisation of the BBC itself – Radio, Television and the Overseas services (now World Service) in London, with separate parallel file sequences generated in each of the Regions. Within that primary arrangement, all the Registries grouped the papers they dealt with into large sections consisting of files in alphabetical order of title with some sub-groups.[7]

In the radio (R) category, large file groupings correspond to the original departments and subsections which created, used and collected them. Many of the files that I consulted originated in the Music Department, presently filed under the heading 'Music General' (R27) and categorized according to the specific tasks and concerns that staff dealt with in the course of their work. These files hold papers on diverse subjects, such as music policy, music programme building, departmental committees, special BBC commissioning projects, the mounting of specific performances, external music organizations to which Music Department staff belonged, and music festivals attended by BBC representatives, to give only a few examples. Similar information concerning both general and specific areas of interest are also held in other categories of files, such as those devoted to various administrative committees, broadcasts originating in concert halls rather than in BBC studios, listener correspondence, papers about employee responsibilities and personnel hierarchies, staff files, etc.

Correspondence, contracts and other documents relating to the hiring of music specialists, such as performers, composers, scholars or critics, are held in the 'contributor files' (RCONT1). I consulted surviving contributor papers relating to Second Viennese School composers, their publishers, performers who specialized in this repertory and speakers who gave talks that included discussions of this type of music. Significantly, most of the RCONT1 files holding information relevant to people that Edward Clark knew personally are incomplete. When he left the Corporation in spring 1936, he apparently took with him letters written to him by his friends. Many of these, including letters to Clark from Schoenberg, Webern and Berg, subsequently found their way to the British Library and are held in the manuscript collection there as Add.ms.52256 and Add.ms.52257. In addition, a few carbon copies of letters written by Clark to various composers are now held in the Northwestern University Music Library manuscript collection, rather than at the WAC. Throughout the text, quotations from letters originally written in German appear only in English, in my translation unless otherwise indicated in the endnote citation. Full transcriptions of all quoted texts, in both English and the original language, appear in my dissertation (Doctor, *The BBC and the Ultra-Modern Problem*).

The task of tracing relevant information at the BBC archives is complicated by paper purges that have been carried out on several occasions since the BBC's foundation. As early as 1926, the first BBC Director-General, John Reith, decreed that 'as a principle he would sooner tear up ten letters and lose one of possible use than keep them all including the nine which can never be wanted'.[8] Because employees were consequently ordered to keep their desks, drawers and files cleared of unnecessary papers, it is particularly difficult to uncover surviving evidence about BBC activities in the 1920s.

One final point about using BBC files needs to be mentioned: although papers relevant to this study were written over half a century ago, all files that I saw were 'vetted' by archive staff, conforming to standard WAC procedure, for papers that cannot be made public because they either contain material categorized as British 'official secrets' or they contain potentially libellous statements. Obviously, the nature of this study did not involve any material that would threaten British national security. However, it is important to record that several files contained papers that I was not permitted to see for the second reason.

In addition to archival files, the WAC holds three other classes of unpublished materials that were vital to this study. The 'Programmes as Broadcast' records, the BBC's programme log, provide an accurate account of what was transmitted each day on every wavelength. This extraordinary collection of lists, begun before the BBC was officially founded, shows exactly what music was broadcast, who performed, what music editions were used and gives exact timings for each broadcast item. Although the BBC has published daily broadcast listings in its weekly magazine, the *Radio Times*, since September 1923, these listings are prepared weeks in advance and often do not reflect what was actually transmitted. The 'Programmes as Broadcast' lists are the only accurate records of BBC broadcasts. An edition of these records exists,[9] but this highly condensed version does not provide the level of detail required for this study.

The WAC's collection of scripts has also proven extremely useful, recording the substance of many broadcast talks. Unfortunately, the original scripts are no longer available for consultation; surviving scripts may only be read from microfilm. The microfilms do not contain scripts for all the talks that were broadcast during the period. The final version of each script read was supposedly collected at the end of the talk, but only a fair percentage are represented in the microfilm records.

Finally, volumes of John Reith's diaries covering the years under consideration were consulted in an attempt to fill in missing details about BBC music personnel and policy decisions. Published excerpts of the diaries exist,[10] but brief references to obscure BBC employees, which have proven very useful to this study, are not included in these extracts. The version of the diaries available at the WAC for research purposes is not the original journal, but a condensation prepared by Reith himself; this condensed version was later vetted by archive staff, who deleted sentences that were deemed confidential according to the libel criterion.

Published primary sources fall into three categories: periodicals published by the BBC, articles and reports published in British newspapers and other periodicals, and books of the time that are relevant to BBC history. The first category primarily consists of the *Radio Times*. This popular, weekly magazine provided essential information, both in its daily programme listings and in the accompanying articles, programme notes and published listeners' letters. The *Radio Times* was the early BBC's primary means of printed communication with listeners, providing publicity about future programmes, as well as details about programmes for the week in which it appeared. Because of its popular nature, the format was frequently changed and different approaches adopted to sustain readers' interest. It had a wide circulation – averaging over 1,300,000 sold per week by 1930, and over 2,600,000 per week by 1936 – and was aimed at readers from all parts of British society. Each issue included at least one article relating to art music.

Two other BBC publications were also consulted. *The Listener*, launched in 1929, was another weekly, founded to circulate edited versions of broadcast talks. Aimed at an intellectual audience, its columns included book reviews, critical discussions of concerts and broadcasts, and feature articles written by specialists on various topics. The BBC yearbooks, first published in 1928, vary in title as the *BBC Handbook*, *BBC Yearbook* and *BBC Annual*. In each volume, the Corporation summarized and publicized its annual programming achievements, technical innovations and newsworthy events or policy decisions. Each yearbook included a lengthy section about music programming, as well as statistics concerning licence distribution, lists of external committee members, and other factual information relating to the BBC and its operations.

The second category of published primary sources encompasses material that appeared in newspapers and music journals. Many newspaper articles that were consulted are held in the substantial press cuttings collections at the WAC. In addition, *The Musical Times* and the *Monthly Musical Record* were scrutinized for the years under consideration, both to gather information about performances and to gain an overview of the British musical climate between the wars. Many reviews of that time were published anonymously or attributed to their authors only by pseudonym or initials. Whenever possible, the identity of these authors has been traced and their names included in citations in square brackets.

Finally, several books reporting on BBC activities were published by BBC staff members during the period. The first wave of books appeared as early as 1924, when the success and popularity of the new broadcasting venture seemed assured; Reith, Cecil Lewis and Arthur Burrows, three of the four central figures in the early BBC hierarchy, published books that year.[11] Three books that appeared slightly after the period in question have also supplied missing details: the 1946 autobiography of Roger Eckersley, the Director of Programmes for much of the period; an account of early BBC experiences written by P. P. Eckersley, the original Chief Engineer; and an alternative view of interwar BBC politics by *Radio Times* editor, Maurice Gorham.[12] In addition, BBC-sponsored books relating to music and music history, such as Percy Scholes's *Everybody's Guide to Broadcast Music*, have proved useful.

Secondary sources relating to this topic are listed in full in the bibliography. Four have provided crucial background information relating to the interwar BBC and its organization. The most important is Asa Briggs's history of the BBC, of which the first two volumes cover the interwar years. Paddy Scannell's social history of British broadcasting provides an account of the general social climate and reaction to the new broadcasting medium. Social insights into early British broadcasting are also explored in D. L. LeMahieu's fascinating study. Finally, Nicholas Kenyon's history of the BBC Symphony Orchestra is a wonderful compilation of material relating to this important ensemble since its formation in 1930.[13]

PART I

# The emergence of BBC music programmes

# 1 The British music industry and the BBC between the wars

From the perspective of the 1990s, two such well-known and predominant institutions as the British Broadcasting Corporation and the Second Viennese School require no introduction: the BBC is so fundamental a part of British contemporary life and culture, and the compositions and idioms of Schoenberg and his colleagues so essential to the twentieth-century development of Western art music that the influence of both today is self-evident. This study of the BBC's early dissemination of music of the Second Viennese circle focuses on a time when this was not yet the case. The reader must shed images of established institutions to rediscover their interwar identities: the BBC's sphere of influence was new and growing, and the impact of Second Viennese School works in Britain were almost entirely dependent on this fledgling medium.

The fundamental purpose of this book is to recapture and examine the BBC's early programme policies and practices concerning the broadcasting of contemporary music, using the music of the Second Viennese School circle as a case study. It concentrates on the organization's initial years as the British Broadcasting Company (1922–6) and its first decade as a Corporation under royal charter (1927–36). Such re-examination seems particularly relevant today, when so much that had come to be accepted and expected with respect to the broadcasting of art music in the United Kingdom is in question.

Early policies, goals and practices can indeed still be perceived today, despite the BBC's many transformations. Interwar Reithian ideals shaped the early stations' priorities, with broadcasts adhering to a fundamental advocacy of lofty educational goals and a mixed programming strategy. Post-war streamlining of wavelengths, intended for specific tastes, led to the formation of the remarkable Third Programme, devoted to exploring the fine arts for six hours each evening; contemporary music broadcasting reached what was perhaps a pinnacle of attention and notoriety on the Third during the experimental years of the 1960s, when William Glock was Controller of Music. Third Programme ideals gradually gave way in the late 1960s as Radio 3 emerged, with art music transmitted all day as well as in the evening. Finally, British licensing of art music on commercial radio in the early 1990s, resulting in Classic FM, introduced such competition for the first time, further transforming the goals, character and programming choices of Radio 3's music broadcasts.[1]

At the roots of this evolutionary development are the original objectives of the men who created British radio. Their decisions not only shaped public attitudes toward art music, but paved the way for general awareness of the latest compositional trends. Collective memory in the latter years of this century has tended to focus on remarkable post-war developments, looking – some with pride, some with horror (and with shifting emphases between these extremes in the past decade) – to the BBC during the Glock years and since to define the Corporation's identity as a radical supporter and disseminator of the new in music. In fact, the BBC established an international reputation for bringing the newest in music into the homes of the British people as early as the 1920s. The considerable achievements of Glock and his successors stand on the shoulders of their predecessors: Reith's idealistic policies led directly to the appointments of the first BBC Music Directors, Percy Pitt and Sir Adrian Boult, who in turn supported and encouraged the unique contributions of the early music programme builders, notably the enigmatic Edward Clark and his practical colleague, Kenneth A. Wright. These men and their associates were fundamentally responsible for the development of the BBC's art music programming, laying the foundation for what later became post-war 'standards'.

What determined the early BBC's approach to contemporary music? Why did policies develop as they did? Who established them and carried them out, making day-to-day decisions about what music to transmit? Who chose which newly composed scores should be aired? How were such scores brought to the BBC's attention? Who made decisions about performers? Who shaped the formats and presentation of art music broadcasts? And how were these emerging policies and practices received – within the BBC, within the music profession and, most importantly, amongst the listening audiences? After all, within just a few years, the BBC was responsible for bringing art music for the first time to the entire British population, on a daily basis and in an easily accessible and affordable format – a phenomenon that could never have been even dreamed of just a few years before.

The following chapters examine these questions in detail, reconstructing the development of the BBC Music Department's personnel structure, programming policies, broadcasting practices and reception concerns, with special focus on programming decisions involving Second Viennese School repertory. For such detailed discussion to be effective, however, it is necessary to have some understanding of historical context. We begin with a brief introduction to significant social and economic issues that defined the nature of the music industry in interwar Britain.

## The changing face of the music industry

The interwar years were a time of extraordinary developments within the music industry, completely changing the fundamental nature and motivations of music-making, not only in the UK but throughout the world.[2] The early decades of this century saw an abrupt move from the established 'Edwardian infrastructure of music consist[ing] of buildings, institutions and processes through which musicians, as producers, and the public, as consumers, came to the market place'.[3] In the new musical order, technological advances enabled the emergence of the modern commercial music industry: the dissemination of music through mechanical means – specifically, sound recordings, broadcasting and film – transformed the role and potentials of music-making in everyday life at all levels of Western society. Participants in the traditional infrastructure continued to play key roles, but the composers, publishers, performers and audiences increasingly served as satellites to new commercial enterprises and priorities. As Cyril Ehrlich has succinctly stated about the twentieth-century music revolution: 'Fundamental patterns of consumption, manufacture and distribution have been realigned, sustaining an enormous growth in the use of music. Mechanized sound has replaced live performance as the normal experience.'[4]

These interwar years were rocky ones for British musicians: within this short period, external economic and social pressures forced sudden, profound shifts to work opportunities within the music industry. During the first decades of the century, silent cinema had rapidly gained popularity, offering musicians extraordinary employment options.

> Far from being silent, it required a ceaseless flow of music which could not yet be reproduced mechanically . . . So long as no soundtrack was available musicians were indispensable; their services required simultaneously everywhere, for most of the year . . . At every level of competence and ensemble, from 'fleapit' pianists or trios with drums to *quasi* symphony orchestras in the principal city theatres, instrumentalists found jobs throughout the country.[5]

However, the arrival of talking films in the late 1920s suddenly changed all that: 'the market collapsed practically overnight . . . Within a few years some 15,000 players lost their jobs.'[6] In addition, the period directly following the 1929 stock market crash brought the national economy into an erratic state.

> Although unemployment, hunger, and severe economic deprivation profoundly affected certain regions of the country . . . other areas of Britain, particularly the South, experienced marked economic growth and a steady rise in the standard of living.[7]

The unpredictable economy contributed to unstable working conditions for many in the music industry. Moreover, in the 1930s, British musicians' interests were threatened by large numbers of European refugees who flocked to safety and what they hoped were work opportunities in the United Kingdom, as the Weimar Republic gave way to the Nazi tide.[8] During this turbulent period, the BBC was born and rapidly gained power, resources and credibility – and, perhaps most significantly in this time of social and economic fluctuation, the BBC had money to spend.

The rapid development of the new music industry was paralleled by profound changes to the way in which British music activities were prioritized, decided and controlled, changes that were avidly fought by men who had achieved positions of authority in the old musical establishment. Success in the new musical world did not necessarily require the skills that had defined the power structures of the old; consequently, the old establishment, based in the music conservatories, performance venues, publishing houses and agencies, found that it was no longer possible to influence in the same way the direction and content of British musical life. Instead, in an incredibly short span of time, men who came from non-traditional – or even non-musical – backgrounds came to control the most powerful new-order institutions, as well as their budgets, and seized responsibility for decisions that affected the lives and livelihoods of a significant percentage of British musicians. The old establishment did not accept this loss of power meekly, and the conflict between those who felt they should be exerting influence and those who actually controlled the new music industry characterizes this period.[9] In particular, within a decade of its formation, the BBC not only became the most significant music disseminator in Britain, it was the foremost employer of British musicians, and the music establishment's attempts to challenge this reality and to exert influence over its ramifications are considered at length in later chapters.

This technical and commercial revolution not only changed the way that music was marketed and consumed, it had a direct impact on the substance of music in terms of the development of new repertoires, such as jazz, and radio and film incidental music. The technological developments and the depth and breadth of their impact on society are responsible at least in part for the division of music audiences into the distinct layers that characterize twentieth-century music reception, initially distinguished in the UK as 'high brow', 'middle brow' and 'low brow'. Within the art music realm, growing accessibility of old repertoires and the ease with which works, both small and large-scale, could be heard – and repeatedly – may well have encouraged the further division of audiences, with strong prefer-

ence for non-contemporary repertories, another distinctly twentieth-
century phenomenon.

Finally, the new opportunites for music composition, performance and
dissemination were paralleled by the development and increasing power
of organizations such as the Performing Right Society, the Mechanical
Copyright Protection Society, the Incorporated Society of Musicians and
the Musicians Union; together with more effective copyright laws following the 1911 Copyright Act, these institutions built up financial structures
that enabled creative artists to share in the financial rewards of the industry's new marketplace.[10] These structures provided the social and economic framework for the development of the 'professional' performing
musician or composer in the modern sense.[11] The BBC played a vital role
in helping to establish the effectiveness and influence of these new organizations, its 'Programmes as Broadcast' records providing detailed information about all transmitted music, enabling accurate distribution of fees.

From the beginning, the BBC was an intrinsic player in the new music
industry, setting new standards and developing new trends as a powerful
employer of musicians, as a commissioning body for new compositions, as
a disseminator of music repertories – inevitably shaping new audiences –
and as a leading distributor of music-related funds. For this reason it is
interesting to consider the early development of the BBC itself, to gain a
sense of why British radio and music programming within it developed in
the precise way that it did.

## A brief introduction to BBC history, 1922–1936

Following World War I, radio in Britain was still experimental, of interest
mainly to the military and the shipping industry, but also to a growing
number of amateur enthusiasts who built their own sets in order to send
and receive transmission signals. In February 1920, the Marconi Company
began to broadcast short, daily programmes of news and music, which
were received by the amateurs and sailors. However, the military disapproved of radio being used for entertainment purposes and the Marconi
programmes were banned in November of that year. After extensive lobby-
ing by the amateur enthusiasts, the Post Office gave the Marconi Company
permission to resume broadcasts, once a week for fifteen minutes from
February 1922. By May, the company was broadcasting non-musical programmes nightly from a powerful station in London called 2LO, by June
musical items were also included, and by autumn 1922, 2LO was heard by
approximately 50,000 people.[12]

As broadcasting increased in popularity, radio grew as a commercial entity. Anyone who wanted to 'listen-in' had to acquire a radio set; thus companies that produced radio equipment promoted broadcasting because it encouraged sales of their products. At the same time there was governmental concern about difficulties that had developed in the United States, where the lack of broadcasting control had resulted in too many stations using the limited wavelength band, adversely affecting reception.[13] In spring and summer 1922, official meetings took place in London to consider these issues. After much discussion and negotiation, the British Broadcasting Company was formed on 18 October 1922, and, in a decision of monumental significance, the government granted it sole right to broadcast in the United Kingdom. On the new monopoly's Board of Directors were representatives of the six most important British manufacturers of radio equipment. BBC broadcasting officially began on 14 November 1922, the day of the General Election. The first orchestral concert was given on 23 December, the same day as the first general news bulletin was read from London and the first broadcast talk was given. At that time the BBC had a staff of four,[14] headed by John Reith as General Manager.

The Company's policy was remarkably simple: on the technical side, to provide a broadcasting service for anyone in the country who cared to listen, and on the programme side, to bring the best of everything into the greatest number of homes. The growth of the Company between 1923 and 1927 was phenomenally rapid on all levels: departmental organization, staff size, building space, technical capability, geographical range, licence and listener numbers, broadcasting hours and programming coverage all expanded as the demand for wireless spread and the expected quality of its output increased. By the end of 1924, eight main stations had been built, which served different regions of the country. By July 1925, when the long-wave station at Daventry (5XX) was opened, 85 per cent of the British population had the capability to receive regional BBC programmes even on crystal sets, the simplest, least expensive early radios. As technological advances broadened transmission range and improved reception quality, the number of BBC licences sold each year increased: in 1924, 1,130,000 licences were sold; by the end of 1926, that number had nearly doubled. Other technical innovations during this period included the development of 'simultaneous broadcasts', where telephone wires linked different stations so that one programme could be transmitted across the country, and 'outside broadcasts', where programmes not confined to a BBC studio were transmitted.

As the BBC's size, responsibility and impact grew, the General Manager, Reith, and the government realized that the nature of the institution should be reconsidered. In 1925, an official committee chaired by the Earl of Crawford was appointed to examine the future of broadcasting; in March 1926, its findings were published, recommending that from the beginning of 1927 the British Broadcasting Company would become a new independent, public body called the British Broadcasting Corporation set up by a royal charter valid for ten years. When the Corporation began on 1 January 1927, Reith became Director-General and there were 773 members of staff.

During the decade under the first Charter, broadcasting played an increasingly significant role in British life and culture; as the BBC's sphere of influence grew, so did the Corporation's staff and hierarchical structure. Briggs describes this relationship as follows:

> On 1 January 1927 the BBC employed 773 people. There were then 2,178,259 wireless-licence holders. On 1 September 1939 the BBC employed nearly 5,000 people and there were 9,082,666 wireless-licence holders. To put the matter simply, in 1927 the BBC was still a small organization, catering for a minority, if a large and growing minority, of the British public. In 1939 the BBC was a large organization, and it was catering for a majority of the British public.[15]

As Table 1.1 demonstrates, by the end of 1926, about 20 per cent of the nation's households owned radios. By December 1933, this number had increased to 50 per cent and by the end of the period under consideration in this study, almost 65 per cent of the population were listening to BBC broadcasts in their homes. In those early years, the absence of other forms of domestic media entertainment and limited programme choice[16] meant that items the BBC chose to transmit were widely heard throughout the country by people of all economic classes and educational backgrounds, encompassing the spectrum of personal interests.

The new Corporation continued to expand throughout the 1930s in terms of size, importance, technical capability and programme sophistication. Since important developments in organizational structure, official policy and programme content are discussed in detail in later chapters, only a few events of historic significance will be mentioned here. On a technical level, the BBC put into effect the Regional Scheme, which enabled listeners in all parts of the country to receive BBC programmes on a minimum of two different wavelengths; this two-programme arrangement remained in effect until the beginning of the war. Musically, the most significant event of the period occurred in summer 1930, when the BBC Symphony Orchestra was formed; soon after, Adrian Boult became its Chief Conductor. On a physical level, the Corporation planned and constructed a

Table 1.1 *Relationship between the number of BBC licences sold annually, the number of British households and the number of BBC staff, December 1926–December 1936*

|      | licences current on 31 December | % increase from previous year | approximate number of licences per 100 households | number of BBC staff |
|------|------------|------|------|-------|
| 1926 | 2,178,259  | 32.4 | 20.0 | 773   |
| 1927 | 2,395,183  | 10.0 | 21.7 | 989   |
| 1928 | 2,628,392  | 9.7  | 23.4 | 1,064 |
| 1929 | 2,956,736  | 12.5 | 26.0 | 1,109 |
| 1930 | 3,411,910  | 15.4 | 29.6 | 1,194 |
| 1931 | 4,330,735  | 26.9 | 37.1 | 1,287 |
| 1932 | 5,263,017  | 21.5 | 44.5 | 1,512 |
| 1933 | 5,973,758  | 13.5 | 50.0 | 1,747 |
| 1934 | 6,780,569  | 13.5 | 56.1 | 2,031 |
| 1935 | 7,403,109  | 9.2  | 60.7 | 2,518 |
| 1936 | 7,960,573  | 7.5  | 64.4 | 3,350 |

The estimated population of the United Kingdom according to the 1931 census was 46,189,445; by the end of 1936, this estimated figure had increased to 47,229,400. For statistical purposes, the BBC estimated that in each British household, there was an average of 4 to 5 people.

The first three columns of statistics were reproduced from 'Licence figures', *BBC Handbook 1939*, 129. The final column was reproduced from Briggs, vol. ii: *The Golden Age of Wireless*, 450.

prestigious, purpose-built London headquarters, Broadcasting House, into which it officially moved on 15 May 1932. On 15 October of that year, the Concert Hall in Broadcasting House first came into use for Corporation-sponsored public concerts, which were also transmitted to listeners across the country. Finally, the last development of note was the renewal of the BBC charter on 1 January 1937. This important event was preceded by a thorough investigation of the Corporation's policies and achievements in its first decade, years in which the very nature of British radio was defined and determined. This review was carried out by a publicly appointed committee headed by Lord Ullswater, and the committee's favourable findings were published in the Ullswater Report of 1936.

Beginning in November 1922, when the British Broadcasting Company was formed, its staff of four began to build an empire in what was basically unchartered territory. It was impossible in those early days for anyone to predict how deeply sound media would permeate contemporary society or how influential the BBC would become – and how breathtakingly swiftly those processes would take place. The questions the early staff faced required groundbreaking and sometimes visionary decisions concerning technical developments, programming choices, presentation formats, and, perhaps most importantly, how to interact with social and economic forces on a national scale. Of these many questions, one in particular was fundamental to the organization during the interwar years: as a publicly funded monopoly, how best could the BBC serve the public and provide for its multiplicity of needs?

These questions could have been answered in many ways, and British radio could have developed along any number of different lines, perhaps similar to the commercial models that characterized early radio in the United States. The specific ways in which these fundamental questions were resolved and the values that the young organization adopted provided a platform for BBC policies, some of which are still recognizable in BBC radio today. This study is a detailed investigation of the way that the early administrators and programmers addressed fundamental questions concerning the broadcasting of art music, particularly contemporary art music, between 1922 and 1936 and the long-term ramifications of their answers.

## 2 BBC personnel, policies and programmes in the 1920s

From the earliest days of the British Broadcasting Company, the medium's pioneers recognized that broadcasting permitted the dissemination of art music on a scale previously unknown: the potential audience was the size of the British population; few had prior knowledge of art music. In a radio talk given in autumn 1923, Percy Scholes, the newly appointed BBC Music Critic and long-time proponent of music appreciation, considered the potential effect of music broadcasting on the British public:

> Up to the present, the great music of the world has been the private preserve of a little band of people who happened to live in the places where it could be heard, and who happened to have money enough to pay to hear it. Henceforth, it belongs to everybody. This means an immense widening of public interest in music, and I believe, a great raising of public taste.
>
> And as taste rises, the programmes of the British Broadcasting Company will rise with them . . .
>
> In five years' time, in my judgement, the general *musical public* of these islands will be treble or quadruple its present size. And the next generation, instead of regarding a symphony as a mysterious contrivance of concentrated boredom, will accept the great symphonies of the world as a part of its regular natural daily and weekly pleasures.[1]

This recognition of broadcasting's power to spread musical awareness throughout the country reflects the fundamental objectives for broadcasting as a whole as they were conceived by the original BBC administrators.

### The controlling hierarchy

During the early years, programme decisions resulted from discussions and resolutions made at all levels of the Company hierarchy. The Company's Board of Directors, representing the six main manufacturers of radio equipment and smaller constituent members, was chaired by Lord Gainford.[2] The board appointed as General Manager (later Managing Director) John C. W. Reith, an engineer who had seen active service during World War I and subsequently worked in the Admiralty and the Ministry of Munitions.[3] Reith was closely assisted by Rear-Admiral C. D. Carpendale, 'his trusted deputy who retired officially but not psychologically from the British Navy'.[4] The military backgrounds of these men and many of their colleagues had a significant impact on the nature of the organization they created. Moreover, in the initial years when Reith and Carpendale were closely involved with employment decisions, both apparently 'agonized over the social status of employees hired for important positions'.[5]

By January 1924, the BBC had grown in size and responsibility, and its organizational structure began to develop, the hierarchical levels, the detailed, paper-based modes of communication and emphasis on accurate record-keeping,[6] and the preoccupation with class and background reflecting in many respects the structures of the British civil service. The Control Committee (later Control Board), the highest decision-making group, was chaired by Carpendale and attended by the heads of the Company's three main divisions: P. P. Eckersley (Chief Engineer), A. R. Burrows (Director of Programmes) and G. V. Rice (Secretary of the BBC). The Organiser of Programmes, C. A. Lewis, also attended the meetings, and the board frequently sought advice from department heads – including Percy Pitt, in charge of music – on specific programming matters. Initially, the Control Board was directly involved with the programming process,[7] but from August 1924 the Director of Programmes assumed primary responsibility.[8]

The implementation of policy decisions was supervised by the Programme Committee (later Programme Board), established in May 1924 and chaired by Burrows.[9] Between twelve and fifteen people attended the meetings, including Lewis, Pitt, Major Corbett Smith (Artistic Director) and J. C. Stobart (Director of Education). Also in attendance was the editor of the *Radio Times*, the BBC's popular magazine; founded in September 1923, it rapidly became one of the highest-circulation weeklies in the country, offering detailed programme listings, as well as articles on all sorts of topics, not least introductions to featured programmes and explanations of BBC policy objectives.[10] The Programme Board met weekly to supervise the 'lay-out and quality of the local Stations' programmes generally', constructing a skeletal schedule for programmes to be aired five weeks later; until March 1925, music programmes were also discussed more specifically by the Musical Committee, a sub-committee of the Programme Board.[11] The full board considered issues of programme presentation and also coordinated programmes simultaneously transmitted from all BBC stations; usually originating from London, these were known as simultaneous broadcasts (SBs) and from August 1924 there were two each week.[12] From autumn 1925, the Programme Board reviewed transmissions of the previous week, considering comments of hired programme critics and listeners' letters.[13] The reviews enabled the board to evaluate the quality of programme content, execution and transmission. They also provided a means by which programmers could consider public responses to broadcasts.

When the BBC became a corporation in 1927, the overall organization changed completely. The profit-seeking Board of Directors was super-seded, under the terms of the royal charter, by a disinterested Board of Governors, 'to be persons of judgement and independence, who would inspire public confidence by having no interests to promote other than the public service';[14] the early Boards of Governors were chaired by the Earl of Clarendon (1927–30), J. H. Whitley (1930–5), Lord Bridgeman (1935) and R. C. Norman (1935–9).[15]

Within the Corporation, there were now five main branches, each of which was divided into departments and sections. At the head of each branch was an Assistant Controller who represented it at meetings of the Control Board: Roger H. Eckersley was in charge of programmes; P. P. Eckersley remained Chief Engineer until September 1929, when he was succeeded by Noel Ashbridge; V. H. Goldsmith supervised the Administrative Branch; W. E. Gladstone Murray headed the Information Branch, which handled publicity and publications; and T. Lochhead was the Chief Accountant.[16] Reith now had the title Director-General and was still assisted by Carpendale, now known as the Controller. This organiza-tional structure was retained until 1933.

The Programme Department (or Programme Branch)[17] also expanded, its organization becoming increasingly complex as programming expecta-tions escalated: increased transmission time, improved transmission and receiving capability, and heightened audience awareness resulted in spiral-ling demands on the branch. Throughout this period, it was headed by R. H. Eckersley, assisted by Cecil G. Graves, who was responsible for 'dealing with the detailed programme communications to all Stations, and forming a linking reference' for the departments and subsections within the branch.[18] Four departments corresponded to the main programme areas – music, productions (including drama), education and talks – each headed by its own director. Other sections dealt with administrative concerns: the copy-right section was 'employed not only in the checking of copyright payments for the thousands of minor items broadcast[,] . . . but in constant negotia-tion for the use of major items of musical, operatic, and dramatic works, . . . [each of which] has to be the subject of careful and special treatment'; the SB section coordinated simultaneous broadcasts with the provincial stations; the programme correspondence section dealt 'with the thousands of letters of appreciation, criticism, comment, and suggestion which pour in from all parts of the country'; and the finance section was linked to the BBC

Accounts Branch.[19] Thus, by 1927 the Music Department and its programme building subsection operated within a large web of programming bureaucracy, which itself was only a part of the larger corporate structure.

The expanded structure of the Programme Branch effected a corresponding amplification of the Programme Board. In January 1927, an *Evening News* article introduced the personnel and explained the board's function. In addition to the chairman, R. H. Eckersley, the core members included the heads of the programme departments, Percy Pitt (music), R. E. Jeffrey (drama), J. C. Stobart (education and religion) and Hilda Matheson (talks), as well as B. E. Nicolls (London Station Director) and George Grossmith (light entertainment).[20] Although membership of the board expanded, its function remained unchanged. Similarly, broadcast preparation became increasingly complex as the BBC grew in size, transmission hours lengthened and technical capabilities improved; nevertheless, the programme-planning process remained remarkably constant throughout the 1920s.[21] Expansion increasingly distanced the central administrators from detailed programme planning, giving the Programme Branch and its subdivisions more effectual control. Ironically, however, as programming conventions solidified, there were fewer opportunities for the programme builders to introduce spontaneous programming ideas, as had been possible in the initial years.

The BBC's hierarchical structure was established in part to ensure that broadcasts reflected the policies and decisions formulated at the organization's core: high level policy decisions were determined by the Control Board; the Programme Committee implemented these policies by overseeing suggestions presented by the individual departments and local stations; finally, each department's proposed schedules incorporated advice from external advisory committees. This brief introduction to the BBC's early decision-making structures provides the foundation for a more detailed examination of the policies that determined and defined music-related programming.

## The central policies

Since the BBC has not preserved many papers from the 1920s, tracing the development of programme and music policies over this decade is a more difficult task than for subsequent years.[22] Nevertheless, it is possible to determine early programming guidelines and goals in two ways: by reviewing surviving policy statements as articulated by the policy makers, and by analysing day-to-day decisions and output as manifest in the broadcasts themselves.

*Specified programme policies for single-programme transmission*

Early policies relating to the music programmes directly emanated from the Company's fundamental programming ethics and goals. The central administrators believed that as the sole broadcasting agency in the country, the BBC was responsible for determining and shaping the role that broadcasting might take in the lives of their audience, a responsibility that they regarded very seriously. During the first years of the Company, they kept the British public informed about current broadcasting issues through articles they contributed to the *Radio Times*. P. P. Eckersley generally explained technical points, innovations and plans, while Pitt contributed articles on broad musical issues. A column by Reith himself often appeared as the lead article, in which he explained the Company's positions and concerns on a variety of topics, effectively providing the public with statements of BBC policy. When asked to articulate these policies explicitly, however, Reith prevaricated, unwilling to impose limits on the rapidly growing and developing organization. Nevertheless, in an article that appeared in March 1924, he encapsulated some of the young Company's basic goals, which served as the guiding force behind the administrators' technical, administrative and programming decisions.

> Remember the appalling difficulties of catering for everyone at once and every variety of taste. To entertain, to interest, to enlighten, in all these ways to bring the very best of everything and to spare no effort to do it, to the greatest possible number; to aim always at the highest standards in every line of achievement in whatever direction it may lie; to exert our every endeavour to secure that the broadcasting service is looked to as giving the best that there is; that the amusement or instruction it provides may be as universally acceptable as is possible to young and old.[23]

From this statement can be inferred the Company's initial policy guidelines. Decisions about technical developments and programme content were based on five simple aspirations: to cater to all tastes; to entertain; to enlighten; to achieve the highest possible standards; and to reach the greatest number of people. The first three of these goals were directly concerned with programming. The BBC's determination to effect them simultaneously was in theory contradictory and in practice controversial. Nevertheless, the pursuit of these basic resolutions served as the cornerstone of the Company's policies and decisions.

Public interest in the new medium's programming possibilities centred on broadcasting's capacity to entertain. However, the BBC administrators recognized that they had the potential to offer a far more significant service: to a previously unknown extent, transmitted programmes could disseminate ideas and cultural values to an audience that represented a significant part of the country's population. In 1924, Reith explained the Company's perception of broadcasting's power:

> Till the advent of this universal and extraordinarily cheap medium of communication, a very large proportion of the people were shut off from first-hand knowledge of the events which make history . . . To-day all this is changed. He who really has something to tell his countrymen, something which it shall be to their profit to hear, can command an audience of millions ready to hand.
>
> An event, be it speech, or music, or play, or ceremony is certainly broadcast for any and all to receive; but it seems to be personal to the individual hearer, and is brought to his very room . . . It is carried to him among all the accustomed and congenial circumstances and surroundings of his own home, and in his leisure hours. It comes in such a way that enjoyment on the one hand, or assimilation on the other, is induced with comparatively little effort.[24]

This belief in the medium's capacity to allow the listener to assimilate 'with comparatively little effort' information, artistic performances or public events that had previously been beyond his or her sphere of influence – in effect, to enlighten – was behind the early administrators' development of the BBC as an educational institution, rather than as an entertainment facility. Reith's attitude toward entertainment was tempered by a broader understanding of the word's provenance:

> I think it will be admitted by all, that to have exploited so great a scientific invention for the purpose and pursuit of 'entertainment' alone would have been a prostitution of its powers and an insult to the character and intelligence of the people . . . A closer inspection of the word 'entertainment' is sufficient to show how incomplete is the ordinarily accepted meaning. To entertain means to occupy agreeably. Would it be urged that this is only to be effected by the broadcasting of jazz bands and popular music, or of sketches by humorists? . . . [Enjoyment] may be part of a systematic and sustained endeavour to re-create, to build up knowledge, experience and character, perhaps even in the face of obstacles. Broadcasting enjoys the co-operation of the leaders of that section of the community whose duty and pleasure it is to give relaxation to the rest, but it is also aided by the discoverers of the intellectual forces which are moulding humanity, who are striving to show how time may be occupied not only agreeably, but well.[25]

This idealized concept of entertainment, which sought to widen listeners' intellectual and cultural horizons and to heighten their critical perceptions, was at the centre of early BBC programming strategy.[26]

During the early years, however, many listeners were only able to receive one BBC signal on their wireless sets; thus, the BBC's programming goals – to cater to all tastes, to enlighten and to entertain – all had to be encompassed within the programme output of each regional station. Inevitably, listeners' programme wishes frequently clashed with the transmitted offerings. For example, the BBC devoted a relatively substantial amount of time to art music, which was unfamiliar and unpopular with the majority of listeners. In February 1924, Reith explained the long-range policies behind broadcasts of such 'high-brow' music. Radio provided the listener,

> night after night, [with] a large variety of pieces from among the world's best composers. With a little advice or a little judgment he can train himself in the enjoyment and appreciation of the particular kind of music which appeals to him. The natural result will be that he will gradually come to have favourite pieces and songs and kinds of music, and will be readier than ever before to take the opportunity of attending concerts where his favourites are to be heard, and where he will also have the companionship of large audiences . . . We say that by popularizing good music, wireless is doing an important service to the musical world, and one which an increasing number in the profession are glad to acknowledge.[27]

Reith thus advocated that enlightenment would lead to entertainment, and in this way Percy Scholes's prediction about the growth of the British art music audience would be fulfilled.

Despite detailed explanations of these idealistic objectives, general criticism of their high-brow orientation continued. In late 1924, Reith once again stated his ideals in his book, *Broadcast over Britain*, but in a more defensive way:

> As we conceive it, our responsibility is to carry into the greatest possible number of homes everything that is best in every department of human knowledge, endeavour and achievement, and to avoid the things which are, or may be, hurtful. It is occasionally indicated to us that we are apparently setting out to give the public what we think they need – and not what they want, but few know what they want, and very few what they need . . . In any case it is better to over-estimate the mentality of the public, than to under-estimate it.[28]

By spring 1925, continuing criticisms prompted the BBC to defend its position in two prominent *Radio Times* articles. In the first, the Company outlined the financial management of the non-profit-making concern, summarizing its technical and programming accomplishments. The article emphasized that the BBC's credibility rested on its success in fulfilling 'the task of providing the whole of the British people with the best available entertainment, thought and culture, at the minimum cost'.[29] The second article, written by the critic J. C. Squire, concentrated on the programming issue and provides insight into listener complaints. Squire asserted that there were two groups of complainants: the vocal minority, who believed the BBC transmitted too much high-brow fare, and the majority, who believed the opposite. After concluding that 'it is impossible to please even the present large public of listeners – with a single programme',[30] Squire suggested that the problem would only be resolved when the BBC developed the capability to transmit alternative programmes.

> I have always believed that discontent will not be allayed or the possibilities of broadcasting fully exploited until at least two complete programmes are sent out side by side from the London Station every day. I am not suggesting an ideal; the ideal would be 'one man – one programme', which is patently impracticable; I am only suggesting an approach to the ideal.[31]

Although the Company engineers, headed by P. P. Eckersley, had been working on developing the technical means to offer alternative programmes, they did not fully achieve this goal for another five years. Given that programme alternatives were as yet unviable, Squire in effect supported the BBC's position.

During winter 1925–6, members of the BBC Board of Directors became concerned about programme complaints and decided to intervene.[32] In December W. W. Burnham, a director representing the interests of small manufacturers of wireless equipment, wrote to Reith in detail, recommending changes to programme policy. He believed that the announcers spoke too much and was concerned that there was 'too much education, too many lectures, and matters of that sort'. In addition, he objected to cultural programming, complaining that there were

> too many uninteresting items, such as Elizabethan music, new fangled songs, weird quartettes and quintettes, groaning Chamber Music, quite unappreciated by the public, readings from unknown poets, etc., which savour very much of the penny reading concerts of olden days, also talks on subjects which are of no interest to 99% of the listeners.[33]

He proposed a new approach to the nightly schedules: no broadcast talks should be scheduled after 7 pm, there should be no talking at all between 8 and 10 pm, and the main programme in that slot should have a more popular orientation.

Reith was unimpressed by Burnham's concerns, recording in his diary that he had received 'a silly letter from W. W. Burnham on programmes, but of the sort to be expected from him'.[34] Nevertheless, at the next meeting, three directors formed a committee with Reith to review programme policy.[35] Two committee members attended subsequent Programme Board meetings – Burnham attended one, and Major Basil Binyon two – in order to make policy suggestions they believed would narrow the gap between programme output and listeners' expectations.[36] Burnham specifically targeted the music programmes, suggesting that different conductors should direct the London station orchestra, programme engineers should have some musical knowledge, music programmes should occasionally be devoted to one composer, and songs should more frequently have orchestral accompaniment. Binyon recommended 'that in the programmes there should be a larger proportion of purely recreative items as opposed to those items demanding sustained concentration', directly challenging Reith's ideals concerning entertainment and programme balance. Binyon reiterated this suggestion at the second meeting he attended, when he also proposed that art music recitals be scheduled earlier in the evening.

The committee prepared a report of their findings, which, as Binyon described to Reith, was drawn 'largely from the proposal submitted at our first meeting and your reply thereto, together with some suggestions submitted by Mr Burnham and myself at a Programme Board, and also some opinions formed by me at the second Programme Board which I attended'; unfortunately, neither the report nor the administrators' response to it survives.[37] The directors' recommendations caused the central administrators to institute changes affecting music programming.

> More outside broadcasts were to be put on at once . . . A new conductor was to be appointed, new arrangements were to be made to ensure 'musical balance and control', and there would be more orchestral accompaniments and fewer gramophone records. No apology was made, however, for sixteenth-century and 'futurist' music: 'a certain amount of this should be included, and the Programme Board does not feel it is being overdone in any way'. Care would also be taken to choose better artists.[38]

In their response to the directors' suggestions then, the administrators concentrated on quality issues affecting performance and transmission standards for the music programmes. They dismissed public criticisms about programme content and the directors' recommendations that the balance of programmes be shifted in favour of lighter entertainment, continuing to defend and implement their fundamental programme goals: to bring the best of everything – enlightening as well as entertaining – into the greatest number of homes.

### Specified programme policies for alternative-programme transmission

The next significant challenge to the administrators' programming objectives occurred in 1927, when the BBC initiated its first experiment in alternative programming. The Corporation had recognized the importance of giving listeners a choice of programmes as early as 1924, ultimately intending that 'all listeners should be able to receive efficiently a minimum of two programmes with inexpensive simple apparatus'.[39] However, it took time to develop the technical capability to transmit alternative programmes which would both reach the entire country and conform to the wavelength restrictions imposed by the European broadcasting authorities.[40] The BBC took an important step toward this goal in August 1927, when the experimental transmitter at Daventry (5GB) was opened, potentially giving listeners within a 100-mile radius a choice of programmes. However, those who were within the receiving area discovered that the experimental transmitter did not provide a level of service equal to the established stations; moreover, listeners outside the Midlands area were unable to benefit from the innovation. It was not until the 1930s, with the establishment of the 'Regional Scheme', that reliable alternative services became available nationally.

While BBC engineers worked on technical developments, the administrators considered alternative programming in terms of programme policy. In effect, their programming strategy remained unaltered. Initially the BBC did not streamline its programme schedules; the assignment of broadcasting material aimed at a specific audience to particular wavelengths was not implemented until after World War II. Before the war, both wavelengths transmitted the full range of programming possibilities. The choice to the listener came from the balancing of the two programmes against each other: when one station broadcast a programme of a serious nature, the alternative provided lighter fare. This was achieved theoretically through the definition of basic programme categories that would enable appropriate alternatives to be balanced against each other.[41] When 'Universal' programmes, defined as music programmes 'which do not require on the part of the listener mental effort for their enjoyment', were aired on one of the wavelengths, 'Speciality' programmes, requiring 'the listener's co-operation', would be broadcast on the other. The latter category was subdivided into 'Speciality (Amusement)' and 'Speciality (Service)', which included time signals, bulletins, weather forecasts, appeals, etc. In addition, spoken programmes could be scheduled as alternatives to music.

Shortly after the experimental station became operational, the administrators questioned whether it was desirable to transmit alternatives all the time. Reith concluded that while 'in the present experimental stage continual alternatives are almost invariably essential, . . . this attitude might have to be modified in the future from the points of view both of policy and finance'.[42] Modification was especially important in the case of music, since experience revealed that one music programme did not adequately balance another on the second wavelength.[43] Later in 1929, as the BBC prepared to shift to the Regional Scheme, the administrators again reviewed their policies. However, during the experimental stage, alternative-programme policies developed as an extension of fundamental programming objectives: on the main wavelength, successive items in the schedule were balanced against each other, in pursuit of the basic goals of enlightening, entertaining and catering to all tastes. Each item in the alternative programme was balanced against that in the main programme, providing contrasting material for the limited number of listeners who could receive it.

## Audience response and responsibility

Reith and the controllers sought to achieve their programming goals in two ways: by controlling the content of the programmes they transmitted, and by influencing the way in which listeners received the broadcasts. Despite their fundamental aim to cater to all tastes, the administrators realized from the outset that no broadcast would be agreeable to every listener; in fact, given the underlying concept of broadcasting programmes the public 'needed' rather than wanted, it was likely that every broadcast would be disagreeable to a portion of the audience. As Burrows explained in a talk transmitted in June 1923:

> We know that by the very nature of our work it will never be possible for us to satisfy at one and the same time every section of our vast audience. Unlike all other forms of entertainment, which only draw to their houses just that section of the public specially interested in their particular type of amusement, we have to cater simultaneously for every grade of society and practically every variety of temperament and taste.[44]

The BBC tried to allay public and press criticisms of its programme policies through published explanations of its objectives. The administrators also developed two other strategies to recognize and respond to these criticisms.

First, the BBC encouraged listeners to express their opinions by writing letters in response to broadcasts. In his talk of 1923, Burrows described what happened after a new programme was aired:

> Next morning, or rather within 48 hours, we receive some hundreds, and at times, some thousands of letters, a number congratulating us and a number, happily more often a much smaller number, asking us 'why on earth we did it'.
>
> Of the letters that reach us regarding programmes, approximately 97 per cent express approval or convey congratulations, whilst 3 per cent are critical and hostile. They are not all addressed to us in endearing terms.[45]

The administrators took such suggestions seriously, believing it was essential to enhance public relations and appraise public opinion. In fact, Burrows gave his 1923 broadcast talk in order to encourage listeners to send criticisms, which the administrators planned to use to review the effectiveness of programme balance.

> We would like to know whether, as at present arranged, we are providing too much classical music of the less popular character, or too little music of this character, too many or too few talks on subjects of general interest, too much or too little music of sentimental character, too much or too little dance music, too much orchestral music or too little orchestral music, too many or too few vocal items, too many or too few instrumental solos.
>
> Now please write your views before we go any further, and post them at the earliest possible moment.

The 1923 campaign represents an early stage in the BBC's postal relationship with its audience. As the following figures show, the Company received an increasing number of letters about its programmes each year:[46]

|      |        |
|------|--------|
| 1923 | 16,000 |
| 1924 | 20,000 |
| 1925 | 25,000 |
| 1926 | 30,000 |
| 1927 | 60,000 |

In addition, many programme-related letters were addressed to the *Radio Times*; by 1929 approximately 500 were received each week.[47] A small number of these were reproduced in the weekly column devoted to listener correspondence, which presented a cross-section of positive and negative responses. The editors often juxtaposed letters which expressed opposing views about the same programme, effectively demonstrating the impossibility of satisfying the needs of each member of the audience with every programme. In January 1926, *The Musical Times* described the BBC's weekly postbag:

> On the whole, the musical policy of the B.B.C. has been thoroughly justified by results, as is shown by the following analyses of letters received at the Company's offices:

Some 8,000 letters a week pour in to the B.B.C. They are carefully clas-
sified, and daily and weekly reports compiled from them to show the tendencies of the public taste. In addition, there are responsible critics in
every centre. For the past six months really adverse criticisms have
amounted to under 5 per cent. For the week ended December 4, 7,600
letters were received by London and the other stations, of which 302 were
adversely critical, as under:

125  condemned dance music.
 65  were general growls.
 52  were against alternative programmes.
 39  condemned talks.
 20  objected to individual artists.
  1  objected to religion.

Here is a striking proof of the public change of attitude towards good music:

Eighteen months ago classical music was definitely unpopular. To-day
there are more enemies of dance music in our correspondence than of
classical. About religion, strangely enough, there is less complaint than
about anything.[48]

Amid the complaints and growls, the BBC used listener correspondence
summaries to extrapolate information about reception trends.

In the days before scientific methods were used to analyse listener
response to programmes,[49] the BBC established the policy of encouraging
programme correspondence as a way of measuring its effectiveness and
keeping in touch with listeners' points of view. By 1924, the Company had
established an elaborate system of dealing with the letters, which enabled
them to consider criticisms as part of the programme-building process;[50]
moreover, personal replies, sometimes written by programme department
heads, were sent to all authors of critical letters. From September 1925, the
Control Board decided 'that the programme criticisms, including a
pr[é]cis from the Programme Correspondence section, should be read at
[Programme Board meetings] instead of being circulated as at present',[51]
increasing the letters' importance within the programming process. By
1927 the system was handled by an entire section of the Programme
Department. A facetious description of this section in the first BBC handbook, as 'a home of lost illusions, inhabited by dreary people of suicidal
tendencies, professing a peculiar cult of Pure Pessimism',[52] provides some
insight into the negative aspects. Nevertheless, the BBC continued to
encourage listeners to send their comments:

It is too much to expect [all listeners] to take it on faith that the sole purpose
of the B.B.C. is to broadcast acceptable programmes in an acceptable
manner, and doubts or perplexities may sometimes engender a spirit of sus-

picion and resentment which need not arise at all. Let such listeners present their problems, and they may be certain that they will receive sympathetic individual attention, and, moreover, that the opinions they may express will be definitely recorded in that register which is so helpful in the appraisement of the public taste.[53]

As the amount of correspondence increased, the administrators considered whether there was a more efficient way to handle the volume; however, the Control Board's conclusion illustrates the value that they placed on the established policy:

> A.D.P. [Assistant Director of Programmes: C. G. Graves] asked whether it was desirable further to curtail the work of the P.C.S. [Programme Correspondence Section], and thereby economise in staff, but it was generally agreed that the goodwill obtained by answering enquiries was worthy of maintenance, and that whilst economy should be effected by the use of standard letters, as already arranged, the full service should be continued.[54]

During the 1920s, personal attention was given to listeners' comments and complaints as an increasingly expensive, but essential, part of the programming process. The practice not only proved an effective aid to public relations, but, more significantly, it permitted the BBC to assess and to respond to problems that resulted from its programming decisions.

One important consequence of the programme correspondence process was that it enabled the BBC to anticipate policy criticisms and to formulate strategies with which to off-set them. One scheme of this type dealt with the two most frequently recurring criticisms of the early years: disaffection with high-brow programmes and complaints about broadcasts that did not suit listeners' tastes led the administrators to develop and propagate the concept of 'correct' listening practices. In this campaign, which was introduced in September 1927 – just after the launch of 5GB – the BBC stressed that listeners must learn to use their radios responsibly:

> If there be an art of broadcasting there is equally an art of listening . . . There can be no excuse for the listener who tunes in to a programme, willy nilly, and complains that he does not care for it. He should decide his broadcast-entertainment for the evening with as much care as he would decide whether to go to see a Bernard Shaw play or a Revue.[55]

In December 1927, P. P. Eckersley further developed this concept in an article published in *Eve, the Lady's Pictorial*. Reminding readers that the BBC was obliged to offer as wide a programme selection as possible, he asserted that no one person should expect to listen indiscriminately to all programmes and derive pleasure from them; that was deemed an abuse of wireless's accessibility. Instead, each listener was responsible for choosing which programmes fell within his or her own scope of interest and for concentrating fully on those programmes during their transmission. He concluded, 'The art of listening is to listen to what you want to listen to – choose something and give it a chance.'[56]

Another article on this subject, written by programme advisor, Filson Young, for the *BBC Handbook 1928*, attributed listener abuse to the ease and affordability with which listeners received broadcasts.

> Every new invention that brings desirable things more easily within our reach thereby to some extent cheapens them . . . We seem to be entering upon a kind of arm-chair period of civilisation, when everything that goes to make up adventure is dealt with wholesale, and delivered, as it were, to the individual at his own door.[57]

Once again, the problem of programme antipathy was ascribed to incorrect listening practices; the listener was encouraged to examine the programme listings, to choose appropriate programmes and to give them complete attention.

> The listener, in other words, should be an epicure and not a glutton; he should choose his broadcast fare with discrimination, and when the time comes give himself deliberately to the enjoyment of it . . . To sum up, I would urge upon those who use wireless to cultivate the art of listening; to discriminate in what they listen to, and to listen with their mind as well as their ears. In that way they will not only increase their pleasure, but actually contribute their part to the improvement and perfection of an art which is yet in its childhood.

Thus, in 1927 the BBC administrators countered criticisms of their policies by promoting the notion that listeners did not use their radios responsibly.

In early 1930, the BBC approached the issue of correct listening more directly. A page of the BBC handbook published that spring prescribed the procedure for 'good listening' in simple terms and emphatic type:

GOOD LISTENING

MAKE SURE THAT YOUR SET IS WORKING PROPERLY *before* YOU SETTLE DOWN TO LISTEN.

CHOOSE YOUR PROGRAMMES AS CAREFULLY AS YOU CHOOSE WHICH THEATRE TO GO TO. IT IS JUST AS IMPORTANT TO YOU TO ENJOY YOURSELF AT HOME AS AT THE THEATRE.

LISTEN AS CAREFULLY AT HOME AS YOU DO IN A THEATRE OR CONCERT HALL. YOU CAN'T GET THE BEST OUT OF A PROGRAMME IF YOUR MIND IS

WANDERING, OR IF YOU ARE PLAYING BRIDGE OR READING. GIVE IT YOUR
FULL ATTENTION. TRY TURNING OUT THE LIGHTS SO THAT YOUR EYE IS
NOT CAUGHT BY FAMILIAR OBJECTS IN THE ROOM. YOUR IMAGINATION
WILL BE TWICE AS VIVID.

IF YOU ONLY LISTEN WITH HALF AN EAR YOU HAVEN'T A QUARTER OF A
RIGHT TO CRITICISE.

THINK OF YOUR FAVOURITE OCCUPATION. DON'T YOU LIKE A CHANGE
SOMETIMES? GIVE THE WIRELESS A REST NOW AND THEN.[58]

A further article on the subject appeared in the *Radio Times* later that
year, written by Filson Young, which squarely blamed the listener for any
dissatisfaction with the programme service.

> What I want to rub in at the moment is that the chief element in broadcast-
> ing is not the artist, not the engineer, not the organizer, but the listener. Yes,
> you! In the long run in matters of supply and demand, people get the service
> they want or deserve. Good listeners will produce good programmes more
> surely and more certainly than anything else. And many of you have not even
> begun to master the art of listening; you have not even begun to try. An
> epicure is not a man who opens his mouth and lets in a stream of nourish-
> ment. He selects, he rejects. The arch-fault of the average listener is that he
> does not select.[59]

Throughout the 1920s, the BBC administrators continued to implement their basic policies of presenting educational as well as entertaining
material. Faced with consistent public criticism of this programming
approach, they defended themselves in two ways: by defining the boundaries of their own responsibilities – proclaiming that they should aim to
provide as wide an array of quality programmes as possible; and by dictat-
ing terms of usage to be practised by the audience – directing listeners to
identify which programmes related to their own personal interests and to
restrict listening to those items. The administrators thus developed a strategy which enabled them to defend and safeguard their fundamental objectives, even when confronted by severe criticism; by formulating and
publicizing rules of correct listening practices, they shifted the responsibility for the criticisms from themselves back to the critics.

### A summary of programme policies during the 1920s: the first BBC Handbook

In 1928, the BBC published the first of what would become an annual
publication in which it reported on all aspects of its policies and objectives, internal organization and external advisors, programmes, processes,

publications and plans, and also provided technical information about transmission techniques, transmitter status and reception tips. This publication was aimed at anyone with an interest in broadcasting, including listeners, amateur radio enthusiasts, critics and officials, and served as a verbal showcase in which the BBC could list its achievements and state its positions. The first publication in the series, *BBC Handbook 1928*, comprised information about 1927.[60] Several of the articles – on administrative structure, programme building procedures, listener criticisms and correct listening practices – have already been discussed. In addition, the handbook contained an important article entitled 'Programme Policy', a summary of the BBC's programming aims.

The article focused on significant issues that had been raised by the administrators and the public during the initial years of broadcasting. The BBC's programming goals – 'to give the public what we think they need, and not what they want' – were reiterated, though in softer terms than previously:

> [The broadcaster], in spite of the valued co-operation of listeners, is necessarily the actual chooser of the programmes. A false step would be taken if, carried away by his sense of what the public needs, he supposes it to be the same as what the public wants. Often – curiously often, a pessimist would have to allow – the two coincide, but it does happen that they disagree.[61]

The article examined this divergence in terms of basic considerations: when planning programmes, the BBC determined which audience interests would be addressed; the programme schedule was structured to cater to all tastes; and contrasting, alternative programmes were provided for those who could receive them. The article pointed out that it was impossible to please every listener with every programme. It defended the decision to include programmes of a serious, rather than purely entertaining, nature, stressing that 'it would be a derogation of duty' if the BBC did not provide opportunities for listeners to increase their cultural awareness. Finally, it justified the decisions and policies that had been enacted according to the BBC credo, 'give the public something slightly better than it now thinks it likes', by looking at the result: 'It must be sufficient to say that a working period of nearly four years has shown that the public becomes not less but more exacting'. Although BBC policies were less stridently articulated in the late 1920s than initially, the Corporation's broadcasting goals remained consistent with the objectives conceived at the outset by John Reith and his Control Board colleagues.

## The programmes

As programming possibilities were explored and developed during the 1920s, the Company's output came to encompass a wide variety of spoken and music programmes. Dramatic presentations, educational programmes, children's hour, religious services, talks, features, news, readings and other spoken series were all transmitted each week, as well as classical music, light music, dance music and gramophone records.

In fact, music accounted for nearly two-thirds of the daily programme output, as shown in Table 2.1. Of the 249 hours broadcast in October 1925, music was heard during 166 hours; almost a fifth of that total was devoted to 'classical' music, while 2/3 of the music total was given over to more popular types. Throughout the 1920s, most music was broadcast live; gramophone records accounted for only 12–15 per cent of the music transmission time and the technique of pre-recording programmes did not develop until the following decade. Significantly, BBC staff who prepared the report in 1926, from which the 1925 figures were derived, began with a category labelled 'Exotic Music', which included both 'Ancient' and 'Futurist' music. At this early date, neither was very well represented in the BBC programmes. Although the percentage of the total music hours broadcast decreased from 67 per cent in 1925 to 60 per cent in 1929, during that same time the percentage of 'classical' music hours increased, from 12 per cent to 19 per cent of the total transmitted hours. The introduction of the experimental alternative wavelength (5GB) from 1927 is responsible for this increase. As Table 2.2 shows, over three-quarters of the 5GB transmission time was devoted to music, as compared to 64 per cent of the total time from the main transmitter, 5XX; during more than 20 per cent of the 5GB transmission hours, art music was aired, in addition to the hours devoted to it over 5XX. Thus, the policy of balancing contrasting material in the experimental programme had the effect of increasing the number of hours during which art music was broadcast.

### Daily programme formats

BBC programme policies directed the programme builders to produce a varied schedule, which provided educationally stimulating material for listeners and appealed to the broad compass of their established tastes and interests. From the beginning of public broadcasting, daily schedules were shaped by a set format, within which various programme types were juxtaposed. Table 2.3 outlines a typical evening's broadcast from the London

Table 2.1 *BBC programme analyses for 1925, 1927 and 1929*

| Category | Details | October 1925 (entire month) | | October 1927 (one week) | | October 1929 (one week) | |
|---|---|---|---|---|---|---|---|
| | | % of total hrs | % of music hrs | % of total hrs | % of music hrs | % of total hrs | % of music hrs |
| Exotic Music | 'Ancient or Futurist' | 0.03 | 0.04 | | | | |
| Classical Music | Opera, Orchestra (Symphony Concerts etc), Chamber Music, Song Recital, Instrumental Recitals | | | | | | |
| | total | 12.02 | 18.05 | 15.79 | 25.07 | 19.32 | 32.15 |
| Medium Music | 'Music which may please all tastes' | 7.42 | 11.14 | | | | |
| Popular Music or Light Music | Orchestra or Band, Musical Comedy, Revue, Star Entertainers, Celebrity etc., Ballad, Recitals, Restaurant and Cinema Music | | | | | | |
| | total | 30.70 | 46.10 | 29.45 | 46.77 | 23.87 | 39.73 |
| Dance Music | | 6.62 | 9.94 | 16.43 | 24.11 | 9.92 | 16.52 |
| Gramophone Records | | 10.20 | 14.71 | 1.29 | 2.05 | 6.96 | 11.58 |
| Drama | | 2.50 | | | | 2.53 | |
| Features | | | | | 1.27 | | |
| Light Entertainment | | | 5.26 | | 3.38 | | |
| Spoken Word | | 2.09 | | 14.71 | | 15.22 | |
| Religion | | 1.20 | | 2.25 | | 3.80 | |
| Children's Hour | | 8.12 | | 5.80 | | 5.70 | |

| | | | |
|---|---|---|---|
| School Broadcasts | 7.09 | 6.65 | |
| Outside Broadcasts (Theatre, Ceremony, Speeches) | | 1.29 | 1.40 |
| Total Hours Broadcast | 248.75 | 77.58 | 78.92 |
| Total Music Hours Broadcast | 165.64 | 48.83 | 47.39 |
| Percentage of Music Hours Broadcast to Total Hours Broadcast | 66.59 | 62.94 | 60.05 |

1925 programme analysis figures are based on those prepared by the BBC in 1926 and reproduced in Briggs, vol. i: *The Birth of Broadcasting*, 390; figures from 1927 and 1929 are based on those in Briggs, vol. ii: *The Golden Age of Wireless*, 35.

Table 2.2 *Analysis of alternative programmes, December 1928–July 1929*

Percentage of programme time devoted to different programme types as broadcast from two BBC stations, Daventry 5XX and Daventry 5GB, between December 1928 and July 1929

| Category | Details | 5XX % of total hrs | 5GB % of total hrs |
|---|---|---|---|
| Music | Serious | 16.77 | 20.36 |
| | Light | 23.57 | 31.43 |
| | Variety | 5.00 | 14.16 |
| | Dance bands | 9.23 | 10.04 |
| | Gramophone records | 9.69 | 0.25 |
| | total | 64.26 | 76.24 |
| Drama | | 1.66 | 3.96 |
| Talks | Talks and debates | 8.87 | |
| | Schools education | 4.56 | |
| | Adult education | 2.50 | |
| | News | 5.07 | 7.17 |
| | Readings | 0.96 | 0.57 |
| | total | 21.96 | 7.74 |
| Religious services | | 4.98 | 1.70 |
| Appeals | | 0.14 | 0.19 |
| Children's Hour | | 5.64 | 8.50 |
| Special transmissions | | 1.36 | 1.67 |

Programme analysis figures are based on those prepared by the BBC in 1929 and published in *The BBC Yearbook 1930*, 56.

station in October 1923; at that time, the nightly programmes began at 7 pm and were based on a format in which a central music concert was flanked by news reports and talks programmes. By autumn 1926, the evening's schedule had expanded both in length and programme range. As Table 2.4 illustrates, music still filled a significant portion of the time, but the first main programme of the evening (at 8.00 pm) was no longer necessarily music-based. The format distinguished between different types of music and specified the optimum times for their transmission. Another outline format, shown in Table 2.5, was publicized in the *Radio Times* in January 1927, shortly after the Corporation came into being.[62] The evening lay-out had again expanded, with the first news read a half-hour earlier, and was regulated even more strictly in terms of programme type

Table 2.3 *Schedule of London programmes for a typical evening in October 1923*

| | | |
|---|---|---|
| 7.00 | first news and weather report | |
| 7.15 | first talk | |
| 7.30 | concert | |
| 9.15 | second talk | |
| 9.30 | second news bulletin | |
| 9.45 | ⌈concert | three times a week |
| | ⌊talk | other nights |
| 10.00 | dance band | |

Information drawn from: BBC WAC, R34/609, undated [ca. Sept 1923]; also from examination of the programmes that were broadcast, as recorded in: *BBC Programme Records 1922–1926*.

Table 2.4 *Schedule of London programmes for a typical evening in October 1926*

| | | |
|---|---|---|
| 7.00 | first news | |
| 7.10 | talk | |
| 7.25 | light music | |
| 7.40 | topical talk or music | |
| 8.00 | programme | |
| 9.30 | talk | |
| 9.45 | music recital | |
| 10.00 | second news | |
| | Mondays, Wednesdays, Fridays | Tuesdays, Thursdays, Saturdays |
| 10.15 | programme | feature |
| 10.30 | | dance music |
| 11.00 | close-down | |
| 12.00 | | close-down |

Information drawn from: BBC WAC, R34/600/3, 18 June 1926.

and entertainment category. The BBC explained that it had 'recast the character of the transmissions in the light of what correspondence from listeners has shown to be the general demand'. The public apparently preferred lighter material at prime listening time; serious items tended to be held until after the second news. Within this framework, the schedules were guaranteed to encompass a varied, but balanced, array of contrasting music programmes.

Table 2.5 *Schedule of London programmes for a typical evening in January 1927*

| | |
|---|---|
| 6.30 | weather and first news |
| 6.45 | musical interlude or London Radio Dance Band |
| 7.00 | first talk |
| 7.15 | piano interlude |
| 7.25 | second talk |
| 7.45 | first evening concert, 'usually of the popular or lighter kind – variety items, concert parties, music, etc.' |
| 8.45* | piano or song recital |
| 9.00 | weather, second news and local announcements |
| 9.15 | third talk. 'This will be of a distinctly greater programme value than hitherto, special topical subjects being dealt with by authoritative speakers. As time goes on these will be supplemented by specially arranged "outside broadcasts".' |
| 9.30 | second evening concert, 'usually of the more serious or "heavier" kind. This will continue until 10.30 three evenings each week, when dance music is relayed; and on the remaining evenings until 11 pm.' |

Information derived and quoted from: 'London and Daventry News and Notes', *RT*, 14 (14 Jan. 1927): 99.

* The 8.45 pm recital was soon deleted from the schedule to allow the 7.45 pm concert to continue uninterrupted until 9.00 pm. This change was announced in 'London and Daventry News and Notes', *RT*, 14 (28 Jan. 1927): 199.

## Projected weekly programme schedules

Outline schedules, similar to those reproduced in Tables 2.3, 2.4 and 2.5, were used by the administrators and programming departments as the basis on which each evening's programmes were planned. The process by which the detailed programmes for each evening grew from these outlines was complicated and required the coordination of the many parts of the Programme Department, as well as the provincial stations. The central administrators contributed to this operation at the weekly meetings of the Programme Board, during which the most prominent programmes to be aired each week were considered and approved. However, the majority of the programmes resulted from decisions made at lower levels.

In the 1928 handbook, the BBC included an article that described the programme building procedure in detail.[63] Each week's schedule was first conceived five weeks in advance, when the most important programmes to

Table 2.6 *Projected programme outline considered by the Programme Board in February 1925*

| Projected SB arrangements for week commencing March 22 | | |
|---|---|---|
| Sunday  (afternoon) | 2LO, 5XX | De Groot – Studio programme |
| (evening) | 2LO, 5XX | 2LO Quartet |
| Monday | 2LO, 5XX | Popular orchestral programme |
| Tuesday | 2LO | Musical comedy programme including a first performance of 'The Red Pen' by Geoffrey Toye |
| | 5XX | Gustav Holst chamber music programme |
| Wednesday | 2LO, 5XX | Old Masters programme |
| Thursday | 2LO | Chamber music programme |
| | 5XX | Sir Frederick [*sic*] Elgar, conducting studio symphony programme |
| Friday | 2LO, 5XX | Grenadier Guards |
| Saturday | | As chart * |

SB denotes simultaneous broadcasts across BBC stations.
* not included in source.
Information drawn from: BBC WAC, R34/600/2, 9 Feb. 1925.

be transmitted from the London station, 2LO, and the high-power transmitter, 5XX were decided.[64] In 1925 this projected schedule was quite simple, as can be seen from Table 2.6, showing a schedule considered by the Programme Board on 9 February. For each day, one or two special programmes were proposed as featured items. Most of these were music-based, and 5XX alternatives were provided for the chamber music programmes. It is interesting to note that the chamber music recital proposed for Thursday evening on 2LO was in the event broadcast over 5XX, replacing the projected symphony programme with Sir 'Frederick' Elgar.[65]

By October 1926, the skeletal outline was more detailed and specified a greater number of projected programmes for each day, as shown in Table 2.7. The outline included weighted recommendations about which programmes should be aired by the regional stations. The two most important transmissions of the week, designated as compulsory simultaneous broadcasts for all stations, were Herbert Ferrer's one-act lyric drama, *The Piper*, broadcast on Monday evening and a studio performance of Rossini's *Il barbiere di Siviglia* aired on Friday.[66] In addition, the schedule encompassed a wide variety of programmes; non-musical items were well represented, but music programmes predominated, including popular items such as light

Table 2.7 *Projected programme outline considered by the Programme Board in October 1926*

*Projected programmes for the week beginning December 5th*

| | | | | |
|---|---|---|---|---|
| Sunday | afternoon | 2LO | 3.30 | Popular Classics – Ansell |
| | | | 5.30 | Reading. Lotus Eaters with Parry's music |
| | | | 5.45 | Missionary Talk |
| | evening | | 8.55 | The Queen's hospital ** |
| | | | 9.15 | Colombo |
| Monday | | 2LO | 7.30 | Orchestral items |
| | | | 7.45 | Debate, OB * |
| | | | 8.30 | The Piper (repeat performance) *** |
| | | | 10.15 | Variety |
| Tuesday | | 2LO | 8.00 | Willie Rouse |
| | | | 8.15 | International chamber concert |
| | | | 10.25 | Layton & Johnstone |
| | | 5XX | 8.00 | Military band and humour |
| Wednesday | | 2LO | 8.00 | Turkish Skotch & music |
| | | | 8.45 | Eton College concert |
| | | | 10.15 | Concert party ** |
| | | 5XX | 8.00 | Chamber music from Edinburgh |
| Thursday | | 2LO | 8.00 | Popular orchestral |
| | | | 8.30 | Vaudeville theatre, OB * |
| | | | 9.00 | Popular orchestral |
| | | | 9.30 | Piano |
| | | | 9.45 | Talk and the Tower Keys, OB |
| | | | 10.15 | Orpheus Male Voice Quartet |
| Friday | | 2LO | 8.00 | The Barber of Seville *** |
| | | | 10.15 | " |
| Saturday | afternoon | 2LO | 3.00 | St Anne's, Soho – Handel programme |
| | | | 4.00 | Concert by Savoy Havana Band |
| | | | 6.00 | Lenghi Cellini and Foden's Brass no.1 Quartet |
| | evening | | 8.00 | 'My Programme' no.7 by George Grossmith ** |
| | | | 10.15 | Recital by Albert Sammons ** |

* strongly recommended for SB    ** practically compulsory SB    *** compulsory SB

SB denotes simultaneous broadcasts across BBC stations.
OB denotes outside broadcasts transmitted from outside a BBC studio.
Information from: BBC WAC, R34/600/3, 28 Oct. 1926.

orchestral classics, dance band music, variety shows, the Orpheus Male Voice Quartet and a recital of Kreisler violin pieces. Art music programmes included, in addition to the two operas, Parry's setting of Tennyson's 'The Lotus Eaters', a concert of Handel choral works and two chamber music concerts, counterbalanced by contrasting alternatives. Against the international chamber concert on Tuesday, featuring the Amar Quartet (with Paul Hindemith on viola) playing works by contemporary German composers, was transmitted 'Military Band and Humour', a military band concert featuring popular classics and a comedian in the interval.

After the Programme Board considered and approved the skeletal outline five weeks before transmission, the plan was circulated to each station. The following process then took place:

1 Each station prepared its own projected schedule, taking into account prior commitments and routine programmes, as well as the simultaneous broadcasts available from London. In making its programming decisions, each station was limited by a weekly budget allowance.

2 The stations then chose artists for each programme, considering the frequency of their previous broadcasts and repertory the artists themselves proposed, verifying that items had not recently been aired and that timings were accurate.

3 Ten days after the Programme Board meeting: the week's projected programmes for each station were assembled as completely as possible, although many specific details would not yet be available. These schedules were circulated to Programme Department sections for consideration and comment, and the Director of Programmes appraised the overall balance.

4 Comments were returned to individual stations, to be acted upon as needed.

5 20 days after the Programme Board meeting (two weeks before transmission): the revised schedule was sent to the *Radio Times* editor, who finalized copy for the published programme listings. The *Radio Times* issue went to press about three days later.

6 A day or two before transmission, late programme amendments were sent to the daily press. Changes were also communicated to the senior announcer, who was responsible for programme presentation. The announcer also ensured that transmissions adhered to the published schedules, deciding when necessary whether to cut off items that overran the allotted time, or whether to begin following items late.

These procedures only represent a fifth of the overall programme building process, since at any one time, the programme builders were involved with five weeks' worth of programmes.[67] Surviving documents indicate that many of the programmes were not finalized in practice until the last moment.

## Transmitted weekly programme schedules

A detailed look at broadcasts during two randomly selected weeks demonstrates more concretely the types of programmes that the BBC planned and presented during the early years. During the week of 18–24 January 1925, the London station broadcast programmes listed in Table 2.8. The only programme to be presented every day, other than the news and weather reports (not shown in the table), was the afternoon children's programme; schools broadcasts were given on weekday afternoons. Around these fixed items, the schedules encompassed a range of programme types and addressed a variety of interests. Thursday's evening schedule provides an example of the diversity: after the first news, two talks were presented, one by the Radio Society of Great Britain and the other on cathedral architecture, followed by a vaudeville programme, readings of six poems by Oxford poets, and a chamber music concert; after another talk and the second news report, the evening's programmes concluded with dance band music transmitted from the Savoy Hotel. Most of the music programmes during the week featured light music, including a military band concert, orchestral light classics, programmes of popular songs from musical comedies, tea-time music from the Trocadero and dance band music from the Savoy. Only two art music programmes were aired: the Tuesday evening studio presentation of Mozart's *Le nozze di Figaro* and the Thursday evening chamber music concert. In response to an unusual, and apparently unanticipated, event, a scheduled talk on Friday afternoon about Malta was changed to a talk on eclipses, as an introduction to the special eclipse transmission on Saturday afternoon, which also did not appear in the published listings.

This schedule for a typical week in early 1925 provides some insight into programme balance during the years when most listeners were able to receive only one BBC signal. Early and mid-afternoon programmes were devoted to lighter music, talks aimed to appeal to housewives, and children's programmes. Just before the first news, a talk on a serious subject was aired. The evenings included further talks on serious and instructive topics, interspersed with feature programmes, ranging from vaudeville and musical comedy to chamber music and opera. Several times a week, the evening ended with dance band music. Various categories of features were transmitted across the week, and throughout each evening, a variety of programme types were juxtaposed. Much of the music was popular or fell into the light classics category; however, as a conspicuous manifestation of the BBC's policy to promote cultural awareness, art music programmes were given prominent attention, often transmitted at prime programming time. Nevertheless, art music was not transmitted every day or even more than a few times a week.

After the launch of the experimental alternative station from Daventry, 5GB, in August 1927, the administrators developed rules for balancing programme output. A comparison of the programmes broadcast from the London station, 2LO, and from 5GB during the week of 2–8 October 1927, shown in Table 2.9, demonstrates the way that the BBC tried to satisfy a wide range of tastes within each schedule while simultaneously balancing the output of the other one. At this experimental stage, 2LO clearly broadcast the main programme material. The London station transmitted for longer hours (from noon to 11 pm or midnight on weekdays, as opposed to 5GB hours, from 3 pm to 11.15 pm) and included a wider range of programme types.

As in 1925, the afternoons in October 1927 were devoted to programmes intended mainly for children and housewives. Musical items were generally of the lighter variety, including dance band programmes, cinema organ recitals, gramophone records and afternoon restaurant music, but most afternoons included at least one art music programme. Over the second wavelength, the afternoon programmes strictly followed the rules of balanced alternatives: on Sunday, when 2LO presented light orchestral music, 5GB broadcast a chamber music concert including Beethoven and Dvořák string quartets; opposite Evensong was aired cinema organ music; against a natural history talk, another chamber concert; a light classical concert was balanced by dance band music; and opposite the operatic concert was a band programme. In most instances, talks were balanced by music, and popular music was balanced by orchestral, military band or chamber music. On weekdays, the children's programme was effectively extended, since it was offered at juxtaposed times on both stations.

Each evening, the 2LO schedule encompassed a variety of short programmes centred around one or two featured items, aired at the prime times of 7.45 pm and 9.35 pm. The featured items throughout the week represented a variety of programme types, including drama, symphony concerts, chamber music and Lieder recitals, live sports commentary, and a popular sing-along. Every evening ended with dance music transmitted from a famous club or hotel. As in the afternoon, the 5GB evening schedule balanced that of 2LO: opposite an abridged Shakespeare play was a

Table 2.8 *London Station (2LO) programming for a typical week, 18–24 January 1925*

| day<br>hours of transmission | important programmes (excluding news and weather reports) | |
| --- | --- | --- |
| | afternoon | evening |
| Sunday<br>3–5.30 pm<br>8.20–10.30 pm | military band concert of light classics<br>Children's Corner (SB) | religious service<br>orchestral concert of light classics from the Piccadilly Hotel |
| Monday<br>3.15–10.30 pm | schools programme<br>talk: 'Vogues and Vanities'<br>afternoon tea music from the Trocadero<br>Children's Corner<br>talk: 'Cupid in Spiderland' | talk: 'Constitutional Law' (SB)<br>songs and popular orchestral music |
| Tuesday<br>1–2 pm<br>3.15–11 pm | songs and light music by the 2LO trio<br>schools programme<br>talk: 'Books to Read'<br>Children's Corner<br>charity appeal | talk: 'Literary Criticism' (SB)<br>'The Opera "Figaro"', Pitt conducting (SB)<br>talk: 'Our Sense of the Ether – Vibrations and Waves, and What they Signify' (SB)<br>dance band music from the Savoy Hotel (SB) |
| Wednesday<br>3.15–10.30 pm | schools programme<br>songs and light music by the 2LO trio<br>Children's Corner<br>talk: 'The Road to Timbuctoo' | talk: 'Spitzbergen Expedition' (SB)<br>burlesque with Willie Rouse<br>talk: 'The Religious Plays of the Middle Ages' (SB)<br>talk: 'The Week's Work in the Garden' (SB)<br>dance music |
| Thursday<br>1–2 pm<br>3.15–11 pm | gramophone record concert of serious and popular music<br>schools programme | talk: the Radio Society of Great Britain (SB)<br>talk: 'Architecture – the Cathedrals of Peterborough, St Alban's, Durham & Norwich (SB) |

| | |
| --- | --- |
| | talk: 'A Talk on Fashion' |
| | afternoon tea music from the Trocadero |
| | Children's Corner |
| | piano solos, including Bach and Liszt |
| | talk: 'The Detectives of Fact and Fiction' |
| Friday | |
| 1–2 pm | songs and light music by the 2LO trio |
| 3.15–10.30 pm | schools broadcast |
| | talk: 'Eclipses' |
| | Children's Corner |
| | Ministry of Agriculture's bulletin (SB) |
| Saturday | |
| 4 pm–midnight | special eclipse transmission |
| | concert by the 2LO octet |
| | talk: 'A Garden Chat' |
| | Children's Corner |
| | talk: 'The Lion City' |

| |
| --- |
| vaudeville (SB) |
| poetry readings (SB) |
| concert: songs by Fauré, Delius, Debussy, Quilter and Gibbs and chamber music by Mozart, Bax and Vaughan Williams (SB) |
| talk: 'A Day in Tutankhamen Land' (SB) |
| dance band music from the Savoy Hotel (SB) |
| talk by Percy Scholes, BBC Music Critic (SB) |
| musical comedy excerpts |
| talk: 'South Africa' (SB) |
| light orchestral music |
| talk: 'General Hints to Poultry Keepers' |
| Burns night programme: 'Folk Songs of Scotland' (SB) |
| talk: 'Hockey Topics' (SB) |
| dance band music from the Savoy Hotel (SB) |

(SB) denotes simultaneous broadcasts across BBC stations.

Programmes as listed in the *Radio Times*, 6 (16 Jan. 1925), 152–64, and in the BBC WAC 'Programmes as Broadcast' records.

Table 2.9 *Programming for a typical week, 2–8 October 1927 (excluding news and weather reports)*

| important 2LO programmes | important 5GB programmes |
| --- | --- |
| SUNDAY | |
| 3.30–5.45 pm | 3–5.30 pm |
|   light orchestra concert |   string quartet and vocal concert, including |
| |   Beethoven op.59, no.1, and Dvořák op.51 |
|   religious talks |   religious talks |
| 8–10.30 pm | 8–10.30 pm |
|   studio religious service |   studio religious service |
|   charity appeal | |
|   light orchestral music from the Grand Hotel, |   Handel's oratorio, *Samson*, from Birmingham |
|     Eastbourne | |
| MONDAY | |
| 12–2, 2.30–6.30 pm | 3–6.30 pm |
|   organ recital from St Michael's, Cornhill | |
|   schools talks |   theatre music by the Rivoli Theatre Orchestra |
|   dance band |   military band concert |
|   talk: 'Planning an Ideal Kitchen' |   children's hour |
|   children's hour | |
|   organ recital from the Astoria cinema | |
| 6.30–11:30 pm | 6.30–11.15 pm |
|   talk: dramatic criticism |   light orchestral concert |
|   The Foundations of Music: Haydn piano sonatas | |
|   talk: German reading | |
|   concert of music by Charles Villiers Stanford, |   military band concert |
|     conducted by Stanford Robinson (his son) | |
|   talk: 'Professors and the Dinner Table' | |
|   concert of chamber music by contemporary | |
|     composers, performed by the Vienna | |
|     String Quartet, including Ravel, Webern |   dance band music from the Riviera Club |
|     op.5, Falla songs, and Schoenberg op.7 | |
|   popular songs | |
| (11–midnight, 5XX only: dance band music from the Riviera Club) | |
| TUESDAY | |
| 12–2, 2.30–6.30 pm | 3–6.30 pm |
|   light music programme | |
|   schools broadcast, including talk by Sir Walford | |
|     Davies: 'Elementary Music' |   organ music from Lozells Picture House |
|   talk: 'Legends of Birds' | |
|   dance band music |   light orchestral concert |
|   children's hour | |
|   dance band music |   children's hour |

Table 2.9 (*cont.*)

| important 2LO programmes | important 5GB programmes |
| --- | --- |
| TUESDAY (*cont.*) | |
| 6.30 pm–midnight | 6.30–11.15 pm |
| talk: 'Filming through Africa' | dance band music |
| The Foundations of Music: Haydn piano sonatas | |
| talk: 'An Evolutionist among the Rocks and Fossils' | |
| variety show | performance of Massenet's *Manon* from the |
| talk by Sir Walford Davies: 'Music and the | Theatre Royal, Glasgow, performed in English |
| Ordinary Listener' | by the British National Opera Company |
| light orchestral classics from the Hotel Victoria | |
| dance music from Ciro's club | abridged performance of Shakespeare's *The* |
| | *Taming of the Shrew* |
| WEDNESDAY | |
| 12– 2, 2.30–6.30 pm | 3–6.30 pm |
| dance band music | |
| luncheon restaurant music | |
| schools broadcast | chamber concert of songs and piano trio music |
| talk: 'Familiar Birds and Beasts of the | by Hurlstone, Wolf and Mozart |
| Countryside' | |
| light classical concert | dance band music |
| children's hour | |
| organ recital from the New Gallery Kinema | children's hour |
| talk on gardening | |
| 6.30–11 pm | 6.30–11.15 pm |
| Ministry of Health talk | 'Old time Dance Music' |
| The Foundations of Music: Haydn piano sonatas | |
| talk: 'Development of Mind and Character: the | |
| Work of Choosing Careers' | |
| recital of Lieder by Hugo Wolf | |
| light orchestral music | symphony concert conducted by Sir Henry |
| talk: 'The Gainsborough Centenary' | Wood, including Purcell Suite, Vaughan |
| musical: 'Miss Hook of Holland' | Williams *A London Symphony*, Tchaikovsky |
| | Rococo Variations and lighter works by |
| | Wagner, Mozart, Rimsky-Korsakov and |
| | Granados |
| | dance music from the Carlton Hotel |
| (11–midnight, 5XX only: dance music from the Carlton Hotel) | |
| THURSDAY | |
| 12–2 pm, 2.30–6.30 pm | 3–6.30 pm |
| concert of new gramophone records of serious | |
| and popular music | |
| speech by the Earl of Birkenhead from the British | |
| Passenger Agents' Association luncheon | |

Table 2.9 (*cont.*)

| important 2LO programmes | important 5GB programmes |
| --- | --- |
| THURSDAY (*cont.*) | |
| Evensong from Westminster Abbey | organ music from Lozells Picture House |
| talk: 'How to Make a Girl's School Outfit' | |
| schools broadcast | band concert of light classics |
| children's hour | |
| dance band music | children's hour |
| 6.30 pm–midnight | 6.30–11.15 pm |
| talk: 'Scouting for the Disabled' | dance band music |
| talk: 'New Novels' | |
| The Foundations of Music: Haydn piano sonatas | |
| talk: 'Pioneers in Astronomy: Tycho Brahe' | The City of Birmingham Orchestra, conducted |
| abridged performance of Shakespeare's *The* | by Boult, including Weber Overture to |
| *Taming of the Shrew* | *Euryanthe*, Butterworth *A Shropshire Lad*, |
| talk: 'Some Personal Sketches' | Mozart Violin Concerto in G Major (with |
| military band music | Jelly D'Aranyi), Sibelius Symphony no.5 |
| commentary of international boxing contest | recital of Schubert Lieder |
| | variety show |
| dance band music from the Savoy Hotel | |
| FRIDAY | |
| 12–2, 2.30–6.30 pm | 3–6.30 pm |
| recital of Beethoven's 'Kreutzer' sonata | |
| organ recital from St Botolph's, Bishopsgate | |
| luncheon music from the Hotel Metropole | |
| schools broadcast | organ recital from St Mary-le-Bow, Cheapside |
| concert for school children with excerpts from | dance band music |
| Schubert and Mozart chamber music | |
| talk: 'A Garden Chat' | |
| children's hour | |
| orchestral music from the Prince of Wales | children's hour |
| Playhouse, Lewisham | |
| 6.30–11 pm | 6.30–11.15 pm |
| talk: 'Seen on the Screen' | The Victor Olof Sextet concert of arrangements |
| The Foundations of Music: Haydn piano sonatas | of light classics |
| talk: 'The Art of the Cinema: the Scenario' | |
| talk by Basil Maine: 'Next Week's Broadcast | |
| Music' | |
| BBC National Concert: The National Orchestra, | musical comedy programme |
| conducted by Sir Henry Wood, relayed from | dance band music |
| the Queen's Hall, including works by Bach and | |
| Beethoven Symphony no.9 | |
| story: 'An Impromptu Dance', told by A.J. Alan | dance music from the New Princes Restaurant |
| (11–midnight, 5XX only: dance music from the New Princes Restaurant) | |

Table 2.9 (*cont.*)

| important 2LO programmes | important 5GB programmes |
|---|---|
| SATURDAY | |
| 1–2, 3–6.30 pm | 3–6.30 pm |
|   dance band music | |
|   concert of operatic excerpts | band concert |
|   children's hour | |
|   dance band music | children's hour |
| 6.30 pm–midnight | 6.30–11.15 pm |
|   talk: 'The National Council of Women and its Work' | light orchestral music |
|   The Foundations of Music: Haydn piano sonatas | |
|   talk: 'Prospects for the Rugby Football Season' | |
|   variety show | dance band music |
|   The Royal Albert Hall Orchestra, conducted by Sir Landon Ronald, relayed from the Queen's Hall, including Beethoven Overture, *Leonora* no.3 and community singing | |
|   dance music from the Savoy Hotel | concert of music by Roger Quilter |

Programmes as listed in the *Radio Times*, 14 (30 Sept. 1927), 569–96, and in the BBC WAC 'Programmes as Broadcast' records.

symphony concert; against boxing commentary was a recital of Schubert Lieder. When 2LO presented art music, 5GB usually offered dance band music. Examination of actual broadcast schedules after the introduction of alternative programmes thus confirms that underlying programme strategies remained virtually unchanged: the main station offered a varied schedule aimed to fulfil the basic programming objectives; 5GB balanced this according to the precepts outlined by the alternative programme policies.

The availability of an alternative programme apparently encouraged the BBC to weight the 2LO schedule with more serious material than would previously have been tolerated. The London station certainly offered a higher proportion of talks in the October 1927 schedules than it had in January 1925. For example, Tuesday's listing included no fewer than six talks, three aired in the afternoon and three in the evening. The many talks broadcast during the week presented information on a range of instructional, educational and informative topics, including drama and cinema criticism, household and gardening advice, scouting, language lessons, musical and literary instruction, art history, natural history, astronomy, politics and sports. All the talks were broadcast over 2LO, none over 5GB. In fact, 2LO seemed to carry the bulk of the serious items while 5GB presented lighter fare. Since a substantial percentage of 2LO listeners were unable to receive 5GB in late 1927, scheduling a higher proportion of serious items over 2LO must have been distressing to many London-area listeners.

Although programming procedures theoretically remained unchanged after the alternative wavelength was introduced, the schedules reveal that alternative options enabled the BBC to increase time devoted to certain types of programmes. This applied most consistently to cultural programming. For example, between 1923 and 1926, dramatic presentations were aired only infrequently; however, during the single week represented in Table 2.9, an abridged performance of Shakespeare's *The Taming of the Shrew* was aired twice, on Tuesday over 5GB and on Thursday over 2LO. The technique of presenting the same programme on alternate stations in close succession became a standard part of BBC programme policy in the following decades. Later called 'diagonalization', it permitted the educational impact of a programme to be increased through repeated hearings and was inexpensive to produce, since little preparation was required for the second performance. In the 1920s, before the development of recording technology, the 'repeat' broadcast was another live performance. The number of art music programmes also increased significantly after 5GB was launched. Whereas in January 1925 the entire week's schedule included only two programmes of art music, in October 1927 there were several every day. Since the total number of broadcast hours also increased, the statistical measure of art music hours compared to total hours does not reflect the significance of what was achieved.

In this way, the advent of alternative programming, even in an elementary form, significantly increased the potency of the BBC's campaign to enlighten and educate. Each week, the demand for popular programming was satisfied in large part through the schedules of the alternative station, expanding the opportunity for serious programming from the more powerful London station. At the forefront of these culturally enhancing broadcast hours were the programmes devoted to art music, the number of which increased as the decade progressed.

PART II

# The Pitt years, 1922–1929

# 3 The foundations of music programming, 1922–1926

Despite the development of complex hierarchical structures and pro-gramme policies, most BBC broadcasts during the 1920s resulted simply from the ideas and impetus of the staff programme builders. In his history of British broadcasting, Asa Briggs summarized the balance between high level decisions and programme output as follows:

> Behind the cavalcade of programmes was a multiplicity of decisions taken within the BBC. Some of the decisions came from above, encouraging as well as restraining: most came from below. Some reflected general programme policy: most bore the imprint only of scriptwriter, producer, and performer.[1]

The focus, content and overall shaping of the programmes were deter-mined largely by individual programme planners in each department, especially when their ideas were consistent with the general principles of high-level policy. Given that the success of the central administrators' objectives were dependent on the individual programme builders, it is useful to consider the hierarchy and duties of the Music Department staff as it evolved during the early years before examining specific programmes which they planned and produced.

## Music Department personnel

Even before the British Broadcasting Company was officially formed, music was a central programming element in public broadcasts. The importance of properly administering music programming was recog-nized in June 1922, when Arthur Burrows, later BBC Director of Programmes, emphasized the need for a music director at the 2LO station. L. Stanton Jefferies, who was already working for the Marconi Company at Chelmsford, was appointed Director of Music at the end of that Summer. In May 1923, the department properly came into being with the part-time appointment of Percy Pitt, composer and opera conductor, as Music Advisor, assisted by Jefferies.

Pitt's influence on the programming policies and personnel decisions of the department, between its formation in 1923 and his resignation at the end of 1929, cannot be over-emphasized. He had studied music in France and Germany in the 1880s; after his return to England, he devoted himself to organizing and conducting opera in Britain. By the 1920s he had acquired an outlook and experience that was unusual for a British musician: his continental training, his detailed knowledge of European musical trends and his leading role as an opera conductor and administrator led to the inclusion of works and the pursuit of musical ideas in BBC programming which differed in significant ways from the focuses and expectations practised and taught in established British music institutions. Nevertheless, the lack of surviving documentation makes the details of Pitt's contribution to the formation of the department and its policies difficult to reconstruct. Burrows briefly described Pitt's responsibilities in 1924:

> Since his resignation from the directorate of music to the British National Opera Company Mr. Pitt has given almost undivided attention to the programmes of the B.B.C. He holds the auditions in the case of artists of repute or particular promise, indicates the conductors most fitted for a special performance, and examines in the light of his wide and special knowledge the musical make-up of every programme, London and provincial. Occasionally Mr. Pitt conducts a night of operatic or symphonic music from the London studio, but his principal work, like that of several others, is now done behind the scenes.[2]

This behind-the-scenes work included contributing to administrative decisions that shaped BBC music policy. Pitt occasionally attended meetings of the Control Board, was a regular member of the Programme Board, and, as the chief of musical matters, would have been a central figure in the Musical Committee during its existence.[3] In March 1925, his responsibilities were further specified in the Programme Board's decision 'that as the Musical Committee was now being dissolved, all operatic and symphonic programmes, should be submitted to the Director of Music for his approval and assistance'.[4] Other surviving clues indicate that Pitt was behind the high proportion of new music broadcasts and the engagement of performers who presented the British public with the latest in European trends. He was also responsible for recruiting other musicians whose interests and approaches to music were similar to his own; some of these ensured that his policies and ideas continued after he himself left the BBC.

While Pitt's work focused on policy decisions and programme planning, Jefferies actually brought the music programmes to fruition. A description of his responsibilities in 1924 shows that in those early Company days, the few staff members were involved in a great variety of tasks, from performing on air to arranging contracts and solving administrative difficulties.

> Mr. Jefferies has not only great ability, but the tirelessness of youth. Nothing disturbs him. He will jump up from a masterful improvisation at the piano

for the amusement of the children to settle a knotty problem in relation to a
tour of contract artistes; will answer almost in the same breath a trunk call
dealing with the reorganisation of an orchestra at a distant station and will
put down the phone to give a really sympathetic hearing to an artiste who
would receive short shrift in many other hands. As a hobby Mr. Stanton
Jefferies finds time between his other duties to produce and conduct musical
plays at the London station.[5]

Jefferies' duties also included arranging for tours of provincial stations by
visiting artists, acquiring a library of music scores, the basis of the present-
day BBC Music Library, and supervising the Music Directors of the provincial BBC stations.[6] By May 1924, Jefferies was assisted by Stanford
Robinson,[7] although in September Robinson moved to the London station
to be the first conductor of the newly-formed Wireless Chorus. In
November 1924, Pitt became full-time Director of Music (sometimes
referred to as Controller of Music).

By the mid-1920s, other musicians were associated with the Company;
these men were not administratively connected with the Music
Department, but nevertheless influenced its policies or programmes. As
the technical capabilities of transmitting orchestral music improved, an
increasing number of broadcasts featured orchestral music or included it
in some way. Although Pitt or guest conductors directed the ambitious
symphony programmes, staff conductors, often members of the Music
Department, met the daily orchestral needs of the station. In May 1924
Dan Godfrey, son of the well-known conductor of the Bournemouth
Municipal Orchestra, moved from being Station Manager at Manchester
to London, where he became the first full-time conductor of the 2LO
Wireless Orchestra; he retained that position until July 1926, when John
Ansell took over.

From 1925 the Music Department was supplemented by a committee of
outside music advisors, the Music Advisory Committee. As early as 1923,
Reith realized that BBC programming and public relations would benefit
greatly from recommendations by experts in fields related to BBC programme output; that year he formed the Central Religious Advisory
Committee, the first of what would become a system of advisory committees representing different areas of expertise. Two years later, the Music
Advisory Committee was convened, initially meeting on 8 July 1925 and
thereafter four times a year. It was chaired by Sir Hugh Allen (director of
the Royal College of Music) and the committee members, solidly and
exclusively chosen from the ranks of the British educational establish-
ments, included John McEwen (principal of the Royal Academy of Music),
Sir Landon Ronald (principal of the Guildhall School of Music), Sir

Walford Davies (University of Wales), Professor Donald Tovey (Edinburgh University), Dr W. G. Whittaker (Armstrong College, Newcastle) and Colonel J. A. C. Somerville (Royal Military School of Music). The committee was convened to advise the Music Department about music policy and to maintain relations between the Corporation and the music profession. At a Control Board meeting soon after its formation, there was concern that press announcements had not emphasized that the committee's function was 'purely advisory and in no sense executive'.[8] The next *Radio Times* included a short statement clarifying this point: 'The functions of the Committee are to give their views and advise on the musical policy of the B.B.C., on the systematic development of musical appreciation amongst the great body of listeners and also on the relations of the musical profession with broadcasting'.[9] From the beginning, however, the committee opposed the unorthodox consequences of Reith's ideals and the Music Department's decisions. Nicholas Kenyon describes the early history of this body as follows:

> In an effort to increase its public accountability, Reith formed a Music Advisory Committee, under the chairmanship of Sir Hugh Allen . . . If Reith thought . . . that the function of this Committee was 'to agree and confirm what [he'd] already decided to do', he was in for a shock. The Committee represented established interests, at the opposite pole from those of Reith's Music Department, and in the years to come it would attempt to interfere in artistic decisions, claiming that the BBC should support only British music and musicians at a time when [the Music Department] was at [its] most adventurously continental. The conflicts were to reach a peak in 1929 when the Committee was nearly disbanded, and were to reassert themselves throughout [later years].[10]

The tensions between the BBC and the music profession underlay Music Department decisions and activities throughout the interwar years. Their ramifications affected the department's programme policies and decisions from the first months of broadcasting, as a detailed examination of early BBC music broadcasts reveals.

## The music programmes

During the Company years, most music programmes were conceived on an individual basis. The first programme planners were severely restricted by technical considerations: early transmission of musical sounds was limited by the primitive microphone technology and, related to that, studio size. Early studio facilities were only suitable for twenty to twenty-five musicians, and station orchestras usually comprised about eighteen players;

hence, many music programmes consisted of works or arrangements that could be performed by small studio ensembles. The problem was discussed at a Control Board meeting in November 1925, when P. P. Eckersley, the Chief Engineer, referred to the necessity of either 're-orchestrating music of the big symphony type to suit . . . smaller orchestras', or finding larger spaces from which to transmit. At that meeting, Reith decisively ruled for the first option, declaring that 'a very large amount of our work should be done by Quartets and Octets, which [are] very popular and very effective'. For special programmes involving larger orchestras, either 'augmentations of the first degree' (up to 45 players) or 'augmentations of the second degree' (anything larger), he conceded that other venues could be used.[11]

The option of using outside performance spaces for special programmes, to overcome studio limitations, became available after techniques for transmitting such 'outside broadcasts' (OBs) were developed. As early as 8 January 1923, an act of Mozart's *Die Zauberflöte* was broadcast from Covent Garden; from that time, acts of operas were frequently aired. This frequency was due, in part, to Pitt's background as an opera conductor; before working for the BBC, he had directed the British National Opera Company, which performed in many opera broadcasts. Outside broadcasts of opera, as opposed to other large-scale genres, were prevalent also because managers of most other established music organizations and performance venues in London refused to cooperate with the BBC during the early years. Led by William Boosey, the managing director of Chappell and Co., the concert organizers believed that the growth of broadcasting would put agents, musicians, venue-owners and music publishers out of business. In a *Daily Telegraph* article published in May 1923, Boosey articulated these fears:

> Music is not machinery, but music by machinery threatens more and more every day to put the musician out of his profession. Those members of the public, who naturally are very glad if they can get something for nothing . . . do not realise that unfortunately in this matter-of-fact world everything has to be paid for, and that if the services of artists are not paid for, their means of livelihood is totally destroyed.[12]

Because of this attitude, the Queen's Hall – which was controlled by Chappell's and was the most important art music venue in London at the time – and artists under Boosey's management, including the Queen's Hall orchestra, were unavailable for broadcasts. Although the Royal Albert Hall was accessible, its acoustic was notoriously bad, making it undesirable for broadcasting.

The uncooperative stance of established concert organizers led the BBC to establish its own series of large-scale symphony concerts. The first took place between February and May 1924 at the Central Hall, Westminster, and consisted of six programmes. Each concert was conducted by a British conductor and conformed to a basic plan. The first half included an overture, a concerto or vocal work with orchestral accompaniment, and a major symphonic work, such as a symphony, a ballet suite or a symphonic poem. The second half included a lighter orchestral work, a group of solo pieces performed by the first-half soloist, and concluded with a rousing orchestral march or overture. The programmes included popular works from the standard repertory, such as Mozart, Glinka and Wagner overtures, excerpts from Borodin's *Prince Igor*, Beethoven and Tchaikovsky symphonies, and a Saint-Saëns violin concerto. Moreover, each programme incorporated works that had been composed during the previous 30 years: the first concert, conducted by Pitt, included D'Indy's 'Istar' Variations (1896) and the Suite from Ravel's *Ma mère l'oye* (1911); the second, directed by Sir Landon Ronald, featured Ronald's own dramatic scena, *Adonaïs* (published 1903) and Elgar's Symphony no. 2 (1911); the third concert, conducted by Eugene Goossens, was a Russian programme, with Prokofiev's Piano Concerto no. 1 (1912) and the suite from Stravinsky's *The Firebird* (1910); the fourth, led by Hamilton Harty, included Respighi's *Antiche arie e danze per liuto*, set 2 (1923); the fifth, directed by L. Stanton Jefferies, included Mackenzie's overture to *Britannia* (1894), Rachmaninov's Piano Concerto no. 2 (1901) and Dukas' *L'apprenti sorcier* (1897); and the final concert, an all-Elgar programme conducted by the composer, included the overture *Cockaigne* (1901), the 'Cello Concerto (1919) and the *Enigma Variations* (1899).

The Music Department presented its second symphony series at Covent Garden during the 1924–5 winter season. This four-concert series was more ambitious than the first and featured guest conductors of international renown. Like the previous series, the concerts presented both well-known and lesser-known orchestral works. However, the programming concept had changed: this series focused on high-quality performances of serious orchestral repertory; less attention was given to recently composed works, little time was given to popular items, and the solo group was eliminated altogether. The first programme, on 10 December 1924, was conducted by Pierre Monteux and included the Lalo 'Cello Concerto, Brahms's Haydn Variations and Strauss's *Don Juan*. On 15 January 1925, Ernest Ansermet conducted Debussy's *Prélude à l'après-midi d'un faune*, Elgar's Violin Concerto and Beethoven's Symphony no. 5. A month later, on 12 February, Bruno Walter conducted a Wagner-Berlioz concert. The series ended on 12 March with a concert devoted entirely to the first

English performance of Edgar Stillman Kelley's oratorio of 1917, *The Pilgrim's Progress*, performed by the Birmingham Symphony Orchestra and two Birmingham choruses, conducted by Joseph Lewis. Through this unusual and enterprising concert series, the Music Department expanded the scope of its programming capabilities and horizons.

In addition to the public symphony concerts, studio broadcasts of standard orchestral repertory became increasingly frequent during the early years. For example, on 26 November 1923, Pitt conducted the Augmented Wireless Orchestra in a programme including Smetana's overture to *The Bartered Bride*, Beethoven's Piano Concerto no. 3 and Schumann's Symphony no. 3 ('Rhenish'); on 19 August 1924, Pitt conducted Rachmaninov's Piano Concerto no. 2 and Beethoven's Symphony no. 2. Some broadcasts featured prominent British composers, such as that on 31 March 1925, in which Elgar conducted the Wireless Symphony Orchestra in his own works. In addition, concerts of mostly standard works, performed by Hamilton Harty and the Hallé Orchestra, were broadcast a few times a month from the Free Trade Hall in Manchester. Some continental concerts were also aired, such as the programme from Amsterdam on 2 April 1925, featuring the Concertgebouw Orchestra conducted by Willem Mengelberg.

Although programmes of opera and orchestral music were aired with increasing frequency, they were nevertheless special events in the schedules, treated as the featured programme of an evening or week and given prominent publicity. Music performed by smaller ensembles was more usual. Chamber music was easier and cheaper to transmit, and was received with better quality by listeners' wireless sets. Each week, the schedules included lighter music programmes performed by chamber groups drawn from the station ensembles (referred to as the '2LO Quartette' or the '2LO Octet' in the programme listings) or by the small station 'orchestras'. In addition, an evening programme was devoted to chamber music a few times a month. For example, on 1 October 1924, violinist Albert Sammons and pianist Ethel Hobday gave a recital including Beethoven's 'Kreutzer' Sonata, op. 47, and Grieg's Sonata, op. 13. On 8 January 1925, a chamber concert was devoted to songs and chamber music works by Gabriel Fauré, including the Piano Quartet in C minor, op. 15. Some of the chamber programmes focused on specified repertories of early music, such as the programme entitled 'Music in the Reigns of Queen Elizabeth and James I' aired on 11 December 1923, that of 31 January 1924 which explored 'Music of the XVI and XVII Centuries', or that presented by Philip Heseltine (Peter Warlock) on 12 December 1924 featuring 'Old English Ayres and Keyboard Music (1597–1622)'.

Between 1922 and 1925, each week's broadcast schedule featured only a few art music programmes. These were frequently geared to enhance the audience's knowledge of standard repertory or to present music of special historical or other notable interest; more often, though, programmes adhered to the engaged performers' suggestions. Although the Music Department produced the series of public symphony concerts in spring 1924 and winter 1924–5, these were exceptional: during the early years, art music programmes tended to be built as individual entities.

## Broadcast music talks and BBC publications

BBC audiences became familiar with art music repertory through the spoken and written word as well as through music broadcasts. The administrators recognized that the successful dissemination of art music depended not only on broadcasting high-quality performances, but also on verbal explanations. By educating listeners about basic music concepts and music history, as well as about specific works that were to be aired, the BBC hoped to encourage listeners' interest and familiarity. Verbal communication was approached in two ways: in print, through the numerous BBC publications, most notably the *Radio Times*, and over the air, through broadcast talks.

The BBC used its weekly house magazine, the *Radio Times*, as a primary means of alerting listeners to the educational, as well as entertainment, value of each week's broadcasts. In addition to the daily listings, each issue included carefully prepared articles about special programmes, as well as announcements of upcoming events and detailed notes relating to specific works. Percy Scholes, the Music Editor, was responsible for music coverage. During the early years, he provided programme notes for three or four key works in a weekly article, usually spanning two columns, called 'Pieces in the Programmes'.[13] Additional announcements about important music programmes were included on the general information pages, 'Official News and Views: Gossip about Broadcasting'. Scholes also wrote books to make music more accessible to listeners, including *Listener's History of Music* (1923) and *Everybody's Guide to Broadcast Music* (1925).

Information about music programmes was also disseminated over the air in broadcast talks. Talks on various topics were transmitted from December 1922; by October 1925, spoken programmes encompassed over a quarter of the total broadcast time.[14] The first talks about music were given by Scholes, in his role as BBC Music Critic. From July 1923, Scholes reviewed current musical events taking place in Britain and on the continent; these talks were given at first weekly and later bi-weekly. Another music appreciation enthusiast who became known for his broadcast talks was Sir Walford Davies. Davies gave his first music talk on 4 April 1924 as part of the new educational programmes intended for school children. His schools talks were so successful that in September 1925 the Programme Board decided that he should give a weekly half-hour talk about music on Tuesday evenings;[15] on 5 January 1926, Sir Walford began his extremely popular series, 'Music and the Ordinary Listener'. Both Scholes's and Davies's talks aimed to educate those whom the BBC introduced to art music; by providing basic instruction about music history, harmony, terminology and other general music subjects, these series were direct implementations of the BBC's educational policies.

Individual talks about music were also broadcast on occasion. For example, on 30 October 1923, the chamber music of Hubert Parry was performed in a special programme about the composer, which included a talk on his life and work by Sir Hugh Allen. On 28 March 1925, a lecture-recital, 'How Beethoven Made his Music', given by Percy Scholes, was broadcast from the Æolian Hall in London. However, these events were infrequent; verbal explanations of specific music programmes were not seen as necessary, since the weekly talks by Scholes were intended to introduce musical items to be broadcast during the next week. An exception to this practice was considered for programmes featuring recently composed music. In May 1925, the Programme Board agreed 'that when a performance of a new work was arranged, it would be a good thing to set aside a few minutes two or three days before such work was given, for explaining the work, its principal tunes, etc.'[16] The board apparently felt that verbal explanation would enhance the comprehensibility of contemporary music for the general public. However, the practice of scheduling explanatory talks immediately prior to musical performances was not instituted until the 1930s.

## British awareness of Second Viennese School works and ideas to 1925

At this point, the discussion should continue with an examination of the BBC's early presentations of contemporary music in broadcast programmes, with special reference to works associated with Schoenberg's circle. However before that, a brief digression is necessary, in order to examine the degree to which the music and ideas of Schoenberg and his colleagues were known in Britain before the BBC Music Department began to take interest in them.

Works from the Second Viennese School repertory were first introduced in Britain before World War I. As Appendix A demonstrates, the first presentation took place on 23 January 1912, when Richard Buhlig performed

Schoenberg's Three Piano Pieces, op. 11, at a recital in the Æolian Hall, London. Over the next 2½ years, eleven performances of seven different Schoenberg works were given in London concert halls, including five presentations of *Verklärte Nacht*, op. 4. The two most significant of these pre-war performances involved the Five Pieces for Orchestra, op. 16. At a Promenade Concert on 3 September 1912, the world première of this work was conducted by Henry Wood, and on 17 January 1914, the second British performance was given, conducted by the composer himself. The reception of Schoenberg's music in Britain during the pre-war years has received attention in a number of articles, most comprehensively by John Irving.[17] This excellent study not only discusses the early British performances of Schoenberg's works, but also documents the publicity accorded to the composer in contemporary periodicals and newspapers, from the first mention in *The Musical Times* in 1905.[18]

With the start of World War I, plans for further British performances involving Second Viennese School repertory abruptly ceased. After war was declared, German and Austrian pieces scheduled for the 1914 Promenade concerts, including Webern's Five Pieces for Orchestra, op. 10, were replaced by French or Russian works. Similarly, throughout the war the prevailing attitude against so-called 'enemy' composers prevented contemporary German music from being heard on British concert platforms.[19] Even after the war ended, anti-German feeling remained strong, as is demonstrated by the following statement made in autumn 1918 by Sir Henry Wood, who had been an advocate of contemporary German music up to 1914:

> German music is at a standstill. Outside Richard Strauss, who is a musical genius, there are no notable German composers. I consider the British School to-day far in advance of the German. Our younger school of composers are much stronger than any of the younger school of German composers . . . Germany has lived on her past tradition, and that tradition is over. I have no use for modern German music. The great masters, of course, will live for ever, and must be played.[20]

Despite the prevailing anti-German attitude, the first post-war British performance of a Schoenberg work, the London String Quartet's presentation of *Verklärte Nacht* on 27 December 1919, was so well received that it had to be repeated the following week. As the *Musical Times* critic reported:

> It was the first time, I believe, that a work of such importance by a living ex-enemy composer had been heard in a London concert hall since 1914. The result was surprising. The Sextet proved so popular as to bring an irresistible demand for its repetition on the following Saturday (January 3), when there

was another overflowing audience, the reception of the work being again enthusiastic. Obviously the intervening years have not served to change public opinion of its merit.[21]

Nevertheless, Schoenberg's music was presented only infrequently during the first half of the new decade. The first British performance of the Chamber Symphony, op. 9, was given on 6 May 1921 in a series of concerts featuring contemporary music that was organized and conducted by the composer's former pupil, Edward Clark. In November of that year another series featuring contemporary works, this time organized and conducted by the British composer, Eugene Goossens, included the first post-war performance of the Five Pieces for Orchestra. In January 1922, *Verklärte Nacht* was given once again at the Chelsea Town Hall. Much attention was given to performances of *Pierrot lunaire*, op. 21, given on 19, 20 and 21 November 1923, the first time this work was heard in Britain. The last Schoenberg performance given in the first half of the decade took place on 20 February 1924, when soprano Dorothy Moulton, a strong advocate of European and British contemporary music, joined the Hungarian String Quartet to present the String Quartet no. 2 during another Goossens chamber concert series.

Schoenberg performances were rare during this period, and works by other composers associated with the Second Viennese School circle received even less British attention: only two relevant performances have been traced. During spring 1922, Egon Wellesz visited London and gave a lecture about his music at the home of his hosts, Dorothy Moulton and her husband, Robert Mayer; to illustrate the lecture, Moulton sang some Wellesz songs.[22] On 17 October 1922, Krenek's String Quartet no. 1 was performed by the McCullagh Quartet at a concert of the newly formed London Contemporary Music Centre. Thus, in the years immediately following World War I anyone in Britain interested in becoming familiar with music of Second Viennese School composers would have been restricted to hearing a handful of works, the majority of which by Schoenberg.

Between 1911 and 1929, many avant-garde works by contemporary composers were introduced to the British public as accompaniments to performances by the Ballets Russes. Sergey Diaghilev and his troupe came to London regularly during those years, except during the war. During the 1920s, they brought works such as Stravinsky's *Pulcinella* and *Ragtime*, Prokofiev's *Chout*, Poulenc's *Les biches*, Auric's *Les fâcheux* and *Les matelots*, Satie's *Parade* and Falla's *El sombrero de tres picos* to the attention of London audiences. The conductors for the London performances included Ernest Ansermet, Adrian Boult and Edward Clark. The Ballets Russes introduced London audiences to the music of a wide variety of living composers, but none of them were associated with the Schoenbergian circle.

Although British performances of works by Schoenberg and his associates were infrequent just after the war, the activities and accomplishments of these composers could be followed in Britain through descriptions that appeared regularly in music journals. Most notably, the monthly periodical, *The Musical Times*, frequently included news about the Second Viennese School composers; in fact, from 1922, some mention of them appeared in nearly every issue. Such information was usually found in the two monthly columns devoted to international news. The first, entitled 'Music in the Foreign Press', included summaries of recent articles, announcements and reviews that originally appeared in non-British music periodicals. The featured material was compiled, translated and annotated by M.-D. Calvocoressi, who frequently included news relating to Second Viennese School composers and European performances of their works. In the other international column, entitled 'Musical Notes from Abroad', correspondents in Vienna and Berlin, Paul Bechert and Adolf Weissmann respectively, reviewed recent musical events of importance; these reports, too, frequently included the latest news about performances of works by Schoenberg, Wellesz, Pisk, Berg, Webern and other members of the circle. It is interesting to note that the Vienna correspondent, Bechert, was initially antagonistic toward Schoenberg and his associates, as can be seen in the following extract from his February 1922 report.

> Let mention quickly be made . . . of Arnold Schönberg, who is preaching musical radicalism at his newly founded Schönberg-Seminar, and himself playing the part of a musical Trotzky [*sic*] in his Society for the Promotion of Private Musical Performances, which is the stronghold of the city's musical extremists, and accessible only to the elect and initiated few.[23]

However, reports in subsequent months depict this critic's conversion into an ardent sympathizer with the creative output and goals of the circle. His personal interest in the musical activities of the group are reflected in the close attention that was paid to events relating to its members, especially when Schoenberg himself was involved. For example, the first performance of Schoenberg's Suite for Piano, op. 25, was described with enthusiasm, although identified by an incorrect opus number.

> The event of the concert was the first performance anywhere of Schönberg's new Pianoforte Suite, Op. 23, which Eduard Steuermann played with so much clarity of conception and lucidity of contrapuntal texture as to make these six pieces almost fully intelligible at first hearing. As a matter of course,

it is well-nigh impossible for the unprepared hearer to perceive much more than the principal 'voice' and a certain symmetry of sequences and imitations. The supreme freedom of Schönberg's contrapunt[al] idiom is here approached with surprising adherence to form almost in the classic sense. The six pieces of the Suite – Prelude, Gavotte, Musette, Intermezzo, Menuet, and Gigue – are clearly discernible as such in their formal architecture.[24]

Similarly, in his December 1924 column, Bechert reviewed Schoenberg's 'very latest work', the Wind Quintet, op. 26, initially comparing it to the compositional style of *Die glückliche Hand* and ending with what is apparently the earliest discussion of the 12-tone technique to be published in England:

In the first-named [*Die glückliche Hand*], it was still possible to trace his ancestry to certain composers of his day; but the Schönberg of our time follows his own path, which separates him from all who have gone before. The Schönberg of old, building upon the foundations of tradition, was a revolutionary of the means and possibilities of his age. In the Quintet he has widened the boundaries of the ground which had sufficed for others. It is the first work in which Schönberg's theory of the twelve-tone scale is convincingly worked out. What makes the twelve-tone scale a complete departure from accepted harmonic fundamentals is the fact that the twelve notes of the scale are reached not by augmentation or diminution of the familiar eight-tone scale, or by alterations of the existing chord combinations; each semitone is an independent entity by itself, and leads its own life, irrespective of its relation to chromatic neighbours. The full significance of the new twelve-tone scale is shortly to be explained by Schönberg in a book which he proposes to devote to this subject. The Quintet, it is understood, merely outlines the possibilities of the new scale, without exhausting them. In its ultimate and most logical application, the new harmonic fundament will, according to Schönberg, demand a twelve-part polyphony, whereas the present work, being scored for five instruments, permits merely a five-part polyphonic texture.[25]

Bechert continued this rather misleading introduction with a somewhat more accurate, though brief, description of how the technique is implemented and what the listener hears in the quintet. Bechert's counterpart in Germany, Weissmann, was less enthusiastic in reporting his first encounter with Schoenberg's new compositional approach. In an article printed in the November 1924 issue of *The Musical Times*, he wrote:

Schönberg's fiftieth birthday was celebrated all over Germany and Austria. His new pianoforte pieces, op. 23, were heard for the first time, and upset most of the hearers. They are an attempt to write polyphonic atonality for the pianoforte, with complete disregard of the instrument. Those who expected effects of sonority were disappointed, and probably those who could take an interest in theoretical experiments performed on the keyboard enjoyed it very much. At all events the pieces as played by Heinz Jolles – a pianist whose programmes are of unusual interest – were not well received, even by the numerous sympathetic hearers who had come to pay Schönberg their tribute of devotion.[26]

Contrary to this example, most coverage of Second Viennese School activities in *The Musical Times* during the first half of the 1920s tended to be favourable and supportive.

Other British periodicals also included relevant information about the compositional and theoretical activities of this group of composers. For example, the January 1922 issue of *Music and Letters*, then in its third year of existence, included an extensive article by the critic and writer on music, Cecil Gray, entitled 'Arnold Schönberg – A Critical Study'.[27] The author was concerned that although Schoenberg's works and ideas were being discussed and debated by musicians and critics throughout Europe, there had previously been no comprehensive English-language attempt to discuss or evaluate his artistic achievement. He aimed to fulfil this goal, providing a summary of Schoenberg's compositions to that time and describing the compositional techniques and harmonic innovations of significant works.

A British music journal that devoted much space to contemporary music discussions was *The Sackbut*, an esoteric monthly of small circulation. The journal first appeared in May 1920 and was edited during its first year by the composer, Philip Heseltine (better known as Peter Warlock), who had published his thoughts about Schoenberg's music as early as 1912.[28] He and his friend, Cecil Gray, founded *The Sackbut* 'to provide an opportunity for the free and unhampered discussion of all matters relating, directly or remotely, to music'.[29] Although no specific discussion of Second Viennese School composers appeared in the early issues of the journal, articles and editorials frequently encompassed contemporary music issues, with explicit approval of those in the advanced avant-garde, including Schoenberg. In 1921, the singer Ursula Greville took over the editorship and contemporary music remained a central focus. For example, the August 1925 issue featured an article by Paul Pisk entitled 'Post-war Tendencies in Austria', which included a discussion of works by Schoenberg, Wellesz, Berg, Webern, Krenek and Hauer.[30] Moreover, over the following two months, the journal published a broad survey of contemporary trends, with essays about compositional activities in many European countries and the USA, written by distinguished musicians. The Austrian article, contributed by Wellesz and published in German, also discussed fellow-composers in the Schoenbergian circle.[31]

In addition to coverage in British periodicals, books and music dictionaries published in London in the early years of the decade encompassed information relating to the Second Viennese School – once again, with emphasis on Schoenberg and his output.[32] Although the British public could not hear many examples of Second Viennese School works between the end of World War I and 1925, interested British musicians and music enthusiasts were able to keep in touch with the activities and ideas of this group of composers through articles and books that were easily accessible to them. Nevertheless, in the period immediately preceding BBC involvement with the music of Schoenberg and his associates, only this fraction of the British public would have known about the ideas and music of the Second Viennese School composers. With the exception of the *Pierrot lunaire* performances of 1923, which received wide coverage in the general press, significant reviews of the few other performances, as well as the reports of European activities, were confined to the specialist music journals.

## Scholes's contemporary music reviews

The BBC first introduced its listeners to the music of living continental composers through Percy Scholes's broadcast reviews. Scholes frequently discussed 'novelties' that he had heard in London concert halls or elsewhere, conforming to current critical practice for printed reviews. Included within the scope of musical novelties was any work outside the standard repertory of the day. During the interwar years, novelties received prominent attention in the press: if a programme included standard repertory works and a novelty, it was likely that the latter would be discussed extensively and the former barely mentioned. Surviving scripts of Scholes's on-air reviews show that contemporary works were treated in this way; given the orientation of the talks toward the ordinary listener, these discussions often included explanations about the works and their compositional significance.[33]

Scholes focused on contemporary trends for the first time on air in August 1923, prompted by the first meeting of the International Society for Contemporary Music (ISCM) in Salzburg. The previous summer, a pilot festival had been held, at which a variety of works by composers from Europe and North America had been presented;[34] the pilot proved so successful that the delegates met at the end to form an international society dedicated to contemporary music performance. The English critic, Edwin Evans, suggested that the central office for the organization be established at the recently formed London Contemporary Music Centre (LCMC), of which he was chairman; this was agreed.[35] Subsequently, he and Edward J. Dent drew up the society's constitution:

> We decided to make the Society a federation of national societies already existing, like the Contemporary Music Centre in London and the *Verein für Privat-Aufführungen* in Vienna; each national section would be autonomous and responsible for its own local activities and finances, but would pay an annual contribution to the central funds. Each section would send a delegate to the general council, and these would elect a jury to choose the festival programmes . . . The absolute integrity and independence of the jury was a fundamental principle . . . Each section was to be responsible for finding artists to perform whatever work might be chosen from their section; if they demanded fees, that was the section's affair.[36]

When Evans offered the use of the LCMC for the central office of the ISCM, he opened a channel between the somewhat isolated British contemporary music scene and new music trends elsewhere. Throughout the interwar period, the ISCM festivals were annual focal points for new developments in Europe and North America. With the international organization based in London, Britain was strongly represented at the festivals by composers and contemporary music enthusiasts – including BBC staff members – throughout this period; moreover, much attention was paid to the organization and its festivals by the British press and the British musical world. It is thus fitting that the first significant notice given to the subject of contemporary music over the air should relate to the first ISCM Festival.

At the 1923 festival, 35 works were performed in six concerts, given between 2 and 7 August, including the following:

Berg: String Quartet, op. 3
Schoenberg: *Das Buch der hängenden Gärten*
Krenek: String Quartet no. 3
Paul Pisk: *Zwei geistliche Lieder*
Walton: String Quartet
Kodály: Sonata for Solo 'Cello
Lord Berners: *Valses bourgeoises*
Prokofiev: *Overture on Hebrew Themes*
Hindemith: Quintet for Clarinet and Strings
Stravinsky: Three Pieces and Concertino for String Quartet
Bartók: Violin Sonata no. 2
Haba: Quartet no. 2 in Quarter-Tones
Honegger: Viola Sonata
Janáček: Violin Sonata
Busoni: *Fantasia contrappuntistica*
Ravel: Sonata for Violin and 'Cello
Milhaud: String Quartet no. 4
Poulenc: *Promenades*
Bliss: Rhapsody

This sample shows that the festival presented works from a variety of countries and compositional styles. The event received ample coverage in the British press, including a supportive concert-by-concert review by Edwin Evans in *The Musical Times*.[37]

In the weekly talk aired on 16 August 1923, Scholes used the festival as a means of introducing the topic of contemporary music to listeners.[38] After explaining the formation, aims and value of the ISCM, he approached the subject of new music in evolutionary terms, reasoning that music must by nature progress over time. He explained that current composers were 'less concerned with producing *romantic-sounding* Tone Poems or *carefully elaborated* Symphonies, than with writing music that shall be *strong in its rhythm and its harmonies*, and *very direct in its utterance*', citing Stravinsky as an example. He also compared new harmonic approaches to past practices: 'In your younger days and mine the beauty of Harmony (i.e. of the combining of notes into a chord) was supposed to lie largely in their agreeing well together, whereas now it is coming to lie in their *refusing to agree*'. Thus, Scholes was not an advocate of 'progressive' compositional methods, as he clarified in his summary:

> Though at Salzburg we have heard a great deal of poor, dull stuff, a great deal of old-fashioned stuff, and a great deal of stuff that was modern in style without being in any way valuable *per se*, yet I, for one, am glad the Salzburg Festival has been held, and is next year to be held again. The Salzburg Festival has revealed to us no new great composer, but it has given evidence of earnest work going on all over the world, and above all, has educated a certain number of intelligent listeners.

This talk would have exposed many listeners to contemporary music issues and trends for the first time. The significant number of Second Viennese works performed at the festival were not specifically alluded to, although Scholes's general grouping of some works into 'the latest and strongest brand of modernist Cayenne pepper' category may well have included the Schoenberg, Berg and Pisk pieces that were performed.

In talks Scholes gave a few months later, Schoenberg received specific attention. The performances of *Pierrot lunaire* given in London on 19, 20 and 21 November 1923, by soprano Marya Freund, reciting in French, and a group of French instrumentalists conducted by Darius Milhaud, received significant notice in the British press,[39] as well as in Scholes's broadcasts. During announcements of upcoming events on 15 November, Scholes mentioned that the first British performance of 'Schönberg's extraordinary work' was to take place;[40] he discussed the work in detail the following week.[41] He had heard the work twice, having attended the first two performances, and reviewed it relatively favourably. He described the French Pierrot character, dispelling possible confusion with the 'comic-singing Pierrot on the Pier' found at British sea-side resorts. He explained the use of

*Sprechstimme*, which he found 'by no means ineffective', and also discussed the unusual instrumentation and the nature of the accompaniment, which he described as: 'very free. Keys are not observed, nor the older harmonies. Some of the music produces a beautiful effect, other is more curious than beautiful'. His overall impression of the work was positive:

> It is at least a clever thing, but whether it is a good one, time only can show. I personally incline to the belief that the work is important as an experiment which will possibly lead to a new form of musical-dramatic art, but that it is not in itself a work which can ever attract the attention of more than a small number of keenly progressive musical people.

Other critics' reactions to the performances were more damning. For instance, Ernest Newman, of *The Sunday Times*, after studying the score extensively and attending two of the performances, gave his opinion quite baldly:

> I cannot imagine anyone who has heard the work two or three times ever wanting to hear it again: I certainly do not. Nothing more needlessly ugly and at the same time so pointless has ever been heard in London; . . . I myself have read through the 'Pierrot Lunaire' many times; indeed, to be able to submit it to *the* great test of music – running it through one's mind on one's walks – I went to the extent of committing a couple of the songs to memory. After all this trouble the music seems to me as ugly and empty as it did at first.[42]

H. C. Colles, the *Musical Times* editor, stated dismissively, 'In this music we are probably on a bypath of the art . . . The beauty of Schönberg, as a minor master, appears largely to lie in his having appreciated how unnecessary his statements would have been'.[43] In assessing Schoenberg's *Pierrot lunaire* for his listening audience, then, Scholes expressed more appreciation for the work and its compositional idiom than did his colleagues.

The next performance of a Schoenberg work in London also received notice in Scholes's talks. On 20 February 1924, the String Quartet no. 2, op. 10, was performed at the Æolian Hall, London, in a series of concerts organized by Eugene Goossens. This first post-war British performance was given by The Hungarian Quartet with English soprano, Dorothy Moulton.[44] Although Scholes's exact remarks about the performance do not survive, a marginal note on the script of his 21 February talk indicates that he did discuss it, along with first performances of works by Armstrong Gibbs and Eugene Bonner given at the same concert.[45] A review by Edwin Evans reveals that in 1924 this string quartet was not seen as a significant part of the twentieth-century canon, but as a transitional work on the way to atonality.

It is not certain that the music really deserves that such great effort should be made on its behalf, for it is in no settled style. It presents the evolution of Schönberg at the stage he had reached on the eve of launching his Op. 11 thunderbolt, not in its provisional consummation, but in a series of conic sections, of which the last suggests hyperbole. Small wonder that he had to call a halt and review his creative prospects.[46]

With the exception of one presentation of *Verklärte Nacht* in 1926, this was the last time that a Second Viennese School work was publicly performed in Britain until 1927.

## Contemporary music broadcasts

In an article that appeared in January 1924, Ernest Newman recognized the unique potential of disseminating new music over the air. Recalling the BBC's cultural-dissemination policy, he demanded that the Company include more unfamiliar works and styles in its music programmes.

> Perhaps some five or six hundred people, at the most, heard the 'Pierrot Lunaire' a few weeks ago; these people may possibly understand our critical wrangles over the work, but I fail to see how the five million other readers of the principal London papers can, or how they can be expected to be inter- ested in these wrangles. Now why cannot the B.B.C. look a little ahead on occasions of this kind, and arrange to broadcast the performance of such a work as 'Pierrot Lunaire'? There is not a music-lover from Land's End to John o'Groats who would not listen eagerly to a thing of this kind . . . It is the unfamiliar music, rather than the familiar, that the B.B.C. could at present give its subscribers with the minimum of expense (for many of these works need only a small number of performers) and the minimum of (at present) damaging comparison; and the Company would be conferring an enormous boon on hundreds of thousands of music lovers all over the country who are curious as to the latest developments in music but have no opportunity to become acquainted with them.[47]

In fact, the music programme planners did broadcast a significant amount of new music during the early years; however, only a small proportion of these works were by non-British composers. As was previously mentioned, both series of symphony concerts featured a number of recently-com- posed works by continental and American composers. On rare occasions, other early programmes included works from this repertory as well. For example, on 30 July 1924, Eugene Goossens conducted the Wireless Symphony Orchestra in an extraordinary programme entitled 'From Bach to Varese', which included the first European performance of Varèse's *Hyperprism*, as well as the 'Berceuse' from Stravinsky's *Firebird*.

Honegger's *Pacific 231*, performed by the Hallé Orchestra, was aired on 20 March 1925 in a simultaneous broadcast from Manchester. A studio piano recital transmitted on 1 April 1925 included one of Poulenc's *Trois mouvements perpetuelles* and 'Reflets dans l'eau' from Debussy's *Images*, Book 1. Moreover, on 15 June 1925, the first British performance of Gershwin's *Rhapsody in Blue* was transmitted from the Savoy Hotel with the composer at the piano. Nevertheless, most of the contemporary works that were included in BBC programmes between 1922 and 1925 were by British composers: the implementation of the cultural dissemination policy during these years had an overwhelmingly national, rather than international, orientation.[48]

The Company's interest in promoting British composers is evident from new music programmes that were broadcast during the first six months of 1924. The first of these, simultaneously broadcast from Cardiff on 20 January, featured the Cardiff Station Symphony Orchestra conducted by Oliver Raymond, performing works by Malcolm Sargent, Eugene Goossens, Herbert Howells, Holst and Joseph Holbrooke. The following month the London station launched a series of programmes that aimed to acquaint listeners with the leading British composers of the day. In the *Radio Times* article introducing the series, Scholes explained its scope.

> On Thursday [28 February 1924], the London Station inaugurates a new and interesting series of brief programmes devoted to British Composers. In time, all the living composers of standing will, I understand, be represented in this series, and in some cases they will be present in person to take part in the performance of their works.[49]

The first 'Hours with Living British Composers' concert was devoted to the Scottish composer, John McEwen.[50] The subsequent recitals were aired at approximately two-week intervals and featured works by John Ireland, Martin Shaw, Vaughan Williams, Arnold Bax, Roger Quilter, Cyril Scott and Frank Bridge respectively. Since these chamber recitals alternated with the concerts in the first symphony series, the orchestral programme devoted to Elgar's music, given on 2 May, augmented the scope of the British composers' series. Public reaction to the series was apparently mixed: the *BBC Handbook 1928* reported that the concerts 'met with a fair amount of support from the public, though it was obvious from the correspondence received at Savoy Hill that many people listening to this series were not accustomed to the modern idiom in music, or, in fact, to Chamber Music at all'.[51]

In the eighteen months following the series, programmes devoted to British works appeared only occasionally in the BBC schedules. One such programme, aired over 2LO on 11 June 1925, was called 'An Hour of First Performances of Chamber Music Works' and included recently-composed pieces by Edgar Bainton, Herbert Bedford, Alan Bush and Frederick Nicholls. Another, aired on 22 July 1925, presented the first performance of Ethel Smyth's opera *Entente cordiale*, performed by students of the Royal College of Music and conducted by the composer.[52] However, it was more usual for art music programmes to consist mostly of standard repertory, with one or two recent British works. To cite only a few examples, the Hallé Orchestra concert simultaneously broadcast from Manchester on 10 November 1924 included the first performance of Hamilton Harty's *An Irish Symphony*; on 16 January 1925, a studio chamber recital included Arnold Bax's Quintet for Oboe and Strings; and on 22 September 1925, a Wireless Symphony Orchestra concert included Harty's Piano Concerto in B minor, with the composer as soloist. In this way, between 1922 and 1925, the BBC gradually established a platform for the dissemination of contemporary British works, bringing composers and music of the nation to the attention of a larger audience than had ever been reached before.

# 4 The music programmes take shape, 1926–1927

By the BBC's fifth season, the Music Department had grown and developed under Percy Pitt's direction. Highly able and enthusiastic staff members were recruited who, like Pitt, often came from backgrounds that were unusual in comparison with other British musicians of the day. Nevertheless, these men took musical charge of what was fast becoming the nation's most powerful disseminator of art music. During the 1926–7 season, they explored and brought to fruition innovative programming ideas; from these initial experiments, the BBC music schedules evolved patterns that became characteristic by the end of the decade.

The first important addition to the Music Department team was Kenneth A. Wright. After completing an engineering degree, Wright worked for the Metropolitan-Vickers Company, one of the original firms behind the formation of the British Broadcasting Company. He became the first director of the BBC Manchester station (2ZY) in 1922 and moved to the London station (2LO) in February 1923 as Assistant Director. After he transferred to the Music Department in August 1926, he became a central figure as Pitt's assistant, substituting when the Music Director was unable to attend administrative meetings, supervising other members of the department and heading the team of music programme builders. A composer of light music whose works were frequently broadcast in the 1920s and 30s, Wright remained in the department until October 1940, when he was promoted to Overseas Music Director. A capable organizer with a strong love of music and a dedication to contemporary music, Wright held a central position within the department throughout his tenure there, maintaining a steady and experienced, yet forward-looking, influence behind the department's personnel decisions and programme plans.

In 1926 another notable figure joined the staff: Victor Hely Hutchinson was hired as a staff pianist and composer, but also assisted the music programme builders. Only twenty-five years old when he began to work for the BBC, Hely Hutchinson received much press attention as his composing and conducting talents were realized and recognized over the following years. He left the BBC later, but returned in 1944 to become Director of Music.

In January 1927, when the Company was re-organized as the British

Broadcasting Corporation, the Music Department expanded still further: Edward Clark joined the department on 4 January and was closely involved with programming decisions throughout the nine years that he worked there. He was particularly known for his promotion of new music. Like Pitt, Clark had received his training on the continent, where he was fascinated by contemporary music trends. Before World War I, he had studied first in Paris, where he fraternized with Debussy, Ravel and Roussel, and then in Berlin, where he was associated with Schoenberg and his circle. He spent much of the war in the Ruhleben Camp, but was released through the auspices of the Red Cross in 1917. Clark then assisted Ansermet and Boult with the Ballets Russes seasons in England and became friends with Diaghilev and Stravinsky. At Pitt's invitation, he joined the BBC in 1924, working initially as Music Director at the Newcastle station. When he moved to the London Music Department in 1927, his vast knowledge of music repertoire, old and new, enabled the BBC to pursue its cultural expansion policy in a way that would not have been possible had any other British person been given the job.

An article which appeared in the *Manchester Guardian* in June 1927 listed each of the music staff members, with a brief description of his BBC responsibilities.[1] Beginning with Pitt, as Music Director, the article surveyed the higher-profile staff members, mentioning in particular Sir Henry Wood, the popular conductor of the Promenade Concerts who was to make his broadcast début in August. Other conductors mentioned include B. Walton O'Donnell (leading the Wireless Military Band), John Ansell (conductor of the Wireless Orchestra) and Stanford Robinson (conductor of the Wireless Chorus). Hely Hutchinson is noted for his compositional skill, and two members of the accompanying staff are listed, Berkeley Mason and Cecil Dixon. The article is less specific about the roles of the less publicly known members of the department. Jefferies had moved to the technical side, working on the balance and control arrangements for music programmes. In addition, the article mentions Wright, although no job description is included for him, David Millar Craig, who worked in the department from April 1926 until he was appointed Music Editor of the *Radio Times* in October 1928, and Edward Clark, noted as a conductor of modern music.

The Music Department acquired one other important recruit at the end of the 1926–7 season. Julian Herbage, a specialist in English music of the seventeenth and eighteenth centuries, did some theatrical conducting before joining the BBC in June 1927, at the age of twenty-three. Herbage worked in the Music Department's programme planning section, alongside Wright and Clark. Thus, by summer 1927 the department's rapidly expanding personnel structure included a core trio of programming experts: Wright, Clark and Herbage were central to BBC music programme planning for the next nine years.

## The music programmes

The recruitment of staff who were dedicated to music programme building had significant effects on the broadcast schedules: programme planning procedures became more structured during the second half of the decade. The advancing technological possibilities of the medium and increasing sophistication of the listeners also influenced programme planning. In the early years, the somewhat haphazard method of planning art music programmes sufficed, since relatively few were aired each week. During the latter half of the decade, long-term music series appeared in the schedules with increasing frequency, structuring the programme output and enabling the department to plan ahead for high-profile events.

A number of programmes transmitted each week consisted of concerts or recitals specifically planned for the allotted broadcast time. These individual events were usually studio based, although outside broadcasts of regional orchestral concerts, operatic performances, festival concerts and the like were also aired. A few programmes from the second half of the decade, shown in Table 4.1, demonstrate the varied repertory and performers that were represented in these individually planned events. The programmes transmitted on 8 October 1926 and 3 February 1928 were typical, each a studio orchestral concert directed by a British conductor. Although a high proportion of works in such concerts was drawn from the standard repertory, the October 1926 concert presented mostly English music, including a violin concerto by the conductor, Geoffrey O'Connor-Morris, with soloist William Primrose (who still performed as a violinist at that time). Prominent foreign conductors also participated in such studio concerts; for example, the symphony programme on 30 September 1927 was conducted by Oskar Fried during his first visit to England.[2] Single-event broadcasts originating outside the studio took place when the BBC chose to transmit important public concerts, such as the first English performance of Rimsky-Korsakov's *Legend of the Invisible City of Kitezh*, broadcast in March 1926 from Covent Garden (where it was performed in concert), or that of the Berlin Philharmonic Orchestra with Furtwängler from the Queen's Hall during their London visit in December 1929. The programmers also marked significant historical events, like the centenary of Beethoven's death on 26 March 1927, with specially planned concerts; the much-publicized all-Beethoven concert was conducted by Zemlinsky

Table 4.1 *Examples of individually planned concerts and recitals broadcast between 1926 and 1929*

| date and performers | sampling of programmed works |
| --- | --- |
| **30 March 1926** (transmitted from Covent Garden, London) | |
| Albert Coates (conductor) | Rimsky-Korsakov: *Legend of the Invisible City of Kitezh* |
| **27 September 1926** | |
| Frederick Thurston (clarinet) | Brahms: Clarinet Quintet op. 115; Frank Bridge: *Idylls* for |
| Spencer Dyke Quartet | string quartet (two only); Haydn: String Quartet, op. 64 no. 5 |
| **8 October 1926** | |
| William Primrose (violin) | Wagner: Overture to *Der fliegende Holländer*; O'Connor- |
| Geoffrey O'Connor-Morris (conductor) | Morris: Violin Concerto no. 2; Butterworth: *A Shropshire* |
| Wireless Symphony Orchestra | *Lad*; Elgar: *Carillon*; Hamilton Harty: *Comedy Overture* |
| **26 March 1927** (transmitted from Bishopsgate Institute, London) | |
| Solomon (piano) | 'Beethoven centenary concert' |
| Alexander von Zemlinsky (conductor) | Overture to *Egmont*; Symphony no. 1; Overture, *Leonora* no. 3; |
| Wireless Symphony Orchestra | Piano Concerto no. 4; Symphony no. 7 |
| **30 September 1927** | |
| Walter Widdop (tenor) | Mozart: Serenade, K525 ('Eine kleine Nachtmusik'); Debussy: |
| Oskar Fried (conductor) | Prelude to *L'après-midi d'un faune*; Beethoven: Overture to |
| Wireless Symphony Orchestra and | *Coriolanus*; Delius: *Brigg Fair*; Liszt: *Faust Symphonie* |
|     Chorus | |
| **12 December 1927** | |
| Miriam Licette (soprano); Aubrey Brain | Brahms: Trio in E flat, op. 40; Mozart: arias from *Le nozze di* |
|    (horn); Arthur Catterall (violin); | *Figaro*; Schubert and Schumann: Lieder; Brahms: Sonata in A |
|    John Wills (piano) | for violin and piano, op. 100 |
| **3 February 1928** | |
| Steuermann (piano) | Weber: Overture to *Der Freischütz*; Beethoven: Piano Concerto |
| Dan Godfrey (conductor) | no. 4; Debussy: *Petite suite*; Brahms: Symphony no. 4 |
| Wireless Symphony Orchestra | |
| **14 October 1928** | |
| Vienna String Quartet | Beethoven: String Quartet in B flat major, op. 130; Brahms: |
| | String Quartet in A minor, op. 51 no. 2 |
| **18 October 1928** (transmitted from the Free Trade Hall, Manchester) | |
| Hamilton Harty (conductor) | Schubert: Symphony in C major [no. 9]; Kodály: suite from |
| Hallé Orchestra | *Háry Janos*; Wagner: 'Siegfried's Rheinfahrt' from |
| | *Götterdämmerung* and overture to *Die Meistersinger* |
| **10 November 1929** | |
| Lev Pouishnov (piano) | Works by Godovsky, Glazunov, Pouishnov, Medtner, Skryabin |
| | and Rachmaninov |
| **3 December 1929** (transmitted from Queen's Hall, London) | |
| Furtwängler (conductor) | Handel: Concerto grosso in D major; Pfitzner: three preludes |
| Berlin Philharmonic Orchestra | from *Palestrina*; Mendelssohn: Overture to *A MidSummer* |
| | *Night's Dream*; Beethoven: Symphony no. 5 |

and featured Solomon as soloist in the Fourth Piano Concerto.[3] In this way, single-event orchestral programmes ranged from unremarked studio performances led by frequently employed conductors to unusual, high-profile events featuring international artists.

Similarly, individually planned chamber concerts and solo recitals involved performances by local musicians, such as those who appeared in the concerts on 27 September 1926 and 12 December 1927, as well as artists of international renown, such as Solomon, Steuermann, Pouishnov or the Vienna String Quartet. International performers who were engaged to appear in higher-profile concerts, either instigated by the BBC or by other British concert societies, often agreed to perform in such broadcasts to make visits to England more financially advantageous. Each week's schedule included a substantial number of programmes of the single-event type, and the planning and production of these programmes involved a significant proportion of the programme planners' time.

As the decade progressed, however, music broadcasts were conceived to an increasing extent as series of symphony concerts, chamber music programmes and solo recitals, geared to explore specific repertories. By developing long-range plans, the music programme builders were able to respond to programming pressures more efficiently; moreover, the plans enabled them to apply high-level BBC policies more effectively to the music programmes. For music, the implementation of the fundamental policy of expanding listeners' tastes and cultural horizons involved two basic goals: building a basic knowledge of standard repertory for those who had little experience with art music, and expanding the repertory base for those who were familiar with standard works. In addition to opera broadcasts, which were aired frequently during the second half of the decade, the music programme builders developed distinctive series that aimed to address these objectives.

## Introducing listeners to the standard repertory canon

The programme builders approached the first goal, to give listeners a grounding in standard repertory, through series of solo and chamber music recitals. The concept was first introduced in January 1926, when they incorporated regular fifteen-minute keyboard recitals into the 2LO schedules, heard around 7.30 pm every day except Sunday. Each week's recitals were presented by a single artist, who performed works chosen from a composer's output in a given genre. In May 1926, the Programme Board decided that the scope of the recitals should be broadened to include vocal, violin and 'cello repertory.[4] In the autumn, the recitals were moved to 9.45 pm, and the *Radio Times* promoted them with prominent announcements and extensive programme notes.[5]

In January 1927, this systematic approach was formalized with the establishment of a new series, 'The Foundations of Music'. As before, short recitals were aired six nights a week, geared toward presenting works from a specific repertory; the recitals were ten minutes in length and were initially broadcast at 7.15 pm, although the exact time later varied. There was an important conceptual change from the 1926 series, as Filson Young, a music programme advisor, explained: 'These performances will not be associated with the name of any particular artist or artists. It is part of its character that the performer should be anonymous – for it is not the performer who is of importance here, but the music'.[6] The basic criterion behind the weekly repertory choice was that it fell into the category of music 'about which the most extreme schools are in agreement, about the merits of which there is no doubt whatever, and which constitutes the foundation from which the whole of modern music is derived and on which it rests'. As Young explained, the goal was to acquaint listeners with fundamental components in the art music canon.

> Those who like to cultivate the opportunities offered by the B.B.C. for enriching their store of musical knowledge and experience will find in these recitals an opportunity such as perhaps is offered, or can be offered, by no other institution in the world. The whole of classical music will, in time, be spread out before them . . . [Listeners] will thus accumulate a library of music which they have actually heard, and while they are listening to and following the most modern developments of the newest school of composers, will feel that, through the medium of this daily offering of musical incense, they are keeping in touch with the past and joining the art of to-day with the foundations on which it rests.

Early series included Bach keyboard music, Mozart, Haydn and Beethoven piano sonatas, Schumann, Brahms, Wolf, Grieg and Strauss songs, and Corelli violin sonatas.

As a verbal complement to the 'Foundations' recitals, the BBC continued to provide basic instruction about music in the regular series of talks given by Sir Walford Davies and Percy Scholes. In autumn 1926, the central administrators decided to introduce another weekly series, in which music broadcasts for the coming week would be introduced.[7] Basil Maine, the well-known music critic of *The Spectator*, was invited to give the talks, which were deemed 'most excellent' after they were initiated.[8] Moreover, music continued to be featured in the *Radio Times*. By autumn 1926, in parallel with general BBC expansion, the house journal had increased in length and sophistication. Scholes's weekly music column, 'Pieces in the

Programmes', was replaced by programme notes about significant works within the daily listings. In a column spanning two full pages near the beginning of each issue, titled 'Both Sides of the Microphone' from October 1927, catchy announcements alerted listeners to programme highlights in the following weeks, including significant music broadcasts. In addition, concert series or music-related programmes of interest occasionally received special notice through feature articles by Scholes or other notable writers on music.

## The new focus on contemporary music

Although the 'Foundations' recitals were aired from the studio, most BBC music series were transmissions of public performances. Public concerts were broadcast for three basic reasons. First, large ensembles could not fit into broadcast studios; the BBC had to transmit symphony concerts from larger halls that were acoustically improved with the presence of an audience. In addition, experience revealed that performers tended to play better before an audience than when just faced with microphones. Finally, since the fidelity of music transmissions was very limited in the 1920s, the BBC encouraged listeners to try to hear original instrumental timbres and created ways that enabled them to do so. As was explained in the 1928 handbook:

> It is commonly admitted that the standard of reproduction and transmission of speech and music in this country is the best in the world. That is to say, our listeners hear a nearer approximation to the original than is possible elsewhere. Such improvement as remains still to be made will be at the receiving end rather than the transmitting. But the B.B.C. desires it to be clearly understood that it does not wish to suggest that this approximation, however near to the original in quality, can ever replace that original . . . It is most important that the wireless listener should not confuse 'tone' as broadcast, with its original, and in order to provide him with more opportunity of hearing music as it really should be heard, the B.B.C. has organised for some seasons past important series of symphony and other concerts given in London and elsewhere, charging such prices for admission as to place the concerts within the reach of almost everyone interested in music.[9]

The BBC encouraged provincial stations to take outside broadcasts of series maintained by their regional orchestras; such transmissions were given by the Hallé Orchestra of Manchester, as well as by orchestras in Belfast, Birmingham, Liverpool, Newcastle and Glasgow. A wide range of standard orchestral works were broadcast in these series, and listeners were encouraged to attend orchestral performances in their local areas.

The most high-profile of the public concerts was a series conceived by the Music Department itself in 1926. It was designed not only to bring high-quality music into the lives of those with little previous experience of it, but also to expand the repertory base of those who might already have a basic knowledge of art music. In July 1926, the Programme Board was briefed about an ambitious series of twelve symphony concerts, which were to be presented during the 1926–7 season at the Royal Albert Hall.[10] This series, which came to be known as the National Concerts, expanded the concept of the earlier BBC public symphony series:

> These Concerts are indeed a realisation of the slogan 'Music for the Masses';
> for not only will they be broadcast simultaneously throughout the length and
> breadth of these islands, and thus be available to everyone who prefers to
> listen at his own fireside, but the Albert Hall will be thrown open at the lowest
> possible prices for those of the public who wish to attend the Concerts.[11]

The Music Department planned high-quality programmes of unusual repertory, to be executed by an orchestra of 150 players under the direction of well-known conductors. Tickets to the performances were offered to the public at affordable prices, from one to four shillings. Publicity for the series was wide-spread, ranging from notices in the *Radio Times*[12] and broadcast announcements to advertisements in buses; in addition to the London press, provincial critics were invited to attend. The enthusiastic publicity department went so far as to propose the introduction of a promotional competition, in which listeners would guess the audience attendance at each concert; however, this idea was dismissed by the Programme Board, which unanimously agreed that 'no such undignified idea should be entertained'.[13] The high value which the BBC administrators placed on the series can be inferred from the board's decision that no provincial station could programme its own symphony concerts in the same week as a National Concert.[14]

The National Concerts took place between 30 September 1926 and 7 April 1927. The programmes included a mixture of standard and contemporary works, reflecting both the interests of the programme builders and the horizon-expanding objectives of programme policy. As Nicholas Kenyon summarized:

> The first-rate programmes for these concerts clearly bear the stamp of the
> combined enthusiasms of Percy Pitt and Edward Clark. There was a
> considerable emphasis on continental music and conductors. Honegger
> came to conduct his oratorio *King David*, and his virtuoso orchestral piece
> *Pacific 231*. Richard Strauss directed his Alpine Symphony; other German
> conductors included the Director for the Leipzig Opera, Gustav Brecher, and

the young Hermann Scherchen, who brought, no doubt with Clark's encouragement, Schoenberg's *Verklärte Nacht*. From Italy there was Bernardino Molinari with music by Casella and Respighi; from France, Ansermet again, conducting Ravel as well as Balakirev and music by Ethel Smyth. English conductors were Hamilton Harty . . ., Albert Coates, Landon Ronald, and Elgar. Gustav Holst conducted the first performance of what must be one of the earliest BBC musical commissions: his choral dance *The Morning of the Year*. The series was rounded off by a Wagner programme under Siegfried Wagner.[15]

With the first series of National Concerts, the Music Department planned and presented exciting and unusual concerts, 'with the object of giving lovers of good music everywhere an opportunity to hear . . . some of the world's finest music, both classic and modern, performed by some of the most famous musicians of Great Britain and the Continent, under exceptionally favourable circumstances'.[16]

As Kenyon's summary indicates, Schoenberg was represented in this series. The seventh concert, given on 3 February 1927, was conducted by Hermann Scherchen, described in the *Radio Times* as 'one of the most energetic pioneers of new musical styles'.[17] The programme, aired from the Albert Hall, included the newly-rediscovered Beethoven overture, *Leonora* no. 2, which was inserted without notice into the programme, replacing the publicized Weber overture. In addition, a Liszt piano concerto, Beethoven's 'Eroica' Symphony, and the orchestral version of *Verklärte Nacht* were performed. This was the first performance of a Schoenberg work to be broadcast by the BBC and, given the absence of advance publicity about the Beethoven, was billed as the programme highlight in the *Radio Times*. The BBC was especially proud to point out that 'this work should sound remarkably well with the large body of string players (over one-hundred) in the National Orchestra'.[18] The programme listing included a full page of explanatory notes, the discussion of *Verklärte Nacht* providing a summary of the Richard Dehmel poem on which the music is based, and a brief stylistic explanation:

> The music of this work, however 'modern' it may at first sound to some hearers, is in reality distinctly descended from the German nineteenth-century style, and actually follows the general lines of statement, development, and recapitulation of tunes. But there are so many tunes, and their treatment is so complex, that the most experienced musician could hardly hope immediately to follow the music in detail without the score. One should, rather, try to appreciate it as a tone-picture, and as an expression of the spirit of the poem, dominated by the atmosphere of the resplendent, moonlit night.[19]

Thus, the BBC expected *Verklärte Nacht* to be somewhat jarring to the listening audience, but tried to soften the impact by placing it within a familiar musical scope. The work was not entirely unknown to British concert audiences, having received London performances in the string sextet version on five previous occasions, the most recent having taken place the previous July at the Royal College of Music.[20] After the BBC concert, the work and the performance were reviewed favourably by the press,[21] although it was felt that the Albert Hall obscured the complex counterpoint, which may also have suffered through the large size of the orchestra. Scherchen conducted the work again a few months later in a 'Light Symphony Concert' broadcast from the studio on 9 June 1927.

## BBC commissioning and the composition competition

The inclusion in the National Concerts of new works by leading continental composers was part of a larger campaign: in 1926 the BBC adopted a more aggressive attitude toward educating the listening public about contemporary music. In addition to scheduling new music broadcasts, the Company launched several projects to encourage the creation of new compositions. These strategies enabled the BBC to offer the British public the opportunity to hear compositional styles that had only rarely been accessible in Britain before then.

In January 1926, the Programme Board expressed its dissatisfaction with the small number of first performances that had been given the previous year and thought about ways in which BBC involvement with newly-composed music might be increased.[22] The board considered the possibility of commissioning new works, since the members recognized that this would 'stimulate the attention of the professional critics with a resultant increase of publicity in the newspapers'; however, Pitt worried that the size of the Company orchestras and studios would be inadequate for performing large-scale commissions. Pitt and Lewis eventually proposed that the BBC hold a festival of concerts during the first two weeks of October 1926, during which prizes would be awarded for newly-composed works in each of six categories: an overture or symphonic poem (£150), a symphony (£300), a short choral work (£250), a 'poem' for voice and orchestra (£150), a work for military band (£100) and a song cycle for voice and orchestra (£50).[23] Although no orchestration limits were specified, each contestant was required 'to provide an arrangement of his work for small orchestra suitable for broadcasting studios'. The competition was planned and sponsored jointly by the BBC and Oxford University Press, represented by Hubert J. Foss. The BBC reserved the right to broadcast the winning works free of performing right charges, and OUP retained the right to publish any of the submitted works. The entries were to be judged by some of the most eminent British composers and conductors of the day, including Elgar, Harty, Allen and McEwen; Foss and Pitt represented the interests of their respective organizations on the adjudication committee. In addition to promoting works by younger composers through the competition, the BBC planned to commission Elgar, Vaughan Williams, Holst and Moeran to write large-scale works to be first performed at the autumn festival.[24] The competition was announced and the rules laid down in the *Radio Times* of 19 March 1926; a shorter announcement was prominently displayed in the following week's issue and further clarification about the rules was included in the issue dated 9 April.[25]

During the course of the summer, the BBC apparently changed its plans with regard to the autumn music festival. By July, the administrators were no longer discussing a festival, but had shifted their focus onto the series that became the 1926–7 season of National Concerts.[26] In the *Radio Times*, the BBC announced the inclusion of these new works in the concerts:

> There will also be played four of the prize-winning works in the British Broadcasting Company's Competition for English composers. They will include the Symphony, the Choral Work, Symphonic Poem, and the Poem for Voice and Orchestra. The Song Cycle and also the Military Band Suite will be reserved for performance under other conditions which will be announced later in *The Radio Times*.
>
> Three of our most distinguished British composers will be represented by entirely new works. Holst is writing a new work specially for these National Concerts . . . and so, too are Dr. Vaughan Williams, England's 'pastoral' composer, as he has been called, and Mr. E. J. Moeran, whose work has in recent years come much to the fore.[27]

Hence, the BBC compressed into a single entity its plans for an autumn festival of new British music and for a series of quality public symphony concerts, perhaps recognizing that it could plan and promote one series more efficiently and successfully than two.

When the initial announcement appeared in the *Radio Times*, the Company obviously intended that winning works from the competition would be included in the National Concert programmes. However, when the competition results were finally publicized in the *Radio Times* of 24 December 1926, it became apparent that plans had changed once again: the BBC made the surprising announcement that no prizes were to be awarded. Of the 240 entries in the six different categories, the adjudicators

> were unanimous . . . in their conclusion that in not one of the classes was there a single work which reached the standard meriting the important

prizes offered. The judges felt that the B.B.C. would be doing harm rather than good to British music if they awarded prizes to works which did not merit them. In the circumstances, therefore, the B.B.C. have, with much regret, applied clause 6 of the rules of the competition, which confers upon the adjudicators the right to withhold the awards in the event of the MSS. falling below the required standard.[28]

The Control Board decided to return the 10s. entry fees to the applicants and to donate a quarter of the prize money to charity, in a show of good faith.[29]

Although the composition competition proved an embarrassing failure, the experience had a positive result in the sense that it drew the BBC into an active role supporting the efforts of British composers. In June 1927, Holst wrote to persuade the BBC to continue to encourage young composers in an enterprising way. In response, the board proposed that the Corporation establish a continuous competition, by which it 'might provide a permanent opportunity for the recognition, financially and by performance, of young composers' works'. Later that year, the administrators decided that notices informing composers that the BBC was willing 'to pay generously for contributions' of new works would be included periodically in the *Radio Times*.[30] Although the continuous competition idea did not materialize, the practice of soliciting newly-composed scores from composers became a fundamental part of the BBC's contemporary music scheme; in fact, during the 1930s, such a large number of scores were submitted annually that the Corporation developed regulations for submission and appointed a panel of experienced readers to ensure that the scores were evaluated fairly and efficiently.

During the 1926–7 season, the BBC administrators supported several other initiatives related to the creation of new music. As mentioned previously, the BBC planned to commission orchestral pieces from Holst, Vaughan Williams and Moeran, to be performed in the National Concert programmes.[31] In March 1926, the Programme Board also began discussing the possibility of commissioning an opera. Pitt reported on 23 March that he was in touch with Edward German, a composer renowned for his light operas;[32] since German's popular and successful works were broadcast frequently, it was not surprising that Pitt would approach him. In April, the board considered the question of the librettist, and agreed that Lewis should discuss the project with Rudyard Kipling. Apparently Kipling was not interested, since in July the Board discussed another possible librettist, A. P. Herbert.[33] In the end, the project never materialized.[34]

In its vigorous quest to promote contemporary music in 1926, the BBC adopted a role as patron, attempting to motivate the creation of new works through commissions and the composition competition. In a separate scheme, the Music Department pursued this same objective within its more usual role as impresario: the programme builders began to plan structured series of contemporary music concerts, encompassing a variety of continental composers and musical styles.

## BBC contemporary concerts

In January 1926, the managers of the New Chenil Galleries in Chelsea expressed interest in offering their venue for broadcast concerts. Reith approved the idea, and during spring 1926, many programmes were transmitted from the galleries, including a series of six chamber concerts given between 26 April and 21 June.[35] In the *Radio Times* of 26 March 1926, the BBC announced the upcoming series of 'Spring Concerts' and explained its objectives in presenting them.[36] The Company organized the concerts as a means of fulfilling its policy 'to provide opportunities for the performance of new or unfamiliar works of merit'. The programmes encompassed unfamiliar works by pre-twentieth-century composers, including Purcell, Bach, Pergolesi and Padre Martini, by European modern composers, such as Honegger, Gruenberg and Medtner, and by British modern composers, including Vaughan Williams, Lennox Berkeley, H. E. Randerson, Patrick Hadley, Rebecca Clarke, Dorothy Howell and Kenneth Wright.[37] The concerts were performed by prominent British chamber musicians. For all but the first concert, only the first halves were transmitted, a practice which disappointed the *Musical Times* reviewer, who considered it a contradiction of the Company's much-publicized cultural-expansion policy:

> The B.B.C. has lately taken to giving select chamber concerts at Chenil Galleries, broadcasting whatever it thought fit for the public ear and reserving the rest for its little gathering of intelligentsia. Thus Pergolesi's 'Stabat Mater' was the public portion at a recent concert, and some careless bright things by young moderns were kept *in camera*. It has been suggested that this was not giving the public what it wanted, nor, considering that the 'Stabat Mater' was not particularly well done, what it ought to have.[38]

Looking at the programmes, it is hardly fair to suggest that listeners were entirely deprived of contemporary works, since at least half the pieces on the transmitted portions of each concert were written by living composers. However, given the programmes for which the second halves have been reconstructed, it does seem as though a significant proportion of the second-half works were by lesser-known British composers. For example, the contemporary works in the broadcast portion of the 31 May programme were by Ravel and Arthur Bliss, while the second half consisted of works by Honegger and three British composers, Gordon Bryan, Patrick Hadley and Rebecca Clarke. Despite their stated policies, the BBC administrators may not have been convinced that the listening audience was ready for such unfamiliar material and, fearing a controversial reception, simply avoided the problem.

Even before the first series had commenced, the BBC administrators' enthusiasm for contemporary music, and the publicity that this type of programming engendered, caused them to initiate plans for a more ambitious series during the 1926–7 winter season. At a Control Board meeting, Lewis proposed that arrangements be made 'for an international series of concerts to take place in October at which some of the more important international artists would be invited to perform . . . Apart from the programme value, the Company would undoubtedly get considerable publicity from these concerts'.[39] In July, Pitt reported to the Programme Board that the programmes had been sketched out and the venue chosen.[40]

In the autumn, the BBC published a special prospectus announcing the upcoming series: six chamber concerts were to be given at the Grotrian Hall in London on the first Tuesday of each month between 5 October 1926 and 1 March 1927; part of each concert was to be broadcast.[41] This series, the first of the BBC Concerts of Contemporary Music, was arranged with the help of Hubert J. Foss of Oxford University Press, who had been involved with the composition competition and may also have assisted with the planning of the spring chamber series. Unlike the spring concerts, with their emphasis on British performers and composers, the winter 1926–7 series focused exclusively on recently-composed music from the continent, including a number of world premières and English first performances, performed by European musicians.[42] Each concert was devoted to the music of one European country, representing new works from Hungary, Italy, Germany, France, Czechoslovakia and Holland; no music from Austria was included in this series. In the prospectus, the BBC clarified its purpose in presenting music by composers unknown to British audiences and performed by unfamiliar artists.

> Each concert will be devoted to the latest phases in the musical development of one of the above-mentioned countries, and practically all the artists engaged, as well as the music itself, will be entirely new to England. In many cases, too, opportunity will be given to hear the actual first performances of works by distinguished contemporary Continental composers – performances the equivalent of which are regarded as events of considerable musical importance at the various European Festivals, e.g. Salzburg, Venice, Zürich, etc.

The BBC further justified the programmes as a necessary part of its public service:

> To us who (notoriously perhaps) stand a little outside the main currents of thought of our Continental neighbours, much of the music may appear strange. But it is that very strangeness which the B.B.C. wishes to lessen; and it feels that in giving this music a chance to be heard is to render an important service to musical England. There is a large public it believes who will be interested to follow the stream of thought in modern music. It has therefore embarked upon this new and original policy, and . . . hopes to prove that music of all kinds has as much appreciation in England as elsewhere.

The press reacted positively to the prospectus. An article announcing the series in *The Spectator*, written by Basil Maine – who was soon to begin his weekly broadcast talks on the BBC music programmes – emphasized the Company's courage and initiative in planning it.[43]

It is interesting to note the BBC administrators' reaction following the first of the concerts. At the Programme Board meeting two days after the Hungarian programme was given, Nicolls, the London Station Director, made a proposal concerning the rest of the series:

> Mr. Nicolls asked for the opinion of the Board as to whether there should not be an alternative programme on the evenings when further concerts of this series were being broadcast. It was unanimously agreed that there should be an alternative, and it was decided that these concerts should be transmitted from London and Daventry alternatively, Daventry transmitting the next concert on November 2nd. It was further decided that these concerts should not be made compulsorily S.B. to Stations.[44]

These decisions, made so quickly and decisively after the first concert, suggest that the board had misjudged the impact that the music broadcast in these programmes would have. Criticisms of the concert included points such as those expressed in the *Evening News* review, entitled '75 Minutes of Chamber Music and NO ALTERNATIVE!':

> Many listeners have commented unfavourably upon the unnecessarily heavy flavour of the first of the big National Albert Hall concerts, and, in last night's chamber music programme from the Grotrian Hall, the same mistake was made.
>
> Yet this 75-minute programme was broadcast last night from every one of the B.B.C. stations, with no alternative. . . .
>
> My strongest objection to this kind of thing is that it creates such a false impression among those who might easily learn to get far more enjoyment out of serious music than they do.
>
> It suggests that the B.B.C. are trying to force modern music down the ears

of listeners; that they are spoon-feeding them with 'cultured tastes'.

    ... With all Mozart, Haydn, and Beethoven to draw on, why try to introduce a million listeners to chamber music by way of quartets receiving their first performance in this country?[45]

Faced with such criticism, the administrators seem to have lost their conviction that 'a large public [would] be interested [in following] the stream of thought in modern music'; in fact, the measures they adopted ensured that the large public would have the option to avoid that stream. The remaining concerts in the series were transmitted alternately from 2LO and 5XX; the fourth, fifth and sixth concerts were broadcast later in the evening, with works from the second half of the programmes chosen for transmission; furthermore, the length of broadcasting time for each programme lessened as the series progressed, until only one 30-minute work was transmitted from the final concert. Thus, although the BBC continued its vigorous campaign to promote the performance of contemporary music during the following seasons, after the administrators themselves had their musical and public-relations horizons expanded during this first season of concerts, they were perhaps more wary of recommending them so whole-heartedly and uncompromisingly for all listeners.

## 5 The first wave of Second Viennese School broadcasts, 1927–1928

From 1928 the administrative side of the Music Department was reorganized frequently to accommodate growing responsibilities as the hours of transmission, technical capabilities and bureaucratic requirements of the Corporation increased. Surviving memos concerning these reorganizations provide a record of the staff members' activities, responsibilities and eccentricities, giving some idea of how programming was planned and effected at the time.

The first documented reorganization establishes the structure of the music programme building section and the varied responsibilities of its members during the 1927–8 season.[1] Wright was the Music Executive, second only to Pitt and supervisor of all details of programme building and of the department's administrative workings. His extensive duties included overseeing: publicity announcements; correspondence with artists; booking slips notifying other administrative sections of artist hire; contracts, pay sheets and weekly work records for the orchestra, military band and chorus; staff records, organisation, leave and salaries; distribution of newly submitted scores to BBC readers for assessment; music copying work and related accounts; the requests for music library acquisitions and music hire; upkeep and accounts for the department's pianos, organs, gramophones and other equipment; and, most importantly, programme building, approving all suggested and finalized programmes, serving as liaison with the Presentation Section, inspecting the *Radio Times* entries, answering questions from the Programme Correspondence Section, and reading and commenting on the weekly talks by Basil Maine, who announced upcoming music programmes, and Percy Scholes, who reviewed recent music events. Wright was assisted by Dorothy Wood with many routine administrative tasks.

Although Wright supervised the Programme Building Section, it initially functioned as an independent entity, headed by Clark and assisted by Hely Hutchinson and Herbage.[2] However, surviving papers reveal that the section was not running smoothly; in fact, during his first year in the department, Clark had proven beyond doubt that he was unsuited to many of the tasks for which he was responsible. In January 1928, Wright finally made a formal complaint to the Music Director. He was deeply troubled by the lack of efficiency in the programme building section, denouncing Clark's haphazard approach.

> Our programmes are always late; Herbage tries his best to put them up but over Chamber Music particularly he is hampered constantly by Clark's habit of half doing jobs by telephone, never confirming them by letter or passing on enough evidence to Herbage to complete the routine side of it . . . A case in point yesterday was the Chamber programme for February 5th. It was not available and was going to press within a few hours. Clark had at least three weeks to think about it.[3]

Moreover, he had serious reservations about Clark's conducting.

> So far as his conducting is concerned, I think you saw that he did not make a marvellous job of the Stravinsky, and certainly Kelley and others have the impression that Stravinsky was very irritated by the amount of time wasted by Clark at the rehearsals. He apparently had to put Clark right very frequently. The same applies to the Bartok. Naturally all this extra rehearsal results in additional expense for orchestra etc.
>
> A further point with Clark is that I think his general 'haziness' of mind is reflected in his conducting in that he never will get that keen clear contact with his orchestra that he is so often discussing. With yourself, for instance, and people like Harty and Ansermet they start off on time with a very clear conception of what they want and no time is wasted. With Clark it takes with his own confession about half a rehearsal to get this 'psychological contact'.[4]

Wright concluded that Clark should no longer be encouraged to conduct for the Corporation or serve as translator to eminent artists who participated in BBC programmes, since he was unable to handle these tasks effectively. In short, Wright believed that Clark's 'personal friendship with and extraordinary adoration of these people [i.e. visiting artists] is a deterrent rather than a help'. Instead of hindering rehearsals through bad conducting and poor translating, Clark should 'buckle down to this programme job and make a much better thing of it'.

Pitt apparently agreed that it was time to sort out the music programme building mess. In February, Wright informed Clark that 'the organisation of your little programme building section is coming under discussion pretty soon'.[5] Throughout March, Wright and the central administrators considered reorganization options.[6] Significantly, C. G. Graves, assistant to the Assistant Controller (Programmes), recognized that 'Mr Clark possesses many admirable qualities . . . His chief fault is that he is not used to routine work and will probably never be any good at it. . . . His incapacity undoubtedly means that more falls on to other people'.[7] This recognition of Clark's talents was reflected in the revised structure of the Music Department.

Under the new scheme, Wright took over Clark's administrative duties, interpreting and implementing the policies and decisions of the

Programme Board and managing the routine details of programming decisions. Herbage was Wright's chief administrative assistant in the section, booking artists, confirming that materials were available and properly timed, checking that the *Radio Times* entries were correct, arranging rehearsals and sound checks, etc. Hely Hutchinson planned the daily 'Foundation of Music' recitals, did research for features programmes, performed as staff accompanist and coach, assisted Sir Walford Davies, did some choral conducting and evaluated submitted manuscripts of lighter music. Millar Craig prepared for Music Advisory Committee meetings, provided translations of texts when required, and did general research work. In June 1928 the group gained a new member: Owen Mase had joined the BBC in 1927 as an accompanist, but transferred into programme planning to provide further administrative assistance.

Relieved of all administrative duties, Clark became the specialist programme builder, providing Wright with ideas for chamber recitals, contemporary music programmes, orchestral features, symphony concerts, and an overview of the next season's programmes. He conducted some orchestral programmes and continued to act as host to visiting artists who were friends of his, such as Stravinsky and Ansermet; however, he was formally prohibited from translating 'at these gentlemen's rehearsals . . . as he is most ineffective in this capacity'.[8] Clark also reported on recent English, American and foreign-language articles and books on music to keep the department up-to-date with the latest ideas and trends, particularly in new music.

Wright clearly defined the boundaries of Clark's responsibilities. He was to specialize exclusively in creative duties, dropping 'responsibility for programmes as a whole and . . . generally giving ideas without undertaking any bookings etc. or commitments of any kind for such special programmes as orchestral features, symphony concerts, international concerts'.[9] Although Clark would make programming suggestions, Wright demanded 'the power of veto' over them; moreover, Wright strictly prohibited him from authorizing bookings:

> So far as executive work is concerned I want you to handle as little as you possibly can. In chamber music work by all means discuss with the artists you want the type of programmes etc. but in no case commit yourself to a booking or even promise a booking except going so far occasionally as to say 'will you just pencil the date', and then get Herbage to requisition the booking. In all such programmes please keep in the closest possible touch with me not only because of the programme aspect but also because of the money allowance.[10]

The spring 1928 restructuring was significant in that Clark's inability to perform routine administrative duties was recognized by BBC administrators; in finding a solution to this problem, the administrators distinguished between creative and administrative tasks for the first time, a distinction that was to become fundamental to large-scale BBC structuring in the 1930s. Clark's supervisors were unhappy that his lack of administrative skills and his disregard of bureaucratic procedures necessitated that an additional staff member – Mase – be hired to make up for his deficiencies. Despite this expensive inconvenience, however, Clark was valued for his extensive knowledge of music repertory and for his passionate interest and expertise in contemporary music. In March 1928, Graves commented,

> It seems a pity that because of a man's administrative inability we have to take on an extra person, but I imagine it is very much the exception to find a musical specialist who does combine administrative talent with creative powers. Myself, I am quite convinced that Edward is too good a man to lose and I think if he worked along-side Wright in the manner suggested, and his undoubted talents are exploited to the full, we shall get very valuable work out of him.[11]

In June, R. H. Eckersley, the Assistant Controller (Programmes), further affirmed the degree to which Clark's contribution to programmes was respected and appreciated:

> Taking a close view of the matter all round, I would recommend a small increase in [Clark's] salary as an appreciation of the help he has been to us musically during the past year and as an earnest of our endeavour to use him to the best possible advantage in the future.[12]

Thus, the 1928 reorganization resulted not only in an enlargement of the music programme planning section, but also in greater specialization of individual duties: responsibilities for planning and producing specific types of art music programmes were assigned to each staff member. Moreover, tighter central control over the section was effected by shifting the authority for programming decisions from Clark to Wright.

## Educating listeners about art music

The expansion of the music department staff in 1927–8 directly paralleled the increasing number, complexity and profile of the BBC music programmes. One of the most significant growth spurts occurred in 1927, when the BBC took over the popular Promenade Concerts, a long-standing public concert series with a performance tradition that was entirely consistent with Reith's educational aims. Founded in 1895, the Proms encouraged 'the creation of a public for classical and modern music'[13] in London long before the BBC pledged to achieve similar goals through broadcasting. This annual festival took place each summer at the Queen's Hall and was managed and backed by William Boosey of Chappell and Co., the lessee of the hall. In March 1927, shortly after the death of the Proms's founder, Robert Newman, Chappell's announced that both the hall and the Proms were threatened by financial collapse. The Royal Philharmonic Society considered saving these vital British institutions, but in fact did not have the financial clout to do so. In a move that marked a significant turning point in British broadcasting history, the BBC did what the musical establishment was unable to do: Reith negotiated with Boosey to take over the Proms. Moreover, he arranged that BBC broadcasts would take place from the previously unavailable, but highly desirable, Queen's Hall, and that the BBC would employ Chappell-controlled artists, such as Sir Henry Wood, who had been prohibited from broadcasting before then.[14] In fact, Sir Henry chose to abandon his previous arrangement with Boosey and became a BBC conductor, initially with a three-year contract.[15]

The first BBC Promenade season took place between 13 August and 24 September 1927. Wood continued as the conductor and concerts were given six nights a week, following Proms tradition. The Queen's Hall arena was still given over to the 'Promenaders', who stood during the concerts, and programming conventions were upheld:

> Wisely, as the event proved, the B.B.C. made no change in the policy which had hitherto guided the concerts: Mondays were, as for years past, 'Wagner Nights', Tuesdays were mainly devoted to Haydn and Mozart, and Friday relied mainly on Beethoven and other classical masters. The great Bach's name stood almost alone on three of the Wednesday programmes, as well as appearing in several others, the end of the programme being given in each case to more modern music, as time-honoured custom ordains.[16]

The presentation of contemporary music included British premières of works by continental composers; nevertheless, the emphasis was clearly placed on recent works by British composers.[17] Part of most concerts was broadcast over the 2LO/5XX or 5GB wavelengths; since the modern works tended to fall later in the programmes, they were often not transmitted. Under the BBC, the Promenade Concerts remained the centre of summer musical activities in London – both in the concert hall and over the air – throughout the interwar years, and in fact continue to fulfil that function to the present day.[18]

As part of the negotiations which led to the BBC take-over of the Proms, the BBC arranged to base the 1927–8 series of National Concerts at the Queen's Hall.[19] Encouraged by the success of the first series, the programme planners expanded the second season to twenty concerts, presented at the prime time of 8.00 pm on Friday nights. The majority of the concerts were performed at the Queen's Hall, though eight were given at the People's Palace in east London. As before, the series was designed to familiarize listeners with large-scale orchestral works; the BBC was satisfied that the new venue arrangements helped to further this goal:

> Performers and audiences alike have hailed with real gratification the change of venue to the Queen's Hall. For generations past the real hub of London's musical activities, the hall has demonstrated, since it opened its doors to the microphone, that it is almost ideally suited for the broadcasting of music in the larger forms, as well as for presenting it to the hearer within its walls. But, with a view to casting their net over an even wider area, the National Concerts of this season are being given partly in the East End, in the People's Palace. The best Symphony Orchestra which can be gathered together, and a number of the most distinguished conductors and artists of the day, are visiting the eastern part of London, in the hope of spreading there also an interest in, and a love for, all that is best in the realm of orchestral music.[20]

Minutes from BBC publicity committee meetings reveal that with these east-end concerts, the BBC specifically aimed to cultivate Jewish audiences.[21] However, in the event, the People's Palace concerts were not as well-attended as the administrators expected them to be, perhaps because the targeted audience would have been otherwise engaged on Friday nights.

Unlike the first series with its international emphasis, the second season of National Concerts focused on British artists and compositions. The programmes were conducted almost entirely by British conductors, including Henry Wood, Landon Ronald, Hamilton Harty, Elgar, Geoffrey Toye, Malcolm Sargent and Pitt;[22] the one exception was the concert on 27 January 1928, in which Schoenberg's *Gurrelieder* was performed, conducted by the composer. Although the *Gurrelieder* was the most ambitious piece of the season, it was not the only work of a continental composer to be performed for the first time in England: Janáček's *Sinfonietta*, Marcel Labey's *Ouverture pour un drame* and Bloch's 'Israel' Symphony were also included in the programmes. However, contemporary music was represented most significantly through British works. The programmes included frequently performed British pieces, such as Butterworth's *A Shropshire Lad*, Delius's *Brigg Fair* and those given at the popular all-Elgar concert; moreover, British novelties were performed, including Edward

Mitchell's *Fantasy Overture*, Stanford's Symphony no. 5 ('L'allegro ed il penseroso') and *First Irish Rhapsody*, Frank Bridge's *The Sea*, Sam Hartley Braithwaite's *Snow Picture*, Moeran's *In the Mountain Country* and Edward German's incidental music to Shakespeare's *Henry VIII*.

The National Concerts included works by living British and continental composers, but in fact the majority of programme time was devoted to music of Wagner, Berlioz, Beethoven, Schumann, Bach, Tchaikovsky, Mendelssohn, Saint-Saëns and Verdi, among others. Since the programme planners expected the People's Palace concerts to be attended by a less-sophisticated audience, a high proportion of the programmes given there consisted of eighteenth and nineteenth-century orchestral standards, with a few British works included to cultivate appreciation for national art; the less-familiar repertory mentioned above was performed at the Queen's Hall concerts.

Insight into what comprised 'standard' repertory at that time in Britain may be discerned from the introductory article in the concert programmes.[23] It first explained the BBC's long-term goal behind the concerts in terms of the fundamental cultural-expansion policy: 'Like all who have the best interests at heart, the B.B.C. is firmly convinced of the truth of the famous dictum, that "the best music is necessary and most popular" if only it be adequately presented'. The notion of popularizing art music led directly to justifying repertory choice: 'The compilers of the programmes for these National Concerts have had no hesitation in including a good deal of music which the unthinking man-in-the-street has hitherto regarded as "severe"'. It might be expected that this 'severe' music referred to the unfamiliar contemporary works, such as Schoenberg's *Gurrelieder*; however, the writer continues:

> Time was, and not very long ago either, when no popular programme would have dared to include the name of the great Bach, the greatest of all masters of music. To the uninitiated the very name was terrifying, and there were even musicians who professed to find his music intellectual and scholarly rather than melodious. For some years now, however, the Promenade Concerts have made it abundantly clear to their own adherents, and the first season of B.B.C. Promenade Concerts to an enormously wider audience, that much of the great Bach's music is full of all those joyous qualities of melody, brightness, and even fun, which make it truly popular . . .
>
> Though probably not to the same extent, Beethoven's name was also apt to sound somewhat austere to the ears of the uninitiated. But his music, too, is becoming steadily more 'popular' in the real sense of the word, as opportunities for hearing it well performed increase. Even the last of his great Symphonies, the Ninth, admittedly the most difficult to appreciate at its real

worth, will inevitably be enjoyed by British audiences, as it already is in its native country, when it is better known.

Thus, even after five years of broadcasting, the BBC entreated the ordinary listener to accept the music of Bach, and even Beethoven. Within this context, Schoenberg's *Gurrelieder* must have seemed very 'severe' indeed.

As a complement to raising public consciousness of art music through high-profile series, such as the National Concerts and the Proms, the BBC began to publish articles which provided general background information for the less musically educated listener. In autumn 1927, C. Whitaker-Wilson contributed articles on well-known composers, such as Mozart, Gluck and Tchaikovsky, in the series 'The Man Behind the Music'.[24] These were designed 'to give a brief but vivid impression of the lives of musical geniuses and so to provide a simply-designed background to their work'. Several months later, in response to public demand, the BBC issued a further series of five lengthy articles, each by a prominent critic, who explained what audiences should listen for when hearing orchestral, vocal, violin, piano and choral music, respectively.[25] In April 1928, another important series of music appreciation articles was launched, entitled 'A Miniature History of Music'; in this seven-part series, Scholes provided a brief introduction to music history and art music genres.[26] Perhaps the most exceptional aid for the listener appeared in the *Radio Times* issue of 22 November 1929, which included a short dictionary of common musical terms.[27] Thus, through articles, programme notes and announcements, the BBC strove to cultivate interest in its art music programmes and to provide basic information, so that the uninformed listener would have a foundation for comprehending them.

## Contemporary music programming

Although the Proms and the second series of National Concerts emphasized the performance of new British music, the BBC developed other outlets to expand listeners' knowledge and awareness of both British and continental contemporary trends. It is interesting to note that the BBC administrators encouraged the Music Department to be in touch with the latest continental developments by providing Clark with the financial means to attend the ISCM Festivals, the annual showcases for contemporary music.[28] Throughout the season, the BBC aired recently-composed works representing different compositional styles in both individually-planned programmes and concert series. For example, Stravinsky and Bartók both visited London during the season. Bartók toured Britain in autumn 1927 and took part in BBC broadcasts on 9 and 19 October.[29] Stravinsky was the soloist in the first English performance of his Concerto for Piano and Winds, performed in a broadcast concert devoted to his works on 19 June 1927. He returned to London during October to make piano rolls, and attended performances of his works by the BBC. He returned again to conduct two broadcasts of *Oedipus Rex* on 12 and 13 May 1928. Prokofiev also took part in BBC broadcasts that season: on 9 December Ansermet conducted the Wireless Symphony Orchestra in a programme which included the orchestral version of the March and Scherzo from *The Love for Three Oranges* and the first English performance of the Piano Concerto no. 2, with the composer as soloist, as well as Stravinsky's *Fireworks* and Ravel's *La valse*. A few days before that, Prokofiev also performed in a chamber recital featuring several of his works.[30] Similarly, concerts of works by British composers were sometimes planned as individual events. Arnold Bax, in particular, was heralded throughout the season as a young British composer of distinction, and several concerts devoted to his works were aired.[31] At the time, Bax was establishing his reputation, and critics tried to place his music within the new-music spectrum of the day:

> This composer occupies a somewhat peculiar position. He is an ultra-modernist, it is true, but not of the flagrant variety. His work, though sometimes extreme, is usually controlled to reasonableness. His big reputation is deserved; and although one cannot always see mind to mind with him, one cannot help being impressed by the genuine and individual nature of his rich gifts.[32]

In its single-event programmes, the Music Department kept listeners up-to-date with music of British avant-garde composers, as well as continental activists.

Most important broadcasts of contemporary works, however, were planned within concert series. During spring 1928, the BBC initiated a series entitled 'New Friends in Music', broadcast over 5GB and consisting of hour-long recitals of piano works by a single composer. Although no documents survive about the planning of this series, it was developed as a strategy to increase the palatability of new music for listeners 'who did not know [the composers] or only knew [them] imperfectly'.[33] The first programme focused on Debussy and was introduced in the previous week's *Radio Times* with a full page of explanatory notes;[34] the concert itself, aired on 21 February, was given as a lecture recital, with Percy Scholes introducing pieces that were subsequently performed. The second concert, devoted to the music of John Ireland, took place on 7 March and received less publicity. The series was given a positive reception in the music press. For example, the broadcasting reviewer in *The Musical Times* recognized the value of presenting newer music within a lecture-recital format:

> When the introduction of new music fails, it is usually because the novelty is
> shot at us (often without preparation), and then heard no more – or, at all
> events, not for a long time. A work that is discussed and explained *briefly*
> (this word is important) at its first hearing, and then given again a week or so
> later, may be counted upon to hit the mark if it is anything of a mark-hitter at
> all.[35]

Nevertheless, the 'New Friends in Music' series lost momentum after the Ireland programme. The third concert was given only after a considerable break, on 31 May, and featured Ravel. The final concert took place on 25 June and was devoted to piano music by Bax.

### Broadcasts of Second Viennese School works

The most important contemporary music programmes of the season were broadcast within the second series of BBC Concerts of Contemporary Music. In these remarkable concerts, and in other broadcasts that season, pieces by members of the Second Viennese circle were heard by British mass audiences for the first time. Of the eight concerts in the series, no fewer than six included works by composers associated with the Schoenbergian circle. Artists brought from the continent to participate in these special concerts also performed works by Schoenberg and his associates in studio recitals.[36]

The second series of BBC Concerts of Contemporary Music took place monthly between 3 October 1927 and 7 May 1928. The concerts represented those composers who were acclaimed on the continent for their innovative, and in some cases controversial, styles.[37] The series did not receive special promotion in the *Radio Times* prior to the first concert in October; however, the *BBC Handbook 1928*, which was published shortly before the second concert, included a discussion of the objectives behind the choice of works. The programme builders resolved that listeners should become familiar with leading composers of the day:

> The special 'International' series it is hoped will succeed in giving a picture of
> what is most valuable in present-day Chamber Music of all countries. It is
> felt that the movement turns round two axes, namely, Schönberg and
> Stravinsky. The Chamber Music of these two composers is very little known
> in England and is represented by key works which are likely to lead to keener
> appreciation of the masters in question.[38]

In addition to Stravinsky and Schoenberg, works by other prominent continental composers were featured in the programmes, including Webern, Bartók, Prokofiev, Schulhoff, Szymanowski, Eisler, Krenek and Hindemith, as well as Honegger, Milhaud and other Les Six composers.

Unlike the first series of contemporary concerts, in which each programme focused on recent music from one country, concerts in the second series consisted of a mixture of composers and styles. Moreover, the recitals were given as studio performances, rather than as public concerts; critics, however, were invited to attend: 'By way of a particularly graceful implicit acknowledgment that broadcasting does not as yet compensate for a direct hearing, the B.B.C. now issues a limited number of invitations to their studios on these occasions.'[39] With few exceptions, the entire programme for each concert was broadcast. The first two concerts were transmitted over the 2LO and 5XX wavelengths; the remaining concerts were broadcast over the alternative wavelength, 5GB, perhaps in response to unfavourable public reaction. The programmes were performed by eminent continental artists, two of whom – Ervín Schulhoff and the Amar-Hindemith String Quartet – had taken part in the previous series; others, including Ansermet, Steuermann and the Vienna String Quartet, had performed for the BBC on other occasions, but were participating in the contemporary music series for the first time.

The first concert in the series was presented by the Vienna String Quartet (later known as the Kolisch Quartet). This ensemble was led by the left-handed violinist Rudolf Kolisch, a pupil of Schoenberg between 1919 and 1922 and the composer's brother-in-law. The quartet was closely associated with the Second Viennese circle and presented many first performances of works by its composing members. Although Pitt was in touch with the group as early as April 1925, concerning fee negotiations for BBC performances,[40] the quartet did not perform regularly for the BBC, or in Britain in general, until the 1927–8 season. The recital on 3 October 1927 included three works by Second Viennese School composers: Schoenberg's String Quartet no. 1, op. 7, Webern's Five Pieces for String Quartet, op. 5 – the first Webern work to be broadcast by the BBC – and the Duo for Violin and 'Cello, op. 7, by Hanns Eisler, a pupil of Schoenberg and Webern who later became an ardent Marxist composer. Surprisingly, the Music Department did not use the *Radio Times* to prepare listeners for the unusual repertory.

Press reception of the concert was favourable, the early Schoenberg and Webern pieces, in particular, positively reviewed. In *The Musical Times*, Eric Blom recognized the transitional nature of the Schoenberg quartet:

The astonishing art and versatility of its writing, and the impassioned beauty of much of the music, grip the hearer and although the work plays for about forty-five minutes without a break, it holds the attention throughout and satisfies both intellectually and emotionally, in spite of the fact that it does not convey an impression of being the last word in the old quartet manner or the first in a new one.[41]

Moreover, he observed the innovative process behind the Webern pieces, which he described as 'decomposition', and was intrigued by the composer's string writing, which he found to be 'not only arresting by its novelty and its wealth of curious effects, but satisfying by reason of Webern's immediate success in handling his medium in a new way that matches the newness of his conceptions'.

In contrast to the positive press response, the programme received a mixed reaction from listeners. The large postbag relating to the concert prompted the BBC to publish a statement in the *Radio Times*, defending new music policies and reminding dissatisfied listeners about the recently-introduced alternative wavelength:

> If the letters of various correspondents are to be taken as an indication of the general opinion, the recent short recital of modern music given . . . by the Vienna String Quartet met with a very mixed reception from listeners . . . One man's meat is proverbially another man's poison – and early Schonberg, it must be admitted, is strongish meat for musical vegetarians to swallow. Those of poor digestion could, however, seek refuge in the alternative programme. There must have been many anxious to get to grips with and understand the new tendencies in music who listened with interest to the whole recital.[42]

The notice also revealed the interesting fact that Stravinsky was present in the studio during the Vienna String Quartet performance.

The fourth concert in the series took place on 9 January 1928. For this programme, Ansermet and a chamber orchestra presented Schoenberg's Chamber Symphony no. 1, as well as Schulhoff's Piano Concerto, Milhaud's *La création du monde* and Stravinsky's Octet. This time, the *Radio Times* provided explanatory notes. Those for the Chamber Symphony used the stylistic standard established by *Verklärte Nacht* to prepare the audience for this somewhat later work:

> Many listeners have already heard some of Schönberg's earlier music, his Sextet . . . having been broadcast a few months ago.
> This *Chamber Symphony*, his Op. 9, dates from 1906 . . . and goes a little farther in modernism than does that tuneful and romantic work . . .
> All that one can expect to get at one sitting is some sense of the music's

moods, perhaps a hint or two of its logical bases, and an idea as to the composer's power of persuading us that he has his goal clearly in sight all the time – and that it is worth the journey to it.[43]

Although the chamber symphony had been performed previously in Britain, this was the first time that it was broadcast, and it was also the first time that a piece dating from after the composer's early, romantic period was transmitted.[44] Although the concert did not receive much critical attention in the press, the performance of the chamber symphony, with its dense texture and dissonant harmonic language, drew initial rumblings about stylistic incomprehensibility.[45] For example, the wireless critic for *The Musical Times* objected to its complexity, although he acknowledged that 'it had some beautiful stuff in it – beautiful in the normal musical way, I mean, for the work was written over twenty years ago, before the composer took the wrong turning'.[46]

Broadcasts of Schoenberg's music continued during the following month. The first work involving the 12-tone technique to be performed both by the BBC and in Britain was heard as part of the 'Foundations of Music' series. The recitals for the week of 30 January to 4 February 1928 were performed by the Polish pianist, Edward Steuermann. Formerly a pupil of Busoni and Schoenberg – his studies with the latter as a fellow-pupil of Edward Clark – Steuermann was a vital figure in the Second Viennese School circle, participating in many first and subsequent performances of Schoenberg, Berg and Webern works. In his group of 'Foundations' recitals, he performed modern piano works of Busoni, Scriabin, Schoenberg, Satie, Reger and Debussy. Although a memo from Hely Hutchinson to Clark dated 31 December 1927 confirms that the Music Department plan for the week had included Steuermann as the 'Foundations' soloist,[47] the *Radio Times* listings for the week announced, instead, that Mrs Norman O'Neill would play 'Modern French Piano Music'.[48] On 26 January 1928, a special memo was circulated to the announcers advising that the change to the printed listings be widely publicized:

> As Mrs. Norman O'Neill's name already appears in the Radio Times it is desirable that as much publicity as possible should be given to the change, and the line we wish to take is that we have been able to get Steuermann as a special treat for listeners and we have, therefore, arranged for Mrs. Norman O'Neill's series of recitals to be postponed.[49]

As part of the 'special treat', Steuermann performed Schoenberg's Suite for Piano, op. 25; originally scheduled for 30 January, the performance of the suite was in fact broadcast on 1 February.[50] This historic event apparently passed unremarked.

Two weeks after this recital, the Vienna String Quartet returned to perform in the fifth of the BBC Concerts of Contemporary Music. Special notice was given in the *Radio Times*, due to the inclusion not only of Schoenberg's String Quartet no. 3, op. 30, written the previous year, but also of Berg's *Lyric Suite* – by far the most radical programme the Music Department had yet planned. Although warning that the programme would be 'distinctly "modern"', the notice reassured listeners, rather misleadingly, that 'the recital on the 13th will be interesting and amusing without being particularly "difficult"'.[51] The notice continued with introductory remarks about Berg, focusing primarily on the formal innovations he had used in *Wozzeck*; Berg's music was virtually unknown in Britain in 1928, since no work of his had yet received a public British performance. Unfortunately, Berg did not become better known on this occasion, since the *Lyric Suite* was not broadcast during the 13 February concert; no surviving documents reveal why the work was suppressed. The broadcast, scheduled for the late hour of 10.15 pm, although it was actually transmitted even later, included only songs by Les Six composers, sung by Claire Croiza, and the Schoenberg quartet.[52] It is interesting to note that the *Lyric Suite* was apparently performed for the small number of critics who had been invited to hear the concert from the studio. The *Musical Opinion* reviewer mentioned the Berg in his review of the concert;[53] moreover, Ernest Newman discussed the work and his general impressions of the concert in eloquent detail.

> The Alban Berg Lyrical Suite (for four strings, played by the Vienna String Quartet) was apparently thought too risky to be broadcast, while Schönberg's third quartet (Op. 30, 1927) was timed to begin at the safe hour of 10.40. As a matter of fact, it began, owing to the delay in completing another transmission, very much later . . . For my part, a curious nervous feeling stole over me as the night wore on. The secrecy and the strangeness of the proceedings seemed to imply something, if not shameful, at least dangerous for us. Here we were, a mere handful of us, hushed and hidden in a padded chamber in a big building in a very quiet part of London, assisting at a mysterious musical rite. I thought of the early Christians resorting to the Catacombs as the only safe place for the exercise of their frowned-upon religion, and I could not repress the fear that the brutal minions of the musical law might suddenly break in on us and arrest us all for indulging in practices that were against the public interest. It would no doubt be useless for some of us to plead, if we were thus raided, that we were not willing participants in the horrid rites, but, strictly speaking the shuddering sacrifices. For we suffered acutely, especially during the Lyrical Suite. Both in this work and in the Schönberg there was so little that was music according to the most liberal definition of the term as we conceive it.[54]

The BBC's pre-concert enthusiasm in introducing the Berg and Schoenberg quartets to the British audience was subsequently diminished into a hushed, partly censored event, transmitted at a time when many listeners would be asleep and only fully accessible to a handful of curious critics. The initial concept behind the concert was thus thwarted by BBC alterations to the broadcast schedule. It is unfortunate that the papers concerning this decision do not survive, as it would be very interesting to see who initiated the change and what provoked that person to do so.

The sixth concert in the BBC contemporary music series on 5 March also included Second Viennese School works. The programme consisted of music for various chamber ensembles, solo piano and voice by Hindemith, Jarnach, Webern, Honegger, Eisler and Prokofiev. It was performed by British instrumentalists and the German soprano Margot Hinnenberg-Lefèbre. Hinnenberg-Lefèbre had become associated with the Second Viennese circle in 1926, when she participated in several continental performances of Schoenberg's String Quartet no. 2 with the Vienna String Quartet. She first performed for the BBC on the night before her appearance in the contemporary music concert, singing Schoenberg's op. 2 songs, 'Erwartung', 'Schenk mir deinen goldenen Kamm', 'Erhebung' and 'Waldsonne'. On 5 March, she sang six of Webern's Stefan George Lieder, from op. 3 and op. 4, and a work by Eisler entitled *Zeitungsausschnitte*. Another Schoenberg performance was broadcast later that same month: on 28 March, the Catterall String Quartet, a British ensemble, broadcast *Verklärte Nacht* in the original sextet version from Manchester. Moreover, the Schoenberg song, 'Schenk mir deinen goldenen Kamm', from op. 2, received another broadcast during the next month: on 27 April, the British soprano, Kathleen Mitchell, sang it in an afternoon recital of piano music and songs.

On 7 May, Steuermann returned to the BBC to perform in the final concert of the contemporary chamber music series.[55] The request to book Steuermann for this concert was made on 29 March, at which time Clark suggested that the artist be asked to perform solo piano works by Schoenberg and Busoni; however, Clark was still trying to finalize the programme on 20 April, when he sent a telegram to the artist urgently requesting confirmation.[56] In the end, Steuermann shared the concert with the Amar-Hindemith String Quartet, and the programme included works by Bartók, Schoenberg, Hindemith and Busoni. In addition to two Busoni Sonatinas, the pianist played Schoenberg's Piano Pieces, op. 11, and what was listed in the *Radio Times* as Schoenberg's 'Five Little Piano Pieces', op. 19, although all six of the op. 19 pieces were aired.[57] The quartet was scheduled to finish with Hindemith's Six Pieces for String Quartet, op. 44, but this work was not broadcast. Once again the *Musical Opinion* critic mentioned the work in his review,[58] indicating that it was played for the invited studio audience only.

The 7 May contemporary music concert was the last broadcast of the 1927–8 season to include music by Second Viennese School composers. The series of contemporary music concerts and individually planned programmes provided the British public with a remarkably rich and varied introduction to the composers and works of this repertory. Moreover, one other Schoenberg performance has yet to be discussed: the most important Schoenberg broadcast – in fact, one of the most important BBC events of the season – took place in January 1928 as part of the National Symphony series.

## The first British performance of Schoenberg's *Gurrelieder*

The first British performance of Schoenberg's *Gurrelieder* was initially envisioned by Clark, who planned to broadcast a version for reduced forces from the BBC Newcastle station, where he was Music Director. The performance did not materialize, however, in part due to Clark's transfer to London in January 1927; moreover, as Clark later explained to Schoenberg, the BBC administrators 'adjudged the performance of the work to be of such importance that they decided it should be done in London'.[59] In February, Clark informed Schoenberg about his recent transfer and relayed a message from Pitt, inviting the composer to conduct the piece on 14 April as part of the first series of BBC National Concerts.[60] Schoenberg responded positively, requesting that enough rehearsals be scheduled to ensure a satisfactory performance. He also inquired about the fee, requesting enough to cover travel expenses for himself and his wife, but, recognizing 'the artistic and moral worth of such an invitation', he would be flexible to secure the performance.[61] By the end of the month, the composer had communicated with both Clark and Pitt advising about the soloists and choruses, recommending that preparation begin immediately, and expressing his disappointment about the allotted number of rehearsals, which was restricted to three.[62] During February and March, the BBC began legal preparations for the performance, negotiating with Universal Edition, Vienna, for the right to broadcast the work; an agreement was reached in which the BBC was granted this right in England for five years.[63] Moreover, Millar Craig was asked to prepare an English translation of the work, which was completed by early April.[64]

Nevertheless, the April 1927 performance did not take place. As Clark explained in a letter to Schoenberg, the change in plans resulted from a Music Department oversight:

> It had escaped peoples' notice that on Friday the 15th (Good Friday), the Chorus was engaged for a special performance of the Dream of Gerontius by Elgar under the composer's direction, which arrangement had been made a considerable time previously. In order to avoid this clash, it was proposed to transfer the concert to the previous Thursday, i.e., April 7th. It was not possible to change the date to a later one because in the following week the Covent Garden Orchestra, which is practically the same as our National Orchestra, began its rehearsals for the Opera Season. I telegraphed you this decision. Then, however, on going into the question of the necessary rehearsals for the performance, and assuming that it was possible at whatever expense (it would have cost £1500) to engage a different chorus (including three male voice choruses) of professional singers, the time was clearly inadequate. A conference of all concerned was then held, and it was decided, to everyone's great regret, that the only thing to do was to postpone the performance of the GURRELIEDER until the next season.[65]

Clark then invited Schoenberg to conduct the work on 27 January 1928, as part of the second season of National Concerts, and the composer accepted the offer.[66] Since Schoenberg had lost engagements through the late cancellation of the April performance, he asked the BBC to make arrangements for rehearsals, artists, fee and binding contract as soon as possible. In the autumn, he received a contract from the BBC, which he signed and returned immediately;[67] at the same time, he sent a separate, private letter to Clark in which he expressed his anxiety about the limited rehearsal arrangements for the performance.

> Yesterday I told Zemlinsky that I shall do the Gurrelieder in London with four rehearsals. He explained that he considered it absolutely *impossible*! I must tell you that I have now developed *very*, very much anxiety. Zemlinsky believes that if the orchestra is ever so good (and he has conducted many orchestras and has 30 years rehearsal experience), then a halfway good performance will not be achieved with under *eight* rehearsals. I must therefore now ask you urgently: make it possible that I am given more suitable [rehearsal arrangements]. You see, I intended to risk the impossible. But I fear that it will not be achieved! Remember: during the summer we spoke of the possibility of a gramophone project to pay for some rehearsals. I ask you most urgently to undertake active steps immediately. For I am very agitated and am alarmed to the highest degree. It would nearly (in fact, even certainly) be a disaster for me if the Gurrelieder should be a failure.[68]

Still unhappy with the number of rehearsals in late December, Schoenberg wrote to Clark suggesting that the BBC schedule a public rehearsal, which could be financed through ticket sales.[69] However, on 8 January, he consented to the existing arrangements and made suggestions about scheduling the chorus and soloist rehearsals after his arrival in London; although his arrival date was still uncertain, it would be sometime between 12 and 16 January.[70]

Schoenberg's fears about the *Gurrelieder* rehearsals were sadly realized, although not for the reasons that he had anticipated. Tensions at rehearsals arose for two fundamental reasons: first, because Clark was incompetent as an interpreter, and his attempts to act in this capacity led to a communication breakdown between the composer and the performers; second, because Schoenberg himself did not conduct the rehearsals in the professional way to which the performers were accustomed. Two days before the performance, the situation had deteriorated to the point that Wright urgently requested Pitt to use his influence as Music Director – as well as his fluent German – to intervene and bring control to the chaotic rehearsal scene.[71] To emphasize his plea, Wright described in detail the difficulties that had arisen earlier that day:

> Robinson [the choral conductor] rang up in a 'state' from Queen's Hall to say that Schonberg had no control over the orchestra and it was completely drowning the singers, and even the chorus when it was singing its loudest . . .
>
> Schonberg particularly asked the chorus to be there at 4.15 p.m. instead of 4.30 p.m. to-day. They are all amateurs in business, are getting very fed up with the performance anyhow particularly since Schonberg has shown at rehearsals that he is a poor conductor, and were most unwilling to try and get off earlier for 4.15 p.m. They did so, however, and every chorister was there at this time. Nevertheless Schonberg continued with the orchestra alone, not making a break till 4.50 p.m. The chorus, of course, could not get to their places till then and were absolutely furious and mutinous. They actually started rehearsing with the orchestra at 5.10 p.m. thus wasting nearly an hour. Further, it was agreed, and Mr Clark understood (Mr Robinson says) that the ladies were not to be called until to-morrow as they also have to get off from business and are singing such a short part of the work.
>
> Schonberg apparently blasphemed about their non-appearance to-day.

Despite the composer's high expectations for this performance, Schoenberg himself created an atmosphere of tension and unprofessionalism by abusing the performers' patience and misusing the precious rehearsal time, ultimately threatening the event's success.

*Gurrelieder* was given exceptional publicity in the *Radio Times*. The first announcement appeared a month before the concert, explaining how the work fit into the composer's *oeuvre*:

*The Song of Gurra*, a choral setting of nineteen poems from the Danish which tell a mediæval love story, is the product of its composer's 'romantic period', when he was following in the great tradition of Wagner, before his later 'modernistic' development. The work is seldom performed, on account of the large number of singers and instrumentalists which it requires . . . The concert on the 27th will be one of the high-water marks of the year's music. The effect of this beautiful work . . . should be unforgettable.[72]

Long feature articles gave more specific explanations of the story and musical style. In an article entitled '140 Players and "Some Big Iron Chains!"', Percy Scholes assured listeners that the work would fall within their musical ken:

*The Songs of Gurra* are not one of Schönberg's latest works. Far from it! They represent his middle period, when his work was but a few degrees more 'modern' than that of Wagner, or, at any rate, of Strauss . . . Take courage, then! This is not the more puzzling Schönberg; it is the Schönberg in his twenties, who has not lost touch with his forerunners, but follows their paths, with, it may be admitted, occasional slight detours.[73]

The week of the concert, the *Radio Times* included a full page article outlining the story and music.[74] Moreover, Basil Maine devoted a significant part of his weekly talk on what he considered to be 'by far the most important musical event next week'.[75] Maine's ambivalent attitude is evident from what he said during the talk, as well as from what he did not say: portions of the original typescript, in which he expressed reservations about Schoenberg's music, were crossed out, indicating that they were not read during the broadcast. For example, in the following excerpt, regard for the composer's technical craftsmanship is negated by misgivings about his stylistic development; however, most of the deprecating remarks were not read – probably to avoid alienating listeners from an event in which the BBC had invested heavily:

Yet in spite of [its] seeming complexity, the basic ideas of the work are comparatively simple. The elaboration of these ideas is the result of intense concentration upon detail. The figuration of each single part is an example of the finest workmanship. . . . For me this early mastery makes the later tragedy of Schonberg all the more poignant. {Not everybody will agree that the last periods of this composer are in any sense a tragedy. My conviction, however, r[e]mains. At Zurich, two years ago, I heard Schonberg's Wind Quintet, a work in which his genius for detail is still apparent. Before hearing the work, I studied the score. It was full of meticulous figures and finely wrought details and had the appearance of beautiful filigree-work, but, translated into sound, it seemed to annihilate all power of receptivity, and to destroy the process of musical thought. It is not that I looked for beauty (in the accepted sense of the term) in this in-growing music, for solace, for romantic warmth, and could find none; for those who have at any time followed after Schonberg in his desert parts have learnt to renounce these fleshly things and in denial to pursue the lonely way without a backward thought. What has been gained by these acts of renunciation? In vain we listen for the note of consistent authority, for Schonberg, with his passion for theory and philos[o]phic enquiry has weakened his creative impulse; he is like a house divided against itself.}

But there is no reason why you should not listen to his music, especially to a work written when he was in the fullness of his power. Listen, then to the 'Songs of Gurra', which is one of the greatest musical works of the last thirty years. Listen and be sad.[76]

The Corporation's intense promotional campaign was equalled by the event itself. Transmitted from the Queen's Hall over all BBC stations except Daventry 5GB, *Gurrelieder* was presented by the huge National Symphony Orchestra, joined by the vocal soloists and enormous chorus. The soloists included some of the best-known British singers of the day: Stiles-Allen (soprano), Gladys Palmer (contralto), John Perry (tenor), Parry Jones (tenor) and Arthur Fear (baritone); the speaker was Arthur Wynn, who worked in the BBC central booking section. The chorus consisted of four separate ensembles brought together for the occasion: The London Wireless Chorus, The Civil Service Choir, Lloyds' Choir and the Railway Clearing House Male Voice Choir. The whole was, of course, conducted by the composer.

The concert received significant attention in the press, both before the performance and after. A measure of the general interest that Schoenberg and this concert aroused is perhaps demonstrated by an exclusive article that appeared in the *Evening News* on the day of the performance, in which the composer himself wrote about modernism in music.[77] Schoenberg's first-hand ideas were relayed to the public also in an interview published in *The Observer* shortly after the concert. The interviewer tried to goad Schoenberg into categorizing his work in traditional 'classic' and 'romantic' terms to which the British public could relate:

You are trying . . . to make me say something I don't want to say. It is my first principle that the reality of music, or the meaning of music, has nothing to do with its sentiments, its expression, its sonority, nothing to do with performance or atmosphere: the one thing that matters is the proportions between the tones . . .

All that we are doing is to find more subtle proportions, and to some extent more complexity – though I hold that harmony is every day growing simpler. It was formerly held that you had to go, as it were, a long way round from a dissonance to a consonance; now you can put them side by side. There is a greater complexity, however, in this: in fugal and contrapuntal music the theme was formerly only two or three bars; now it may be a dozen or more. But there is no break in tradition – music is always the same. When you try to make these antitheses and comparisons, it is as though you started a discussion by saying, 'Well, the sun does go round the earth after all, doesn't it?'[78]

The BBC's extensive preparation for the event was clearly effective, as measured by the generally positive critical response, not only in evaluating the performance, but also in praising the Corporation for having the initiative and resources to present such a work. Many of the critics wrote lengthy and thoughtful reviews, which reflected an informed knowledge of the work and style and which, for the most part, applauded the carefully prepared performance. For example, after pointing out the work's out-moded harmonic style and formal weaknesses, Eric Blom of the *Manchester Guardian* commended it:

> When all is said, one remains under the spell of Schönberg's immense crea-tive power. His inexhaustible invention, his mastery of thematic combina-tion and his grasp of climax, his ingenious musical – as distinct from literary – use of the *leitmotiv*, his sureness in the handling of instrumental and vocal resources – all this and much more make of the 'Gurrelieder' a work as great in quality as it is in bulk.[79]

Although critics pointed out the weak performances of Parry Jones and Stiles-Allen, who sang the long love-scene in Part 1, they tended to approve the performance of the gathered forces as a whole, prominent in the latter parts of the work.[80]

Nevertheless, some critics objected to the event. The reviewer for the *Evening Standard* based his objections on financial grounds:

> Some of those who listened last night, either at the Queen's Hall or over the wireless, to Herr Schönberg's highly impressive Wagner and water, must have wondered, as I did, whether any Continental nation would have subsidised a British composer to the extent of about £2000 . . .
>
> I cannot help thinking that now that State help, in an indirect form, is at last being given to music, it might have been given more judiciously. Two thousand pounds would put several symphony concerts on their legs, and to 'blow the lot' (if a colloquialism may be pardoned) on an orgy of Schönberg is hardly a wise proceeding.[81]

Similarly, the *Musical Times* critic, writing several weeks after the perfor-mance, queried the apparent lack of lasting impact:

> Indeed, there is significance in the suddenness and promptitude of the silence that followed a performance so eagerly anticipated and so industriously written up before-hand. One felt that the B.B.C. was doing well in giving us a chance of hearing a work that seemed likely to establish itself as a masterpiece . . . ; but before the evening was over doubt began to arise as to whether, after all, so costly an enterprise had been worth while – for, to be frank, the first twenty minutes proved boring, and even at the interval nothing had been heard that justified so vast an assemblage of performers . . . The production is reported to have cost £2,000. What couldn't be done for neglected English works – not one, but a dozen – for that sum! Will the B.B.C. do it?[82]

Finally, Ernest Newman, writing for the *Glasgow Herald*, had serious misgivings about the performance for artistic reasons, a criticism he levelled more at the mediocre standard of British solo singers, than at the work, the chorus or the orchestra. He ended his critique by imploring listeners to give the work another hearing.

> If any Scottish listener-in, then, received an unfavourable impression of the 'Gurre-Lieder' last Friday, I beg him to suspend judgment on it until he has heard it again – if he ever does hear it again! – in a more representative performance. I am sorry to have to say this, for I am grateful beyond words to the B.B.C. for having produced the work and for having taken such pains over it; but the composer's interests must come before that of anyone else concerned, and the composer certainly suffered on this occasion.[83]

Despite these weaknesses, the composer himself was apparently pleased with the final outcome of the enterprise. After returning home, Schoenberg wrote a letter to Clark expressing not only his pleasure with the performance and the executants, but also his gratitude to Clark, Pitt and the BBC for programming the work:

> In London I found neither the time nor the opportunity to thank everyone who worked toward the realization of my Gurrelieder performance.
> Before all – and this is the chief purpose of this letter – to [thank] you! It is really very wonderful that you have testified to my work by standing up for it with great honesty and devotion. I was especially pleased by that and always think with pleasure about the moment when with great warmth you said: 'What a powerful kind of music the old Gurrelieder still are!' That was genuine and made me very happy.
> So I thank you, therefore, from my heart for the wonderful days that you arranged for me and ask you to give my deepest thanks to all the participants.
> Before all to the BBC and here, especially, to Mr Percy Pitt.[84]

The BBC was equally happy with the performance, considering it to be among the most important BBC events of the year. The *BBC Handbook*

*1929* review of first English performances presented during the 1927–8 National Concert season concluded:

> Easily [the] first in importance [was] the 'Gurrelieder', by Arnold Schönberg, who came over from Germany himself to conduct rehearsals and performance of his truly monumental work. Everything that could be done by way of careful rehearsal was done, with the whole-hearted enthusiasm of all concerned, and the performance was one of those events which make musical history.[85]

Moreover, the article was illustrated solely by a full-page photograph of Schoenberg with his wife, further evidence of the enormous impact that the composer and his work had on the season as a whole.

During the first season in which the BBC prominently exhibited the music of Second Viennese composers, no fewer than 13 different works were aired: two by Eisler, two by Webern and nine by Schoenberg, representing all of his compositional styles to that time. Many of the performances were given by musicians who were themselves associated with the Second Viennese circle: Scherchen, the Vienna String Quartet, Steuermann, Hinnenberg-Lefèbre, and of course Schoenberg himself were among the most authoritative musicians of the day for performing the repertory. Moreover, British musicians participated in several of the performances, revealing a willingness to incorporate music by these composers into their repertories. In this way, the 1927–8 broadcast season is notable for the wide array of Second Viennese School works that was presented, for the high standard attained in the performance of those works, and for the significant attention and appreciation that was accorded to some of the performances, most notably the first British performance of Schoenberg's *Gurrelieder*. These factors established a surprisingly high level of public tolerance toward this repertory, especially compared to that accorded to other contemporary composers and styles that were represented during the season.

## The emergence of the ultra-modern 'problem'

The BBC promoted contemporary music in an emphatic and pervasive way during the 1927–8 season, not only by including a relatively high percentage of recently-composed works in its music broadcasts, but also by incorporating educational information about new music in broadcast talks and publishing articles in the *Radio Times* explaining and justifying its new music policy. As the season progressed, however, the general public began to have serious doubts about its interest in learning about this type of music. The attitude gradually shifted from one of curiosity to one ranging from boredom and disapproval to ardent dislike and anger. As the BBC's campaign increased in intensity, and as the music included in the programmes appeared more frequently and included an increasing proportion of difficult, ultra-modern works, public outcry against these programmes blossomed.

During the Company years, the BBC responded to adverse public reaction with encouraging remarks in publications and talks supporting its contemporary music policy. For example, in a talk given in August 1924, Scholes considered a question posed by a listener who had been 'trying to find out what the modern composers are "getting at"'. Scholes encouraged this listener, and others who were baffled by modern music, to: 'Listen patiently, and listen to as much modern music as you can, and hope that time and your own musical sense will sift the good from the bad. Remember that Music never has stood still, and be sure that it never will stand still'.[86] On occasion, the BBC printed complaints about new music broadcasts in the *Radio Times* column devoted to listeners' letters. An example appeared in February 1925, from H. J. B. of Totley Rise, near Sheffield, who objected to the BBC's programmes of modern music and poetry. After expressing his impressions of the modern composer in a feeble poetic attempt of his own, he pleaded that the BBC should discontinue this type of programme in the future. In response, the editor pointed out that some listeners had an interest in learning about contemporary art forms: 'It is realized that to certain listeners modern music is anathema. On the other hand, however, there are many who not only enjoy this type of matter, but who like to hear it, whether they themselves are appreciative or not'.[87] Nevertheless, as the number of broadcasts of ultra-modern music increased, the negative reaction to this type of programming increased proportionately. The BBC began to take offensive, rather than merely defensive, steps to counteract the negative response and to justify its policies.

## Misunderstanding chamber music

To some extent, negative public feeling resulted from a general misconception concerning chamber music. Negative reactions to chamber music were evident in letters published in the press throughout the 1920s. Chamber music came to represent the highest of high-brow elitism and was widely deplored by a large proportion of the public. In part, this attitude can be attributed to the BBC's practice of equating chamber music with contemporary music. From the first series of public chamber concerts promoted by the BBC, the spring 1926 series given at the Chenil

Galleries in Chelsea, the term 'chamber music' was used, quite legitimately, to refer to concerts performed by chamber ensembles; as was discussed earlier, these concerts included music by twentieth-century composers, as well as rarely performed, earlier chamber works. However, the BBC continued to label its subsequent series of recently composed works as 'chamber-music concerts'. In this way, listeners heard the latest continental works and associated what they heard with the term 'chamber music'. As the public attitude against new music developed, the attitude toward chamber music in general became tarnished.

The chamber music problem is attributed to a different cause by Scannell and Cardiff.[88] They compare the relatively popular reception of symphony concerts to the unfavourable reception of chamber music recitals and conclude that the schism resulted from the accessibility of programme music, as embodied by symphonic music, and the inaccessibility of absolute music, as represented by chamber music. The authors reasoned that the twentieth-century break from established traditions, such as tonality and composing for large-scale orchestras, by composers such as Stravinsky and Schoenberg exacerbated this divide. In summary, Scannell and Cardiff attributed 'the differences between the BBC policy-makers, the Music Department and the listening public' to the differing agendas of the three groups:

> The policy-makers thought of . . . the 'Beethoven–Brahms–Tchaikovsky standard' as defining the norm for 'good' music, as setting the level of taste and appreciation to which the ordinary listener might, with time and effort aspire. We have seen evidence that the self-improving listener, under the kindly tutelage of Sir Walford Davies or Percy Scholes, might indeed cultivate a liking for such music. The trouble was that this norm was not that of the Music Department, for whom the standard symphonic repertoire was somewhat old hat and vulgar. Chamber music, classical and modern, as the embodiment of absolute music was the norm of the Music Department. This negation of market values in music inevitably entailed an indifference to general considerations of the needs and circumstances of the general listening public.

There are a number of flaws in this argument. The surviving evidence concerning music programme building during the 1920s – as seen in the minutes of the policy-makers' meetings, the memos directed from them to the Music Department, the memos between programmers within the department, and the programmes themselves – indicates that: (1) Far from opposing the programming of contemporary chamber music, the policy-makers supported and encouraged its performance as a direct implementation of their own fundamental policy to enlighten and educate the listening audience. (2) Although the programme builders incorporated a higher proportion of recently-composed works into music transmissions than was included in contemporaneous concert hall programmes, the majority of art music broadcasts – of both orchestral and chamber music – featured music by pre-twentieth-century composers. The same men who Scannell and Cardiff believe found the standard repertory 'old hat and vulgar' often conducted this type of music for studio broadcasts. Furthermore, as has been demonstrated, 'the norm' of the day made even the music of Bach and Beethoven difficult for a significant proportion of the listening audience. A distinction between the interests of the policy-makers and the Music Department was not evident during the 1920s. Although a schism between the programming desired by the audience and supplied by the BBC did exist, it did not result from a difference in 'norms' between the Music Department and the public, but from the idealistic policies of the administrators and the tolerance levels of the audience. (3) The idea of associating programme music exclusively with symphonic works and absolute music with chamber works is unsound; Scannell and Cardiff, both specialists in media studies, may be unfamiliar with the musicological meanings and historical associations of these terms.

An article in the *BBC Handbook 1928* exemplifies the misunderstanding concerning chamber music. The average listener's view of it is characterized as 'something remote, intangible, incomprehensible to all but a few mad enthusiasts who for a quite inconceivable reason would sit for an hour on end in an uncomfortable seat listening to four people amusing themselves with four fiddles, to the complete disregard of anyone else who happened to be present'.[89] From the first, the BBC recognized that broadcasting provided the ideal opportunity to break down this prejudice, 'that the programmes ought to be built in such a way that the strangers might be attracted to the new sound, and bright and cheery Quartet movements of Haydn, Mozart and early Beethoven were ideal for this purpose'. However, the article's summary of important chamber music events during the BBC's first four years emphasized only broadcasts of recently-composed music. The author recalled the programmes of music by living British composers that had been transmitted in 1924,[90] the Chenil Gallery concerts in spring 1926, which 'included the first performances of some important works as well as revivals of old and recent Chamber Music', and the international concerts at the Grotrian Hall the following season, in which 'practically all the artists engaged, as well as the music itself, were entirely new to England, and in many cases, too, opportunity was given to hear the actual performances of works by distinguished contemporary continental composers'. Although many recitals of standard chamber repertory had been broadcast over these years, the article made no mention of them.

Hence, concerns about chamber music compounded as the British public's incomprehension of the BBC's 'chamber music' broadcasts proliferated – that is, as listeners found themselves unable to relate to the contemporary works that the BBC transmitted in its chamber music series. As one listener later pointed out:

> It has been in my mind for some time past to write to you on the subject of the almost universal condemnation of Chamber Music, which puzzles musicians and bewilders your musical director. From time to time I have arguments about it with people who took no interest in music and knew nothing about it until they obtained wireless sets, and I ask them whether they like *Andante Cantabile* by Tchaikovsky, the Beethoven setting of *The Lost Chord*, and one or two other well-known things, and always receive a surprised answer in the affirmative. When I tell them that these are examples of Chamber Music I am scorned, and informed that Chamber Music is that awful noise like cats squealing that they hear on the wireless, labelled 'Chamber Music' in the programme. Now the fact is that the programme compilers are to blame for this; they reserve the description 'Chamber Music' for the music of modern 'advanced' composers and very rarely apply it to the Chamber Music of the classical or more orthodox composers whose compositions are almost always described simply as trios, quartets, or quintets.[91]

Within the first years of broadcasting, the schism between 'accessible' standard works and 'difficult-to-understand' newer music developed, and the resultant difficulties were compounded by the unfortunate association with the term 'chamber music'.

## The Stravinsky–Bartók controversy

The BBC soon recognized that a public relations problem was developing with regard to its contemporary music programming. This problem especially concerned the music of Stravinsky and Bartók, whose works featured prominently in the season's programmes, and the Corporation began to take defensive action. For example, on 12 July 1927 the London première of Stravinsky's *L'histoire du soldat* was 'read, played and danced' at the Arts Theatre Club in London and broadcast over 2LO, 5XX and some regional stations. Conducted by Clark, the performance was promoted in the *Radio Times* with a full page of explanatory notes by Sacheverell Sitwell.[92] Another article appeared two weeks later, written by Scholes:

> As I am writing before the actual broadcast takes place, I cannot say whether
> the performance was a good one or whether I thought the work a master-
> piece. But as I know the B.B.C.'s audience pretty well by now, I feel that I can
> say, and with confidence, that a large number of listeners thought the work a
> very bad one and that the moment the performance ended – or before! – a
> fair number of them sat down and wrote vigorously to the B.B.C. and to me
> about it – as though somehow we had created Stravinsky![93]

Scholes compared uncomplimentary nineteenth-century criticisms of Wagner – in 1927, an extremely popular composer in Britain – with current criticisms of Stravinsky, encouraging listeners to think carefully before passing judgement on 'ultimate' value. The BBC thus changed tactic from merely responding to specific listener complaints to anticipating the inevitable hostility that such performances provoked, hoping to convince listeners to adopt more tolerant attitudes.

As the number of letters from unenthusiastic listeners accumulated, the BBC tackled the problem directly in December 1927 with a lead *Radio Times* article by Scholes, entitled 'Is Bartok mad – or are we?'. Although Bartók's music astonished and confused many listeners, the problem 'in the main, [was] not Bartok's composing but their hearing. *The human ear is a very conservative member*'.[94] Scholes encouraged listeners to have patience with Bartók and other contemporary composers: the more that listeners encountered and listened to this type of music, specifically through the auspices of BBC programmes, the more familiar it would become; in other words, greater exposure to contemporary music would achieve the desired result of broadening listeners' horizons of expecta-tions. The article drew an overwhelming response from the public and representative letters were reproduced in the *Radio Times*. Although one listener agreed with Scholes's view that listeners ought to be 'prepared to give modern music a fair hearing', a number of the respondents were in sympathy with the views of Eric Lewis: 'If Bartok, Stravinsky and Co. were administered in somewhat smaller doses, it might be possible to persuade the patient to "keep them down". The "treatment" so far has been rather too drastic'.[95]

By the end of the 1927–8 season, more contemporary works were trans-mitted than had been performed in Britain in any season at least since the war. Many listeners were fed up and pressed the BBC to reconsider its pro-gramme policy. Taking a new approach, the BBC turned the controversy itself into a publicity drive, in which adverse public reaction was cited as the basis for further discussion and expanations. In the *Radio Times* issue of 18 May 1928, the lead article was an overview of recent compositional trends by Scholes, entitled 'The Music of Today'.[96] In this article, the seventh and last in a series surveying music history, Scholes discussed leading contemporary composers, in effect placing the season's contemporary music programming into historical perspective. In a short introduction, the editor briefly summarized the problems:

> On no question is public opinion more sharply divided than on that of Modern Music. 'Is Bartok Mad?' asked Percy A. Scholes in a recent article, and drew to the Editor thousands of letters from listeners in every part of the country. But what do the famous Hungarian and his contemporaries stand for? And how do they stand in relation to each other? In this, the Seventh and concluding, Chapter of his 'Miniature History of Music' Mr. Scholes deals with the aims and achievements of the composers of our own time.

Scholes divided contemporary composers into two basic groups, which he labelled the 'New Romantics' and the 'Anti-Romantics'; the former included those composers 'who are carried along by the as yet unspent Romantic impulse of the last century', and the latter, 'those who resist that impulse and are, indeed, many of them in active revolt against it'. Although acknowledging that 'this division is not absolute, and that some composers have produced works that would entitle them to consideration under both heads', Scholes assigned Strauss, Elgar, Scriabin and, perhaps surprisingly, Schoenberg to the first group, while he considered Bartók and Stravinsky to be members of the second. No other composers associated with the Second Viennese circle were mentioned in the discussion.

Scholes's assignment of Schoenberg to the first group was consistent with a general perception of Schoenberg and his work that was symptomatic of that composer's reception in Britain at that particular time. As Scholes explained:

> Schönberg, too, is, it seems to me, a Newer Romantic. His early string sextet, *Resplendent Night* . . . and his *Songs of Gurra*, whatever traces of his own personality they may show, are quite in the Wagner tradition. Both these pieces have been broadcast by the B.B.C. upon 'state occasions', when thousands of the readers of this journal were listening, and they will probably be able to confirm that view from their recollections.

The enormous attention accorded to the broadcasts of *Verklärte Nacht* and *Gurrelieder* resulted, during the 1926–8 period, in a general perception of Schoenberg as a late romantic composer, rather than as a radical innovator. Although the Suite for Piano, op. 25, and the String Quartet no. 3 had also been broadcast, the almost surreptitious presentation of these later works was certainly eclipsed, as far as the general public was concerned, by the high-powered publicity accorded to the earlier ones. In the article, Scholes acknowledged Schoenberg's more recent works, mentioning that the composer 'uses a harmony (or a deliberate dis-harmony) so novel, and to less tolerant ears so excruciating, that the essential romanticism of his feeling may escape many listeners'; Scholes nevertheless perceptively maintained that even those disharmonious works remained 'generally or always romantic in feeling'. However, the subtlety of the romantic qualities of Schoenberg's later works was less at issue than the fact that most listeners remained unaware of the composer's atonal and 12-tone developments.

Despite adverse publicity and public reception, by the end of the 1927–8 season the BBC had established a high standard for contemporary music dissemination: individually-planned broadcasts and concert series included a significant percentage of interesting and unusual new works by British and continental composers, often performed by internationally-renowned artists who specialized in the repertory they presented. More specifically, the music of the Second Viennese School and the performers closely allied with that circle were admitted to the British broadcasting sphere in a powerful and pervasive way.

# 6 Refining the music programmes, 1928–1929

The extensive reorganization of the Music Department in spring 1928 gave it enough scope and man-power to fulfil its obligations until the end of the decade, and the music personnel remained fairly stable during the 1928–9 season. In contrast, a large number of high-ranking personnel left other BBC departments during the first half of 1929. Among the long list of resigning officials were: Eric Dunstan, senior 2LO announcer; Cecil Lewis, one of the original four BBC employees;[1] C. E. Hodges, organizer of the Children's Hour; Rex Palmer, first director of the London station; R. E. Jeffrey, director of dramatic productions; Mr Thornton, supervisor of outside broadcasts; and Mr Scanlan, chief research engineer. As the resignations were announced in the press, questions were raised as to why so many important officials were resigning; the reported reasons included low pay and the bureaucracy.[2] Many of these men left the Corporation to work for gramophone and film companies.

## Personnel shifts

The resignation controversy reached a climax at the end of the season, with the announcement that Captain P. P. Eckersley was leaving his position as Chief Engineer of the BBC. Eckersley may have been the best-known and most popular figure in broadcasting at that time, known from the earliest radio days for his entertaining programmes aired from the Writtle station and subsequently for his many talks and articles about radio technology and broadcasting. A fundamental participant in the founding and building of the BBC, particularly in its technical development, Eckersley was a powerful influence within the hierarchy, a member of the Control Board and in charge of the engineering side of the Corporation. As the *Manchester Guardian* noted in its report about the resignation, 'No official reason for the step is given, but personal questions are said to be involved'.[3] It later became clear that Eckersley's resignation was connected with his impending divorce. Director-General Reith, a devout Christian, would not tolerate divorce among his employees, believing that BBC staff should set an example for the public. As Eckersley wrote in 1941:

It is seldom appreciated that ours is officially a Christian country, ruled over by a King who is called 'Defender of the Faith'. Sir John Reith, as both a Christian and the head of a national organization, had the right to order my dismissal and the integrity to uphold his convictions. It might nevertheless have been thought that a national conscience which sees no ideological obstacle to an alliance with an officially anti-Christian country, and which permits atheistic schoolmasters to prepare boys for confirmation, might have found a way to accept the services of a technician who only wanted to readjust his private life.[4]

The Eckersley resignation rocked the BBC to its structural core, aggravating the already strained relations between Reith and the BBC Board of Directors, and leading to a public inquiry into the Corporation's personnel procedures. The event affected the Music Department on a more personal level. Neither the newspaper articles or Eckersley's autobiographical account reveal the precise provocation that led to the divorce. *The Times*'s report of the divorce hearing clarifies this point: 'In this undefended petition Mrs. Stella Eckersley, *née* Grove, of Finchley-road, prayed for the dissolution of her marriage with Mr. Peter Pendleton Eckersley on the ground of his adultery with Mrs. Dorothy Clark at addresses in Brick-street, Piccadilly, and Hyde Park-mansions'.[5] Edward Clark and his first wife, known as Dolly, married in 1921 and were separated by 1925.[6] Although the affair between Eckersley and Dolly, which led to the divorce, is discussed in detail elsewhere,[7] little information survives about the effect that this highly publicized affair had on Clark. However, given the fact that he held a prominent position in the same institution as Reith and Eckersley – and Dolly, who was a BBC secretary – and that the affair led to Clark's divorce as well, it is probable that he was affected, and in an adverse way, by his association with the scandal.

In any case, Clark's position at the Corporation came under severe scrutiny once again in the early months of 1929. In fact, he came very close to being dismissed, not because of his links with the Eckersley affair, but through neglect of his BBC work. Although the reorganization of the previous spring had specifically brought Clark's responsibilities in line with his skills, by the end of the year, continued mishaps on his part resulted in another departmental crisis, once again forcing Wright to make a formal complaint to Pitt.

> As you had requested, I am submitting on the attached a few cases occurring in the last three weeks which illustrate the various remarks which have been made recently with regard to Mr Clark's fatal knack of muddling most things with which he is actively concerned and which had thrown considerable

extra work and trouble on members of this Department. As a consequence in making this report I know I am backed very strongly by the feelings of several of my colleagues thus irritated.

  The important corollary is that there is definite distrust and bias on anything which is in Clark's hands; there is a constant uncertainty as to whether things will or will not go right. This means lack of efficiency and the best solution would seem to be a still more severe detachment from Clark of anything in the nature of executive duty.[8]

Clark's transgressions included habitually submitting programmes late, spending work-time on external conducting projects rather than in the office, avoiding altogether his responsibility to come up with ideas for suitable feature programmes and, perhaps most acutely, neglecting to inform his colleagues about specific arrangements he had made for broadcasts planned for January and February 1929 before going on an extended holiday.[9] There was also strong evidence that Clark, who suffered from rheumatism in late 1928, had abused sick-leave privileges.

Considerable ill feeling is evidenced here at his behaviour in connection with his sick leave. I myself was convinced that he needed it. He had seemed thoroughly out of sorts for weeks and had been more than usually 'distrait', yet we now find that on December 10 he conducted a Symphony Concert with two rehearsals in Prague, and actually before he left London (December 5) when he normally carried his right arm in a sling he had conducted a Chamber Orchestra at a private concert in the Boulestin Restaurant.

By mid-January 1929, Wright admitted that matters had improved, but was still unhappy with Clark's irregular working habits.

[Clark] cannot understand the necessity for absolute regular hours and this is one reason for the strong resentment on the part of everyone else in Room 58. They feel that if a man is given a job involving work in the office, such as the Chamber Concerts which Clark is doing, he ought to be there regularly . . . to receive the many telephone calls directed to him, to undertake programme changes necessitated by unforeseen alterations, to give Mase his publicity or to be referred to on general matters, as frequently happens (for his knowledge in certain directions is extensive) . . . He seems to need the unhealthy fillip of urgency to produce anything, and then it usually has to be altered.

  The only solution we can find is the possibility of putting Clark in the Research Department, where in accordance with existing routine he can be allotted his Chamber Concerts without the responsibility for any routine whatever.[10]

Further discussion raised another question about Clark's competence. In the past, it had been recognized that he was unable to handle paperwork adequately; now, for the first time, administrators also questioned whether his programming ideas were useful, or even legitimately conceived. As the Programme Executive, Graves, reported to R. H. Eckersley,

> There is a doubt . . . as to whether Clark would be any use in an advisory capacity, and it is apparent from what both Pitt and others say that much of his knowledge is not first-hand at all, and that he passes on recommendations to us without really knowing anything about the subjects concerned, i.e. if Scherchen or Schonberg or Ansermet say something to him he takes it as gospel.[11]

Given the choice of dismissing Clark altogether or employing him to provide suspect advice, Graves naturally seemed inclined toward the former.

In subsequent months, however, this serious allegation was discounted, both by co-workers within the BBC and by respected colleagues outside the organization – including Adrian Boult, who was appointed BBC Music Director shortly thereafter.[12] In March, Wright reported that Clark's work and attitude had improved so remarkably that he no longer felt it was necessary for the transfer to be considered.[13] Despite a rather lukewarm assessment of Clark's attributes by Pitt,[14] Eckersley's final recommendation to Reith reveals that he too strongly advocated Clark's continued employment within the Music Department.

> Even with his lack of executive instinct, I am sure his specialised knowledge is of great value. He is an excellent builder of programmes, and is doing very good work in connection with the forthcoming Promenade season. If we want our output to be fully representative, we should, I feel sure, be unwise to part with him, and I will make myself responsible for seeing, if he stays with us, that he fully justifies his position. I am afraid, in an organisation like the Music Department, we may in stimulating the artistic side have to put up with individuals who lack executive ability. If, however, the work is properly regulated it should be possible to get the proper value out of the individual without penalising the work of the department as a whole.[15]

Reith seemed unconvinced by Clark's conversion:

> [It is] inexplicable to me that such conduct should so long have been tolerated except in terms of a state of affairs which conveys a serious reflection on those responsible for discipline and work.
>
> If you were keeping him, I presume you would give him a proper dressing down, and probably put him on two or three months trial with strict watch . . .
>
> Mr Wright . . . and Mr Pitt . . . have obviously many residual reservations, and I could feel little confidence in such a complete reformation as would be necessary. His conduct has been disgraceful and some of it apparently

deliberate. Apart from this, his judgment and knowledge do not seem to be of a high standard.

It is a thoroughly bad case and I will give no opinion, so you may settle it yourself.[16]

Nevertheless, Eckersley, buoyed by his conviction of the programme builder's ultimate value, maintained his position, and, Clark, as a direct consequence, retained his.[17]

One other significant staffing change of 1928–9 deserves mention: Percy Scholes relinquished his positions as BBC Music Critic and *Radio Times* Music Editor at the beginning of the season. As early as 1926, the Programme and Control Boards had considered whether the weekly critical talks might be more effective with a fresh speaker. Reasons for dissatisfaction may be inferred from their complaints about Scholes's programme notes, which they felt should address 'a more musically-cultured public'.[18] Only when Scholes resigned in September 1928 did Ernest Newman, a highly respected writer, critic and speaker, take over as BBC Music Critic. Newman's intellectual musical standpoint contrasted sharply with Scholes's popular approach, as well as with Walford Davies's educational one. The decision to appoint Newman as official critic revealed a significant shift of emphasis: initially, it had been desirable for the BBC to educate a 'beginning' audience about art music, and Scholes, with his extensive music appreciation experience, had been the obvious candidate for the task. By the end of the decade, however, the programmes and audiences had changed. Believing that music talks should cater to the sophisticated, as well as the ordinary, listener, the administrators turned to Newman.

The shift at this time toward acknowledging and providing for listeners' intellectual needs may also be seen in the BBC's decision to launch a second weekly house magazine. In addition to the *Radio Times*, the Corporation began to publish *The Listener* in January 1929 to meet public demand for reprints of important broadcast talks. Music coverage was abundant, the magazine regularly including reviews of recent concerts and broadcasts, reviews of books about music, announcements of upcoming broadcasts and articles on current musical topics, all by notable critics and other members of the music intelligentsia. With *The Listener*, the BBC provided a broader base of information about art music, as discussed by leading music thinkers and writers of the day.

## The music programmes: series planning

By the end of the decade, a significant proportion of broadcast time was devoted to art music, and music programmes were developed more and more within series. Seasonal planning of high-profile series enabled the Music Department to control large-scale programming concerns, ensuring that a broad repertory range was encompassed and that standard works were not repeated too often. Series programming also lengthened the time available for negotiating with performers and for publicizing events.

During the 1928–9 season, the Queen's Hall and People's Palace symphony concerts were divided into two separate series. The National Concerts were renamed 'The BBC Symphony Concerts' and took place at the Queen's Hall, performed by the so-called BBC Symphony Orchestra[19] and the Hallé Orchestra. The programme planners returned to the high-profile programming and publicizing approach of the first National Concert season: the twelve concerts were designed to attract a high level of interest, offering unusual works and well-known artists. The programmes reflected a synthesis of the previous two seasons' emphases: British performers and composers were well-represented on the programmes as in the second season, but they were balanced by concerts which featured international artists and contemporary continental repertory, as in the first. For example, the opening programme had a British focus, with Beecham conducting works by Delius and Lord Berners, as well as Schumann's Symphony no. 3; the second concert featured Szigeti giving the first English performance of Alfredo Casella's Violin Concerto. In the fourth concert, Granville Bantock conducted the first performance of his new work, *The Pilgrim's Progress*, while in the sixth, Ansermet conducted Debussy's music to *Le martyre de Saint Sébastien* and Stravinsky's *The Rite of Spring*. The final concert was especially significant: Sir Henry Wood conducted the first English performance of Mahler's Symphony no. 8. The Queen's Hall series was a showcase within the BBC's art music programmes, offering listeners the opportunity to hear concerts in which unusual, large-scale works were presented by top-quality performers.

The new People's Palace series served a different purpose: these concerts aimed to bring the orchestral experience to new audiences, and most of the programmed works were drawn from the standard repertory. The eight-concert series, conducted by Sir Landon Ronald and Percy Pitt, took place weekly during April and May 1929, on Thursday nights to avoid the previous season's Friday evening mistake. The programmes were given full-page coverage in the *Radio Times*, including extensive programme notes. This approach to cultivating new audiences for symphonic music proved successful, as The *Radio Times* reported:

> Listeners will remember the popular concerts that were given by the BBC early this year at the People's Palace in the Mile End Road, E. They were, in

their way, a kind of second Proms – without the Promenaders: there was the same joyousness about them and healthy enthusiasm. To be present at any of those crowded concerts was to realize what a moving experience music can be when accepted simply as music – without prejudice or partisanship and unswayed by the fashions of the moment.[20]

The programme builders also developed other types of art music programmes as sets of series. One of the most discussed featured the Bach cantatas, one presented each Sunday from May 1928.[21] The programmers aimed to broadcast all the cantatas in this way, as a means of overcoming popular prejudice against Bach's music. In another notable series, an opera was presented each month, broadcast twice in its entirety.[22] A lead *Radio Times* article listed twelve that were transmitted between September 1928 and August 1929, including W. Vincent Wallaces's *Maritana*, Debussy's *Pelléas et Mélisande*, Rimsky-Korsakov's *Coq d'Or*, Wagner's *Der Fliegender Holländer* and Delibes's *Le roi l'a dit*.

## Contemporary music programming

In 1928–9, the BBC continued its contemporary music policy of the previous season, promoting, explaining and defending new music transmissions in publications and broadcast talks. Feature articles on the subject appeared in the *Radio Times* throughout the season, written by both advocates and opponents. The Corporation also printed many letters relating to the debate in the 'What the Other Listener Thinks' column. By publicly acknowledging and exposing the different sides of the issue, the BBC exploited the debate as a means of developing public awareness and understanding of the issues.

### *The new music debate escalates*

The BBC launched the new season with a *Radio Times* article entitled 'Is Modern Music Inferior?', part of a series providing 'Points of View' on different topics.[23] It was written by Edwin Evans, a founding member of both the LCMC and the ISCM, and a noted critic, who was intimately familiar with British and continental trends in music and knew many composers and performers of the day. By inviting Evans to contribute this article, the BBC deviated from the usual practice of having Scholes serve as spokesman on musical matters. The Corporation may have felt that an authority would carry more weight in the spiralling debate, or perhaps Scholes's upcoming resignation motivated the Corporation to introduce specialist writers on musical topics. In any case, Evans directly challenged the many listeners who had expressed their dislike of recent musical trends, emphasizing that the diversity of new compositional styles was an essential indicator of growth and progress: '[Art] is fertilized by the frontiers between different cultures, nations, creeds, types, and ultimately individuals. The unprecedented diversity of contemporary music is a sign that the art is in a healthy condition of unimpeded fertility'.

Evans's article sparked a chain reaction in the *Radio Times*. One respondent, H. A. Scott, an ardent Elgar enthusiast, categorized those who wrote 'hopelessly unattractive' music as attention-seeking sensationalists.

> One of the most curious features of modern music is indeed the way in which some of the biggest reputations are enjoyed by composers whose music is least often performed. Schönberg supplies one case in point and Stravinsky another. Each is commonly regarded as a composer of the first importance, but the actual compositions of both are found so unpalatable, not merely by the vulgar herd, but by the musical public in general, that it is the rarest of occurrences for any of them to be played![24]

Scott's article was, in its turn, refuted in a letter to the editor, written by J. L. N. O'L.

> Astonishment has given way to eloquence after reading a column in a recent issue of *The Radio Times* which expresses a view of modern music as unbalanced as it is misleading. Elgar's music, which alone provides your contributor with pleasure amongst that of twentieth-century composers, is *not* modern. Some of it is recent. . . . The rich beauty of *The Fire Bird*, the sober greatness of *Œdipus Rex*, and the warm humanity of what Bartok's music I have heard, do not exist for him, and when even a few can appreciate modern music, one is entitled to suspect that the fault lies, not with the composer, but with an unresponsive listener.[25]

This listener's view was heartily supported by Ernest Newman in his broadcast talk the next day:

> In this week's 'Radio Times' there is what I think a very sensible letter of reply from someone who signs himself J. L. N. O'L., who urges that we should give contemporary music its chance. I agree with him. Whether you like all the music you hear on the wireless or not is not the point. The point is that modern music is here. It has come to stay, and you will have to reckon with it, whether you like it or not. You cannot dispose of it by taking your earphones off and burying your head in the sand and trying to persuade yourself that because you are not listening to this music it does not exist. It does exist, and you must get used to it now or later. The sooner you get used to it the better you will be able to discriminate between what is genuine in the new music and what is merely bogus.[26]

A few months later, the debate escalated into a full-scale controversy as a result of two BBC incidents. On 18 January, Ansermet presented a public concert in the BBC symphony series, in which Debussy's music to *Le martyre de Saint Sébastien* and Stravinsky's *The Rite of Spring* were performed. The latter inspired cries of incomprehensibility and anguish (belying the 16 years since its first hearing), as well as strong letters supporting Stravinsky's music.[27] Two weeks later, on 1 February, another forthright *Radio Times* article appeared, entitled 'What the New Composer is Driving At'. Headed with a direct editorial order, 'An Article by Edwin Evans which You Should Read', the editor briefly outlined its purpose:

> It may be that many listeners who have grown to look upon Modern Music as unpardonable will be persuaded to forgiveness by the accompanying article. With admirable simplicity Mr. Edwin Evans explains not only what the modern composer is driving at, but also the attitude which the liberal-minded listener should adopt towards the new style of composition.[28]

The BBC no longer hoped to compel all listeners to adopt a sympathetic attitude toward contemporary music, but the educational campaign continued for the sake of the 'liberal-minded'.

Evans directed the article at the listener who was curious, but confused, about new musical trends: 'subconsciously he may even be annoyed to think that here is something others enjoy in which he cannot share ... he would like to fathom the mystery, if only he knew how'. Evans explained the schism between composer and audience in socio-economic terms, drawing parallels with the visual arts.

> Since the artist always is, and must be, ahead of the plain man (who otherwise would have no need of artists), it follows that the less control the plain man exercises over the artist the more the latter will push ahead, and the fewer people there will be to follow him. Thus in the aristocratic eighteenth century he wrote in such a way that the ordinary educated man could keep pace with him, but in the democratic twentieth the audience that can stay the course has shrunk into a kind of aristocracy, not of birth or of rank, but of people prepared to make the necessary effort to understand a composer who is not 'everybody's money'.

Nevertheless, the 'plain man' should not disregard or avoid new music, since 'the claim of the new is that it bears a close relation to the age in which we live, and therefore to ourselves ... If it proves difficult to assimilate, the receptive faculties should rise to the occasion, not evade it'. Furthermore, the difficulty of assimilating new music resulted from new compositional processes:

> The established method underwent searching tests, with the result that it was found to be, not wrong, but incomplete. And most of the experiment in musical craftsmanship has been in the direction, not of upsetting, but of completing it. All the factors have been dissected in turn: the scale, harmony, rhythm, timbre. As light had been dissected by painters, sound was, and is still being, dissected, taken to pieces and put together again in hundreds of different ways.

Thus, listeners had to work harder to decode and to comprehend the composer's message. Finally, Evans attributed the composer–audience schism to the increased use of discord.

> But this is an old story. It began when counterpoint was first invented. Always the composer went on ahead, determined to make the voices sound as independent parts. But though the listener was baffled for a time, his ears became gradually accustomed to the new sounds and heard them as one, so that the composer had perforce to steal another march upon him. That is what has happened, is happening, and, so far as we can see, will continue to happen so long as there is music.

As was perhaps expected, the article elicited vigorous public response, especially given its publication so soon after the *Rite of Spring* performance. The BBC fuelled the controversy by publishing a significant number of letters – both pro and con – in the *Radio Time*s until the end of March.[29] The Corporation used the opposing views of its correspondents as tacit justification of its policy: for every printed letter that strongly objected to the transmission of a contemporary work, there was an equally adamant one defending listeners' rights to hear it. For example, the 22 March issue devoted nearly a column to letters responding to the 4 March concert of Bartók works performed by the composer with violinist Zoltán Székely.[30] Under the headings, 'Anti-Bartok', 'Pro-Bartok', '– And Anti once again', the BBC presented letters from three listeners who communicated their views in some detail. The first questioned whether the BBC truly represented contemporary music in broadcasts featuring extremist composers.

> Is it fair to other composers of serious contemporary music, among whom are some of our own sane nationals, to give the listening public who are not really instructed in the matter, the impression that last night's unmitigated 'tripe', must be taken as a sample of what some of our really fine moderns are doing.

This listener concluded with a three-stanza poem, describing his or her personal impressions of Bartók's music. The second letter defended the right of contemporary music enthusiasts to hear such broadcasts.

> I beg those who consider themselves 'really musical' (e.g., the cinema organ lovers) not to begrudge us, the 'degenerate Bartokians', say, an hour a fortnight for us to wallow in our depravity, which leaves countless hours for brass bands, ballad concerts and suchlike.

The third writer vividly described his or her experience in listening to the final work in the broadcast.

> It seemed to me as though the pandemonium of a pianistic Babel had been suddenly released. One could neither determine its key (minor or major), time, or melody, in short it was nothing more than a vast clinker of syncopation and discord, with a bewildering sequence of acciaturas [sic] and gargantuan thumpings of the bass, leading up to its pitiful finale.[31]

Throughout the spring of 1929, the BBC represented different points of view relating to the contemporary music controversy in the *Radio Times*. Although many letters were negative, expressing the confusion and outrage that was no doubt felt by a large proportion of listeners, even the hostile letters implicitly supported the BBC's horizon-expanding policy, since the writer had in fact listened to at least part of the objectionable broadcast. Whether listeners liked the music or not was in some ways immaterial; the very fact that they had listened – the fact that the controversy itself was taking place – was proof that the BBC contemporary music policy was having an effect: the Corporation was indeed bringing new and unfamiliar music to sections of the public that would otherwise have been ignorant of it.

### Broadcasts of Second Viennese School works

Throughout the weeks that these views were being exchanged, contemporary music was planned and transmitted according to criteria established during the previous season. Recently-composed works were discussed in broadcast talks and performed in individually-planned studio recitals, as well as in series. For example, the 'New Friends in Music' programmes continued sporadically in spring 1929, featuring piano works of living composers. Stravinsky was featured on 20 March and Eugene Goossens on 21 June. Scholes briefly discussed the works before he performed them or played them from gramophone recordings.

Once again, the most important new music broadcasts took place within the series of BBC Concerts of Contemporary Music, conceived using the same guidelines and format as for the previous season.[32] The performances took place at a new venue, the Arts Theatre Club in London. The BBC administrators began to take an interest in this theatre in 1927, sponsoring R. H. Eckersley's membership there from February of that year.[33] In spring 1928, it was used for broadcasts of chamber music and concerts performed by The Arts Theatre Chamber Orchestra conducted by Clark, who became the club's music director in spring 1928.[34] The BBC was particularly pleased with its find:

> The Arts Theatre Club is the most friendly and comfortable of all theatrical clubs, and its little theatre a perfect setting for venturesome production. And now it has added Chamber Music Concerts to its other amenities.[35]

As before, the contemporary music series consisted of eight programmes, presented between 3 September 1928 and 3 April 1929 to invited audiences of critics and new music enthusiasts; all the concerts were broadcast over the 2LO and 5XX wavelengths. They were performed by internationally renowned artists, many of whom were new music specialists. Several had already taken part in BBC broadcasts of contemporary music, including the Vienna String Quartet, Margot Hinnenberg-Lefèbre, Scherchen, Steuermann, Bartók and the Amar-Hindemith Quartet. Continental composers represented in the second season were to be featured once again: plans included works by Schoenberg, Webern, Krenek, Ravel, Falla, Bartók, Hindemith, Honegger and the Les Six composers. Moreover, an emphasis was placed on British composers and artists that had been lacking previously: compositions by Goossens, Bridge, Bliss, Delius and Bax were planned for inclusion, as were performances by the Brosa String Quartet, Leon Goossens and Arnold Bax.

As part of the aggressive campaign to communicate with the public about contemporary music, Wright explained the programming criteria for the series in a *Radio Times* article, which appeared just prior to the first concert. Illustrated with a photograph of Schoenberg, the article aimed to 'help listeners to appreciate the endeavour which the B.B.C. is making to introduce leading contemporary composers to a wider public'.[36] To make the programmes more accessible, the programme builders juxtaposed works by three distinct categories of contemporary composers: those who the Music Department considered to be 'definitely established', those who were 'more established' and those who were 'more experimental' or 'less accepted':

> One has to mention only Stravinsky, Schönberg, Prokofief, Kodaly, Milhaud, de Falla, Ravel, Honegger, Busoni, and Bartok among the more 'established' composers represented, and among the more experimental, or shall we say less 'accepted', Hindemith, Eisler, Koechlin, Szymanowsky, Alban Berg, Auric, and Harsanyi . . .
> The general system of the programmes will be similar to that of last season

> in that they will revolve round the two composers who are the axes of the
> modern movement, Schönberg and Stravinsky. In a similar way, too, they
> will be constructed in such a fashion that one may hear side by side an
> important or 'key' work by a definitely established composer such as
> Debussy, Ravel, Reger, Fauré, Busoni, and a more experimental work by a
> younger man who nevertheless is building on the foundations laid down by
> the older masters.

New British works made up another essential category. Wright's explanation permits unusual insight into the Music Department's programming
perceptions and strategies during the latter years of the 1920s. The article
concluded with a vague hope – or perhaps a plea – that the new format
would engender a less hostile reception from listeners.

In broadcast talks relating to specific concerts in the series, the BBC
Music Critic, Ernest Newman, furthered the Corporation's campaign.
While Wright justified the series from a programming point of view,
Newman challenged listeners with a cultural-expansionist argument.

> Now whether, after hearing this music, you like it or dislike it, is a matter for
> each individual, I think, but you are not playing the game unless you hear it at
> any rate once. If there is anything in it depend upon it it will catch hold of you
> sooner or later. If you decide that there is nothing in it – you may be right or
> you may be wrong – at least your conscience is clear. At least you have not
> condemned it unheard. Therefore during this performance on Monday do
> not switch off in a temper the moment you hear something that annoys you;
> endure to the end; bear your sufferings – if you are suffering – like men. The
> B.B.C. is doing wonderful work for us in broadcasting these advanced
> modern works. It is putting it within the power of every man to form a judg-
> ment for himself, instead of taking his opinions ready made from the critics.[37]

The following week, Newman continued with this line of thought, emphasizing that the attention he gave to a work was no guarantee of its musical
value.

> It does not at all follow that because I ask you to listen in to [a] particular work
> I am recommending it to you as an excellent piece. On the contrary, I shall
> occasionally suggest that you are listening to a work of which I do not think
> very much myself, and which I am pretty sure you will not like . . . The only
> way we can get to the truth of the matter is by hearing as much of the new
> music as possible . . . I am not tipping you winners. As often as not I shall be
> talking mainly of 'also rans', but I shall not be responsible for non-starters.[38]

Despite the emphatic BBC propaganda, the vigorous disputes about
contemporary music suggest that the *Star* critic may have expressed the
views of many in his response to the announced programmes:

> In spite of friendly warnings the B.B.C. will not be checked in its wild career; it is resuming its concerts of ultra-modern music on Monday evening. The program reads like a replica of one given at Siena recently, which proved too much even for the strongest musical digestions. Even some of our most advanced critics wilted.
>
> A sympathetic and understanding attitude to the latest developments is most becoming to an influential body like the B.B.C., but I wonder how many listeners-in really want a whole evening of the latest masterpieces (that they are masterpieces goe[s] without saying) or like it when they get it.[39]

The reference to Siena pertains to the previous ISCM Festival, which took place there in September 1928. Members of the Vienna String Quartet presented Webern's String Trio at the festival, and the performance provoked a small riot, which received attention in Britain as elsewhere in Europe. The second of the BBC Concerts of Contemporary Music, as announced in the *Radio Times* and other BBC publicity, was to include this work, as well as Arthur Bliss's Quintet for Oboe and Strings, Hindemith's *Die Serenaden* and Schoenberg's Second String Quartet.[40] In a talk two days before the event, Newman prepared listeners for the difficult programme, focusing especially on the trio. His comments were not encouraging.

> Webern, who was a pupil of Schönberg, is now about 45, and a man of such wide musical knowledge and accomplishment that we must treat him with the utmost respect, but I find myself, like most other people, utterly unable to follow his music. I can tell you nothing about this Trio, because after repeated study of it I still cannot follow his mental processes at all . . . In plain words, I am completely beaten. Perhaps it is his mind is a thousand years ahead of mine; anyhow it works along lines so remote from mine that there is no chance of the two ever meeting. I can only suggest that you listen to the Trio for yourselves . . . But be very careful; the work begins so quietly that it may have proceeded for a little while before you are aware it has begun. The train may be at Crewe before you have got in at Liverpool.[41]

The programme took place on 15 October, performed by the Vienna String Quartet, Margot Hinnenberg-Lefèbre and the English oboist Leon Goossens. However, in the end, the first two movements of the Bliss Quintet and the entire Webern Trio were not transmitted; only the audience at the Arts Theatre Club heard them. The BBC was still promoting the trio in the *Radio Times* of 5 October, prepared before the Siena news arrived in Britain, but when the broadcast schedules were published the following week, the work was not listed with the rest of the concert. As with the *Lyric Suite* performance the previous February, the BBC apparently felt it necessary to 'censor' Webern's extreme musical style, perhaps worried by the possibility of provoking a reaction similar to that in Siena.

In fact, the ISCM controversy aroused great interest in the Webern Trio, and many listeners were disappointed and angry that the work was not aired. Newman complained at length, both in his next broadcast talk[42] and in his widely-read column in *The Sunday Times*.

> We have had some curious and some sad experiences during the week; the saddest of all was the experience we were denied. Hitherto I have attended every one of the B.B.C.'s chamber concerts in the flesh. Last Monday I thought I would try listening in, to see how some of this modern music must strike the ordinary man...
>
> The work all of us most wanted to hear was that string trio of Alban Berg's [*sic*] that nearly caused bloodshed at Siena... I was anxious to know what it really sounded like, for I have never been able to make head or tail of it from the score. But the B.B.C. announcer calmly tells us the trio cannot be given! That is cruel enough to us millions of listeners-in; but to be told later that the trio was actually played but not broadcast is positively twisting the poisoned knife in the wound. Why, we ask plaintively, should a couple of dozen people in the Arts Theatre be granted a privilege and given a pleasure that are denied to the rest of us? Can it be that music of this sort is regarded as morally bad for us? If so, why should a handful of favoured beings be permitted to enjoy it in secret?... I respectfully suggest that I have as much right to hear bad music through my receiving set as my colleagues have to hear it in the Arts Theatre.[43]

Not surprisingly, critics who heard the complete concert at the Arts Theatre Club had varying views of the trio. Whether reacting positively or negatively, however, they all seemed baffled by Webern's compositional style. For example, in a favourable review of the concert, the *Daily Telegraph* critic assessed the Webern as 'a strange work indeed, the unintelligibility of which is intensified by the almost unrelieved pianissimo maintained throughout'.[44] Others tried to describe its effect:

> In Anton Webern's Trio for strings (1927) – we no longer distinguish things by their keys – you may hear curious sounds: a butterfly on the window-pane, a newly-sharpened slate pencil doing a sum, a good length ball taking the leg-bail, the 'fünf-gezackte Kamm' passing through Hafis's hair, and others. It felt like being tickled with a blade of grass in unexpected places.[45]

Despite the general curiosity about the trio, provoked by the ISCM reports and BBC promotion, the Corporation once again chose to suppress transmission of an ultra-modern work rather than risk pushing its critics too far.

The excitement over the Webern left little energy or space for comments concerning the Schoenberg string quartet. It is interesting to note that the *Observer* critic found it remarkably accessible – at least, compared to the Webern.

> We had Schönberg's Op. 10, that once astonished and enraged us, and now it
> sounds euphonious, like a belated classic, almost like – perilously like –
> Brahms, at least, until the voice enters, where Brahms, who still liked to give
> the singer something he would enjoy singing, is left nowhere.[46]

Having been denied the opportunity of hearing the Webern, Newman was
unable to compare the works' styles. He focused instead on the effect of
atonality on the average listener.

> The theorists may talk as they like about some of the new developments –
> polytonality, atonality, abnormality, triviality, bestiality, or any ality you will
> – but they will not get very far until they have swept away our present sense
> of hearing and endowed us with another. They naïvely confess that the atonal
> composers, when writing their music, take particular pains to avoid anything
> that may suggest tonality. Well and good: the composers may be able to per-
> suade themselves that they are really thinking atonally. But it is difficult for
> the rest of us to avoid the impression, generally speaking, that what we are
> getting is ordinary tonal music deliberately put a little out of drawing, as it
> were: and all the while we are listening, one part of our sub-conscious is sur-
> reptitiously putting the drawing straight again.[47]

Newman continued to ruminate about Schoenberg's contribution to
music history in a broadcast talk he gave a few weeks later.

> [Schoenberg] is still respected as the pioneer of a good many modern devel-
> opments, respected as a teacher, and as a person of an inspiring influence,
> but even his partisans have to bow to the logic of events, that he has so far
> failed, although now about 54, to produce a single work in his later style that
> has captured the heart of the general musical public. His theories are admir-
> able, but his practice is doubtful.[48]

Despite the fact that most British audiences had yet to hear 'a single work
in his later style', they were nevertheless informed by a highly respected
and influential critic that Schoenberg's atonal compositions were ineffective and without credibility.

The fourth BBC Concert of Contemporary Music, on 3 December 1928,
featured Hermann Scherchen conducting the first performance in
England of a work by Josef Matthias Hauer, the chamber oratorio,
*Wandlungen*, op. 53. The work had received its première the previous July
at the Baden Baden festival, to great acclaim. As the British composer and
conductor, Eugene Goossens, reported:

> Hauer's 'Wandlungen' was the occasion for a spontaneous demonstration by
> the audience. It is a work for six solo voices, choir, and small orchestra, and is
> the latest result of this Composer's experiments with the 12-tone scale. As I
> invariably look upon musical laboratory-work with suspicion, I am content

to pass over the 12-tone business and to record the simple fact that, as music, the work was extremely impressive, though marred by shocking bad vocal writing. There were a few crude moments, but the polyphonic beauty of the closing pages was quite memorable. Theories or no theories, it's the music that counts, and the ovation to Hauer was a tribute not to his theories, but to his musicianship. [49]

Clark, who also attended the première,[50] apparently decided that the piece merited immediate placement in the contemporary concert series. The programme, as announced in the *Radio Times*[51] and the official concert programme, also included Hindemith's Chamber Music no. 1, Ernst Krenek's *Symphonic Music* for nine instruments, op. 11, and a Janáček song cycle, *Říkadla*.

In accordance with the BBC policy that large-scale vocal pieces be sung in English, Clark initiated processes for commissioning and gaining the rights for translations of the Janáček and Hauer texts.[52] The subsequent negotiations, which continued until late November, provide interesting insights into each organization's view of its sacrificial role as contemporary music disseminator. In October, Richard Howgill, the BBC copyright assistant who handled the matter, requested formal permission from Universal Edition (UE), Vienna, the publisher of both works. UE granted permission, on condition that it could include the translations in its publications. Howgill pointed out that this was disadvantageous for the BBC: 'In order to perform these works satisfactorily in this country it is necessary for us to go to the expense of having the translations made, and we feel that if you want them placed at your disposal you should be prepared to pay for them.'[53] He suggested that UE should instead be showing gratitude to the BBC.

> We venture to say that it is to your advantage to have your modern publications performed in this country, and as we are perhaps the only organisation to bring them before the notice of the public we consider that you should bear this in mind in framing your terms for performance, translation, etc.[54]

While acknowledging these laudable achievements, UE felt that organizations like the BBC should be more appreciative of its willingness, as a purely commercial concern, to make available for performance works that reaped little or no financial benefit.

> As you are certainly aware, we are among the few publishing-houses which have intensively taken up modern work and which make extremely great material sacrifices in propaganda for contemporary work. Nor should it be forgotten that we are a private concern, that we have no obligations either towards contemporary composers or to the public, that we draw no subsidy of any sort and that we are only enabled to bring out new works by the sums

which come to us as profit in already published works. Only through modern minded conductors, broadcasting companies, theatre managers, etc., who take notice of our propaganda for modern work and pay us accordingly, are we in a position to continue to direct our activities to furthering modern production.[55]

In the end, David Millar Craig, the same translator who prepared the English text for the BBC performance of Schoenberg's *Gurrelieder*, translated both works at a total cost of £10. UE bought the rights to the translations from the BBC, reducing the total rental fee for the score and parts by that amount.

Prior to the concert, the usual notice appeared in the *Radio Times*, attempting to incite interest in the unfamiliar music while preparing listeners for the potentially strange musical styles. Moreover, the comparison with Wagnerian accessibility problems was made once again:

> [Hauer's] ventures in atonality, though their dissonances may be a trifle disconcerting to the conservative ear, are vividly interesting. He has even elaborated a new type of musical notation ... The concert on the 3rd should be of special interest to the musical enthusiasts. The 'modernity' of it may trouble some of the more formally minded. Still, there was a time when Wagner was one too much for the ordinary music-lover.[56]

Newman gave a more concrete explanation of Hauer's compositional technique in a talk on 1 December. To relate the style to something within the experience of British listeners, Newman equated Hauer's approach to that of Schoenberg:

> [Hauer] has written a fair amount of music in styles of his own based on theories of his own. He is an out-and-out attonalist [*sic*]. That is to say, he completely throws over the traditional conception of music as being founded on certain relations between the 8 diatonic notes of the scale and the 5 subordinate semi-tones. He is an adherent of what is called the 12 tone scale, the scale usually associated in most people's minds with Schönberg. It would take me a long time to make clear to you all that is implied in this scale. Roughly speaking, it means that of the twelve equal degrees of the octave, the twelve semi-tones, one note is just as good as another. The old notions of dominant, sub-dominant and so on, go by the board.[57]

Although Newman was unimpressed with Hauer's music and theories, he concluded with his usual plea that listeners should at least listen objectively to the performance.

> Hauer has published some remarkable treatises, from which at any rate I get the impression – I say it with all respect – that he is a fanatic with whom it is

difficult to argue because of the complete way in which his fanaticism absorbs him. He seems to regard practically all the music of the last two thousand years or so as a mistake . . . According to Hauer, the only music worthy of the name is attonal music, the possibilities of which he regards as infinite. Whether you like or dislike this work of his which you will hear on Monday, please believe me that he is a completely sincere man of considerable ability of a sort. I am not attempting to influence your opinion about the work at all; I am only asking you to listen to it with an open mind.

Although pre-concert publicity promoted four programme items, the performance included just the Krenek, the Hindemith and the Hauer, and only the latter two were broadcast. The Janáček was omitted at the last moment, because rehearsal time was inadequate for preparing such a difficult programme. The change was not apparent to the broadcast audience, as Newman reported in his *Sunday Times* review:

The B.B.C. programme for the concert of modern chamber music did not pan out quite as was intended. Owing to the difficulty of rehearsing so many new works, we who were in the Arts Theatre were told, the Janacek 'Nursery Rhymes' were to be dropped. The two works to have been broadcast were the Janacek and Hauer's 'Wandlungen'; so that the shelving of the former left room for another work. But whether it was Hindemith's 'Kammermusik No.1' or Krenek's 'Symphonic music for nine solo instruments' that was broadcast I do not know: some listeners in whom I have consulted on the point missed whatever announcement there may have been, and they confessed that neither Hindemith nor Krenek meant anything in their young lives, and they couldn't tell one from the other if their eternal salvation depended on it.[58]

The Hindemith and Krenek works were received by the critics with neither animosity nor enthusiasm. The *Manchester Guardian* reviewer considered Krenek's *Symphonic music* 'as curiously deficient in imaginative vitality. The work contains much that awakens one's interest, but there is none of that natural communicativeness that will keep it awake for any stretch of time'.[59] Newman assessed it somewhat more favourably:

It is perfectly lucid in expression and quite well organised in the matter of form; and its dissonances have no terrors for ears that have been through some of the experiences of recent years. Krenek is sensible enough to strew the more purely thematic writing with plenty of simple rhythmical effects – hammered triplets on the same note, and so on – and it is no doubt the sure hold that these afford the mind that gives the listener the sense of solid organisation in the work. What we cannot be sure of is that there is much really good musical thinking in it, or, as with Hindemith, very much more than a quite infectious delight in a coltish kicking-up of the heels.

While the musical language of these works was familiar enough that they could be listened to and evaluated in traditional ways, the Hauer oratorio perplexed the critics, not only musically, but textually. The BBC had not bothered to provide the invited audience or listening public with the text or translation, and the sung words were unintelligible. The *Manchester Guardian* critic complained:

> The most difficult item to apprehend at a first hearing was Josef Matthias Hauer's 'Transmutations'... No help was given in the way of printed words in the programme or intelligent diction on the singers' part, and one could make nothing of what the Gree[k] characters and the presumably Greek chorus had to convey... That this work of Hauer's was barely intelligible may be due to our total neglect of that composer in England so far, but the fact that one could get neither enjoyment nor much interest out of it looks suspiciously like a deficiency in himself.

Newman felt that the work may have suffered from a poor performance. Even with the text, which he had borrowed from someone who had attended the Baden Baden première, he was unable to understand or assess the piece.

> I have the suspicion... that in spite of the skill of the players and the undoubted competence of Hermann Scherchen, who was conducting, the performance was a very inadequate one. The large body of solo singers no doubt did their conscientious best; but they were evidently ill at ease, and for the most part could not give the work what is the most vital pre-essential to music of this kind – dead certainty of intonation... I confess, however, that the bulk of the music was incomprehensible to me. But the instrumental passage before the solo of Antigone and the music of Antigone herself (beautifully sung by Miss Barbara Pett Fraser), had so much genuinely fine expression in it that I hesitate to believe that all the rest is as bad as it sounded. In this case again I should have welcomed a second performance the same evening.

This concert represents a pattern that had evolved with regard to the BBC contemporary concerts: recently composed works that were structured in discernibly traditional ways and that were constructed on a tonal foundation were received with some degree of comprehension, if not necessarily with enthusiasm. Atonal works, with less immediately accessible forms and textures, were listened to stoically, but were heard with little or no understanding, even by critics such as Newman or Edwin Evans, who were eager to learn about and have access to the latest compositional styles and trends.[60] Perhaps if the BBC had chosen to provide verbal explanations at the time of performance and had given repeat performances, as

Newman suggested, the broadcast dissemination of ultra-modern repertory would have been received in less inflammatory and more meaningful
ways. However, the monthly presentation of extremely difficult works –
over the air, in a single hearing, with little explanation and often with inadequate rehearsal – led to unfavourable critical notices and resistance by the
general public.

The next concert in the contemporary series, on 7 January 1929, featured Steuermann. In August 1928, the pianist wrote that he had recitals
booked in London in October and wondered whether there was any possibility of a BBC engagement at that time.[61] Clark highly recommended to
Wright that he be engaged.

> Personally I consider Steuermann to be the best of the Busoni pupils, and I
> know this opinion is shared by those who know his work best. He has not
> made the career of an international virtuoso, and has no intention of doing
> so, but when it comes to *playing* – His performance of the Hammerklavier
> Sonata was one of the outstanding pianistic events I have heard for a long
> time.[62]

Wright responded cautiously, invoking a new policy concerning foreign
artists.

> Confirming the decision of our Music Committee on September 5th, we are
> to use Steuermann at the time mentioned only if it is not at the expense of an
> English artist who is available and can give an equally attractive programme
> contribution.
>
>   It is felt that we are tending once again too much on the engagement of
> foreigners, and while it is realised that most of these are very talented and
> distinguished in one way or another, we must see that they do not encroach
> too much upon our own artists' work.

In the end, Steuermann was engaged to perform a programme of classical
works in October and the contemporary music concert in January.
Nevertheless, this exchange represents an early manifestation of a policy
approach that was urged by some Corporation policy-makers. This
nationalist tendency became a significant issue in the 1930s, dampening
not only the hiring of foreign artists, but also the amount of continental
contemporary music that could be aired by the BBC.

Preparing for the 7 January concert posed great difficulties for the programme building section, primarily because Clark went on holiday in
December and neglected to inform his colleagues of the programme plans.
As early as 6 November, Steuermann asked Clark to confirm that he would
perform Busoni's *Elegies* and Schoenberg's Five Piano Pieces, op. 23;[63] nevertheless, on 13 December, Wright had to send a desperate telegram to dis-

cover what works Steuermann had agreed to play. Wright also sent a furious letter to Clark at his holiday address in Vienna, revealing that these programme details were not the only information Clark had failed to hand over to his supervisor; in fact, he had left many projects in irretrievable states of limbo.[64] In addition to requesting information that was desperately needed to keep the department running, Wright, not surprisingly, expressed his frustration in trying to work around Clark's negligence and idiosyncrasies.

> I would point out how extremely awkward it is for us working under these conditions. You are the only one who had the information, you knew you were going away for over a month, and here are the Radio Times and other publicity people asking for details so that they may give you publicity and we have to look blank and say we have nothing . . .
>
> I am sorry to worry you with these things, but frankly I think you ought [to] have let me have the [details] without chasing around after you before you left. I am not the only one involved. [T]here is strong irri[t]ation here about this lack of liaison, or whatever one likes to call it, and particularly over the letter I have had from Bechert with reference to Malko . . . I therefore suggest you take immediate steps to clear yourself in the matter or else put it right.

Clark was with Steuermann when Wright's telegram arrived, and apparently contacted him immediately. Nevertheless, details for the 7 January concert were rediscovered too late to be included in the *Radio Times*. The short article simply stated the truth:

> The next recital of 'The Contemporary Chamber Music' season will be relayed from the Arts Theatre Club, Great Newport Street, on Monday evening, January 7. This will be given by Steuermann, the pianist, and Claire Croiza, soprano. Details of their programme have not yet reached me.[65]

In addition to Steuermann's solo contributions – the Busoni and Schoenberg pieces – the programme was to include French songs by Roussel, Ravel, Caplet, Poulenc, Milhaud and Honegger, sung by Claire Croiza and accompanied by Hely Hutchinson. However, the programme had to be changed at the last moment when Croiza became too ill to perform. Steuermann's portion was unchanged, but the singer was replaced by the International String Quartet, a British-based ensemble, performing Vaughan Williams's *Phantasy Quintet* for strings and Bernard van Dieren's String Quartet no. 6;[66] the latter was not broadcast. Two days before the concert, Wright followed standard procedure for last minute programme changes, arranging for the following to be aired:

> We regret to announce that through illness Madame Croiza will be unable to appear in our Concert of contemporary music at the Arts Theatre Club

to-morrow evening at 8 p.m. The programme has consequently been read-justed and will consist of the Busoni and Schönberg pianoforte pieces played by Steuermann, as already announced, together with Vaughan Williams' String Quintet played by The International String Quartet with a second viola.[67]

Wright also intended to send the corrected programme to the announcer responsible for the concert, but – to add yet another mishap to the series that had plagued this programme – he neglected to so. The announcer described the embarrassing consequences of this oversight.

It was my duty to announce the programme for above.

(1) There was no announcement sent down.
(2) No apology framed re the absence of Claire Croiza.
(3) I made the announcement – in my own words – from the 'P. as. B' and apologised re. Croiza. The order of my programme read

 1. String Quartet
 2. Steuermann

The programme was a difficult one to announce, and made me feel *foolish and angry*, when the programme was begun by Steuermann. Surely this should have been otherwise?[68]

Wright acknowledged the error and apologized to those concerned.[69]

During this concert, a Second Viennese School work in the latest style, Schoenberg's Five Piano Pieces, op. 23, was finally broadcast at prime-time. Nevertheless, the daily press devoted little space to the Schoenberg, focusing instead on the chamber works. In his *Manchester Guardian* notice, Eric Blom sarcastically celebrated the fact that a British work should at last receive attention in the contemporary concert series.

The B.B.C. had to change their plans for this evening's programme . . . They had to fall back on something so relatively unenterprising as a second perfor-mance of Mr Bernard van Dieren's latest string quartet, and for once seemed unable to avoid including an English work . . . It must have disappointed those hearers all over the country who were listening-in tonight in breathless anxiety to be made conversant with all the latest tendencies, which are thus delivered to them in monthly instalments, but in rural districts it is sure to have awakened the pleasant feeling that the music which is loved by country-folk contributes something towards the modern metropolitan cults as well as the celebrations of Paris and Vienna. One fancies that the B.B.C. did a good deal by broadcasting this work to give English people at large confidence in the rest of these exacting chamber music programmes.[70]

With respect to Schoenberg's op. 23, Blom seemed more impressed with Steuermann's ability to perform the difficult pieces from memory than with the nature of the work, concluding that 'nothing would be easier than to do precisely the same kind of thing at the piano for hours without the least technical aim or effort of coherent thinking. Without being an out-and-out Schonbergian it is impossible to see any difference between these disconnected sounds and the most recklessly haphazard improvisation.' Cecil Gray of *The Daily Telegraph* had a slightly more positive response.

> The [Busoni] proved distinctly interesting, if a trifle unequal both in style and content. The same could hardly be said of the latter, which are in Schönberg's latest and most ruthless manner. However unpleasant to listen to considered simply as sound, it is nevertheless impossible to deny their power and logic, particularly in the second and third pieces.[71]

Unlike his colleagues, Ernest Newman, in *The Sunday Times*, viewed the Schoenberg pieces as artifacts of a now-discarded compositional experiment: 'The Five Piano Pieces of Schönberg seemed to come to us from a vanished epoch, so old-fashioned and so futile do they sound nowadays. It is hard to believe that a few enthusiasts once saw in them the dawning of a new epoch in music.'[72]

Blom's review for *The Musical Times* concentrated primarily on the Schoenberg piano pieces, only mentioning the other works at the end of the article.[73] Although he revealed a basic awareness of Schoenberg's new compositional approach, he condemned it and expressed his dissatisfaction that it was given so much broadcast time.

> The almost invariable presidency of Schönberg, represented either by his own work or that of his disciples, makes one suspect the influence of predilections excusable and interesting in a particular person, but not altogether natural to a corporation.

Without specifying Clark by name, Blom challenged the repertory pattern of the series, which, not surprisingly, reflected the influence and interests of the programme builder primarily responsible for it. He also focused on the specific case of Schoenberg's op. 23:

> The objection to these pieces is not that they are nonsense, for one does not for a moment call Schönberg's sincerity in question, but that they are written in an idiom in which no man not forewarned can trust himself to tell sense from nonsense. A composer has a right to make a new language for himself, but even the newest language must have a vocabulary susceptible to some sort of grammatical treatment and a syntax. Schönberg's new Dance Suite for pianoforte, Op. 25, for instance, is written in a highly formalised new idiom, though even there it is questionable whether the ultimate test of the ear will justify a theoretically interesting system. Op. 23 quite definitely yields nothing to study or to hearing.

Clark's repeated effort to broadcast recent repertory from the Second Viennese School was at least partially successful: although the prime time broadcast of Schoenberg's op. 23 had little impact on the wider listening audience, the event was accorded notice, if not understanding, enthusiasm or sympathy, within the British musical community.

Several broadcasts of Schoenberg and Berg works that took place outside the 1928–9 BBC Concerts of Contemporary Music are worthy of note. Berg's music was finally introduced to listeners on 24 October 1928, in a studio recital featuring the German pianist, Dr Ernst Bachrich, a pupil of Schoenberg from 1916 to 1919 and a member of the Second Viennese circle. Bachrich performed a Smetana polka and Berg's Piano Sonata, op. 1. Although this was a studio concert transmitted over the alternative wavelength, Newman devoted a significant portion of a talk to introducing the composer and his op. 1, recommending that listeners 'interested in modern musical development might do well to listen to this Sonata'.[74] After placing its style within a familiar context in the usual way – 'You will notice how Wagnerian it is; it will set you thinking of "Tristan"' – Newman justified subsequent Second Viennese School developments.

> Now, if you had followed Schönberg from the beginning of his career you would have got the impression in his early days that here was a gifted young man who was destined to take up the old German tradition, and to carry it a stage further. Then at a later stage you would have found Schönberg turning his back on it, or the greater part of it, and wanting none of it. He realised that there was no future for himself, or anyone else, on those lines, because everything that could be said had been said so effectively by Wagner that whoever tried to work in the same vein would be only echoing Wagner. And so Schönberg decided to take a line of his own, and when he revolted he took his pupils with him.
>
> Now, I should like you to test this theory for yourselves by listening to Alban Berg's Sonata . . . The Sonata shows a really fine imagination, a gift for continuous thinking, and a sensitive feeling for style . . . This Sonata when we hear it will help to explain a good many things that have happened in the music of the last 20 years.

Newman's personal interest in Berg and his music accorded unusual attention to this routine studio broadcast.

Second Viennese repertory featured in two other studio broadcasts during the 1928–9 season. First, *Verklärte Nacht* was broadcast again on 17 December 1928. More interestingly, perhaps, the Vienna String Quartet returned to the BBC in February 1929 to perform a programme similar to the one they gave on 13 February 1928. The studio recital replaced a concert broadcast of *Pierrot lunaire* that was planned for 12 February 1929. In

Wright's angry letter to Clark of 14 December 1928, he referred to: 'Pierrot Luniare [*sic*] (February 11 and 12)'. Clark was arranging for the work to be performed at the Arts Theatre Club on those dates and suggested that one of the concerts be transmitted. When the BBC contacted the theatre manager, Lionel Barton, about this plan, he replied: 'Clark and I did not fully go into the question of Pierrot Luniare and I am afraid I shall have to have all the available dates before saying whether we could do it'. Wright felt that Clark had misrepresented the theatre's commitment to the performance.

> You told me quite definitely it was decided upon and asked me to fix February 12 here again so that you might wire Bechert,[75] although I never signed off that wire; I dont know if you sent it. I wish you would take up the matter at once with Barton for although personally I do not care two hoops whether we do it here on February 12 or not a decision one way or the other ought to be given and it is frankly the Arts Theatre and not the B.B.C. who is holding it up. [76]

In the new year, Wright informed the artists that the theatre was unavailable on the suggested dates, and the project was postponed until the following season.[77]

The programmers replaced the *Pierrot lunaire* broadcast on 12 February with a studio recital of comparable works, performed by the Vienna String Quartet. Although the *Radio Times* indicated that the quartet were to play only Bartók's and Schönberg's Third String Quartets,[78] the 'Programmes as Broadcast' records show that two movements from Berg's *Lyric Suite* – 'Andante amoroso' and 'Allegro misterioso' – were also performed. Once again, programme changes led to a significant event taking place with negligible notice: the long-postponed transmission of Berg's *Lyric Suite* was realized, at least in part, but without warning and, given the late broadcasting time, probably without much of an audience.

Newman discussed the recital in a 'Music Criticism' talk, in which he reviewed recent broadcasts.[79] He did not mention the Berg, reserving comment on Second Viennese School matters for the Schoenberg quartet. Having heard the work three times and studied the score, Newman apparently felt ready to express his opinion: 'I found it disappointing, and unquestionably boring. I am conscious of the technical ingenuity of the writing, but it seemed to me poor stuff. I have no use for technical ingenuity when it is expended on ideas that are mostly ugly or commonplace'. More importantly, he made a general pronouncement about Schoenberg's latest idiom:

> For my part I am getting thoroughly tired of music the writers of which expect too much of us. It is impossible for us at first to be sure there is not

something in it, impossible to be sure that the fault for our failure to like it is not in ourselves, unless we study it carefully. When I have done this, when I have given hours and hours to a difficult score like this Schönberg and then had to come to the conclusion that it was never worth all the trouble that I too conscientiously took over it, I feel that I have been a bit of a fool.

Like Blom in his assessment of Schoenberg's op. 23, Newman concluded that Schoenberg's compositional method was worthless and ineffectual; even after repeated hearings and analysis, it did not yield tangible meaning or pleasure . He concluded:

> Once bitten, twice shy; I shall take no such trouble over any future work by Schönberg. No composer has the right to expect so large a proportion of a busy man's time to be spent trying to discover whether he has written sense or nonsense. I am content to wait now for the verdict of time as to the value of Schönberg . . . I shall leave Schönberg to the little international clique of admirers that has tried to force him on us all these years, and I shall get on to something that interests me more, and gives me more pleasure – and I have a suspicion that you feel about this matter very much as I do.

Although transmissions of early, romantic works by Second Viennese School composers still received favourable attention, by 1929 greater exposure to recent works of Schoenberg, Berg and Webern in BBC broadcasts led important and influential British critics, such as Newman and Blom, to denounce publicly and vehemently this difficult musical idiom.

# 7 Pitt's final season, 1929–1930

The last season of the decade coincided with major upheaval within the inner circles of the BBC Music Department. Like the rest of the Corporation, the department suffered from a spate of resignations of well-known radio personalities around this time. In addition to Scholes's resignation in September 1928, the other man known for educating listeners about music, Sir Walford Davies, ceased to give his popular music talks in November 1929; his 'Music and the Ordinary Listener' series was taken over for a time by Dr George Dyson.[1] The most-publicized resignation, however, was that of Percy Pitt from his position as Music Director at the end of 1929. This fundamental change had far-reaching implications for the department as a whole, inherently affecting its structure, programming and outlook.

Pitt was not happy about leaving the BBC. Rumours that he was to resign began to circulate as early as March 1929, when the press reported that he was 'likely to relinquish his post at the end of the year';[2] however, this information was immediately refuted: 'The B.B.C. stated yesterday that the report that Mr. Percy Pitt has resigned his position as music director of the corporation is inaccurate.'[3] In May, rumours of Pitt's resignation were again reported:

> The British Broadcasting Corporation has decided that its officials shall automatically retire on reaching the age of 60. This decision will affect certain of the present staff, of whom the best known is probably Mr. Percy Pitt, the Director of Music, who will be 60 years of age on January 4th of next year . . .
>
> Mr. Pitt's retirement has been rumoured for some time, and only recently he denied that he had resigned. It is understood that his retirement will take place at the end of December.[4]

Once again, the rumour was denied, although the denial was viewed with suspicion:

> The fervour of denial at Savoy Hill demonstrated that there was something in the rumour that Mr. Percy Pitt could not be prevailed upon to continue the conduct of the work of the B.B.C. Music Department after the end of this year. Readers of these notes will have known that the succession has been a close thing between Sir Hamilton Harty and Dr. Adrian Boult, with Beecham stock intervening every now and then . . .[5]

By June, Pitt's resignation was confirmed, as was the identity of his successor, Adrian Boult.[6] It was originally planned that Boult would assume his role as Music Director immediately after Pitt formally left the BBC on 31 December 1929; however, in December, the BBC announced that Boult would not take up his new post until 15 May 1930.[7]

The confused publicity surrounding Pitt's resignation might suggest that there was indecision behind the scenes about whether he was to leave. However, a Control Board minute from October 1929 clarifies that the central administrators had had no doubt since April that the Music Department's leadership would change, and they had apparently initiated the action:

> Controller [C. D. Carpendale] asked the position in regard to Mr. Pitt, and A.C. [Assistant Controller: Goldsmith] replied that he had been given notice on 6th April for his services to terminate on 4th January next.[8]

Nevertheless, rumours continued even after Pitt's resignation had taken effect. On 3 January 1930, the *Daily Telegraph* reported that the resignation had been due to ill-health, only to rescind that claim: 'We are asked to say that it is not the fact, as stated yesterday, that Mr. Percy Pitt resigned from the post of musical director of the B.B.C. on account of ill-health. Mr. Pitt, we are glad to say, is in excellent health.'[9]

Pitt's final year as Music Director was marred by his impending resignation; he resented what he believed was unfair treatment by the Corporation.[10] Nevertheless, the outstanding achievements of his years as Music Department head remained untainted. Between 1923 and 1929, he built into the Music Department a core programming staff which had the vision, imagination and experience to implement musically the fundamental BBC policy of educating listeners and expanding their cultural horizons. His concepts and convictions were supplemented by the experiences, ideas and industry of Wright, Clark and Herbage, assisted by Hely Hutchinson and Mase. Pitt's legacy to the BBC included the formation of this dedicated group, who fulfilled the ever-increasing demands in programme quantity, quality and variety that the Corporation required. Furthermore, initiatives devised by Pitt and his staff and encouraged by the central administrators' policies during the BBC's formative years resulted in music programmes that were often extraordinary for their time.

## The music programmes

Music broadcasts during the 1929–30 season followed the now-established programming pattern of previous years, with the Queen's Hall symphony concerts at the cornerstone. The 22 programmes, presented on Friday nights at 8.00 pm, nearly doubled the number given the previous year. Many of the conductors from earlier seasons returned, including Beecham,[11] Wood, Ronald, Ansermet and Scherchen. The series encompassed a wide range of repertory, balancing standard works with recently-composed British and continental music. Some of the works which would have been unfamiliar to the listening audience were Strauss's *Sinfonia domestica*, Hindemith's *Kammermusik* no. 5 with the composer as viola soloist, Walton's *Sinfonia concertante* for piano and orchestra, Bartók's Piano Concerto no. 1 with the composer as soloist, Bax's Symphony no. 2, Sibelius's *Tapiola*, Toch's Piano Concerto, Reger's *Variations and Fugue on a Theme of Mozart* and a repeat of Mahler's Symphony no. 8. In one of the more unusual programmes, Ansermet conducted Vaughan Williams's *Flos campi*, Debussy's *La mer*, Honegger's *Rugby* and Stravinsky's *Song of the Nightingale*. In another, Perez Casas conducted an all-Spanish programme, including Falla's *Noches en los jardines de España* and Oscar Espla's *La noch buena del diablo*.[12] At the end of the series, two extra programmes were given: a Good Friday concert conducted by Wood consisting of excerpts from *Parsifal*, and a performance of Mendelssohn's *Elijah* conducted by Stanford Robinson.

The People's Palace concerts continued during winter 1929–30. Like the first series, these symphony concerts were conducted by Ronald and Pitt and most of the soloists were British. In addition, regional symphony concerts continued to be broadcast as regularly presented series. The Hallé concerts from Manchester were featured every other week on Thursday nights. On other Thursdays, concerts were relayed by the Birmingham orchestra from the city's Town Hall, and on many Tuesday nights, concerts by the Liverpool Philharmonic Orchestra were transmitted from The Philharmonic Hall. Every Thursday afternoon at 3 pm, orchestral concerts were presented from The Pavilion in Bournemouth. This fascinating series of concerts, conducted by Sir Dan Godfrey, was aimed at a middle-class, sea-side resort audience and often featured first performances of orchestral works by lesser-known British composers, many of whom were women. Interestingly, the series of Bach cantatas continued each Sunday, with the BBC proudly claiming that 'no feature of the week's programmes has a larger body of supporters than the Sunday cantata'.[13] Similarly, the 'Foundations of Music' recitals continued to be presented on a regular basis. Finally, monthly presentations of opera were continued during the 1929–30 season.[14]

By the end of the 1920s, then, large-scale series were established as the primary means by which the music programme builders developed long-range programming schemes. This approach enabled the Music

Department to implement the BBC's fundamental cultural-expansion policies: through increasingly sophisticated programme options – such as the unusual public symphony concerts, the popular orchestral concerts, full-length opera performances, the 'Fundamentals' recitals and the Bach cantatas – radio provided ordinary listeners with frequent opportunities to acquaint themselves with the musical spectrum of the day.

## Contemporary music programming

During Pitt's final season as BBC Music Director, contemporary music programming also followed the precepts and patterns established during the previous two seasons. However, the intensive publicity campaign that had been sustained throughout the 1928–9 season was discontinued in autumn 1929. The BBC adopted a new strategy of passivity, no longer promoting or justifying its contemporary music policy to the British public. Although occasional letters from new music enthusiasts were printed in the *Radio Times*, there were no feature articles and few talks tackling the subject. At the end of the season, vituperative audience response to an all-Schoenberg concert briefly returned the issue to public attention. Nevertheless, for most of the 1929–30 season, the BBC outwardly limited its new music activities to broadcasting recently-composed works.

### *BBC commissioning of new works for radio*

In contrast to this subdued public approach, new music activities continued behind the scenes as before: members of the Music Department staff retained a keen interest in new works and compositional trends. In spring 1929, Clark informed the department about a scheme that had been initiated in Germany, in which radio companies commissioned young composers to create pieces specifically for broadcasting. That year alone, works had been commissioned from twelve composers, including Franz Schreker, Max Butting, Kurt Weill, Josef Matthias Hauer and Ernst Toch. Clark strongly recommended that the BBC launch such a scheme.

> Our programmes are generally considered to be the best, but in the present instance the Germans have undoubtedly got ahead of us. Might I suggest that we discuss the possibility of giving certain of our composers commissions to write similar kinds of works especially for wireless transmission, such as would take into account and solve the difficulties which are inherent in the mechanism of radio. It would be a profitable thing for all concerned if the young creative musical forces were associated with our work and the experi-

mental results would be invaluable to all those musicians who write and arrange things for the broadcast repertoire, as time goes on more and more people are becoming dependant [*sic*] on wireless for their hearing of music.[15]

In May, the Music Department approved a similar project,[16] an important step since the BBC had avoided commissioning new works since the failed attempts of 1926. Department staff considered which characteristics would guarantee a works' appropriateness for broadcasting, determining that the new pieces should be 'orchestral or chamber or both (with or without small Chorus) really light in character and suitable for the microphone'. Clark prepared a list of composers who might be invited to participate in the project.

In January 1930, Clark and Herbage submitted proposals from three British composers who were willing to write a work for 'small chorus, small orchestra of not exceeding fifteen, and soloist'. William Walton proposed to write *Nebuchadnezzar, or The Writing on the Wall*, setting an Osbert Sitwell text. Constant Lambert was interested in composing *Black Majesty (The Emperor of Haiti)*, using his own adaptation of a book by that name. Victor Hely Hutchinson suggested *The Town*, to a text by Cecil Lewis. In a memo to Boult and Eckersley, Wright provided details about commissioning fees,[17] and explained that the new works were expected to be 'musically entertaining, and usable fairly extensively and not merely rarely . . . They should, further, be more of the type that continental stations would like to broadcast, as indicative of our work in this sphere'.[18] He also mentioned an unexpected complication:

> Immediately Clark had discussed matters with Walton, he 'spilled the beans' to the Press, stating that he had been definitely commissioned – at least, that is the story in the papers. We do not want to quarrel with him, and by the time these suggestions have been approved, and letters sent to the composers, it will be almost a new story.

Wright did not foresee any difficulties from early publicity, although the BBC had not planned to inform the press until all plans were finalized.

On 1 April, Herbage again broached the subject with the Music Director:

> A Concert of the 'Music for Broadcasting' commissioned by the German Broadcasting Company will be given here under the direction of Hermann Scherchen on May 7th, and we feel that this is the most suitable time to announce our commissions to British composers and so secure the widest publicity and reclame for the B.B.C.'s part in the development of music specially written for broadcasting.[19]

With the launch date only five weeks away, the programme builders still awaited official approval for the commissions. In fact, Eckersley had suggested an alternative scheme to the Director-General a few days earlier, proposing that the BBC offer a £100 prize for the best composition of the year, 'in the nature of a Nobel prize for music in this country'.

> I feel it to be one of our duties to stimulate as far as possible the work of the British composer. Attempts have been made in the past to effect such stimulation by the commissioning of works, and, on occasions, by competitions. I am not sure that these methods are satisfactory. It is too easy to commission a work and then find the results not worth while. The same applies to competitions with money prizes and we have had experience of this.[20]

Reith did not take to the idea: 'I don't feel vy. enthusiastic because of our fiascos, and there must be a good many such prizes already'.[21] Moreover, Boult reminded Eckersley of Clark's project.

> This particular commissioning scheme seems to have been embarked on sometime ago, and I gather . . . that we are pretty well committed. Under these circumstances would you be willing to sanction it pending our discussion of the whole idea?[22]

Eckersley grudgingly agreed that the Music Department 'must go ahead with the present commitment to Walton & Lambert'.

Despite Boult's urgings, however, official approval was not finalized before the broadcast of German works.[23] The *Radio Times* notice included a detailed description of the main piece, *Der Lindberghflug* composed by Hindemith and Weill.

> It is designed absolutely for the radio – feeding the mind's eye with words as its music feeds the ear, using the additional artifice of 'effects', and building from it all something 'rich and strange'.[24]

The notice also alluded to the possibility of broadcasts of similar English works: 'A whisper has reached us (how authoritatively informed we do not know) that certain young English composers may be expected soon to join in this attractive adventure.'

At the end of May, Clark informed Boult that Walton had returned from Italy and the commissioned score was nearly complete. European conductors who had seen the work, which was now called *Belshazzar's Feast*, were anxious to perform it, and Clark recommended that the BBC take immediate steps toward arranging the première.[25] However, only on 6 June, over a year after the project was first discussed, did Richard Howgill, the Copyright Assistant, finally send Walton a letter of invitation:

> The payment we would suggest is £50 for the sole broadcasting rights, to cover the interests of both yourself and your collaborator, and this leaves the mechanical rights and all other performing rights in your hands. We shall be glad to hear that you are agreeable to these terms in order that we can complete the matter and arrange for the first performance.[26]

At this point, serious problems surfaced: the BBC's prolonged delay had led to a misunderstanding on Walton's part as to the type and length of the commissioned work. Far from being a piece 'really light in character and suitable for the microphone', *Belshazzar's Feast* was a large-scale oratorio of significant length and serious nature. Walton referred the matter to his publisher, Hubert J. Foss of Oxford University Press, who relayed the composer's point of view to the BBC.

> The B.B.C. seem to have misunderstood about the length and nature of the work they commissioned me to do for them. Though I am only about half-way through, I can foresee more or less exactly how long it will last. Its duration will be a little over the half hour – certainly not more than 40 minutes. The material required for its performance is a chorus (not less than 16 and preferably about 24 or 32), two soloists (baritone and mezzo-soprano), speaker and small orchestra – its title being BELSHAZZAR'S FEAST. It is in four sections, connected by the speaker.[27]

Foss suggested that the Corporation pay the composer £100 for sole broadcasting rights to the work for ten years.

When reporting the situation to Graves, the Assistant Director of Programmes, Howgill clearly disapproved of the unprofessional manner in which the Music Department had handled the commissioning project:

> I must mention that we seem to be very definitely committed over the matter although I did not write to Walton until the 6th of this month when the composition of the work had been in train apparently for some time. Walton refers to having been commissioned to do the work and states that he definitely refused a better offer in order to get on with it, which points to his having been asked to go ahead before arrangements were ready. I do not think the matter ought to have been mentioned to him in such a way as to give him a reason for starting before we were able to agree about the payment and the nature and length of the work required. If it was, our hands are tied as regards negotiation and it seems that all we can do now is to endeavour to get it for, say, £80 instead of £100 . . .
>
> The commissioning of original musical works is not, in my opinion, very satisfactory and you will probably agree that unless the initial stages of negotiation are properly handled it is even less so.[28]

Graves concurred, firmly blaming Clark for the mix-up: 'It was quite clear from the [papers] that before D.P. [Director of Programmes: Eckersley] had agreed the scheme Clarke had got Walton in train. Will you impress on him that only Howgill can be at all committal in any matters of this kind'.[29] However, Wright adamantly defended his colleague:

> Clark assures me that nothing was ever said to Walton that implied a definite commission. On the contrary, when [Walton] was going away to Italy early this year and asked if he could get on with it he was told that that was a matter for himself to decide and that although this department was recommending the commissioning of the work it had not had any official sanction whatsoever. When he returned from Italy the work was half written. I might add that the subject was well in his mind as an attractive possibility at the time that we first approached him with regard to a commission of some kind.[30]

Moreover, Wright blamed Walton for diverging from the original commissioning concept and recommended that the BBC refuse to take financial responsibility.

> With regard to the time and price for 'Belshazzar's Feast', Mr Howgill agreed with Clark, Herbage and myself that the work should be from 20 minutes to half-an-hour and a reasonable price would be £50. Walton's original idea was just inside half-an-hour which is still of the magnitude envisaged by Mr Howgill for the £50 figure. If Walton has found 40 minutes necessary it is his concern, and, in fact, we view it with disfavour, having felt always that 30 minutes should be the maximum for broadcasting purposes. If Mr Howgill has to go higher than £50 I submit that it should be on the intrinsic value of the work considered on the half hour basis still, and not because Walton on his own account has gone well beyond the limits first discussed.

Walton maintained his position that the work was in fact a direct result of the BBC offer and, furthermore, complained that 'while in Italy I wrote repeatedly to the B.B.C. to Mr. Clark to get the commission put in writing but had no reply. Naturally enough, having started the work, I wasn't very willing to stop and start something else, though having no confirmation from the B.B.C.'[31] Nevertheless, the BBC was unwilling to pay more than £50, especially given the fact that *Belshazzar's Feast* was inappropriate for its intended function. Walton finally agreed to write 'something else as his commissioned work, and offers us, quite independent of commission, the first performance of 'Belshazzar's Feast.'"[32] In the end, he never composed a work to fulfil the commission; moreover, the Corporation did not take up the offer for the oratorio's first performance.[33]

Similarly, the work solicited from Constant Lambert did not come to fruition. During the negotiations for Walton's work, Howgill asked the Music Department about the status of Lambert's commission. Mase confirmed that 'we are not committed in writing to Lambert, but I feel that morally we are, as he has obviously understood from various conversations that he would be commissioned'.[34] However, in November 1930, Foss informed Howgill that Lambert was no longer interested.

> [Lambert] has asked me to write and say that after thinking it over at considerable length with great care, he thinks there is very little chance of his being able to devote his attention to a choral work for some considerable time. In his present mood he finds that a choral work has little attraction for him.[35]

Lambert offered the BBC a newly completed concerto for piano and eight instruments in lieu of the agreed choral work, but the Music Department decided that would not be acceptable.

> The whole point of the commission was of music for broadcasting. In it not merely the possibilities (and vagaries) of microphone technique would be exploited, but the subject of the text should be such as to appeal to the masses irrespective of the actual music. That is why the 'Lindberghflug', though perhaps doubtful on purely musical or artistic grounds, did make a sensational appeal in Germany to the masses, and we thought that Lambert's original suggestion based on the book 'Black Majesty' was excellent for our purpose.[36]

In fact, Lambert never completed his choral work based on *Black Majesty*.

Finally, the commission to Hely Hutchinson was obstructed for different reasons. In September 1930, Boult considered when the programme builder might be granted leave for this work, now planned as 'a sequence of songs and orchestral pieces based on G. K. Chesterton's book "The Flying Inn"', but Eckersley felt the Music Department could not spare him for the three weeks he needed.[37] Wright urged the administrators to reconsider:

> You do realise, don't you, that Mr Hely Hutchinson is on an all-inclusive contract, it being felt that one of the most valuable parts of his work has always been his inventiveness, particularly his compositions written for, and ideally suited to, microphone work. It seems hardly fair, if we want an important work like this from him, to ask him to attempt to do it under unfavourable conditions, or during his holiday when he should be resting.[38]

In 1933, Hely Hutchinson published three songs based on Chesterton texts;[39] however, it is not clear whether these settings were part of Hely Hutchinson's commissioned radio work, or whether that work was ever completed or broadcast.

The Music Department eagerly supported Clark's initial suggestion that they commission young British composers to create new musical works of popular character, especially written for the new medium of radio.

However, the lack of coordinated procedure led to a series of errors and misunderstandings, which ultimately resulted in the project's failure. In the end, none of the composers provided the BBC with a light, choral work, suited to the microphone. Moreover, by stubbornly adhering to the original commissioning concept, the BBC completely missed the significance of the work that Walton did produce, in effect rejecting one of the foremost British works from the first half of this century. As in its earlier attempts to become involved with the creation of new musical compositions, the Music Department's commissioning aspirations once again led to embarrassing failure.

### The covert campaign to educate listeners

Although the BBC avoided blatant debate or defence of its contemporary music policy during most of the 1929–30 season, it bolstered its position in less direct ways. For example, at judicious intervals the Corporation published letters from contemporary music enthusiasts in the *Radio Times*. The week before a broadcast featuring Second Viennese School repertory, the following appeared:

> I am glad to see your winter programme of contemporary and other chamber music. I trust that the great number of complaints which you are bound to receive will not affect your policy in this direction. I belong to that small but ever-growing body of people who make a point of listening to certain programmes rather than hearing them, as I fear a great number of your listeners do. I have, however, no desire to deprive this very large section of the public to its rightful amusement, and I hope this section will not desire to deprive us, the very small section, of ours.[40]

Similarly, the issue of 4 April 1930 – distributed a few days before an all-Schoenberg concert – contained a similar letter.

> I see a number of letters objecting to the production by the B.B.C. of modern music. Does *no* one ever write to you thanking you for it? I should like to put on emphatic record my gratitude to the B.B.C. for giving us examples of Stravinsky, Hindemith, Schonberg, Krenek and others; not to mention the work of numerous contemporary British composers who are making the present the most remarkable musical era in the history of this country. Much of the modern music may not be great. I am not arguing values. But the object of this letter is to thank the B.B.C. very warmly, on behalf of those of us who are living contemporaneously, and not in a past age, for the priceless opportunity it gives us of hearing contemporary music.[41]

On the same page, this view was reinforced by the reprinting of a remark recently made by Compton Mackenzie, the editor of *The Gramophone*:

> The halfwits who write nearly every week to *The Radio Times* about chamber music as if it were a kind of eczema on the programme of the B.B.C. are, of course, not worth bothering about, though I think it is a pity to give publicity to their letters, which are on par with the rude noises children make in omnibuses.

Mackenzie's comment was less subtle, perhaps, than the letter of thanks, but its very crudeness underlined the point. The BBC used it to reinforce its covert efforts to stave off criticism of the upcoming concert.

In addition to these letters, new music was touched on in several broadcast talks during the season. Newman's bi-weekly talk on 27 September 1929 tackled the problem of contemporary harmony.

> I want tonight to talk to you a little about a subject which is evidently exercising the minds of a great many people, judging from the correspondence I have had. You will remember that a fortnight ago I read a letter from a lady at Ilford protesting against the 'noises' that were made by the B.B.C. under the guise of music . . . Evidently this has upset a great many people. It is impossible, of course, in a quarter of an hour, to cover the whole range of modern harmony, but let us try to get to one or two of the fundamental points connected with it.[42]

Newman briefly explained different modern harmonic approaches, basing his discussion on specific pieces. He aimed to convince listeners that 'a chord that sounds horrible in itself may not be horrible in its context . . . Let us try, if we can, to get at the composer's meaning, because once you have got his meaning you will not be likely to be upset by an apparent harshness in his harmony'. His final example was a 12-tone work, identified only as follows: 'It is by a young Polish composer; it is a series of fifteen variations on a Theme dedicated to Arnold Schönberg'. However, instead of providing concrete information about the compositional system or harmonic language, Newman simply complained about his inability to come to terms with the 12-tone technique.

In another talk on 22 November 1929 – given shortly after a concert featuring Second Viennese School works – Newman defended himself and the BBC from listener protests in the usual way. He argued that the BBC was simply facilitating a natural process.

> Whether music is good music or bad music is decided in the long run, not by the critics, but by the great mass of orderly, sensible people who make up the musical public – in a word by yourselves. If, after a reasonable amount of hearing of this music, you say that you do not like it, sentence of death is pronounced on it . . . You are the tribunal, and there is no appeal from your decision. But no honest tribunal will pronounce judgment without hearing the evidence.[43]

Finally, he reminded listeners that 'it is impossible to over-estimate the service the B.B.C. has done the country in broadcasting all this modern music. But for the B.B.C., millions of you would never have heard it'. The BBC thus indirectly circulated its now-familiar arguments, continuing to justify and defend the broadcasting of this highly unpopular material.

A third talk on contemporary music was given on 17 January 1930 by Peter Latham, a University of London harmony and counterpoint lecturer. 'Is Modern Music Bad?' was not only broadcast, but it was reproduced, in shortened form, in the next week's issue of *The Listener*.[44] Latham gave a brief explanation of dissonant harmony, like Newman, encouraging listeners to hear new music for themselves.

> [The amateur] may say, 'I don't like Holst's music', but he must not say, 'Holst's music is bad', unless he can produce weighty arguments to confute the many who have pronounced it good, and given reasons for their verdict . . . I know that he is genuinely anxious to come to terms with modern music, and I know also how difficult he finds it. I should like to help him if I can, not to explore the whole subject – we have not time for that – but to remove a difficulty or two from his path.

In its attempt to reduce controversial public debate, the BBC found subtle ways, such as this article, to support its contemporary music broadcasts during the 1929–30 season. Nevertheless, the debate re-emerged with a vengeance in spring 1930, as described below, and the BBC returned to more direct means of defending its new music policies and activities.

## Broadcasts of Second Viennese School works

Following the general trend to underplay new music transmissions, the 1929–30 BBC Concerts of Contemporary Music took place with little public ceremony. Unlike the previous year, in which they were broadcast over the main wavelengths, 2LO and 5XX, this series was aired over the alternative wavelength, 5GB. The decision to limit the broadcasts in this way resulted from internal BBC objections to them. In response, Wright wrote the first of what would become annual spring statements in which he defended the Music Department's commitment to the series.[45] Admitting that the concerts were aimed at a small audience, he conceded that 'it is bad policy to thrust these minority programmes down people's throats, but this is an argument not against the programmes but in favour of continuing them on 5GB instead of 2LO or S.B. ' Moreover, he proposed the interesting, but unprecedented, idea of transmitting the concerts over the long-wave transmitter, 5XX, in conjunction with 5GB.

> We are admired on the Continent among musicians for our progressive policy in this matter, and 5GB is inaudible usually to these people. Could the policy of putting them on 5XX, though not 2LO, be considered, or is it an important and unchanging policy to keep 5XX and 5GB always different?

This suggestion was not implemented.

Wright also responded to the administrators' strong objections to the uncompromising nature of the music, rejecting the idea of mixing familiar and unfamiliar material in the programmes.

> We cannot agree . . . to this policy being applied to the solitary hour of Contemporary Music once a month. People either listen or do not listen to these, and any amount of coaxing b[y] a less strange work would not make much difference.
>
>  It is agreed, apparently, that the publicity value of these special concerts in the presence of critics etc. is great. It should be realised that we would not get them there unless the whole programme was exceptional in interest, i.e. it cannot afford to be diluted.

It is interesting to note that Wright responded directly to the BBC Music Critic's disparaging remarks about the idioms represented – comments that apparently induced the central administrators to question the series' value.

> Newman may have disapproved strongly of some of the works, but he has been one of the strongest supporters of the B.B.C. policy of giving this new music a hearing. Whether this hearing is going to kill or make this music can only be a matter of private conjecture and the proof of time.
>
>  Newman is not the man to seek for guidance in choosing these programmes. He is not in sympathy with music representative of composers activity to-day, but he is a fine critic and for that reason his views are always interesting.

Wright concluded with a brief allusion to the cultural-expansionist argument, emphasizing once again the important service the BBC provided with this series: 'Modern music will be a staple diet only when it ceases to be "modern", and by bringing it forward we are helping it to cease to be "modern" and "strange".'

Wright's memo was apparently effective, since the 1929–30 series of contemporary concerts went ahead. Eight concerts were presented monthly between 7 October 1929 and 5 May 1930. The programmes emphasized many of the same composers, musical styles and international artists as in earlier seasons: an all-Bartók concert was performed by the composer and Szigeti, a programme featuring Stravinsky's *Les noces* was conducted by Ansermet, two French and German concerts were given, one involving Hindemith as a performer and the other conducted by Scherchen, and there was an all-British programme. The remaining three concerts featured Second Viennese School repertory, performed by Steuermann, Hinnenberg-Lefèbre, the Pierrot Lunaire Ensemble of Vienna, and Anton Webern, in his British conducting début.[46]

The music staff felt that airing the programmes from the Arts Theatre Club had been a success in 1928–9, and requested that it be rehired for the new series.

> We do want the music critics and others who are interested to come and whose goodwill we are very glad to keep, to be comfortable, and they certainly were not in the Studio. At the Arts Theatre there is nice room for them and the music can be heard to advantage as in a concert hall, while the broadcast itself is definitely good. It would be a great pity to try to go back to the Studio for the next series, especially as the audience of musicians particularly interested and even the number of critics themselves is definitely on the increase.[47]

The Programme Board approved the theatre's continued use, and its Managing Director, Bernard Isaacs, was approached about booking dates.[48] He asked for an increase in fee, from £15 to £20 per concert, and was only willing to book the first half of the series at that time; the BBC agreed to these terms.[49]

In September, Herbage drew up a preliminary plan for the series, based on discussions with Clark, which included estimated costs for each concert. He proposed that programmes with audience drawing power be performed at the Kingsway Hall in London.

> The cost of the Arts Theatre is £21 per broadcast, of which it is not possible to get any back by the sale of tickets: the cost of the Kingsway Hall would be £31/10/–, and the necessary advertising, tickets, etc. need not be more than £10/10/– to £15/15/–. Thus, if we took an average of only £30 on these concerts, we would be saving money and also would probably not come up against the difficulties of accommodation and balance that a concert like 'Les Noces' would certainly encounter at the Arts Theatre Club.[50]

This raised an important policy question. The BBC had not risked opening the contemporary concerts to the public since the first season in 1926–7. Would the Corporation now risk enabling the general public to hear the concerts properly from the hall and in their entirety? Although Wright felt Herbage had underestimated the costs, he supported the idea.[51] The Booking Manager also agreed that the suggestion was financially feasible, and the plan was officially approved at a November meeting of the Programme Board.[52]

In the end, the concerts in the second half of the series were held at the cavernous Central Hall, Westminster, rather than at the more intimate Kingsway Hall.[53] The huge number of seats in the Central Hall would not be filled by those willing to pay to hear unfamiliar music. Rather than justifying the larger venue through box office takings, as Herbage and Wright had originally envisaged, the BBC chose to distribute free tickets in a widely advertised campaign.[54] However, the *Evening News* critic gave what he believed were the real reasons behind such apparent generosity:

> A B.B.C. authority told me the truth about the tickets given away for those concerts of very modern chamber music. 'We always gave away some', he said – 'not many, because at the Arts Theatre there was not much room. Now our concerts of contemporary chamber music are to be at the Central Hall, Westminster, which has 1,000 seats. For acoustical reasons we want as many as possible of those 1,000 seats to be occupied. We are glad for keen students of music to hear these concerts, and doubly glad because they damp down the echo, which is a little excessive if the hall is quite empty'.[55]

To improve acoustical clarity, the BBC was forced to sacrifice the projected financial returns.

At the beginning of the season, the BBC did not publish introductions to the series as previously. Instead, a short notice appeared in the *Radio Times* after the first programme, briefly outlining the remaining concerts;[56] further promotion was limited to advertising and introducing each programme.

The first concert to feature Second Viennese School repertory took place on 4 November 1929. Since the Arts Theatre Club was unavailable that day, it took place at the Grotrian Hall.[57] Steuermann and Margot Hinnenberg-Lefèbre performed a programme that was built around Schoenberg's song cycle, *Das Buch der hängenden Gärten*, op. 15. Steuermann also played Eisler's and Berg's op. 1 Piano Sonatas and Busoni's *Fantasia contrappuntistica*; all except the last work were broadcast.

Clark first began to discuss this programme with Steuermann in April 1929, shortly after hearing a work by one of Steuermann's pupils.

> I have just come back from Geneva, where one of the best things I heard was the Set of Variations on a Theme of Schönberg by Victor Ullmann. We have not yet made definite plans for next year's concerts, but, if it were possible to fit it in, would you be prepared to include this little piece in a programme?[58]

By August, Clark was able to inform Steuermann of the date of the concert and its main item.

On November 4th, we would like you and Margot Hinnenberg Léfebre to give a recital containing the 'Georgelieder'. As these would last 25 minutes, I would suggest that you complete the programme with two groups, one before and the other after the Schoenberg.

What do you suggest for this? The first group might contain a modern sonata, or perhaps, if it were not too long, also the variations by Ullmann. For the last group what do you think about the Fantasia Contrapontistica?[59]

In the end, Steuermann began with the Berg and Eisler sonatas, rather than with the Ullmann. Unusually for a BBC event involving Second Viennese School repertory, the 4 November concert was performed as planned, without any crises affecting programme content or performer participation.

Publicity focused on the Schoenberg song cycle, briefly alluding to the composer's background.

Like Wagner before him, Schönberg has shown a terrifying propensity to make as many enemies as friends; and no one remains indifferent to him – he is too positive a genius for that. Although the storm around his name has now somewhat subsided, and indiscriminate admiration and passionate abuse have given place to a more reasoned acceptance of Schönberg as a vital composer, critics are still loath to 'place' him: he stands alone.[60]

The song cycle was compared to the relatively popular *Gurrelieder*, without clarifying the disparity in style between the two works. In a broadcast talk introducing interesting events of the week, Basil Maine focused on the Schoenberg and was more forthcoming about its idiom.

When the composer was about thirty-five years old, he broke through the shell of Romanticism and began composing in an altogether new manner. The songs which are to be sung on this occasion represent him in the transition stage, with a marked tendency towards new ideas, but not yet completely emancipated. (I use the word 'emancipated' from the composer's and not from the public's point of view.)[61]

The *Radio Times* programme listing briefly introduced the three works that were to be transmitted. Comments about musical styles were expressed in unemotional terms, the sonatas summarized as 'fairly representative of present day tendencies', and the song settings described neutrally: 'dating from about 1908, [they] are as strongly individual as anything he has given us'.[62] The language and descriptions in BBC notices were less provocative than previously – though the innocuous statements may nevertheless be interpreted as mild warnings.

As might be expected, critical notices were mixed. Whereas Cecil Gray in *The Daily Telegraph* was impressed with the Schoenberg, concluding, 'in short, a magnificent work, one of the masterpieces of modern music, ideally interpreted',[63] Jack Westrup of *The Daily Mail* was equally convinced of its worthlessness:

> The chief weakness of the music lies in an almost colourless monotony which is rarely relieved by moments of dramatic intensity. This monotony was intensified by the singing of Mme. Margot Hinnenberg-Lefebre, which became hard and unmusical when it broke away from a veiled and husky *mezzo voce*.[64]

Gray found that the juxtaposition of the two sonatas gave him the rare, but welcome, opportunity for comparison: 'The two sonatas showed that although their composers are influenced by Schönberg, they are by no means mere imitators, but possess distinct personalities of their own and have something definite to say.' Not surprisingly, Westrup expressed an opposing view: 'Romanticism was also apparent in some immature and rambling sonatas by pupils of Schönberg.' In his *Sunday Times* review, Ernest Newman acknowledged the significance of hearing works previously unperformed in England, but remained unimpressed.

> As my opinion of the songs is based not on a casual hearing but on considerable study of them, I can only conclude either that Providence has denied me the faculty for appreciating this kind of art – except, of course, in its purely technical aspect – or that the Schönberg circle has standards of æsthetic value of its own that the rest of us have some difficulty in understanding.[65]

The second concert of the series to include Second Viennese School repertory took place at the Arts Theatre Club on 2 December. The programme was presented by a small chamber orchestra conducted by Anton Webern. This concert was the first the composer conducted in Britain and was the first of nine BBC performances he gave between 1929 and 1936.[66] Fortunately, a number of letters and telegrams exchanged by Clark and Webern regarding the programming of this concert survive: the excesses of Webern's side of the correspondence provide fascinating insights into his programming ideas and thought-processes; the sparsity of Clark's side is inevitably less revealing, though it does substantiate his reputation for neglecting correspondence.

Clark first approached Webern about conducting for the BBC by telephone when on Christmas leave in Austria in 1928.[67] In July 1929, he formally invited Webern to conduct in the 'series dedicated to the "New" music', giving a choice of possible dates. The concert should last 1¼ to 1½ hours, could involve as many as eighteen instrumentalists and would be allotted three rehearsals. He requested that the programme include Webern's recently composed Symphony, op. 21, but asked the composer to propose other works:

The 'New' need not be taken too strictly. The Symphony is there as an important novelty. It is necessary only that the programme be built to some extent contrastingly. If I could only recommend an English work to you; or possibly a French one. But, it is best if I leave you to make suggestions.[68]

Clark asked Webern to recommend a soloist, mentioning the Czech singer, Ružena Herlinger, singing Mahler Lieder and Webern's op. 13 songs, as a possibility.

Webern's enthusiastic reply, dated 8 July 1929, spanned seventeen sides of writing paper, encompassing his thoughts, almost in a stream of consciousness way, as he considered many programme options.[69] Although delighted with the invitation, Webern objected to most of the BBC stipulations. He ruled out 4 November, since he needed to be in Vienna preparing a Workmen's Symphony Concert around that time, and also had reservations about 2 December.

> The matter is as follows (please, this is *confidential*!!!): The League of Composers in New York applied for the *first performance* of a chamber orchestra work from me (*for a rather considerable sum*) for the *beginning of December* (1929); now, I offered them my Symphony. If they accept – I expect the answer to my offer at the end of July or the beginning of August at the latest – then we can do the Symphony in London only in the second half of December.

The timing complicated programme options, since with- and without-symphony contingencies had to be considered. Moreover, Webern worried about the nature of the programme:

> It seems to me, that this, my début in London, could be an event of the most far-reaching consequence for my future life! I am anxious therefore – so far as it depends on me – to shape it the best way possible. And that is why I believe the programme-question in this case is of extremely great, even decisive, importance for me.

In light of this, requests for additional performers and rehearsals were recurrent motives throughout the letter. He confided that he had originally hoped to do Mahler's Symphony no. 4 for his London début, but this was impossible with a chamber group of eighteen musicians.

Webern considered different programme options, carefully counting the number of musicians that would be required for various works, as well as the total timing. He was happy to have Ružena Herlinger sing Mahler Lieder, but emphatically rejected the idea of including his op. 13 songs.

> My Lieder op. 13 will not work. It seems to me (please, confidentially) *risky*, for one thing because of Fr H. , but also, particularly, because of the small number of rehearsals that are at my disposal. With three rehearsals, I would

have had for these songs alone *much* too little [time] ... And, dear friend, (I speak from the most far-reaching experience) if such a work cannot be completely successful (or approximately so), then it is better to leave it. No, nothing is more harmful for our music than such half successful performances. What experiences Schönberg, Berg and I have had already!

He suggested that Herlinger sing one or two songs from his *Geistlichen Lieder*, op. 15, instead. In lieu of his Symphony, he recommended his Five Orchestral Pieces, op. 10, not yet performed in London. He enthusiastically described the qualities that he believed made this work particularly suited to radio performance.

Dear friend, you will be persuaded: just this piece with the bells will sound especially beautiful on radio ... I am perfectly convinced that it is all *radio-music*! Nothing can be more suitable for radio! I am so anxious to learn whether I am right, that I would like above all else to do this piece. Dear, good Clark, if you had heard these pieces when I did them in Zürich! (everyone immediately wanted to hear this third piece with the bells again. Hence, a 'success', don't you think. I am writing this so that you will not worry too much about it.) All these sounds are extremely delicate but very intense. *Lightly ff*!!! Therefore, as if created for radio.

Webern considered a Milhaud chamber symphony and Arthur Bliss's *Conversations*, expressing preference for the Milhaud. He also pondered at length about doing a Schoenberg piece.

Of Schönberg there would be so much for this type of small ensemble: the Chamber symphony, the Serenade, the Wind quintet and the Suite (*with* piano) op. 29. But it is only [possible] to think seriously about the Chamber symphony if I am given musicians who have already played it and if I am given at least *one rehearsal* more!!! And then, one could probably only consider three movements from the Serenade: perhaps the *third* (*variations*), the fifth: 'Tanzscene' and the sixth 'Lied (ohne Worte)'. But I still am not sure whether Schönberg would be the right thing.

He concluded that the limitations ruled out the Schoenberg options. In fact, to accommodate the restrictions he suddenly shifted his entire frame of reference:

I suggest now a work, which I consider extraordinarily suitable (considering our situation) and which also lies very much at my heart; nothing 'modern', I suppose, but also nothing directly 'classical', a wonderful work: the Serenade op. 15 in A major for small orchestra by *Brahms*!!!

Do you know it? Has it been played much in London? Probably no more than here; that is, as much as not at all. (If I did it today in Vienna, it would be a downright novelty.) It is an infinitely tender, lovely work.

Finally, Webern proposed one other programme possibility, informing his friend about a new Second Viennese School work:

> But now, to close, another very important but strictly confidential matter:
> Berg is writing a concert-aria for Frau Herlinger. I still know nothing about which orchestra it is for (whether large or chamber orchestra), but if the latter were the case, how wonderful it would be to integrate this piece into our programme arrangements.

In fact, Berg's concert aria, *Der Wein*, was given its first British performance by the BBC several years later.[70] Webern ended this letter, really an essay in programme planning, with the post-script: 'I have never before written such a long letter!' – and added a marginal note with a final programme suggestion: Schubert's Octet.

One would think that such a massive effort would have warranted an immediate response; moreover, Webern apparently wrote a second letter in July with additional programming ideas.[71] However, on 18 August, Webern urgently requested that Clark inform him of the BBC's decisions about the concert's date and programme content, since he had not yet received a response.[72] By that time, Webern had accepted conducting engagements in Frankfurt and needed to know about the London plans in order to make travel arrangements. It is not clear whether Clark responded to this letter; the official BBC contract and letter of confirmation for the concert were certainly not sent until much later, in early October.[73] These documents confirm that Webern was to receive 40 guineas to prepare and conduct a chamber orchestra concert, to take place on 2 December at the Arts Theatre Club. The programme was to include Milhaud's Chamber Symphony no. 1 ('Le printemps'), four Mahler songs, Webern's op. 10 and the Brahms A major Serenade.

On 6 November, Webern wrote Clark again, concerned that he might need an entry permit to show British officials upon arrival on the 27th. He also provided information about orchestral scores and parts, to ensure that the BBC would have the correct materials on time.[74] He repeated this information in two increasingly frantic letters sent on 12 and 18 November;[75] in fact, the BBC did not even apply to the Ministry of Labour for the entry permit until 19 November.[76]

By that time, Webern was burdened with yet another anxiety, which he communicated in a quickly scrawled, pencil note to Clark: 'Just now, Frau Herlinger telegraphed me that she must cancel for *London*. She is ill, has hemorrhaging of the vocal chords and may not sing for many weeks.' He then proposed: 'I am for putting *nothing else* in *place of the Lieder*!!! The programme is still *long* enough for the purpose!' The composer proved his point in a table, in which he indicated his preferred, though unorthodox, order of the revised programme – first the Milhaud, then the Brahms, and finally his op. 10. The table also included Webern's rather inflated timings of the three works: 10, 40 and 12 minutes respectively.

> With the songs, the programme would actually have been too long. Thus, dear friend, we stay with this. I consider it best. At this point in time, another solution will not be found. And I gain rehearsal time for my pieces![77]

While Webern's letter made its way to the BBC, Clark sent two urgent telegrams, asking for suggestions of a replacement English singer, but the composer reaffirmed his desire to drop the Mahler altogether.[78] The BBC accepted this plan, although the items were presented in the more expected order of Milhaud, Webern and Brahms.

Webern arrived in London on 28 November, the night before his first rehearsal, recording in his diary: 'Arrived in London about 10.30 pm. Met by Clark. With him to the Strand Palace Hotel in the city. Then to a party. Very tired'. In a letter to Schoenberg, he revealed that throughout his London stay, 'Clark devoted himself to me in a touching manner', accompanying him for all meals and during his free time. The conductor devoted the entire first rehearsal to his op. 10 pieces, which apparently met 'with little understanding on the part of the orchestra'. According to Moldenhauer, 'The difficulty no doubt lay in the fact that Webern's English was insufficient, making it necessary for his extensive and explicit comments to be related to the musicians by an interpreter'.[79] At the second rehearsal on 30 November and the final dress rehearsal on the morning of the concert, the conductor worked on all three pieces.

The 2 December concert received more attention in the *Radio Times* than had the Schoenberg concert in November. The pre-concert announcement focused on Webern's '"Five Pieces" (Op. 10), one of which must surely constitute a record for brevity; it consists of six bars only, scored for a skeleton orchestra. Apparently, von Webern does not believe in padding out his ideas'.[80] The event's importance from the BBC's point of view can be deduced from the fact that photographs of Webern and Herlinger, placed in the centre of the page, illustrated the programme listings.[81] There were also extensive explanatory notes, a *Radio Times* honour reserved for significant events.

> The earliest and one of the most devoted of the Schönberg disciples, he has developed a very distinct idiom of his own. He has an amazing gift of conveying the most vivid impressions by the slightest of means, and many of his

most expressive pieces are so short as to seem like a mere flash of light, a brief whisper of the wind as it passes. And yet each holds within its momentary compass a wonderful wealth of thought and feeling; though it may take but a moment to give its message, it is a message which stays long after in the listener's mind. Of these five pieces for Orchestra it has been well said that 'each is a moment of lyric ecstasy'.[82]

In vivid contrast to *Radio Times* apologies for Schoenberg's music, the Webern notes were expressed in a positive, enticing way.

Despite such special treatment, the programme change seriously affected the concert's reception. Even though Webern's orchestral pieces were repeated for the benefit of those who were in the theatre,[83] the entire event lasted less than an hour, and this brevity, rather than the musical content or even the quality of the performance, was the focus of critical comment. Even a thoughtful critic like Newman viewed the event as a triviality. His entire *Sunday Times* review consisted of the following:

> The 'Symphony' of Milhaud, lasting about six minutes, and the 'Five Orchestral Pieces' of Webern, lasting in all five minutes, gave an air of mild humour to the B.B.C. chamber concert last Monday. The Milhaud is only a juvenile attempt at a joke; the work dates from about the beginning of the silly season (1917). Webern's experiments in the combination of sounds *qua* sounds are theoretically interesting, but they fit into no definition of music as the world has hitherto understood the term. Those of us who moved on from the Arts Theatre to the Wigmore Hall at the end of the eleven minutes found more substantial musical fare in the Brahms recital of Mme Elena Gerhardt.[84]

Many critics left before the Brahms, depriving the conductor of his long-awaited chance to prove himself in London. Despite Webern's high expectations and careful attempts to ensure that his London début would be a success, the event was received almost as a joke.

Newman gave more attention to the music in a talk broadcast a few days after the concert, describing Webern's unique sound world.

> The fact is that Webern does not ask you to listen to his music in the ordinary way, or to judge it by the ordinary standards. There is rarely anything in a work of his that you can detach and quote as a theme; what we get is not thematic writing but a succession of sounds, now in this instrument, now in that, combining to make a shifting web of pitches and colours. There is little or nothing corresponding to an 'idea' as that term is commonly understood in music.[85]

Perhaps predictably, Newman concluded that the idiom eluded his personal boundaries of comprehension.

> I confess that I have given up the attempt to see into the minds of some of these composers of the Schönberg School. They are undoubtedly very intelligent men, but in practical music their intelligence seems to run on lines along which the rest of the world cannot follow them.

Webern's diary reveals that he was not very happy with the concert: 'My pieces came out well. About the same as in Zürich. Yet better there. Brahms was played dryly. Milhaud not very good either.'[86] In contrast, Clark was pleased with Webern's visit, as he wrote to Schoenberg: 'We are enormously happy over Webern's success as composer and conductor.'[87] No direct evidence of BBC internal response survives, but decisions to invite Webern to conduct in subsequent seasons implies satisfaction with his initial appearance.

The third and last programme in the contemporary series to include Second Viennese School repertory took place on 7 April 1930 at the Central Hall, Westminster. Devoted exclusively to Schoenberg, the programme featured a complete performance of *Pierrot lunaire*, op. 21, as well as the Suite for Piano, op. 25, and the Chamber Symphony, op. 9, in Webern's arrangement for *Pierrot* instrumentation. The concert was given by the Pierrot Lunaire Ensemble of Vienna, a group who toured together to present Schoenberg's song cycle. The seven performers included the actress, Erika Wagner, Rudolf Kolisch (violin and viola) and Benar Heifetz ('cello) of the Vienna String Quartet, Franz Wangler (flute and piccolo), Viktor Polatschek (clarinets), Steuermann (piano), and the conductor, Erwin Stein. The ensemble had initially planned to present *Pierrot lunaire* in London in February 1929, but the event was postponed. The following August, Clark advised Steuermann: 'I am glad to say that it will at last be possible to have the "Pierrot Lunaire" Ensemble, for which the date of April 7th has been fixed.'[88]

Unfortunately, most of the papers documenting the negotiations for the 7 April concert do not survive.[89] In January 1930, *The Listener* published a list of notable music broadcasts, and at that time the programme included Schoenberg's Suite, op. 29, and *Pierrot lunaire*.[90] An extant letter from February indicates that the BBC was unwilling to pay more than £120 to the ensemble, but offered additional contracts to individual performers: Kolisch's string quartet and the clarinetist were engaged for one concert, Steuermann was offered a solo recital, and Erika Wagner another engagement.[91] By March, the Chamber Symphony and Piano Suite had replaced the Suite, op. 29, in the programme plans. However, the terms of the additional contracts were causing difficulties, probably due to disparity in fees. Steuermann was engaged for his usual fee of 35 guineas for a broadcast recital, while Polatschek and Erika Wagner were only offered 15 guineas. Steuermann soon reported: 'From my telegram, you know that the "diplomatic endeavors" have been successful.'[92] The studio broadcasts took place on 6 April. At 5.15 pm Steuermann played Beethoven's Diabelli Variations, and at around 9.00 pm the Kolisch Quartet[93] performed Beethoven's String Quartet, op. 132, Erika Wagner recited passages from Goethe and Shakespeare, and Steuermann joined members of the quartet for Brahms's Piano Quartet in A major.

BBC promotion of the 7 April concert returned to high-profile tactics not used since the previous season. The intense publicity campaign stressed the special opportunity of hearing *Pierrot lunaire* performed by dedicated artists.

> Schönberg's admirers have always been untiring in their efforts to spread the gospel of his work; and, since 1920, a band of distinguished musicians in Vienna have devoted themselves entirely to the performance and propagation of this amazing and fearfully difficult work, undertaking concert-tours with it, and broadcasting it. Of what other piece of music, we wonder, can the same be said?[94]

Schoenberg's controversial history was exploited to attract listeners' curiosity.

> Of all the *enfants terribles* of modern music Schönberg is undoubtedly the most worth while. He is also one of the most formidable of them all – formidable in that the idiom he employs is so intensely his own, so astonishingly new. Far more controversy has centred round his name than round that of any other recent composer: but Schönberg goes on his own way, rigorously selective of his material, intensely self-critical, and debtor to no man.[95]

These tactics were intensified during the week of the concert. Remarkably, on the *Radio Times* cover, the concert was designated as one of the week's four most outstanding programmes. Inside, it was promoted in three separate places: in the daily schedules, in the column highlighting notable musical events of the week,[96] and in a full-page feature article, 'The Moon-Struck Pierrot Comes to London' by Erwin Stein. Stein explored the work from musical and poetic points of view, in the context of its reception history:

> Even works of art must bow to destiny, but only few have known so much of destiny's caprice as Schönberg's music, and especially *Pierrot Lunaire*. The thing has already become an absurd tradition; a new work by Schönberg is hailed as incomprehensible and ugly, until after a lapse of one or two decades, the public realizes that it is beautiful and spiritual. It happened so with *Die Verklärte Nacht* and even with the *Gurrelieder*.[97]

*Pierrot lunaire* had at first been similarly received with incomprehension and anger, but later, 'on a whole generation of younger musicians it has had a fruitful influence. For them it denotes a turning away from the academic theory of music, and, especially the principle of composing for a small *ensemble* specially gathered for the work, founded a new method'. Schoenberg's op. 21 was generally unknown in Britain, since it had not been heard there since the Milhaud performances more than six years before. This comprehensive introduction – written by the conductor and the composer's friend and advocate – added substantially to the BBC's effort to convince unenthusiastic listeners to give the programme a fair hearing.

Not surprisingly, the broadcast received mixed reviews and incited a new wave of protests against BBC new music policies. Richard Capell of *The Daily Mail* encapsulated his feelings in his review, 'Last Night's Wireless Infliction'. For him, the event was an entirely negative experience – a judgement apparently shared by many in the concert audience.

> Not all who had thought they could stand an evening of Schönberg held fast. A bold front was put up in the first part of the programme, but the British line wavered in the course of 'Pierrot Lunaire'. At one moment the deserters were so many that it looked as though we were in a general retreat.[98]

He believed that the musical style was unsuitable for the British psyche.

> Schönberg's music is, outside Central Europe, incomprehensible. It belongs to countries where people are overdone and fed up with normal music. Outside Berlin and Vienna this art is meaningless, and the subtle Schönberg a bore.

Eric Blom, in the *Manchester Guardian*, was similarly unimpressed. Although he acknowledged the high level of performance, he condemned the music and the acoustics of the hall. For the Chamber Symphony, 'the Westminster Central Hall, which is anything but a chamber, all but ruined the superb playing of the five artists'. Of *Pierrot*, he grudgingly admitted:

> To pretend at this time of day that this work is not music would be childish. It is one of the most artfully wrought scores in existence, and it always sounds astonishingly well. It is true that to the ear the extreme thematic ingenuities which the score reader may discover with the aid of a microscope are almost entirely lost, but they at least never make the music sound dull or crabbed. It is always alive and amazingly, almost excessively, suggestive.[99]

Many of the critics deplored the *Sprechstimme*. Capell described Erika Wagner's performance as 'plaintive miaowing'. Blom believed that the problem was not with the performer, but with the technique itself.

> Miss Erika Wagner gave a masterly reading of the song speech, but even she could not make one feel that this experiment in semi-musical declamation really succeeded. Whenever the tone drops into speech with impossible long-sustained vowels, it detaches itself from the fabric like a thread that had escaped the weaver's attention.

Ernest Newman, in his *Sunday Times* review, felt that the reciter had not adhered to the composer's instructions.

> The performance of the 'Pierrot Lunaire' was an excellent one on the part of the players, and, I thought, a poor one on the part of Madame Erika Wagner, who, I believe, is an actress, not a musician, by profession . . . This combination of instrumental music with a vocal part that is neither sung nor spoken, but something between the two, is to my ears and mind an infliction too painful for words. But if we are to have it at all, we may as well have it as Schönberg intended it . . . The fact remains that he has indicated specific pitches for the voice, and we ought to be made aware of them, however fleetingly. Mme Wagner simply played fast and loose with the great majority of these indications, to the vast annoyance, I am sure, of people who were following with the score.[100]

At the end of his review, Newman launched yet another attack on Schoenberg's atonal idiom.

In contrast to these mostly negative press reports, one entirely favourable review bears mentioning. Perhaps predictably, this critique appeared in the BBC publication, *The Listener*, written by the well-known writer on music and new music devotee, M. D. Calvocoressi. The full-page report explained Schoenberg's career and how the three works on the programme represented different stages of it.

> The course of his evolution is from post-Wagnerian romanticism to a strictly abstract, architectural conception of music, an art exploiting relations of lines and forms rather than deliberately expressive effects. But the romantic spirit is strong in him. The new, ever-increasing thirst for abstract form-building is evinced quite clearly in the Chamber Symphony, built out of four typical themes which are used in a variety of carefully thought out, strictly worked out developments and combinations. And yet the whole work is imbued with romantic qualities.[101]

Calvocoressi's discussion of *Pierrot*, too, emphasized its romantic foundations, describing it as 'the last stage of [Schoenberg's] romantic evolution'. Ignoring surface elements that were the focus of other critics' comments, he stressed the work's compositional significance: 'The combination of daring experimentalism and strict formal discipline is as striking here as in any other of Schönberg's works.' Calvocoressi discussed the Piano Suite in terms of its 12-tone construction – a fact that had been ignored in other reviews and BBC articles. He included a neat, one-sentence explanation of the 12-tone system, mentioning that it 'compels the composer to move within the limits imposed by the abstract, purely architectural notion of music built up on a theme consisting of the twelve notes of the chromatic scale in any chosen (but invariable, once chosen) order'. The article concluded:

> The novel problems set by his recent works have come to confront us long before most of us had begun to feel quite at ease with the older ones. There may have been comparatively few landmarks in his earlier works: but in the new diction and style conditioned by 'twelve-tone composition' there are fewer – one is tempted to say practically none. So that most of us, just now, are setting against the latest works the interrogation marks that we were setting, eighteen or twenty years ago, against 'Pierrot Lunaire' or the Chamber Symphony. But even so, there are some of [us] who feel quite definitely that Schönberg's latest achievements correspond to an unformulated, yet manifest necessity.

Calvocoressi strongly advocated Schoenberg's right to compose music in this manner, and, tacitly, the BBC's right and obligation to bring this type of music to the British public. In accordance with the intellectual bias of *The Listener*, the author offered a thought-provoking, musicological explanation of the concert – undoubtedly a calculated defence against anticipated public reaction to the difficult music.

If the BBC expected an outcry after the Schoenberg concert, it certainly was not disappointed. The programme provoked many listeners to send in their opinions, and letters were reproduced in the *Radio Times* for three months after the concert took place.[102] The BBC responded through two *Radio Times* articles. The first, which appeared in the 25 April issue, took particular exception to Capell's review, 'Last Night's Wireless Affliction'.

> Its critic seemed to have lost sight of the fact that it is impossible to *inflict* anything upon people who have a means of escape – in this instance, either recourse to the National programme or the second alternative, which never seems to occur to listeners, of switching off the set for an hour and reading a book.[103]

The appearance of a second article a full five weeks after the event indicates the extent of the continuing debate. A leading feature in the *Radio Times* of 16 May, 'Modernist Music, or "Devastating the Home"' was a full-page essay written by W. J. Turner, music critic for *The New Statesman*.[104] The article primarily attacked the press for its reaction to modern artistic trends, again singling out Capell's review.

> The reason that certain newspapers are so ready to attack the B.B.C. for being 'high-brow' or for being too 'advanced' or 'educational' is, firstly, that they think this pleases the largest public and represents its opinion . . . The great universal humbug and deceit of our time is the notion that what pleases the greatest number is the best. It is all part of the idolatory of quantity in place of quality; and this substitution of size and numbers for quality and value is a necessary result of following the line of least resistance.

Turner concluded with an explicit statement of the BBC's cultural-expansionist policy.

> As Wordsworth said, every great poet has to create the taste by which he is enjoyed, and this is true in music as well as in poetry. Those works of art which win immediate acclamation from the critics and immediate acceptance by the general public are as a rule mediocre productions, the work of clever men who repeat what has already been done in a slightly new and fashionable dress. The great creators are wholly different. Their work is difficult and inaccessible, and sometimes its inaccessibility is due to a combination of simplicity and profundity that make it unremarkable among its bizarre and deliberately advanced contemporaries.

Although the Corporation began the 1929–30 season with a low-profile approach to new music programming, the strength of adverse reaction, particularly to the all-Schoenberg concert, forced it to return to a more aggressive stance. The BBC not only defended its policy, but openly accused certain critics of irresponsibility for attacking its decision to bring contemporary music to the British public.

Second Viennese School repertory was also heard in several broadcasts that took place outside the 1929–30 BBC Concerts of Contemporary Music. On 22 December 1929, shortly after the Webern concert, the Vienna String Quartet performed Schoenberg's Third String Quartet for the third consecutive season. Ružena Herlinger, having recovered from her illness, participated in a chamber recital on 4 March 1930. She sang a group of German-language songs that included Schoenberg's 'Waldsonne' from op. 2. *Verklärte Nacht* was once again performed in its sextet version by British musicians on 25 April. Moreover, Paul Pisk was represented in the BBC programmes for the first time on 3 July, his Suite for Piano performed by Friedrich Wührer. Finally, Krenek's *Little Symphony*, op. 58, was presented in a studio orchestra concert conducted by Sir Henry Wood on 2 March.

The 1929–30 season was marked by the BBC's efforts to reduce criticism of its new music policies. Despite internal doubts, the Concerts of Contemporary Music continued, following the pattern established previously; however, most of the concerts took place with little ceremony and far fewer broadcasts of new works were scheduled outside this series.

Nevertheless, the Corporation was a victim of its own success. By spring 1930, the contemporary music campaign had genuinely expanded many listeners' horizons of expectations to include an awareness of modern European musical trends. However, the short-term effect of this awareness was vehement objection to its being forced upon them. Percy Pitt's final year as BBC Music Director was characterized by a growing negativity toward contemporary music idioms, both by BBC administrators and by the public at large.

## Pitt's legacy

Within just a few years of the launch of public broadcasting in the UK, wireless became the primary disseminator of art music to the British population. As early as spring 1926, the BBC began to feature music by living European composers in high-profile broadcasts. This programming strategy was extraordinary for its time, since little attention was paid to this repertory in British concert halls. This visionary strategy resulted from two basic factors: the central administrators' belief in the value and necessity of a cultural-expansionist programme policy, and Pitt's particular interest in recent compositional trends. In 1927, Pitt's decision to transfer Clark – with his unique knowledge of contemporary repertory, his personal musical biases and loyalties, and his extraordinary contacts – to London raised the music broadcasting potential to a new level. This propitious combination of elements ensured that new music became an intrinsic component within the broadcast schedules.

Clark's personal interest in the music and personalities of the Second Viennese School led to the regular inclusion of works associated with this repertory in BBC broadcasts. As Table 7.1 demonstrates, between February 1927 and July 1930, a period of just three and a half years, the BBC mounted 39 performances of 28 different works by Schoenberg, Webern, Berg, Eisler, Pisk, Krenek and Hauer. These performances were heard by a significant proportion of the nation's population, at a fidelity extraordinary for its time, considering that the transmissions took place within the first decade of BBC operations. During the 1927–8 season, attention was

Table 7.1 *Works by Second Viennese School composers and their associates, performed in BBC concerts and broadcasts between 1927 and spring 1930*

**Schoenberg**

     songs from op. 2: 'Erwartung', 'Schenk mir deinen goldenen Kamm'**, 'Erhebung' and 'Waldsonne' **

     *Verklärte Nacht*, op. 4 *****

     *Gurrelieder*

     String Quartet no. 1, op. 7

     Chamber Symphony, op. 9 (also performed in the Webern arrangement for *Pierrot* instrumentation)

     String Quartet no. 2, op. 10

     Three Piano Pieces, op. 11

     *Das Buch der hängenden Gärten*, op. 15

     *Six Little Piano Pieces*, op. 19

     *Pierrot lunaire*, op. 21

     Five Piano Pieces, op. 23

     Suite for Piano, op. 25 **

     String Quartet no. 3, op. 30 ***

**Webern**

     selected songs from op. 3 ** and op. 4

     Five Pieces for String Quartet, op. 5

     Five Pieces for Orchestra, op. 10

     String Trio, op. 20 (not broadcast)

**Berg**

     Piano Sonata, op. 1 **

     *Lyric Suite* (not broadcast; two movements broadcast on a second occasion)

**Eisler**

     Piano Sonata, op. 1

     Duo for violin and 'cello, op. 7

     *Zeitungsausschnitte*, op. 11

**Pisk**

     Suite for Piano

**Krenek**

     Five Piano Pieces, op. 39

     *Symphonic Music* for nine instruments, op. 11

     *Potpourri*, op. 54 (not broadcast)

     *Little Symphony*, op. 58

**Hauer**

     *Wandlungen*, op. 53

     **    work performed on two different occasions
     ***    work performed on three different occasions
     *****    work performed on five different occasions

focused on Schoenberg's early works, and they had a relatively favourable reception, especially compared to Bartók and Stravinsky broadcasts of that year. However, during the final seasons of the decade, works from the atonal and 12-tone periods gradually came into prominence, and composers of the Second Viennese circle were soon categorized within the ranks of the incomprehensible ultra-modernists.

# PART III

# The early Boult years, 1930–1936

# 8 Boult's initial seasons, 1930–1931, 1931–1932

The new decade brought far-reaching changes to the BBC on many levels, with profound consequences for the Music Department and music broadcasts. Significantly, the Corporation's size and physical requirements had outgrown the premises at Savoy Hill, and on 15 May 1932, the BBC officially moved into Broadcasting House, a new specially built facility at the top of Regent Street. In addition to providing more space, the atmosphere of efficiency and structure contrasted with the Savoy Hill environment. The young BBC had developed from the inspiration of individuals, deriving its identity from the impetus and spontaneity of employees' specific personalities and talents. The vast Corporation of the 1930s was a bureaucratic, controlling monument, symbolically represented by the new building's edifice.[1] Within the physical and hierarchical structures, procedure, planning and professionalism were increasingly emphasized and relied upon to produce the high quality programmes and technical developments that were by this time expected of the BBC. Maurice Gorham later described this change with cynical directness:

> All th[e] pre-occupation with appearances – interior decoration, specially designed furniture, faked-up studios, busts in foyers, and floral decorations by a lady of title – was symptomatic of the worst phase in the BBC's history, which began with the move to Broadcasting House. From 1932 to 1939, when the war saved the BBC from itself, was the great Stuffed Shirt era, marked internally by paternalism run riot, bureaucracy of the most hierachi[c]al type, an administration system that made productive work harder instead of easier, and a tendency to promote the most negative characters to be found amongst the staff. Externally it was similarly marked by aloofness, resentment of criticism, and a positive contempt for the listener.[2]

## The BBC of the 1930s

From an administrative point of view, the Corporation's continuous growth resulted in a sprawling structure, in which each large branch and each section within each branch became increasingly isolated from other areas. The Music Department's decisions and policies were thus less dependent on and cognizant of actions and discussions taking place in other parts of the Corporation. One consequence of the BBC's escalating bureaucracy is beneficial to this study: more documentation survives for the 1930s, and it is easier to reconstruct the discussions, attitudes and outcomes relating to specific issues and concerns.[3]

On the technical side, introduction of the Regional Scheme in March 1930 brought programme alternatives to the entire country for the first time. Although experiments for transmitting two programmes had been in effect since August 1927, the reception area for the experimental wavelength (Daventry 5GB) had been limited to the Midlands. With the new system, twin-wave transmitters enabled all listeners to receive BBC signals on two wavelengths, designated the National Programme (261 metres) and the Regional Programme (356 metres in London). Material transmitted over the National wavelength was planned and produced in London and was available to everyone. The Regional programmes also originated to some extent from London, but often included regional variants from local stations. The basic tenets of alternative programme planning, as conceived in 1927, continued to apply.[4]

The programming objectives in the 1930s remained true to the ideals the Company sought to achieve back in 1922, aiming to bring high-quality broadcasts to an audience potentially the size of the entire nation, using the most up-to-date transmission techniques. By the turn of the decade, the scope of the Corporation had expanded beyond all expectation, inevitably resulting in new ways in which these objectives were approached and expressed. Policy statements were less idealistic and open-ended than in the early years: they dictated the BBC's terms of operation, plainly defining the limitations of the medium, which listeners were expected to accept and tolerate. The tenth anniversary issue of the *BBC Yearbook* included such a statement, reflecting the imperious professionalism of the 1930s BBC:

> As to the choice and execution of the music itself, of whatever genre, practice is governed by three main principles: (a) the different kinds of audiences must be satisfied; (b) the music must be, in each kind, the best; (c) standards of performance must, in each kind, be as high as possible. With regard to (a) the chief point to note is that, although over the week, or the evening, 'something for everybody' is the ideal, this is sought for not by making particular musical programmes serve general purposes, but by treating each as an artistic entity addressed to a definite class of listener, the number of such programmes being governed more or less by the estimated proportions of the different classes among listeners. As to (b) and (c), the listener must judge as to whether the standards have been attained; but allusion may be permitted to the fact that once the broadcaster assumes responsibility, as he must in practice, for the quality of performance (as distinct from transmission and the selection of works), he is necessarily led to form his own organisations for most of the ensemble work in each category.[5]

Policy statements like this read almost like legal contracts between the BBC and the listener, clearly defining and controlling what listeners might expect, while promoting the Corporation's achievements.

In May 1935, the central administrators prepared a report that was submitted as evidence to the public committee chaired by Lord Ullswater, appointed to review BBC operations prior to the first renewal of the Corporation's charter. In this vital paper, the administrators once again articulated the basic tenet of BBC programming:

> Programme policy on the larger issues has from the outset been determined by the conviction that listeners would come to appreciate that which at first might appear uninteresting or even alarming. The B.B.C. has in fact aimed at providing a service somewhat ahead of what the public would demand were it possible for such demand to be made articulate and intelligible. On a basis of recreative entertainment a powerful cultural influence has been developed.[6]

The restatement of Reith's policy as Ullswater Committee evidence demonstrates the degree to which this fundamental objective guided the second decade of BBC activity, as it had the first. The administrators specifically cited the dissemination of art music as an outstanding success of this policy.

Nevertheless, day-to-day attitudes and decisions, which influenced and controlled the character and content of music programming, gradually altered during the 1930s. External factors, such as programme expectations and social context, also changed. Between 1930 and 1936 two prominent issues preoccupied the policy-makers. First, discussions centred on the degree to which British music and musicians should be promoted, and foreign music and musicians excluded, in BBC programmes. Second, they debated the extent to which box-office considerations should affect programme content and balance. These arguments significantly affected the BBC's broadcasting of contemporary music during these years.

## Personnel shifts

Requests for additions to the Music Department staff were made frequently during the 1930s. These pleas resulted not only from the natural growth rate of the organization, but also from a basic conflict between old and new management goals. The core music staff had been hired in the mid-1920s and was suited to the BBC work ethic of that period, with its emphasis on spontaneity, diversity and creativity. By the 1930s, the expanding enterprise led to a more business-like, cost-efficient management basis. New priorities and procedures led to seemingly unmanageable work-loads; staff were responsible for more broadcast time and were expected to produce programmes of higher quality and sophistication. Requests for further assistance were analysed according to the priorities of individual officials: the pressures and responsibilities at each level led the representative at that level to emphasize either economic (Nicolls), administrative (Beadle and Mase) or artistic (Wright and Boult) points of view. Whichever individual dominated the decision-making process at a particular time determined the emphasis and nature of the final outcome.

The beginning of the decade coincided with a change at the highest level: Adrian Boult's accession as Music Director in May 1930 inevitably affected the way in which music programme planning and other matters were handled and decided. His activities are well documented, confirming that he was personally involved with many high and low-level decisions, that he directed and shaped the department's priorities and programmes.

The department's programming potentials were also transformed that spring with the establishment of the BBC Symphony Orchestra. For the first time, the Corporation had a full-size, resident orchestra of outstanding quality at its disposal. In addition to being the country's foremost impresario, the BBC founded and controlled a premier performing ensemble with a vast audience base. As the decade turned, central administrators, senior members of the department and the director-to-be were deeply involved with planning and hiring top-quality musicians for the orchestra; moreover, the BBC was negotiating with the proposed conductor of this ensemble, Sir Thomas Beecham. The complex intrigue and delicate arrangements required in developing these projects have been fully explained elsewhere; the orchestra plans were eventually brought to successful fruition, but the negotiations with Beecham were abandoned.[7] Thus, Boult became Music Director of a complex and busy organization, responsible for planning and producing most of the nation's art music broadcasts; he simultaneously assumed responsibility for organizing, shaping and launching what was soon to be recognized as one of Britain's finest orchestras. Specialized administrators for the orchestra were also appointed that spring, including Richard Pratt as Orchestra Manager and W. W. Thompson as Concerts Manager; Joseph Lewis was transferred from the Birmingham station in July to become the orchestra's assistant conductor.

Further departmental reorganization directly affected the programme building hierarchy. In March 1930, Wright outlined three main restructuring objectives: to prepare for Boult's accession, to alleviate overworked staff, especially himself and Herbage, and to improve the administrative side of the department.[8] Wright proposed to give up his place at the hub of programme building to become Boult's assistant, responsible for 'the general run of the organisation and all matters of personnel etc., relieving Music Director of as much trouble as possible in these matters'. He recommended that Herbage become the 'Programme Organiser', responsible for programme building, and that Mase assist Wright with administration. As Wright wrote to the Director of Programmes:

> I have from time to time made the remark that I have felt Mase had definite ability of an executive nature, but also definite limitations, and further that he had behaved sometimes in a way which has prejudiced the friendliness and co-operation of some of his colleagues. I have great pleasure in stating that there is already seen a decided improvement in his relations with these colleagues, and I have every hope that after a few more personal chats between me and all concerned the suggested scheme will work well. There is, however, an important point: that I and not Mase should retain the personal touch with everyone in the department on matters of staff duties, leave, salary etc., as I know many of our people would resent going to him instead of to myself.[9]

Wright's plan was eventually approved, but with certain provisos. Mase would be promoted, but was 'to have no musical duties whatsoever. He should definitely be informed that his appointment is probationary . . . The Music Director will report on his capacity to hold this job after three months and if the report is not satisfactory we may have to consider putting in an outsider to do the work'.[10] Herbage was also to be promoted, but again with misgivings:

> While we appreciate the good work that has been done by Herbage, we realise that he is very young and inexperienced for the important position that it is proposed he should hold. We realise that in agreeing that Herbage should handle this job we are taking a risk. We are prepared to experiment, however, and it is up to Herbage to prove his worth. He should be informed that this is the situation and it should be impressed upon him how necessary it is for him to work with due recognition of the importance of the job and his own comparative lack of qualifications to hold it.

There were objections from the very top about assigning Wright the title 'Assistant Director of Music'. The central administrators discussed this matter at extraordinary length over a period of three weeks, and finally agreed that Wright would be called Principal Assistant to the Music Director, Mase would take over the title Music Executive, and Herbage would be Programme Organiser as originally proposed.[11]

Just a year later, in May 1931, Boult made a decision that altered his position at the BBC and had far-reaching ramifications on the organization as a whole: while retaining his responsibilities as Music Director, he simultaneously took on a second job as Chief Conductor of the BBC Symphony Orchestra. His time was divided between overseeing the music broadcasts and learning scores, rehearsing and conducting, as demanded by the orchestra's busy schedule. Kenyon has described the balance of responsibility:

> The system could not possibly have worked had it not been for Boult's skill in delegation attested to by those who worked in the Department during the 1930s. Allocation of responsibilities was absolutely firm, and once fixed was adhered to. Boult never interfered with his subordinates' work; he was always available for consultation when necessary, but confined his own responsibility to policy decisions, the direction of the Orchestra, and the representation of the Music Department within the BBC. He persevered . . . right through the 1930s, finally relinquishing the Directorship only in 1942 when wartime conditions made the combination of planning and conducting almost impossible.[12]

The BBC administrators recognized that the department would need a second authority figure to assist Boult and to make decisions in his absence. In a memo to Reith, Eckersley outlined his views:

> I should expect [Boult] to be in general artistic charge of the work and to have a big say in musical policy and programme making. I see no reason why Boult should not on general occasions preside over the weekly Music Department's meeting, and attend the meetings of the M.A.C. [Music Advisory Committee]. I would suggest, therefore, that the title of Assistant Music Director be given to the person appointed in charge of the administrative work, and that this man should nominally be responsible to Boult, though in practice he would work almost entirely to me direct.[13]

Eckersley considered which members of the department might be suitable and named four contenders: Wright, Mase, Hely Hutchinson and O'Donnell, the conductor of the BBC Military Band.

> Hely Hutchinson fills the bill in many ways, but he is somewhat young and I am not sufficiently sure of his qualities of leadership. Mase is an excellent administrative man, but has not sufficient personality to be able to deal with major issues. Wright suffers from the same disability. O'Donnell, a first-class trustworthy member of the staff, has his heart primarily in conducting, and I should be sorry to see him forced to forego his work with the Military Band.

Although Eckersley recommended that the Corporation search outside the department, his colleagues apparently disagreed. Two weeks later they decided to appoint Mase to the post.[14]

The administrators anticipated that their decision would be unpopular.

After all, Wright's record as a dedicated, responsible and fair supervisor made him the obvious candidate for the job. However, his working methods and personality, which befitted the BBC operation of the 1920s, no longer suited the Corporation image of the thirties. As Eckersley specified:

> Whoever is in administrative charge of the programmes will have to be in a position to interview important people and, if necessary, put things over them. He will have to take important urgent decisions with or without Boult's knowledge and will have to represent the department at all sorts of conferences.[15]

The administrators were interested in a strong, decisive figure, who could handle the wide-ranging business interests of the department with tough efficiency. Mase had been criticized just a year earlier for his ruthless relations with other employees and, perhaps more crucially, his inability to make competent musical decisions; yet, he was selected for the job. Letters between Boult and Eckersley reveal that they were anxious about Wright's reaction. However, Boult reported, 'Wright took his knock very well indeed: was in fact a bit relieved I think!', and observed that 'one or two people have warned him that if he wasn't careful Mase would climb over his dead body, but he never worried much, and Mase is several years his senior'.[16] The administrators felt it was necessary to prepare a decisively worded announcement for distribution to staff, and Eckersley, Graves and Carpendale took some care in drafting it.[17] The final version was signed by Carpendale, the Corporation's second-in-command:

> The experience of the past year, since Mr. Boult became Music Director, has made it clear that it is impossible to combine in one person the full administrative and musical duties of this appointment, and it has been decided to appoint an Assistant Music Director, who will take immediate seniority after Mr. Boult and will act as his deputy in the office on all occasions when he is absent.
>
> It has been decided to appoint Mr. Mase Assistant Music Director forthwith.[18]

A week later, Mase's former position as Music Executive was filled by Arthur Wynn.[19]

The BBC was apparently criticized in 1931 for the music staff's lack of professional credentials, provoking an article in the next BBC yearbook. The Corporation argued that

> the musical programmes . . . are broadcast for the benefit of the general public . . . There is, therefore, every justification, both from the point of attracting the listener to the most significant music and from that of catering

for his simple but quite important and legitimate pleasures, for subjecting purely musical arrangements to the scrutiny of laymen experienced in assessing the public taste.[20]

The BBC nevertheless assured the public that the Music Department staff, from Boult down to those who booked the artists, were all trained and experienced professionals, describing their achievements in a confusing, not to mention exaggerated, paragraph (the square-bracketed material has been added for clarification):

> Excluding Dr Boult and the regular B.B.C. conductors . . . there are five offi-
> cials concerned with the general administration of the musical programmes
> [Wright, Clark, Herbage, Mase and Hely Hutchinson], and of them all five
> are composers whose works have had public performance; two are also
> concert pianists [Mase and Hely Hutchinson]; three have been conductors,
> apart from broadcasting [Clark, Herbage and Hely Hutchinson]; one has
> been a singer, actor, and producer [Herbage]; two have won musical scholar-
> ships at Oxford and Cambridge [Hely Hutchinson and Herbage], one of
> whom afterwards held a professorship at Cape Town Conservatoire [Hely
> Hutchinson]. Another has also had long experience of musical administra-
> tion at a famous publishing house [unclear to whom this refers], and another
> has studied on the Continent under musicians of the calibre of Schonberg
> [Clark]. There remain the managers of the B.B.C.'s Queen's Hall Concerts
> [Thompson] and of the B.B.C. orchestra [Pratt], and two officials engaged in
> booking artists. Both of the former are trained musicians and of the latter
> one came to the B.B.C. from the concert industry [Tillett]; the other from the
> Beecham Opera Company in which he was a principal [Wynn].

This odd, not to mention vague, manner of portraying the music staff accounted – in some cases, several times – for each individual's proficien-cies, even attributing some which were lacking. Although Clark studied composition with Schoenberg, he never had any works performed publicly and certainly did not categorize himself as a composer. Mase's career as a performer was as an accompanist rather than as a 'concert pianist'. Most importantly, the list all but ignores Wright, perhaps reflecting that, despite his creditable success as a composer, his musical background was, in fact, that of an amateur. In this way, the BBC attempted to justify the respon-sibility that was given to those men who determined the nature and content of the nations' music broadcasts, emphasizing their qualifications as experienced musicians.

## Contemporary music programming, 1930–1931

Music programming practices from the 1920s were maintained to a large extent during the 1930–31 season. Several established series were continued, including the 'Foundations of Music' recitals. More significant, perhaps, were two series featuring the new orchestra. The BBC Symphony Concerts became the Corporation's music showcase, in which high-profile orchestra concerts were presented publicly at the Queen's Hall on Wednesday nights and broadcast in their entirety. The programmes included a mixture of standard works and 'novelties'. Contemporary music was promoted on occasion, as in the all-Stravinsky programme on 28 January 1931, conducted by Ansermet and with the composer as soloist. Works by British composers were also featured, including Vaughan Williams's *Sea Symphony* (5 November), Walton's *Portsmouth Point* (21 January), Bliss's *Morning Heroes* (4 February) and Bax's Symphony no. 2 (29 April).[21] The other new orchestral series was broadcast from the studio on Sunday nights and offered more popular fare.[22]

## Presenting programmes of new music

At the beginning of the season, music programme presentation once again became the subject of discussion. In September 1930, the broadcasting critic of *The Observer* recommended that the Corporation modify its manner of introducing music programmes: 'More talks immediately before the performance of the music are needed; and I think that good gramophone records of the works might be used as well as piano examples'.[23] The BBC defended its usual practices:

> The B.B.C. does not believe that any good and general purpose would be served by prefacing its musical programmes, or even items in those programmes, with explanatory talks on the music about to be heard. The enjoyment of music is, or surely should be, an end in itself; an entertainment, first and foremost. To anticipate the listener's enjoyment by inflicting upon him someone else's ideas as to what the music means, how it is built, and so on, is only to confuse his sense of values when he comes, immediately afterwards, to listen to it himself.[24]

Curiously, the BBC conceded that verbal explanation of a contemporary work might be advantageous, but 'such talks must come at other times. Dissection belongs to the laboratory. Only in the rarest instances (Stravinsky's *Le Sacre* or Schonberg's *Pierrot Lunaire*) might it be advisable to bring the talks into direct juxtaposition with the music concerned'. In retrospect, this attitude seems odd, but the Corporation had used this approach for years, with explanatory remarks provided instead in Percy Scholes's, Ernest Newman's and Basil Maine's weekly talks.

This self-serving reaction was deemed unacceptable not only by the *Observer* critic,[25] but by Percy Scholes himself. Writing from Switzerland, he urged the Corporation to improve its presentation of new music.

They have been utterly regardless of the state of mind of a public unaccustomed to the sounds of the music of its own day. Sometimes, too, one of the most difficult works in the programme has been chosen as its opening item, so that thousands of listeners have 'switched off' and never heard the rest . . . But, above all, little or nothing has been said or done, microphonically to prepare a sympathetic atmosphere; works which might have attained a degree of comprehensibility if the musical themes or tunes had been previously known have been left without any guiding thread for the listener to clutch, so that, indeed, he has never even discovered that there were any themes at all.[26]

The BBC again defended its position, claiming that Scholes was out of touch with the average listener's interests and needs.

Does it necessarily help the listener to preface a musical performance with a lecture? The majority of people are not 'musical'; that is what musicians never seem to realize; or, if they do, they mistake the method of overcoming the still persisting ignorance and mistrust of serious music. Should the average man, switching on his set for a concert, encounter a lecture, he will find his opinion of music as a high-falutin' business confirmed, and switch off again.[27]

Rather than being out of touch with the listener, the former broadcasting critic was simply out of touch with current trends in presentation tactics. When Scholes was central to the Corporation's music-disseminating activities, spreading cultural enlightenment was more important than satisfying popular demand. In the 1930s, the balance shifted: although the central administrators still pursued their horizon-expanding policy, they now believed that popular reaction had to be addressed to some extent. Cultural and artistic merit were still taken into account, but they were no longer the sole or even the primary considerations in music programme building. The BBC dismissed the *Observer* critic's sensible suggestion, fearing that pre-concert talks would generate adverse, anti-elitist reaction to controversial and unpopular new music programmes. It is ironic that this exchange of ideas took place in autumn 1930, when few programmes devoted to new works were in fact aired.

In spring 1932, the BBC launched a new series of talks, which aimed to explain basic musical concepts to non-specialist listeners. Aired weekly on Monday evenings between 11 April and 4 July, these half-hour talks, entitled 'Music, Old and New', were written and read by Victor Hely Hutchinson.[28] The scope and purpose were outlined in the *Radio Times*.

This series of twelve talks is intended for music lovers who wish to broaden and deepen their musical knowledge and appreciation. The talks will be simple, and copiously supplemented with gramophone records and pianoforte illustrations. One of the chief points about the series is that classical and modern music will be dealt with on an equal basis, and perhaps many prejudices will be removed when it is discovered how little the fundamental principles of the two differ.[29]

In the talks on 18 and 25 April and 2 May 1932, Hely Hutchinson discussed keys and their relationship to music composition over the centuries. He concluded with a brief illustration of atonality, using Schoenberg's op. 19 piano pieces as examples.

> As the bonds of key have become progressively loosened the next step is that they should disappear altogether and all notes in a work be related directly and completely to the inner musical concept. This [type] of musical composition is called atonal, and it is the most controversial subject in music today. First let me make it clear that atonality does not mean the abandonment of melodic line, of harmony or form, but only of key. The notes in the atonal style of writing are not related to one main key-note. I must say at once that it is a subject on which experts disagree and so I can only give my own personal opinion for what it is worth, but my own reaction is that I cannot see the difficulty in accepting atonality as a legitimate and useful style of musical writing, either theoretically or practically . . . I have here two very short pieces by Shoneberg [sic], the most prominent exponent of atonality, from *Six Little Piano Pieces*, Nos. 3 and 5. I will play them without comment and you will see if you like them and if you appreciate their message.[30]

Shortly after Hely Hutchinson's series, the BBC Talks Department decided that it was no longer expedient or effective for Newman to continue the bi-weekly critical talks that he had been delivering since 1928; they were suspended for the 1932–3 season.[31] Significantly, the Corporation decided to replace them with explanations to be given nearer to the performances under discussion – finally adopting the strategy that had been recommended by the *Observer* radio critic and Percy Scholes two years before.

## Broadcasts of Second Viennese School works

The BBC's commitment to contemporary music was actively supported by the new Music Director, and, after an initial hiatus, new works permeated the 1930s broadcast schedules. Links between the Music Department and continental composers strengthened throughout the decade as political tensions in Central Europe reduced or eliminated performance opportunities there, particularly of ultra-modern music, and forced musicians from the continent to seek refuge in the UK. By the middle of the decade, for example, the BBC was one of the few organizations in Europe to present Second Viennese School works on a regular basis. Wright took over from Clark as the primary BBC contact with foreign musicians, and, like Clark, he developed personal friendships with many of them.

The 1930–1 contemporary concert series followed a significantly different planning and programming pattern than previously. Comprehensive building of the fifth series began much later than usual, and the concerts themselves did not commence until January 1931. It seems reasonable to assume that the transition to Boult's direction of the Music Department, the founding of the new orchestra and the planning of its first season took up the programme builders' time and concentration during spring and summer 1930, leaving little opportunity for proposing, planning and preparing other series.

In fact, only two Schoenberg works were broadcast before the new year. On 29 November, soprano Emmy Heim sang a group of German Lieder that included Schoenberg's 'Jane Gray' from op. 12. The other event was more significant: the eighth of the BBC Symphony Concerts took place on 10 December 1930, conducted by Scherchen. The first half of the programme was dedicated to Beethoven, and the second half to the first British performance of Schoenberg's *Pelleas und Melisande*, op. 5. An introductory *Radio Times* article focused entirely on the Schoenberg. Briefly outlining the composer's early career, the article equated *Pelleas* with works that were familiar to the British public. 'The *Songs of Gurra*, the *Resplendent Night*, and the present *Pélleas* were all written on the big scale . . ., but since then he has changed his tactics so considerably that his latest compositions are scored for a very minimum of players'.[32] The programme was well-received by the concert attendees, the London critics and the broadcast audience. Although the *Daily Telegraph* critic was unimpressed, he remarked on its surprising reception:

> At the B.B.C. concert in Queen's Hall last night a new work by Schönberg was brought to our hearing for the first time in London – true it has been in existence for some eight and twenty years, but we knew it not – and only about a dozen folk quitted the hall ere its last note had sounded! And when that note had faded away a large section of the audience still remained to applaud.[33]

In contrast to 1930, 1931 was an extraordinarily busy year for new music activities in Britain. Schoenberg, Berg, Webern and Stravinsky all visited England during the initial months, and many eminent composers, performers and new music enthusiasts came in July to attend the International Society for Contemporary Music (ISCM) Festival, held in Oxford and London. The six months before that saw the revitalization of the BBC's commitment to new music dissemination, through the Concerts of Contemporary Music.

The music programme builders proposed a six-concert series, to be given between January and June 1931. The concerts were to be presented before invited audiences as before, and they were to take place in the Corporation's No.10 studio, a converted warehouse on the south side of Waterloo Bridge. Significantly, the programme builders felt the need to justify

> the desirability of continuing the series for the fifth year, in view of the B.B.C.'s association, in this country and abroad, with the production of Contemporary Music. Opinions may have differed with regard to the actual music, but the concerts have included a high proportion of things that have been accorded places of honour as first productions abroad, including certain British works.[34]

This consideration had special significance in 1931, since England would become the international focal point for new music in July. In fact, the series was specifically organized 'to lead up to the 1931 I.S.C.M. Festival, in which the B.B.C. is interested, politically and financially'. The Music Department not only hoped to encourage public recognition of the festival's musical and cultural significance, but also needed to ensure that BBC interests in it would be appreciated and well-received.

The programmes proposed for the series differed from previous seasons. Most importantly, for the first time the series was designed to focus on orchestral rather than chamber works. The new orchestra made it financially advantageous to plan orchestral concerts, since its members were on annual BBC contracts while chamber ensembles had to be hired specially for each appearance. Although a few guest conductors were considered, it was proposed that Boult would conduct most of the broadcasts. The programmes emphasized British composers to an extent that had not been evident since the mid-1920s; it can be assumed that this significant change reflected the interests and influence of the new Music Director. Moreover, the proposal did not include the European composer-performers featured in the past, such as Bartók and Hindemith. Only one Stravinsky work was suggested: *Les noces*, which had been given the previous season. However, two of the proposed programmes were devoted to Second Viennese School repertory, one to be conducted by Schoenberg, featuring the first British performance of *Erwartung*, the other by Webern. The proposed series was thus oriented around two poles: works by modern British composers, and works by Schoenberg and Webern.

During November and December 1930, the proposal was reworked and refined. Wright clarified that we should like to play the important works twice. In the event of a late broadcast, they could be played over beforehand, and if the broadcast is early, say at 8 p.m., then the repetition would be made in the studio afterwards. This would cost no more, and would enable the Press and others present better to understand the music. This does not, of course, apply to standard or well-known works.[35]

The idea of presenting *Les noces* was withdrawn, since it proved impossible to schedule it during Ansermet's visit; another British-based programme was planned in its place. Finally, Clark's idea of inviting Ravel to perform his Piano Concerto in the final concert was vetoed by Wright: 'I am not keen on having Ravel, who would be expensive, as he plays atrociously: I would much rather see an English artist invited to do it'.[36]

In the end, the six programmes balanced British contemporary trends with those of Europe.[37] British music was featured in no less than half the concerts, and except for Margot Hinnenberg-Lefèbre, Schoenberg and Webern, all the performers and conductors were British. The programmes were designed to acquaint listeners with previously unexplored styles, with a work each by Conrad Beck and Igor Markevich, and with a concert devoted to Manuel de Falla. Except for the Schoenberg and Webern programmes, the series as a whole tended to be less abrasive and less focused on inaccessible, atonal idioms than previously. Perhaps the British works and the Falla concert were designed to show listeners that contemporary repertory included a range of accessible styles, as well as ultra-modern works. The BBC may have hoped that this would encourage the British public to be more favourably disposed to the ISCM Festival.

The first concert of the series took place on 9 January 1931 and featured Schoenberg conducting his own works. Plans for Schoenberg's second BBC appearance had begun over a year before, in September 1929, when Clark invited him to conduct during the 1929–30 season. As proof of his devotion, Clark proudly listed the many Schoenberg works that had already been broadcast, and expressed his wish to schedule Schoenberg's op. 17.

> At the beginning of the season, I brought forward my long-held wish for us to present *Erwartung* under your direction. Now, as I've been told that Frau Hinnenberg knows the part, the plan's realization is not in doubt, and it has been received with the greatest interest by everyone here. The work will undoubtedly make its full impact on radio, in a dramatic as well as a musical sense, and I consider it wholly suited to satisfying the general public, which should be fairly familiar with your other works by now.[38]

Clark also promised that Schoenberg's newly-completed, one-act opera, *Von heute auf morgen*, would be considered for the 1929–30 season,[39] explaining that the programmes would complement each other.

First, we do the concert with *Erwartung* – indeed, if it suits you, perhaps in December. The success of this evening will prepare for the performance of the new work, which we could then probably put on early in the year. Meanwhile, it would be performed in Germany; a great deal will certainly be written about it in the English press, which we will use as publicity. I would try to come to the première and would report on it.

I believe it would be right to proceed in this practical way. Since *Erwartung* will be sung by Frau Hinnenberg, who knows German well, nothing stands in the way of an early performance, while a certain time will still be needed to translate and study the roles for the new work. Besides, I confess, I've been itching for a long time to hear the monodrama and, as described, the performance with us would be solidly done, under the most favorable conditions.[40]

Schoenberg proposed that the *Erwartung* programme also include his orchestration of a Bach Prelude and Fugue and his op. 8 orchestral Lieder. He suggested that the concert take place on 5 or 6 December 1929 – the same time that Webern was scheduled to conduct for the BBC. By mid-October, the plans were still vague and Schoenberg was becoming frantic, uncertain about the date, the availability of the soloist, Margot Hinnenberg-Lefèbre, and the proximity of the London concert to the opera's première in Frankfurt.[41] Although no documentation survives, the Music Department apparently decided that it was best to postpone Schoenberg's programme, and no further mention is made of it during the 1929–30 season.

The following summer, Clark and Schoenberg began to plan anew for the *Erwartung* concert. A surviving postcard verifies that Schoenberg expected to conduct a BBC concert in October.[42] This news surprised Wright, who took it as evidence that Clark had promised Schoenberg not one, but two concerts. The Music Department had agreed that the composer should conduct in January, but 'No question of 2 performances so far as I know of. ACB [Boult] is surprised and averse'.[43] In August, the BBC formally invited both Schoenberg and Hinnenberg-Lefèbre to participate in a concert on 9 January 1931, at which *Erwartung* and the Bach arrangement would be presented.[44]

Surprisingly, the Music Department still seemed uncertain about the January concert three months later, when Wright asked Boult to confirm the programme plans.

Would you add your comments with regard to 'Erwartung' as if you do not approve of this particular work, there is still the Schönberg commitment, and any change of programme should be discussed immediately, as it will involve readjustments of the rehearsal scheme? Erwartung only lasts 1/2 an hour and would be preceded by Schonberg's recent orchestration of 2 Bach fugues and preludes.[45]

The concert was also threatened by Hinnenberg-Lefèbre. She had never been happy with the 9 January date, since she was committed to singing *Gurrelieder* in Nürnberg on the 6th. In addition, the singer requested a hefty £80 fee, twice the amount she usually received from the Corporation. When the BBC proposed changing the date to the 8th to avoid transmitting such a difficult and controversial programme on a Friday evening, it became impossible for her. On 10 December, the situation reached a crisis point, with the Music Department sending the singer no fewer than three telegrams.

> Much regret January 8 only possible date Schonberg *Erwartung*. Also owing high cost of concert we cannot pay you more than 40 guineas stop Please wire acceptance otherwise must postpone concert indefinitely.[46]

Clark then offered Hinnenberg-Lefèbre the full fee, on condition that she also sang a programme of standard repertory songs. The *Erwartung* concert was returned to 9 January, with three rehearsals scheduled for the 8th and 9th. These conditions were agreed by the artist, and the programme was finalized at last.[47] Wright was not pleased with the outcome, complaining that 'we have by accident rather than design got Schonberg on a Friday'.[48]

The first of the season's Concerts of Contemporary Music was viewed by the Music Department as the centrepiece of the week's music programmes,[49] and a significant amount of *Radio Times* space was devoted to drawing listeners' attention to the event. A short article in the 26 December issue justified not only this concert, but the series as a whole.

> Controversy in itself is not necessarily a sign of health; but in this particular connection we believe it does reveal a dawning awareness that there may be something, after all, in this difficult music. England remains so obstinately in the rearguard, however, in this matter, that it seems to require some such drive and integrity as that which lies behind these concerts to shake us into this awareness.[50]

The favourable reception of Schoenberg's *Pelleas* was also exploited, since listeners' commendations of the 10 December programme arrived just in time to be published in the *Radio Times* of 2 January. For example, a letter from Paul A. McEwen of Nottinghamshire was conspicuously reproduced:

> I have just been listening to Schönberg's 'Pelleas and Melisande' (alas! that I couldn't be there) and must write to thank somebody, so I thank the B.B.C., again and again, for giving us this first performance here. But why only the first performance? Why not the hundredth? It is exquisite, wonderful – it must be – whatever the critics say. Please let us have it again, and often.[51]

That issue's music column was entitled 'Schönberg to Conduct his Own Music this Week', and was illustrated with a severe drawing of the composer in the centre of the page.[52] Two lengthy paragraphs introduced the guest conductor as 'one of the dominating figures of our generation: the disciples who look to him as their master include in their ranks a large number of the foremost musicians – composers and performers – of the world, and his influence on the course of music is a far-reaching one'.[53] The article also included a detailed and vivid description of *Erwartung*'s drama. Although the *Radio Times* programme listing indicated that only two works would be presented, in fact an additional piece was performed and broadcast: Schoenberg's *Friede auf Erde*, op. 13, was sung by the Wireless Chorus conducted by Stanford Robinson. The work had been given during a studio broadcast on 7 January, as a lead up to the all-Schoenberg concert; the programme builders apparently decided to repeat it, since the Bach transcription and *Erwartung* by themselves made for a short programme.

In reviews, most space was devoted to the performance of the mono-drama, and reaction ranged, as usual, between critics who dismissed the work outright as musically meaningless and critics who dismissed it after more careful thought. For example, the *Evening News* critic wrote:

> It may seem to the plain man who is no bigot in the matter of music that modern composers of the extreme order, just like the ultra-futurists among the painters, are obsessed with the one idea – that of producing something utterly different. Sometimes in ignoring everything that has gone before, especially works that stand to-day as masterpieces, the new composers do achieve something that reaches our perceptions and convinces as to its quality. More often there is such a wilderness of wild disorder in their strivings for expression that the plain man loses all patience.[54]

Many critics found that the excessiveness of the idiom was manifest most annoyingly in the work's duration. The *Daily Telegraph* reviewer complained that 'the music goes through terrible agonies for half an hour and more, expressive to the last ounce. And at the end the listener-in, unfamiliar with the work as a stage play . . . must confess himself (to say the least) dissatisfied with the experience'.[55] In contrast, Newman reluctantly admitted that aspects of the performance were interesting.

> One could admire . . . – the remarkable musicianship of the singer, Madame Hinnenberg-Lefebre, the brave way the B.B.C. Orchestra tackled a most difficult score, the constant, if sometimes perverse, ingenuity of the writing, and so on. But I cannot see the work ever becoming a world-beater. The writing for the voice is too near the style of ordinary speech to convey much musical

pleasure. The orchestral part is frequently more impressive to the eye than to the ear: that is to say, it looks the last word in harmonic ingenuity, not to say preciosity, but in performance we find that very often the actual notes really do not matter so much as the colour wash of tone in which the phrase is bathed. The orchestration, considered in and by itself, is truly remarkable: it is to this, more than to anything else, that the work owes whatever power it has to give us a sense of blood-and-thunder drama. But when we boil it all down to its musical essentials we cannot persuade ourselves that the musical thinking in it is really first-class.[56]

Only Constant Lambert hailed the concert as a success.

Even to those who are familiar with his style, Schönberg's work is extremely baffling on paper, and only actual performance can reveal the ingenuity and beauty of his music. Although I do not consider 'Erwartung' as belonging to Schönberg's best period, there is no doubt that it is a *tour de force* without parallel. The ease and assurance with which he manipulates the complex textures of the orchestra are amazing, and the technical mastery of this music must surely impress the least sympathetic listener.[57]

The composer, too, was pleased with the performance, writing to Clark from Berlin. He was especially impressed by the new orchestra.

The orchestra rehearsals brought me great happiness. I can say that I have perhaps never yet rehearsed such a difficult work so effortlessly. I want to *thank you most sincerely for all of this!*[58]

Clearly, Schoenberg's second performance for the BBC did not have the impact of his *Gurrelieder* performance two years before; nevertheless, the personal appearance of this well-known and controversial figure as conductor of his own works enabled the Corporation to launch its new series of contemporary concerts in a conspicuous and auspicious way.

Just days after Schoenberg's performance, Berg visited England for the first time, although not on BBC business. He was one of the international jurors who gathered at the Cambridge home of the ISCM President, Edward J. Dent, between 11 and 15 January to decide which works would be selected for that year's festival. Comprehensive discussions of Berg's experiences in England appear elsewhere,[59] but it is worth noting the small part that Clark played in this visit. In a letter written the previous December, Berg had informed his friend that his travel plans permitted a few hours in London on 11 January, if it were possible for Clark to meet him then. In fact, Berg became ill, his arrival was postponed and the meeting was cancelled. After the composer's adjudication duties were completed, however, he spent a day seeing London in Clark's company before returning home.[60]

Although Clark spent little time with Berg during this visit, he managed to relay news, which Berg, and Schoenberg as well, subsequently passed on to Webern: the Music Department intended to invite Webern to conduct for the BBC during spring 1931. Since he had not heard directly from the Corporation, Webern wrote to Clark on 4 February, expressing excitement at the prospect of conducting in London again and listing dates he had free.[61] He was especially pleased that he might be engaged for two performances.

> As Berg told me, you are even planning two evenings for me: one with a Schönberg [piece], a classical [piece] and a work by me, and the other as a 'Viennese' evening (with Schubert, Joh. Strauss etc.)? That would be brilliant.

He had already thought about possible programmes, but – remembering that he had previously made many suggestions that were ignored – he specified, 'I request a detailed reply, if necessary.'

This letter provoked Clark into action. He had already obtained approval to invite the composer to conduct a contemporary concert, but only after receiving the letter did he formally propose that Webern conduct a second programme of light Viennese classics. Clark stressed that Webern's strengths lay in his interpretation of standard repertory, rather than in conducting esoteric, contemporary works.

> Webern is an admirable conductor who was by way of coming into his own at present in Vienna and who might, in future, be useful to us as conductor in a general way . . . The suggestion was made in the belief that the Viennese programme would be in itself first rate and popular with all, and would serve the purpose of introducing this musician to the widest audience.
>
>   Webern is on the staff of the RAVAG and conducts regularly in their symphonic programmes. Further, he has conducted the Arbeiter Symphonie Concerts for some years past where his performances in particular of Mahler's Second and Eighth Symphonies have established him in the eyes of musicians in Vienna as one of the outstanding young conductors of the day.[62]

Clark also wrote to Webern, confirming the contemporary concert and allowing for the possibility of a second programme. He proposed options for the new music concert.

> I suggest a work of yours, either the Symphony or the piece for string orchestra of which Berg told me while he was in London. Further the Schoenberg Musik zu einer Lichtspielszene, and together with this we might do the transcription of the Lied der Waldtaube for Chamber Orchestra.[63]

Webern responded with an enthusiasm that was reminiscent of his reaction to the first invitation – though not nearly so long-winded. He was pleased at the prospect of travelling to England in May, preferring the middle of the month to avoid conflicts with other engagements. He also approved most of Clark's proposals.

> Your suggestions please me very much. Have you perhaps already
> Schoenberg's agreement that I will do his 'Lichtspielmusik' for you? (It could
> be that he intends to reserve it for himself.) Naturally, nothing would be
> better than to be able to perform just *this piece*. Of mine, I suggest the
> arrangement of my first quartet for string orchestra. The Symphony should
> come at the music festival of the ISCM.[64]

Webern continued with some interesting comments about his arrangement of the op. 5 pieces.

> I believe the score (of the arrangement) will interest you very much.
> Compared with the string quartet it has become something completely new;
> even though no notes were changed, still some shifting took place. And for
> all that, within it I arrive at *15 divisions of the strings*. It is an uninterrupted
> succession of tutti, half-sections, single desks and soloists, and I need for it as
> large an ensemble of strings *as possible. As large as it could possibly be.*

He was less happy about conducting the chamber orchestra arrangement of 'Lied der Waldtaube' from *Gurrelieder*. Since the first two works involved full orchestra, he felt that the third should as well. Moreover, he worried that the duration of the proposed programme, which he calculated at around 45 minutes, was too short, and wondered if he might conduct a symphony instead.

> It would also be opportune for me to be able to conduct a *large* symphonic
> work. Perhaps in place of the 'Waldtaube', a *classical* symphony! For example,
> the *Eroica* or perhaps still better the *5th of Beethoven*! What do you think? Or
> how would *Mahler's 1st* be? For me as conductor, it would be extraordinarily
> favourable. Wouldn't that really work? What an unprecedented four move-
> ments! They could only cause a sensation. I am convinced that the people in
> the west are only still against Mahler because they have not yet heard him
> properly.

With the Mahler Symphony, the programme would last about 80 minutes, or with a Beethoven symphony, around 65 minutes. Webern saw a satisfying coherence in conducting two Viennese programmes.

> With this program: *Schoenberg, W. , Mahler* we would have a purely *Austrian*
> (*Viennese*) evening. Since for the *second* concert intended for me you plan a
> kind of *cheerful Viennese evening*, both concerts would be linked through this
> splendidly!!! Two Viennese evenings of great contrast, but related.

The composer specified the required number of rehearsals for various options: four for the contemporary concert with Mahler, or three with Beethoven, and one for the light music programme. Finally, he broached the subject of his fee, requesting £80 for the two concerts.

At the end of the month, Webern received an official BBC contract, which confirmed his engagement for the two performances. However, the proposed fee incited him to write Clark again.

> I am somewhat disappointed about the honorarium set for me in it: £63 for *both* concerts. Since I had received £42 for *one* concert last time, this time I calculated approximately double that sum, therefore around £80. Is it possible any longer to change this?[65]

He was also frustrated that Clark had not replied to his previous letter, leaving him in ignorance about programme details a mere month before the concerts were to take place. He seized the opportunity to reiterate his wish to conduct a symphony.

> I asked you *most urgently* not to add a piece for *chamber orchestra* to the two initial works, since we need for these a *large* orchestra, but suggested as a complement, a *classical* symphony! (you had also related the programme to me in this way through Berg) I ask you to tell me the decision as soon as possible!!! And request once more that you refrain from the Waldtaube, and make the *5th symphony* of Beethoven possible. Also, with the 'Waldtaube', the programme would be too *short*! . . . With the Beethoven 5th, it would work out just splendidly. With two novelties of this kind, the idea of a 'contemporary music concert', I believe, is amply fulfilled.
> Only give an immediate answer!!!
> Beethoven 5th
> Dear friend; I beg you many times for this!!!

Webern requested an immediate response to queries concerning the number and times of the rehearsals, whether he would need an entry permit, and whether he should bring concert dress, since he was uncertain if the concert was to be performed in public.

Clark still failed to reply to Webern's frantic questions. However, on 10 April the BBC Booking Section sent the composer a routine letter concerning the 8 May concert, confirming that the programme consisted of the orchestral arrangement of Webern's op. 5, the chamber orchestra arrangement of Schoenberg's 'Lied der Waldtaube', and Schoenberg's op. 34; times for two rehearsals were also specified.[66] Webern responded with a rather impatient letter to his friend.

> Now, since there is no possibility that I will conduct a classical symphony on the second of my evenings – I received news from the BBC yesterday – I will perform the 'Waldtauben-Lied', certainly with no less pleasure; but I am

*astonished* that up to today I have heard not *a single word* about the *reason* why my wish is unfulfilled.[67]

He also responded with anger to the proposed rehearsal schedule, which he interpreted in terms of both concerts. Since two rehearsals were listed, he inferred that he had been assigned one for each concert – a substantial reduction from his request for four or five.

> After all the detailed explanation which I gave you about the number and type of rehearsals that are necessary in my view, now I have learned . . . that only *one* rehearsal per concert has been scheduled. This I can only take as a *misunderstanding*! Was it done with your knowledge? No, dear Clark, that is *absolutely* too few! How should I bring about *well* in a *single* rehearsal *three* such difficult pieces as the 'Lichtspielmusik', my 'Five pieces' and the 'Waldtauben-Lied', which is especially exacting in the arrangement for chamber orchestra? That would not even be demanded of anyone here in Vienna . . . I must request urgently, with all emphasis, that *at least* another, third, rehearsal be granted to me.

Webern again requested clarification of the many unresolved questions and asked Clark to make his hotel reservations.

On 17 April, the BBC issued a new contract offering the composer 70 guineas for the two concerts.[68] Webern immediately wrote to thank Clark:

> I am very happy and thank you very much for having procured this increase for me. Now I also hope to receive *favourable news* relating to the rehearsals!!! . . . Dear friend, 3 rehearsals for both concerts is the least. ! 4 ! ! 4 ! (Four!!!)[69]

On the 21st, the Booking Section sent Webern another routine letter, this time confirming the programme and rehearsal schedule for the concert of lighter music on 7 May. A few days later, Webern's entry permit was also posted to him.[70] Webern at last realized that he had misinterpreted the rehearsal situation and wrote to Clark yet again.

> From a fresh BBC letter, I infer that I was mistaken in my belief (complained about to you in my letter before last) that only *one* rehearsal per concert would be assigned to me, and that *two* rehearsals are intended for the second evening. So, I will have in *all three rehearsals* . . . Now I am already calmer! But, dear friend, won't a *fourth* rehearsal be possible, which I put down to you from the beginning as necessary? Perhaps *Friday the 8th in the morning*? or on the *afternoon of the 6th*?[71]

Webern requested that a piano rehearsal be organized with the singer, Enid Cruickshank, a Scottish contralto with whom he had not worked before. He also asked that players with important parts (the pianist, harmonium player and solo violist) look over their music thoroughly before the rehearsals. He was to leave Vienna the morning of 5 May, arriving at Victoria Station on the evening of the 6th, and requested most emphatically: 'I ask you many times *to await me at the station*!' All arrangements were finalized in telegrams over the next few days.[72]

Over a four-month period, Webern had attempted to influence the shape of his programmes and the manner of their preparation. Throughout the course of the one-sided discussion, the composer's ideas and demands were ignored, and the contemporary programme was designed and rehearsed exactly as Clark had originally conceived it. Including Beethoven's Fifth Symphony in the one series reserved for new repertory was never a viable option. Clark could simply have informed Webern of that fact; ignoring the composer's suggestions and questions was neither considerate nor professional. However, in the end, Clark's negligent, haphazard approach achieved the desired effect: Webern came to London as a special guest of the BBC and conducted a concert of Second Viennese School works, two of which were completely new to British audiences.

Webern's concerts were given the usual pre-concert publicity. The *Radio Times* emphasized that although 'Webern is known as Schönberg's most uncompromising pupil', he was going to conduct a programme to appeal to the general public, as well as one devoted to contemporary music.

> Such versatility is not surprising, for Herr Webern, as conductor of the *Wiener Arbeitersinfonieconzerte* (Vienna Workmen's Concerts), has made a big reputation for himself as an interpreter of such classical and romantic composers as Beethoven, Brahms, and Mahler.[73]

In this way, the BBC tried to improve Webern's image by associating him with repertory that was generally popular. The daily listings for 8 May were illustrated with photographs of Webern and Enid Cruickshank,[74] and a section of the weekly music column described the composer's op. 5.

> The five pieces of his own with which he begins this programme are not quite on such a miniature scale as those which were last broadcast, and the first, in a brisk tempo, is of quite usual length, with a quiet alternating section. No. 2 is a very brief lyrical impression, which the viola introduces, and the third hurries along so rapidly as to occupy only some thirty-five seconds in performance. The fourth is also very short and extremely difficult in its subtlety. The last is in a very slow measure, and it, too, makes severe demands on the imaginative gifts of the players, as of those who hear it.[75]

The article concluded with a brief allusion to the more popular programme.

> But that even so modern a composer and conductor as Webern is in no way out of sympathy with the tuneful music of other days, will be obvious to all who hear his programme of Viennese music on the National wavelength on Thursday, at 7.45. It includes two of the great classics of the ball room, of which Vienna today is as proud as ever it was.

The concerts were thus promoted as a double-bill of contrasts, as opposing sides of Webern's musical character: the appealing conductor of romantic favourites on the one hand, and the uncompromising composer of fleeting, wispy music on the other. Surprisingly, no reviews of the contemporary concert appeared in the usual London papers.

The BBC's contemporary music series of 1930–1 was shorter than in previous years and emphasized British composers and artists at the expense of European styles; nevertheless, attention accorded to Second Viennese composers remained strong, with Schoenberg and Webern both appearing as guest artists and represented compositionally as well. In general, however, the presentation of Second Viennese School repertory in BBC programmes declined significantly during this season; just nine works were broadcast in total, one by Webern and the rest by Schoenberg. Moreover, except for Margot Hinnenberg-Lefèbre and the composer-conductors, the performing members of Schoenberg's circle were not invited to give broadcasts, as previously. The Corporation's decision to broadcast less continental new music during the 1930–1 season may well have been a conscious attempt to counterbalance the high proportion of contemporary music that was to be performed, and in some cases broadcast, at the summer's ISCM Festival.

## Preparing audiences for the ISCM Festival

The BBC took other steps to prepare the British public for the festival. In spring 1931, the Corporation relaunched the 'New Friends in Music' talks, which aimed to make recent compositional trends more accessible to non-specialist listeners. The new series encompassed six 30-minute talks, broadcast weekly between 20 February and 27 March. Each programme was devoted to a significant living composer and was written and read by an eminent musician or music critic. The first talk, focusing on Ravel, was given by Constant Lambert; Stravinsky was considered in the second by Edwin Evans; then Strauss by Malcolm Sargent; Holst by Adrian Boult; Bax by Percy Scholes, and Holst again by Victor Hely Hutchinson. The reintroduction of the series at this time undoubtedly aimed to improve public receptivity of contemporary trends.

The composers and styles covered in the talks in fact avoided idioms and issues that were difficult for the average listener. In contrast, the BBC Music Critic, Ernest Newman, directly addressed listeners' concerns about such inaccessible idioms in a talk he gave in January 1931. Listener response was so positive that he wrote to the BBC Director of Talks, Hilda Matheson, strongly recommending that the Corporation tackle the subject in a systematic way.

> I am more than ever convinced of the necessity of a few talks of the kind I outlined to you long ago – designed to help intelligent and earnest listeners to do their own thinking about modern developments, to get some sort of standard of good and bad, and generally to discover the cultural and other causes of the confusion of the day, with the hope of finding their way about in the maze. Once more I feel that while you have given listeners an enormous amount of explanation of rudimentary things that hardly need explanation, you have done too little for the large class of listeners who have quite a good grasp of the older music, but are hopelessly at sea with the new.[76]

Matheson informed Newman of the 'New Friends in Music' series,[77] but those talks did not provide the type of information that Newman had in mind.

> The special talks you mention should be very interesting: but none of these can possibly cover the ground I had in mind. None of these composers is 'ultra-modern', as the stock term goes – not even Stravinsky. My idea was a course that would deal with the *general situation* in modern music & art generally, individual composers being used merely by way of illustration here & there. Mainly there is a desire of this kind on the part of thoughtful listeners who have no means of getting the necessary enlightenment for themselves. However, I quite see the difficulties in the way of such a course.[78]

Newman's idea was taken no further.

In May 1931, Lionel Fielden, an assistant in the BBC's Adult Education Department, proposed that the issue of ultra-modern music be addressed another way. He invited Newman to participate in a panel of eminent British musicians and writers for a 50-minute broadcast discussion.

> I should very much like to make this a really hot debate on the merits of ancient and modern composers. People are always writing, as you know, to ask for more talks on modern music, and I think it would be great fun to have an attack on, and defence of, it. It might be illustrated by excerpts by both sides. I have talked about it to Boult, and he is quite keen on the idea.[79]

Although Newman approved the idea in principle, he did not believe that the format would work. In a long letter to Fielden, he explained his objections, revealing many of his personal feelings towards contemporary music.

> There is really no such thing as 'modern music', except in the sense of music
> written recently. Modern musicians are of all sorts; they work in different
> ways, have different ideals and different techniques; no one formula can be
> found to cover them all . . . There is no such thing as 'modern music' in the
> sense of a music fundamentally different, over the whole field, from the old
> music. So I am afraid the discussion would be futile, because no definition of
> the subject of debate is really possible.[80]

He also felt that the unavoidable use of technical terms would make the
discussion inaccessible to non-specialist listeners.

> Once the debaters got down to brass tacks, they would be talking miles above
> the heads of the ordinary listener. They could only prove some point or other
> by a musical demonstration of it, and not only would this take time, but the
> affair would inevitably tend more and more to become a talk rather than a
> debate. In a word, the subject is too vast and too vague for debate in this off-
> hand way, and the moment it began to address itself to realities it would take
> the plain man out of his depth.

Fielden tried to get Newman to change his mind, but the critic adamantly
held his ground.[81] Fielden eventually conceded, despondently reporting, 'I
have now put in a discussion on betting instead, which I suppose will
amuse most people'.[82]

Although the broadcast debate fell through, the BBC had already laid
the foundations for audience appreciation of the ISCM Festival. During
the first half of the year, the Concerts of Contemporary Music were
designed for this purpose. In the weeks immediately preceding the festival,
'New Friends in Music' and other talks intensified the effort. It is impossible to say whether these tactics achieved the desired effect.

## The ISCM Festival, July 1931

During the week of 21–8 July 1931, the ISCM Festival took place for the
first time in England, the country in which its president, Edward J. Dent,
and its headquarters were based. It was no coincidence that the British
Section volunteered to host the festival in the first year of the BBC
Symphony Orchestra's existence. As the Chairman of the British Section,
Edwin Evans, explained,

> It had long been the desire not only of the British but of all Sections to hold a
> Festival in this country, but until now we have been placed at a disadvantage.
> Whereas other countries could offer such amenities as municipal concert-halls
> and orchestras, or State opera houses, with perhaps a Ministry in the back-
> ground to ensure that everything was done to help the national prestige by

welcoming the international guests, England could offer nothing of the kind until the British Broadcasting Corporation founded its splendid permanent orchestra and most generously offered its services, together with those of the National Chorus, to the British Section of the I.S.C.M. At the same time, the University of Oxford offered the Society the hospitality of its historic buildings. With these two promises of support, the British Section felt that it could commit this country to a Festival without fear of humiliating comparisons.[83]

Several of the Music Department staff had close ties with the society: Clark had been the official BBC observer since 1927,[84] and both he and Wright regularly attended the annual festivals, including the 1930 gathering at Liège.[85] It seems likely that these BBC representatives offered the use of the BBC orchestra and choruses to the Chairman of the British Section.[86]

Although the Music Department recognized the festival's significance and felt it merited a high level of BBC attention, others failed to agree. For example, Wright requested that the BBC Talks Director, Hilda Matheson, schedule an introductory talk.

> This Festival is an occasion of such wide interest on account of its undoubtedly international importance that we feel a special talk period should be reserved at once if possible for a talk on it, by someone like Professor Dent who is the President of the Society which gives the Festival annually. If this could be latish in the evening all the better. Are there any possibilities, please?[87]

However, Boult planned to mention the festival in one of his bi-weekly talks, and Matheson felt that was adequate coverage.[88] The Music Department disagreed: special attention was warranted to safeguard the BBC's financial interests. Even Mase pointed out:

> It is a very important occasion – the Festival is but rarely held in this country & we are spending a large sum. Both musically & financially we want all the notice taken possible. Would you reconsider? We should be very grateful.[89]

Eckersley supported the Music Department's point of view, explaining that it was up to the BBC to uphold Britain's reputation.

> The British Government . . . seem to be doing nothing, and I think this is rather a slur on us as a musical nation. I think, therefore, that anything extra that we (the B.B.C.) could do to help would be a good gesture, and for this reason and because of the importance of the occasion I think we ought to give a special talk on the Festival and what it stands for.[90]

He recommended that Matheson invite an official of the society to give the talk. In the event, Dent refused,[91] but Evans gave it on 18 July, the Saturday before the festival commenced.[92]

It was equally challenging to convince the British public of the festival's significance. Throughout July 1931, the BBC sustained an intensive campaign informing listeners about new music issues, about the ISCM, about the British festival – emphasizing the BBC's crucial role within it, of course – and about events that were to be broadcast. A *Radio Times* editorial of 3 July gave a brief explanation of the festival's history and purpose: to 'safeguar[d] the interests of modern music, by securing the best of it a hearing under nearly ideal conditions and with unusual publicity. Its avowed aim is to encourage young composers and to spread an interest in the new music'.[93] The article pointed out the significant attention that had been given to British works at previous ISCM gatherings and justified the BBC's involvement as a natural extension of its cultural-expansionist policy.

> Considering the incalculable part played by broadcasting in the spread of musical culture, it is both natural and right that the B.B.C. should be taking an active interest in this important expression of present-day musical activities . . . All who take an intelligent interest in music have here the best possible opportunity for hearing what 'the vanguard' is doing.

The 17 July issue led with an article by Edwin Evans, explaining the ISCM's history, its current membership, the system and criteria behind music selection, and details about the specific works to be heard in Oxford and London.[94] Evans's article mirrored his introductory talk, which was reprinted in the 22 July issue of *The Listener*.[95] In addition, other *Radio Times* articles promoted specific ISCM events.[96] This extensive publicity demonstrates the strength of the BBC's commitment to the festival's success.

As a supplement, the BBC devoted the leading articles in the 10 and 24 July *Radio Times* to discussions of contemporary music reception. In 'Music that Expresses Contemporary Life', Robin Hey asserted that ordinary listeners related to contemporary music more easily than music critics.

> The musical layman, approaching music as he does, is likely to be fairly prompt in response to this expression of the *Zeitgeist*. It is not, necessarily, that he is more in tune with the 'spirit of the age' than is the critic; it is simply that, since art means less to him than life, he is more freely iconoclastic about it and, further, he is more able to sense where it reflects the colours of the life about him . . . The critic should look less scornfully on the layman's enthusiasm for the modern music. Let him be humble about it. That enthusiasm may not be very intelligent, but it is undoubtedly sincere.[97]

This article introduced a new strategy by which the BBC tried to induce public acceptance of new music. By implying that the silent majority were generally enthusiastic and that they triumphed over close-minded music critics, the BBC encouraged listeners to be open to festival broadcasts and to disregard any negative criticisms. In the following issue, the BBC published a response by a well-known broadcasting critic, W. R. Anderson, to sustain listeners' interest during the festival's second week.[98]

The festival itself encompassed eight concerts, two of which presented English music of previous centuries. As can be seen from Table 8.1, the other six events presented 29 recently-composed works from 13 different countries, four by composers associated with the Second Viennese circle: Wellesz's *Drei geistliche Chöre*, op. 47, Webern's Symphony, op. 21, Jozef Koffler's String Trio and Otto Jokl's Sonatina for Piano, op. 21.[99] The eleven pieces that were broadcast were performed by the Corporation's orchestra and choruses. The first concert took place in Oxford on the afternoon of 23 July, but works from the programme were not broadcast until that evening; in the days before pre-recording, this meant that the musicians travelled to London and repeated a condensed version of the concert from a BBC studio.[100] Also broadcast were parts of the orchestral concerts on 27 and 28 July, transmitted live from the Queen's Hall in London.

The festival as a whole received wide coverage in both the daily press and specialist journals.[101] Unusually, the BBC published a festival retrospective in the *Radio Times*.

> The part recently played by the B.B.C., in making it possible for this year's Festival of the International Society for Contemporary Music to be held in England, serves to emphasize the possibility of a new era in English corporate musical life ... This year, by dint of the B.B.C.'s loan of both orchestra and chorus, it has been possible to perform these difficult compositions to the credit of the Festival and the approval of the public.[102]

*The Listener* also included a comprehensive review, by Eric Blom. Each work in each concert was critiqued in a sentence or two, briefly encapsulating the compositional style, the musical impression and the quality of performance. The outstanding works received a bit more attention; by general consensus, these appeared to be the Delannoy String Quartet, the Cartan Sonatina, Vaughan Williams's *Benedicite* and Roussel's Psalm setting.[103]

The critics reached similar conclusions in their assessments of the Second Viennese School works. Although the Wellesz choral pieces were received favourably, they were dismissed with little comment as anachronistic. Not surprisingly, the Webern Symphony received a significant amount of attention, as in Blom's review:

> One recognised almost nothing that was like music of any accustomed kind and hardly even the twelve-tone theme on which it is based in some

Table 8.1 *Contemporary music programmes of the ISCM Festival, Oxford and London,*
*July 1931*

| **Thursday, 23 July 1931** [†] | | Sheldonian Theatre, Oxford |
|---|---|---|
| Lev Knipper | USSR | * *Malen'kaya liricheskaya suita* ('Little Lyric Suite'), op. 18 |
| Roger Sessions | USA | Piano Sonata no. 1 |
| Józef Koffler | Poland | String Trio |
| Jean Huré | France | * *Ame en peine* for chorus |
| Egon Wellesz | Austria | * *Drei geistliche Chöre*, op. 47 |
| Jan Maklakiewicz | Poland | * *Pieśni japońskie* ('Japanese Songs') for soprano and chamber orchestra |
| Ernesto Halffter | Spain | * *Sinfonietta* in D major |
| **Friday, 24 July 1931** | | New Theatre, Oxford |
| Ralph Vaughan Williams | Great Britain | *Job* |
| Ervín Schulhoff | Czechoslovakia | *La somnambule* |
| Constant Lambert | Great Britain | *Pomona* |
| **Saturday, 25 July 1931, morning** | | Holywell Music Room, Oxford |
| Paul Hindemith | Germany | *Wir bauen eine Stadt* |
| **Saturday, 25 July 1931, evening** | | Sheldonian Theatre, Oxford |
| Marcel Delannoy | France | String Quartet |
| Otto Jokl | Austria | Sonatina for Piano, op. 21 |
| Jean Cartan | France | Sonatina for Flute and Clarinet |
| Eugene Goossens | Great Britain | Sonata no. 2 for Violin and Piano |
| Mario Pilati | Italy | Piano Quintet |
| **Monday, 27 July 1931** | | Queen's Hall, London |
| Roman Palester | Poland | *Muzyka symfoniczna* |
| Anton Webern | Austria | Symphony, op. 21 |
| Virgilio Mortari | Italy | Rhapsody for orchestra |
| Vladimir Dukelsky | Russian-American | * Symphony no. 2 |
| Constant Lambert | Great Britain | * Music for orchestra |
| George Gershwin | USA | * *An American in Paris* |
| **Tuesday, 28 July 1931** | | Queen's Hall, London |
| Juan José Castro | Argentina | *Tres trozos sinfonicos* |
| Fernand Quinet | Belgium | *Trois mouvements symphoniques* |
| Karol Szymanowski | Poland | *Pieśni kurpiowskie* ('Kurpie Songs') for chorus |
| Ferencz Szabo | Hungary | *Farkasok dala* ('Song of the Wolves') for chorus |
| Ralph Vaughan Williams | Great Britain | * *Benedicite* for soprano, chorus and orchestra |
| Vladimir Vogel | Russian-German | * Two Studies for orchestra |
| Albert Roussel | France | * Psalm 80, op. 37, for tenor, chorus and orchestra |

The names of the musicians who participated in these programmes are included in Eric Blom's review of
the festival: 'The Listener's Music: Music of the Month', *The Listener*, 6 (12 Aug. 1931): 251.

* indicates that the work was broadcast.

[†] The 23 July concert took place in the afternoon in Oxford with the broadcast given at 8.55 that evening
from a London studio. The transmitted works were not performed in concert order; the broadcast order
was: Knipper, Maklakiewicz, Huré, Wellesz, Halffter.

unfathomable way. What one did recognise, though, was a superior mentality and a sense that art is something not to be toyed with. No doubt this is music to study with the score. There must be a solution to the problem of finding the picture among its scattered fragments of sound, and one feels that it is a picture worth attention.

Other critics were less willing to admit the idiom's musical value. In *The Musical Mirror and Fanfare*, Ralph Hill complained that

> we are faced with a pattern of sounds based on entirely new laws and principles, which apparently bear little or no relationship to what we understand by the terms melody, harmony, and tonality . . . The æsthetic results defy analysis and Schönberg admits that the way to understand it is only through perfect faith. Thus criticism is silenced once and for all, and in future reason is to be superseded by intuition – a retrogressive movement with a vengeance!

Similarly, Harry Farjeon of *The Sunday Times* refused to sanction the validity of this musical language.

> So far is this series of isolated sounds from spelling to the ear a tune or recognisable theme, that to follow the intricate workings, in which excessive ingenuity is displayed, by merely listening once to them, is practically impossible. This is a queer conception of music – something written to look at on paper. Needless to say, it is as destitute of emotional significance as hieroglyphs in an unknown tongue must always remain.

*The Star* reported that eminent composers in the audience also seemed unmoved by the new Webern work: 'I could make neither head or tail of the music, but as Dr Vaughan Williams was also restless I did not mind'.[104]

The international launch of Webern's Symphony, op. 21, was not broadcast. Nevertheless, the Symphony's idiom and significance were debated in the daily British press; moreover, the composer's use of the 12-tone technique brought that term into those widely-read pages for the first time. By enabling the ISCM Festival to take place in England and by bringing the event to national attention, the BBC conveyed the British musical community and general public to the cutting edge of musical styles and controversies of the day.

## The 1931 Promenade Concerts

Two further performances of Second Viennese School works were given under the auspices of the BBC during summer 1931. These were presented within the Promenade Concerts, the first time works from this repertory were broadcast in this highly popular series.[105] At the 22 August concert,

Webern's Passacaglia, op. 1, received its first British performance by the BBC Symphony Orchestra under Sir Henry Wood. The work received the usual publicity accorded to Proms novelties, and the composer was introduced once again in the *Radio Times*.

> Besides taking so important a place among the composers of today, he is also a distinguished conductor, and a Doctor of Philosophy, whose writings have contributed much to the understanding both of old and of new music; and, despite the ultra-modern tendencies of his own work, he is as enthusiastic as any on behalf of the lighter music which Vienna has always claimed as peculiarly its own.[106]

Not surprisingly, critics were uninterested in Webern's light music enthusiasms in their assessments of this early orchestral work. Eric Blom simply dismissed it as a juvenile exercise.

> [This] was an Op. 1 submitted to our judgment too late, unless it were given simply for the sake of comparative study. The later work heard at the I.S.C.M. Festival showed us in a finished product what this composer aimed at from the start, and proved that the aim was worth while; the early effort was merely an interesting surveying of a territory of which the explorer hardly knew what was immediately ahead of him.[107]

Although Webern's op. 1 was widely heard at its British première, in the wake of the ISCM Festival its musical impact was negligible.

Berg was also represented at the 1931 Proms. Six of his *Seven Early Songs* were performed on 15 September by Margot Hinnenberg-Lefèbre and the BBC Symphony Orchestra, under Sir Henry Wood. Initially, the Booking Manager, Tillett, invited the soprano to perform the Three Fragments from *Wozzeck* rather than the songs; remembering previous negotiation difficulties, he carefully specified the terms of the fee.[108] The singer accepted the invitation in principle, but requested that she give a second, classical programme for a total fee of £80. Tillett countered with an offer of 60 guineas, suggesting that 'an appearance with our Orchestra at the Queen's Hall would be an excellent advertisement for you for other outside concerts'.[109] In the end, Hinnenberg-Lefèbre accepted the BBC's terms: she agreed to sing the *Wozzeck* excerpts and a group of Lieder with piano accompaniment at the Proms, as well as a studio recital of Scarlatti, Bach, Haydn and Mahler.

However, on 20 August, the Concerts Manager, W. W. Thompson, informed the singer of alterations to the Promenade programme.

> Owing to the length of the concert in question, . . . we think it would be advisable to omit your piano group from the second half. We hope therefore

you will be agreeable to include only the 'Wozzeck' Fragments and accept our apologies for having given you any unnecessary bother.[110]

On 1 September, Clark sent a telegram with further changes.

Regret infinitely must replace Wozzeck because necessary extra rehearsals are an impossibility stop Suggest instead Berg early songs. Please telegraph which titles to choose. Total duration 15 to 17 minutes.[111]

The soprano suggested orchestral Lieder by Krenek, but Clark insisted on the *Seven Early Songs*. She eventually agreed to sing all but the 'Liebesode'.[112] The programme change was made so belatedly that Proms publicity notices advertised the *Wozzeck* Fragments. The *Radio Times* programme note also focused on the opera.

Berg's most important work is the opera *Wozzeck*, a type of music-drama different from any yet conceived. In it he has exploited his main innovation, the pitched spoken word in the place of the lyric treatment usual in opera. To judge by its extravagant reception abroad, he has made a success of his invention. The songs to be heard tonight will give some idea of the means by which Berg gets his remarkable effects in *Wozzeck*, an opera which we are not very likely to hear in London. For one thing, it is far too new; for another, far too morbid. In any case, it is said that a singer takes a year, at least, to learn the music, and that is longer by nearly a year than is usually allowed an opera singer in England.[113]

Like the Webern Passacaglia, the early songs of Berg were received with disappointment by British critics. Eric Blom summarized his feelings in a single sentence.

Alban Berg's Songs with orchestra, given on the 15th (Margot Hinnenberg-Lefèbre), are early examples of a lyrical vein he has long outgrown: they reached us too late to compensate us for the promised extracts from the remarkable opera, 'Wozzeck'.[114]

Nevertheless, the Berg performance sparked a chain of letters in *The Musical Times* over subsequent months. Berg's modernity, as exemplified in the *Seven Early Songs*, was debated by the composer and writer on music, Kaikhosru Sorabji – a frequent *Musical Times* correspondent, who was not renowned for tact, tolerance or subtlety – and other readers. The debate was started by James C. G. Graves of Bedfordshire, who objected to the 'appalling noise, [which] wandered on, with a flourish or so here and there, in an incoherent manner with excruciating harmonies complete'; he concluded by appealing for an explanation of the composer's idiom.[115] Sorabji's response, published under the heading 'Alban Berg is Not

Alarming', ridiculed the need to explain an idiom that so clearly derived from Wagner and Strauss. He condemned Graves as a victim of press suggestions 'that the works of Alban Berg, particularly "Wozzeck", are of a hair-raising "modernity", whatever that preposterous and idiotic word may mean'.[116]

This argument documents a reception pattern that was well established by this time: because non-specialist listeners were warned by the BBC and music critics that the Second Viennese idiom was outside normal musical experience, most found works from the repertory to be incomprehensible. Since the *Radio Times* introduced the Berg in a paragraph that focused on *Wozzeck*, 'different from any [opera] yet conceived', James G. C. Graves, and probably many others, listened to the early songs in that spirit and rejected them as too distanced from previous experience and expectations – even though they probably were not.

## Contemporary music programming, 1931–1932

During summer 1931, the BBC brought a wealth of new music to the British public, including no fewer than four British premières of Second Viennese School works. Contemporary music activities were understandably reduced in subsequent months. Plans for the 1931–2 season were initiated in February 1931, when Wright asked Clark to prepare a list of new works to be considered for broadcasting.[117] Clark proposed seven recently composed works by British composers for the Wednesday night symphony concerts, and eleven works by continental composers for the contemporary series, including Schoenberg's Variations for Orchestra, op. 31 and Berg's Three Fragments from *Wozzeck*.[118]

When the first contemporary concert appeared in the projected schedules in autumn 1931, the Director of Programmes objected to Boult:

> I think it unlikely in the present circumstances that such a series will be sanctioned, and I should like to discuss the matter with you or Mase before anything further is done. Speaking unofficially at the moment, I must warn you that various measures of economy will have to be put into force very shortly, and we shall have to concentrate on essentials a great deal more than in the past.[119]

The central administrators' reactions to the heavy dose of new music during spring and summer 1931 may now only be guessed, but it may be significant that a short time later they questioned for the first time the BBC's commitment to contemporary music dissemination. Of course, Eckersley's memo may simply reflect the difficult economic climate of the time. In general, British organizations sought ways to eliminate inessential expenditure, and criticisms of BBC extravagances were rife in the press at this particular time, including specific references to broadcasts of new music .[120]

Wright responded immediately, submitting a formal proposal for the series to Boult. Interestingly, he defined the department's current interpretation of 'contemporary' to allay the administrators' fears about the nature and significance of the chosen works.

> Our recent policy for concerts of Contemporary Music has been to concentrate on those masters who have been accepted as having advanced the scope and art of musical composition. We have, as a general rule, neither included those composers who are writing music to-day which, from its type, might have been written thirty o[r] forty years ago, nor the experimental work of those young pioneers who, while attempting to find new paths, have not yet found an ultimately satisfactory form of expression.[121]

He also addressed Eckersley's threat to cancel the series.

> In the past [these concerts] have been attacked, as we knew they would be, but they have been one of the chief 'planks' of our musical policy, and have carried into the repertoire of ordinary concerts a good deal of music and composers whose names are now accepted. Our collaboration in the successful Festival last July was another link in the progression of our work in this field, and has obtained for us excellent publicity in the press of many countries, which must have resulted in increasing the prestige of the B.B.C., of its Orchestra and its permanent Conductor.

Wright proposed an eight-concert format, to be given monthly between November 1931 and June 1932, encompassing both orchestral and chamber programmes and presented once again from the BBC's No.10 studio. The concerts fell into two categories: composer programmes, devoted to works of a single composer, and national programmes, with works by different composers from the same country. Five of the proposed concerts came to fruition, devoted to Schoenberg, Delius, English music, Russian music and so-called German music (including works by Austrian and German composers). Busoni and Bartók concerts and a programme of recent choral music were added later. As previously, three programmes included Second Viennese School works. The contemporary series included less British music; as Wright explained: 'it should be remembered that there are many outlets for new English works, catering for all styles and types of work'. In fact, a significant amount of recent British music was incorporated into the high-profile BBC Symphony Concerts.

The series changed conception in another notable way. Many of the programmes featured soloists and conductors of international repute, who were not necessarily contemporary music specialists. These included Joseph Szigeti and Solomon, as well as Sir Henry Wood and Sir Thomas Beecham. Bartók returned to perform his Rhapsody for Piano and Orchestra, op. 1, but no other composer-performers were represented. A number of continental composers participated in other broadcasts: Strauss conducted two programmes of his works during October, Milhaud conducted a studio concert of his music in March, Bartók participated in a second recital of standard repertory in March, and Prokofiev performed in two programmes in April.[122]

### Broadcasts of Second Viennese School works

None of the Second Viennese School composers participated in broadcasts of their works during the 1931–2 season, although Wright initially proposed that the 'Schonberg Programme, consisting of "Verklärte Nacht" (a very early work), and the Orchestral variations, Op. 31 (a late work, played extensively on the Continent) . . . be conducted by the composer because of the interest shown in his personal visits'.[123] No correspondence has been traced concerning this plan, and it is not clear whether an invitation was issued. Since ill health involving emphysema forced the composer to spend autumn 1931 in the dry climate of Barcelona,[124] any invitation may have been declined.

The Schoenberg concert launched the 1931–2 series of contemporary concerts. It took place in a week featuring three broadcasts of his works: on 13 November, the all-Schoenberg programme took place, conducted by Boult; on 15 November, Enid Cruickshank sang the op. 2 songs in a chamber music recital; and on 18 November, Boult conducted the Five Pieces for Orchestra, op. 16, in a BBC Symphony Concert. In the span of a week, the Music Department gave listeners the opportunity to hear important works from Schoenberg's early, middle and late periods.

The 13 November concert, featuring *Verklärte Nacht* and the Variations, op. 31, received the usual *Radio Times* attention. One article outlined Schoenberg's life history, emphasizing the disturbances his music had provoked in the past.[125] The programme was advertized as one of the important events of the week, albeit backhandedly: 'Anti-moderns need not fret; *Verklarte Nacht* is romantic, almost Wagnerian, and, if the *Variations for Orchestra* prove tough, there's the Military Band on the National.'[126] Surprisingly, there were no articles or programme notes to help listeners comprehend the difficult music.[127]

This lack of preparation was at least partly to blame for the programme's poor reception. In his *Time and Tide* review, Edwin Evans identified the omission as an important public relations error.

> I have no doubt that the B.B.C. is 'in for' another flood of indignant protests, and not exclusively from the lay public . . . So far as I have been able to discover, they had no more warning than is implied in the name of Schönberg. The Variations were just sprung upon them without an intimation of the kind of music they were, unless perhaps the official musical critic of the B.B.C. included a warning in his weekly talk, which I did not hear.[128] Now, when those Variations were first performed on December 2, 1928, by the Berlin Philharmonic under Furtwängler, they occasioned a hostile demonstration . . . The audience of the Berlin Philharmonic is one of the most adept in Europe . . . If that audience found the variations too tough for its digestion, surely the millions who may have been tempted to turn on their sets at 8.30 p.m. – a likely hour – on Friday, the 13th – an ominous date – could not be expected to rejoice.[129]

Certainly, London critics did not give the impression of rejoicing in their reviews. Most focused on the contrast between Schoenberg's early romantic style and his latest style, which that they did not understand or like. Ferruccio Bonavia in *The Daily Telegraph* gave an interesting account of Schoenberg's influences.

> Ever since he realised that 'Verklärte Nacht', in spite of its title, was not quite free from the mists of romanticism, Schönberg has avoided romantic expression with a persistence which is almost an obsession. In his search for originality he has sought help of Debussy and Stravinsky. He has since turned to the dodecaphonic system – unsuccessful in this quest, too, since the system is the discovery of another. Whether the variations owe their existence to dodecaphony or to some other more recent discovery is of little importance. The sad reality is that as music they are simply inadmissible.[130]

Although Ernest Newman once again despaired of coming to terms with Schoenberg's recent style,[131] the *Manchester Guardian* critic wrote in surprisingly favourable terms.

> The Variations, indeed, are admittedly a pretty hard nut to crack, but one has heard many modern works both more baffling and infinitely more cacophonous. While it is obviously impossible on a single hear[ing] and without a study of the score to pass any final judgment on a work of such complexity and novelty of idiom, the fact remains that this preliminary impression was a highly favourable one.[132]

He continued with an informed discussion of the work's construction.

> It is the only large orchestral work that Schönberg has written for many years and the first to embody in this medium the æsthetic principles and methods

of construction which he promulgated in his manifesto of 1924, entitled 'Composition in Twelve Tones',[133] and which in practice had hitherto been carried out in works written for various chamber music combinations only. The introduction is of an harmonic rather than of a contrapuntal character, and is chiefly concerned with the presentation in embryonic form of several thematic fragments which are eventually welded together into the theme – which, incidentally, is of a surprisingly mellifluous and almost romantic type. The subsequent variations primarily consist in the application to it of every conceivable form of contrapuntal torture, known and unknown – canon, inversion, cancrizans, and others unspecifiable; and the finale is a kind of elaborate summing-up of all that has gone before . . .

The work chiefly impressed one by virtue of its closely knit logic and continuity of texture. Even if certain phrases fell harshly on the ear, one's interest never flagged from first bar to last. There can be little doubt, indeed, that this work takes rank among the most important achievements of its composer, and consequently of modern music.

This cogent, interesting and enthusiastic description reveals that this critic was familiar with Schoenberg's writings and theories, demonstrating that by 1931, specific information about his theoretical and compositional developments was in fact available in Britain to those who were interested in pursuing it.

In contrast to the meagre preparation for the all-Schoenberg concert, the BBC provided substantial pre-concert information about the Five Pieces for Orchestra, op. 16, broadcast on 18 November. The attention was probably thought necessary because it was performed at one of the popular symphony concerts, which usually presented standard orchestral repertory. In addition to the Schoenberg, the concert, conducted by Boult, included Locatelli's *Concerto da camera* no. 10, Bach's First Concerto for Keyboard and String Orchestra with Walter Gieseking as soloist, and Beethoven's Symphony no. 7. The *Radio Times* announcement concentrated solely on the Schoenberg and was juxtaposed with a paragraph about his *Harmonielehre*.

A favourite question from the anti-Schönberg school over here is: why does no one come forward and tell us, simply and sympathetically, what Schönberg's music is all about? Such critics should be immediately put on to Schönberg's own book: 'Harmonielehre'. There, in the simplest terms imaginable, they would find exactly what Schönberg's attitude to music is. The book is, in many ways, more important than any work on music published this century; and yet it remains unpublished in this country. Is it true, then, after all, that we are not sufficiently intelligent about music to want to know what perhaps the major creative musician of our time has to say about it?[134]

Another *Radio Times* article, by Edwin Evans, gave a thoughtful account of Schoenberg and his career. Published on 13 November – the day of the all-Schoenberg broadcast – this overview described the different stages of the composer's musical development, demonstrating that he derived musically and culturally from late nineteenth-century romanticism.[135] Finally, the programme listing for the concert included half a page of programme notes, including three paragraphs on the op. 16 orchestral pieces.[136]

Despite the difference in publicity, the pattern of critical response was not unlike that for the op. 31 Variations. This work had been introduced to British audiences nearly twenty years before, but was nevertheless received with disfavour. For example, Ernest Newman wrote:

> Speaking for myself, I can only say that while the work once more interested me as a cerebral exercise, it gave me practically no musical pleasure. I was rather astonished to find, however, that even on the intellectual side I could not work up the interest I felt in it twenty years ago. I suppose the explanation is that at that time all this sort of thing was delightfully fresh to us, an adventure thrilling in itself and promising in the vistas it opened out for music, while the years between have shown that the promise has not been fulfilled, the vistas not realised.[137]

Even the reviewer for the BBC's journal, *The Listener*, expressed disappointment:

> The Five Pieces were an entirely new departure, and they continue to sound strange after nearly twenty years, not because we fail to see what the composer is aiming at, but because we cannot yet persuade ourselves that music as a whole must needs follow the path which Schönberg for his own part treads with the determination of a leader.[138]

Once again, the *Manchester Guardian* critic dissented from the majority opinion: 'The conclusion to which one comes concerning the composition as a whole is that it is a powerful but unequal work containing much that is purely experimental and not always successfully so, but also much that is of quite exceptional beauty and originality.'[139] In fact, most of his column was concerned with factors behind Schoenberg's unpopularity:

> It cannot be explained simply by the fact that he makes sounds to which we are not accustomed. In 1909 that might well have been so, but to-day this characteristic is by no means a bar to popular favour – rather the reverse, indeed. There are no stranger instrumental combinations and effects in the Five Orchestral Pieces than there are in much 'jazz' music and its derivates, and there is no more of harmonic dissonance than is to be found in modern works that are comparatively popular, such as 'Pacific 231' of Honegger or

'The Music of the Machines' of Mossolov, which never fail to bring the house down whenever they are performed.

It would seem, in fact, that the public will tolerate almost any degree of cacophony provided it has an illustrative intention, and it is probably the recognition of this fact that has induced the composer to attach titles to each movement after having left them for over twenty years in austere anonymity.

The week of performances in which Schoenberg's early, middle and late styles could be heard and compared marked a low point in British interest in his music and ideas. *Verklärte Nacht*, previously a popular concert work, was dismissed as old-fashioned and unrepresentative. The Five Orchestral Pieces were criticized for their experimental nature and for the fact that they remained 'difficult' after twenty years. The new Variations for Orchestra were condemned by many for their incomprehensibility, the repellence of their aural impact and their 12-tone construction. In following weeks, a single response to the broadcasts was chosen for publication in the *Radio Times*, written by a listener billed as sympathetic to modern music.

> Schönberg's Op. 16 is sheer decadence in the most degenerate form I have yet experienced. Heaven forbid that you should ever again include such balderdash as this in any of your programmes, and if ever you are tempted to do so I would plead here and now that the wonderful 'all-in policy' of the B.B.C.'s entirely praiseworthy and comprehensive fare, as served up in its broadcast programmes, is not justified in putting to such base use the wonderful instrument it has created – the B.B.C. Symphony Orchestra.[140]

By November 1931, then, even self-proclaimed new music enthusiasts had lost patience with the Corporation's preoccupation with this particular composer.

Two other Schoenberg broadcasts took place during the 1931–2 season, but received little or no comment. On 15 February 1932, mezzo-soprano Anne Thursfield sang two songs, 'Traumleben' from op. 6 and 'Waldsonne' from op. 2, in a chamber music recital. The April concert of contemporary music featured unaccompanied choral works by living composers, and included Schoenberg's *Friede auf Erde*, op. 13, in addition to music of Vaughan Williams, Kodály, Delius, Poulenc, Ravel and Bax.

In contrast, the penultimate concert in the contemporary music series, on 13 May 1932, was devoted to music by Second Viennese composers and received significant promotion by the BBC. Works by Krenek, Webern and Berg were performed by the BBC Symphony Orchestra, conducted by Sir Henry Wood. Webern's Passacaglia, op. 1, and Berg's Three Fragments from *Wozzeck* were carry-overs from the 1931 Promenade Concerts, in which the Webern was performed, but the Berg was postponed. These works were publicized as the main attractions, with Krenek's Theme and 13 Variations, op. 69, receiving minimal attention.[141] Webern's op. 1 was reassuringly promoted as 'normal in proportions and character', but the BBC warned:

> Even the earliest exercises of a Webern are remote from the easy view of music most of us take. But the purpose of these concerts, it should be remembered, is not quite the same as that of the usual run of concert broadcasts. They are expressly designed to give those who take their music seriously an opportunity to become acquainted with music which, though it is not yet generally accepted, is honestly believed to be important both as an expression of our time and as the accepted music of the future.

The Corporation also published a full-length article by R. K. Silver, 'Those "Contemporary" Concerts', which once again outlined the series' scope and purpose.

> Given irregularly in a converted wharf over by Waterloo Bridge; they are attended by a handful of critics and enthusiasts; and they are broadcast. In that last statement lies the true measure of their significance. For when the majority of listeners, in anger, distaste, or boredom, have switched off their sets or tuned to another wavelength, there remain several hundreds who genuinely wish to hear what the more adventurous musical minds of their time have to say; and in those several hundreds . . . lies an ample justification for the concerts . . .
>
> In Vienna, in Berlin (and other German cities), in Paris, it is taken for granted that the advance-guard of music, for instance, shall be considered seriously, and it provides no occasion for startled comment that there should even be societies devoted entirely to the propagation of such music; but in London it is otherwise.[142] It is not the least of the merits of these 'Contemporary Concerts', then, that they have been able, by virtue of an economic security and a consequent aloofness from the biased condemnation of philistines, to bring England into line at last with those countries who have the mental courage to take their music seriously.[143]

In contrast to such defensive strategies, the BBC promoted Berg's Three Fragments positively. Although *Wozzeck* had not yet received a complete, or even partial, performance in Britain, continental productions had been discussed and praised in the British press. The work's reputation enabled its promotion as an event of general interest and importance.

> Though this opera was written in 1914–20, and has become generally recognized as the most significant opera of our time, it is entirely unknown over here; the present performance of the three fragments is, we believe, the first

English performance even of extracts from it. In *Wozzeck* Alban Berg was the first to prove that the new, so-called 'atonal' music (decried by its adversaries as 'the technique for miniatures') could be used as the foundation of a dramatic work of the grandest style.[144]

The *Radio Times* programme listing was illustrated with a scene from the Berlin production, depicting Wozzeck and Marie.[145] However, the BBC failed once again to provide any musical or dramatic explanation for the *Wozzeck* excerpts.

Nevertheless, the 13 May contemporary concert was received with interest and enthusiasm. Unusually, an internal Music Department critique of it survives. BBC staff who attended the performance were asked to provide the Music Executive with written comments. Herbage wrote:

> I heard this in the studio, so my report is not of much use. As we had surmised, the Krenek turned out to be rather a makeweight. The Wozzeck fragments and the Passacaglia made a profound impression. Sir Henry Wood and the orchestra were at the top of their form, and May Blyth's tackling of her difficult part deserves much credit.[146]

The Krenek was generally characterized as an insubstantial, eclectic mixture. Constant Lambert complained that it 'embraces every modern style from Elgar to Schönberg and falls between thirteen stools. Nothing is more boring that this excessive variety'.[147] In contrast, the Webern and, particularly, the Berg were received with sympathy. The *Daily Telegraph* critic wrote that 'even in fragments, and deprived of its proper setting, this music had a strength and imaginative vigour that made a very definite and lasting appeal'.[148] Lambert went even further:

> Alban Berg is in a totally different category. There is no composer in Europe more sure of himself or with greater technical ability. His most daring flights 'come off' with surprising ease, and, considering their complexity, his harmonies and orchestration are really very lucid. Although strongly influenced by Schönberg, Alban Berg is in no sense a rigid atonalist, and much of his music is no more difficult to listen to than Ravel . . . The exacting vocal part was very well sung by May Blyth, and the orchestra sailed through the extreme intricacies of the score as though they were playing William Tell. It is high time we were allowed to hear the whole of 'Wozzeck'.

At the time that interest and patience with Schoenberg's music was on the wane, curiosity was aroused concerning Berg and his output, particularly once the power and beauty of his first opera were sampled in Britain for the first time.

The 13 May broadcast was the last of the 1931–2 season to include Second Viennese School works. However, one other event deserves mention here. In May 1932, Egon Wellesz visited England at the invitation of Oxford University, which awarded him with an honorary doctorate. As Benser has explained, the honour was conferred for his work as a composer, rather than for his musicological research into Byzantine music.[149] Wellesz was chosen at the suggestion of Sir Hugh Allen, professor of music at Oxford, director of the Royal College of Music and chair of the BBC Music Advisory Committee. As an expression of his appreciation, the composer dedicated a recently composed cantata, *Mitte des Lebens*, op. 45, to Oxford University. It is interesting to note that Edward J. Dent also received an honorary doctorate from Oxford at this time for his contributions to musicology.

This event strengthened Wellesz's bonds with England. Not only did this affect his decision to emigrate there in 1938, when the political climate in Austria became untenable for him and his family, but the attention he received encouraged him to try to promote further British interest in his music – most notably, through the auspices of the BBC.

Boult's first seasons as BBC Music Director were marked not only by the successful launch of the BBC Symphony Orchestra, but also for the many broadcasts devoted to exploring ultra-modern music. In 1931 and 1932, particularly, transmissions from the ISCM Festival, from the Promenade Concerts, from the BBC Symphony Concerts and, of course, from the BBC Concerts of Contemporary Music signalled that the new director had embraced and fortified the new music policies established by his predecessor.

# 9   Transition to the new régime, 1932–1933, 1933–1934

In the years immediately following the BBC's move to Broadcasting House, the inner workings of the organization, now a decade old, were reviewed and reconceived. During 1933–4, the corporate restructuring was put in place, the new management reshaping original values and goals in line with the efficiency and output that were expected of an organization that was no longer viewed as an experiment but as the establishment.

## Personnel shifts and policy clashes

During the 1932–3 season, staff arrangements within the Music Department were still in transition from the old régime to the new. Several personnel changes were effected, mostly to deal with imbalances in daily operations. For example, in autumn 1932 music programming demands stretched resources to breaking point. Increased work-loads caused staff to work many extra hours to fulfil basic programming requirements, and Mase worried that quality was declining.

> The building . . . of the major programmes alone requires the greatest thought, knowledge and research, and must of necessity take much time . . . The question, so urgent, of bringing the ordinary programmes up to a relative level hangs far behind through the real limit of human capacity for constructive and detailed thought in a given time. Now we are even getting behind in efficient planning of big things.[1]

The excellence of the senior staff was not at issue. Mase acknowledged that 'the Department possesses the brains, knowledge, and initiative, indeed I do not know how we would find an equal body to combine real musical ability with knowledge and experience of the needs and opportunities of broadcasting'. He requested a new junior position to take over routine duties and a Music Executive to replace Arthur Wynne, who was soon to move to the Booking Department. He also asked that Richard Howgill of the Copyright Department be available on a regular basis for consultation on musical matters. Howgill, a composer and expert on music copyright, already served on the New Music Subcommittee with Clark and Hely Hutchinson,[2] and Mase felt that 'in music his knowledge, artistic sense, and quiet sanity are noteworthy'. Boult concurred that departmental expansion was urgently required, but wondered 'whether the re-organization you propose really goes far enough. It is *essential* that the people who are doing creative work (and in this I include programme-making) should have *ample* time to think things over'.[3]

Although Eckersley approved these requests, Carpendale demanded specific descriptions of staff responsibilities,[4] and G. C. Beadle prepared a statement which provides insight into the programme planning section at that time.[5] The programmes were still planned by Wright, Herbage, Clark and Hely Hutchinson, with the additional help of the assistant conductor, Joseph Lewis. While Hely Hutchinson continued to be responsible for the 'Foundations of Music' series and Lewis planned lighter mid-day broadcasts, the bulk of the music programmes were planned by Wright, Herbage and Clark. Beadle listed the number of events for which they were responsible annually:

| | | | |
|---|---|---|---|
| 18 | Public Symphony Concerts | 350 | Studio Orchestral Programmes |
| 6 | Festival Concerts | 150 | Military Band Concerts |
| 24 | Sunday Symphony Concerts | 100 | Theatre Orchestra Concerts |
| 49 | Summer Promenades | 150 | Programmes for the Wireless |
| 13 | Winter Promenades | | Singers |
| 8 | Contemporary Music Concerts | 100 | Studio Chamber Concerts |
| 6 | (or possibly 14) Public Chamber Concerts | 26 | Studio Operatic Programmes |

Some of these figures were apparently inflated: the Wireless Singers did not participate in so many broadcasts, and the Theatre Orchestra programmes were transferred to another section soon after this memo was written.[6] Nevertheless, it is clear that by 1932 the BBC annually transmitted a large number of music broadcasts, which the senior music programme builders were responsible for planning and producing.

Beadle's memo also explained the programme builders' duties in some detail. (1) They chose music for the programmes, ensuring artistic excellence and avoiding repetition with other broadcasts within the same time period. (2) They found interesting new works and researched old music, both to expand the repertory and to ascertain that editions were accurate and suitable. (3) They arranged details of performers' employment, aside from the formal contract. (4) They were responsible for providing accurate timings of all works and programmes. (5) They provided the *Radio Times* editors with all information relevant to the music programmes. Multiplied by the number of broadcasts produced each year, the enormous responsibility and pressures that they shouldered becomes evident. The Assistant Controller, Goldsmith, assured Carpendale that the section was running as efficiently as possible, and the combined evidence finally convinced him. Howgill received official permission to advise the programme builders, and on 2 January 1933 Hubert Foster Clark was appointed to the staff.[7]

Three months later, Mase again requested staff help. Foster Clark spent much time working on the new Empire programmes, leaving the programme builders to face the same pressures as before. Mase suggested that the studio assistant, Leslie Woodgate, take over responsibility for light music broadcasts.

> Woodgate knows a good deal about the kind of music our lighter programmes have to contain, although it has unfortunately been proved that he is not the best man actually to *perform* it. The proper building of the lighter programmes and the supervision of their artists is one of our most incessant labours and it is undoubtedly the side of our work that has received very much less individual attention than it urgently needs . . . By putting him in charge of these lighter programmes[,] his full attention to it should do much towards remedying their poor quality, about which I have been greatly exercised.[8]

Boult concurred, and Woodgate was added to the programme building staff.[9]

## The Music Advisory Committee: protecting British interests

More significant, perhaps, were changes to staff structure that were provoked by the Music Advisory Committee. 1933 was the first year for which sufficient papers survive to reconstruct matters relating to the committee, and they reveal that tensions between it and the Music Department were approaching boiling point. The eight-man committee was still chaired by Sir Hugh Allen, and included Dr E. C. Bairstow, Sir Walford Davies, Sir J. B. McEwen, Sir Landon Ronald, Colonel J. C. Somerville, Dr W. G. Whittaker and the President of the Incorporated Society of Musicians.[10] A notation in Reith's diary for January 1933 reveals that friction had already arisen: 'Lunched with Landon Ronald and discussed the Allen, McEwen troubles, vis-à-vis Mase and the musical troubles'.[11] Doubts about Mase's ability to execute his responsibilities as Assistant Music Director were compounded by difficulties with members of the committee.

The issues behind the tensions are hinted at in a memo from Mase to Boult, dating from February 1933. Mase felt that the problems stemmed from the committee's attitude to new music.

> Is it not true that there is hardly one member of our committee who has any real sympathy with, true understanding of, or live interest in present day

musical developments? We get from them as a body almost exclusively negative criticism of most of our activities and we should so welcome a broader,
more constructive attitude which, I feel, can only be created by the addition
of men who are perhaps more in touch, actually and spiritually, with the
creative thought of to-day.[12]

Disagreement arose, at least in part, from fundamental differences in programming priorities. Cursory comparison of BBC output with advertisements for other concerts in *The Daily Telegraph* and *The Musical Times*
reveals that the BBC consistently presented a higher proportion of new
works, particularly from the continent, than did other British organizations of the time. Perhaps it is not surprising that this programming tendency was unpopular with the Music Advisory Committee, who
represented the interests of British musicians.

A logical solution was to appoint new members to the committee who
were in sympathy with the Music Department's views and objectives. Mase
put forward five candidates: the composer, Arthur Bliss; the music academic and president of the ISCM, Edward Dent; the critic, Ernest
Newman ('the doyen of critics, who has proved to be of sane but wide sym-
pathies'); and the composers, Edgar Bainton and Sir Granville Bantock.
Boult approved Mase's first choice:

> I sounded Arthur Bliss today on music programmes, and found him an even
> finer ally than I thought. As I expect you know, he listens a good deal and
> follows the *Radio Times* carefully. He would I'm sure be a very good MAC
> man – not that he will always be on one side, but he will always be *construc-
> tive*.[13]

Reith apparently agreed to Bliss's candidacy at that time,[14] and the idea was
still under serious consideration a month later.[15]

The conflict between department and committee centred on a fundamental policy question: did the programmes adequately represent British
musical interests – both of composers and performers? This basic question
led to four main areas of difference, which remained at the centre of policy
discussions for several years. The first concerned programme balance,
with the department supporting a high proportion of contemporary
music and the committee tending toward standard repertory. The second
focused on the nationalism issue, with the committee representing the
interests of British professional musicians, and the department opting to
provide performances of quality, without regard to nationality. The third
concerned the qualifications of the music staff; the committee doubted
that staff members had the professional experience necessary to plan the
nation's music broadcasts. Finally, though less tangibly, the sphere of

influence of the Music Advisory Committee came into question, with the members anxious to be involved with programming and staff decisions, and the BBC opposing any extension of the committee's powers.

A lengthy memo written by Boult in February 1933 illustrates many of these points.[16] At Music Advisory Committee meetings and at a private meeting involving Boult, Allen and McEwen, the latter had represented the view that the BBC should support native composers and musicians more visibly. As Boult reported:

> Sir John McEwen's participation at our second talk produced the usual wrangle, during which I am afraid I found it impossible to conceal my irritation, about foreign artists and compositions and our 'senseless predilection for Vienna and Berlin'. I repeatedly made the point that English professionals were, generally speaking, not good enough for our most important performances, and that for our less important things we were encouraging them as far as we possibly could.[17]

The Music Director was sympathetic to promoting British musicians, but was unwilling to do so at the cost of the BBC's standards of excellence. The advisory committee also demanded that a panel of professional musicians be appointed to take part in programme building, reflecting doubts about staff qualifications.

> Sir John repeatedly referred to our 'incompetent' staff, meaning thereby that they had not been musically trained . . . I feel certain that the basis of the whole thing is a feeling that so few of our music staff have been completely trained as musicians. It is no use our saying that they have by this time had a complete training in broadcasting – this they simply do not understand.

Boult's final point demonstrates the fiery emotions that were aroused by this conflict.

> When I retaliated by using the word 'insult' they became rather hot. Allen said that if he had had any idea that I should have looked upon it as an insult he would never have backed the proposal, and would prefer to retire from the M.A.C. I said that I could not look upon it as other than an insult, though I was quite prepared to swallow it, and see what could be done . . . The matter was left rather in mid-air owing to the general explosion on the subject of the insult. I have written a personal note to Allen [suggesting] . . . that it was now up to him (Allen) to bring the matter up at an M.A.C., but I do not think he will accept this suggestion until I have withdrawn the word 'insult', which I have no intention of doing.

The dispute intensified in April and May, when Sir Landon Ronald published three articles in the *News Chronicle*, in which he attacked the

British music industry for neglecting native composers and musicians.[18] In the second of these, he accused the BBC of 'giving a plethora of foreign works, new and old' in its spring series of BBC Symphony Concerts. He devoted the third to criticizing the foreign orientation of the London Music Festival, a Corporation-sponsored event mounted in May 1933. Ronald maintained that the festival should promote British music and musicians.

> You may understand why I expressed surprise when I read the word 'London' attached to this musical festival. *True, it takes place in London, but in every other respect it is about as English as Frankfurter sausage!* . . . As programmes I have no fault to find with them artistically, but patriotically and as a member of a profession which is admittedly in an extremely bad way, *I deplore and deprecate such a preponderance of the foreign element in a 'London' Festival.*

Not surprisingly, Boult confronted Ronald at the next gathering of the Music Advisory Committee on 11 May, and reported to Eckersley:

> As I told you yesterday, I tackled Sir Landon Ronald at the Music Advisory Committee Meeting on the three points in his last two articles (1) that the B.B.C. has pursued its policy of playing a plethora of foreign work, old and new; (2) that the London Music Festival was not English; (3) that we had engaged a German soprano to sing with three English singers in the Ninth Symphony next week . . . The main discussion centered round the first of these points. Sir Landon changed his ground considerably and joined us with the other concert-giving organizations in a general attack on the absence of English music in London programmes. I did all I could to dissociate the two, and think I made an impression on the Committee.[19]

Moreover, the committee clearly affirmed that British music and musicians should be promoted in broadcasts, even at the expense of programme quality. Again Boult reported:

> Discussing the Bruno Walter question in D.G.'s room two days ago, [Allen] almost took the side that it would be better to have second-rate direction of the Orchestra if it was British, than first-rate direction if it was foreign, and a remark of the same kind at the Meeting on Thursday evoked a reply from me somewhat on these lines – 'Do you really mean that you would prefer us to employ a second-rate Britisher in place of a first-rate foreigner at a concert of first-class importance?' Allen's own reply was qualified somewhat, but I have an impression that others murmured 'Yes', and I certainly noticed Sir Edward Bairstow saying 'Yes, by all means'.[20]

This attitude directly challenged the fundamental policy behind BBC programming: to bring the best quality music and performances into listeners'

homes. Boult recognized that the committee's view had far-reaching implications.

> Now this seems to me to be worthy of consideration by the D.G. from the
> policy angle, if not by the Board of Governors, that is to say if the M.A.C., or
> those whose judgment we really respect, seem unanimous on the point: Are
> we really to give our listeners the second best because it is British, and if we
> are to do this, exactly on what occasions are we to do this, and on what occa-
> sions may we still feel free to think internationally?
>
> If the principle of putting professional interests before those of our listeners
> is once admitted, I feel we should very carefully distinguish the limits to which
> this principle is to apply . . . If we are going to stick to our policy of considering
> our listeners' interests first without regard to nationality of performer or work
> performed, then I feel we should clearly say this to the M.A.C., and, if neces-
> sary, incorporate it in 'The Radio Times' or 'The Listener' articles.

The tiff between Ronald and Boult sparked significant repercussions.
Reith had to intervene to prevent Ronald, a long-standing friend, from
resigning from the committee. He recorded in his diary on 22 May that he
'lunched with Sir Hugh Allen in connection with a row between Landon
Ronald and Boult, Boult having been very rude to Ronald, and he [Ronald]
having sent in his resignation'; a week later he again 'lunched with Landon
Ronald at the Carlton – this about Boult having been rude to him at the last
meeting of the Music Advisory Committee'.[21]

After the turbulent May meeting, the BBC initiated two courses of
action to address the nationalism issue. First, it collected data in defense of
its record. Boult provided evidence that in both studio and public concerts, the BBC had a significantly better record than other concert-produc-
ing organizations for presenting works by living British composers. A table
comparing the proportion of British and foreign contemporary works
broadcast illustrated that in studio recitals there were $2\frac{1}{2}$ times as many
British contemporary works to foreign, in the Queen's Hall concerts nearly
three times as many, and in the Promenade concerts over $2\frac{1}{2}$ times as
many. Boult also showed that an overwhelmingly higher proportion of
British musicians were hired than foreign ones.[22]

In addition, the central administrators decided that the BBC should
sponsor a festival of British music to enhance its image as a benevolent
patron of national art. Eckersley described the scheme to Reith:

> With regard to the proposal of a series of concerts to be devoted to British
> music, to be conducted by British conductors and to include only British
> artists, I think this would be a very good gesture at the present moment and
> one that surely would have the whole-hearted support of the M.A.C.

> I wonder if you could give your official sanction to this, if you approve it of course, at once.[23]

Reith approved the idea, and a series of six concerts, a showcase of British works and British artists, were planned, to be presented at the Queen's Hall between 1 and 12 January 1934.

The overall situation became more complicated in late May 1933, when the central administrators recognized that Mase was not working out as Assistant Music Director. Executive posts throughout the Corporation were restructured around this time, resulting in positions of greater responsibility, and the administrators reassigned him to the Music Executive post, to take effect on 1 October 1933.[24] The question of who might be suitable as Boult's 'creative' assistant became a matter of priority. Eckersley suggested Francis Toye, the music critic for the *Morning Post* who often contributed articles to *The Listener*, but when Boult strongly backed Bliss, supported by Reith,[25] Eckersley had no objections.

> I'm perfectly in favour of having Arthur Bliss as A.M.D. He is a good man – I know him pretty well. I take it he is not biassed in favour of modern music. I wonder if he'll come. He – or his wife – is very comfortably off without working. He's just as good a choice as Francis T.[26]

Once it was decided to offer Bliss the internal position, Reith approved Dent as his choice for the additional man to the Music Advisory Committee.[27] It is not clear whether the BBC formally invited Dent; he certainly did not join the committee.

Boult approached Bliss about becoming his assistant, but the composer was unwilling to consider a full-time position that would interfere with his creative activities. He proposed that he be appointed as part-time '"Musical Programme Advisor" whose function it would be to attend all weekly meetings of the Programme Committee and any others that are called for Emergency Situations – and to be responsible to [Boult] for the suggestions made and decisions taken at [the] meetings with regard to all musical programmes'.[28] Eager to have Bliss on almost any terms, Boult responded: 'He is, I think, the only person in the country with whom I could confidently share this responsibility'.[29] Nevertheless, the Music Advisory Committee recommended the appointment of a small committee of advisors in lieu of an Assistant Music Director,[30] while Nicolls, thinking that Boult's double position might eventually be split, lobbied for a full-time assistant:

> I think a possible alternative would be for Bliss's help to come via the M.A.C. (i.e. membership as suggested, and some special work or functions), and

> Boult to have a personal assistant who should be selected as a possible suc-
> cessor in a few years time. I visualise the eventual relationship between Boult
> and the internal Music Director as that between, say, the War Office and a
> Commander-in-Chief in the field (Boult).[31]

While Bliss's appointment was under discussion, the Music Advisory
Committee reconvened for its June meeting. This was even more conten-
tious than the one in May, leading Reith to consider whether the committee should be disbanded altogether.

> A most ridiculous and unpleasant meeting and I determined that different
> arrangements must be made in the future. We shall either take on an
> Assistant Music Director or have a programme consultative committee of
> three, abolishing the M.A.C., or having them meet only twice a year.[32]

Reith and the central administrators hoped that Bliss's appointment as
Assistant Music Director would solve the problem, but Bliss's refusal
forced them to consider other options. They decided that a separate body,
consisting of professional musicians, should be appointed to advise the
programme builders. Boult asked that the search for his assistant be discontinued.

> The more I think about it, the more I feel that, now that M.A.C. seem to
> think the new programme advisory sub-committee, (or whatever it is to be
> called) will fill the bill *from the point of view of the profession* & public, there is
> no need to bring in anyone else, & I should be quite ready to go on with Mase
> as A.M.D. The point of lack of support & the publicity that I mentioned is
> fairly well met by the new sub-committee, & as time goes on, the need surely
> will become less & less. I am sure our internal machinery can be made to
> work all right this way.[33]

At the end of June, the Music Advisory Committee approved that 'a
Programme Committee of three should be instituted to assist in the building of the B.B.C. general musical programmes',[34] and the Music Department began to plan seriously for the creation of what would be known as
the Music Programme Advisory Panel. Boult felt that the panel should play
a central role in music programming, having direct say about short and
long-term plans. The group would meet each week with the programme
builders to discuss specific programmes under consideration, as well as
seasonal plans for the public concert series.[35]

In July, the committee chairman, Allen, submitted to Reith the names of
six eminent musicians as potential candidates, including Sidney
Waddington, Benjamin Dale, Aylmer Buesst, George Dyson, Harold
Craxton and Julius Harrison.[36] By August, the candidates had been nar-

rowed to three: Bliss, Waddington and Dale. The Music Director's primary choice was Bliss, 'a regular and very keen listener and reader of the "Radio Times". I should say, indeed, that he probably listens nearly as much as the whole of the Music Advisory Committee put together'.[37] However, the central administrators worried that Bliss's independence would make him unreliable.[38] As second choice, Boult recommended Waddington, an opera conductor, composer and harmony teacher at the Royal College of Music.

> He is a very generous-minded musician, whose personal modesty has kept him from achieving a position of greater importance than that which he now holds. He has very wide sympathies, but is perfectly prepared to tell you, for instance, where he thinks a movement in a Beethoven symphony is weak, whilst recognising its enormous value. He is a person who is very much liked by his pupils, and I consider a most easy person to work with. At the same time, he holds quite definite opinions about things.

The Music Director was less impressed with Dale, a composer and composition teacher at the Royal Academy of Music.

> He is a much respected member of the staff of the Royal Academy, but I consider that his knowledge would be less wide and his judgment less well-balanced than that of Mr Waddington. He has written some good music, but I cannot help feeling that, like most composers, he might be apt to misunderstand and misjudge his contemporaries.

In the autumn months, Reith, Allen, Boult and Eckersley tried to decide whether the panel should consist of two or three members, and who exactly should be appointed to it.[39] Notes prepared by Eckersley clarify the degree to which Royal College–Royal Academy allegiances influenced the decision.

> *Bliss* is Royal College almost entirely (except that he taught composition at academy for one or two terms[ )].
> *Waddington* – entirely College – but very good.
> *Dale.* Academy entirely – but useless from our point of view –
> *Craxton.* Very busy man – gives piano lessons. Used to be academy. maybe still.
> *Harrison.* out. Landon Ronald.
> *Buesst.* out.
> *Dyson.* useful but college[40]

It was finally decided to invite Bliss, Waddington and Dale to serve on the panel, and they all accepted.[41] They would meet with the music programme builders every Tuesday afternoon, starting on 24 April 1934.[42]

This basic arrangement proved to be highly satisfactory and remained in operation until the beginning of the war.

Although Reith, Boult and the central administrators fought hard against the Music Advisory Committee's demands, the dispute provoked a number of programming and personnel changes that may be viewed as BBC concessions to the music profession. The issues of increased programme input and staff qualifications were addressed through the formation of the Music Programme Advisory Panel. Safeguarding of British interests led to projects such as the British music festival. In fact, the nationalism issue continued to be debated throughout the decade, exacerbated by the political situation in Europe, which forced increasing numbers of foreign musicians and composers to seek refuge, and performance opportunities, in Britain. In defence, the BBC continued to prepare statistics and publish statements proving that their promotion of British talent was more than sufficient.

## The new BBC organization, 1933–1934

During 1933, the BBC as a whole underwent extensive restructuring. Originally conceived by Reith, plans for a new organization were discussed at the highest levels from March.[43] As Briggs explained, 'there was a careful and detailed examination of the role of every officer in the BBC and of almost every operational process'.[44] In August, fundamental changes were implemented at each corporate level, every area designated as either administrative or creative. The BBC as a whole was divided into two parts: the Administration Division, under the direction of Carpendale, now known as Controller (Administration), and the Programme Division, under the direction of a newcomer to the BBC, Colonel Alan Dawnay, the Controller (Programmes). Each division consisted of four branches: within the Administration Division were Engineering (directed by Noel Ashbridge), Finance (T. Lochhead), Internal Administration (Basil Nicolls) and Business Relations (V. H. Goldsmith); within the Programme Division were Empire and Foreign Services (directed by C. G. Graves), Talks (Charles Siepmann), Publicity and Publications (W. E. Gladstone Murray) and Entertainment (R. H. Eckersley). In accordance with this bipartite structure, the weekly meetings of the Control Board were replaced by 'D.G.'s Meetings' (i.e., Director-General's Meetings), at which Reith met with the two division heads, the Director of Business Relations, the Chief Engineer and the Chairman of the Board of Governors.[45]

Maurice Gorham later recalled the difficult realities of this new arrangement:

In 1933 . . . Nicolls became the first Director of Internal Administration. What it meant was that the head of every section, department, and branch had as his right-hand man an executive responsible for money, accommodation, staff, salaries, and all the business and facilities side of his job, and this executive worked not for him or for his chief but for Nicolls . . .

This system of divided control lasted right through the pre-war phase, and it made Nicolls, who became Controller (Administration) [in 1935], the most powerful figure in the BBC. Under that system, in my opinion, it became progressively harder to get the work done. The machine was manned by people who had every incentive to say No and none to say Yes, and who were suspicious of every demand because they did not know enough to see the reasons for it.[46]

## *The music programme building review: devaluing the personal approach*

General BBC restructuring initiated a review of the Music Department just as it was adjusting to a new Assistant Music Director. Despite discussion the previous season to discontinue this post, Aylmer Buesst, a conductor who had worked with Pitt at the British National Opera Company and with Boult at the Royal College of Music in the 1920s, was appointed to it on 1 October 1933. As usual, the programme builders were under pressure, and the department requested additional staff. As Wright explained in September:

> The main creative work of the Department has for some years sprung from a small group, led by myself, known as the Programme Committee. Earlier in the year you authorised its re-institution under the title of 'The Programme (Planning) Committee' in order to facilitate the continuance and development of the work in closer contact with yourself.
>
> In the very beginning this Committee had no official status. It was the spontaneous coming together of people to solve programme problems as they arose . . . The Committee has gradually extended the co-ordinated planning of our series of concerts; first, Sunday Orchestral Concerts, and subsequently Contemporary Concerts, and others, have been dealt with in this way. The absorption of its individual members in their ordinary routine work has allowed them to meet only on the most urgently important matters, and then out of office hours.
>
> With the reorganisation of Music Department into Creative and Administrative Sides, this Committee, as the nucleus of the former, will be building all the types of programme that must be handled in a co-ordinated, progressive manner, both with regard to resources (artists etc.) and repertoire.[47]

Increasing responsibilities and the impending resignation of Hely Hutchinson necessitated another appointment.[48] Wright envisaged that the new person would assist Herbage with the more than 450 orchestral programmes that were transmitted annually by late 1933.

By mid-October, the music programme builders were under even greater pressure, exacerbated by a lapse in Wright's health and by Clark's month-long holiday leave.[49] Buesst fervently supported Wright's request for assistance, and Herbage explained how far behind schedule they had become.

> This week we are due to build in detail the final programmes for 1933 – next Monday we embark on the detailed building of the first week of 1934. The Queens Hall Symphony Concerts and Public Chamber Concerts, are, of course, complete and the January Concerts of British Music practically so. With these exceptions, no other main series is in any way near completion.
>
> For the Sunday Orchestral Concerts in the New Year only a rough scheme of conductors and soloists with a few 'key' works has been prepared. The May Festival is in a quite indefinite state. The Contemporary Series is still under discussion with regard to at least one whole programme, and practically none of the concerts are built in detail. Our Studio Opera scheme has hardly taken definite shape. Foundations of Music, for which we hoped to have a five-years plan, have not been even considered beyond the end of December. Bach Cantatas are only fixed up to December 17th. All the above series should already have been plotted in detail, the estimates where necessary agreed, and the artists at least 'pencilled' if not definitely booked.[50]

The Entertainment Executive, G. C. Beadle, brought the critical situation to the attention of the Director of Internal Administration, Basil Nicolls. Although Nicolls reacted swiftly, reassigning Foster Clark to creative duties on a full-time basis, the department was not satisfied. Beadle prepared a comprehensive summary of each programme builder's responsibilities, providing a glimpse into the workings of this vital group of seven: the core three, Wright, Herbage and Clark, assisted by Buesst, Woodgate, Lewis and Foster Clark.[51] Wright still served as the fulcrum: 'He indicates in advance to other programme builders the type of programmes required; he guides them to some extent during the process of building, and all the programmes, when built, have to be passed by him'. He built important recitals and some of the light music programmes, assisted by Woodgate, and served as the link between the Music and Presentation Departments. Herbage, second in command, planned the more important orchestral series, working closely with the Orchestral Manager: 'It is [Herbage] who decides whether sufficient orchestral resources are available to play a work at any given moment. This requires a great deal of

investigation, not only into the resources available, but also into the possibility of giving each work an adequate performance with those resources'.
Clark continued to build contemporary, chamber and light classical concerts. In addition, he conducted some orchestral programmes and maintained a link with European music and musicians. As Chairman of the
Programme Committee, Buesst was responsible for supervising the planning of the high-profile concert series. As Boult's assistant, however, his
main duty was to take on the director's routine work, such as correspondence, interviews and 'a good deal of the musical politics in which Boult
inevitably becomes involved'. It was also planned that Buesst would
oversee the Music Programme Advisory Panel, once it was convened. In
addition to helping Wright with light music, Woodgate was responsible for
building organ recitals. Lewis built the orchestral programmes he himself
conducted, and Foster Clark helped with military band broadcasts and
music programmes for the Empire Service.

Nicolls disagreed with Beadle's assessment, disputing facts and statistics
that were the basis of Beadle's argument. He outlined specific ways that the
new organizational structure might improve work-load distribution.

> The re-organisation does not turn a person who was previously considered a
> musician into a layman, and it was never intended to [imply] . . . that no one
> on the executive side can do any creative work. If a hard and fast rule of that
> kind was allowed, it would have to be applied equally to the creative side, a
> great many of whom are still doing what is really executive work – indeed, a
> great deal of the work done by Mr Wright and others would appear on the
> face of it to be executive . . . The essence of the re-organisation is that the
> creative people should be left alone to plan and think and that all the results
> of their thoughts should be carried out by the executive people.[52]

With masterly manipulation of statistics, he concluded that Wright,
Herbage and Clark working full-time and Woodgate half-time were
together only responsible for 16 hours of programming each week, which
seemed reasonable. He maintained that O'Donnell and Lewis were not
achieving their potentials and that Buesst and Mase were deployed ineffec-
tively.

> It was stated several times during the work of the re-organisation that
> [Buesst] would specifically replace Mr Hutchinson in the sense of doing
> nearly all the office work that Mr Hutchinson did, and a little, but not much,
> of the conducting . . . Mr Buesst is intended to be Personal Assistant to Dr
> Boult on creative work. Mr Mase is intended as Music Executive to carry out
> for Dr Boult a very great deal of the work he previously did for him. He
> should, for instance, interview disgruntled artists, musicians, etc., by way of

> keeping them off from Dr Boult – in fact he should do everything of that
> kind in order to leave Mr Buesst free for definite creative programme work.

In Nicolls's view, if the programme builders revised their jobs to conform
with the new scheme and if all staff worked to full capacity, the section
would be under less pressure and would be more effectual. He agreed 'to
Mr Foster Clark being re-transferred to the creative side on the grounds
that he was wrongly transferred away from it in the reorganisation', but
determined that any further change must wait until the section reached a
higher standard of efficiency. The emphasis on bureaucracy and efficiency
– through the views expressed, the approaches applied, even symbolically
through the memo's inordinate length – is a significant indicator of the
management's shift toward corporate values at this time.

Another momentous decision outlined in Nicolls's memo concerned
staff members and conducting:

> In my view, it is not primarily the job of members of the staff, other than
> those taken on definitely as conductors, to conduct. I take it that Dr Boult,
> Mr O'Donnell, Mr Lewis and the Chorus Master are the only members of the
> department who are ex officio entitled to conduct. I realise that others want
> to conduct and that it is of value to their creative work if they do themselves
> conduct occasionally, but I think that it would be quite reasonable to limit
> them all to a normal maximum of one concert a month, except when holiday
> arrangements demand otherwise. This will have the effect of freeing them for
> their legitimate work. It is obvious, of course, that this will not save money,
> but conducting as such is a legitimate programme charge and is essentially
> an outside artist's job, and it should not be allowed to take the staff away
> from their normal work of programme building.

This attitude demonstrates a profound change in priorities. In the 1920s,
the music programme building section evolved from a nucleus of practising, knowledgeable musicians. Programming decisions depended on their
broad musical experiences and connections, and they had the flexibility
and skill to perform on air at short notice if necessary, as well as to address
creative and administrative duties. However, in the corporate hierarchy of
the 1930s, practical musical skills were no longer viewed as a primary
requirement for programme builders. Administrators felt that the recurring problems within the Music Department would be resolved if staff
focused on their 'legitimate' work – building programmes – and stopped
wasting time in peripheral activities such as performing. Despite the fundamental recognition that creative work should be treated differently from
administrative routine, the increasing size of the Corporation inevitably
distanced the end-product from those who planned and produced it.
Nicolls capped this trend by restricting programme building responsibil-

ities to within office boundaries, limiting staff duties to well-defined, quantifiable tasks: to plan and produce an average number of programmes each week.

This view did not take into account the personal or emotional factors that in fact underlay the department's successes: intangible, time-consuming and inefficient personal contacts and networking had been the basis on which the programme builders recruited performers and discovered new works, activities which led to the BBC's unusual music programmes. Nicolls was unwilling – or perhaps unable – to tolerate those working methods within the new BBC structure, just as he no longer recognized as significant the value of having experienced and practising musicians in an office staff. Primarily concerned with getting the work done efficiently in terms of time, personnel and cost, Nicolls's conducting decision serves as an excellent example of the priorities that were espoused and implemented within the Corporation during its second decade of existence.

Beadle discussed Nicolls's ideas with Boult and Eckersley, considering how best to express the Music Department's disagreement with the philosophy underlying his reasoning.[53] In another lengthy memo, he reiterated his conviction, backed by Boult, that the music programme builders' responsibilities should be kept within realistic limits:

> With regard to Wright, Herbage, and Clark, I have the assurance of Dr Boult that even with such assistance as Buesst is able to afford, they ought not to be called upon to build more than the following:-
>
> | | |
> |---|---|
> | Queen's Hall Concerts | 18 |
> | January Concerts | 6 |
> | May Festival | 6 |
> | Promenade Concerts | 49 |
> | Sunday Symphony Concerts | 24 |
> | Contemporary Concerts | 8 |
> | Public Chamber Concerts | 12 |
> | Studio Chamber Concerts | 70 (approx.) |
> | LSO or equivalent | |
> |    Sunday Concerts | 25 (approx.) |
> | Foundations of Music | |
>
> . . . The list involves about 412 hours per annum, distributed amongst three people. It is equivalent to about 137 hours per man per year, or, allowing for holidays, say three hours a week.[54]

He emphasized the impossibility of reducing their responsibilities to simple terms expressible through statistical calculations on paper: the quality of their work was wholly dependent on unquantifiable, but essential, elements that required time to cultivate and sustain.

> Calculated mathematically, this figure seems absurdly low, but to do the job properly, these people have to undertake a great deal of study, they ought to go about hearing recitals and concerts, and they have to keep in close touch with the outside musical world, which necessarily occupies, or should occupy, a good deal of their time.

Beadle strongly argued against Nicolls's inclination to try to limit the programme builders' jobs to mere office work, insisting that he recognize, value and grant time for the essential personal and creative aspects of their tasks.

In yet another lengthy reply, Nicolls tediously reviewed the correspondence that each programme builder handled each week as an indication of his efficiency, concluding that 'there is a certain amount of secretarial power being wasted on the creative side'.[55] He especially praised Clark's efficient letter-writing record: 'Mr Clark seems to be working ideally as a creative person, as he has practically no correspondence.' This conclusion demonstrates the futility of measuring efficiency in this way, since Clark was world-renowned as a terrible correspondent, who neglected to answer even the most urgent letters to the despair of many eminent composers and performers.

In the new year, changes to Music Department organization were finally approved as follows: Foster Clark was transferred to the creative side of the department; Woodgate became the Chorus Master; Woodgate's duties as light music programme builder were taken over by a new recruit, Arnold Perry; Wynn was transferred to the head of the Artists Booking Section; his administrative work in the department was taken over by Miss Cole; and Lewis left the official staff, continuing on an artist's contract.[56]

The extensive exchange of memos that resulted from Wright's initial request for programme building help in September 1933 provides a sense of the bureaucratic emphasis that the new building, the new organization and the newly-appointed central administrators imposed on even a relatively imbedded part of the vast corporate structure. Nicolls was a strong advocate of this bureaucratic approach to BBC management, and his new position gave him power over Music Department matters. His attitudes exemplify administrative priorities that were adopted and espoused by the BBC throughout the 1930s.

## Contemporary music programming

At the start of the 1932–3 season, the BBC launched its contemporary music campaign with a leading *Radio Times* article, 'Fair Treatment, Please, for Modern Music'. The full-page essay, written by Hubert J. Foss of

Oxford University Press, was illustrated with pictures of Wagner and Liszt, 'musical rebels of the nineteenth century', and of Schoenberg and Stravinsky, 'leaders in the so-called revolutionary movement of today'.[57] Foss argued that listeners were prejudiced by terminology.

> There is no doubt that to announce today a concert of 'contemporary' or 'modern' music means that one incurs suspicion on many sides. Into such disrepute have simple terms come with the musical public . . . The phrase, 'contemporary', 'modern', 'new' music, has a misunderstood but living secondary meaning of 'highbrow', incomprehensible music, which relates to standards unknown of the ordinary man, is self-consciously original, and has no appeal for the general.

These attitudes originated in the second half of the nineteenth century, when 'new matter was coming into music which it was hard to accept'. Foss proposed that it was the listeners' task to learn how to access such new ideas, to overcome the natural tendency to favour the familiar and to reject the unfamiliar. They should avoid comparing new works to musical styles of the past. 'Let us at least judge the new music by its achievement, and not by its difference from other schools or standards'. This prominently placed plea renewed the BBC's campaign to encourage new music awareness, paving the way for the 1932–3 season.

Plans for the BBC Concerts of Contemporary Music were proposed by Wright in October 1932.[58] As previously, there were to be eight concerts, aired monthly on Friday nights between November and June before an invited audience in the new Broadcasting House Concert Hall, which had only come into use on 15 October. Four of the programmes were planned to focus on music from a specific country, including Britain, Austria, Hungary and the Soviet Union. One concert was to be performed by the BBC's top choral group, the Wireless Singers, while another would present recent organ music – the first time this repertory was included in the contemporary series, in honour of the new Concert Hall organ. There was a decided emphasis on British works, no doubt as a result of pressure on the Music Department to promote national music. In addition to the all-British concert, the proposed programme of Van Dieren's works 'of course counts as a British concert',[59] and the choral programme would 'include some British music'. For the March concert, Wright proposed that the BBC mount what may well have been its first multi-media event, a performance of Hindemith's *Lehrstück*.

> It should be a very good stunt to do, and the audience which has to take part in the choruses, should be strengthened with the Wireless Chorus. The words are thrown on a screen, the accompaniment is by three instruments (it

is published in such a way that almost any three instruments can do this, but for our performance we should arrange for the best possible accompaniment). Only those sections of most interest from the listener's point of view would be chosen, but for the audience present the dancing and acting could be done either by amateurs or on a film. We should have to get Productions Department on to this programme early.

Wright's proposal was largely realized, though some details were altered.[60] For example, well-known performers that had been suggested – Nicolai Malko, Myra Hess and Sir Henry Wood – did not take part. In addition, a concert featuring Bartók playing his own music was replaced with Zoltán Kodály conducting a concert performance, in English, of his opera, *Skékely fonó* ('Spinning-Room'). Although Clark was undoubtedly involved with the initial designing of the programmes, for the first time Wright, Herbage and Tillett, the Booking Manager, corresponded with artists regarding programmes, rehearsals and fees. This may explain why there were uncharacteristically few discrepancies between the planned and performed programmes.

### Broadcasts of Second Viennese School works, 1932–1933

The contemporary concert on 23 December 1932 was the first broadcast of the season to include Second Viennese School repertory. The programme featured unaccompanied choral works by Szymanowski, Beck, Hindemith, Poulenc, Stravinsky and Bax, and included carols, drinking songs and folk songs in mood with the Christmas season. The BBC also invited German pianist Else Kraus, a strong advocate of Schoenberg's piano music, to present two groups of solo piano works. She performed a Piano Sonata by Norbert von Hannenheim, a Romanian composer who studied with Schoenberg in Berlin from 1929 to 1932, as well as Schoenberg's early Piano Pieces, op. 11, and his more recent Piano Pieces, op. 33a and op. 33b.

*Radio Times* attention consisted of a brief notice listing the representative composers. Specific works were neither listed nor discussed. Only oblique reference was made to the non-choral part of the programme: 'Elsa Krauss [*sic*], who is *the* Schönberg pianoforte player, will enliven the concert'.[61] The daily programme listing omitted mention of the Hannenheim Sonata and only briefly alluded to Schoenberg's career.[62] In contrast, the piano works were accorded significant space in reviews. Kraus's performance was praised, but both works were panned. Scott Goddard of the *Morning Post* avoided direct discussion of musical idioms:

> The pianoforte solo work was divided between a series of very angular pieces by Schönberg and a sonata largely similar in style by von Hannenheim, all of this played with great skill by Miss Kraus. Whatever may have been the difficulties of this music for the listeners, these evidently did not exist for the pianist, who seemed to be in complete command of their intricacies.[63]

The *Glasgow Herald* critic also preferred the performance to the music.

> A good deal of the music, particularly that which Madame Else Kraus played on the piano, was an appeal to mental processes that the ordinary listener cannot apply, however musical he may be in the ordinary sense. The merits of Schoenberg's piano pieces, for instance, have to be taken on trust as measured by the standards of the composer's little world. But before we can acknowledge masters in music of this or any other kind, we must discover some impulse or inspiration in it that overrides the rules and soars above the barriers of its castle, and nothing of the kind could be observed in the Schonberg music that we heard to-night, or in the Sonata by Hannenheim that followed it.[64]

The critic further complained 'that the B.B.C. has pursued its propaganda for this composer to more than adequate lengths, and that it is time he was dropped in favour of somebody more interesting'. The programme builders clearly did not share this view. From February 1933, music of Schoenberg and his circle was transmitted with remarkable frequency.

The sequence of broadcasts began on 5 February, when Clark conducted the world première of Schoenberg's recently completed transcription of a 'cello concerto by the eighteenth-century composer, Matthias Georg Monn. The solo part was played by Antoni Sala, and the afternoon studio concert took place without excitement or notice. Although no documentation survives, it seems likely that this performance took place in the presence of the composer. Three days later, Schoenberg himself conducted a BBC concert, and Clark apparently arranged the concerto performance so the composer could hear it.

Schoenberg's concert on 8 February was the twelfth in that season's prestigious Wednesday night BBC Symphony Concerts, broadcast live from the Queen's Hall. Boult conducted most of the programme, which included a Weber overture, Strauss Lieder sung by Elena Gerhardt, and Beethoven's Symphony no. 3. Between the Strauss and the Beethoven, Schoenberg conducted the first public performance in Britain of his Variations for Orchestra, op. 31.[65] In contrast to the studio broadcast in November 1931, the BBC prefaced this performance with much explanation. The *Radio Times* daily programme listing devoted half a page to the concert, with a substantial paragraph about Schoenberg and his career.[66]

More importantly, the editorial pages included an extensive article by Constant Lambert. Lambert compared Schoenberg to Debussy, whose music was by then familiar and appreciated in Britain.

> Schönberg and Debussy are the two great revolutionaries of modern music, and Debussy, underneath his disarmingly quiet manner, is actually the greater revolutionary of the two. He did not so much discover a new world of sound as a new way of using sound. The actual quality and texture of sound in Schönberg's music is, at a first hearing, much stranger than anything in Debussy, but Schönberg uses this new material in a comparatively academic way. Thus the work we are to hear on Wednesday, though revolutionary enough in its appeal to the ear alone, is actually a very logically-constructed set of variations, a form which Debussy would have rejected as being too conventional.[67]

Lambert also compared Schoenberg's post-war style to Bach fugues.

> The morbid sensibility and mathematical technique of Schönberg may seem contradictory, but we must remember that they are only an extreme statement of a contradiction to be found already in Bach. After all, the combination of introspective romanticism and academic formalism in Bach's 'Forty-Eight' does not prevent their being one of the glories of music.

The BBC thus provided listeners with musical points of reference to increase the accessibility of Schoenberg's difficult Variations.

As a promotional feature, the Corporation invited London critics to attend a rehearsal conducted by Schoenberg on 7 February, increasing the likelihood of newspaper publicity. On 8 February the concert received an unusual amount of press attention, alerting listeners that a significant, if not necessarily pleasurable, event was to take place that evening. Perhaps the most sensational notice appeared in the *Daily Herald*:

> At about 2.30 yesterday afternoon I went to the Queen's Hall to watch Schönberg rehearse his 'Variations for Orchestra'.
>
> The great B.B.C. symphonic body of well over a hundred British players was busy tuning-up; an electric air of expectancy filled the orchestra tiers.
>
> 'When are they beginning?' I asked a musical official after two or three minutes.
>
> 'Beginning?' he whispered aghast. 'Good heavens, they've been rehearsing since 2.15'.
>
> This is not a joke. Nothing is more detestably easy than trying to be funny at the expense of modern art. It is a truthful record of what actually happened ...
>
> Tune in on 261.6 metres this evening, but don't let the children (or your nervous auntie) near the wireless. Don't think that you need new valves, or that the batteries are wearing out.

It is just Arnold Schönberg conducting his 'Variations for Orchestra' before the elite of musical London in the Queen's Hall.[68]

The concert programme included detailed notes by David Millar Craig, describing the work's structure and orchestration, illustrated with musical examples. The programme also contained an article by M.-D. Calvocoressi, 'On Tackling Schönberg's Music'.[69] To prepare the radio audience, the BBC scheduled an introductory talk immediately before the transmission and invited Newman to give it. He accepted with tempered enthusiasm: 'You *do* pick out the nice jobs for me! Talking about the Schönberg will be no joke, but I shall be delighted to tackle the job if you can lend me the score for three days.'[70] Newman's doubts about Schoenberg's post-war style were once again reflected in this important talk. Excerpts appeared in the next day's *Daily Herald*.

> 'It will last for 20 minutes', said the highbrow critic, 'and you may feel that you might be better employed.
>
> 'I have studied the score very hard, every note of it. As musical mathematics or musical chemistry, it is a marvel . . .
>
> 'Schonberg faces life as he sees it, without making any money, and neglected by the world. His conscience is clear and his purpose pure.
>
> 'I urge you to repay his honesty by your patience'.[71]

Schoenberg's Variations were received by the British press in a surprisingly favourable light. Significantly, many of the critics particularly mentioned the work's 12-tone construction. As Edwin Evans explained:

> The theme consists of the twelve notes of the chromatic scale arranged in a certain order. It is then inverted, transposed, turned upside down and back to front, its rhythm modified in numerous ways, and all these different versions employed to make a web of sound.
>
> To say that this is mathematics, not music, means nothing, for all our music began with combinations of notes which, in their day, were considered just as ingenious and just as mathematical. But we have become accustomed to those, and not yet to these.
>
> With a little study – which of course the layman cannot be expected to give – they soon begin to clear up, and then one realises that Schönberg is a very great artist, though possibly his successors may profit more than himself by his discoveries.[72]

This association with the composer's recent idiom did not evoke the usual reactions of incomprehension and distaste. As Richard Capell wrote:

> Schönberg's Op. 31 is, no doubt, music of the torture chamber, but the listener is not tortured. Never is Schönberg's orchestral music – only his piano and vocal music is – ugly and repellant [*sic*]. The new Variations put music to

the thumbscrew and the rack, but the result has for the listener a certain fascination like the literature of flagellation and witchcraft.[73]

The concert hall audience apparently also received the work with interest and enthusiasm.

> The thunderous applause at the close of the work may have been prompted largely by the feeling that an extraordinarily difficult undertaking had been carried through without mishap, but the demonstration also indicated that a great many people had found real interest and enjoyment in what they had just heard.[74]

Although there were some negative notices, general response to this important programme was remarkably positive.[75] The combination of presenting a large-scale Second Viennese School work conducted by the composer, at a high-profile concert with extensive pre-concert publicity resulted in a momentous and surprisingly successful BBC event.

Not everyone was pleased, however, as *The Music Teacher* reported:

> Sir John Reith, Director of the B.B.C., speaking on the day after the Schönberg broadcast, said:
> 'I am going to a meeting of the Musical Advisory Committee (of the B.B.C.) over which I preside two or three times a year. If you (members of the Radio Manufacturers' Association) have any message to send them concerning the Schönberg music which was broadcast last night, I will gladly take it. I shall certainly have some comments of my own to make. Such music does not leave me cold – I wish it did – its effect is very much the reverse.'[76]

Reith's diary corroborates that he did speak to the Radio Manufacturer's Association on the day in question and later attended a Music Advisory Committee meeting, of which he only recorded: 'Many things discussed, but quite pleasantly'.[77] The numerous broadcasts of Second Viennese School works in the following weeks suggest that if he did raise objections, they did not affect short-term programme plans.

On 13 February, in a public concert transmitted from the Concert Hall, the Kolisch Quartet performed Haydn and Schubert string quartets and Berg's *Lyric Suite*, the first time this work was broadcast in its entirety. As always, the quartet performed from memory. The proximity to the Schoenberg concert inevitably led critics to compare the two composers' styles. Lambert, a Schoenberg enthusiast, wrote:

> This, like Schonberg's variations, is one of the most successful of atonal works, though Berg is by no means so strict a theorist as his master. The allegro mysterioso in particular is a movement of the greatest originality and

beauty of sound. I am by no means a theoretical upholder of atonality, but a movement like this must surely convince the most academic critic.[78]

The *Manchester Guardian* critic preferred Berg's style.

Strange as this latter work is in harmony, and baffling as many of its ideas are bound to be until a patient study of the score can throw light on them, there are more links with the older music than can be discovered in Schönberg's writings, and it is probable that Berg will bring us all to a clearer understanding of the new musical tendencies in Europe than Schönberg himself or his pupils Webern and Wellesz are likely to do, in spite of their strenuous propaganda . . . In the case of Berg's music there is a more universal expression and more graciousness in the delivery of his message.[79]

Positive reception of Berg's music, initiated the previous season, thus continued with this performance. At a studio broadcast on 25 February, the Kolisch Quartet presented Schoenberg's String Quartet no. 1, but this event received no critical attention.

Berg reached the headlines again on 8 March, when Sir Henry Wood conducted the first public performance in Britain of the Three Fragments from *Wozzeck* at a BBC Symphony Concert. The soloist was soprano May Blyth, who had sung the work in the studio broadcast of May 1932. The programme also included Beethoven's Overture to *Egmont*, Haydn's Symphony no. 31 in D major, Bach's Violin Concerto no. 2 in E major, with Adolf Busch as soloist, and Strauss's *Tod und Verklärung*.

As for the Schoenberg Variations, the BBC prepared for the *Wozzeck* excerpts with a vigorous publicity campaign. A full-page *Radio Times* article by Eric Blom explained the opera's musical structure and dramatic scenario.[80] On the day of the concert, *The Listener* also included a full-page feature, by M. D. Calvocoressi. This thoughtful article placed the work in its historical context, as the most succesful of modern operas. Calvocoressi emphasized the importance of the performance for British audiences, who had few opportunities to experience operas by living composers. He also considered the work's atonal construction.

None of the means of expressing moods, character, action, and so forth, which in operatic music from olden days to the present time had grown and changed without ever ceasing to be recognisable, and which we are accustomed to, are used any longer. Failing the usual foundation of the structure and the usual association-compelling means of expression, the questions arise: what does the composer build on (which is his business)? and what do we listeners get instead of all that is given up (which is decidedly our business)?[81]

Calvocoressi concluded that the human qualities portrayed in the drama provided an expressive foundation for the work, which transcended the complexities and strangeness of the music.

> Berg uses a language unfamiliar to us, but so thoroughly human in accent as to be intelligible and acceptable forthwith. Practically all those who have heard 'Wozzeck' speak with enthusiasm of its dramatic effectiveness and of the convincing quality of the music. The work has, in the course of the past eight years, proved its vitality by living.

The concert programme included a lengthy dramatic description, illustrated by music examples and the texts.[82] Explanation was also provided in a broadcast talk by Edwin Evans given immediately before the concert. In pointed contrast to Calvocoressi's sophisticated arguments, Evans used simplistic language and images.

> There's an exclamation which occurs several times in the opera: Wir ar[m]e Leute! A free translation would be 'We poor devils'. Wozzeck is a poor devil. He's a private soldier . . . He's reprimanded by his captain. To earn a few pence he lets the regimental doctor, who's a charlatan, try experiments with his food. The drum-major steals his girl from him, and when he objects, thrashes him into the bargain. Everybody's hand is against him. In the end he becomes so exasperated that he murders his girl and drowns himself. As you see, it's not a cheerful subject.[83]

He also reassured listeners about the accessibility of Berg's music.

> Schonberg's admired by a large number of musicians and rejected by others, but even his admirers wouldn't claim that he's popular. Yet his pupil, using the same method, has won a popular success. I can assure you that it is so. I've known musicians whom I should call conservative, who were prejudiced against Schonberg and his method of composing, and who came away from a performance of 'Wozzeck' wholly convinced and deeply impressed . . . Whereas Schonberg had to invent his method, and must therefore have been much preoccupied with its technical aspect, his pupil, Alban Berg, so to speak grew up with it, so that to him it's a completely spontaneous mode of expression, like a language one's spoken from childhood.

Unlike the studio broadcast the previous season, this public performance was accorded more than adequate pre-concert preparation and explanation.

Not surprisingly, the concert reviews devoted most space to the Berg. The critics tended to write favourably – although with some reservations, since the full opera was not yet known to many of them. Constant Lambert requested:

If the rest of Wozzek [*sic*] comes off as well as these three fragments I cannot understand why we are denied a hearing of the opera in this country. Berg, in 'Wozzek' at least, is not a strict atonalist by any means, and his music is far easier to follow at a first hearing than that of his master Schönberg. I cannot understand anyone who has not been frightened off by Berg's reputation as a bogey-man failing to appreciate the direct expressiveness of these fragments. Above all, Berg is a supreme master of orchestral colour. The military march in No. 1 and the chromatic passage in No. 3 are memorable moments even in these days of orchestral virtuosity. The latter is perhaps too much of a 'stunt' in the concert hall, but it must be strangely impressive in the theatre.[84]

The *Evening Standard* reviewer also reflected on Berg's accessibility.

Here is a case of the pupil not outstripping his master in their mutual idiom but showing less extravagance . . . Berg's music is far more *schön* than that of Schönberg. There is tenderness in it and true beauty. When 'nasty' things happen, one feels that there is a good reason for them.[85]

Even Newman grudgingly admitted that Berg's work transcended his criticisms of Schoenberg.

What was abundantly clear was that the music does possess the uncompromising eloquence of originality. Berg may have actually set out to build upon the crass, elaborate theories of his master, Schönberg. For him, they are proved compatible with art.[86]

The excerpts from Berg's opera were received with relative favour and enthusiasm, even though they were presented in the season's conservative symphony series. The performance also made a profound impression on the BBC administrators: during summer 1933, the Corporation began to make plans to mount the British première of *Wozzeck* in its entirety.

The final broadcasts of the season with Second Viennese School associations took place on 21 and 23 April, when Webern returned to conduct for the BBC. Plans began in September 1932, when Boult approved a list of conductors for the season's Sunday Orchestral Concerts, including Webern for the 23 April concert.[87] He was officially offered the engagement, and accepted it on 7 October.[88] The proposed programme included Beethoven's Overture to *Prometheus*, Webern's arrangement of the Schubert Dances, D. 820, and – satisfying the composer's long-standing request – Mahler's Symphony no. 4, with British soprano Elsie Suddaby as soloist. The Music Department also planned for Webern to conduct a contemporary concert. Wright's series proposal specified:

*Friday, April 21st: Orchestral*, conducted by Webern. Austrian Programme, to include Krenek's 'Dürch [*sic*] die Nacht', with Hedda Kux, specially recommended from the Vienna Festival. Alban Berg's Kammerkonzert with Steuermann (piano) might be given. Soloist, first movement, Kolisch (violin); second movement, Steuermann; third movement, both. In addition, Kolisch and Steuermann would probably play an agreed sonata.[89]

When details were confirmed in December, the programme consisted of three movements from Berg's *Lyric Suite*, arranged for string orchestra by the composer, Krenek's song cycle *Durch die Nacht* with soprano Hedda Kux,[90] and Berg's Chamber Concerto for Piano, Violin and 13 Wind Instruments.[91]

In March, Steuermann and Kolisch were formally contracted for the contemporary concert, as well as for a second duo recital on 20 April.[92] The Booking Manager also sent an urgent letter to Webern, requesting that he sign and return his contract.[93] Instead, he queried the rehearsal and fee arrangements, and a detailed explanation revealed that the contemporary programme was apportioned an unprecedented ten rehearsals in four days, while Sunday's concert was assigned three rehearsals in two days, resulting in a gruelling schedule for the conductor. Webern was offered 60 guineas for the two concerts.[94] The BBC sent Webern his entry permit at the end of March, but the arrangements were still not settled. The composer demanded a 70 guinea fee, as he received previously, and suggested a programme change.

> Referring now to the programme for Friday, 21 April, I must ask you to note that despite the abundant rehearsal allocation, a performance of the *second movement* of Berg's *Lyric suite* cannot be considered, since, even with *as many* rehearsals again, the difficulties of time can probably not be overcome. After discussing it with the composer, therefore, I will confine myself to the *first* and *third* movements and cannot depart from this decision under any circumstances. Since these two movements should not be too difficult, some of the *rehearsal time* provided for the *Lyric suite* could be used for the Chamber concerto.[95]

Webern was willing to perform the 'Andante amoroso' and 'Adagio appassionato' in the string orchestra version, but not the difficult 'Allegro misterioso'. The BBC sent a new contract, awarding Webern a 70 guinea fee and agreeing to drop the movement; however, the rehearsal schedule could not be varied.[96] Despite these late negotiations, the arrangements for Webern's 1933 engagements were made with relatively little fuss or anxiety, compared to previous occasions.

The only surviving communication between Webern and Clark pertaining to these concerts was written on 11 April. Webern relayed his and Steuermann's arrival time in London on the 17th and requested that reservations be made for them at the Strand Palace Hotel. He also commented about the omission of the 'Allegro misterioso'.

> I just wrote again that I will not do the second piece from the *Lyric suite*.
> Whoever performs that today, *cheats* deliberately. And that cannot be expected of me!!!
> It is impossible for it to be *really* brought about with orchestra. Up to now, it could only *really* be played by the Kolisch people. Everything else is and can only *be nonsense*!!! I hope, then, that the first and third movements will succeed all the more beautifully. So I already look forward to London, even if there will be downright *insane* work this time. (Has anyone before held an eight-hour orchestra rehearsal in one day? For such works?!)[97]

The Webern concerts received little pre-concert attention. A press release for the contemporary series sent to critics in February 1933 listed works that were to be performed, without any explanatory comments.[98] The *Radio Times* programme listing for 21 April briefly introduced Berg – 'an Austrian composer forty-seven years old, and the most gifted of the pupils of Arnold Schönberg, his only master, lives quietly in Vienna, composing, teaching, and writing' – and gave the titles, with short descriptions, for the *Lyric Suite* movements.[99] The Krenek listing gave the song titles without commentary. Similarly, Webern was listed as conductor, with no biographical notes. However, a brief paragraph about his career was included in the programme listing for 23 April.

> Early in his career [Webern] came under the influence of Schönberg, the first and one of the most distinguished of whose pupils he was, and the most loyal of whom he has remained. His compositions, which are few in number – some of them have been heard by listeners – are concentrated in structure, intensely expressive, and subdued in tone, and have earned for him the description of 'composer of the pianissimo espressivo'. As a conductor in Vienna, particularly of the well-known Work-People's Concerts, he has made a big reputation, both in the ultra-modern music of which he is a disciple and in the great classics.[100]

Critical response to the Webern concerts was similarly subdued. Even new music advocates were unenthusiastic about the 21 April programme. Evans wrote in the *Daily Mail*:

> One of [the works] consist[s] of three movements of the Lyric Suite . . . and, though 'advanced', does not present considerable difficulty. But the other, a concerto for piano, violin, and thirteen wind instruments, in which Herren Eduard Steuermann and Rudolf Kolisch were the soloists, is so recondite as to require some preliminary initiation.
> Miss Hedda Kux sang a song-cycle by Ernst Krenek . . . This setting of a

rather melancholy text, 'Durch die Nacht' (Through the Night), was easier of apprehension, though the choppy nature of the accompaniment, played by a chamber orchestra, tended to mask its romantic derivation.[101]

Newman described the Berg as 'dry, though, of course, not deficient in the peculiar cerebration that is his characteristic'. He was equally dismissive of Webern's conducting: it 'appeared to do ample justice to what had as little emotional significance as a musical cross-word puzzle'.[102] William McNaught was one of the few critics who worked up enough interest to condemn the concert outright:

> Neither of these works gave any impression of short-cutting the cares and labours of artistic production.
>    Their detail was minute and exact, their technical elaboration of an order that exercised the highest faculties.
>    The music bore every sign that the craftsman's part in it had been ordered by a real and insistent idealism.
>    Yet the effect was antagonising and tedious.[103]

In contrast to Schoenberg's conducting success just weeks earlier, Webern's BBC engagements had little, if any, impact on the British musical scene.

Nevertheless, the experience was important to members of the Second Viennese circle. In an effusive letter to Schoenberg, written on 3 May 1933, Webern expressed his satisfaction with the London concerts.

> In London this time it was especially satisfying, though strenuous. In six days I had to hold *33 hours* of orchestra rehearsals and give two concerts. I believe that Berg's works turned out very well, at any rate they were clean through-out. They also met with great success. The first concert was for an invited audience in the hall of the BBC House. *The orchestra is really splendid.* How they played Mahler's Fourth! There was at times a quite fabulous sound, really and truly quite ideal. Marvellous in sonority. My Schubert Dances, too, came out very beautifully. The orchestra seems to have really enjoyed them. I might also report in all modesty that, from all appearances, I have had a very far-reaching effect on the orchestra (acclamations during and at the end of the rehearsals, a spontaneous storm of applause after the *Prometheus* Overture, and after the second concert a veritable ovation). In short, dearest friend, I was really very, very happy.[104]

Webern also mentioned that he believed Clark's loyalty to the Second Viennese group would lead to further BBC engagements, a welcome pros-pect since opportunities in Vienna were dwindling.

> Clark seems to have been happy, too. It is not easy to deal with him from a distance, but on the spot he is always a really splendid fellow, who knows

absolutely and exactly what is involved, and who is full of the deepest faith in you and in us, too. Now I hope for a fortuitous continuation of my engagements there and also that eventually there can be more than only one a year. I need this so urgently. Things here really are becoming more and more impossible. Steuermann and Kolisch played splendidly.

Berg was pleased by the performance, which he heard over the air, writing to Clark on 13 May: '*Thank you* for your good offices which made possible and brought to fruition the beautiful Berg–(Křenek) concert that gave me so much pleasure'.[105]

The ambivalent reception of these concerts was not helped by a *Radio Times* article of 21 April. Entitled 'Symphony *versus* Cacophony', the full-page discussion was headed with the provocative prediction: 'C. Whitaker-Wilson, debating the problem of Ultra-Modern Music, foresees the day when we shall hear a full organ and full orchestra holding every note of the scale at once for half an hour at a time'.[106] Whitaker-Wilson argued that current compositional trends did not derive from the traditions of the accepted canon.

> Now we come to the present-day music, of the type I have called ultra-modern. I have examined the scores of such music. I have analysed the dissonances. I have found dissonances to exist for which I cannot account, using the system by which music has been evolved. The chords are unfigurable; they cannot be 'rooted'; they contain combinations which prove to me that scholarship and musicianship, in the accepted sense, are wanting.
>
> Even so, it is not my purpose here to sweep ultra-modern music aside as worthless. To do that is to weaken my case against it. For the moment I will accept it as sincere, but I arraign its composers in that they have departed from the tradition of their forefathers, that they have either designedly or through ignorance caused sounds to be heard that are not justifiable on any musical grounds whatever.

The author categorized the traditional line of musical development as Symphony, based on the word's Greek root meaning agreement in sound. Modern-day developments, epitomized by Schoenberg's op. 31 Variations, were classed as Cacophony, meaning bad sound.

> So long as we recognise the fact that Symphony and Cacophony cannot be combined so long as we take steps to honour both *but to separate them*, no harm can result. Let us be honest in this matter. Let the B.B.C. organise a series of Cacophony Concerts, either at Queen's Hall or Broadcasting House, setting aside a special time in the programmes for them. We should then be able to choose between a Symphony Concert on the National and a Cacophony Concert on the Regional.

Not surprisingly, the extreme views expressed in this article sparked a new *Radio Times* debate. The next week, a full-page rebuttal by C. Henry Warren appeared. Claiming that Whitaker-Wilson's arguments derived from an unwillingness to accept the spirit of the times, Warren concluded:

> It is, in fact, utterly beside the point to draw this hard and fast distinction . . . between 'Symphony' and 'Cacophony'. All music in which, according to [Whitaker-Wilson's] ear, the sounds do not agree is cacophony . . . Discord and Ultra-Modern Music are, for him, synonymous. He looks at a modern score and sees basses which he cannot figure, chords to which he cannot give a name. It must be most discouraging. All the same, why not forget for a moment the figured bass and the academically correct chord? Why not simply listen, for a change, to the music?[107]

Listeners' contributions to both sides of the argument were printed for weeks afterwards. The BBC thus concluded the 1932–3 season as it had begun, with prominent Radio Times discussion of the new music issue. The number of letters that the controversy sparked whenever it resurfaced demonstrates the passion that it aroused in the British public – and was sufficient justification for the BBC's continued involvement with it.

Pieces by two other composers from the Schoenbergian circle were considered for performance during the 1932–3 season, but were not actually broadcast. Roberto Gerhard's *Five Catalan Folk Songs* for soprano and orchestra were scheduled for transmission on 15 January 1933, as part of the Winter Promenade series. Gerhard himself was going to accompany Concepció Badiá D'Agusti during the second half of the concert. However, the last-minute illness of the singer led to postponement. Soprano Sophie Wyss sang the British première of the Gerhard songs on 5 October 1933 as part of the summer Promenade Concerts.[108]

Wellesz also hoped that one of his works would be selected for broadcasting that season. When Boult conducted the Vienna Philharmonic Orchestra in February 1933, Wellesz submitted to him scores of his opera, *Scherz, List und Rache*, op. 41, and his cantata, *Mitte des Lebens*, op. 45. He subsequently wrote to cultivate interest, but neither work was broadcast during spring or summer 1933.[109] Only one broadcast of a Second Viennese School work did take place then: on 20 August, contralto Enid Cruickshank sang three songs from Schoenberg's op. 2 and op. 3.

## Broadcasts of Second Viennese School works, 1933–4

During the following season, interest in Berg's music continued to gain momentum, culminating in an extremely significant event: the BBC's mounting of the first British performance of *Wozzeck* in March 1934. In contrast to the huge amount of publicity that surrounded that particular concert, the BBC re-adopted a non-interventionist policy in general: although new works were transmitted frequently throughout the season, the BBC avoided provoking controversy. Many of the music programmes followed prescriptive patterns established in previous years. The stream-lined format and routine presentation of the BBC Concerts of Contemporary Music typify this trend.

Planning discussions for the 1933–4 series began relatively early. In August 1933, shortly after the Music Department and the Music Advisory Committee clash over British representation, Wright submitted a proposal to Boult for eight concerts, to take place monthly between 24 November 1933 and 29 June 1934.

> You will see that in nationalities there is plenty of variety and that British music occupies 25 per cent. of the time. In view of the large amount of British music in other series of concerts, including some three important new works, it would not be far wrong to say that 50 per cent. of the new music we are producing is British.[110]

In fact, two of the proposed concerts were devoted to British works. The remaining six presented music by Russian, Swiss, Hungarian, Austrian, German and American composers, with entire programmes devoted to Stravinsky, Honegger, Bartók, Schoenberg and Hindemith. The proposal was largely realized, although the Hindemith programme was replaced by a second Russian programme, conducted by Nicolai Malko.[111] For the first time, Clark performed in the series, conducting both the American and the British programmes. Benjamin Britten was the only composer to have works performed in two concerts: *A Boy was Born*, op. 3, was presented during the British choral concert, and the *Sinfonietta*, op. 1, was given in the eighth programme.[112] Also performed were Stravinsky's *Mavra* and *Les noces*, Bartók's *Cantata profana* (world première) and *Két portré* ('Two Portraits'), Varèse's *Octandre* and Honegger's *Cris du monde*.

The first concert of the series, an all-Schoenberg programme, was presented during a two-week period in which a number of Second Viennese School works were aired. At a studio broadcast on 20 November 1933, British pianist, Helen Perkin, played Berg's Piano Sonata, op. 1, as well as Wellesz's 'Tanzstück' and 'Pastorale'.[113] On 1 December, the Kolisch Quartet presented a public chamber concert, including the variation movement from Krenek's String Quartet no. 5, op. 65, Webern's Five Pieces for String Quartet, op. 5, and Beethoven's Quartet in A minor, op. 132.

Background information was presented in the *Radio Times* programme listing and in an essay by Ernst Schoen in the 'Notable Music of the Week' column.[114] Avoiding the educational approach, Schoen played on shock potential:

> When [the Quartet] play the older music, they are at one with their audience; where the newer music is concerned, a hostile audience, often bitterly hostile, is the least they have come to expect. I have been present when this Quartet was overwhelmed with applause, and again when it was showered with invective.

He described Webern's music in dramatic terms.

> It must always remain a mystery how a composer can, as Webern is doing, make use of whatever instruments and sounds are available to him, to create such painful and wild musical exclamations and scraps of melody, undefinable in words . . . The adventurous listener should plunge head first into the brief sensation offered by Webern's composition, as into dangerous and unfamiliar waters; for this is stark music, unsocial, with a shape and a spirit of its own, naked and lonely, the strange sounds of nature imprisoned in a score. Thus may the listener experience a moment of intense artistic revelation, stripped of all artifice, and therein find his reward.

Perhaps surprisingly, the concert generated several positive reviews in the British papers, with the *Observer* critic even remarking that he would like to hear the Webern again.[115]

Between the 20 November piano recital and the 1 December quartet concert, two BBC events were to feature Schoenberg conducting his own works. The all-Schoenberg programme in the contemporary concert series was planned for 24 November, and a BBC Symphony Concert with the world première of his arrangement of Handel's *Concerto grosso*, op. 6 no. 7, for 29 November. The idea to present the *Concerto grosso* was initiated when Schoenberg sent Clark a desperate postcard from Paris in May 1933. He and his family had just fled from Germany, and he had lost his teaching position at the Berlin Academy. He requested Clark's assistance.

> I want to ask you now: 1. Can I count on one or the other concerts at the BBC? 2. Do you know of a publisher for my 'cello concerto (Oxford-Press???) 3. I am writing for radio a concerto for string quartet and orchestra and a 'Conc. gr. by Handel'. I am also searching for a publisher for these, and a concert-engagement. 4. Do you know a Jewish, English publisher, who would be interested in a Jewish drama by me? It was written in 1925–6 and deals with a Jewish national uprising, which I already recognized as a necessity at that time. 5. I have almost finished an opera 'Moses und Aron' and have a volume of collected writings.[116]

That Schoenberg should seek Clark's help in a moment of crisis was not without precedent. When the composer, facing severe financial difficulties, had moved to Berlin in 1911, Clark had helped him search for teaching opportunities there. When Schoenberg appealed to his former student on this occasion, Clark came through once again, this time with conducting offers from the BBC.[117]

In Wright's proposal for the contemporary series, he suggested that *Pierrot lunaire* receive another performance: 'This was done three seasons ago and I think a repetition now would be justified. There is no need to bring over the composer at this time'.[118] The BBC nevertheless decided to invite Schoenberg to conduct, perhaps influenced by Clark's news about his circumstances. An article previewing the BBC Symphony Concerts announced that he would conduct his *Concerto grosso* arrangement in a programme including Schubert's Symphony no. 5 and Bruckner's Symphony no. 9.[119] The proposed contemporary programme consisted of the Suite, op. 29, and *Pierrot lunaire*.[120] Unlike the April 1930 broadcast, performed by an entirely foreign ensemble, pressures in 1933 to engage fewer foreign artists clearly influenced the BBC's decision to engage a mixed Austrian and British ensemble, including Erika Wagner as reciter, members of the Kolisch Quartet to play the string parts, and Steuermann as pianist.[121] The British contingent was drawn from the BBC Symphony Orchestra: Robert Murchie was invited to play flute and piccolo, Frederick Thurston and Ralph Clarke, clarinets, and Walter Lear, bass clarinet.

The routine arrangements for the 24 November concert seemed smoothly on course. A chatty paragraph about *Pierrot lunaire* appeared in the *Radio Times*, as did a full-page article by Cecil Gray, explaining Schoenberg's compositional background.[122] A press release to music critics stressed the unusual opportunity that the programme offered:

> 'Pierrot Lunaire' is one of the most original works ever written; it would probably be played more frequently were it not so very difficult and were there not so few executants to do it justice. Yet whenever it is played it is received with marked success and, despite its modernity and difficulty, it has proved to be one of the most easily understood and assimilated works of modern times.[123]

However, an ominous notice appeared in the *Manchester Guardian* of 1 November:

> As Arnold Schönberg is prevented from appearing at the Queen's Hall Symphony Concert on November 29, and in view of his wish to direct the first performance of his Concerto Grosso, it has been decided to revise the

programme. The soloist will be Alfred Cortot, and the full symphony orchestra will be conducted by Adrian Boult.[124]

On 22 November, just two days before the concert, the BBC circulated another press release:

> The B.B.C. announces that Constant Lambert has undertaken at short notice to conduct the performance of Arnold Schönberg's 'Pierrot Lunaire' which is being performed in the Concert of Contemporary Music on Friday next, November 24. The composer's Three Pieces, Opus 11, played by Eduard Steuermann, will be substituted for the Suite for E flat Clarinet, Clarinet, Bass Clarinet, Violin, Viola, Violoncello and Pianoforte, Opus 29 (1927).[125]

Since the only offer of European work that Schoenberg received was from the BBC, he decided to pursue more promising opportunities in the United States and sailed from France to New York on 25 October 1933. According to Stuckenschmidt, he declined the BBC offer before his departure.[126] Strangely, on 9 November, the Corporation applied for an entry permit for him, the cancellation news apparently not circulating to the appropriate offices.[127]

With the deletion of Schoenberg's op. 29, the first contemporary concert of the season consisted entirely of pre-World War I works, a fact that was noted in several reviews. The *Times* critic asked:

> How long does music remain contemporary? Last night the B.B.C. began a new series of 'Concerts of Contemporary Music' with some of the earlier works of Arnold Schönberg. Three piano pieces, Op. 11, and still more, five shorter and easier pieces, Op. 19, called up memories of the long-past pre-War days when we picked them out carefully on the piano and felt very up to date in taking these first steps in what was then called 'Modern' music.[128]

Although *Pierrot lunaire* had impressed British critics with its innovative characteristics and unusual sounds in April 1930, by November 1933 it was barely classed as a novelty. As Edwin Evans pointed out in *The Daily Mail*: 'It is the most accessible of the music Schönberg has written since he turned his back upon his early works. But still it remains music for a comparatively small circle.'[129]

The response to this concert demonstrates the degree to which the BBC had achieved its goal to improve British awareness of new music trends. The significant attention paid to Schoenberg between January 1928, when he conducted the *Gurrelieder*, and autumn 1933, when he emigrated to the USA, brought his name and reputation, at the least, into households throughout Britain. As Richard Capell remarked:

> British listeners by the million are today familiar with this esoteric com-
> poser's name, and in particular with that of his masterpiece, 'Pierrot
> Lunaire'; and British listeners by the million, we have no doubt, make haste
> the moment the name is announced to turn the knobs in quest of other fare,
> Puccini or Jack Hylton, or even a Talk, or even Foundations – anything, in
> fact, rather than contemporary esotericism.
>
> And yet we hold that the B.B.C.'s cult of Schönberg and his like counts to
> its credit as much, or almost, as any of its so various enterprises.
>
> It would, no doubt, be an easier and more acceptable policy to broadcast
> nothing but popular music . . . As for 'contemporary' music – that contem-
> porary music which has in the actual hall an interest so lively and stimulating
> that, whatever we may say about it afterwards, no opportunity is willingly
> missed of spending forty minutes or so in the company of Schönberg or
> Stravinsky, Berg, Bartok, or Casella – well, it is a penance by one's own fire-
> side.[130]

Although Capell confirmed that the British public was aware of
Schoenberg, he questioned whether the BBC had succeeded in broadening
audience horizons in purely musical terms, attributing the communication breakdown to shortcomings in the broadcasting medium of the time.

The November 1933 concerts thus represented an important turning
point in the history of the BBC's dissemination of Schoenberg's music.
Some works from his atonal period were finally received in Britain as
familiar and accepted repertory. Nevertheless, this was the last invitation
the composer received to participate in British broadcasts, this was the last
time before World War II that a recent Schoenberg work was broadcast in a
high-profile BBC public concert,[131] and this was his last work to be broadcast in 1933–4. In effect, Schoenberg's departure from Europe coincided
with a waning of interest in his music by the Music Department.

1934 began with the BBC's British Music Festival, which took place
between 1 and 12 January. The pro-British, anti-foreign values symbolized
by this festival characterized the programming of the entire season, effectively limiting broadcasts of Second Viennese School works, aside from
those related to *Wozzeck*, to three broadcasts. On 10 February 1934, Ružena
Herlinger returned to give the first British performance of Berg's *Der Wein*
at a studio orchestra concert conducted by Robert Heger.[132] Wright first
proposed inviting Herlinger to sing this work in October 1933, having
heard her perform it in Vienna in 1931.[133] He needed Boult's permission to
engage an artist on the BBC's 'Reserve International List', and eventually
received it. Herlinger accepted the engagement enthusiastically, though she
requested a fee of 20 guineas in place of the BBC's lower offer.[134] This
British première took place quietly, without public or critical notice.

The April 1934 contemporary concert was devoted to American works and included a movement by Adolph Weiss, who had studied with Schoenberg during 1925–6, as well as works by Henry Cowell, Virgil Thomson and Edgard Varèse. The Andante from Weiss's Chamber Symphony was the first work by this composer to receive BBC attention. Both this piece and Varèse's *Octandre* were repeated for those in the Concert Hall, but the repetitions were not broadcast.

Finally, on 18 June 1934, Paul Pisk presented three of his piano pieces in a studio chamber music broadcast. The idea to invite Pisk to broadcast came from Herlinger, but Wright worried about the new restrictions: 'We are so besieged with enquiries from foreign artists of all kinds that we cannot accept more than one suggestion in a dozen, and unfortunately in June we have commitments already to certain other foreign composers to take part in recitals of their music'.[135] Nevertheless, Herlinger's suggestion was effected for political reasons. Wright recognized that Pisk, a Social Democrat, had been persecuted and was experiencing financial hardship.

> You will probably remember that he is a member of the L.S.O.M. group in Vienna, and suffered particularly badly in the recent disturbances. Although he personally has never taken any part in political affairs, he actually got imprisoned and what not.
>
> Madame Herlinger . . . begs us to consider engaging Pisk for a short recital of his music, as the fee which would probably be about 12 guineas, would be such a godsend to him.

Pisk presented the Toccata from his Concert Piece, op. 7, the complete Small Suite, op. 11, and the March from his Great Suite, op. 17. Despite the philanthropic aspect, members of the Music Department were unimpressed with this composer's works, deciding 'that they were not of sufficient value to justify a repetition'.[136]

Webern was once again engaged by the BBC during the 1933–4 season, though he did not conduct any Second Viennese School works. The Corporation contacted him in August 1933 about the possibility of conducting a Sunday Orchestral Concert in the new year. Webern clarified the dates on which he would be available, and also wrote to Clark requesting a second BBC engagement.[137] He mentioned some programme possibilities:

> Of my own works, sometime I would like to conduct the Four songs with orchestra, op. 13 (with a singer from here, perhaps *Hanna Schwarz* . . . ), and naturally: *(above all) 6 pieces for orchestra, op. 6, Berg,* 3 orchestra pieces, op. 6, *Schönberg:* 5 orchestra pieces, op. 16 (Peters) – *but he will probably want to conduct these himself*!!!

In September, Wright sent further details to Webern: 'The idea for the Sunday Concert was to perform Mahler's Lied von der Erde with a suitable introductory item, but even this is not yet settled'.[138] Webern approved this idea, suggested Schubert, Brahms, Mozart and Beethoven pieces for the rest of the concert, and again requested a second engagement.[139] Wright soon relayed the disappointing news that it was not possible to offer Webern a Sunday Orchestral Concert after all, but only a less prestigious orchestra concert. Moreover, 'it will unfortunately not be possible to offer you two concerts, owing to the very bad condition of things still in this country in the artistic profession, which means that our engagements to foreign artists must be strictly regulated and limited'.[140]

Only in February was a mutually agreeable date for the broadcast agreed.[141] Webern was contracted to conduct Schubert's Symphony no. 4 ('Tragic') and the 'Nachtmusik' movements from Mahler's Symphony no. 7 on 25 April, for a fee of 40 guineas. Although Webern signed and returned the contract, he sent Clark a letter begging for an increase to £50. The political upheavals in Austria had seriously affected his financial situation, and the relative currency values meant that the honorarium would barely cover travel and hotel expenses.[142] However, Wright responded with a firmly worded letter:

> We must regretfully decline to increase the amount of forty guineas already agreed. This fee is considered a fair one, arrived at with due regard to your value in our programmes, of which we are fully appreciative, and the fees paid to other guests, including foreign conductors. We feel that we would not be justified in increasing this fee, even had you raised the matter at once instead of signing the contract for the present amount.
>
> You will appreciate, I feel sure, that we have to regard the matter from the business point of view, and can really concern ourselves only with the question of programme value and fair comparison of fees among all conductors. While we are most sympathetic to those who, like yourself, have suffered under the unfortunate conditions obtaining in other countries, these facts cannot very well weigh in a business argument in assessing a fee. Besides, these same unfortunate world conditions have made life very difficult for British artists, and the general distribution of fees from our programme allowance must be considered from their point of view also.[143]

Webern accepted this decision, although he was more cautious in subsequent negotiations with the BBC. The composer once again asked Clark to make hotel arrangements and to meet him at Victoria station upon arrival.[144] The concert took place with no further mishaps or attention.

This survey reveals that Schoenberg, Webern and others in the Second Viennese circle were less conspicuously represented during the 1933–4 season. However, the attention accorded to Berg more than made up for this deficiency. On 14 March 1934, the BBC mounted the first British performance of *Wozzeck*. This was not just the most important BBC event of the season; it was one of the most significant BBC events to take place during the first decades of the Corporation's existence.

## The first British performance of Berg's *Wozzeck*

The BBC's decision to tackle as large and complicated a project as producing *Wozzeck* developed over a number of years. The opera's exceptional reception in Europe after its première in 1925 made it a likely target for Music Department interest. In 1930 Clark and Wright attended a staged performance in Aix-la-Chapelle to assess whether it would be appropriate for broadcasting.[145] Two years later, the Music Department reviewed its broadcast opera policies. A committee chaired by the Presentation Assistant, Wellington, and including Clark, proposed a wide-ranging opera scheme for the 1932–3 season. In addition to broadcasting Covent Garden productions and six studio operas, the committee suggested that the BBC transmit six operas from the continent, including '2 of original works or works of special musical interest (e.g. Wozzek [*sic*])'.[146] In fact, Berg's opera was not relayed to British audiences that season, although the BBC had broadcast excerpts from it twice by summer 1933.[147] The blandness of the operatic broadcasts during the 1932–3 season provoked Mase, then Assistant Music Director, to complain to the Director of Programmes, Eckersley:

> It seems a pity to run a whole season without anything novel or exceptionally interesting in it. We have proved over and over again from the public angle that while one must not push new works it is essential for a good scheme to have at least one interesting and unusual event. For instance, the opera which has made more stir during recent years than any other is Wozzeck which is undoubtedly, in view of all critics and the continental public, a great and interesting work. It seems a pity that it could not have been included in this season in this country. It would be wrong to fill a season with new works, but we feel sure that at least one interesting and good novelty, already proved elsewhere, ought to be included.[148]

In August 1933, the BBC finally began to plan a *Wozzeck* performance. Mase wrote to both Berg and the London agent for Universal Edition, Jean Michaud of Universal Music Agencies, informing them of the Corporation's interest and asking about the possibility of a performance on 14 March 1934.[149] Berg responded immediately, mentioning that Willi

Reich's pamphlet about the opera was being sent to the BBC and asking about the English translation of the text. Berg had personally checked the Russian, Czech and French translations and was anxious to do so for the English version.[150] Although the BBC began to prepare a translation, the idea was soon abandoned, as Boult reported to Eckersley:

> We have come to the conclusion that the problems connected with doing 'Wozzeck' in English are insuperable. To begin with, the translation (which has been prepared by Mr Calvocoressi) of one scene, makes it appear that, like some German Songs, it is almost impossible to achieve a translation that is not ridiculous. Further, the size of the name part makes it very difficult to think of an English artist who could do justice to it.[151]

Eckersley approved this decision: 'I am not one of those who want to follow the work at a concert. From a broadcasting point of view I [don't believe] it will make an enormous amount of difference! This sounds rude to singers – but it is difficult to follow words in a big orchestral show'.[152]

This was not the only problem to develop during the initial stages. The publishers demanded an exorbitant £200 for hire and performance fees, comparable to what they had received for the staged Berlin performances. Mase negotiated with Michaud, who eventually agreed to half that figure.[153] In addition, the time-consuming arrangements hindered the already overworked staff, as Wright pointed out in October: 'the casting and general organisation of work of "Wozzeck" . . . presents problems more difficult than any production of the kind we have yet tackled'.[154] By December, the astronomical costs of mounting the opera became apparent; the administrators had not applied for nearly enough funding. As Mase nervously explained:

> The Creative side have now supplied me with the full implications and cast of the above. In the estimates at the beginning of the season when the work was put in, not much was known about it except its fame and the number of artists was said to be two or three, and an estimate was made at £108 to cover the cost of these. Their full investigation in casting now shows that it is the most difficult musical work ever written and that a large number of artists and understudies are required and a chorus.[155]

Not only did the opera unexpectedly involve many performers, but Boult decided that its success depended on a fully qualified coach.

> M.D. has formed the certain opinion also that the engagement of a coach for a long period to coach the artists in their parts and to assist the chorus is essential. In this last direction we are fortunate that Mr Kurt Prerauer is in

> England and he produced it in Berlin and other parts of Germany at least ten times and is the most efficient coach for this very difficult work one could possibly find. I do not anticipate we shall have any difficulty with the Home Office in getting permission for him to undertake it as there is no Englishman who knows the work. It will mean his coaching the artists practically daily from the beginning of January until the final rehearsals in the second week in March.
>
> I have approached Mr Prerauer tentatively and he would accept a fee of 100 guineas for this two and a half month's work. This, I think, is exceptionally reasonable as he is one of the men most essential for producing the work at all.

Mase informed the central administration that the opera's personnel costs would be £576, instead of the estimated £108. On a more positive note, he reported that the projected performance had generated a great deal of public interest.

> 'Wozzeck' is the work which has caused immense interest in our Series and we are the only people who can produce it in this country. When it was suggested that Covent Garden should produce it they said it was impossible as it would take 30 full rehearsals with orchestra.
>
> We have started rehearsing our Orchestra at odd convenient times already, and therefore the strain on orchestral rehearsal at the last minute will not be excessive.

Nevertheless, Eckersley was unimpressed by the Music Department's mishandling of the project, as he wrote to Boult:

> It seems to me that the Music Department have been seriously at fault in regard to the inclusion of the Wozzeck work. The point as I understand it is that it was not known at the time of putting it into the programmes what an extraordinarily expensive show this would be, and consequently there is no money earmarked for it. Surely it should not have been included without more definite knowledge of what it involved? As it is there is likely to be considerable difficulty at this late hour in getting authority for the extra money.[156]

Less than a week later, Mase reported that the financial problems had been resolved, although he did not explain by what means.[157]

Once these hurdles were overcome, preparations proceeded relatively smoothly.[158] The opera was transmitted from the Queen's Hall on 14 March in the BBC Symphony Concert series. It was conducted by Boult, and the soloists included Richard Bitterauf in the title role, May Blyth as Marie, Parry Jones as the Captain, Tudor Davies as Andres, Mary Jarred as Margret, Percy Heming as the Doctor and Walter Widdop as the Drum-

major.[159] Given the investment in time and money for this one performance, it is not surprising that the Corporation mounted an unusually
intense publicity campaign, launched on 11 February, when Boult conducted a Sunday Orchestral Concert including the popular Three
Fragments from *Wozzeck*, as well as Webern's arrangement of the Schubert
Dances, D. 820. The performance featured soprano May Blyth, who was to
sing Marie on 14 March.

The BBC also devoted a remarkable amount of space to *Wozzeck* in its
publications. Three tactics were used to encourage listeners' interest. First,
the BBC emphasized that the broadcast offered a truly unique opportunity
for British audiences.

> This will be an event of considerable moment in the musical world, for the
> opera, though it has been played hundreds of times in Germany and made a
> *furore* in New York, has never been done over here. Nor, so far as we know, is
> it likely to be, in this country, whose chief Opera House is used for opera for
> a month or two in the summer and for half-crown hops, charity balls, and
> prize-fights during the rest of the year.[160]

Second, the BBC tried to stimulate listeners' curiosity through gruesome
descriptions of the story.

> Wozzeck himself is a soldier of the post-Napoleonic period who suffers from
> (a) inferiority complex and incipient insanity, (b) a bullying Drum Major
> who cuts him out with (c) Marie, his faithless girl. There are plenty of sensa-
> tional scenes, including a murder (by Wozzeck of Marie), a wild drinking-
> bout in an inn, and poor Wozzeck's accidental death by drowning in the
> pond into which he threw Marie; but you needn't fear for your nerves that
> night. After all, you won't actually see any of these harrowing scenes.

Finally, the Corporation publicized the extraordinary amount of time and
effort involved in the broadcast.

> The music of *Wozzeck* is exceptionally difficult to sing and to play, and
> rehearsals have been going on for some time; in fact, the principals have been
> at it since early in January. The rehearsals for the original production in
> Vienna[161] involved 320 hours of solid study; roughly a fortnight of *Wozzeck*
> without stopping for a second, or the equivalent of 140 performances.

By implication, any performance that required, and received, such intensive preparation by professionals must be worth experiencing.

In the week of the performance, the *Radio Times* featured a two-page
article by Edwin Evans, illustrated with pictures from staged productions,
which explained the history of the opera and provided a scene by scene
synopsis of the plot. Evans also described the work's musical idiom.

The composer uses Schönberg's twelve-tone system, but not slavishly. It is his servant, not his master. Many think that Berg has given a more convincing justification of Schönberg's theories than that master himself, but that may be because his sense of the theatre gave him an advantage which Schönberg, in his 'absolute' music, has lacked. The score is a marvel of skill and ingenuity. The musical substance is developed in a hundred different ways, and always with an effect corresponding to that required by the drama. In a sense it represents an entirely new technique of opera.[162]

Another extensive article, of a more philosophical nature but also illustrated with scenes from staged performances, appeared in *The Listener*. In it, M. D. Calvocoressi considered the artistic impact of the opera, unusual among modern works for its communicative powers.[163] Finally, an explanatory talk about the work was read by Leslie Heward just before the broadcast.[164]

Given such publicity, it is surprising that BBC administrators would contemplate anything that might detract from the broadcast's drawing power. Nevertheless, at the Programme Board meeting on 8 March, the Presentation Director, Wellington, 'asked whether it would be proper, in the preliminary announcement, to refer listeners to the alternative on the other wavelength. "Wozzeck" was not likely to appeal to a very wide audience. After discussion, it was agreed that this should not be done, as it might suggest an element of apology'.[165]

The general press gave the performance a significant amount of pre-concert attention. As early as 1 March, *The Daily Telegraph* published a short article, giving factual information about the BBC's preparation and a brief history of the opera's previous successes.[166] As the 14th approached, the concert received mostly positive notice in other daily papers. Even the article entitled 'Prepare to Hear "Wozzeck": It Needs Two Years' Rehearsal: And Then It's Wrong!', which appeared in *Era* on 7 March, admitted: 'This is just another of those musical events for which we must compliment the B.B.C., for without the aid of the Corporation it is hardly likely that the work would have been presented in England at all'.[167] The extensive promotion ensured that the 14 March performance was anticipated with curiosity and interest.

Not surprisingly, the concert generated an enormous number of reviews, debates, listeners' letters and editorial remarks. In the four days after the event, the BBC collected more than twenty-five lengthy articles published in response to the première.[168] It was unanimously agreed that the work had received an admirable performance and that the piece made a favourable impression. Even J. A. Forsyth, critic for *The Star* who almost invariably responded to modern music with sensational negativism, discovered that, 'although many of the sounds are curious and at time unpleasant, the music is extraordinarily clever, and never offensive, as is so much of the modern stuff'.[169] Richard Capell of *The Daily Telegraph* felt that 'the work, though not seeming so novel in style as it would have done before so much of Schönberg's music had been heard here, remains excessively difficult'.[170] Nevertheless, Edwin Evans reported in *The Daily Mail* that the music's effect on those in Queen's Hall was profound.

> Some may have withheld judgment at the outset, not certain whether what they felt to be sophistication was not going to become tedious before the end of the evening. But as the work proceeded the tension increased, and long before the catastrophe was reached it was plain that the music had gripped the audience.[171]

Many critics, including Eric Blom of the *Birmingham Post*, wondered whether a similar impact could have been made on the radio audience.

> An opera performance at two removes from the stage is not likely to be effective even where a familiar work is concerned; but when a dramatic composition, written in an idiom strange to the average music lover, is heard over the microphone sung in a foreign language, the listener's difficulty in grasping what is going on is perhaps more easily imagined than overcome.[172]

Only one criticism of the event was common to nearly all the reviews, and it concerned the limitation of hearing *Wozzeck* in a concert, rather than a staged, performance. Capell maintained that the work could not succeed without its dramatic context.

> However ungrateful it is to say so, the performance was radically an æsthetic mistake. 'Wozzeck' is an opera, an opera by a librettist of genius (Büchner), with music by a highly intelligent but academic composer, a composer of the utmost integrity, but theory-ridden and low-spirited ... A concert performance must depend wholly on the music, and Berg's music, so effective as a whispering, rustling, or sometimes horrified and strident accompaniment, does not stand on its own feet.

Even critics who were more favourably disposed to the music, such as Constant Lambert of the *Sunday Referee*, felt that the impact of the performance was marginalized.

> It is a grotesque comment on English musical life that Alban Berg's 'Wozzeck', the finest opera of recent years, should have received its first English performance not on the stage at Covent Garden but in concert form at the Queen's Hall. Brilliantly effective though it was in this form, a great deal is inevitably lost without the stage action.[173]

More severe remarks soon began to appear. *The Daily Telegraph* published a forthright article demanding a staged performance.

> The B.B.C. had gone to enormous expense and trouble over this performance – which was not wholly unsuccessful, for many who had never before taken Schönbergian music seriously were interested . . . What the B.B.C. obviously should have done was to collaborate with Covent Garden in producing 'Wozzeck'. A fortune must have been spent on last Wednesday's concert, but it will not have been wasted if – singers and players having now learnt the tricky music – that performance is regarded as a stage on the way towards giving the interesting composition in its proper form.[174]

Lambert directly blamed the Covent Garden management for the dissatisfying experience.

> While it is deplorable that the Holy Vehm who rule at Covent Garden show not the least interest in recent musical development, it is consoling to think that the B.B.C. have more intelligence, more enterprise, and more taste. I am told that the B.B.C. have offered 'Wozzeck' to Covent Garden, and have received the cold shoulder, in spite of the fact that the opera is cheap and easy to mount.[175]

Within the BBC, the concert was viewed as a huge success. At the Music Department meeting the day after the performance, 'It was unanimously agreed that much of the success of the singers in "Wozzeck" was due to the coaching by Kurt Prerauer. It was strongly felt that for "Boris" and any future operatic performances, the services of a coach would be invaluable'.[176] Boult received enough letters from listeners asking for a repeat performance that he requested Buesst to consider scheduling it; nevertheless, when an opportunity for the repeat arose a few weeks later, the Music Department presented Hindemith's *Das Unaufhörliche* instead, perhaps because another option was by then under serious consideration.[177] Just two days after the concert, Buesst – Assistant Music Director and husband of May Blyth, who had performed Marie – circulated a proposal for a staged production to interested parties, including Boult, the music programme builders, the Concerts Manager, the Orchestra Manager, the Director of Entertainment, Eckersley, and the Controller (Programmes), Dawnay.

> In view of the B.B.C.'s declared policy of collaborating with other National institutions, I suggest that it would be a fine thing for the B.B.C. to offer to Covent Garden the orchestra, cast and conductor for a couple of stage performances, on such business terms as could easily be determined by our Administrative side. This would afford the general public a long over-due opportunity of judging from a proper angle the most outstanding work of the post-war epoch.[178]

Dawnay conceded in a marginal note: 'In principle, I think the idea is a good one.'

Berg himself was strongly in favour of another British performance of his opera. He heard the transmission from Austria and immediately wrote to thank Boult:

> I am longing to tell you how yesterday's *Wozzeck* performance delighted me. In the relay from Sottens (Geneva) I heard *clearly*, and so I can judge on how high an artistic level and with what rare success the performance went forward. But I can also measure – as no one else could – what an immense preparation must have preceded this concert. It equalled the finest stage-performances with the work in the regular repertory. And so I must tell you of the one thing in this performance which did *not* please me but made me sad: that this immense amount of work, perseverance, talent and genius – in a word, that such *love* for one work (without which such success would never have been possible) – was put together only for this *one* performance, to remain only in memory when the last chord had died away.[179]

In his reply, Boult cautiously hinted that the BBC was considering another performance.

> Please excuse a typed letter in English to thank you for your most kind and delightful letter, which I enjoyed reading more than I can say . . .
> I quite agree with you how much it is to be deplored that the work cannot remain in the repertoire, but I certainly have hopes that we shall be able to find some opportunity for repeating the performance, though this is of course very uncertain in the present difficulties in our London concert life.[180]

As a further token of appreciation, Boult was presented with a full score of the opera by Universal Edition.[181] Berg also wrote to Clark: 'I want to take the opportunity to say how deeply happy the BBC Wozzeck has made me. To my admiration for the BBC is now added that for the marvellous Mr Boult.'[182]

During April 1934, the Music Department began to explore the possibility of joining forces with Covent Garden for a staged production. In a memo of 13 April, Mase tried to determine where the BBC administrators stood with respect to such a project, pointing out that before the broadcast, the Covent Garden management had rejected the possibility of producing *Wozzeck*.

> The next step is really to ascertain whether [Covent Garden] would be willing to put it on with our assistance in their next season, since it is obviously too late for this year. If they consented, well and good, if not, what would be the views of the authorities as to our taking Covent Garden to give one or two performances of it quite apart form the Covent Garden people? If

> it is not possible for us to give it on the stage at all, we are, I understand, to give another concert performance in our next symphony series.[183]

The Presentation Director, Wellington, confirmed that another concert performance of *Wozzeck* could be transmitted during the 1934–5 season, 'in view of the success of this year's broadcast'. If Covent Garden was willing to produce the opera – Wellington made no mention of BBC collaboration here – the BBC would relay it; however, it would not assume sole sponsorship of a staged performance.

> It is doubtful whether a broadcast audience would get a better performance from Covent Garden than from the Queen's Hall, and the disadvantages of competing with existing organisations in a field which does not demonstrably profit broadcasting are undoubted.[184]

Wellington was undoubtedly responding to negative reaction that had erupted in the wake of rumours concerning the BBC's staging of the opera.

> The 'Sunday Chronicle' is able to disclose that [the BBC] are to enter into direct competition with the theatres of the West End by producing 'Wozzeck' in full stage opera form over a six weeks' season.
>
> And the West End Managers' Association is up in arms about it. One possibility freely discussed in theatre circles is that the Musicians' Union and British Equity will forbid their members to play in the performance.[185]

Perhaps in light of these strong objections, the Entertainment Executive, Beadle, favoured the collaboration option: 'Looking at it from the point of view of musical propaganda, I should have thought an operatic performance at Covent Garden would be better than a Concert Hall performance at the Queen's Hall, particularly in view of the fact that the latter has already been done.'[186]

In June 1934, Wright visited Vienna and met twice with Berg to discuss a second BBC performance, considering ways that Berg could be present. As Wright relayed to Boult,

> I said that it might be possible to repeat the work next season, but that nothing was of course settled. He would very much like to be privileged to be present during the official rehearsals and performance on another occasion, and realising that we could scarcely bring him over purely for that said that he would like:
>
> (a) To accompany a group of songs in a recital.
> (b) To give a short microphone interview, if we wish, before the performance of the opera to help with the publicity.
>
> It seemed to me that it was quite a good idea to bear in mind, since newspaper interviews and so on would bring a fresh angle on the publicity question which we were unable to explore last time.[187]

Wright also reported on a reception he had attended in honour of Berg, at which he had met representatives of Universal Edition, including Kalmus and Stein, and many musicians associated with the Second Viennese circle, including Pisk, Krenek, Wellesz, Jalowitz and Zemlinsky.[188] Wright had been 'asked to convey many messages of greeting and of hearty congratulation on the artistic work steadily going forward under the aegis of the B.B.C.', as well as instructions from Berg:

> Alban Berg repeated his request that at the next performance of the Bible Scene from 'Wozzeck', Marie should speak those portions which on the occasion of the complete opera performance we allowed Prerauer to persuade her to sing. He emphasised that the actual pitch indicated by the score need not be rigidly adhered to, so long as the general inflectional curve was realised.

By the end of June, progress had been made with Covent Garden. Mase and Geoffrey Toye, the managing director of the Royal Opera, found a way to divide the burden of responsibility.

> [Toye] thinks something might be possible on the lines of our providing orch., conductor & artists and they house, scenery & production. He is talking to Beecham about it next week. End of April seems a suitable time (beginning of CG Season) and that would probably suit us best too. He thinks 2 performances, so do I. [189]

Nevertheless, when Michaud, Universal Edition's London representative, prompted the BBC for news just a few days later, he received no direct reply.[190] By August, Wright felt it was time to convene a committee to deal with logistical questions. He was particularly adamant that he and Clark should be involved: 'Mr Woodgate has never seen the opera on the stage, whereas Mr Clark and I have three times, and I believe the former has been to rehearsals as well in Vienna.'[191] On the day that Wright circulated that memo, 14 August 1934, Sir Henry Wood conducted the BBC Symphony Orchestra in a Promenade Concert that included Respighi's *Fontane di Roma*, a Tchaikovsky aria with baritone Percy Heming, Bax's Fantasy for viola and orchestra with Lionel Tertis, Debussy's *La mer*, and the *Wozzeck* Fragments, with soprano May Blyth.

On 23 August, Wright was finally able to send hopeful news to Berg:

> We are looking into the question of the possibility of giving 'Wozzeck' at Covent Garden. At the moment it is quite impossible to say if the plans we have in mind will mature, but at least we would like to be ready with a definite proposal should circumstances prove propitious . . . [We] need scarcely say how happy we shall be if we can follow up the successful concert performance of 'Wozzeck' with a really fine opera house performance.[192]

He also confirmed that the BBC would bring the composer to London.

> You mentioned how much you would like to come over with your wife in the event of our performing 'Wozzeck' again. It is agreed in principle that we should invite you to accompany a recital of your songs in the studio during the same period, and this would enable you to be here at the time. You could assist us materially in Press interviews, etc., in obtaining publicity for the performance of the opera.

Berg replied enthusiastically:

> It would of course be wonderful if the richly deserved resurrection of the magnificent BBC performance of 'Wozzeck' were to be celebrated at Covent Garden, and I for my part would willingly do all in my power towards it. In other words, come to the final rehearsals, possibly give a lecture, give interviews, etc, etc. Naturally also accompany lieder and make myself useful in other ways. Gentlemen, I am entirely at your disposal![193]

He gave casting advice and recommended that Carl Ebert – the German-born production manager at the newly-established Glyndebourne Festival – be engaged as director, if there was no suitable British candidate.

Over the following months, many memos and other correspondence relating to casting, estimated costs, scenery arrangements, producers and rehearsals for the staged production were exchanged within the BBC. [194] In December, just four months before the performances were to take place, Wright met with Boult and the proposed director, Dr Otto Erhardt, to clarify the status of the project.

> [Boult] said that the whole matter was unfortunately still undecided, but the sketch of rehearsals had been drawn up in order that on a decision being reached to include the opera no general upset of other plans would be involved. He also mentioned that the sketches for an English made set for the opera appeared good. I asked that those of us on this side who knew most about opera in general and 'Wozzeck' in particular and especially yourself and Mr Clark should be consulted on all creative matters, such as production, setting, etc., in fact, everything, as it has musical implication in which we might be able to help. I understand that Music Ex. is centralising all the known information with regard to the scheme.[195]

The plans steamed on during January 1935, and Erhardt travelled to Vienna to discuss production details with the composer.[196]

Nevertheless, financial negotiations between the Music Department and Covent Garden began to break down in January. Kalmus of Universal Edition, Vienna, wrote an urgent letter to Boult in support of the project, emphasizing its importance to Berg, who did not yet know of the problems.[197] Despite all the hard work and enthusiastic ideas, Covent Garden

and the BBC could not reach agreement and, a few weeks later, the project
was abandoned. On 12 February, the decision was explained to the Music
Programme Advisory Panel:

> Covent Garden had refused to contribute anything in the nature of expenses,
> although the demands made by the B.B.C. in this respect had been very rea-
> sonable, consisting merely of scenery and costumes, which, in view of the
> amount of money contributed to them by the Corporation seemed perfectly
> fair.
>
> The Panel unanimously wished it to be recorded that they deplored the
> breakdown in the negotiations, and urged that it be not allowed to fall
> through altogether.[198]

Two days later, Boult informed Kalmus and Erhardt that the staged production was to be postponed.[199] On 19 February, Berg wrote to Boult
about other BBC performances planned for that spring, and concluded:

> I hear that the Covent Garden performance of 'Wozzeck' is suddenly facing
> difficulties. That astounds me, since after all that has happened so far one
> was entitled to assume that the event could be regarded as absolutely certain.
> I do not need to tell you how taken aback I was by this news. Not only for the
> obvious reason that the chance to utilize this fabulous BBC performance
> would be lacking, but also for more personal reasons: The news of the stage
> performance of 'Wozzeck' has been for weeks, nay, months *so generally*
> known and circulated in all European and American newspapers that a
> failure to happen or a cancellation of this performance would be seen
> throughout the world as a direct humiliation for me.
>
> I do not mind saying this *in front of you*, Mr Boult, since I know that there
> is scarcely anyone who understands as well as you what the performance of
> Wozzeck a year ago in the BBC has meant for the work and for modern music
> generally; the present stage performance represents the culmination of this
> achievement, this idea – an idea which apparently seems to be missing in the
> German-speaking world.[200]

Boult's reply provides a complete explanation of what happened:

> I cannot tell you what a grief it has been to think that this prospective perfor-
> mance of 'Wozzeck' has fallen through. I am more than sorry that the matter
> should have been spread about so much beforehand, but, as sometimes
> happens, the basis on which the agreement was being made seems to have
> been built on a misunderstanding. I think there is no harm in my telling you
> privately what the issue was: the arrangement as we understood it was the
> Covent Garden was to be responsible for the stage and the B.B.C. for the
> Orchestra and the singers. Now Covent Garden are saying that they never
> intended to undertake any expense in connection with the stage and scenery,
> and you will readily understand that we as a broadcasting authority could

never justify before Parliament an expenditure on scenery and dresses for the benefit of the seeing audience.

We have been offered a smaller theatre by the authorities of the Old Vic, which you may have heard of as doing wonderful work for Opera in the poorer quarters of London. We will let you know how these negotiations proceed, and in any case, though I can make no promises, I certainly hope that the full score of 'Wozzeck', which was so kindly presented to me by Doktor Kalmus, will not remain unopened much longer.[201]

Although the BBC explored other possibilities, including a more economical version for reduced orchestration, the staged performance was never realized.[202] In fact, *Wozzeck* did not receive a staged performance in Britain until January 1952, when it was produced at Covent Garden under the direction of Erich Kleiber.

The 1932–3 and 1933–4 seasons witnessed a decisive swing in BBC interest away from Schoenberg and toward his former pupil, Berg. The latter's compositional style attracted BBC notice because of its relative accessibility, its emotional power and its commercial possibilities. Since *Wozzeck* was unlikely to be produced by another British institution, the BBC's exclusive association with this influential work led to highly favourable press attention. Thus, although a significant number of works by other members of the Second Viennese circle were broadcast during this period, they were overshadowed by the attention accorded to Berg. Of the nine occasions on which Berg's works were broadcast during these seasons, no fewer than four involved *Wozzeck*, with three presentations of the concert excerpts and one of the complete work. The long-awaited staging of the opera failed to materialize in spring 1935; nevertheless, the negotiations, arrangements and publicity relating to that performance and others involving Berg's music in the 1934–5 season only served to increase BBC and British interest in this remarkable composer.

# 10   Policies and politics, 1934–1935, 1935–1936

By the mid-1930s, many political, economic and sociological characteristics of the decade were already established, although the full consequences of these trends were not to be realized for some time to come. The rapid rise to power of political extremists, and the reactions to this phenomenon, led to tensions and pressures of shifting populations, as well as ideological stances emphasizing national interests, in place of the international cosmopolitanism of the previous decade. The British Broadcasting Corporation approached its tenth year at the end of 1936, and these forces led to external and internal reassessments of the parameters and goals of this large, complex and extremely influential organization.

Significantly, the entire BBC came under public scrutiny during these years. In spring 1935, the Ullswater Committee, representing the three major political parties, was appointed by Parliament to review the BBC's broadcasting activities and to recommend the direction broadcasting should take after the royal charter expired on 31 December 1936. During this time of public assessment, the BBC was anxious to verify that each division, branch and section was running smoothly and efficiently. Departmental structures and programming policies, particularly concerning the broadcasting of contemporary music, were seriously questioned. Because the various arguments and issues are symptomatic of the BBC's maturing position within British social and cultural life during this period, they are considered in detail in this chapter.

## Personnel shifts

Within the Music Department, the organization and duty allocation of the creative sections were examined, from the Music Director's position down, in a series of reviews. Significantly, Boult requested that the department's status be upgraded to that of a branch. The central administrators were adamant that before that could be considered, efficiency had to be improved. The move toward improving standards provoked the now familiar requests for additional staff help. Around this time, there was also general recognition that Boult's dual role as Chief Conductor and Music Director had become untenable: the central administrators were determined to appoint a separate administrative leader.

*Restructuring the programme building section, spring 1935*

During 1934–5, minimal staffing changes occurred within the music programme building section;[1] however, dynamics within it deteriorated significantly in autumn 1934 and quality of work reached unacceptably low
levels. Mase brought the situation to the attention of the Entertainment
Executive, Beadle, who reported:

> All this [Mase] believes to be due to lack of co-ordination and leadership.
> There is nobody in the Department prepared to take decisions and stick to
> them . . . The trouble as I see it is that the musicians we have who are really
> capable of getting a job of work done in the way it should be done, are not
> placed in positions where they can make themselves adequately felt. The
> people I have in mind are Howgill; W. W. Thompson; in perhaps a lesser
> degree, Wright and Herbage; and in spite of certain well-known disadvan-
> tages, Mase.[2]

Beadle's assessment reveals another instance in which staff with strong
administrative skills – Howgill, the Programme Services Executive, and
Thompson, the Concerts Manager – were valued above those perceived as
having more artistic inclinations. Beadle warned that the situation had
degenerated to the point that Wright was applying for a transfer. The
memo served as a catalyst for action. Just four days later, the Director of
Internal Administration, Nicolls, informed Boult:

> From to-day Mr Buesst is to be superseded as A.M.D. and . . . temporarily Mr
> K. A. Wright will act in his place until further notice. Mr Buesst will continue
> in the Music Department, if he so wishes, with programme building and
> other duties.[3]

An unsigned memo, probably prepared by Wright, outlined the specific
responsibilities of the programme builders up to September 1935.[4] The
section then consisted of Wright, Clark, Herbage, Buesst, Phillips, Perry,
O'Donnell and Woodgate. As Assistant Music Director, Wright supervised
the section's work. He attended various meetings, sometimes in Boult's
place, including weekly departmental and advisory panel gatherings, acted
on central administrative decisions, and continued as the main link with
the Presentation Department. Significantly, Clark was now number two in
the section, displacing Herbage. He was responsible for orchestral programmes and attended meetings, including those of the Music
Department and the Music Programme Advisory Panel. Clark also met
with the Presentation Director and the editors of the *Radio Times* and *The
Listener*, attended auditions and continued to provide information about
music events on the continent. Herbage, now Wright's assistant and third

in the hierarchy, was responsible for the 'Foundations of Music' series, as well as for the research and development of early music programmes, often dealing with issues of performance practice. Herbage, too, met with the Music Programme Advisory Panel, and also with Wright and Clark 'on all important series and questions of musical policy', the core of the section thus remaining intact.

Following his demotion, Buesst served as department representative at rehearsals of visiting artists and conductors, at concerts and for social occasions. He heard auditions, conducted, took part in meetings of the Music Programme Advisory Panel, and read manuscript scores submitted to the Corporation. Phillips built the solo and chamber music recitals, as well as the contemporary concerts, military band concerts and less important orchestral programmes. Perry was responsible for the light music programmes, organ recitals and brass band concerts. He was involved with studio opera and also attended auditions. Finally, Woodgate was involved with choral programming, and O'Donnell conducted military band programmes, and assisted with string auditions and with some orchestra concerts.

In March 1935, Mase asked Beadle for more staff to help with light music and organ programmes, with the 'Foundations of Music' series and with orchestral programmes.

> The stage has been reached and passed where the work has become too great, and we are behind on many of the programme schemes. It is necessary to have another man to assist in order that Mr Clark may be more available for the bigger schemes. At present, the hand to mouth necessity of studio programmes renders consultation with conductors and artists, and research of works and their requirements, etc., much too perfunctory, and proper advance planning is not possible . . . It is much too haphazard, and innumerable things are not properly covered.[5]

A new studio opera section was being formed at this time, which would also need suitable staff.[6] Wright and Mase proposed a completely new structure that would resolve all these problems. The programme building section would be divided into four subsections each consisting of a team, headed by a core programme builder, which was responsible for planning programmes in specific genres.[7] The first team, headed by Clark, would build orchestral, military band, brass band and choral programmes. The second, led by Herbage, would handle chamber music programmes and all recitals. The third, devoted to opera, was to be headed by the conductor, Clarence Raybould. The final team, dealing with light music, would consist of new recruits. The plan required four additional staff members.

In April, Nicolls recommended that the scheme be implemented, approving the formation of the opera section and the hiring of three assistants.[8] A month later, the reorganization was approved, full details of the secondary staff structure were worked out over the summer months,[9] and the reorganization took effect in September 1935. Buesst was no longer employed on a full-time basis, retained only on 'a programme contract . . . covering occasional conducting and reading'.[10] New staff included: Maurice Johnstone, a new recruit, appointed as Clark's assistant; the well-known entertainer and arranger, Leslie Bridgewater, appointed in October 1935 to head the light music subsection; Horace Dann, who had worked in the balance and control section of the Music Department since 1932, became his assistant; and finally, A. C. Lewis, another new recruit, assisted Herbage.[11] This comprehensive restructuring was implemented to relieve pressure and to increase efficiency and quality of output – both prerequisites for the department's eligibility for elevation to branch status.

## Dividing Boult's position

The other condition – that of dividing Boult's job into two positions – was also under discussion during these months. This option was considered as early as 1933,[12] but only in 1935 did the central administrators take action. In March, Nicolls confirmed that Boult would retain the post of Chief Conductor, while a new administrative head of the Music Department would be sought.[13] The appointee would initially hold the title Deputy Music Director; once he proved himself, he would be promoted to Music Director. Nicolls outlined the ideal candidate's qualities:

> For our D.M.D. we want a man who:
> (i)    is preferably not an executant (conductor, composer, etc.);
> (ii)   has the encyclopaedic knowledge of a Tovey;
> (iii)  has a decisive mind and is able to control staff;
> (iv)   has artistic integrity;
> (v)    must be recognisable by the Profession and the public to some extent as a suitably qualified musician.

The first item again demonstrates Nicolls's prejudice against creative artists in administrative roles, though he grudgingly conceded that a musician was required for this particular position.

In August, when the staff reorganization had been successfully implemented, Boult again brought up the matter of his own position. In spring 1933 he had unequivocally recommended Arthur Bliss as the best person for the job of Assistant Music Director, and reiterated this opinion now:

> There is no question that by far the least dislocation would be caused by the introduction of Mr Arthur Bliss. I think he could be persuaded to come for a time at any rate. The staff know him and like him, and it would be of enormous value that a man whose name is now being recognised in Europe and America as a composer of real importance should join us in an administrative capacity.[14]

Eckersley agreed with this recommendation.

> I think the idea of appointing Arthur Bliss as Music Director is a good one. I do not know from first hand knowledge anything of his powers administratively, but I have always found him businesslike, quick to take a decision, and incisive in his outlook and manner. The field from which we could draw a Music Director is very limited and I know of only two or three other names which could be considered as possibilities, so that this makes the Bliss suggestion all the more attractive.[15]

However, Wright strongly opposed the idea for two fundamental reasons. First, he believed that Boult's experience made him uniquely qualified for the job:

> Our appointment, which combines Music Director and Chief Conductor, represents the greatest musical responsibility in the world, and Dr Boult is the one man we can imagine holding that job down. He has grown up in it five years, and has helped to build up the edifice.[16]

Wright also opposed change at that time, because he believed the staff reorganization would relieve pressure on the Music Director. Wright himself would

> be free to be in touch with everything concerning our work without having to bury myself in details, and make it my business to keep Dr Boult informed of every important point, getting his reaction where necessary. A development of my 'verbal précis' technique will under the new conditions enable me to do this and to keep a great deal of correspondence, memoranda, articles etc. from Dr Boult's desk. If, supposing a new Music Director be appointed, Dr Boult is still nominally in charge, he still would need this 'feeding' with information, which I submit can be done better by one who has grown up in every phase of our work than by an outsider, however quick and a musician he may be.

Moreover, Wright suggested that 'the haunting feeling of responsibility for everything that is going on in programmes, in artists' booking, in research, etc.', should be reassigned to the Music Programme Advisory Panel. He proposed that Bliss be appointed the panel's chairman and take over responsibility for regional music policy.

> Perhaps [Bliss] could carry both the Panel and this Regional job of contacting and giving practical help and encouragement around the country: the linking of the two responsibilities could only be an additional advantage.

Finally, Wright recognized that the changed focus of his own duties would result in insufficient supervision over music programme building. He made one further recommendation:

> I foresee the desirability before long of creating an important programme-centralising position in the Department, and am convinced that Mr Edward Clark should be the man for promotion. He might be called 'Music Programme Director' or 'Music Programmes', and, assisted by a good man (Johnston[e]) should continue to do all work on the draft, fed by his immediate colleagues, and also be responsible for his orchestra-band-chorus group as now. It would emphasise his position as third senior in the Department, and again free me from more routine detail.

Boult's, Eckersley's and Wright's recommendations were evaluated by the central administrators. Dawnay advised Reith that Boult's job should be divided, as Boult and Eckersley proposed, and agreed that Bliss was the best candidate. He also suggested Geoffrey Shaw, a respected music educator, and Francis Toye, the writer on music who had been considered for the position in 1933.[17] The administrators approved the recommendations, stipulating that before they were made public, the Board of Governors should be notified.[18] The Governors also agreed, 'provided a satisfactory candidate for the [Music Director] position could be found'.[19]

Not surprisingly, the Music Advisory Committee were less willing to give consent: 'Sir Hugh Allen urged that such re-organisation was a matter of the utmost importance, both to the B.B.C. and the musical world, and asked that the Committee should be fully consulted before any appointment was made.'[20] Members were unanimously agreed in their verdict – one of the rare occasions for which this was true.

> D.G. reported fairly fully on the last meeting of the Music Advisory Committee at which Mr Graves took the chair, and also on a meeting which he had had with Sir Landon Ronald, Sir John McEwen and Sir Hugh Allen. He said that ultimately they all supported the idea of a split in the Music Department, but that they were unanimous in saying that the new Director should not be Arthur Bliss. They had no constructive suggestion to make.[21]

The committee eventually approved the decision to divide Boult's position, with the proviso that 'the consideration of names of likely candidates for the post of Director of Music should be considered by a Sub-Committee consisting of Sir Hugh Allen, Sir John McEwen, and Sir Landon Ronald'.[22]

The search for a musician with the appropriate qualities finally began. In late February 1936, Reith interviewed Boult's long-time friend, R. S. Thatcher: 'An hour with one Dr. Thatcher, Music Master at Harrow, for Music Directorship. He told Graves I gave him a gruelling time. I think he might do.'[23] The advisory subcommittee continued to propose alternative suggestions, as Reith recorded in his diary on 3 March:

> Ronald to see me, followed by Allen quarter of an hour later. They proposed that Wright and Mase should be Music Director jointly, the Panel meets weekly, a Sub Comte. of the M.A.C. fortnightly and the M.A.C. monthly. I kept my patience and they departed very shortly quite satisfied that Thatcher shd. be Music Director on his own.[24]

The following day, he interviewed another eminent musician: 'Lunched . . . with MacEwen [sic] and Marchant, the St Paul's organist who would like to be considered for our Music Directorship; a nice fellow and quite a good man but not as good as Thatcher.'[25] Reith reported to the Board of Governors:

> He had done all he could to get suitable candidates for this job, but . . . after consultation with the three musical knights the only possibilities seemed to be Dr Marchant, the Organist at St Pauls, and Dr Thatcher, Music Master at Harrow. Chairman [R. C. Norman] and Mrs Hamilton [another Governor] to see these two.[26]

The Governors interviewed the candidates, but were not satisfied that either had the required qualities.[27] The central administrators proposed that the Assistant Director of Programme Administration, Howgill – respected both as an experienced administrator and a talented composer – be transferred into the department as Boult's assistant.

> Possibility of moving Mr Howgill to Music Department considered, Dr Boult retaining final responsibility. Doubt was expressed as to whether that would be acceptable to the Music Profession. C(P) explained that in his opinion experience of broadcasting carried a great deal of weight in such an appointment, but if there were an outsider with outstanding qualifications he would still consider appointing a new man.[28]

The decision to divide Boult's position was finally abandoned. On 29 April 1936, the Board of Governors officially sanctioned this:

> Decided that the previous decision to separate the functions of Conductor of the Orchestra and Director of the Music Department could not be implemented as it had been impossible to find a candidate to fulfil all the requirements of Music Director; that the organisation should remain as at present, Dr Boult being relieved of administrative work, and a new Deputy Music Director being appointed.[29]

The Board determined that Thatcher should be offered that appointment. Significantly, Mrs Hamilton, the Governor most closely associated with Music Department concerns, 'refrained from voting on the proposal to appoint Dr Thatcher, she being in favour . . . of Mr Wright being retained as Assistant Music Director'. Despite this vote of confidence for the long-serving Wright, Thatcher was appointed and began his BBC work in January 1937.[30] At last, Boult had the assistance he had been seeking, as he recalled in his memoirs:

> It was not until 1937 when Reginald Thatcher, an old Oxford friend, who was then Director of Music at Harrow, came in as Deputy-Director that I could really feel that the responsibility could be shared, particularly in the upward direction of Administration.[31]

Boult remained at the helm of the orchestra and the department, assisted by Thatcher, a respected and capable member of the music profession. This arrangement remained in effect into the war years.

## The Music Programme Advisory Panel

During the 1934–5 season, the Music Programme Advisory Panel became a vital part of music programming procedure. Each Tuesday, the panel members joined the programme building staff in looking over a projected weekly schedule under consideration for future transmission. The panel routinely discussed a variety of issues pertaining to the music pro-grammes, frequent topics including: (1) seasonal planning for the regular music series, such as 'Foundations of Music' recitals, symphony concerts, Promenade concerts, public chamber music recitals and contemporary concerts; (2) setting dates and discussing repertory for BBC-sponsored music festivals; (3) considering the creation of new series or festivals, or ways to mark special events through the music programmes; (4) planning for BBC Symphony Orchestra tours; (5) inviting various performers and conductors to broadcast; (6) planning broadcasts of new or early works; (7) requesting certain composers to submit pieces for transmission; (8) discussing the presentation of music listings in the *Radio Times* and other BBC publications; (9) considering speakers for talks relating to specific programmes or series; and (10) discussing practical problems, such as audition procedures or the overabundance of artists approved for broad-casting.[32] The panel often concluded their meetings by listening to a broadcast or a Blattnerphone recording.[33]

In July 1934, the official duties of the panel were expanded to include reading and evaluating scores submitted for broadcasting consideration.[34]

The score submission procedure resembled a competition: composers submitted manuscripts, which were then evaluated by Music Department staff or external readers. Each score was either rejected or approved for broadcasting. If accepted, the work received a rough rating indicating whether the BBC should sponsor a performance, in the case of an outstanding score, or whether it should be broadcast only if proposed by an engaged performer.[35] The number of submitted scores increased each year, presenting the Music Department with two practical problems. First, the scores had to be evaluated fairly and swiftly. In the days before easy copying methods were available, composers often needed their manuscripts for other performance opportunities. Second, the programme builders had to find ways to accommodate accepted works within the broadcast schedules. Excerpts from panel discussions in autumn 1934 illustrate the difficulties:

> Mr Bliss asked to be informed as to the position in regard to works which although not great were nevertheless worthy of performance, and questioned whether such works could not be dealt with in a more direct way instead of being held over until the prescribed period. The difficulties of fitting works into programmes even after they had been accepted for performance was explained.
>
> It was asked whether composers at any time had been encouraged in the belief that by writing for a smaller orchestra or for a special combination of instruments their works would have a greater chance of performance. Mr Herbage deprecated this idea and considered it most inadvisable in every way, it being the B.B.C.'s function to encourage creative work in any form ... Many works are unfortunately just too good to be entirely rejected, yet not sufficiently so to have hope of success. Really good works could always be used, but their number was so very limited.[36]

Procedures remained unchanged over subsequent months, and the practical difficulties did not diminish.[37] The panel was particularly concerned at the lack of broadcast opportunities, since many of the selected works had been submitted by talented British composers. Representation of British musical interests had been a fundamental aim behind the panel's formation; by score reading and by challenging Music Department attitudes and procedures, the panel demonstrated its commitment to promoting these particular interests.

From the first meeting of the panel, Bliss proved a dominant force, recommending that the Corporation take immediate steps to publicize programme policies and to enhance public perceptions of music broadcasts and the BBC Symphony Orchestra.[38] In August 1934, he wrote to Boult, strongly advocating measures to achieve these goals. In a suggestion that greatly overstepped his jurisdiction, he emphasized the need for a major alteration to the Music Department's organization and policy structure: in its present state, Bliss believed, the department was impeded by the decisions and policies of central authority.

> It is quite plain to me as a member of the Advisory Panel that things are not going right in the Music Department. The trouble lies not inside but outside the department. The members of the programme committee are keen, loyal and amazingly efficient and disinterested where their work is concerned. One really feels the greatest respect for them. BUT they are being continually thwarted and checked on the main policies which determine the future of music by higher authority – They have no power . . .
>
> Difficulties of all kinds would be minimised if *you* were Director of the whole Music Dept. responsible *only* to the Director-General. It is absolutely necessary that Music be an independent entity under yourself.[39]

The central administrators were perturbed by this letter. Not only did they disagree with the main principles, but the discussions about splitting Boult's position and elevating the department to a branch were confidential, and they doubted that Bliss could come to such conclusions from his panel work. However, Boult denied having spoken to him on the subject.[40] As Eckersley wrote to the Controller of Programmes, Dawnay:

> A highly mischievous letter, written apparently without any kind of knowledge of the problems of broadcasting as a whole – It assumes that music qua music must as a sine qua non have entirely preferential treatment as opposed to all the other activities which go to build the whole programmes.[41]

Dawnay prepared the official response, the strongly worded conclusion demonstrating its tone:

> I trust that what I have said . . . will have made it clear that it would not be possible or right, either in theory or in practice, to give special preferential treatment within the organisation to any one department. There is no question in the minds of those responsible here of any deliberate thwarting or checking – to use your own expression. If matters are not always decided in accordance with the recommendations of those directly responsible within the Music Department, you may be certain that an adverse decision has been taken only with the general broadcast programme in mind, and in the interests of listeners as a whole. I am certainly not aware of any 'continual thwarting'. On the contrary, I should have said that within its own sphere the recommendations of the Music Department are nearly always accepted.[42]

Nevertheless, Bliss firmly asserted his right to criticize the Corporation's fundamental policies.

> As I see it, the only raison d'etre for the existence of the Advisory Panel is the opportunity it gives to offer constructive comment such as a new comer into any organization can often profitably do. My letter to Dr Boult was therefore the first of several that I intend sending to the Music Director during my temporary appointment. Whether he passes the recommendations to higher authority is entirely at his discretion.[43]

Bliss was thus responsible for widening the panel's prerogative, and meetings regularly included discussions of policy matters, which the music staff welcomed. As Wright reported to Boult: 'While they all want not to lose contact with detailed programmes of importance, they like general discussions on policy matters: I told them frankly that we had been extremely glad of their support in these matters.'[44] In striking contrast to the volatile Music Advisory Committee, the panel worked closely and harmoniously with Music Department staff. It is interesting to note that two years later, the central administrators worried that the panel's influence had become too great. Graves, then the Controller (Programmes), expressed his reservations:

> For some time I have been bothered about the functions of this body which are to scrutinise the week's programmes and to comment thereon. It was set up on the initiative of the M.A.C. and its primary use is to act as a buffer between us and the music loving public, i.e. when we are criticised by certain sections of listeners we can always say that programmes have passed scrutiny of three qualified musicians not connected with the B.B.C. I have always felt that the Music Department use the Panel far more than they need or should . . . It is for the B.B.C. itself to make these decisions, though there is, of course, no objection to asking the Panel for its views.[45]

However, Grave's assistant, Wellington, defended the panel's vital role in departmental activities:

> [Thatcher] makes the observation . . . that in this committee of three he has a consultant panel of great wisdom, experience and range, and that he goes out of his way to make the utmost use of this reservoir of experience. In other words he picks their brains as extensively as possible, but does not leave *decision* with them, though naturally he often takes their advice. This seems to me to be a very wise attitude, of which I am sure you will approve.[46]

In a wide-ranging and satisfactory way, the Music Programme Advisory Panel thus fulfilled a highly significant function: its members not only served as representatives of the music profession within the Music Department, but offered ideas and experience that were recognized, valued and encouraged by department staff and by central administrators of the BBC.

## Music programming policy

During the mid-1930s, the fundamental policy behind BBC music pro-gramming – to bring programmes of the highest quality to listeners – con-tinued to be challenged on nationalist grounds. Another aspect of the Corporation's basic tenet was also undermined around this time: the early BBC view that 'few know what they want, and very few what they need' was no longer acceptable to high-level administrators of the mid-1930s. They endorsed the idea that programme popularity and accessibility – meas-ured in box office sales, since the BBC did not measure audience size or reaction in other ways until 1938 – should be a significant factor in pro-gramme building. Tensions once again increased, since some members of the Music Advisory Committee and the music programme builders ada-mantly disagreed with this view.

The issue was first raised in June 1934 when the Concerts Committee, a group of BBC staff 'responsible solely for the administration and manage-ment of B.B.C. public concerts',[47] prepared a report on the 1933–4 Queen's Hall Symphony Concerts. Criticism focused on the consistently disap-pointing attendance levels, and the report recommended ways to remedy this problem. The committee's main premise was that 'it would be a mistake to continue public concerts without more care to ensure their success as such', and success would be ensured if new programming tactics were implemented. Two points directly affected the programming of con-temporary music . First, the committee recommended that box office con-siderations influence the planning of the concerts. Large-scale works that were completely unfamiliar – particularly new works – should not be included, although the committee conceded that 'good box office pro-grammes could be devised by the programme builders without rigid adherence to well-known works'. In other words, the programmes did not have to consist entirely of familiar favourites, but a balance should be achieved between well-known and unknown repertory. Second, the char-acter of each concert series should be better defined in terms of large-scale planning.

### The BBC's responsibility to the box office and the music profession

The Music Advisory Committee discussed the Concert Committee's rec-ommendations at length in June 1934.[48] Its members agreed that the overall programme scheme would be improved by long-term planning, but opposed other points; most significantly: 'The [Music Advisory] Committee considered that the B.B.C. could afford to ignore box office considerations, and that to adopt such a policy would be retrograde.' Beadle, the Entertainment Executive and chairman of the Concerts Committee, disagreed, clarifying the central administrators' view: 'Though the Corporation did not look upon its public Symphony Concerts as money making ventures, it was important to ensure that they were successful as public concerts.'[49] On another point, the advisory committee concurred that attractive programmes should not be limited to the familiar.

> The Committee thought that if this measure was adopted, the distinctive character of the B.B.C. Public Symphony Concerts would be lost. They stressed the attention devoted by press critics to the new and unusual works hitherto included in B.B.C. Public Symphony Concerts. The performance of these works elsewhere would not attract the same amount of attention.

The Concert Committee's report thus provoked the Music Advisory Committee to formulate and express its views on these significant issues, instigating a debate that continued to the end of the decade.

In autumn 1934, tensions between the BBC and the Music Advisory Committee escalated over the nationalism and box office issues. At the October meeting, the question of excluding foreign artists from broadcasts was re-opened:

> Some members said they felt it was the duty of the Corporation to give the best programmes possible from an artistic point of view with the exclusive use of British artists. This was diametrically opposed to the views of others who felt that the best programmes could only be given without any restrictions as to nationality.[50]

Boult responded with a practical compromise, which was already Music Department procedure:

> The Public Concerts, both Symphony and Chamber, were the peak points of our year's musical work and that it was considered proper to include in them the finest artists procurable. Where artistic considerations were equal, preference would always be given to British artists.

Before the next meeting, the Music Department collected statistics about foreign artists who had participated in the previous season's public concerts. Of the soloists, 255 had been British and 47 of other nationality.[51] The number of British and foreign conductors, singers and other soloists who had performed in BBC Symphony Concerts between the 1930–1 and the 1934–5 seasons was also tabulated,[52] provoking Boult to stress quality considerations once again:

> It would be possible for the Corporation to employ only British Artists for all its work. This would inevitably lower the standard of performance, and

therefore also the importance of the Concerts. Thus an appearance at the Corporation's Concerts would gradually come to have less value and give less prestige to those employed there. If Foreign Artists are to be used, they must come into the programmes on the basis of the use of the finest available artist for each occasion.

At the Music Advisory Committee meeting on 14 December, discussions of these issues heated into unpleasant exchanges. In a subsequent report, Eckersley outlined the committee members' specific views on the foreign artists question.

> McEwen, although I believe he has since denied it, did actually say that he thought it was the duty of the B.B.C. to use British artists only in public as well as studio work. Sir Hugh Allen, Waddington, and Dale, were, to an extent, on his side, not so much saying that we should never use foreign artists but that our first and real responsibility was towards British artists, especially at public concerts. Walford Davies and Bliss, on the other hand, were entirely in favour of using the best artists irrespective of nationality. We are all agreed that where standards are equal, British artists should be given preference, but I am wholly in favour of a policy in which art and not nationality comes first.[53]

Discussion also focused on the box office question, and Eckersley once again sided with Boult:

> I agree with what M.D. has to say about building programmes to attract audiences and that in general terms a successful concert and a successful broadcast can only be achieved by virtue of a full house. This does not mean that we shall omit to do new and other works which may not have so general an appeal. There is plenty of room to include these and at the same time build popular and interesting programmes.

Eckersley recommended that the Director-General quell further arguments by presenting official policy statements on these issues at the next meeting. He assured Reith, 'if any member of the committee finds himself unable to agree with [them], he always has his own remedy, but I do not think it will come to any resignations'. Boult prepared both statements. In the draft statement concerning foreign artists, he reiterated his position:

> The Corporation is working every year towards a closer inter-relation of its various programme series, and inevitably its public activities must be maintained as the peak series of the year. It is felt that this can only be adequately done by the employment, in these series, of the finest solo artists that can be found for any given work. Throughout the whole range our endeavour is to use British artists whenever artistic considerations are equal.[54]

The statement was accompanied by statistics clearly illustrating that over the previous five seasons, the BBC had more than adequately supported native musicians. Boult also argued that international artists' broadcasts provided models of excellence for local musicians, encouraging improvement of British performance standards. Boult's statement on the box office question was brief:

> The Corporation considers it essential for its own prestige and for the maintenance of a high standard of orchestral playing, that it should give public concerts.
>
> Both these objects will be unfulfilled if these concerts fail to draw large paying audiences. An empty or papered hall would show that the concert has been badly organized, which fact would neither add prestige to the Corporation nor encourage the Orchestra to continued improvement.
>
> The Corporation further believes that Box Office returns are an indication of the feeling of listeners. A programme which fails to fill Queen's Hall correspondingly fails to draw the interest of a large wireless audience.

At the Music Advisory Committee meeting on 14 February 1935, the foreign artists policy was circulated and accepted with little comment.[55] However, the committee took exception to the statement on box office policy.[56] Discussion of this matter continued for months, not only in meetings of the external advisors but also internally, amongst BBC staff.

In January 1935, Nicolls complained to the Director-General that the Music Department had presented public concerts that were inappropriate for the intended audience. On each occasion, the programmers refused to alter the programme plan, and the concert failed to draw a sufficient audience. In fact, in 1933–4 the failure of certain public concerts featuring large-scale contemporary works led Nicolls to ban contemporary music from public concerts.

> At the end of last season, after the fiasco with the Hindemith Oratorio in the May Festival, I made the ruling that, generally speaking, exotic works should be done in the studio and not in the Queen's Hall. Perhaps it is wrong to say that I made the ruling, because to a certain extent that would have been ultra vires, but I refused to agree to a proposal for taking the Central Hall, Westminster, to do concerts of contemporary music in and generally let it be understood that the inclusion of works like the Hindemith in the Queen's Hall programmes would be contested administratively.[57]

Nicolls and Boult agreed that public concerts should attract the general public, but whereas Boult believed that programmes could include unfamiliar repertory, Nicolls stressed: 'Everyone recognises that the public concerts would be incomplete without occasional novelties and experiments, but I maintain that programmes should be built in such a way as to ensure the effect of the experiments being minimised by attractive items in other parts of the concert'. Nicolls actively endorsed and campaigned for a policy which aimed simply to cater to public appeal, while the music programmers upheld the right to build programmes on musical grounds.

The Concerts Committee was asked to state its position on this question. Not surprisingly, perhaps, the committee disagreed with everyone else.

> It is hardly necessary to point out that the Concerts Committee are wholly out of sympathy with the wishes of the M.A.C. and they hold very firmly to the view that public concerts are not worth giving at all unless they are successful from the box office point of view . . . The programmes should be composed largely of works which have stood the test of time, and are popular, firstly because they are good, and secondly because they are well-known. But there is a second category of works which, in the opinion of the Concerts Committee, deserves some place in the programmes. These are works which, by reason of their merit, deserve performance under the most favourable circumstances (viz. 'Wozzeck') but which are not popular at the moment because they are not well-known. The inclusion of this second category in due proportion is considered by the Committee to be good box office policy, in spite of the fact that the first performances of such works must necessarily be of an experimental nature, and involve reduced houses.[58]

In fact, the committee believed that a dearth of unusual items on the programmes would have serious long-term effects on the series' drawing power.

> A strict adherence to the first category of works might ensure full or nearly full houses for a time, after which the Corporation's concerts would probably begin to earn the reputation of being too conservative, out-of-date, and dull. The younger generation and the trained musicians would tend to lose interest, and the box office would eventually suffer. The judicious inclusion of modern and unfamiliar works is therefore, in the Concerts Committee's opinion, good business *in the long run*. It operates as an insurance for the future, and gives each series a certain 'aliveness' which it would otherwise lack.

The committee recommended a practical solution, in which programme content should be balanced to satisfy both short-term and long-term interests. Eckersley concurred with this view:

> I feel that Nicolls may be going too much to the right and the M.A.C. too much to the left, and personally recommend a middle course which to my mind is well put in Beadle's memo of February 7th, to which Boult also subscribes.[59]

The diversity of views led Boult to draft further statements of the department's official policy on this subject. He considered the relation between the BBC's fundamental programme policy – 'to give the listener the widest possible field of music as a whole with the great classics in preponderant proportion' – and box office success.

> The Box Office is by far the most reliable indication that we have of the feeling of our audience. Our endeavour is to guide their opinion . . . We are not watching the Box Office in the sense that a commercial manager does and must do, but from the point of view of giving us an indication how best our guiding policy can be pursued.[60]

Boult wrote to each member of the Music Advisory Committee to this effect just prior to the meeting on 6 June. Nevertheless, the committee's discussion resulted in an extreme recommendation: that BBC public concerts be reduced to just one a month.[61] The malevolence of the dissenting members led Reith to express disapproval, recording in his diary: 'M.A.C. in the afternoon as trying as usual, and I had to say a few things definitely, particularly on the music profession's jealousy of the B.B.C. and in the matter of our public concerts.'[62] The Music Department ignored the suggestion, and the matter receded from the Music Advisory Committee agenda after this time. In fact, the dissident members of the committee continued to air their grievances, but in a public forum, submitting damaging statements about BBC music policy to the Ullswater Committee in June and July 1935.

Although the box office question incited emotional discussions from June 1934 to June 1935, its effect on BBC policy was negligible: different views provoked the administrators to clarify their positions verbally, but their policy statements were consistent with previous practices and the shape and objectives of BBC public concerts remained the same. Nevertheless, the discussions led to subtle changes in programme planning. Once the discussions had taken place and the box office record thoroughly examined, the music staff and central administrators were sensitive to the issue in a way that had not burdened them previously. This new awareness made the Music Department more careful about programming new works in public concerts during the second half of the decade.

## The Five-Year Plan

As a consequence of the Concerts Committee report of June 1934, a large-scale planning scheme was developed in which high-profile music broadcasts were conceived and shaped for a period of years, rather on a season-to-season basis.[63] In October, Eckersley convened a committee, consisting of those responsible for music programming policies, including himself as chairman, Beadle, Boult, Wellington (the Presentation Director), Mase, Buesst, Wright and Herbage. The group was formed 'with the object of framing future music plans, and in particular a recommendation to Controller (P) for a planned music scheme covering a period of five years',[64] a scheme known as the Five-Year Plan. The committee met on two occasions, after which Eckersley prepared draft reports, which were amended by Boult, Beadle, Wellington and Reith. This process enabled the BBC to formulate a comprehensive, formal statement concerning the nature and substance of its music programmes for the first time.

The committee examined the high-profile public concert series – the symphony concerts, May Festival, winter and summer Promenade concerts, provincial concerts, foreign tours, public chamber concerts and contemporary concerts – to determine whether the number, frequency and format of each was favourable. It recommended that the symphony series be increased from twelve concerts to sixteen to encompass a broader scope and offer more interesting programmes.[65] The committee also suggested that the chamber music series be expanded, from six concerts to twelve. Public perception of chamber music was still poor in 1934, as it had been in the 1920s. Music staff argued that 'Chamber Music, possibly the purest form of the musical art, had almost gone out of fashion. Nobody but the B.B.C. could afford to run Chamber Music Concerts. It was therefore the B.B.C.'s duty to music to undertake propaganda on its behalf'. The Presentation Director worried that the BBC's sponsoring of so many preset public concerts, or 'fixed points', increased the difficulty of balancing the programme schedules. Boult suggested that the concerts be planned and performed, but not necessarily transmitted. Eckersley 'doubted whether this could be allowed', and later admitted that he strongly disagreed with Boult's radical proposal.[66] Of the contemporary series, 'it was unanimously agreed that these concerts served a very valuable purpose, and that 8 should be given per season'.

Less prominent BBC music programmes were also scrutinized and discussed. For perhaps the first time, a policy was formulated with regard to studio programming:

> It was unanimously recommended by those present that in view of the unavoidable fixity of all public concerts, it was more than ever necessary to maintain the principle of flexibility so far as all studio work was concerned.[67]

The committee determined that the procedure for planning these programmes should be better organized. 'It was agreed that a large stock of ready built programmes should always be in hand. Hitherto programme building had, generally speaking, been a last-minute affair. Insufficient time and thought was devoted to it.' Last-minute panic was also to be avoided through the hiring of additional programme building staff.

In December, Eckersley prepared draft reports on the scheme, addressing three main areas: recommendations for the public concert series, a statement on studio programmes, and a suggestion that the BBC publish a pamphlet promoting the music programmes two or four times a year.[68] The endorsement of the contemporary concerts clearly had more to do with upholding the BBC's reputation than with musical values.

> These concerts appeal only to a minority, and are laughed at by the majority. They do nevertheless serve a very valuable purpose. Extreme modernity is nearly always an object of ridicule and execration, but it is generally the livest spot in any art. Musically we could never hope to be taken really seriously if we were completely to ignore it.

W. E. Gladstone Murray reviewed the report for the central administrators and recommended that they reject Boult's proposal concerning public chamber concerts.

> There is no compelling reason why we should give so many of these public Concerts and so stand to be shot at for competing with private interests. I am not, however, in a position to judge of the opinion, apparently strongly held by M.D. , that there should be 12 or none . . . Perhaps Music Department should be asked to consider again whether within six concerts some useful artistic purpose cannot be served. If the answer is still negative, then I would be disposed to say none rather than 12.[69]

However, Murray condoned the continuation of the contemporary series:

> D.E. tells me that he has no information as to whether any of our first performances are ever repeated; whether, in fact, we effectually introduce any contemporary music. Even so, however, 8 per annum of this kind are probably justified on general policy grounds.

The final report was presented to the Board of Governors on 16 January 1935, and the Governors provisionally accepted the Five-Year Plan.[70] Reith clarified that the Board approved sixteen symphony concerts and six public chamber concerts.[71] No specific comment was made concerning the contemporary music programmes. The Music Department prepared a concise version of the report, entitled 'Planning Ahead', for the Music Advisory Committee.[72] The committee approved the plan, with the proviso that 'the Corporation's public activities should only be arranged after full consideration of the plans of other musical organisations'.[73]

In many ways, the Five-Year Plan simply substantiated basic procedures that the programme builders had developed gradually for shaping the music broadcasts they planned and produced. The review caused the policy-makers to scrutinize the content and nature of the music programmes and question the validity of previously accepted practices. In particular, in discussions about the public chamber concerts and contemporary music series, the administrators revealed unfavourable attitudes. Nevertheless, the Music Department's enthusiastic promotion of these concerts prevailed, supported by Reith's fundamental programming ethic. Just a few years later, when war-time conditions invalidated previously established policies, the balance of opinion shifted and less popular music programmes – especially those featuring ultra-modern works – were temporarily phased out.

## The Ullswater Committee, evidence and recommendations

During the first half of 1935, the BBC as a whole underwent its second large-scale public examination.[74] With the expiration of the Corporation's first charter at the end of 1936, the Ullswater Committee was formed to review the BBC's activities over the previous decade,

> to consider the constitution, control, and finance of the broadcasting service in this country and advise generally on the conditions under which the service, including broadcasting to the Empire, television broadcasting, and the system of wireless exchanges, should be conducted after 31 December 1936.[75]

The appointment of the committee was announced in Parliament on 17 April 1935, and on 1 May the committee publicly declared that it was 'prepared to receive evidence or representations in writing from any person or organisation'.[76] During June and July, the committee accepted evidence from 79 witnesses, including Sir Edward Bairstow and Frank Eames (of the Incorporated Society of Musicians), Sir Hugh Allen (of the Royal College of Music), Sir John McEwen (of the Royal Academy of Music), Sir Landon Ronald (of the Guildhall School of Music), George Dyson, Sir Thomas Beecham, Sir Walford Davies, Sir Hamilton Harty and Boult. The committee completed its report in February 1936, and it was issued to the public on 16 March.

The Ullswater Committee's review of the Corporation's music-related activities involved many policy issues that had preoccupied the central administrators, the Music Department staff and the advisory committees during the preceding years. A full examination of the highly charged debates that surfaced during the Ullswater investigation, involving many pages of written and oral testimony, is available elsewhere;[77] however, brief consideration of the issues raised and the positions taken by different factions provides an effective conclusion to the present discussion of BBC music policy to spring 1936.

The music-related evidence submitted to the committee encompassed two distinct points of view: representatives of the music profession criticized the effects of broadcasting on music-making at amateur and professional levels, while the BBC defended its record, supported by those who approved its art music broadcasts. The BBC submitted the first written evidence, considered by the committee on 3 May 1935.[78] The Corporation outlined its achievements as a public service utility. In terms of programming, the statement focused on its cultural-expansionist policy:

> Programme policy on the larger issues has from the outset been determined by the conviction that listeners would come to appreciate that which at first might appear uninteresting or even alarming. The B.B.C. has in fact aimed at providing a service somewhat ahead of what the public would demand were it possible for such demand to be made articulate and intelligible.

Anticipating the music profession's objections, the statement also included a short paragraph defending the right and necessity for the Corporation to continue to sponsor its own public concerts.

Over subsequent weeks, many organizations and individuals submitted statements and gave testimony to the committee. On 19 June, Reith seemed satisfied with its progress, recording in his diary:

> Lunched with Mrs Hamilton and Attlee,[79] at the Forum Club. Attlee said he did not think much damage was being done to [us] by the procession of more or less hostile and axe-grinding witnesses, and that he did not think we need bother ourselves to stimulate witnesses of the other sort.[80]

However, the next day, the Incorporated Society of Musicians (ISM) submitted a statement that greatly angered him, especially since it was signed by Sir Edward Bairstow, of the Music Advisory Committee, and was apparently supported by other committee members, including Sir Hugh Allen.

> A most monstrous document has gone to the Committee from the I.S.M. and I rang up Allen about it, but of course he was too embarrassed to say anything and he is playing a double game, as they all are. I saw Walford Davies in the afternoon and he rang up Eames, the Secretary, to get a copy of it, but Eames refused to give it to him. He sent a wire to Bairstow, the President who signed it, but he had got no reply by Saturday. This shows what a dirty game they are playing if they are not prepared to let an ex-President of the Society see it.[81]

In its statement, the ISM grudgingly acknowledged the BBC had 'enabled a vast number of people to realise for the first time the value of music as a source of pleasure, and it has created widespread interest in the art. We believe that broadcasting will increasingly stimulate a desire for wider and more intimate knowledge of Music'.[82] The rest of the document strongly criticized music broadcasting. The ISM's primary complaint concerned centralization:

> The administration has become increasingly centred in London, has reduced regional broadcasting activity to a minimum, and has subjected all the actual and potential activities in the provinces to an over-riding authority which is not, and cannot be, under the present form of administration, in close and constant touch with the main centres of interest and population outside London.

The society recommended that six independent and autonomous units be established in different parts of the country, each to provide a broadcasting service suited to its region.

The ISM also recommended that the music profession be granted greater power within the Corporation, on a constitutional basis. First, external advisors should be given statutory powers, since existing committees 'have neither the authority nor the corporate responsibility of a Statutory Advisory Council which we submit should be established and form a constituent part of the constitution under the new conditions'. In addition, one of the BBC Governors should be a music specialist, 'responsible to the Board of Governors for the music policy of the Corporation ... We suggest that it should be a full-time and salaried office and that the Prime Minister might agree to receive from institutions representative of music in its various activities a list of names of his consideration when appointing a Governor with this special responsibility'. Finally, to protect the interests of professional musicians, the ISM recommended that BBC administrative staff be banned from taking part in music broadcasts, that the BBC be prohibited from giving public concerts and that less attention be given to non-British contemporary works:

> We submit that in the selection of such works an anti-national bias is at times discernible. This bias is probably due to the predominant influence of London, and to the superficially cosmopolitan pretensions of some of its more active cliques. The selection of performers sometimes shows a similar bias quite irrespective of quality.

Thus, the ISM's evidence encompassed the most significant concerns that the Music Advisory Committee had raised with the BBC administrators during preceding months. This view was supported by evidence submitted by other respected musicians,[83] but was strongly refuted by those who defended the BBC's music activities, including Sir Walford Davies and the Music Director himself.

Sir Walford's evidence was significant not only because of his professional integrity and his national popularity, but also because of the vital role he had played in making music accessible to listeners through his educational broadcast talks. His statement, submitted on 26 June, emphatically affirmed the extraordinary opportunities that broadcasting had provided for the entire country.

> The Corporation as a Public Service, apart from giving information and amusement, can now let the whole country overhear the very finest minds in action – whether through spoken word or music. The possibilities of this on a scale still unattempted seem so vast that I do not find it enough to say that the invention of Broadcasting is to music what the invention of Printing was to the dissemination of knowledge. It is far more . . .
>
> I wish to state here that in my judgment the advance made in right directions by the Corporation during the last ten years is little short of miraculous, and though still very far short of all our desires, and of the practical and immediate possibilities of development, any suggestion that the charter should not be renewed is to me, as a musician, unthinkable.[84]

Davies recognized that modern developments inevitably led to changes in traditional practices; that 'many resentments from those hitherto responsible for supply are to be expected, some real and public-spirited, some shadowy and ego-centric. And many real hardships, in the transfer from the old kind of supply to the new, need to be met.' To encourage smooth transition to the new conditions, he recommended the establishment of a working alliance between the Corporation and the music profession to discuss music broadcasting issues and to develop a compensation scheme for professionals who suffered financially as a result of the BBC's success. Davies also recommended that music programmes be planned in a more systematic manner.

In contrast to Davies's dignified stance, Boult's statement was fired by months of frustration. The vehemence with which he condemned previous testimony astounded the committee members, as Reith recorded in his diary:

> Boult, having been kept waiting over an hour was only with the Committee for about a quarter of an hour. He so flabbergasted them by saying that the other people had been telling lies that they asked him to write a memorandum and go back next week.[85]

Boult's written statement was equally candid.

> I am astonished at the inaccuracy of the statements of most of my colleagues
> in the musical profession who have given evidence before the Committee. In
> spite of the fact that the majority of them have for many years been taken
> closely into our councils, they still show an extraordinary lack of under-
> standing of the primary purpose for which the British Broadcasting
> Corporation exists, and they still appear to be phenomenally ill-informed of
> the Corporation's musical activities.[86]

In particular, he expressed his dissatisfaction with the views and recommendations of the Music Advisory Committee:

> As Music Director of the Corporation I place a high value on the disinter-
> ested advice of the senior members of the music profession, but I seldom get
> that advice from the Music Advisory Committee, of which Sir Hugh Allen,
> Sir John McEwen and Sir Landon Ronald are all members . . . More often
> than not the members occupy their time at the meetings trying to bully the
> Corporation into adopting courses of action which they think would be to
> the benefit of the music profession, but without due regard for the
> Corporation's programme standards, or for the interests of the listening
> public. That Committee has tried to insist on the Corporation broadcasting
> a far larger quota of British music than is merited by the quality and quantity
> of that music. It has tried to make the Corporation employ practically none
> but British artists, thus preventing listeners from hearing the pick of the
> world's musical talent, and disregards altogether the fact that even now only
> an extremely small percentage of the artists employed are of foreign nation-
> ality.

Boult also attacked those who criticized the BBC's public concerts:

> The Corporation's musical policy, with which a certain number of public
> concerts are inseparable, is rapidly acquiring for this country a very high
> musical reputation. British professional musicians will ultimately benefit by
> it. If the Corporation's public concerts were stopped or seriously reduced
> that policy would be nullified, and the musical reputation of this country
> would have to depend on individuals and organisations less capable than the
> Corporation of performing this great task.

Boult's passionate statement publicly denounced the Music Advisory
Committee's stand on issues that had impeded BBC music policy decisions for several years. The blunt and direct manner of his statement left
no room for doubt concerning the Corporation's official response to the
serious criticisms that had been levied against his department's activities.[87]

In its published report, the Ullswater Committee recommended that the

BBC's royal charter be renewed for another decade from 1 January 1937.[88] In general, it approved the Corporation's policies and practices:

> We feel that a great debt of gratitude is owed to the wisdom which founded the British Broadcasting Corporation in its present form, and to the prudence and idealism which have characterised its operations and enabled it to overcome the many difficulties which surround a novel and rapidly expanding public service . . . Our recommendations are directed towards the further strengthening and securing of the position which the broadcasting service in Great Britain has happily attained in the few years of its history.[89]

Five paragraphs, numbered 95–9, focused exclusively on music-related issues, endorsing the BBC's music policies and procedures. The committee especially noted the unparalleled success the Corporation had had in the dissemination of art music:

> The purpose which a broadcasting organisation should regard as paramount is that fine music, played under the best conditions, may be heard and appreciated over the whole country to the vast extent which broadcasting alone has made possible. To this end, performance is rightly supplemented by educational courses and explanatory and introductory talks. We support the policy of a full development of studio performances by the BBC orchestras and their judicious use in public concerts not necessarily confined to London, together with the relaying of the best performances of outside organisations in any important class of music.[90]

Moreover, the committee supported Boult's position, concluding that broadcasting had helped, not harmed, the music profession,

> by affording employment to performers; by offering to composers a prospect of the performance of suitable works; by relaying, as mentioned above, the best performances and contributing towards the cost; by pursuing a considered scheme of collaboration with active and efficient local societies, in order to supply what each region most requires for its own musical development; and by other methods, such as visits, lectures, and broadcast announcements directing attention to local musical enterprises.[91]

By the mid-1930s, the BBC had become the leading force in British music. Its power and influence as the largest employer of musicians in the country led, perhaps inevitably, to a power struggle with members of the music profession, who fought to gain some control over the Corporation's music-related decisions. After years of resentment and debate, the Ullswater Committee's review ultimately quashed the music profession's objections to BBC policies and practices. The Ullswater Report strongly supported the BBC's approach to music broadcasting and recommended unequivocally that it continue for another ten years.

## Contemporary music programming

While the central administrators and high-level staff in branches and departments throughout the BBC were focusing their energies on the policies and politics induced by new organizational structures, new management strategies and the Ullswater review, programmes continued to be broadcast in the usual way, following the now well-established patterns.

### Broadcasts of Second Viennese School works, 1934–5

The 1934–5 Concerts of Contemporary Music were first discussed in May 1934, as part of the Concerts Committee's review of box office issues. The committee recommended that new orchestral works be programmed in the contemporary concerts, rather than in symphony series,[92] as a way of diminishing their negative impact on the public and the BBC's finances. In an ironic twist, the department hailed the decision as an opportunity to bring the concerts fully into the public domain and to present more ambitious works. In the series proposal, submitted to Boult in July, each of the eight programmes required an orchestra, and several involved chorus as well. The introduction reflects the programme builders' expanded vision:

> We suggest below a scheme of eight concerts as in former years, but with this difference that all deserve a genuine public hearing in the sense of a public concert in a public hall. Further, all require the use of a section of the B.B.C. Orchestra, this being dictated partly by the present tendency of composers to write almost exclusively orchestral music, as can be seen from the recent Contemporary Music Festival[93] programmes as compared with a few years ago. It is also necessitated by the works suggested, some of which are on a scale not possible, or not worth while in the private type of programme given in No.10 Studio or the B.B.C. Concert Hall.[94]

Buoyed by *Wozzeck*'s success, the proposal included two modern operas that had enjoyed success on the continent: Shostakovich's *Lady Macbeth of the Mtensk District* and Bartók's *Bluebeard's Castle*. Also proposed were Hindemith's newly-completed *Mathis der Maler* Symphony, Janáček's *Glagolitic Mass*, two programmes devoted to recent British music and one to American music. Significantly, music of the Schoenbergian circle was not featured: 'It will be noted that the "Central European" group has purposely been omitted from this series'; Berg and Schoenberg were represented in other BBC series instead.

Since the Concert Hall at Broadcasting House could not accommodate works involving large chorus and full orchestra, the committee suggested the Central Hall, Westminster, as the performance venue. However, the

Director of Internal Administration, Nicolls, baulked at the £40–50 per concert hiring fee, stipulating instead:

> The Music Department, having agreed to include in the Contemporary series important orchestral choral works which are likely to prove a box office loss at the Queen's Hall, should make out its programmes without any reference to considerations other than artistic ones, and that the series then should be broadcast as far as possible entirely from the Concert Hall or Maida Vale, an outside hall being taken for special works only when absolutely necessary.[95]

The question of venue and programme costs was debated for weeks. Nicolls reiterated that 'agreement will not be given to our embarking on a series of unnecessary losses through performing this sort of music in public when it is possible to do it in the studio'.[96] Since the Maida Vale studio could only accommodate an audience of 150, Beadle argued that it was worth hiring the Central Hall, Westminster.

> About £350 would be spent for the benefit of an audience of about 700 persons, who are sufficiently interested in music of this kind to attend the performances when no charge is made for admission. On the face of it the case is a weak one, in spite of which I recommend it, because it has big policy implications. The production of unknown contemporary music on a big scale is a thing which noone [sic] but the B.B.C. can do, and I think it is very important that a large number of people should know that we do it. Public performances in the Central Hall before audiences of seven or eight hundred or more, will achieve this object in a way which a performance in the Maida Vale studio before about 150 people would not.[97]

But Nicolls stubbornly upheld his view: 'The audience is incidental to the broadcasting and we are not justified in extra expense to meet a possible bigger demand for free seats. Those who cannot get seats can listen at home.'[98] The concerts were scheduled for the Maida Vale studio.[99]

The ambitious plans were eventually scaled down to manageable proportions.[100] Neither of the operas were presented, but Hindemith's *Mathis der Maler* Symphony, conducted by the composer, and Janáček's *Glagolitic Mass* were performed as planned. Prokofiev participated in the series, conducting a programme devoted to his music. The remaining concerts included American music, British music, two mixed programmes, and a radio adaptation of Kurt Weill's *Dreigroschenoper* – jokingly listed as 'The Tuppeny-Ha'penny opera' – conducted by Clark.

For the first time, only one work associated with the Second Viennese School was presented in the season's contemporary concerts. The programme for 12 April 1935 included Hanns Eisler's *Little Symphony*, op. 29.

The pre-concert press release correctly reported that the composer had dissociated himself from the Schoenbergian circle.

> Ansermet's programme also includes an unfamiliar 'Little Symphony' by Hanns Eisler, one of Schönberg's younger pupils . . . The Symphony to be played on April 12 is a recent work in which Schönberg's influence has considerably diminished, making way for the reflection of the composer's own personality.[101]

Broadcasts of Second Viennese School repertory were presented instead within other series, the Sunday Orchestral Concerts, the BBC Symphony Concerts and the Promenade Concerts, as well as in studio recitals. Despite continued restrictions on the hiring of foreign artists, most of the performances were given by continental specialists and received little publicity or attention. The first of these was aired on Armistice Day, 11 November 1934, in a late afternoon studio chamber music recital. The programme featured The Prague String Quartet playing Dvořák and Schumann, and soprano Ružena Herlinger singing Webern's 'Eingang' from op. 4 and 'Kahl reckt der Baum' from op. 3, as well as Beethoven Lieder.[102]

Schoenberg's music was by no means ignored during the 1934–5 season, but broadcasts were confined to the most accessible works, presented and received without controversy or even comment. On 16 November, a chamber concert presented by the Kolisch Quartet and Margot Hinnenberg-Lefèbre began with the Second String Quartet. The concert was performed publicly in the Concert Hall at Broadcasting House, but only the latter parts of the programme – Schubert Lieder and Schubert and Beethoven string quartets – were transmitted.

In January, *Verklärte Nacht*, op. 4, was broadcast twice. On 18 January, the work was presented in a lunch-time concert from Birmingham, performed by the Birmingham Philharmonic String Orchestra conducted by Johan Hock. On 20 January, Frank Bridge conducted it in a Sunday Orchestral Concert that also included Haydn's Symphony no. 99, movements of Rimsky-Korsakov's suite from *Coq d'or* and his own rhapsody, *Enter Spring*. On 27 February, Boult included Schoenberg's arrangement of Bach's Prelude and Fugue in E flat major ('St Anne') in a BBC Symphony Concert transmitted from Birmingham's Town Hall.

In a Sunday Orchestral Concert on 10 March, Clark conducted *Gurrelieder* Part I in the version for reduced orchestra. Soloists included soprano May Blyth, contralto Enid Cruickshank and tenor Parry Jones. The programme was introduced in the *Radio Times* with a half-page article by Edwin Evans, explaining the story and musical background.[103] The final Schoenberg broadcast of the season took place on 18 March. In a studio chamber music recital, the Kolisch Quartet presented a programme that began with Schubert's Quartet in D minor ('Death and the Maiden') and concluded with Schoenberg's String Quartet no. 3. Surprisingly, this late night recital was publicized with a substantial article in the *Radio Times* 'Notable Music of the Week' column.[104] However, it was presented just two days before one of the most important events of the season – the British première of symphonic excerpts from Berg's new opera, *Lulu* – and the composers' connections were emphasized in juxtaposed articles introducing the string quartet and the new opera.

The decision to programme the Symphonic Excerpts from *Lulu* in March 1935 was undoubtedly linked to the London staged performance of *Wozzeck* planned for the following month. Having waited nearly a decade after *Wozzeck*'s première to reap the benefits of its success, the BBC was eager to be involved with *Lulu* from the beginning. In September 1934, Wright wrote to Berg:

> We cannot at present say anything more definite with regard to the projected performance of 'Wozzeck' on the stage, but we can confirm that we are hoping to give the Suite of Five Symphonic Pieces from 'Lulu' on March 20th at Queen's Hall under Dr Boult's direction.[105]

In November, Wright sought Berg's advice about the vocal part.

> With regard to the movement demanding a high soprano voice, would you kindly give us as accurate an idea as possible of the type of voice and the style of singing required, quoting Austrian and German equivalents, from which we hope to be able to judge whom to invite from our own English artists to undertake it?[106]

Berg did not recommend specific voices, but merely confirmed that the part required a 'high, versatile soprano', mentioning that a vocal score of the movement was being sent by the publishers.[107] In February, the composer sent a long letter to Boult recommending Julia Nessy, if an English soprano had not yet been engaged, and providing detailed instructions about the fourth movement.[108] Boult replied:

> I am so sorry that we did not know that Madame Nessy was to be in England on March 20th, as we should have been delighted to make use of her services. Under the circumstances, however, we felt that Miss May Blyth, who sang the part of 'Marie' with such distinction last year, would be able to do full justice to the part. As you know, there is always a certain pressure on the B.B.C. in favour of engaging English singers, where possible, and so we have engaged Miss Blyth, who is an excellent musician, and who is learning the part. I do most earnestly hope that her performance will satisfy you.[109]

Berg approved the BBC's choice of singer.[110]

The much-heralded BBC Symphony Concert on 20 March included, in addition to the Berg, a new symphony by Gian Francesco Malipiero, a Frescobaldi toccata transcribed by Malipiero, Mozart's Violin Concerto no. 5, K. 219, with soloist Jascha Heifetz, and the second suite from Ravel's *Daphnis et Chloé*. The BBC began to publicize the programme as early as October 1934, in a preview of the Symphony Concert series.

> On March 20, three works new to England will be played. In two of them Malipiero, one of Italy's foremost composers, has had a hand. But the most interesting promises to be the extracts from Alban Berg's new opera, *Lulu*. After the great success of his *Wozzeck*, much is expected of Berg, and anything new from him is eagerly looked for.[111]

In March, publicity began in earnest. As with *Wozzeck*, the BBC attempted to attract curiosity by hinting at perversions in the plot.

> The libretto of the opera is founded on two plays by Frank Wedekind, *The Earth Spirit* and *Pandora's Box*, and if *Wozzeck* was no *Peter Pan*, *Lulu* sounds to us like a glimpse of the real underworld. Lulu, apparently, begins by being tried for the murder of her husband, but that isn't the half of it.[112]

A more accurate *Radio Times* description by Scott Goddard was published under the heading, 'An Erotic Opera'. Goddard pointed out that Berg's music had only gained recognition with time: 'Knowledge of the music and, still more, of the tale has brought at least some understanding of the meaning of *Wozzeck*. Some listeners are already able to bear *Wozzeck* with an almost sympathetic interest, while a smaller minority in this country are really appreciative.'[113] He surmised that this history underlay Berg's early release of parts of his second opera: 'The composer has issued this Symphonic Suite so that the public may approach *Lulu* by short stages and hear five excerpts from the opera before getting down to the complete work.' Since the opera had not been performed and the score and libretto were not yet available, Goddard had to guess how Berg might have adapted the original plays:

> Berg, in his opera, will assuredly have made his writing fulfil one of music's greatest possibilities: the portrayal of generalised states of being; in this case the conflict between the spiritual and animal in Lulu, between the divine and the demonic. On that plane the sordid drama can be transformed and the musical setting can lift the whole idea into the atmosphere of high tragedy, in which understanding born of pity has more freedom to exercise its influence on listeners.

Another full-page article about Berg and his operas, written by M. D. Calvocoressi, appeared in *The Listener* on the day of the performance.[114]

The *Lulu* Excerpts were not received with the same enthusiasm that had greeted BBC performances of *Wozzeck* or the *Wozzeck* Fragments. Critics complained of the difficulty of hearing the work without its dramatic context. As Edwin Evans remarked in *The Daily Mail*,

> This is almost entirely cerebral music, worked out with extraordinary cleverness. As in the case of 'Wozzeck', it may be that in the atmosphere of the theatre it generates a genuine dramatic emotion, but at a first hearing in the concert-room one is too much occupied with its permutations and combinations to let one's imagination wander into the incidents of the opera.[115]

The ambivalent response of the Queen's Hall audience was also attributed to this disconnectedness. The *Times* critic wrote:

> Last night's audience, which included many composers and other musicians, accorded the composer his due, but at the end the applause was hardly lukewarm. We are inclined to agree with the judgment of the audience, for there was nothing in this music to stir the emotions or arouse sympathy ... [This] style of writing has been with justice criticized as incapable of portraying anything but morbid and sordid ideas, but it was surely perverse to descend quite so low into the mire of neuro-pathology.[116]

In marked contrast, Berg, Boult and the Music Department staff hailed the performance as a triumph. Wright expressed his admiration in a letter to the composer.

> I must take this opportunity of saying how much I was impressed with the performance of last Wed. at Queens Hall under Dr Boult, of the suite from 'Lulu'. Were you able to hear it? Miss May Blyth worked very hard at the songs and sang them really well. Probably Dr Boult will write to you himself to say how much he enjoyed the experience of conducting the Suite. We made a private recording of the work (only to hear ourselves, of course), and he says that listening to it now as one of the audience, he is beginning to realise what it is all about! In point of fact we all thought he conducted it superbly and we hope that he will one day be able to direct the complete opera in London.[117]

Ten days after the broadcast, Berg wrote a warm letter of thanks to Boult.

> For a long time now I have been wanting to thank you for the Lulu-Symphony. I was able to hear it fairly well and I observed with pleasure how wonderfully it was again prepared and put together and how splendid the orchestra seems to have sounded. Deepest thanks to you, Mr Boult, and your colleagues for this latest support for my work. That this is happening in England especially – and not in my own country, where these pieces have not been performed and no one thinks of performing them – makes me doubly happy and proud![118]

Finally, Boult thanked the composer for his appreciation of the performance, admitting that, 'without the authoritative guidance of anyone like Mr Prerauer I was not always certain that I was interpreting your wishes correctly'.[119] The conductor also wrote of the usefulness of the BBC's private recordings.

> Mr Wright has told you how very much more the work meant to me after the performance when I heard it reproduced by our recording process. It has taught me a most valuable lesson about modern music, for the conductor is so immersed in the mechanics of the performance that he cannot, as it were, get far enough away from the work to judge it at the same time.

The Berg performance was the apex of BBC broadcasts of Second Viennese School repertory that season. Nevertheless, in April 1935, three further programmes included works by members of the circle. On 14 April, Julian Clifford included the Webern arrangement of Schubert's German Dances, D. 820, in an afternoon orchestra concert. On 30 April, the same conductor directed a studio broadcast that included two of Berg's *Seven Early Songs*, 'Liebesode' and 'Traumgekrönt', sung by soprano Rose Walter. However, the most significant of the broadcasts took place on 25 April, when Webern made his annual pilgrimage to London to conduct three of his own works.

On 28 February, Webern wrote to Clark, arranging to repay his friend for settling his English tax bill.[120] The composer took the opportunity to ask about BBC work.

> I would only like to take advantage of your willingness to pay this amount in the interim if a fresh BBC engagement for me may still come about this season or in the near future, as you promised in Vienna at Christmas.
> How does that stand now?
> I hope to hear from you about it soon![121]

During Clark's visit, they had discussed the possibility of two broadcasts. One was to include works by Webern himself, such as the newly completed arrangement of the ricercare from Bach's *Das musikalische Opfer*.

> My Bach fugue was finished long ago and the orchestra material is already *available from UE*! Therefore, nothing more lies in the way of this first performance. Our arrangement was: Schubert, B minor symphony, Bach fugue, after that my orchestra pieces, op. 6 (six pieces) and Passacaglia.

The second consisted of Brahms's Piano Concerto in D minor, with Steuermann as soloist, and Beethoven's Symphony no. 8.

On 9 March, Webern confirmed that he had received a contract to conduct an orchestra concert on 25 April, but was distressed by the 40 guinea fee.

> Due to the recent depreciation of the pound, nearly half of the total would slip away for the travel expenses alone! To that are still the costs of staying, taxes to the British Board of Assessment (for my previous engagement with you, I have still £5 to pay), the time spent, etc. What would remain would be too negligible a total and not acceptable. Therefore, I must request most urgently that you increase the honorarium to at least 50 guineas.[122]

Wright soon reported to Clark:

> Dr Boult agrees under the circumstances that it would be a very nice gesture to make to Webern to increase his fee to 45 guineas. Call it 'special' in view of the fact that on some other occasion he may not have to spend so long in this country rehearsing etc., and also international currency conditions may adjust themselves.[123]

On 22 March, the BBC sent Webern a routine letter confirming the rehearsal schedule and the programme,[124] prompting him to write another urgent, but lengthy, letter to Clark.

> Yesterday I received from the BBC the programme details for correction and to my astonishment, found specified there my
> > *5 pieces op. 10.*
> But, in our discussion, I had not meant these pieces, which I already performed at the BBC in 1929, but the
> > *Six orchestra pieces op. 6.*
> I set great store by performing just these [pieces] with the wonderful BBC Orchestra at last![125]

Webern provided details about his op. 6 pieces and was particularly specific about the bells called for in two of the movements: 'It is important to me to have several low bells – *as low as possible*. In two pieces, an impression of *far distant, low* country bells (unspecified pitches) must be made.' He had revised the orchestration a few years before, and since material for the new version was still in preparation, he offered to send a copy of the manuscript score for consideration. Webern also asked Clark to find inexpensive accommodation for him in London.

On 10 April, not yet knowing the BBC's decision, Webern sent Clark a telegram: 'Telegraph whether opus 6 or 10'. Clark replied simply, 'Opus 10 please'.[126] Once again, Webern's passionate pleas to the BBC were ignored; the programme was given exactly as the BBC had planned. On 25 April 1935, at the late hour of 10.15 pm, Webern conducted a studio orchestra concert that consisted of Schubert's popular Symphony no. 8 and his three works, the Five Orchestral Pieces, op. 10, the Passacaglia, op. 1, and the world première of the Bach fugue arrangement. Significantly, the choice of Webern selections conformed to programming practice of the season: the broadcast only presented Webern's earlier or more accessible works, avoiding the controversial styles of those written since the war.

Although the April broadcasts were the last of the season to include music by members of the Second Viennese School, two further works were presented during the summer. On 24 August 1935, Julian Clifford conducted Schoenberg's *Begleitmusik zu einer Lichtspielszene*, op. 34, during a studio orchestra concert. Interestingly, even this performance, a studio event involving a British conductor and a British orchestra, came under scrutiny, because the music was by a foreign composer. The Music Programme Advisory Panel minutes reported:

> Mr Bliss felt it was a pity Schönberg's Musik für Lichtspielszene could not be replaced in Mr Clifford's concert on August 24th by one of the new English works. Mr Clark explained that Mr Clifford has for some considerable time wished to include this particular work and in point of fact on examining the list of new English works none was found to be suitable in type or orchestration for this concert. Mr Wright pointed out that this very experience was typical of the difficulties confronting programme builders when attempting to solve such a problem.

Finally, on 9 September, the *Wozzeck* Fragments were given again at a Promenade Concert, conducted by Sir Henry Wood and sung by soprano May Blyth. Since the concert took place on a Monday night, reserved for Wagner's music according to Proms tradition, only the first half of the concert, featuring Wagner works, was transmitted.

### Broadcasts of Second Viennese School works, 1935–36

During 1935–6, the BBC presented a wider range of works from the Second Viennese School repertory than it had the previous season. Schoenberg was again represented by safe, accessible pieces, though post-war works by Koffler and Wellesz were given attention. The BBC seemed more inclined to transmit works by members of the circle who were less known in Britain, thus avoiding the controversies sparked by broadcasts of Schoenberg and Webern. No such precautions were necessary in the case of Berg: performances of his music were highlighted at the start and the end of the 1935–6 season.

The first of the season's BBC Symphony Concerts took place on 23 October 1935. Conducted by Boult, the programme was designed to feature the 'three B's', Bach, Beethoven and Brahms, German masters whose works were universally accepted within the art music canon. To this group was added a fourth B – Berg – this composer symbolizing similar values for early twentieth-century music. Pre-concert publicity remarked on the four-B nature of the programme, but focused entirely on the first British concert performance of Berg's string orchestra arrangement of three movements from the *Lyric Suite*.[127] The *Radio Times* announcement firmly placed Berg within the Schoenbergian sphere: 'The music is striking and original, and satisfactorily applies the technical and æsthetic principles of that great figure in modern music, Arnold Schönberg, under whom Berg studied.'[128] *The Listener* included detailed comments about the work's idiom.

> All three pieces are excellent examples of the style of Berg's maturity, and also of the features that characterised his music from the outset – principal being an abundance of melodic invention and the suppleness of the harmonic texture.
>
> The music is in the twelve-tone system, and therefore, in theory, atonal. In actual fact, however, not the slightest impression of instability, vagueness or arbitrariness is conveyed. The logic, consistency, and purposefulness are unmistakable, although not obvious in the same way as they would be in a tonal scheme. They will be easily felt even by listeners unfamiliar with the twelve-tone idiom, for Berg is giving us no abstract, purely formal music. Here, as elsewhere, his object is frank poetic or dramatic expression.[129]

The work's musical style was also described in a broadcast talk given by Newman directly before the transmission. He focused on the difficulties that Berg's atonality might pose for the listener.

> [I can] only recommend you to listen carefully to this music, with the hope that, strange as the idiom may sometimes be to you, you will feel something of the warmth of the emotion of the *andante amoroso*, something of the passion of the adagio, and the charm of the cobweb texture of the 'mysterious' allegro . . . I can't, myself, believe that atonal music is destined to have much of a future: indeed, most of the composers who were attracted to it as a theoretic possibility a few years ago now show signs of abandoning it, at any rate in its more thorough-going form. But since the thing *is* in the air today, and since the language of music as we have hitherto known it is inevitably destined to change a good deal in the future, you may as well listen to representative works in this idiom when you get the chance; and you must be left to decide for yourselves whether they please you or not.[130]

Reviews were enthusiastic, generally devoting equal space to each of the four B's. Many commented on Berg's romanticism, as Newman wrote in his *Sunday Times* column:

> The Berg work, one thinks, might become fairly popular if it were given regularly; its atonality is not pronounced enough to be a bar to the plain man's

comprehension of the music. But the work falls between two stools: Berg seems to be writing most of the time with one eye on his master Schönberg and the other on the Wagner of 'Tristan'. Here, as elsewhere, one doubts whether his atonalism was ever much more than an act of piety towards Schönberg; one feels that Berg, in his heart of hearts, is a true son of German romanticism of the Wagner-Strauss-Mahler type.[131]

Criticisms centred on the string orchestra arrangement. For example, the *Times* critic remarked:

Perfectly played by a quartet who have mastered every detail, it has a strange attractiveness even to ears quite unable to analyse its structure. Less perfectly played by a large body of strings, it loses its attractiveness and certainly does not become more intelligible.[132]

Nevertheless, Boult's presentation of this work at the opening of the BBC's most prestigious concert series proved a success. The accessibility of the *Lyric Suite* movements confirmed Berg's growing reputation in Britain as an ultra-modern composer who need not be avoided.

The season's BBC Concerts of Contemporary Music began soon after. The 1935–6 series consisted of eight concerts, presented at monthly intervals between 1 November and 19 June.[133] They were transmitted over the National wavelength from the Concert Hall at Broadcasting House, where they were given before an invited audience. There was a discernible national emphasis, with four programmes including at least one British work. Five concerts were devoted to a single composer, including Krenek, Markevich, Malipiero, Berg and Lennox Berkeley. Significantly, the anchors of previous seasons, such as Schoenberg, Bartók, Stravinsky and Hindemith, were absent: works by these and many other living composers were broadcast that season, but not under the auspices of this series.

The first contemporary concert, on 1 November 1935, featured vocal music by Ernst Krenek sung by Viennese soprano, Hertha Glatz, accompanied by the composer, and by the BBC Singers conducted by Leslie Woodgate. The previous May, Krenek and Clark had corresponded about the possibility of a BBC broadcast of Krenek's music, but nothing materialized.[134] In September, Krenek wrote to Clark again after they had met in Prague and considered a broadcast of vocal music by Krenek and Theodor Wiesengrund-Adorno.[135] Clark extended a formal invitation,[136] and Krenek proposed a programme including either his *Concerto grosso* no. 2, op. 25, or his *Symphonic Music* for nine solo instruments, op. 11, followed by songs from op. 9, op. 53 and op. 71. Since Adorno, then resident in Oxford, had initially suggested that Krenek come to England, Krenek also hoped to give a performance of Adorno's op. 3 songs in London, perhaps in a second broadcast.[137] In early October, Wright and the composer arranged the programme, which, in the end, featured only his own vocal music: 'Räume', 'Rätselspiel' and 'Die frühen Gräber' from op. 9, 'Ein anderes' from op. 53, *Gesänge des späten Jahres*, op. 71, and *Reisebuch aus dem österreichischen Alpen*, op. 62.[138]

The 1 November concert was linked to a Sunday Orchestral Concert two days later, in which the BBC Orchestra conducted by Sir Henry Wood presented Krenek's *Concerto grosso* no. 2, op. 25. Even though the all-Krenek programme was the first contemporary concert of the season, presented in tandem with another important Krenek performance, the events received little pre-concert publicity. *Radio Times* coverage consisted of a short introduction:

> Though born at Vienna in 1900 of Czech family, Ernst Krenek is considered one of the leading composers of the younger German school. He studied composition under Franz Schreker in Vienna and in Berlin, where he now lives. 'He appears to be swayed', says Edwin Evans, 'by strictly musical, not to say even technical, impulses, and rarely, if ever, allows his course to be deflected by emotional or temperamental considerations. He takes the "linear" view of polyphony, which prevails in so much recent German music, and is in fact one of its most uncompromising adherents.'[139]

Krenek had been associated with the Schoenbergian circle for several years, even referring specifically to 'our circle' in a letter he wrote to Clark in December 1935,[140] but this fact was not mentioned.

Superficial comparison with Schoenberg's music was made in a more detailed *Listener* article, which related the works featured in the broadcasts to Krenek's compositional development. The op. 9 songs represented Krenek's early style.

> His work at this time shares with a few pieces from Schönberg's middle period the distinction of being the only real example of what one might call anarchy in music. The catchword is 'linear counterpoint'. With utter disregard of harmony each voice goes its own way – a threatening, independent way which has nothing to do with classical counterpoint.[141]

The second, so-called 'normal', period, due to his use of traditional harmony, was represented by the *Reisebuch aus den österreichischen Alpen*. Finally, the *Gesänge als späten Jahres* was from his third period, marked by a mature return to atonality. The BBC thus offered background information only in *The Listener*, aimed at the British cultural elite; there was no attempt to attract the notice of the public at large.

The all-Krenek concert received the usual critical attention. For a few reviewers, such as William McNaught in the *Evening News*, the programme had offered little of musical interest.

> Krenek is too serious, his music too glum and awry and generally uncongenial to the musical temperament.
>
> One thing the concert made certain. He is not exploring hidden avenues down which future generations will gaze in content. There is no mystery in his music. He is revolving within the confines of a temporary convention, and everybody can see what he is up to and where the value of it stops short.[142]

McNaught did enjoy hearing Hertha Glatz, whose 'voice and style were so lovely that one could have listened to her singing Schubert for hours'. Other critics found positive things to say about Krenek's choral music, at least. As Jack Westrup wrote in *The Daily Telegraph*:

> Both the songs and the unaccompanied choruses were inspired by a serious determination which impressed though it did not always attract. At a first hearing the picturesque treatment of the theme of 'Die Jahreszeiten['] appeared more inviting than the songs, in which philosophical speculation seemed to play a part in shaping the generally spare and severe musical structure.[143]

In *The Sunday Times*, Newman attributed this accessibility to the unaccompanied choral medium.

> Some part songs . . . (admirably sung by the B.B.C. Singers under Leslie Woodgate) proved attractive enough to make us wishful to hear them again. A composer cannot (without, of course, signing his own death warrant), monkey with a body of unaccompanied voices as he can with the piano or the orchestra. In the a cappella medium Krenek has to keep more on the rails; and the result in the present instance is a set of choruses that formed a restful oasis in the general desert of last night's music.[144]

In fact, Krenek's choral pieces were sung again by the BBC Singers later that month in a concert presented at the Royal Academy of Music in London. No direct evidence survives about the impact of these performances on BBC staff, but his music was broadcast with relative frequency from this time until the beginning of the war.[145]

The high-profile performances of Berg's *Lyric Suite* movements in October 1935 and the Krenek concerts in November were followed by numerous BBC presentations of Second Viennese School works, given as unobtrusive studio broadcasts. In an evening studio recital on 30 November, violinist Dea Gombrich aired music of Bach and Bartók, as well as the first performance of a violin and piano arrangement of the

Adagio from Berg's Chamber Concerto for violin, piano and thirteen wind instruments.[146] On 7 December the Boyd Neel String Orchestra, conducted by Neel, presented a studio concert that included the first British performance of Józef Koffler's *Wariacje na temat serii dwunastotonowej* ('Variations on a 12-Tone Series'), op. 9; this was the first time a piece by this composer was broadcast by the BBC.[147] In a Sunday Orchestral Concert the following day, Ernest Ansermet conducted the BBC Orchestra in a programme that included another performance of the three movements from Berg's *Lyric Suite*, arranged for string orchestra.

The new year featured several Schoenberg broadcasts. A performance of *Pelleas und Melisande*, op. 5, was scheduled for the BBC Symphony Concert on 22 January 1936. In preparation for this significant event, a lengthy article appeared in the *Radio Times* explaining the work's history, musical style and dramatic programme.[148] However, following the death of George V on 20 January, the concert was postponed along with all scheduled programmes between 21 and 28 January. *Pelleas und Melisande* was eventually aired in a studio concert conducted by Boult on 5 February. Four days previously, on 1 February, the Boyd Neel String Orchestra gave the first British broadcast of Schoenberg's Suite in G major for string orchestra. The *Radio Times* attempted to reassure listeners frightened by the mere appearance of the composer's name:

> The Suite for Strings is Schönberg's latest work, and received its first performance in New York under Otto Klemperer some weeks ago. It marks yet another phase in Schönberg's development, for it is quite unlike anything he has written before, except perhaps the recent 'Cello Concerto. But whereas the concerto was an attempt to construct something entirely new on an old work of Monn, the present Suite is quite original in material, although classical forms are used.[149]

The same ensemble presented a second broadcast of this work on 14 April 1936.

One other Schoenberg work was transmitted during the 1935–6 season. In an afternoon studio recital on 6 April, the British composer, Edmund Rubbra, performed Schoenberg's *Six Little Piano Pieces*, op. 19. Later that evening, Malcolm Sargent conducted the BBC Orchestra in a studio broadcast of Kodály's *Szinházi nyitány* ('Theatre Overture'), five of Berg's *Seven Early Songs* – 'Sommertage', 'Im Zimmer', 'Schilflied', 'Traumgekrönt' and 'Die Nachtigall' – and three dances from Falla's *El sombrero de tres picos*. The Berg songs were sung by soprano Hanna Schwarz.

Near the end of the season, on 25 May 1936, the last studio broadcast of a work by a composer associated with the Second Viennese circle took place: Egon Wellesz's Piano Concerto, op. 49, was performed by pianist John Hunt and the BBC Orchestra, conducted by Julian Clifford. Compared with his Viennese colleagues, Wellesz's music had received little BBC attention over the years, a fact that was raised for discussion several times. In October 1933, Wellesz visited England to give a series of lectures on opera at the University of London.[150] Before this prestigious event, Universal Edition's London agent sent the BBC a score of his symphonic poem *Vorfrühling*, op. 12. The Director of Entertainment, Eckersley, asked Boult about the composer's significance and received a positive response:

> I am very glad to say that he is a very well known person all over the musical world, a charming personality and quite a good talker and lecturer with a very fair command of English, not without accent of course. He was chosen by Sir Hugh Allen to represent Vienna, the city of Haydn, when he was giving honorary degrees (Mus. Doc., Ox.) on the occasion of the Haydn celebrations at Oxford.[151]

Interest in the composer was renewed in spring 1934, when scores of Wellesz's Oxford cantata, *Mitte des Lebens*, op. 45, and his recently finished Piano Concerto were sent to the BBC for assessment.[152] Although the Music Department 'noted' the works in May – that is, listed them as possibilities for future broadcasts – neither was then scheduled.[153]

In June 1934, the Austrian Minister in London wrote to Boult about Wellesz's apparent neglect in England. The Music Director replied:

> I think you will like to know, confidentially, I am again going into the question of Professor Wellesz and his music. He is such a charming person, whom I have known for so many years, that it grieves me very much that his work is neglected here. On the other hand we cannot quite feel that his music is of the kind of importance that would justify its inclusion in England, though I am having a fresh examination of some of it, and much hope that something may mature.[154]

Wellesz himself complained about the lack of British attention toward his music, and particularly toward the Oxford cantata, in a letter to the BBC Governor, Mary Agnes Hamilton; Mrs Hamilton immediately wrote to Boult:

> I have a long letter from Dr Egon Wellesz, who is very much upset about his Cantata. I think the simplest plan is to send his letter on to you. You have done so much in giving us the chance of hearing important new works – a real part of the BBC's function, to my mind – that I am sure you will forgive my troubling you personally in the matter.[155]

Boult replied candidly:

> Wellesz is a composer who, though a pupil of Schoenberg, is not, we feel,
> cutting any special ice or writing any works of an importance which justifies
> our taking special notice of them, particularly as their impression, as far as I
> can see, on an English audience is bound to be one of dullness. If it would
> interest you I could send you the reports of readers like Mr Howgill, with
> which I am bound to say I agree, though I cannot claim to have made any-
> thing like such a study of Wellesz' work as our readers have . . .
>
>     Sir Hugh Allen put me in a very awkward position during Wellesz' last visit
> by inviting me to meet Wellesz at lunch and in front of the composer asking
> me to arrange for the performance of some of his works by the B.B.C. If I had
> known Wellesz a little better I should have been inclined to say that nothing
> would induce me to do so under pressure of that kind . . .
>
>     P. S. I should like to say that I know and like Wellesz very much personally.
> It is unpleasant to have to keep one's personal feelings out of things of this
> kind.[156]

Howgill's assessment of Wellesz's cantata does not survive, but Clark had
submitted a scathing report in September 1932.

> This was played over to us by the composer during the summer. My impres-
> sion was that however suitable the work might be to an academic occasion
> such as the presentation of a Doctors Degree honoris causa to an eminent
> historian of Byzantian Music, it was unlikely to prove palatable to any of our
> publics which look primarily for musical interest in the programmes we
> present to them.[157]

Thus Boult, the BBC score readers and even Clark were unable to recommend Wellesz's *Mitte des Lebens* for broadcasting.

    Mrs Hamilton wrote to the Music Director again in August 1934, urging
that he reassess the BBC's position.

> I plead, for 2 reasons, for a reconsideration of the question of our perform-
> ing some work of his. The first is frankly political: convinced that, at the
> present juncture, there is a very real value in any gesture we can make of
> friendship towards Austria.
>
>     The second is different and perhaps rather more personal. I like Dr
> Wellesz, and felt after talking with musical people in Salzburg and elsewhere
> that his work deserves a hearing . . . He did not, of course, say anything
> himself on this issue; but I feel quite distinctly that he is a little hurt.[158]

Boult was inclined to accede to this influential Governor's second request
and suggested that one of Wellesz's light operas might be suitable for
broadcasting.[159] Buesst reported that another Wellesz work was already
under consideration:

Walter Frey has himself ask[ed] to be allowed to play the Piano Concerto, and we are endeavouring to arrange for this to take place in December. The exact date will be negotiated. By this means Wellesz will have the satisfaction of having a major work performed by an artist of repute, which is, I imagine, sufficient recognition of a composer whose music we do not feel would offer great attraction to our public.[160]

By November 1934, the plan had changed:

Now it has been decided to offer this Concerto to John Hunt for a definite performance in the studio, everyone is anxious to get it over. There is no obstruction, though it seems to be generally agreed that on purely musical grounds it does not deserve this honour.[161]

Boult was finally able to assure Mrs Hamilton that a Wellesz broadcast would soon take place, though he still had reservations:

Personally I am delighted about this, but am bound to say I find it not quite easy to square with my conscience. There is so little room for foreign novelties in our programmes that I feel we should most carefully choose only the most suitable composers, and of these I reluctantly feel Wellesz is not one.[162]

Despite Boult's assurances that the concerto would be presented in the near future, another year passed before the performance was finally realized, on 25 May 1936. This late night broadcast, transmitted from the studio, received an unusual amount of pre-concert publicity. The *Radio Times* outlined Wellesz's distinguished career:

Egon Wellesz, composer and musicologist, studied under Schönberg, Bruno Walter, and also under the famous musical scholar and historian Guido Adler. In 1913 he was appointed Lecturer and Musical Historian at Vienna University. He has made a special study of old Byzantine music and has written many important essays on the Baroque period. As a composer, he follows in the wake of Schönberg, although it must be pointed out that he has not blindly followed his master's footsteps. Like many composers of this school, Wellesz's early works show certain influences of Mahler and Reger.[163]

A lengthy article by M. D. Calvocoressi also appeared in *The Listener*.[164] In retrospect, the unusual attention accorded to this low-profile event seems to reflect political manoeuvring, rather than genuine appreciation for the music.

The last concert to be discussed here is the BBC Concert of Contemporary Music that was presented on 1 May 1936. Webern conducted this important concert, the programme of which consisted of only two items: two movements from the *Lyric Suite* in the string orchestra arrangement, and the Berg Violin Concerto, performed by Louis

Krasner.[165] The concerto, Berg's last completed work, had received its world première on 19 April in Barcelona as part of the 1936 ISCM Festival; the BBC performance was given just two weeks later. Webern also conducted a second broadcast on 3 May, a studio orchestra concert featuring Bruckner's Symphony no. 7.

Since the events leading up to these performances have been described in detail elsewhere,[166] only a summary is given here. In October 1935, Wright approached Webern about the possibility of a BBC engagement to take place in April 1936; they agreed that he would conduct the Bruckner symphony. In November, Wright invited Webern to conduct two programmes, the Bruckner on 3 May and a contemporary concert on 1 May. Delighted with this proposal, Webern sent a lengthy response with suggestions for the contemporary programme, including Berg's new Violin Concerto.

> The concerto is committed to a definite soloist, Herr Krasner in America, who has commissioned the work from Berg and so has the sole performing right for a fixed period. The concerto is Berg's most recent work and was composed this summer. I can tell you that it is *quite certain* that Herr Krasner will be in Europe at the time of our concert date and is ready to perform the work.[167]

A few weeks later, Berg died. Within hours, the BBC had heard the news and sent a telegram to his widow:

> We have learned with profound regret of your sad bereavement stop The whole musical world in extending to you its deepest sympathy will join in deploring the passing of so great a composer and so fine a man.[168]

Wright also expressed his regret in a letter to Webern:

> I must refer to the very sad loss the musical world in general and you and your friends in particular have suffered at the sudden and irreparable death of Alban Berg. He was much admired in this country, and we do not remember any composer, great or small – and he was undoubtedly very great – who at the same time held such an essentially simple outlook, and was of such a lovable disposition.[169]

Clark went to Vienna and attended Berg's funeral.

The ISCM Jury, meeting shortly after Berg's death, determined that the première of the Violin Concerto would take place at the Barcelona Festival in April.[170] On 11 January, Webern sent an extensive letter to Clark, expressing his grief and his wish that the 1 May BBC concert be dedicated to Berg's memory.[171] The Music Department adopted this idea: 'We are anxious for Webern to make his Contemporary Concert on May 1st a memorial concert to Berg, and from the point of view of suitability and interest the Violin Concerto will be most valuable.'[172]

Meanwhile, Krasner's European agent, Hanna Graf, contacted the Music Department.[173] She had heard from Universal Edition and Webern that the BBC planned to broadcast the concerto; since Krasner owned exclusive performance rights, the BBC had to engage him as soloist. The Music Department had misgivings about hiring an artist whose playing was unknown to them.[174] Wright also warned the booking office that the fee might be extortionate: 'We will probably be prepared to cut it in half. Evidently Krasner, or someone on his behalf, has paid a considerable sum of money to commission Berg to write this work.'[175] The surprisingly low 15-guinea fee may have convinced the BBC to finalize the engagement, and a contract was issued on 11 March.

The following day, Webern wrote to Clark again, approving the contemporary concert programme. However, as in 1933, when he had previously conducted the *Lyric Suite* movements for the BBC, he refused to include the *Allegro misterioso*:

> My recommendation that only the *first* and *third* pieces should be performed has gone by the board!
>
> It is impossible for me to conduct the second!
>
> It is a virtuoso piece for four soloists and can scarcely be mastered even so.
>
> However good the orchestra may be, the performance of the piece can only be seen as an experiment! An attempt in some degree to approach the wonderful sound of the (quartet) solo strings.
>
> No, I will not and cannot have anything to do with it and will always refuse to conduct this piece.
>
> Even in connexion with our commemoration![176]

The Music Department accepted Webern's decision without dispute – and without informing him that the strings of the BBC Orchestra had already performed the movement twice that season.

Unusually, the BBC decided to begin the memorial concert with an introductory talk about Berg and his contribution to music. Webern recommended that Adorno be invited to present the talk, but Maurice Johnstone informed him that 'experience has shown us that the best results are always obtained by employing an English speaker who is thoroughly accustomed to microphone work, and therefore we are arranging for one of our regular announcers to give the talk'.[177] On 23 April, just a week before the event, the Director of Programme Planning, Wellington, wrote a furious memo demanding to know how the decision to transmit a spoken eulogy had been made without the knowledge, participation or approval of him or the Controller (Programmes), Graves.

> The decision to have an 'introductory announcement' is surely one in which I might be supposed to have an interest. I gather that it is intended to last for five minutes. I have had to say definitely that the B.B.C. as such cannot pronounce eulogies on the dead in this way and that we must get an Ernest Newman to do it for us. That will complicate the presentation of the programme in the Hall as he will presumably have to speak from another studio.[178]

In fact, the pre-concert eulogy, described in the *Radio Times* as an 'Introductory Announcement', resulted from a series of errors and mis-communications within the Music Department. As Wright explained:

> Alban Berg died at Xmas & Steuermann came at the end of January and suggested an all-Berg concert in order appropriately to place the new concerto. This in principal [*sic*] was agreed by Panel & D.M. [Boult] after we had had some difficulty in tracing the violinist who has the sole right to perform it. There was not suggestion of any special presentation in the form of a 'Eulogium', but naturally a well thought out announcement to be discussed between us & your side in due course. I then fell ill, and in my and Edward Clark's absence Maurice Johnstone had a letter from Webern referring to the introductory talk. Dr Boult 'phoned a message to my house, and I replied that I had not corresponded on, or agreed to, a special talk, and certainly not by Webern. But the inclusion of the words 'Introductory Announcement' was done by Johnstone on a telephoned instruction of Clark . . . and this is the first I have known of it.[179]

George Barnes of the Talks Department invited Newman to give the disputed talk.[180] He mentioned that the content should 'consist more or less of a funeral oration on Berg rather than a description of the music which is to be played', since a talk earlier that evening would provide an introduction to Berg's music.[181] Barnes apologized that the invitation was so late:

> I feel that I owe you an apology for asking you at such short notice, especially when you are so busy on your Wagner book. The fact is, let me confess it at once, that a mistake has been made. Box and Cox each thought that the other had written to you four weeks ago. I hope that your enjoyment on hearing that such a situation can arise in the B.B.C. will overcome your irritation at being invited so late!

In fact, it had only been decided the day before that Newman should give the talk. Newman responded that he would 'undertake the melancholy task with pleasure'.[182]

In his eulogy, Newman tried to explain why Berg was universally mourned.

> As a rule, when a composer's death evokes widespread regret it is because, no matter how young he may have been when he died, he has endowed the

world with a number of works that have already taken their place in the repertory. But this was not so in Berg's case . . . Never in all history has there been such general regret at the death of a composer who meant so little to the public as a whole.[183]

Newman felt that Berg provided an essential link between traditions of the past and ultra-modern idioms.

Many of us have felt all along during the last twenty years or so that Schönberg had posed a problem rather than solved it . . . Now Berg's works show him to have been aiming more and more, as time went on, consciously or unconsciously, at a working compromise between old and new. What really went on inside him it is impossible for us who did not know him personally to say: but I think it probable that as the years moved on, bringing experience with them, he became a little doubtful of Schönbergianism in its more extreme form, though his loyalty to his beloved master might not allow him to confess it, even to himself. I think there was always a certain disunion within him, his teacher's theories pulling him one way, certain of his own instincts another.

Newman concluded that Berg's linking role explained the great sense of loss felt at the news of his death.

His death has been a matter of equally profound regret to musicians of all parties. The Schönbergians honour him as the most gifted composer of their circle, the one who seemed most likely to become a permanent world-figure, and most likely to win over the plain musical man to their theories and their practice; while the rest of us see in him a composer who, in time, would have solved, if anyone could, the difficult problem of accommodating the new musical language to the old.

The memorial concert was received with interest, though without detailed comment, in the British press. Most reviewers focused on the work's suitability as a requiem for the composer and the traditional qualities that made it accessible to listeners, even on first hearing. William McNaught, in the *Evening News*, simply reported:

This was a Violin Concerto that the composer dedicated to the memory of a young friend, and which has proved to be his own requiem. One does not need to possess an ear attuned to the modernist idiom to recognise that this work is one of the finest of its products.[184]

In *The Daily Telegraph*, Richard Capell explained the work's structure and musical characteristics in more detail, but likewise concluded:

By his 'programme' and by the use of the chorale . . . Berg has given this work a shape and a human appeal beyond the more academic compositions of the school to which he belonged. What the lasting effect of the concerto may be it would be rash to guess, but it is assuredly one of the major symphonic works of the new Vienna.[185]

The music programme builders concurred with the general feeling that the new work was a significant addition to the modern repertory. A few days after the broadcast, Wright recommended that the BBC immediately organize its first public performance in Britain. He reported to Herbage:

> In view of the extremely important nature of the above work and the general trend of the press criticisms I have seen . . . I have got Louis Krasner (who has all the performing rights for a further two years) to promise that he will not offer the work to or agree to play it for, any other London Society next season without first getting in touch with us . . . I feel that if we can place it in one of Dr Boult's concerts with something of more general attraction we need have no hesitation in booking Krasner for it. He is a good musician and plays the work very well, though perhaps not so superlatively as it may deserve.[186]

The first British public performance of the work was given at the Queen's Hall on 9 December 1936 in a BBC Symphony Concert conducted by Sir Henry Wood, with Louis Krasner as soloist.

Although British critics reviewed Berg's concerto favourably, some had been less impressed by the quality of the performance. Capell had attended the Barcelona première, conducted by Scherchen, and did not think the second performance had been as well executed.

> A more perfect performance than was given last night – Webern is not the conductor he might be – might have rendered the elaboration of the chorale more convincing, and one feels bound to say that the magical effect achieved last week under Scherchen of the final cadence and exquisitely consoling resolution in B flat was hardly matched, in spite of the artistry of the B.B.C. players.[187]

This view was shared by certain members of the BBC staff, including the Music Executive, Mase, who wrote to Boult:

> Although only an Executive, I took the trouble to spend two half hours at Webern's rehearsals with the orchestra. It is my emphatic opinion that under no circumstances should he ever be engaged as a conductor.[188]

Boult passed the memo to Wright with the comment: 'This wants careful thought. Orch. Manager [Pratt] is inclined to agree.' However, Wright defended Webern:

> Music Executive had already informed me of his views about Webern's conducting, but I also made a point of going to two rehearsals and the whole of

the Contemporary performance, and think that while Webern's technique such as it is, goes to bits when he is excited and he no doubt worries the orchestra, he obtained a remarkably good performance of the Concerto. This was due, I think, to the fact that the orchestra realised that he understood and loved every note of the work, and his funny little explanations of the varying dynamics and flexibility of tempo were quickly interpreted by the orchestra correctly. There should be no question, I think, of bringing Webern every year, but I should like you, if you will, to talk to Bliss also, as he was present at the first full rehearsal for the Concerto with me, and I do not like to see so fin[e] and sincere a musician condemned outright without very serious consideration.[189]

Nevertheless, when Webern applied for another engagement the following spring, the Music Programme Advisory Panel – of which Bliss was a key member – turned down the application. The minutes record:

> The Panel could not recommend his engagement as a conductor, but it was suggested that his newly revised Six Pieces for Orchestra might be considered for a Contemporary Concert, and his orchestration of Bach's Fugue from the Musikalisches Opfer for a Sunday Orchestral Concert.[190]

Although Webern's music continued to be broadcast, Webern himself was never again invited to conduct for the BBC. The performance of the Berg Violin Concerto in May 1936 marked the ending of an era: it was the last BBC contemporary concert of Second Viennese School repertory to be planned with the cooperation of Edward Clark, and it was the last to involve the personal participation of Anton Webern.

By the end of the 1935–6 season, BBC interest in Berg's music had completely supplanted that previously granted to his teacher and mentor, Schoenberg. Attention accorded to Second Viennese School repertory was unquestionably dominated by the season's broadcasts of Berg works. No fewer than three presentations were given of the string orchestra arrangement of the *Lyric Suite* movements, conducted by Boult, Ansermet and Webern, all noted for their interpretations of contemporary repertory. The powerful response to the composer's final composition, the Violin Concerto, both in the British press and within the BBC, strengthened Berg's popularity in British music circles. This composer's expressive idiom and his discernable links with Wagner and German Romanticism dissolved some of the barriers that had become associated with Second Viennese School repertory in the decade since it was introduced to the British public through BBC broadcasts.

# 11 Clark's legacy

A significant change to Music Department personnel in March 1936 defines the end of the period considered in this study: Clark resigned from the BBC. Wright's confidence in Clark's abilities had led to promotion in spring 1935, and Clark was considered for further promotion in the autumn. Nevertheless, the programme builder's position reached a crisis point in early 1936.

The central administrators were incensed when Clark failed to spend his time and their money as expected during a trip to the continent, in which he organized the BBC Symphony Orchestra's spring tour of Europe and met with Toscanini to discuss the May Festival concerts. In February, Nicolls wrote a scathing memo, complaining that the trip had been planned at the last minute, that Clark had changed his travel plans, staying away a week longer than proposed and missing the winter Proms in London, and that he had not completed his report on time. Nicolls angrily concluded:

> I objected very strongly to this visit occurring at Christmas, to my being first asked to agree to it about four days before Christmas, to the fact that Mr Graves was rung up at Fallodon about the matter – in other words, I objected to the whole way in which the matter was handled by the Music Department. I agreed to the proposal finally for reasons which I will not put on paper. I consider that that agreement has been seriously abused.[1]

Boult replied with an equally adamant memo:

> I most emphatically consider that Mr Clark carried out the intentions of his foreign visit in a most thorough and satisfactory manner. He certainly took longer over it than I (or he) anticipated, but in following through his movements step by step, as I have carefully done, I can see that the extra week was as unavoidable as it is justified. Quite apart from a rough report he prepared for me immediately on his return, I know from his replies to many searching musical and technical questions both from his colleagues and from the Panel, that he brought back an expert view of the whole situation in each centre visited which, even if not completely written down, is most comforting to have behind so important a set of programmes, subject to the most searching criticism here and abroad.[2]

Boult verified that Clark had maintained contact with Wright at each stage of the journey and summarized his delicate negotiations, pointing out how awkward it had been to discuss programmes with Toscanini at the very time that BBC administrators were being difficult about his fee. He accounted for Clark's time in each city, justifying especially the extended period in Vienna.

> [He] certainly took longer there than he expected because (1) there were more people to see there than anywhere else, (2) the situation musically is extremely difficult, yet it is a very important centre, (3) not all the people were available right away, (4) he quite rightly attended Alban Berg's funeral, while the unexpected disaster to the musical circle scarcely predisposed his friends to plunge enthusiastically into discussions about our orchestral tour.

Boult concluded by criticizing Nicolls for his interference.

> I am afraid I entirely fail to understand the last paragraph of Controller (A's) memorandum of February 6th. Ample reason was given him then, and is repeated here, as to why the visit occurred at Christmas and as to the lateness of arrival in Controller (P's) office of the application, and I must absolutely rebut his charge that the authority had been abused. If the Corporation could bring itself to understand a little more of the way great artists are handled by their managers and by big firms like the gramophone companies, the much abused Music Department might save valuable time now expended in dealing with inquisitions of this kind.

Nicolls conceded that if Boult was satisfied, he had no more to say about it.[3] Once again, administrators who valued routine and accountability severely criticized Clark's irregular working habits. But once again, Clark's advocates – those who appreciated his unique qualities over his practical deficiencies – came to his rescue.

Unfortunately, these same supporters were unable to sanction Clark's behaviour only a month later. The programme builder discovered that last minute changes had been made, while he was ill and without his approval, to the programmes he had carefully built for the European tour. He tried to discuss the matter with Boult.

> I cannot accept something in which I don't believe. The morning after I heard the news, I rose from my sick bed . . . at 7 a.m. I sent a telegram to Dr Adrian Boult at Broadcasting House, asking him to meet me before the usual meeting at 10.30. I arrived at 10 and was told that Dr Boult was not there.
> It was impossible for me to wait, my legs had no strength. I sat down and wrote out my resignation. I was compelled to resign.[4]

The resignation letter was received by the Corporation on 16 March.[5] Clark was not merely upset by the programme alterations, though:

> Had I been consulted I should at once have pointed out mistakes of pro-gramme building in the new Paris programme, which in certain fatal

respects is ill balanced and ill advised. I should have continued to defend
those grand old BBC lines of inspiring & progressive musical policy and
should have exposed the last-minute revival of the 'box-office' shibboleth –
as though that had not been fully examined & a straight course set.

He felt compelled to resign because the changes had been made without
reference to him.

I find myself unable to accept the manner in which the matter was dealt with.
I was given the job of preparing the project of a programme scheme for this
Tour. I don[']t think you will doubt that I put forward my best suggestions
for its greatest success, or that I spared any pains either in collecting material
here and on the continent or in piloting the scheme (once we had established
it) through all the rocks and shallows of the countless committees etc we
have to navigate – by far the most arduous task for the programme builder
these days. I understood that this was all successfully accomplished and
everything definitely agreed and promulgated.

   That these three months work be washed out, that the course be reversed
even at the eleventh hour after everyone concerned therewith had already
given his assent, I will not criticize. But for this to be done without the
person responsible for the original (and accepted) scheme being either
referred to or even informed is a procedure which I am afraid I can neither
comprehend nor accept. It is clear that I could never again undertake any
further such commissions and must therefore retire.

In the week before Boult responded, he discussed the situation with senior
Music Department staff.[6] In the end, Boult accepted the resignation without
dispute, because he seriously disagreed with Clark's perception of the extent
that a programme builder should control programmes he planned.

I need not go into all my reasons now, but I should like to say that I ultimately, and with great regret, came to the conclusion that the grounds you
have put forward seem to me to show such a misconception of your position
vis-à-vis the Corporation, and mine, and of the nature of the charges to
which you take exception, that no other course was possible.[7]

Boult nevertheless expressed his personal appreciation for Clark's BBC
work:

Now I want to put on record, however inadequately, the great debt that we
owe to you for your conduct of B.B.C. programmes of music since you first
went to Savoy Hill. It is very impressive to hear, wherever one goes, things
said of our programme policy like those which were said at the Milhaud
lunch recently – and it cannot be forgotten that the original idea of the
B.B.C. Orchestra scheme was yours. Formal letters of thanks will no doubt
reach you from the Corporation, but I want you to have this as well, and I
know that what I have said is felt by everyone in Music Department.

The Corporation paid him a further three months' salary, plus severance pay equal to nearly half his annual earnings, and he did not work out his notice.[8] The news reached the London newspapers on 28 March, and – in the week of German elections confirming Hitler's power-base – made the front page of at least one major newspaper.[9] Clark's BBC duties were taken over by his assistant, Maurice Johnstone.

In June 1936, Newman wrote to Reith on Clark's behalf, asking whether the programme builder might present a case for regaining his position.[10] After consulting Graves and Boult, Reith replied in the negative.

> [Graves and Boult] are not surprised to hear that Edward Clark is regretting his resignation, and, in fact, they expected he would do so. When his resignation was accepted all aspects were, of course, carefully considered, including the possible loss to us of his specialist knowledge of modern music. Mr Clark certainly had exceptionally wide knowledge and experience on that side, but I understand from Mr Graves that he hopes that, after making allowances for a period of adjustment, you will be able to agree that the programmes have not suffered to anything like the extent which might have been anticipated.[11]

Thus, Clark's rocky career in the BBC came to an untimely end. Although he regretted his heated decision, Corporation administrators who had battled with his unorthodox methods for years were unwilling to consider reinstatement. Clark occasionally conducted and gave talks for the BBC in later years, but he was never again a member of the Corporation staff.

Clark's resignation marked the end of an era in the BBC Music Department. Since the programme building section had been formed nearly a decade earlier, the three core members, Wright, Clark and Herbage, had worked together to build the music programmes, shaping the musical tastes and experiences of the British listening public. Clark's expansive knowledge of art music repertory and his intimacy with the European new music network provided the BBC with a unique source of experience. The Music Directors' specialist interests and the BBC's horizon-broadening policies had encouraged Clark to bring an enterprising and original approach to music broadcasts. Wright and Herbage maintained the programming conventions and contacts that Clark had helped to establish until war was declared, after which music programme policies and planning methods were drastically changed.

## Conclusion

By the mid-1930s, the BBC was the most important music impresario operating in Britain. As transmission capabilities improved and the number of listeners increased, the Corporation's programmes reached the widest audience of any music-disseminating organization in British history. This increase in external power and influence was matched by extensive growth of the Corporation's structure, responsibility and expectations. In the Music Department alone, Boult directed a substantial music-generating operation, managing the outstanding BBC Symphony Orchestra and the many other BBC orchestras and choruses, hiring artists and ensembles of both local and foreign origin, purchasing performances of other music organizations, both in Britain and on the continent, and, finally, coordinating all these elements into daily music broadcasts that offered variety, quality and satisfaction.

Throughout the many changes that accompanied the Corporation's rapid growth, responsibility for planning art music broadcasts remained in the hands of Wright, Clark and Herbage, who created programmes along lines they established in the late 1920s, encompassing a spectrum of musical genres and styles. However, as the significance and influence of the programmes grew, there was, perhaps inevitably, a parallel increase in interference in policies and programming practices, both from within the BBC and from without. Internally, men like Nicolls, with different broadcasting objectives, came to control Music Department finances and ultimately redefined programming options. At the same time, the severe economic and political conditions of the 1930s resulted in intense pressure on the programme builders to support British music and musicians at the expense of the international outlook encouraged in earlier years.

The BBC cultivated in its music staff men who were unusually knowledgeable and well connected with new music forces, compared to many British musicians of the day. Pitt, Boult, Clark and Wright shared an interest in contemporary music, and their enthusiasm and dedication to it inspired senior administrators to support and encourage its presentation in BBC broadcasts, through performances, talks and prominent publicity. New music programmes disseminated otherwise unattainable cultural experiences to the British population, and the administrators viewed this as an important and appropriate means of executing their fundamental horizon-expanding policies. However, the effect of bringing difficult compositional styles of works written during the previous twenty-five years to many who had little or no experience, background or familiarity with even standard art music repertory was understandably controversial. Critics of these policies frequently cited contemporary music broadcasts as notorious examples of the BBC's excesses in forcing unwanted programming on the innocent and incomprehending public.

Nevertheless, the Music Department sustained the BBC's commitment to contemporary music, as well as to music of other less-familiar repertories. An examination of works by composers associated with the Second Viennese circle transmitted during the years of Boult's directorship when Clark was still involved with programme building, from autumn 1930 to May 1936 (listed in Table 11.1), emphatically demonstrates this point. Over 85 performances of 59 different works by Schoenberg, Berg, Webern, Wellesz, Pisk, Koffler, von Hannenheim, Gerhard, Weiss, Krenek, Eisler and Hauer were presented during this period. After a decade of devoting broadcast time to Second Viennese School works,[12] the BBC had certainly succeeded in its cultural-expansionist goal to make the listening public aware of its existence.

In the early 1930s, as at the end of the previous decade, Schoenberg's music was the focal point of BBC attention. However, the inaccessability of his 12-tone idiom, as epitomized in the BBC performances of the Variations for Orchestra, op. 31, finally drove critics and the public to reject this music outright. With Schoenberg's permanent departure from Europe in autumn 1933, BBC interest in his post-war output quickly waned. Attention shifted to his friend and colleague, Berg, who had been all but ignored by the BBC during the 1920s. Broadcasts of Berg's music prevailed from the time that excerpts from *Wozzeck* were first transmitted in 1932. By mid-1936, his major post-war works, from *Wozzeck* to the Symphonic Excerpts from *Lulu* to the Violin Concerto, had been broadcast by the Corporation at least once, to much critical acclaim. In fact, the BBC exploited Berg's music, recognizing that it provided a much-needed link between the familiar and the new, a link which served as a foundation for appreciation, and perhaps even for comprehension, of ultra-modern music by British audiences.

It is hard to imagine today that BBC music programming began as a one-man operation, with L. Stanton Jefferies providing all music-related services for the infant broadcasting company. From that basic beginning, the Music Department rapidly grew into a specialized team of music broadcasting experts. The staff's diverse and unusual knowledge, experience and artistic values soon established a music programming tradition, founded on Reith's idealistic broadcasting goals: to entertain, to educate and inform, to bring the art music spectrum – both familiar and unfamiliar, old and new, accessible and difficult, standard and controversial – into the homes of the British public on a daily basis. This cultural-expansionist approach to broadcasting played a vital role in shaping the British public's musical tastes, and has remained the basis of BBC art music dissemination for three-quarters of a century.

Table 11.1 *Works by Second Viennese School composers and their associates, performed in BBC concerts and broadcasts between autumn 1930 and spring 1936 (performances of arrangements of works by other composers are not included)*

**Schoenberg**
songs from op. 2: 'Erwartung',** 'Erhebung', 'Schenk mir deinen goldenen Kamm',**
    'Waldsonne'**
song from op. 3: 'Hochzeitslied'
*Verklärte Nacht*, op. 4 ***
*Gurrelieder*, Part I
'Lied der Waldtaube' from *Gurrelieder*
*Pelleas und Melisande*, op. 5 **
song from op. 6: 'Traumleben'
String Quartet no. 1, op. 7 **
String Quartet no. 2, op. 10 (not broadcast)
Three Piano Pieces, op. 11 **
song from op. 12: 'Jane Gray'
*Friede auf Erden*, op. 13 ***
Five Orchestra Pieces, op. 16
*Erwartung*, op. 17
*Six Little Piano Pieces*, op. 19 **
*Pierrot lunaire*, op. 21
String Quartet no. 3, op. 30
Variations for Orchestra, op. 31 **
Piano Pieces, op. 33a and op. 33b
*Begleitmusik zu einer Lichtspielszene*, op. 34 **
Suite in G major for string orchestra **

**Berg**
Seven Early Songs: 'Nacht', 'Schilflied',** 'Die Nachtigall',** 'Traumgekrönt',*** 'Im
    Zimmer',** 'Liebesode', and 'Sommertage'**
Piano Sonata, op. 1
songs from op. 2 (not specified)
*Wozzeck*
Three fragments from *Wozzeck* ***** (one performance was not broadcast)
Chamber Concerto for piano, violin and 13 wind instruments ('Adagio' also
    performed in arrangement for violin and piano)
*Lyric Suite*
Three Movements from the *Lyric Suite*, arr. for string orchestra **** (on two
    occasions, only two movements were performed)
*Der Wein*
Symphonic Excerpts from *Lulu*
Violin Concerto

**Webern**
Passacaglia, op. 1 ***
song from op. 3: 'Kahl reckt der Baum'

Table 11.1 (*cont.*)

**Webern** (*cont.*)
song from op. 4: 'Eingang'
Five Pieces for String Quartet, op. 5 (also performed in the arrangement for string orchestra)
Five Orchestra Pieces, op. 10
Symphony, op. 21 (ISCM 1931; not broadcast)

**Krenek**
songs from op. 9: 'Räume', 'Rätselspiel' and 'Die frühen Gräber'
Concerto grosso no. 2, op. 25
*Die Jahreszeiten*, op. 35
song from op. 53: 'Ein anderes'
Piano Sonata no. 2, op. 59
*Reisebuch aus dem österreichischen Alpen*, op. 62
'Variations' from String Quartet no. 5, op. 65
Theme and 13 Variations, op. 69
*Durch die Nacht*, op. 67a
*Gesänge des späten Jahres*, op. 71

**Wellesz**
piano pieces: 'Tanzstück' and 'Pastorale'
*Drei geistliche Chöre*, op. 47 (ISCM 1931)
Piano Concerto, op. 49

**Pisk**
piano pieces: 'Toccata' from Concert Piece, op. 7; Small Suite, op. 11; 'March' from Great Suite, op. 17

**Koffler**
String Trio (ISCM 1931; not broadcast)
*Variations on a 12-tone Series*, op. 9

**Hannenheim**
Piano Sonata

**Gerhard**
Six Catalan Folk Songs for soprano and orchestra

**Weiss**
'Andante' from Chamber Symphony

**Eisler**
*Little Symphony*, op. 29

**Hauer**
songs: 'An die Hoffnung' from op. 21; 'Der gute Glaube' from op. 6; op. 12: 'Ehemals
    und jetzt', 'Abbitte', and 'Die Heimat'

    **   work performed on 2 different occasions
   ***   work performed on 3 different occasions
  ****   work performed on 4 different occasions
*****   work performed on 5 different occasions

# Appendix A    British performances of Second Viennese School works, January 1912 – May 1936

This appendix provides a chronological list of broadcast and concert performances of works by Second Viennese School composers that took place in Britain between 1912, when the first occurred, and May 1936, the end of the period under investigation. Most of the performances were traced through announcements and reviews, primarily found in *The Musical Times*, the *Monthly Musical Record*, the *Radio Times* and the BBC 'Programmes as Broadcast' records. Since other performances, not mentioned in these or other consulted sources, probably took place, this list is undoubtedly not comprehensive; however, it includes the most significant British performances of Second Viennese School works during the period, and provides a representative idea of which works received attention and the frequency with which such performances took place.

Each entry in the list contains information about a broadcast or concert which included one or more works from the Second Viennese School repertory, as defined in the introduction. The entry gives details about what was performed, the names of performers, the place and date of performance and other relevant information. Each entry includes as much information as was possible to trace; in some cases the sources were vague or incomplete in their coverage of an event, and details may be missing.

**1912 Jan. 23**
*place of performance:* Steinway Hall, London                broadcast:        concert: ✓
*work(s) performed:* Schoenberg    *Three Piano Pieces, op. 11
*performed by:* Richard Buhlig (piano)
*notes:* *1st British performance

**1912 Sept. 3**    Promenade Concert
*place of performance:* Queen's Hall, London                broadcast:        concert: ✓
*work(s) performed:* Schoenberg    *Five Pieces for orchestra, op. 16
*performed by:* Queen's Hall Orchestra
*conductor:* Sir Henry Wood
*notes:* *1st performance

**1913 Nov. 1**
*place of performance:* Bechstein Hall, London          broadcast:     concert: ✓
*work(s) performed:* Schoenberg    *String Quartet no. 1, op. 7
*performed by:* Flonzaley Quartet
*notes:* *1st British performance

**1914 Jan. 15**    meeting of the Music Club
*place of performance:* Grafton Gallery (private concert),        broadcast:     concert: ✓
     London
*work(s) performed:* Schoenberg    * *Verklärte Nacht,* op. 4
                     Schoenberg    selection of early songs
*performed by:* London String Quartet, and singers Juliette Autran and Frederick Austin
*notes:* *1st British performance
     The string players were: A. E. Sammons, Thomas W. Petre, H. Waldo Warner, and C.
     Warwick Evans, with James Lockyer (viola), Cedric Sharpe ('cello). The Schoenberg
     songs were not identified.

**1914 Jan. 17**
*place of performance:* Queen's Hall, London          broadcast:     concert: ✓
*work(s) performed:* Schoenberg    Five Pieces for orchestra, op. 16
*performed by:* Queen's Hall Orchestra
*conductor:* Schoenberg
*notes:* Schoenberg was invited to conduct by Edward Clark, at Sir Henry Wood's
     suggestion.

**1914 Jan. 23**
*place of performance:* Bechstein Hall, London          broadcast:     concert: ✓
*work(s) performed:* Schoenberg    * *Verklärte Nacht,* op. 4
*performed by:* London String Quartet with James Lockyer (viola) and Cedric Sharpe
     ('cello)
*notes:*    *1st public British performance

**1914 Feb. 20**
*place of performance:* Bechstein Hall, London          broadcast:     concert: ✓
*work(s) performed:* Schoenberg    *Verklärte Nacht,* op. 4
*performed by:* London String Quartet

**1914 March 12**
*place of performance:* Royal College of Music, London        broadcast:     concert: ✓
*work(s) performed:* Schoenberg    *Verklärte Nacht,* op. 4

**1914 March 13**
*place of performance:* Bechstein Hall, London          broadcast:     concert: ✓
*work(s) performed:* Schoenberg    'Erwartung' and 'Waldsonne' from op. 2
*performed by:* Fanny Copeland (soprano) and Geoffrey O'Connor-Morris (piano)

**1914 March 19**
*place of performance:* Leighton House, London                    broadcast:        concert: ✓
*work(s) performed:* Schoenberg    *Verklärte Nacht*, op. 4
*performed by:* London String Quartet

**1914 March 27**
*place of performance:* Steinway Hall, London                    broadcast:        concert: ✓
*work(s) performed:* Schoenberg    *Six Little Piano Pieces*, op. 19
                     Schoenberg    two piano pieces from op. 11
*performed by:* Leo Ornstein (piano)

**1914 June 10**
*place of performance:* London                    broadcast:        concert: ✓
*work(s) performed:* Schoenberg    *String Quartet no. 2, op. 10
*performed by:* London String Quartet with Carrie Tubb (soprano)
*notes:* *1st British performance

**1919 Dec. 27**
*place of performance:* Æolian Hall, London                    broadcast:        concert: ✓
*work(s) performed:* Schoenberg    *Verklärte Nacht*, op. 4
*performed by:* London String Quartet with James Lockyer (viola) and Cedric Sharpe
    ('cello)
*notes:* Repeated by demand on 3 January 1920. 'The first time . . . a work of such
    importance by a living ex-enemy composer had been heard in a London concert hall
    since 1914.'

**1920 Jan. 3**
*place of performance:* London                    broadcast:        concert: ✓
*work(s) performed:* Schoenberg    *Verklärte Nacht*, op. 4
*performed by:* London String Quartet with James Lockyer (viola) and Cedric Sharpe
    ('cello)
*notes:* A repeat of the 27 December 1919 performance, by popular demand.

**1921 May 6**    orchestral concerts organized by Edward Clark
*place of performance:* Æolian Hall, London                    broadcast:        concert: ✓
*work(s) performed:* Schoenberg    *Chamber Symphony, op. 9
*performed by:* included Charles Woodhouse (violin), John Barbirolli ('cello), Leon
    Goossens (oboe), Aubrey and Alfred Brain (horns)
*conductor:* Edward Clark
*notes:* *1st British performance. Series of four concerts performed at Queen's Hall and
    Æolian Hall, which included recent works by French, German and English
    composers, many of them first English performances.

**1921 Nov. 9**   Goossen's Orchestral Concerts
*place of performance:* Queen's Hall, London                     broadcast:    concert: ✓
*work(s) performed:* Schoenberg    Five Pieces for orchestra, op. 16
*conductor:* Eugene Goossens
*other works performed:* by J. R. Heath, Ravel, Strauss, Bliss and Delius
*notes:* Part of a series of concerts organized and conducted by Goossens, which
    included many recent works.

**1922 Jan. 12**
*place of performance:* Chelsea Town Hall, Chelsea                broadcast:    concert: ✓
*work(s) performed:* Schoenberg    *Verklärte Nacht*, op. 4
*performed by:* Philharmonic Quartet with Ernest Tomlinson and Ambrose
    Gauntlett

**1922 Spring**
*place of performance:* private concert at the home of           broadcast:    concert: ✓
    Robert Mayer
*work(s) performed:* Wellesz songs
*performed by:* Dorothy Moulton (soprano)
*notes:* During a visit to London, Wellesz gave a lecture about his music, illustrated by
    these performances of his songs sung by Mayer's wife, Dorothy Moulton. It is not
    known which Wellesz songs were sung.

**1922 Oct. 17**
*place of performance:* London Contemporary Music Centre    broadcast:    concert: ✓
*work(s) performed:* Krenek    String Quartet no. 1
*performed by:* McCullagh Quartet
*other works performed:* Cecil Hazlehurst: *The Masque of Fear*; Cliffe Forrester: *Dance
    Fantasy*; Alfred Wall: Piano Quartet
*notes:* The performance was heard by Edward J. Dent, who wrote to Krenek in
    appreciation.

**1923 Nov. 19**   Kensington New Music Club
*place of performance:* Kensington Town Hall, London             broadcast:    concert: ✓
*work(s) performed:* Schoenberg    *Pierrot lunaire*, op. 21
*performed by:* Marya Freund (soprano), J. Wiéner (piano), L. Fleury (flute/piccolo),
    H. Delacroix (clarinet/bass clarinet), H. Denayer (violin/viola), P. Mas ('cello)
*conductor:* Darius Milhaud
*other works performed:* by L. Vinci and Schumann
*notes:* *1st British performance. Performed in French. (See also 20 and 21 November.)

**1923 Nov. 20**   Music Society
*place of performance:* St John's Institute, London          broadcast:     concert: ✓
*work(s) performed:* Schoenberg   *Pierrot lunaire*, op. 21
*performed by:* Marya Freund (soprano), J. Wiéner (piano), L. Fleury (flute/piccolo),
    H. Delacroix (clarinet/bass clarinet), H. Denayer (violin/viola), P. Mas ('cello)
*conductor:* Darius Milhaud
*other works performed:* by L. Vinci, Schumann
*notes:* Performed in French. (See also 19 and 21 November.)

**1923 Nov. 21**
*place of performance:* Chelsea          broadcast:     concert: ✓
*work(s) performed:* Schoenberg   *Pierrot lunaire*, op. 21
*performed by:* Marya Freund (soprano), J. Wiéner (piano), L. Fleury (flute/piccolo),
    H. Delacroix (clarinet/bass clarinet), H. Denayer (violin/viola), P. Mas ('cello)
*conductor:* Darius Milhaud
*other works performed:* by L. Vinci, Schumann
*notes:* Performed in French. (See also 19 and 20 November.)

**1924 Feb. 20**   The Goossens Chamber Concerts
*place of performance:* Æolian Hall, London          broadcast:     concert: ✓
*work(s) performed:* Schoenberg   String Quartet no. 2, op. 10
*performed by:* Hungarian String Quartet with Dorothy Moulton (soprano)
*other works performed:* first performances of works by Armstrong Gibbs and Eugène
    Bonner
*notes:* Second concert in the Goossens chamber music series.

**1926 July 1**   College Concerts
*place of performance:* Royal College of Music, London          broadcast:     concert: ✓
*work(s) performed:* Schoenberg   *Verklärte Nacht*, op. 4
*performed by:* Jack Sealey, Leila Hermitage, Mary Gladden, Joyce Cook, Helen Just and
    Audrey Piggott
*other works performed:* Schubert, Beethoven, Veracini, Dunhill and Arne songs, and
    Renaissance madrigals.

**1926 Dec. 7**   BBC International Chamber Concerts of New Music
*broadcast over:* 2LO (8.15–9.30 pm)          broadcast: ✓ concert: ✓
*place of performance:* Grotrian Hall, London
*work(s) performed:* [Krenek   String Quartet, op. 12]
*performed by:* Amar Quartet: Licco Amar, Paul Hindemith, Walter Caspar and Rudolf
    Hindemith
*other works performed:* actual programme: Jarnach: *String Quartet, op. 16; Reger:
    String Trio, op. 77b; and Hindemith: *String Quartet, op. 22 (not broadcast)
*notes:* *1st English performance. Although the first English performance of Krenek's
    'String Quartet, op. 12' was listed in initial announcements, the Reger String Trio
    was performed instead. Third concert of the series, this one focusing on recent
    works by German composers.

**1927 Feb. 3**   National Concert
*broadcast over:* 2LO (8.0–9.15 pm)                                                                    broadcast: ✓ concert: ✓
*place of performance:* Royal Albert Hall, London
*work(s) performed:* Schoenberg   *Verklärte Nacht*, op. 4
*orchestra:* National Orchestra
*conductor:* Scherchen
*other works performed:* by Beethoven and Liszt
*notes:* The Schoenberg was performed in its string orchestra arrangement. Pouishnov
   took part in the concert.


**1927 June 9**   Light Symphony Concert
*broadcast over:* 2LO (8.0–9 pm, 9.37–10.30 pm)                                          broadcast: ✓ concert:
*work(s) performed:* Schoenberg   *Verklärte Nacht*, op. 4
*performed by:* soloists in other works: Dr E. Schipper (baritone), R. Murchie (flute)
*orchestra:* Wireless Symphony Orchestra
*conductor:* Scherchen


**1927 Oct. 3**   Concerts of Contemporary Music, series ii, concert 1
*broadcast over:* 2LO&5XX (9.35–11.24 pm)                                                    broadcast: ✓ concert:
*work(s) performed:* Webern      Five Pieces for string quartet, op. 5
                     Schoenberg   String Quartet no. 1, op. 7
                     Eisler       Duo for violin and 'cello, op. 7
*performed by:* Vienna String Quartet
*other works performed:* Ravel: *Cinq mélodies populaires grecques*; Falla: popular Spanish
   songs
*notes:* Sarah Fischer (soprano) also performed. According to the *Radio Times*,
   Stravinsky attended the performance.


**1927 Nov. 7**   Concerts of Contemporary Music, series ii, concert 2
*broadcast over:* 2LO&5XX (9.35–10.38 pm)                                                    broadcast: ✓ concert:
*work(s) performed:* Krenek   Five Piano Pieces, op. 39
*performed by:* Emma Lubbecke-Job (piano)
*other works performed:* by Stravinsky, Hindemith, Koechlin, Honegger and Milhaud
*notes:* The performed programme was altered from the announced programme, due to
   the last-minute change in pianist from Marcelle Meyer to Emma Lubbecke-Job.
   Thus, the Krenek was not originally planned for performance on this programme,
   but was a late addition. The Pro Arte String Quartet also performed.


**1928 Jan. 9**   Concerts of Contemporary Music, series ii, concert 4
*broadcast over:* 5GB (8.30–10.0 pm)                                                              broadcast: ✓ concert:
*work(s) performed:* Schoenberg   Chamber Symphony, op. 9
*conductor:* Ansermet
*other works performed:* Schulhoff: Piano Concerto, with the composer as soloist;
   Milhaud: *La création du monde*; and Stravinsky: Octet

**1928 Jan. 27**    National Concert
*broadcast over:* 2LO&5XX (8.0–9.15 pm, 9.25–10.33 pm)          broadcast: ✓ concert: ✓
*place of performance:* Queen's Hall
*work(s) performed:* Schoenberg    \**Gurrelieder*
*performed by:* A. Wynn (speaker), Stiles Allen (soprano), Gladys Palmer (contralto),
     J. Perry (tenor), Parry Jones (tenor), F. Phillips (baritone)
*orchestra:* National Symphony Orchestra
*chorus:* National Chorus of London, Wireless Chorus, Civil Servic Choir, Lloyds Choir,
     Railway Clearing House Male Voice Choir
*conductor:* Schoenberg
*notes:* *1st British performance

**1928 Feb. 1**    The Foundations of Music
*broadcast over:* 2LO&5XX (7.14–7.27 pm)          broadcast: ✓ concert:
*work(s) performed:* Schoenberg    *Suite for Piano, op. 25
*performed by:* Steuermann (piano)
*notes:* *1st British performance. The series for the week was listed in the *Radio Times* as
     '"Modern French Piano Music" played by Mrs Norman O'Neill'; in fact,
     Steuermann performed contemporary piano pieces by Busoni (30 Jan.), Scriabin
     (31 Jan.), Schoenberg, Satie (2 Feb.), Reger (3 Feb.) and Debussy (4 Feb.).

**1928 Feb. 13**    Concerts of Contemporary Music, series ii, concert 5
*broadcast over:* 5GB (10.30–11.35 pm)          broadcast: ✓ concert:
*work(s) performed:* Schoenberg    String Quartet no. 3, op. 30
                         Berg          *Lyric Suite* (not broadcast)
*performed by:* Vienna String Quartet
*other works performed:* songs by Auric, Debussy, Milhaud and Poulenc (the Poulenc
     was not announced in the *Radio Times* listings)
*notes:* The *Radio Times* announcement for this concert included Berg's *Lyric Suite* as
     part of the programme; although this work was not broadcast, it was performed in
     the studio and was mentioned in reviews. Claire Croiza (soprano) also performed.

**1928 Feb. 14**    Gerald Cooper Concerts          broadcast:    concert: ✓
*work(s) performed:* Schoenberg    String Quartet no. 2, op. 10
*performed by:* Vienna String Quartet with Ružena Herlinger (soprano)

**1928 March 4**    Chamber Music
*broadcast over:* 2LO&5XX (9.09–10.35 pm)          broadcast: ✓ concert:
*work(s) performed:* Schoenberg    'Erwartung', 'Schenk mir deinen goldenen Kamm',
                         'Erhebung' and 'Waldsonne' from op. 2
*performed by:* Margot Hinnenberg-Lefèbre (soprano)
*other works performed:* a Mozart aria and Haydn, Grieg and Debussy string quartets
*notes:* The Virtuoso String Quartet also performed.

**1928 March 5**   Concerts of Contemporary Music, series ii, concert 6
*broadcast over:* 5GB (8.30–10.0 pm)                                    broadcast: ✓ concert:
*work(s) performed:* Webern    six songs from op. 3 and 4
                    Eisler    *Zeitungausschnitte*, op. 11
*performed by:* Margot Hinnenberg-Lefèbre (soprano), Kathleen Long (piano) and
    other instrumentalists
*other works performed:* by Hindemith, Honegger and Prokofiev
*notes:* The performed programme was altered from the announced programme, which
    included a work by Jarnach in place of the Hindemith. (See Table B.3 for more
    details.)

**1928 March 28**   The Catterall Quartet Chamber Music Concert
*broadcast over:* 2LO&5XX (7.45–9.0 pm)                                 broadcast: ✓ concert: ✓
*place of performance:* Memorial Hall, Manchester
*work(s) performed:* Schoenberg    *Verklärte Nacht*, op. 4
*performed by:* Catterall Quartet with Stewart Redfern (viola) and Carl Fuchs ('cello)
*other works performed:* Tchaikovsky: Sextet for strings

**1928 April 27**   'An Afternoon Concert'
*broadcast over:* 2LO&5XX (4.0–5.0 pm)                                  broadcast: ✓ concert:
*work(s) performed:* Schoenberg    'Schenk mir deinen goldenen Kamm' from op. 2
*performed by:* Kathleen Mitchell (soprano), Hilda Bor (piano)
*other works performed:* included piano works by Bach, Chopin, Liszt and Ravel, and
    songs by Weingartner, Vaughan Williams, Hely Hutchinson, Foss, Turnbull and
    Milford
*notes:* Ernest Potts (bass) also performed.

**1928 May 7**   Concerts of Contemporary Music, series ii, concert 8
*broadcast over:* 5GB (8.30–10 pm)                                      broadcast: ✓ concert:
*work(s) performed:* Schoenberg    Three Piano Pieces, op. 11
                    Schoenberg    *Six Little Piano Pieces*, op. 19
*performed by:* Steuermann (piano)
*other works performed:* by Bartók, Hindemith and Busoni
*notes:* The Amar-Hindemith String Quartet also performed. The final work on the
    programme, Hindemith's Six Pieces for string quartet, op. 44, was performed in the
    studio but was not broadcast.

**1928 Sept. 20**    Promenade Concerts
*place of performance:* Queen's Hall, London                broadcast:        concert: ✓
*work(s) performed:* Bach-Schoenberg    *Schmücke dich*
                    Bach-Schoenberg    *Veni creator*
*notes:* This Promenade Concert was not broadcast.

**1928 Oct. 15**    Contemporary Chamber Music, series iii, concert 2
*broadcast over:* 2LO&5XX (8.02–9.02 pm)              broadcast: ✓ concert: ✓
*place of performance:* Arts Theatre Club, London
*work(s) performed:* Schoenberg    String Quartet no. 2, op. 10
                    Webern        String Trio, op. 20 (not broadcast)
*performed by:* Vienna String Quartet with Margot Hinnenberg-Lefèbre (soprano)
*other works performed:* by Bliss and Hindemith
*notes:* Webern's String Trio, op. 20, was initially announced for broadcasting, but in
    the event was only performed for those critics who heard the concert from the
    theatre. Leon Goossens (oboe) also performed.

**1928 Oct. 22**
*place of performance:* Grotrian Hall, London              broadcast:        concert: ✓
*work(s) performed:* Schoenberg    Chamber Symphony, op. 9, arranged for piano
*performed by:* Steuermann (piano)
*other works performed:* Reger: *Variations and Fugue on a Theme of J. S. Bach*, and
    Beethoven: Piano Sonata, op. 106

**1928 Oct. 24**    A Recital
*broadcast over:* 5GB (9.30–10.0 pm)                broadcast: ✓ concert:
*work(s) performed:* Berg    Piano Sonata, op. 1
*performed by:* Dr Ernst Bachrich (piano)
*other works performed:* Strauss songs and a Smetana polka
*notes:* Stiles Allen (soprano) also performed.

**1928 Oct. 26**
*place of performance:* Wigmore Hall, London              broadcast:        concert: ✓
*work(s) performed:* Schoenberg    'Ghasel' and 'Alles' from op. 6, 'Erwartung' and
                                'Waldsonne' from op. 2
                    Webern        nos. 1, 2 and 5 from op. 3, and 'Der Tag ist
                                vergangen' and 'Gleich und gleich' from op. 12
*performed by:* Ružena Herlinger (soprano) and Steuermann (piano)
*other works performed:* Debussy: *Proses lyriques*, and Mahler songs

**1928 Dec. 3**    Contemporary Chamber Music, series iii, concert 4
*broadcast over:* 2LO&5XX (9.38–10.30 pm)                    broadcast: ✓ concert: ✓
*place of performance:* Arts Theatre Club, London
*work(s) performed:* Hauer    *Wandlungen*, op. 53
                   Krenek    *Symphonic Music*, op. 11 (not broadcast)
*performed by:* Leonie Zifado (soprano), B. Pett-Fraser (mezzo), Doris Owens
    (contralto), T. Purvis (tenor), L. White (baritone), S. Dyson (bass)
*conductor:* Scherchen
*other works performed:* Hindemith: Chamber Music no. 1
*notes:* The Krenek was announced for this concert and appeared in the concert
    programme, although it was not listed in the *Radio Times* and was not broadcast.
    Janáček's *Říkadla* was listed in the *Radio Times*, but the Hindemith, which was not,
    was actually performed.

**1928 Dec. 4**    Music Society
*place of performance:* Tufton Street, London                    broadcast:    concert: ✓
*work(s) performed:* Zemlinsky    String Quartet
*performed by:* Vienna String Quartet
*other works performed:* by Schubert and Brahms

**1928 Dec. 17**    Chamber Music
*broadcast over:* 2LO&5XX (9.35–11.0 pm)                    broadcast: ✓ concert:
*work(s) performed:* Schoenberg    *Verklärte Nacht*, op. 4
*performed by:* Samuel Kutcher, George Whittaker (violins), Raymond Jeremy, James
    Lockyer (violas), Cedric Sharpe, Edward Robinson ('cellos)
*other works performed:* Brahms: Sextet in G major, and Beethoven piano works
*notes:* Eugen d'Albert (piano) also performed.

**1929 Jan. 7**    Contemporary Chamber Music, series iii, concert 5
*broadcast over:* 2LO&5XX (8.0–9.0 pm)                    broadcast: ✓ concert: ✓
*place of performance:* Arts Theatre Club, London
*work(s) performed:* Schoenberg    Five Piano Pieces, op. 23
*performed by:* Steuermann (piano)
*other works performed:* by Vaughan Williams, Busoni and Van Dieren
*notes:* Claire Croiza (soprano) was supposed to sing Roussel, Ravel and Caplet on this
    programme; however, she became ill, and the International String Quartet with
    Raymond Jeremy (viola) performed instead.

**1929 Feb. 12**    Chamber Music
*broadcast over:* 5GB (10.15–11.15 pm)                    broadcast: ✓ concert:
*work(s) performed:* Schoenberg    String Quartet no. 3, op. 30
                   Berg        two movements from the *Lyric Suite*
*performed by:* Vienna String Quartet
*other works performed:* Bartok: *String Quartet no. 3
*notes:* *1st British performance
    The Berg movements were not listed in the *Radio Times*, although they were
    performed and broadcast. At one time, Schoenberg's *Pierrot lunaire*, op. 21, was
    planned for this concert.

**1929 Feb. 13**   Gerald Cooper Concerts              broadcast:   concert: ✓
*work(s) performed:* Schoenberg   String Quartet no. 2, op. 10
*performed by:* Vienna String Quartet with Ružena Herlinger (soprano)
*notes:* This performance may have taken place on this date in 1928, but 1929 is more
  likely.

**1929 Nov. 4**   Contemporary Chamber Music, series iv, concert 2
*broadcast over:* 5GB (8.0–9.0 pm)            broadcast: ✓ concert: ✓
*place of performance:* Grotrian Hall, London
*work(s) performed:* Berg       Piano Sonata, op. 1
                    Eisler      Piano Sonata, op. 1
                    Schoenberg  *Das Buch der hängenden Gärten*, op. 15
*performed by:* Margot Hinnenberg-Lefèbre (soprano) and Steuermann (piano)
*other works performed:* Busoni: *Fantasia contrappuntistica* (not broadcast)

**1929 Nov. 28**
*place of performance:* London            broadcast:   concert: ✓
*work(s) performed:* Hauer   Suite no. 7
*performed by:* Szigeti (violinist in Mozart concerto)
*orchestra:* Philharmonic Orchestra
*conductor:* Scherchen
*other works performed:* by Schubert, Beethoven, Mozart and Bartók

**1929 Dec. 2**   Contemporary Chamber Music, series iv, concert 3
*broadcast over:* 5GB (7.45–9.0 pm)          broadcast: ✓ concert: ✓
*place of performance:* Arts Theatre Club, London
*work(s) performed:* Webern   Five Pieces for Orchestra, op. 10
*conductor:* Webern
*other works performed:* Milhaud: Chamber Symphony no. 1 ('Le Printemps') and
  Brahms: Serenade, op. 16
*notes:* Webern's British conducting début in England. Mahler songs were also
  programmed, but were omitted when the singer, Ružena Herlinger, became ill.

**1929 Dec. 22**   Chamber Music
*broadcast over:* 5GB (4.15–5.45 pm)          broadcast: ✓ concert:
*work(s) performed:* Schoenberg   String Quartet no. 3, op. 30
*performed by:* Vienna String Quartet
*other works performed:* Beethoven: String Quartet, op. 130; also Schubert, Brahms and
  Schumann songs
*notes:* Robert Maitland (singer) also performed other works.

**1930 Jan. 30**
*place of performance:* Manchester                    broadcast:    concert: ✓
*work(s) performed:* Krenek    *Potpourri*, op. 54
*orchestra:* Hallé Orchestra

**1930 March 2**
*broadcast over:* 2LO&5XX (9.05–10.30 pm)            broadcast: ✓ concert:
*work(s) performed:* Krenek    *Little Symphony*, op. 58
*performed by:* Marcelle Meyer (piano)
*orchestra:* Wireless Symphony Orchestra
*conductor:* Wood
*other works performed:* by Mozart, Beethoven, Liszt and Wagner

**1930 March 4**    'Chamber Music'
*broadcast over:* 5GB (9.0–10.15 pm)                broadcast: ✓ concert:
*work(s) performed:* Schoenberg    'Waldsonne' from op. 2
*performed by:* Ružena Herlinger (soprano)
*other works performed:* by Bach, Handel, Mozart, Beethoven, Ibert, d'Indy, Wolf,
    Reger, Marx and Korngold
*notes:* The Aeolian Players also performed.

**1930 April 7**    Contemporary Chamber Music, series iv, concert 7
*broadcast over:* London Regional (8.37–10.15 pm)    broadcast: ✓ concert: ✓
*place of performance:* Central Hall, Westminster
*work(s) performed:* Schoenberg    Suite for Piano, op. 25
                Schoenberg    *Pierrot lunaire*, op. 21
                Schoenberg,    Chamber Symphony, op. 9 (arr. for Pierrot
                arr. Webern    ensemble)
*performed by:* Vienna 'Pierrot Lunaire' Ensemble: Erika Wagner (reciter), Rudolf
    Kolisch (violin/viola), Benar Heifetz ('cello), Franz Wangler (flute/piccolo), Viktor
    Polatschek (clarinets) and Steuermann (piano)
*conductor:* Erwin Stein

**1930 April 25**    Chamber Music
*broadcast over:* National (9.40–11.0 pm)            broadcast: ✓ concert:
*work(s) performed:* Schoenberg    *Verklärte Nacht*, op. 4
*performed by:* Marjorie Hayward and Pierre Tas (violin), Rebecca Clarke and Dorothy
    Jones (violas), May Mukle and Allen Ford ('cellos)
*other works performed:* by Brahms and Pizzetti
*notes:* Anne Thursfield (mezzo-soprano) also performed.

**1930 May 22**
*place of performance:* Grotrian Hall, London        broadcast:    concert: ✓
*work(s) performed:* Krenek    *\*Reisebuch aus dem österreichischen Alpen*
*performed by:* Thelma Bardsley (singer)
*notes:* \*1st British performance

**1930 July 3**     Chamber Music
*broadcast over:* London Regional (8.0–9.10 pm)                    broadcast: ✓ concert:
*work(s) performed:* Pisk    Suite for piano
*performed by:* Friedrich Wührer (piano)
*other works performed:* Piano pieces by Reger, and works for wind quintet by
    Klughardt, Randerson, Blumer, Scarlatti-Greenbaum and Stainer
*notes:* The London Wind Quintet also performed.

**1930 Aug. 26**     Promenade Concerts
*place of performance:* Queen's Hall, London                  broadcast: ✓ concert: ✓
*work(s) performed:* Krenek    *Potpourri*, op. 54 (not broadcast)
*conductor:* Wood
*other works performed:* by Mendelssohn, Verdi, Saint-Saëns, Weelkes, Gibbons,
    Bennett and Tchaikovsky.
*notes:* The Krenek was performed in the second half of the programme, which was not
    broadcast.

**1930 Nov. 29**
*broadcast over:* London Regional (9.00–10.15 pm)                   broadcast: ✓ concert:
*work(s) performed:* Schoenberg    'Jane Gray' from op. 12
*performed by:* Emmy Heim (soprano)
*other works performed:* Mozart quintet, Schubert songs, Bruckner quintet and a
    Vaughan Williams quintet
*notes:* The International String Quartet and Anne Wolfe (viola) also performed.

**1930 Dec. 10**     BBC Symphony Concert–viii
*broadcast over:* National (8.00–10.01 pm)                   broadcast: ✓ concert: ✓
*place of performance:* Queen's Hall, London
*work(s) performed:* Schoenberg    *Pelleas und Melisande*, op. 5
*orchestra:* BBC Symphony Orchestra
*conductor:* Scherchen
*other works performed:* Beethoven: the *Grosse Fuge*, op. 133, and Piano Concerto no. 3
    with Lamond as soloist
*notes:* *1st British performance

**1931 Jan. 7**
*broadcast over:* National (9.40–11.00 pm)                   broadcast: ✓ concert:
*work(s) performed:* Schoenberg    *Friede auf Erden*, op. 13
*chorus:* Wireless Chorus
*conductor:* Stanford Robinson
*other works performed:* Mozart and Beethoven string quartets
*notes:* The Roth String Quartet also performed.

**1931 Jan. 9**    Concerts of Contemporary Music, series v, concert 1
*broadcast over:* National (9.37–10.43 pm)                    broadcast: ✓ concert: ✓
*place of performance:* Studio 10, London
*work(s) performed:* Schoenberg            *Erwartung*, op. 17
                    Bach, arr. Schoenberg    *Prelude and Fugue in E flat ('St. Anne')
                    Schoenberg            *Friede auf Erden*, op. 13
*performed by:* Margot Hinnenberg-Lefèbre (soprano)
*orchestra:* BBC Symphony Orchestra
*chorus:* Wireless Chorus
*conductor:* Schoenberg
*notes:* *1st British performance
    *Friede auf Erden* is not listed in the *Radio Times*, but was performed according to the
    'Programmes as Broadcast' records.

**1931 Jan. 21**    Active Society for the Propagation of Contemporary Music
*place of performance:* Glasgow                    broadcast:    concert: ✓
*work(s) performed:* Schoenberg    Three Piano Pieces, op. 11
*performed by:* Erik Chisholm (piano)
*other works performed:* Kodály: Cello Sonata op. 4; Bartók: Violin Sonata no. 2; Pijper:
    Violin Sonata; and Van Dieren: *Sonata tyroica* for violin
*notes:* Edward Dennis (violin) and Basil Hogarth ('cello) also performed.

**1931 Feb. 2 or 3**    Courtauld-Sargent Concert
*place of performance:* London                    broadcast:    concert: ✓
*work(s) performed:* Bach, arr. Schoenberg    Prelude and Fugue in E flat ('St Anne')
*orchestra:* Philharmonic Orchestra
*chorus:* Philharmonic Choir
*conductor:* Klemperer
*other works performed:* Beethoven: Symphony no. 9

**1931 Feb. 28**
*broadcast over:* London Regional (9.00–10.15 pm)                    broadcast: ✓ concert:
*work(s) performed:* Schoenberg    String Quartet no. 1, op. 7
*performed by:* Kolisch Quartet
*other works performed:* Haydn string quartet, and songs
*notes:* Gladys Ripley (contralto) also performed.

**1931 Mar. 30**    Active Society for the Propagation of Contemporary Music
*place of performance:* Glasgow                    broadcast:    concert: ✓
*work(s) performed:* Webern    Four Pieces for violin and piano, op. 7
*performed by:* Edward Dennis (violin) and Erik Chisholm (piano)
*other works performed:* Bloch: Violin Sonata; Delius: Violin Sonata no. 3; and Bartók:
    Violin Sonata

**1931 May 8**     Concerts of Contemporary Music, series v, concert 5
*broadcast over:* London Regional (9.02–10.02 pm)               broadcast: ✓ concert:
*work(s) performed:* Webern          *Five Pieces for string orchestra (arr. of the Five
                                     Pieces for string quartet, op. 5)
                  Schoenberg     *Begleitmusik zu einer Lichtspielszene*, op. 34
                  Schoenberg     'Lied der Waldtaube' from *Gurrelieder*
*performed by:* Enid Cruickshank (contralto)
*orchestra:* BBC Orchestra
*conductor:* Webern
*notes:* *1st British performance
     Schoenberg's op. 34 was performed, and broadcast, twice.


**1931 May 27**
*place of performance:* Wigmore Hall, London               broadcast:    concert: ✓
*work(s) performed:* Berg          Piano Sonata, op. 1
                  Schubert-Krenek   Sonata in C
*performed by:* John Hunt (piano)


**1931 July 23**     ISCM Festival 1931
*broadcast over:* London Regional (8.59–10.19 pm; from               broadcast: ✓ concert: ✓
     London)
*place of performance:* Sheldonian Theatre, Oxford (at 3 pm)
*work(s) performed:* Wellesz          *Drei geistliche Chöre*, op. 47
                  Józef Koffler   String Trio (not broadcast)
*performed by:* members of the International String Quartet
*chorus:* Wireless Singers
*conductor:* Stanford Robinson
*other works performed:* For a full listing of the programme, see Table 8.1.


**1931 July 27**     ISCM Festival 1931
*broadcast over:* London Regional (6.36–10.29 pm)               broadcast: ✓ concert: ✓
*place of performance:* Queen's Hall, London
*work(s) performed:* Webern     *Symphony, op. 21 (not broadcast)
*orchestra:* BBC Orchestra
*conductor:* Scherchen
*other works performed:* For a full listing of the programme, see Table 8.1.
*notes:* *1st British performance

**1931 Aug. 22**    Promenade Concert
*broadcast over:* London Regional (8.00–9.25 pm)                    broadcast: ✓ concert: ✓
*place of performance:* Queen's Hall, London
*work(s) performed:* Webern    *Passacaglia, op. 1
*performed by:* C. Supervia (soprano), W. Widdop (tenor) and Clifford Curzon
    (piano)
*orchestra:* BBC Symphony Orchestra
*conductor:* Wood
*other works performed:* by Beethoven, Handel, Schubert-Liszt, Saint-Saëns, Strauss
    and Hérold
*notes:* *1st British performance

**1931 Sept. 15**    Promenade Concert
*broadcast over:* National (8.00–9.40 pm)                    broadcast: ✓ concert: ✓
*place of performance:* Queen's Hall, London
*work(s) performed:* Berg    'Nacht', 'Schilflied', 'Die Nachtigall', 'Traumgekrönt', 'Im
                Zimmer' and 'Sommertage' from *Seven Early Songs*
*performed by:* Margot Hinnenberg-Lefèbre (soprano)
*orchestra:* BBC Symphony Orchestra
*conductor:* Wood
*other works performed:* by Mendelssohn, Debussy, Cyril Scott, Massenet and
    Schubert
*notes:* The programme was originally to have included the Three Fragments from
    *Wozzeck* in place of the Berg songs.

**1931 Nov. 13**    Concerts of Contemporary Music, series vi, concert 1
*broadcast over:* London Regional (8.00–9.00 pm)                    broadcast: ✓ concert:
*work(s) performed:* Schoenberg    *Variations for Orchestra, op. 31
                Schoenberg    *Verklärte Nacht*, op. 4
*orchestra:* BBC Orchestra
*conductor:* Boult
*notes:* *1st British performance

**1931 Nov. 15**    'Chamber Music'
*broadcast over:* National (4.16–5.32 pm)                    broadcast: ✓ concert:
*work(s) performed:* Schoenberg    'Erwartung', 'Waldsonne', 'Schenk mir deinen
                goldenen Kamm' and 'Erhebung' from op. 2
*performed by:* Enid Cruickshank (contralto)
*other works performed:* Bax: Viola Sonata; Brahms: 'Der Tod, das ist die kühle Nacht';
    Delius: arr. of Violin Sonata no. 2
*notes:* The *Radio Times* mistakenly listed the second Schoenberg song as 'Der
    Wanderer'. Lionel Tertis (viola) and Harriet Cohen (piano) also performed.

**1931 Nov. 18**    BBC Symphony Concert
*broadcast over:* National (8.16–10.16 pm)                    broadcast: ✓ concert: ✓
*place of performance:* Queen's Hall, London
*work(s) performed:* Schoenberg    Five Orchestra Pieces, op. 16
*orchestra:* BBC Symphony Orchestra
*conductor:* Boult
*other works performed:* Locatelli: *Concerto da camera* in E flat; Bach: Keyboard
     Concerto no. 1 in D minor with Gieseking as soloist; Beethoven: Symphony no. 7

**1932 Feb. 1**    'Chamber Music'
*broadcast over:* National (9.52–11.14 pm)                    broadcast: ✓ concert:
*work(s) performed:* Berg    songs from op. 2
*performed by:* Emmy Heim (soprano)
*other works performed:* Wolf and Mahler songs; also chamber works by Brahms and
     Bax
*notes:* Marjorie Hayward (violin), Rebecca Clarke (viola), May Mukle ('cello) and
     Kathleen Long (piano) also performed.

**1932 Feb. 15**    'Chamber Music'
*broadcast over:* National (9.44–11.02 pm)                    broadcast: ✓ concert:
*work(s) performed:* Schoenberg    'Traumleben' and 'Waldsonne'
*performed by:* Anne Thursfield (soprano)
*other works performed:* Schumann and Reger songs; also chamber works by Mozart
     and Beethoven
*notes:* The Kutcher String Quartet also performed.

**1932 April 22**    Concerts of Contemporary Music, series vi, concert 6
*broadcast over:* London Regional (8.15–9.15 pm)                    broadcast: ✓ concert:
*work(s) performed:* Schoenberg    *Friede auf Erden*, op. 13
*chorus:* Wireless Chorus
*conductor:* Stanford Robinson
*other works performed:* by Vaughan Williams, Kodály, Delius, Poulenc, Ravel and Bax

**1932 April**
*place of performance:* St John's Institute, Westminster          broadcast:    concert: ✓
*work(s) performed:* Berg    *Lyric Suite*
*performed by:* Kolisch Quartet
*other works performed:* Haydn Sunrise Quartet

**1932 May 13**    Concerts of Contemporary Music, series vi, concert 7
*broadcast over:* London Regional (8.35–9.50 pm)                    broadcast: ✓ concert:
*work(s) performed:* Berg          *Three Fragments from *Wozzeck
                     Webern    *Passacaglia*, op. 1
                     Krenek    Theme and 13 Variations, op. 69
*performed by:* May Blyth (soprano)
*orchestra:* BBC Orchestra
*conductor:* Wood
*notes:* *1st British performance

**1932 Dec. 23**   Concerts of Contemporary Music, series vii, concert 2
*broadcast over:* London Regional (9.02–10.21 pm)                     broadcast: ✓ concert: ✓
*place of performance:* Concert Hall, Broadcasting House
*work(s) performed:* Schoenberg          Three Piano Pieces, op. 11
                        Schoenberg          Piano Pieces, op. 33a and op. 33b
                        von Hannenheim   Piano Sonata
*performed by:* Else C. Kraus (piano)
*chorus:* Wireless Chorus
*conductor:* Cyril Dalmaine
*other works performed:* choral works by Szymanowski, Conrad Beck, Hindemith,
    Poulenc, Stravinsky and Bax

**1933 Jan. 12**   Winter Promenade Concerts
*broadcast over:* London Regional (8.00–9.25 pm)                     broadcast: ✓ concert: ✓
*work(s) performed:* [Gerhard    Five Catalan Songs for soprano and orchestra]
*place of performance:* Queen's Hall, London
*conductor:* Wood
*other works performed:* by Smetana, Duparc, Saint-Saëns, Grieg, Mendelssohn,
    Scriabin, Ravel, Chopin and Arensky
*notes:* *1st English performance. The Gerhard songs were not performed, due to the
    last-minute illness of the soloist, Concepció Badiá D'Agusti. Juan Manén (violin)
    also performed.

**1933 Feb. 5**   'Orchestral Concert'
*broadcast over:* National (4.15–5.30 pm)                     broadcast: ✓ concert:
*work(s) performed:* Monn-Schoenberg    Concerto in G minor
*performed by:* Antoni Sala ('cello)
*orchestra:* BBC Orchestra
*conductor:* Clark
*other works performed:* Dittersdorf; Britten: *Sinfonietta*; Ravel: *Le tombeau de Couperin*;
    Delius-Fenby: *Caprice and Elegy*

**1933 Feb. 8**   BBC Symphony Concert–xii
*broadcast over:* National (8.15–9.14 pm)                     broadcast: ✓ concert: ✓
*place of performance:* Queen's Hall, London
*work(s) performed:* Schoenberg    *Variations for Orchestra, op. 31
*performed by:* Elena Gerhardt (soprano)
*orchestra:* BBC Symphony Orchestra
*conductor:* Schoenberg and Boult
*other works performed:* Weber: Overture to *Euryanthe*; Strauss Lieder; and Beethoven:
    Symphony no. 3
*notes:* *1st public British performance. The Schoenberg was introduced with a
    broadcast talk given by Ernest Newman, who warned: 'It will last for twenty
    minutes and you may feel that you might be better employed elsewhere'.

**1933 Feb. 13**    BBC Chamber Concerts–ii
*broadcast over:* National (8.00–8.56 pm)                    broadcast: ✓ concert: ✓
*place of performance:* Concert Hall, Broadcasting House
*work(s) performed:* Berg    *Lyric Suite*
*performed by:* Kolisch Quartet
*other works performed:* Haydn and Schubert string quartets
*notes:* The Schubert string quartet was not broadcast.


**1933 Feb. 25**    'Chamber Music'
*broadcast over:* London Regional (9.00–10.15 pm)              broadcast: ✓ concert:
*work(s) performed:* Schoenberg    String Quartet no. 1, op. 7
*performed by:* Kolisch Quartet
*other works performed:* Haydn: String Quartet, op. 76, no. 6, and Beethoven: 32
    Variations in C minor
*notes:* Josefa Rosanska (piano) also performed.


**1933 March 8**    BBC Symphony Concert–xv
*broadcast over:* National (8.16–10.22 pm)                    broadcast: ✓ concert: ✓
*place of performance:* Queen's Hall, London
*work(s) performed:* Berg    *Three Fragments from Wozzeck
*performed by:* May Blyth (soprano)
*orchestra:* BBC Symphony Orchestra
*conductor:* Wood
*other works performed:* by Beethoven, Haydn, Bach and Strauss: *Tod und Verklärung*,
    op. 24
*notes:* *1st public British performance. Adolf Busch (violin) also performed.


**1933 April 21**    Concerts of Contemporary Music, series vii, concert 6
*broadcast over:* London Regional (9.01–10.23 pm)             broadcast: ✓ concert:
*place of performance:* Concert Hall, Broadcasting House
*work(s) performed:* Berg    'Andante amoroso' and 'Adagio appassionato' from the
                        *Lyric Suite*, arr. for string orchestra
                Berg    Chamber Concerto for piano, violin and 13 wind
                        instruments
                Krenek  *Durch die Nacht*, op. 67a
*performed by:* Hedda Kux (soprano), Rudolf Kolisch (violin) and Steuermann
    (piano)
*orchestra:* BBC Orchestra
*conductor:* Webern
*notes:* Originally, the 'Allegro misterioso' from the *Lyric Suite* was also scheduled, but
    Webern cancelled it from the programme.

**1933 April 23**    Sunday Orchestral Concert–xxiii
*broadcast over:* London Regional (9.08–10.22 pm)                    broadcast: ✓ concert:
*work(s) performed:* Schubert, arr. Webern    German Dances, D.820
*performed by:* Elsie Suddaby (soprano)
*orchestra:* BBC Orchestra
*conductor:* Webern
*other works performed:* Beethoven: Overture to *Prometheus*, and Mahler: Symphony
    no. 4

**1933 June 29**
*place of performance:* Royal Academy of Music, London          broadcast:    concert: ✓
*work(s) performed:* Schoenberg    *Verklärte Nacht*, op. 4
*performed by:* Frederick Grinke (leader)

**1933 July 24**    'Chamber Music'
*broadcast over:* National (9.49–10.58 pm)                    broadcast: ✓ concert:
*work(s) performed:* Hauer    Hölderlin settings: 'An die Hoffnung' from op. 21, 'Der
                                gute Glaube' from op. 6, and the complete op. 12:
                                'Ehemals und jetzt', 'Abbitte', and 'Die Heimat'
*performed by:* Emmy Heim (mezzo-soprano)
*other works performed:* by Bloch and Brahms
*notes:* Lionel Tertis (viola) and Solomon (piano) also performed.

**1933 Aug. 20**    'Chamber Music'
*broadcast over:* London Regional (9.05–10.30 pm)              broadcast: ✓ concert:
*work(s) performed:* Schoenberg    'Erwartung' and 'Schenk mir deinen goldenen
                                Kamm' from op. 2, and 'Hochzeitslied' from op. 3
*performed by:* Enid Cruickshank (contralto); Eda Kersey (violin), Cedric Sharpe
    ('cello) and Gerald Moore (piano) performed as a string trio in other works
*other works performed:* by Beethoven, Berlioz, Ireland and Schubert

**1933 Sept. 17**    'Chamber Music'
*broadcast over:* London Regional (9.06–10.30 pm)              broadcast: ✓ concert:
*work(s) performed:* Krenek    Piano Sonata no. 2, op. 59
*performed by:* John Hunt (piano)
*orchestra:* London String Players
*conductor:* Herbert Menges
*other works performed:* by Avison arr. Warlock, Bach, Sibelius and Suk

**1933 Oct. 5**    Promenade Concert
*broadcast over:* National (7.57–9.40 pm)                    broadcast: ✓ concert: ✓
*place of performance:* Queen's Hall, London
*work(s) performed:* Gerhard    *Six Catalan folk songs for soprano and orchestra
*performed by:* Sophie Wyss (soprano)
*orchestra:* BBC Symphony Orchestra
*conductor:* Wood
*other works performed:* Smetana: Overture to *The Bartered Bride*; Elgar: Violin
    Concerto; Schubert: Symphony no. 8
*notes:* *1st British performance. The Gerhard songs were scheduled for performance
    on 15 January 1933, but were postponed at that time. Albert Sammons (violin) also
    performed.

**1933 Nov. 20**    'A Pianoforte Recital'
*broadcast over:* London Regional (8.00–8.27 pm)                    broadcast: ✓ concert:
*work(s) performed:* Berg        Piano Sonata, op. 1
                Wellesz    'Tanzstück' and 'Pastorale'
*performed by:* Helen Perkin (piano)
*other works performed:* by Schubert and John Ireland

**1933 Nov. 24**    Concerts of Contemporary Music, series viii, concert 1
*broadcast over:* London Regional (9.00–10.15 pm)                    broadcast: ✓ concert: ✓
*place of performance:* Concert Hall, Broadcasting House
*work(s) performed:* Schoenberg    Three Piano Pieces, op. 11
                Schoenberg    *Six Little Piano Pieces*, op. 19
                Schoenberg    *Pierrot lunaire*, op. 21
*performed by:* Erika Wagner (reciter), Rudolf Kolisch (violin/viola), Benar Heifetz
    ('cello), Robert Murchie (flute/piccolo), Frederick Thurston (clarinet), Walter Lear
    (bass clarinet) and Steuermann (piano)
*conductor:* Constant Lambert
*notes:* Schoenberg's Suite, op. 29, was originally announced and listed in the
    *Radio Times* for performance, but was replaced by the op. 11 and op. 19 piano
    pieces.

**1933 Nov. 29**    BBC Symphony Concerts
*broadcast over:* National (8.15–10.30 pm)                    broadcast: ✓ concert: ✓
*place of performance:* Queen's Hall, London
*work(s) performed:* [Handel arr. Schoenberg    *Concerto grosso*]
*orchestra:* BBC Symphony Orchestra
*conductor:* Boult
*other works performed:* by Mendelssohn; Beethoven: Piano Concerto no. 1 (with Alfred
    Cortot as soloist); and Bruckner: Symphony no. 9
*notes:* This programme was originally to have included Schoenberg's arrangement of
    the Handel *Concerto grosso*, conducted by Schoenberg, and Schubert's Symphony
    no. 5. When Schoenberg could not come to Britain to perform, the work was
    omitted from the programme.

**1933 Dec. 1**   BBC Chamber Concert–iv
*broadcast over:* London Regional (9.03–10.25 pm)          broadcast: ✓ concert: ✓
*place of performance:* Concert Hall, Broadcasting House
*work(s) performed:* Krenek    'Variations' from String Quartet no. 5, op. 65
                    Webern    Five Pieces for string quartet, op. 5
*performed by:* Kolisch Quartet
*other works performed:* Beethoven: Quartet in A minor, op. 132

**1934 Feb. 10**
*broadcast over:* London Regional (8.00–9.06 pm)          broadcast: ✓ concert:
*work(s) performed:* Berg    *Der Wein
*performed by:* Ružena Herlinger (soprano)
*orchestra:* BBC Orchestra
*conductor:* Robert Heger
*other works performed:* by Schubert and Korngold
notes: *1st British performance

**1934 Feb. 11**   Sunday Orchestral Concert–xiii
*broadcast over:* London Regional (9.05–10.30 pm)          broadcast: ✓ concert:
*work(s) performed:* Berg              Three Fragments from *Wozzeck*
                 Schubert arr. Webern   German Dances, D.820
*performed by:* May Blyth (soprano)
*orchestra:* BBC Orchestra
*conductor:* Boult
*other works performed:* by Gluck and Beethoven: Symphony no. 2

**1934 March 14**   BBC Symphony Concert–xv
*broadcast over:* National (8.24–10.35 pm)          broadcast: ✓ concert: ✓
*place of performance:* Queen's Hall, London
*work(s) performed:* Berg    *Wozzeck
*performed by:* Parry Jones (The Captain), Richard Bitterauf (Wozzeck), Tudor Davies
    (Andres), May Blyth (Marie), Mary Jarred (Margret), Percy Heming (The Doctor),
    Walter Widdop (The Drum-Major)
*orchestra:* BBC Symphony Orchestra
*chorus:* The Wireless Chorus
*conductor:* Boult
*notes:* *1st British performance
    Performed in concert. Plans for a staged performance at Covent Garden in spring
    1935 never came to fruition.

**1934 March 23**    Concerts of Contemporary Music, series viii, concert 5
*broadcast over:* London Regional (9.01–10.09 pm)        broadcast: ✓ concert: ✓
*place of performance:* Concert Hall, Broadcasting House
*work(s) performed:* Weiss    'Andante' from Chamber Symphony
*orchestra:* section of the London Symphony Orchestra
*chorus:* Wireless Male Voice Quartet
*conductor:* Clark
*other works performed:* Cowell: *Sinfonietta*; Virgil Thomson: *Capital, Capitals*; Varèse: *Octandre*
*notes:* Programme of American composers. The Weiss and Varèse were repeated for those who heard the programme at the Concert Hall.

**1934 June 18**    'Chamber Music'
*broadcast over:* National (9.37–10.46 pm)        broadcast: ✓ concert:
*work(s) performed:* Pisk    'Toccata' from *Concert Piece*, op. 7
                    Pisk    *Small Suite*, op. 11
                    Pisk    March from *Great Suite*, op. 17
*performed by:* Paul Pisk (piano)
*other works performed:* Mozart and Moeran string quartets
*notes:* The Stratton String Quartet performed other works.

**1934 Aug. 14**    Promenade Concerts
*broadcast over:* London Regional (7.58–9.32 pm)        broadcast: ✓ concert: ✓
*work(s) performed:* Berg    Three Fragments from *Wozzeck*
*place of performance:* Queen's Hall, London
*performed by:* May Blyth (soprano)
*orchestra:* BBC Symphony Orchestra
*conductor:* Wood
*other works performed:* by Respighi, Tchaikovsky, Bax and Debussy
*notes:* Percy Heming (baritone) and Lionel Tertis (viola) also performed as soloists.

**1934 Nov. 11**    'Chamber Music'
*broadcast over:* National (5.32–6.49 pm)        broadcast: ✓ concert:
*work(s) performed:* Webern    'Eingang' from op. 4 and 'Kahl reckt der Baum' from
                    op. 3
*performed by:* Ružena Herlinger (soprano)
*other works performed:* Beethoven Lieder; Dvořák and Schumann string quartets
*notes:* The Prague String Quartet also performed.

**1934 Nov. 16**   'Chamber Music'
*broadcast over:* London Regional (8.50–10.01 pm)          broadcast: ✓ concert: ✓
*place of performance:* Concert Hall, Broadcasting House
*work(s) performed:* Schoenberg   String Quartet no. 2, op. 10 (not broadcast)
*performed by:* Kolisch Quartet, Margot Hinnenberg-Lefèbre (soprano)
*other works performed:* Schubert Lieder and quartet movement; Beethoven Quartet,
    op. 130, and the *Grosse Fuge*, op. 133
*notes:* The Schoenberg was performed at the beginning of the programme, which was
    not transmitted; only the Schubert and Beethoven pieces were broadcast. The
    Kolisch Quartet arranged for Julia Nessy to sing, but Hinnenberg-Lefèbre had
    already been engaged.

**1935 Jan. 18**   Friday Mid-day Concert
*broadcast over:* National (1.15–2.02 pm)          broadcast: ✓ concert: ✓
*place of performance:* Queen's College, Birmingham
*work(s) performed:* Schoenberg   *Verklärte Nacht*, op. 4
*orchestra:* Birmingham Philharmonic String Orchestra
*conductor:* Johan Hock
*other works performed:* Elgar: *Introduction and Allegro*

**1935 Jan. 20**   Sunday Orchestral Concert
*broadcast over:* Regional (9.25–10.45 pm)          broadcast: ✓ concert:
*work(s) performed:* Schoenberg   *Verklärte Nacht*, op. 4
*orchestra:* BBC Orchestra
*conductor:* Frank Bridge
*other works performed:* by Haydn, Bridge and Rimsky-Korsakov

**1935 Feb. 27**
*broadcast over:* Regional (7.30–9.50 pm)          broadcast: ✓ concert: ✓
*place of performance:* Town Hall, Birmingham
*work(s) performed:* Bach, arr. Schoenberg   Prelude and fugue in E flat ('St. Anne')
*orchestra:* BBC Symphony Orchestra
*conductor:* Boult
*other works performed:* by Brahms, Delius, Ravel and Busoni: Two Studies for *Dr Faust*

**1935 March 10**   Sunday Orchestral Concert
*broadcast over:* Regional (9.20–10.28 pm)          broadcast: ✓ concert:
*work(s) performed:* Schoenberg   *Gurrelieder*, Part I
*performed by:* May Blyth (soprano), Enid Cruickshank (contralto) and Parry Jones
    (tenor)
*orchestra:* BBC Orchestra
*conductor:* Clark

**1935 March 18**   'Chamber Music'
*broadcast over:* National (10.05–11.16 pm)          broadcast: ✓ concert:
*work(s) performed:* Schoenberg   String Quartet no. 3, op. 30
*performed by:* Kolisch Quartet
*other works performed:* Schubert Quartet in D minor ('Death and the Maiden')

**1935 March 20**    BBC Symphony Concert
*broadcast over:* National (8.30–10.46 pm)                    broadcast: ✓ concert: ✓
*place of performance:* Queen's Hall, London
*work(s) performed:* Berg    *Symphonic Excerpts from *Lulu*
*performed by:* May Blyth (soprano)
*orchestra:* BBC Symphony Orchestra
*conductor:* Boult
*other works performed:* by Frescobaldi; Malipiero: *Sinfonia; Mozart: Violin Concerto
    no. 5, K.219, with Jascha Heifetz as soloist; Ravel: Suite no. 2 from *Daphnis et Chloé*
*notes:* *1st British performance

**1935 April 12**    Concerts of Contemporary Music, series ix, concert 7
*broadcast over:* National (10.20–11.33 pm)                    broadcast: ✓ concert: ✓
*place of performance:* Concert Hall, Broadcasting House
*work(s) performed:* Eisler    *Little Symphony*, op. 29
*performed by:* Marie Korchinska (harp); Bradbridge White and Martin Boddey
    (tenors), Stanley Riley and Samuel Dyson (basses)
*orchestra:* 'An orchestra'
*conductor:* Ansermet
*other works performed:* Christian Darnton: Concerto for harp and wind instruments;
    Stravinsky: Octet; Stravinsky: *Renard*

**1935 April 14**
*broadcast over:* Regional (4.30–5.27 pm)                    broadcast: ✓ concert:
*work(s) performed:* Schubert, arr. Webern    German Dances, D.820
*orchestra:* BBC Orchestra
*conductor:* Julian Clifford
*other works performed:* by Boieldieu, Malipiero, Delius, Rimsky-Korsakov and
    Schubert

**1935 April 25**    'Symphony Concert'
*broadcast over:* National (10.18–11.15 pm)                    broadcast: ✓ concert:
*work(s) performed:* Bach, arr. Webern    *Ricercare from *Das musikalische Opfer*
                Webern        Five Orchestra Pieces, op. 10
                Webern        Passacaglia, op. 1
*orchestra:* BBC Orchestra
*conductor:* Webern
*other works performed:* Schubert: Symphony no. 8 ('Unfinished')
*notes:* *1st performance

**1935 April 30**
*broadcast over:* Regional (9.02–10.03 pm)                    broadcast: ✓ concert:
*work(s) performed:* Berg    'Liebesode' and 'Traumgekrönt' from the *Seven Early Songs*
*performed by:* Rose Walter (soprano)
*orchestra:* BBC Orchestra
*conductor:* Julian Clifford
*other works performed:* by Haydn, Gluck, Grétry, Mozart and Stravinsky: Suite from
    *Pulcinella*

**1935 Aug. 24**
*broadcast over:* National (10.00–11.00 pm)                    broadcast: ✓ concert:
*work(s) performed:* Schoenberg   *Begleitmusik zu einer Lichtspielszene*, op. 34
*orchestra:* BBC Orchestra
*conductor:* Julian Clifford
*other works performed:* by Haydn and Brahms

**1935 Sept. 9**    Promenade Concerts
*broadcast over:* National (8.00–9.30 pm)                    broadcast: ✓ concert: ✓
*place of performance:* Queen's Hall, London
*work(s) performed:* Berg    Three Fragments from *Wozzeck* (not broadcast)
*performed by:* May Blyth (soprano)
*orchestra:* BBC Symphony Orchestra
*conductor:* Wood
*other works performed:* by Wagner
*notes:* The Berg was in the second half of the programme, which was not broadcast.

**1935 Oct. 23**    BBC Symphony Concert–i
*broadcast over:* National (8.30–10.53 pm)                    broadcast: ✓ concert: ✓
*place of performance:* Queen's Hall, London
*work(s) performed:* Berg    *Three movements from the *Lyric Suite*, arr. for string
                                    orchestra
*orchestra:* BBC Symphony Orchestra
*conductor:* Boult
*other works performed:* by Bach; Beethoven: Violin Concerto with Carl Flesch as
    soloist; Brahms: Symphony no. 1
*notes:* *1st public British performance

**1935 Nov. 1**    Concerts of Contemporary Music, series x, concert 1
*broadcast over:* National (10.25–11.17 pm)                    broadcast: ✓ concert: ✓
*place of performance:* Concert Hall, Broadcasting House
*work(s) performed:* Krenek    songs and choral works
*performed by:* Hertha Glatz (contralto), Ernst Krenek (piano)
*orchestra:* BBC Singers
*conductor:* Leslie Woodgate
*notes:* The concert was devoted to vocal music by Krenek. For details of the exact works
    performed, see Table B.11.

**1935 Nov. 3**    Sunday Orchestral Concert
*broadcast over:* Regional (9.25–10.53 pm)                    broadcast: ✓ concert:
*work(s) performed:* Krenek    *Concerto grosso* no. 2, op. 25
*performed by:* Egon Petri (piano)
*orchestra:* BBC Orchestra
*conductor:* Wood
*other works performed:* by Mozart; Liszt: *Malédiction* for piano and string orchestra;
    Busoni: Concert piece for piano and orchestra; and Berlioz.

**1935 Nov. 30**   'Violin Recital'
*broadcast over:* Regional (9.30–10.02 pm)                    broadcast: ✓ concert:
*work(s) performed:* Berg    *Adagio for violin and piano from Chamber Concerto for
                             violin, piano and 13 wind instruments
*performed by:* Dea Gombrich (violin)
*other works performed:* Bach and Bartók
*notes:* *1st performance of this version. The name of the pianist was not listed.

**1935 Nov.**
*place of performance:* Royal Academy of Music                broadcast:    concert: ✓
*work(s) performed:* Krenek    *Die Jahreszeiten*, op. 35
*orchestra:* BBC Singers
*conductor:* Leslie Woodgate
*notes:* This same choral work was performed at the BBC Concert of Contemporary
    Music on 1 November 1935.

**1935 Dec. 7**
*broadcast over:* Regional (8.30–9.32 pm)                     broadcast: ✓ concert:
*work(s) performed:* Józef Koffler    *Variations on a 12-Tone Series*
*performed by:* Stiles Allen (soprano)
*orchestra:* Boyd Neel String Orchestra
*conductor:* Boyd Neel
*other works performed:* by Abel-Carse, Marcello, Delius, Lotter, Tchaikovsky and
    Johann Strauss
*notes:* *1st British performance

**1935 Dec. 8**   Sunday Orchestral Concert
*broadcast over:* Regional (9.21–10.44 pm)                    broadcast: ✓ concert:
*work(s) performed:* Berg    Three movements from the *Lyric Suite*, arr. for string
                             orchestra
*orchestra:* BBC Orchestra
*conductor:* Ernest Ansermet
*other works performed:* by Haydn and Debussy

**1936 Feb. 1**
*broadcast over:* Regional (8.30–9.32 pm)                     broadcast: ✓ concert:
*work(s) performed:* Schoenberg    *Suite in G major for string orchestra
*orchestra:* Boyd Neel String Orchestra
*conductor:* Boyd Neel
*other works performed:* by Bach, Bach arr. Vaughan Williams and Arnold Foster, and
    Mozart
*notes:* *1st broadcast performance

**1936 Feb. 5**
*broadcast over:* National (8.00–9.30 pm)                    broadcast: ✓ concert:
*work(s) performed:* Schoenberg    *Pelleas und Melisande*, op. 5
*orchestra:* BBC Orchestra
*conductor:* Boult and Darius Milhaud
*other works performed:* by Haydn, Berlioz, Wagner, and Milhaud: *Chants populaires hébraïques*
*notes:* The Schoenberg was originally to have been given at a BBC Symphony Concert on 22 January 1936, but following the death of George V on 20 January, all scheduled broadcasts were cancelled until after the funeral on 28 January.

**1936 April 6**    'A Pianoforte Recital'
*broadcast over:* National (3.15–3.45 pm)                    broadcast: ✓ concert:
*work(s) performed:* Schoenberg    *Six Little Piano Pieces*, op. 19
*performed by:* Edmund Rubbra (piano)
*other works performed:* by Froberger, Zipoli and Debussy

**1936 April 6**
*broadcast over:* Regional (9.00–9.55 pm)                    broadcast: ✓ concert:
*work(s) performed:* Berg    'Sommertage', 'Im Zimmer', Schilflied,' 'Traumgekrönt', and 'Die Nachtigall' from *Seven Early Songs*
*performed by:* Hanna Schwarz (soprano)
*orchestra:* BBC Orchestra
*conductor:* Malcolm Sargent
*other works performed:* by Kodály, Falla and Holst

**1936 April 14**
*broadcast over:* National (8.00–9.00 pm)                    broadcast: ✓ concert:
*work(s) performed:* Schoenberg    Suite in G major for string orchestra
*orchestra:* Boyd Neel String Orchestra
*conductor:* Boyd Neel
*other works performed:* by Vivaldi, and Britten: *Simple Symphony*

**1936 May 1**    Concerts of Contemporary Music, series x, concert 7
*broadcast over:* National (10.29–11.21 pm)                    broadcast: ✓ concert: ✓
*place of performance:* Concert Hall, Broadcasting House
*work(s) performed:* Berg    *Violin Concerto
                    Berg    Two movements from *Lyric Suite*, arr. for string orchestra
*performed by:* Louis Krasner (violin)
*orchestra:* BBC Orchestra
*conductor:* Webern
*notes:* *1st British performance
    This concert was designated as an 'Alban Berg Memorial Concert' by the BBC.

**1936 May 25**
*broadcast over:* National (10.18–11.17 pm)                    broadcast: ✓ concert:
*work(s) performed:* Wellesz    Piano Concerto, op. 49
*performed by:* John Hunt (piano)
*orchestra:* BBC Orchestra
*conductor:* Julian Clifford
*other works performed:* by Berlioz and Liszt

# Appendix B    BBC Concerts of Contemporary Music, 1926–36

Table B.1 *The BBC spring series of chamber music concerts, April–June 1926*

all six concerts were broadcast at 8.30 pm over 2LO from the New Chenil Galleries, Chelsea

**26 April**
Steuart Wilson (tenor)
The London Chamber Orchestra
Anthony Bernard (conductor)

| | |
|---|---|
| Bach | Brandenburg Concerto no. 1* [first three movements only] |
| Vaughan Williams | Songs from *Hugh the Drover*\* ['First time in new arrangement'] |
| Honegger | *Pastorale d'été*\* |
| Lennox Berkeley | *Introduction and Dance*†\* |
| Bloch | *Concerto grosso*†\* |
| Peter Warlock | *An Old Song* |
| Louis Gruenberg | *The Daniel Jazz*†\* |

**3 May** \*\*
Leon Goossens (oboe)
Jean Pougnet (viola and violin)
Ambrose Gauntlett ('cello)
The Music Society String Quartet (André Mangeot, Doris Pecker, Henry J. Berly and
John Barbirolli)

| | |
|---|---|
| Purcell | *Fantasia upon One Note* for string quintet* |
| Vaughan Williams | Phantasy Quintet* |
| Mozart | Quartet for oboe and strings* |
| Randerson | *The Fields Breathe Sweet* for violin, viola and oboe††\* |
| Eugene Goossens | Phantasy Sextet |

**17 May**\*\*
Tom Goodey (tenor)
Arthur Catterall (violin)
John Wills (piano)

| | |
|---|---|
| Mozart | Violin Sonata in A major, K.395* |
| Medtner | *Sonata vocalise*\* |
| Delius | *Légende* for violin and piano* [replaced Medtner: *Three Nocturnes*, op. 16, originally announced] |
| Wolf | Lieder* |
| Brahms | Violin Sonata in A major |

Table B.1 (*cont.*)

**31 May**
Anne Thursfield (soprano)
The Aeolian Players (Joseph Slater, flute; Constance Izard, violin; Rebecca Clarke, viola; Gordon Bryan, piano)

| | |
|---|---|
| J. C. F. Bach | Sonata in C major for flute, violin and piano* |
| Padre Martini | Sonatina in D major for viola and piano* |

Songs with obligatos:

| | |
|---|---|
| Ravel | *La flûte enchantée* (with flute)* |
| Fauré | *Clair de lune* (with flute and piano)* |
| Arthur Bliss | *Two Nursery Rhymes* (with viola and piano and with viola)* |
| Beethoven | Serenade for flute, violin and viola, op. 25* |
| Honegger | Rhapsody for flute, violin, viola and piano† |
| Gordon Bryan | songs: 'Phantom' and 'The Persian Coat' |
| Patrick Hadley | *The Woodlanders*†† |
| Rebecca Clarke | *Chinese Puzzle* |

**14 June**
Vivienne Chatterton (soprano)
Dorothy Helmrich (contralto)
The Chenil Chamber Orchestra
The Wireless Ladies' Chorus
John Barbirolli (conductor)

| | |
|---|---|
| Pergolesi | *Stabat Mater*\* |
| Dorothy Howell | *Nocturne*††\* |
| Kenneth Wright | *Sleepy Tune*\* ['First time with new arrangement'] |

Songs with orchestra:

| | |
|---|---|
| Elizabeth Poston | *Aubade* |
| Muriel Herbert | *Fountain Court* |
| Maurice Besly | *The New Umbrella* |
| [one more, never specified] | |
| Purcell | Suite |

**21 June** ***
Dale Smith (baritone)
Sidonie Goossens (harp)
The Virtuoso String Quartet (Marjorie Hayward, Edwin Virgo, Raymond Jeremy, Cedric Sharpe)

| | |
|---|---|
| Beethoven | String Quartet, op. 18 no. 3* |
| Eric Fogg | *Ode to a Nightingale*†††\* |
| John Foulds | *Aquarelles* for string quartet†††\* |

† first English performance    †† first performance    ††† first London performance
* denotes works that were transmitted, as listed in the BBC WAC 'Programmes as Broadcast' records. Works that were not transmitted (no asterisk follows the title) are reconstructed from press reviews. No programmes for these concerts survive at the BBC WAC.

Table B.1 (*cont.*)

*Notes* (*cont.*):

** On 4 May 1926, a General Strike began which lasted until 12 May; the general resumption of work did not occur until 17 May. Since the strike stopped the publication of newspapers, no reviews of the 3 May concert and few of the 17 May concert were published. Hence, it is nearly impossible to determine the parts of the programmes that were not broadcast. One work performed during the second half on 3 May, the Goossens Phantasy, was mentioned in *The R.C.M. Magazine* 22/3 (1925–6), 98.

*** have been unable to determine the works performed during the second half of this concert.

Table B.2 *The First Season of BBC Concerts of Contemporary Music, 1926–7*

all six concerts were broadcast over 2LO or 5XX from the Grotrian Hall, Wigmore Street, London

| *date and performers* | *performed works* | *broadcast wavelength and time* |
|---|---|---|
| **5 October 1926** <br> Maria Basilides (singer) <br> The Hungarian String Quartet | **Hungary** <br> Dohnányi: String Quartet in A minor[††][*] <br> Kodály: songs[*] <br> Kodály: Serenade for two violins and viola, op. 12[*] <br> Bartók and Kodály: songs <br> Antal Molnár: *Quartetto breve*[††] | 2LO, 8.15–9.30 pm |
| **2 November 1926** <br> Kathleen Lafla (singer) <br> The Venetian String Quartet | **Italy** <br> Mario Labroca: String Quartet[†][*] <br> Malipiero: *Le stagioni italiche* <br> Francesco de Guarnieri: String Quartet no. 2[†][*] <br> Respighi: *Quartetto dorico* | 5XX, 8.15–9.30 pm |
| **7 December 1926** <br> The Amar Quartet | **Germany** <br> Jarnach: String Quartet, op. 16[†][*] <br> Reger: String Trio, op. 77b[*] <br> Hindemith: String Quartet, op. 22[†] | 2LO, 8.15–9.30 pm |
| **4 January 1927** <br> Léon Bleuzet (oboe) <br> Yvonne Ereizenem-Bleuzet (piano) <br> Dora Stevens (soprano) <br> Harold Craxton (piano) | **France** <br> Koechlin: Sonata for oboe and piano[†] <br> Debussy: *Quatre mélodies inédites*[†][*] <br><br> Taulet: oboe solos[†][*] <br> Honegger: songs[*] <br> Paul Ladmirault: *Esquisses* for piano[†††][*] | 5XX, 9.30–10.30 pm |
| **1 February 1927** <br> Ervín Schulhoff (piano) <br> The Zika String Quartet | **Czechoslovakia** <br> Jirák: String Quartet in C minor, op. 9[†] <br> Václav Kaprál: Piano Sonata no. 3 <br> Schulhoff: String Quartet no. 1 <br> Schulhoff: *Cinq jazz-studies concertantes*[*] <br> Dvořák: String Quartet in D minor, op. 34[*] | 2LO, 9.30–10.20 pm |
| **1 March 1927** <br> Willem Pijper (piano) <br> J. Feltkamp (flute) <br> Henrik Rijnberger (violin) <br> Marix Leovensohn ('cello) | **Holland** <br> Pijper: 'Cello Sonata no. 2[†] <br> Dresden: Flute Sonata[†] <br> Pijper: Violin Sonata no. 2[†] <br> Ketting and Pijper: piano works <br> Zagwijn: piano works <br> Voormolen: Piano Trio[†][*] | 5XX, 9.35–10.05 pm |

[†] first English performance    [††] first performance    [†††] 'probably first public performance in England'
[*] denotes works that were transmitted, as listed in the BBC WAC 'Programmes as Broadcast' records. Works that were not transmitted (no asterisk follows the title) are given as listed in the concert programmes. All transmitted works were definitely performed; however, there may have been alterations to the non-transmitted parts of the programmes, which will not be reflected in this table.

Broadcast times shown are to the nearest five-minute increment.

Table B.3 *The second season of BBC Concerts of Contemporary Music, 1927–8*

all eight concerts were given as studio broadcasts from the London station

| *planned programme* | *performed programme*[1] |
|---|---|
| **3 October 1927**     [The programme was performed as planned.] | 2LO and 5XX, 9.30–11.25 pm |
| Sarah Fischer (soprano) | Eisler: Duo for violin and 'cello, op. 7 |
| The Vienna String Quartet | Ravel: *Cinq mélodies populaires grecques* |
|  | Webern: Five Pieces for string quartet, op. 5 |
|  | Falla: arrangements of popular Spanish songs |
|  | Schoenberg: String Quartet no. 1, op. 7 |
| **7 November 1927**[2] | 2LO and 5XX, 9.35–10.40 pm |
| Marcelle Meyer (piano) | Emma Lubbecke-Job (piano) |
| The Pro Arte String Quartet | The Pro Arte String Quartet |
| Stravinsky: Concertino for string quartet | Stravinsky: Concertino for string quartet |
| Stravinsky: Three Pieces for string quartet | Stravinsky: Three Pieces for string quartet |
| Stravinsky: Piano Sonata | Hindemith: solo piano pieces |
| Stravinsky: *Piano-Rag-Music* | Koechlin: String Quartet no. 1 |
| Koechlin: String Quartet no. 1 | Krenek: Five Pieces for piano, op. 39 |
| Poulenc: *Napoli Suite* for piano | Honegger: Sonatina for two violins |
| Honegger: Sonatina for two violins | Milhaud: String Quartet no. 7 |
| Auric: Three Fragments from *Les fâcheux* (arranged for piano) | |
| Milhaud: String Quartet no. 7 | |
| **5 December 1927**[3] | 5GB, 8.30–10.00 pm |
| Lina Llubera (soprano) | |
| Serge Prokofiev (piano) | Serge Prokofiev (piano) |
| The Hungarian String Quartet | The Hungarian String Quartet |
| Szymanowski: String Quartet, op. 37 | Szymanowski: String Quartet, op. 37 |
| Prokofiev: Piano Sonata no. 3, op. 28 | Prokofiev: Piano Sonata no. 3, op. 28 |
| Prokofiev: songs | Prokofiev: solo piano pieces |
| Kodály: String Quartet no. 2, op. 10 | Kodály: String Quartet no. 2, op. 10 |
| Prokofiev: solo piano pieces | Prokofiev: solo piano pieces |
| Myaskovsky and Stravinsky: songs | |
| **9 January 1928**     [The programme was performed as planned.] | 5GB, 8.30–10.00 pm |
| Ervín Schulhoff (piano) | Schoenberg: Chamber Symphony no. 1 |
| Ernest Ansermet (conductor) | Schulhoff: Concerto for piano and chamber orchestra |
|  | Milhaud: *La création du monde* |
|  | Stravinsky: Octet |
| **13 February 1928**[4]     [The programme was performed as planned.] | 5GB, 10.30–11.35 pm |
| Claire Croiza (soprano) | {Berg: *Lyric suite*} |
| The Vienna String Quartet | Auric, Debussy, Milhaud, Poulenc: songs |
|  | Schoenberg: String Quartet no. 3, op. 30 |

Table B.3 (*cont.*)

| planned programme | performed programme[1] |
|---|---|
| **5 March 1928** | 5GB, 8.30–10.00 pm |
| Margot Hinnenberg-Lefèbre (soprano) | |
| Robert Murchie and Frank Almgill (flute), J. C. Pantling (oboe), Frederick Thurston (clarinet) | |
| Samuel Kutcher (violin), Ernest Tomlinson (viola), Victor Watson (double bass) | |
| Kathleen Long and Victor Hely Hutchinson (piano) | |
| Honegger: Rhapsodie for 2 flutes, clarinet and piano | Hindemith: Sonata for two flutes, op. 31 no. 3 |
| Webern: Six Stefan George Lieder, from op. 3 & 4 | Jarnach: Piano Sonatina, op. 18 |
| Jarnach: Piano Sonatina, op. 18 | Webern: Six Stefan George Lieder, from op. 3 & 4 |
| Eisler: *Zeitungsausschnitte*, op. 11 | Honegger: Rhapsodie for 2 flutes, clarinet & piano |
| Prokofiev: Quintet for oboe, clarinet, violin, viola and double bass | Eisler: *Zeitungsausschnitte*, op. 11 |
| | Prokofiev: Quintet |
| **2 April 1928** | 5GB, 8.00–9.30 pm |
| Marcelle Meyer (piano) | |
| The Roth String Quartet | |
| Harsányi: String Quartet | Harsanyi: String Quartet |
| Stravinsky: Piano Sonata | Stravinsky: Piano Sonata |
| Stravinsky: *Piano-Rag-Music* | Stravinsky: *Piano-Rag-Music* |
| Poulenc: *Napoli Suite* for piano | Poulenc: *Napoli Suite* for piano |
| Auric: Three Fragments from *Les fâcheux* | Auric: Three Fragments from *Les fâcheux* |
| Schulhoff: String Quartet no. 2 | (arranged for piano) |
| | Honegger: String Quartet |
| **7 May 1928**[5] | 5GB, 8.30–10.00 pm |
| Steuermann (piano) | |
| The Amar-Hindemith String Quartet | |
| Bartók: String Quartet no. 1, op. 7 | Bartók: String Quartet no. 1, op. 7 |
| Schoenberg: Three Piano Pieces, op. 11 | Schoenberg: Three Piano Pieces, op. 11 |
| Schoenberg: 'Five Little Piano Pieces', op. 19 | Schoenberg: 'Six Little Piano Pieces', op. 19 |
| Hindemith: String Trio, op. 34 | Hindemith: String Trio, op. 34 |
| Busoni: Piano Sonatinas, nos. 1 and 11 | Busoni: Piano Sonatinas, nos. 1 and 11 |
| Hindemith: Six Pieces for string quartet, op. 44 | {Hindemith: Six Pieces for string quartet, op. 44} |

[1] For five of the programmes, the advertised programme listing differed from the actual performance: for each concert, the originally-announced works, as listed in the 'final' programme (found in BBC WAC R79/2/2) and in the *Radio Times*, is shown in the 'planned programme' column; the concert that was actually broadcast, as listed in the BBC WAC 'Programmes as Broadcast' records, is shown in the 'performed programme' column.

[2] The 7 November alterations were due to the last-minute withdrawal of Marcelle Meyer from the performance. She later presented most of the works she was to have performed at this concert on the 2 April 1928 programme.

[3] The 5 December alterations resulted from the absence of Lina Llubera, Prokofiev's wife, from the performance.

[4] Although Berg's *Lyric Suite* was initially announced for performance on the 13 February programme, the work was not broadcast. Reviews of the concert indicate that it was performed for the critics who attended the concert at the studio.

[5] For the 7 May concert, although the final Hindemith work was probably performed in the studio, it was not broadcast.

Broadcast times shown are to the nearest five-minute increment.

## Table B.4 *The third season of BBC Concerts of Contemporary Music, 1928–9*

all eight concerts were given before an invited audience at the Arts Theatre Club, London, and broadcast over the 2LO and 5XX wavelengths

| *planned programme* | *performed programme*[1] |
|---|---|
| **3 September 1928**<br>Ninon Vallin (soprano)<br>The Brosa String Quartet<br>Cecil Dixon (accompanist) | concert start: 8.15 pm; broadcast time: 8.15–9.15 pm<br>Bax: String Quartet no. 2<br>Debussy: songs from *Trois chansons de France*, *Le promenoir des deux amants* and *Trois ballades de Villon*<br>Goossens: String Quartet, op. 14<br>{Falla: songs from *Trois mélodies* (Gautier texts) and *El amor brujo*; four Spanish Folk Tunes}<br>{Bridge: String Quartet no. 3} |
| **15 October 1928**[2]<br>Margot Hinnenberg-Lefèbre (soprano)<br>Leon Goossens (oboe)<br>The Vienna String Quartet | concert start: 7.45 pm; broadcast time: 8.00–9.00 pm |
| Bliss: Quintet for oboe and strings<br>Webern: String Trio, op. 20<br>Hindemith: *Die Serenaden*, op. 35<br>Schoenberg: String Quartet no. 2, op. 10 | {Bliss: movts 1 & 2 from Quintet for oboe and strings}<br>Bliss: movt 3 from Quintet for oboe and strings<br>Hindemith: *Die Serenaden*, op. 35<br>Schoenberg: String Quartet no. 2, op. 10<br>{Webern: String Trio, op. 20} |
| **5 November 1928**<br>Walter Gieseking (piano)<br>The Pro Arte String Quartet | concert start: 8.00 pm; broadcast time: 8.00–9.00 pm<br>Fauré: String Quartet, op. 121 (posth.)<br>Hindemith: Piano Music, op. 37 (part 1)<br>Ravel: Sonata for violin and 'cello<br>{Ravel: *Le tombeau de Couperin*}<br>{Milhaud: String Quartet no. 4} |
| **3 December 1928**[3]<br>L. Zifado (soprano), B. Pett-Fraser (mezzo-soprano), D. Owens (contralto), T. Purvis (tenor), L. White (baritone), S. Dyson (bass)<br>Hermann Scherchen (conductor) | concert start: 8.30 pm; broadcast time: 9.40–10.30 pm |
| [Hindemith: Chamber Music no. 1, op. 24 no. 1]<br>[Krenek: *Symphonic Music* for nine instruments, op. 11]<br>Janáček: *Říkadla* ('Nursery Rhymes') for voices and instruments<br>Hauer: *Wandlungen*, op. 53 | {Krenek: *Symphonic Music* for nine instruments, op. 11}<br>Hindemith: Chamber Music no. 1, op. 24 no. 1<br>Hauer: *Wandlungen*, op. 53 |
| **7 January 1929**[4]<br>Claire Croiza (soprano)<br>Edward Steuermann (piano)<br>Victor Hely Hutchinson (accompanist) | concert start: 8.00 pm; broadcast time: 8.00–9.00 pm<br>Edward Steuermann (piano)<br>The International String Quartet<br>Raymond Jeremy (viola) |

Table B.4 (*cont.*)

| planned programme | performed programme[1] |
|---|---|
| Roussel: *Deux poèmes de Ronsard*, op. 26 | Busoni: Elegies for piano |
| Ravel: *Trois poèmes de Stéphane Mallarmé* | Vaughan Williams: Phantasy Quintet for strings |
| Busoni: Elegies for piano | Schoenberg: Five Piano Pieces, op. 23 |
| André Caplet: *Le vieux coffret* | {Bernard van Dieren: String Quartet no. 6} |
| Schoenberg: Five Piano Pieces, op. 23 | |
| {Poulenc: *Le bestiaire*} | |
| {Milhaud: *Catalogue de fleurs*, op. 60} | |
| {Honegger: Chanson (Ronsard text); *Les Pâques à New York: Trois fragments*} | |
| **4 February 1929** | concert start: 9.35 pm; broadcast time: 9.40–10.40 pm |
| Claire Croiza (soprano) | {Ravel: *Trois poèmes de Stéphane Mallarmé*} |
| Emil Telmanyi (violin) | {Delius: Sonata no. 2 for violin and piano} |
| Arnold Bax (piano) | Fauré: songs from *La bonne chanson* |
| Victor Hely Hutchinson (accompanist) | Bax: Sonata no. 3 for violin and piano (1st performance) |
| | Poulenc: *Le bestiaire* |
| | Milhaud: *Catalogue de fleurs*, op. 60 |
| | Roussel: 'Ciel, aer et vens' from *Deux poèmes de Ronsard*, op. 26 |
| | Honegger: Chanson (Ronsard text); *Les Pâques à New York: Trois fragments* |
| **4 March 1929**[5] | concert start: 8.00 pm; broadcast time: 8.00–9.00 pm |
| Zoltán Székely (violin) | **Bartók programme** |
| Béla Bartók (piano) | Rhapsody for violin and piano |
| | Suite for piano, op. 14 |
| | *Allegro barbaro* |
| | Sonatina for piano |
| | Three Rondeaux on Folk Tunes |
| | arr. Szigeti: Hungarian Folktunes [arr. of *Gyermekeknek* ('For Children'), orig. for piano] |
| | arr. Székely: Rumanian Folkdances [orig. for piano] |
| | {Piano Sonata} |
| | {'Three Open Air Pieces' [presumably three pieces from the *Out of Doors* suite]} |
| **3 April 1929**[6] | concert start: 8.00 pm; broadcast time: 8.00–8.55 pm |
| Marcelle Meyer (piano) | |
| The Amar-Hindemith String Quartet | The Amar-Hindemith String Quartet |
| Martinů: String Quartet no. 2 | Martinů: String Quartet no. 2 |
| Stravinsky: Serenade in A for piano | Hindemith: Sonata for solo viola, op. 25 no. 1 |
| Hindemith: Sonata for solo viola, op. 25 no. 1 | Hindemith: String Quartet no. 4, op. 32 |
| Nikolas Nabokov: Piano Sonata | |
| {Hindemith: String Quartet no. 4, op. 32} | |

[1] For four of the programmes, the advertised programme listing differed from the actual performance: for each concert, the originally-announced works, as listed in the 'final' programme (found in BBC WAC

## Table B.4 (*cont.*)

*Notes* (*cont.*):

R79/2/2) and in the *Radio Times*, are shown in the 'planned programme' column; the concert that was actually broadcast, as listed in the BBC WAC 'Programmes as Broadcast' records, is shown in the 'performed programme' column. All of the programmes included one or two works which were listed in the concert programme and were apparently performed for the audience invited to the Arts Theatre Club, but which were definitely not broadcast; these works are enclosed by curly brackets {}.

[2] For the 15 October concert, although the Webern trio was performed for the invited audience at the Arts Theatre Club, it was not broadcast.

[3] For the 3 December concert, the programme listed in the *Radio Times* did not include the Hindemith or the Krenek, although both were listed in the concert programme. The Janáček was not performed at all.

[4] The 7 January alterations were due to the last-minute withdrawal of Claire Croiza from the performance due to illness. She performed instead on the 4 February programme.

[5] For the 4 March programme, the *Radio Times* and concert programme listed 'Two Rhapsodies' as the first item, although only one rhapsody was broadcast; it is not clear whether Rhapsody no. 1 or no. 2 was performed. Moreover, the *Radio Times* listed the *Allegro barbaro* as the final movement of the Suite for Piano. Finally, there were two short transmission breakdowns during the broadcasting of this programme: from 8.17–8.19 pm and from 8.21–8.25 pm; it is impossible to determine which piece was being performed at the time.

[6] Marcelle Meyer apparently did not show up to perform at the 3 April concert; according to the 'Programmes as Broadcast' records, at 8.30 pm, halfway through the broadcast, the announcer apologized for the non-appearance of the pianist. Hence, only the works for strings were presented.

Broadcast times shown are to the nearest five-minute increment.

Table B.5 *The fourth season of BBC Concerts of Contemporary Music, 1929–30*

all eight concerts were broadcast over the alternative wavelength[1]

| planned programme | performed programme[2] |
|---|---|
| **7 October 1929**[3] at the Arts Theatre Club<br>Claire Croiza (soprano)<br>Paul Hindemith (viola)<br>Emma Lubbecke-Job (piano)<br>Frederick Waterhouse (heckelphone)<br>Ernest Lush (accompanist) | concert start: 8.00 pm; broadcast time: 8.00–9.00 pm<br>Hindemith: Sonata for viola and piano, op. 11, no. 4<br>Milhaud: *Les soirées de Pétrograde*<br>Hindemith: *Kleine Sonate* for viola d'amore and piano, op. 25 no. 2<br>Roussel: 'Sarabande' from *Deux mélodies*, op. 20; 'Ode à un jeune gentilhomme' from *Deux poèmes chinois*, op. 12; *Jazz dans la nuit*, op. 38<br>Debussy: *Chansons de Bilitis*<br>{Hindemith: Trio for viola, heckelphone, piano, op. 47} |
| **4 November 1929**[4] at the Grotrian Hall<br>Margot Hinnenberg-Lefèbre (soprano)<br>Edward Steuerman (piano) | concert start: 8.00 pm; broadcast time: 8.00–9.00 pm<br>Eisler: Piano Sonata, op. 1<br>Berg: Piano Sonata, op. 1<br>Schoenberg: *Das Buch der hängenden Gärten*, op. 15<br>{Busoni: *Fantasia contrappuntistica* for piano} |
| **2 December 1929**[5] at the Arts Theatre Club<br>Ružena Herlinger (soprano)<br>Anton Webern (conductor)<br><br>Milhaud: Chamber Symphony no. 1<br>Mahler: Four Orchestral Lieder<br>Webern: Five Pieces for orchestra, op. 10<br>Brahms: Serenade in A major, op. 16 | concert start: 7.45 pm; broadcast time: 7.45–8.40 pm<br>Anton Webern (conductor)<br><br>Milhaud: Chamber Symphony no. 1, 'Le printemps'<br>Webern: Five Pieces for orchestra, op. 10<br>Brahms: Serenade in A major, op. 16 |
| **6 January 1930** at the Arts Theatre Club<br>Maria Basilides (contralto)<br>Joseph Szigeti (violin)<br>Béla Bartók (piano) | concert start: 8.30 pm; broadcast time: 8.30–9.25 pm<br>**Bartók programme**<br>Rhapsody no. 1 for violin and piano (new version)<br>Four Hungarian folksongs<br>Elegy no. 2 for piano<br>Two Burlesques for piano<br>Sonata no. 2 for violin and piano<br>{Three songs from *Falun* ('Village Scenes')}<br>{*Nine Little Pieces* for piano}<br>{arr. Szigeti: Hungarian folktunes [arr. of *Gyermekeknek* ('For children'), orig. for piano]} |

Table B.5 (*cont.*)

| planned programme | performed programme[2] |
|---|---|
| **3 February 1930** at the Central Hall, Westminster | concert start: 8.30 pm; broadcast time: 8.30–10.05 pm |

Kate Winter (soprano), Linda Seymour (contralto), Parry Jones (tenor), Roy Henderson (bass)
Samuel Kutcher, George Stratton, George Whittaker, Victor Olof (violins)
Victor Hely Hutchinson, Ernest Lush, Lyell Barbour, Leslie Heward (pianos)
Robert Murchie (flute), Haydn Draper (clarinet), Richard Newton (bassoon), Ernest Hall (trumpet)
Douglas Cameron ('cello), Victor Watson (double bass)
John Lees (timpani) James Gillegin, John Hanrahan, Frederick Wheelhouse, Arthur Ure (percussionists)
The Wireless Chorus
Ernest Ansermet (conductor)

> Vivaldi: Concerto in B minor for four violins
> Vivaldi, arr. Bach: Concerto in A minor for four pianos
> Gabriel Popoff: Septet for flute, clarinet, bassoon, trumpet, violin, 'cello and double bass, op. 2
> Stravinsky: *Les noces*

| **3 March 1930** at the Central Hall, Westminster | concert start: 8.30 pm; broadcast time: 8.35–10.15 pm |
|---|---|

George Parker (baritone)
John Ireland, Arthur Alexander, Angus Morrison (pianos)
Robert Murchie (flute), Frederick Thurston (clarinets),
Walter Lear (saxophone), Ernest Hall (trumpet),
Ambrose Gauntlett ('cello), Charles Bender (percussion)
Edith Sitwell and Constant Lambert (speakers)
Leslie Heward (conductor)

> Ireland: Ballade for piano
> Ireland: songs
> Lambert: Piano Sonata
> Walton: *Façade*

| **7 April 1930** at the Central Hall, Westminster | concert start: 8.30 pm; broadcast time: 8.35–10.00 pm |
|---|---|

Edward Steuermann (piano)
The Vienna Pierrot Lunaire Ensemble:
   Erika Wagner (reciter), Rudolf Kolisch (violin and viola),
   Benar Heifetz ('cello), Franz Wangler (flute and piccolo),
   Viktor Polatschek (clarinet and bass clarinet)
   Edward Steuermann (piano)
   Erwin Stein (conductor)

> **Schoenberg programme**
> arr. Webern: Chamber Symphony, op. 9
> Suite for Piano, op. 25
> *Pierrot lunaire*, op. 21

Table B.5 (*cont.*)

| planned programme | performed programme[2] |
|---|---|
| **5 May 1930**[6] at the Central Hall, Westminster<br>Quentin MacLean (organ)<br>Hermann Scherchen (conductor) | concert start: 8.30 pm; broadcast time: 8.35–10.10 pm |
| Milhaud: *L'homme et son désir*, op. 48<br>Hindemith: Concerto for organ and orchestra, op. 46 no. 2<br>Weill: Suite from *Die Dreigroschenoper* | Milhaud: *L'homme et son désir*, op. 48<br>Max Butting: *Heitere Musik für kleines Orchester*, op. 38 (Radiomusik II)<br>Hindemith: Concerto for organ and orchestra, op. 46 no. 2<br>Weill: Suite from *Die Dreigroschenoper* |

[1] The alternative wavelength was known as 5GB until 8 March 1930, when it became the London Regional wavelength.

[2] Many of the programmes included one or more works which were listed in the concert programme and were performed for the attending audience, but which were definitely not broadcast; these works are enclosed by curly brackets {}.

[3] For the 7 October concert, although the final Hindemith work was listed in the *Radio Times* programme schedule, it was not broadcast; however, reviews indicate that the trio was performed at the theatre.

[4] For the 4 November concert, although the Busoni *Fantasia contrappuntistica* was listed in the *Radio Times* programme schedule and in the pre-prepared 'Programmes as broadcast' record, the latter listing was crossed out by hand, indicating that it was not broadcast. However, reviews indicate the work was performed for the attending audience.

[5] For only one concert in the series, on 2 December, did the advertised programme differ significantly from the actual performance: the originally-announced works are shown in the 'planned programme' column; the concert that was actually broadcast is shown in the 'performed programme' column. The alterations were due to the last-minute withdrawal of Ružena Herlinger from the performance due to illness.

[6] For the 5 May concert, the Max Butting work was performed, and broadcast, although it was not included in the pre-announced programme or in the *Radio Times* programme listing.

Broadcast times shown are to the nearest five-minute increment.

Table B.6 *The fifth season of BBC Concerts of Contemporary Music, January–June 1931*

All six concerts were given before an invited audience from the BBC's No.10 studio. The concerts were transmitted over the London Regional wavelength, except for the 9 January concert, which was transmitted over the National wavelength. All orchestral works were performed by members of the BBC Symphony Orchestra.

| *planned programme* | *performed programme*[1] |
| --- | --- |
| **9 January 1931**[2] | concert start: 9.35 pm; broadcast time: 9.35–10.45 pm |
| Margot Hinnenberg-Lefèbre (soprano) | Margot Hinnenberg-Lefèbre (soprano) |
| Arnold Schoenberg (conductor) | Wireless Chorus, Stanford Robinson (conductor) |
|  | Arnold Schoenberg (conductor) |
| **Schoenberg programme** | **Schoenberg programme** |
| Bach, arr. Schoenberg: Prelude and Fugue in E flat ('St Anne') | Bach, arr. Schoenberg: Prelude and Fugue in E flat ('St Anne') |
| *Erwartung*, op. 17 | *Friede auf Erden*, op. 13 |
|  | *Erwartung*, op. 17 |
| **13 February 1931** | concert start: 9.00 pm; broadcast time: 9.10–10.25 pm |
| Megan Thomas (soprano) |  |
| Steuart Wilson (tenor) |  |
| Clive Carey (bass) | Albert Sammons (violin) |
| Ralph Vaughan Williams (conductor) | William Murdoch (piano) |
| Adrian Boult (conductor) | Ralph Vaughan Williams (conductor) |
| Holst: *Savitri* | Goossens: Sonata no. 2 for violin and piano |
| Vaughan Williams: *Job* | Vaughan Williams: *Job* |
| **6 March 1931** | concert start: 9.00 pm; broadcast time: 9.00–10.30 pm |
| John Armstrong (tenor) | Van Dieren: String Quartet no. 5 (first performance) |
| Emma Lübbecke-Job (piano) | Warlock: *The Curlew* for tenor, flute, English horn and string quartet |
| Robert Murchie (flute) |  |
| Terence Macdonagh (English horn) | Hindemith: *Konzertmusik* for piano, brass and two harps, op. 49 |
| Frank Bridge (conductor) |  |
| **31 March 1931** | concert start: 9.00 pm; broadcast time: 9.00–10.20 pm |
| Brosa String Quartet | Bridge: *Enter Spring* |
| Frank Bridge (conductor) | Conrad Beck: Concerto for string quartet and orchestra |
|  | Bridge: *There is a Willow Grows Aslant a Brook* |
|  | Igor Markevich: *Concerto grosso* for orchestra |
| **8 May 1931**[3] | concert start: 9.00 pm; broadcast time: 9.00–10.00 pm |
| Enid Cruickshank (contralto) | Webern: Five Pieces for string orchestra (arr. of the Five Pieces for string quartet, op. 5) |
| Anton Webern (conductor) |  |
|  | Schoenberg: 'Lied der Waldtaube' from *Gurrelieder* |
|  | Schoenberg: *Begleitmusik zu einer Lichtspielszene*, op. 34 |

Table B.6 (*cont.*)

| planned programme | performed programme[1] |
| --- | --- |
| **24 June 1931** | concert start: 8.45 pm; broadcast time: 8.35–9.55 pm |
| Manuel de Falla (harpsichord and conductor) | **Falla programme**<br>*El amor brujo* |
| Mary Hamlin (soprano) | Concerto for harpsichord, flute, oboe, clarinet, violin and 'cello |
| Frank Titterton (tenor) | *El retablo de maese Pedro* |
| Roy Henderson (baritone) | |
| Sir Henry Wood (conductor) | |

[1] For the programmes on 9 January and 13 February, the advertised programme listing differed from the actual performance: for each concert, the originally-announced works, as listed in the 'final' programme (found in BBC WAC R79/2/3) and in the *Radio Times*, are shown in the 'planned programme' column; the concert that was actually broadcast, as listed in the BBC WAC 'Programmes as Broadcast' records, is shown in the 'performed programme' column.

[2] The original plans for the 9 January programme only included the Bach transcription and the monodrama, and only these works were listed in the official concert programme and the *Radio Times* daily programme listing; however, the 'Programmes as Broadcast' records indicate that Schoenberg's op. 13 choral work was also performed. This piece, which had been given in a studio broadcast on 7 January, may have been repeated on the 9th to increase the length of the concert.

[3] For the 8 May programme, the 'Programmes as Broadcast' records list the Webern as 'Four movements for String quartet, op. 5, arr. for string orchestra', suggesting that only four of the five movements were in fact broadcast. The same records indicate that Schoenberg's op. 34 was performed, and broadcast, twice.

Broadcast times shown are to the nearest five-minute increment.

### Table B.7 *The sixth season of BBC Concerts of Contemporary Music, 1931–2*

All eight concerts were given before an invited audience from the BBC's No.10 studio. The concerts were transmitted over the London Regional wavelength, except for the 20 May concert, which was transmitted over the National wavelength. All orchestral works were performed by members of the BBC Symphony Orchestra.

| performers | programme[1] |
|---|---|
| **13 November 1931**<br>Adrian Boult (conductor) | concert start: 8.00 pm; broadcast time: 8.00–8.55 pm<br>**Schoenberg programme**<br>*Verklärte Nacht*, op. 4 (string orchestra version)<br>Variations for Orchestra, op. 31 |
| **18 December 1931**<br>Odette de Foras (soprano)<br>Arthur Benjamin (piano)<br>Constant Lambert (conductor) | concert start: 9.00 pm; broadcast time: 9.00–10.15 pm<br>Lambert: Suite from *Romeo and Juliet*<br>Patrick Hadley: *Ephemera* for soprano and small orchestra<br>Lambert: Concerto for piano and nine intruments<br>Lambert: *Seven Poems by Li-Po* for soprano and small orchestra<br>Bliss: *Rout* |
| **22 January 1932**<br>Joseph Szigeti (violin)<br>Adrian Boult (conductor) | concert start: 8.00 pm; broadcast time: 8.00–9.20 pm<br>**Busoni programme**<br>*Lustspielouvertüre*, op. 38<br>Violin Concerto in D major, op. 35a<br>*Turandot*, suite from the music to Gozzi's drama, op. 41 |
| **5 February 1932**[2]<br>Solomon (piano)<br>Nicolai Malko (conductor) | concert start: 9.00 pm; broadcast time: 9.00–10.25 pm<br>Shostakovich: Symphony [no. 1]<br>Mossolov: Piano Concerto no. 1, op. 14<br>Vogel: Two Etudes for orchestra |
| **4 March 1932**<br>Béla Bartók (piano)<br>Sir Henry Wood (conductor) | concert start: 9.00 pm; broadcast time: 9.00–10.25 pm<br>**Bartók programme**<br>Suite no. 1 for orchestra, op. 3<br>Rhapsody for piano and orchestra, op. 1<br>*A csadálatos mandarin* ('The Miraculous Mandarin'), op. 19 |
| **22 April 1932**<br>Wireless Chorus<br>Stanford Robinson (conductor) | concert start: 8.15 pm; broadcast time: 8.15–9.15 pm<br>Vaughan Williams: Motet, *O vos omnes*<br>Kodály: *Este* ('Evening')<br>Kodály: Two Hungarian folk songs<br>Schoenberg: *Friede auf Erden*, op. 13<br>Delius: *Wanderer's Song*<br>Poulenc: *Chanson à boire*<br>Ravel: *Trois chansons*<br>Bax: *Mater ora Filium* |

Table B.7 (*cont.*)

| performers | programme[1] |
|---|---|
| **13 May 1932** | concert start: 8.35 pm; broadcast time: 8.35–9.40 pm |
| May Blyth (soprano) | Krenek: Theme and 13 Variations, op. 69 |
| Sir Henry Wood (conductor) | Berg: Three Fragments from *Wozzeck* |
| | Webern: Passacaglia, op. 1 |
| **20 May 1932** | concert start: 8.00 pm; broadcast time: 8.00–9.15 pm |
| Sir Thomas Beecham (conductor) | Delius: *A Village Romeo and Juliet* |

[1] For the first time in the history of the BBC Concerts of Contemporary Music, all the programmes during the 1931–2 season were performed as originally planned.
[2] For the 5 February concert, the precise number of the Shostakovich symphony was not specified in the programme, the *Radio Times* listing or the 'Programmes as Broadcast' records. However, the *Radio Times* programme notes suggest that the work performed was the first symphony, and this fact is confirmed by the concert reviews.

Broadcast times shown are to the nearest five-minute increment.

## Table B.8 *The seventh season of BBC Concerts of Contemporary Music, 1932–3*

All eight concerts were given before an invited audience in the Concert Hall at Broadcasting House and were transmitted over the London Regional wavelength. All orchestral works were performed by members of the BBC Symphony Orchestra.

| performers | programme[1] |
| --- | --- |
| **25 November 1932**[2]<br>Megan Foster (soprano)<br>Frida Kindler (piano)<br>International String Quartet<br>The Wireless Singers<br>Stanford Robinson (conductor)<br>Berkeley Mason (accompanist) | concert start: 9.00 pm; broadcast time: 9.00–10.15 pm<br>**Van Dieren programme**<br>Theme and Variations for piano<br>Two Poems for speaker and string quartet, op. 17:<br>    'Ballade pour prier Notre Dame' and<br>    'Recueillement'<br>*Deus meus ad te luce vigilo*, motet for chorus<br>'Bälow', 'With margerain gentle', 'Mädchenlied'<br>    and 'Schöne Rohtraut' for voice and piano<br>String Quartet no. 5, op. 24 |
| **23 December 1932**<br>Else C. Kraus (piano)<br>The Wireless Chorus<br>Cyril Dalmaine (conductor) | concert start: 9.00 pm; broadcast time: 9.00–10.20 pm<br>Szymanowski: Six Polish Folksongs<br>Schoenberg: Three Piano Pieces, op. 11, and Piano<br>    Pieces, op. 33a and op. 33b<br>Conrad Beck: *Es kummt ein schiff geladen*, carol for<br>    chorus<br>Norbert von Hannenheim: Piano Sonata<br>Hindemith: *Der Tod* for men's chorus<br>Poulenc: *Chanson à boire* for men's chorus<br>Stravinsky: *Podblyudnïya* ('Saucers') for women's<br>    chorus<br>Bax: *This worldes joie*, motet for chorus |
| **20 January 1933**<br>Victor Hely Hutchinson (piano)<br>Ernest Lush (piano)<br>Adrian Boult (conductor) | concert start: 8.15 pm; broadcast time: 8.15–9.30 pm<br>Jacques Ibert: *Escales* for orchestra<br>Bliss: Concerto for two pianos and orchestra<br>Roussel: Symphony in G minor, op. 42 |
| **17 February 1933**<br>International String Quartet<br>Anthony Collins (viola)<br>Eugene Cruft (double bass)<br>Ralph Clarke (clarinet)<br>Richard Newton (bassoon)<br>Ernest Hall (trumpet) | concert start: 9.00 pm; broadcast time: 9.05–10.15 pm<br>Britten: *Phantasy* in F minor for string quintet<br>Christian Darnton: String Trio<br>Erik Chisholm: Double Trio for violin, 'cello,<br>    double bass, clarinet, bassoon and trumpet |
| **24 March 1933**<br>The Wireless Chorus<br>members of the Wireless<br>    Military Band<br>BBC Orchestra<br>Adrian Boult (conductor) | concert start: 9.15 pm; broadcast time: 9.15–10.05 pm<br>Hindemith: *Lehrstück* (in English) |

Table B.8 (*cont.*)

| performers | programme[1] |
|---|---|
| **21 April 1933**[3]<br>Hedda Kux (soprano)<br>Rudolf Kolisch (violin)<br>Steuermann (piano)<br>Anton Webern (conductor) | concert start: 9.00 pm; broadcast time: 9.00–9.45 pm<br>Berg: Two movements from the *Lyric Suite*, transcribed for string orchestra by the composer<br>Krenek: *Durch die Nacht*, op. 67a, for soprano and chamber orchestra<br>Berg: Chamber Concerto for piano, violin and 13 wind instruments |
| **26 May 1933**<br>Enid Cruickshank, Harold Williams, Parry Jones, Ina Souez, Betty Bannerman and and Roy Henderson (vocal soloists)<br>Zoltán Kodály (conductor) | concert start: 9.00 pm; broadcast time: 9.00–10.30 pm<br>Kodály: *Székely fonó* ('Spinning-Room', sung in English) |
| **23 June 1933**<br>Thalben-Ball (organ)<br>Elsie Suddaby (soprano)<br>Marie Goossens (harp)<br>Edward J. Robinson ('cello)<br>Adolf Lotter (double bass)<br>The Wireless Chorus<br>Cyril Dalmaine (conductor) | concert start: 9.00 pm; broadcast time: 9.00–10.20 pm<br>Joseph Jongen: Sonata for organ<br>Bax: *Of a Rose I sing*, carol for chorus and instruments<br>Herbert Howells: Psalm Prelude no. 1 for organ ('Lo the poor crieth')<br>Karg-Elert: 'The Mirrored Moon' and 'Hymn to the Stars' from *Seven Pastels* for organ<br>Delius: *To be Sung of a Summer Night on the Water* for chorus<br>Edward Bonnel: *Cloches dans le ciel* for organ<br>Louis Vierne: Impromptu for organ<br>Marcel Dupré: *Carillon* for organ<br>Vaughan Williams: *Benedicite* for soprano, chorus and organ |

[1] The programmes during the 1932–3 season were performed as originally planned, with a few minor changes, explained in footnotes 2 and 3.

[2] For the 25 November programme, 'Recueillement' was listed before 'Ballade' in the concert programme and the *Radio Times* programme listing; however, the 'Programmes as Broadcast' records indicate that the two works were performed as shown above. In addition, only the first two movements of the String Quartet no. 5 were broadcast, although the entire work was performed for those in the Concert Hall.

[3] For the 21 April concert, three movements from Berg's *Lyric Suite* were originally planned for performance: 'Andante amoroso', 'Allegro misterioso' and 'Adagio appassionato'. However, Webern decided not to perform the 'Allegro misterioso' because of ensemble difficulties in the string orchestra version.

Broadcast times shown are to the nearest five-minute increment.

Table B.9 *The eighth season of BBC Concerts of Contemporary Music, 1933–4*

All eight concerts were given before an invited audience in the Concert Hall at Broadcasting House and were transmitted over the London Regional wavelength.

| performers | programme |
|---|---|
| **24 November 1933**[1]<br>Erika Wagner (reciter)<br>Rudolf Kolisch (violin/viola)<br>Benar Haifetz ('cello)<br>Robert Murchie (flute/piccolo)<br>Frederick Thurston (clarinet)<br>Walter Lear (bass clarinet)<br>Edward Steuermann (piano)<br>Constant Lambert (conductor) | concert start: 9.00 pm; broadcast time: 9.00–10.15 pm<br>**Schoenberg programme**<br>Three Piano Pieces, op. 11<br>*Six Little Piano Pieces*, op. 19<br>*Pierrot lunaire*, op. 21 |
| **22 December 1933**<br>Kate Winter (soprano)<br>Betty Bannerman (contralto)<br>Mark Raphael (baritone)<br>Wireless Chorus<br>BBC Orchestra<br>Adrian Boult (conductor) | concert start: 9.15 pm; broadcast time: 9.15–10.10 pm<br>Honegger: *Cris du monde* |
| **26 January 1934**<br>Parry Jones (tenor)<br>BBC Symphony Orchestra<br>Nicolai Malko (conductor) | concert start: 9.00 pm; broadcast time: 9.00–10.15 pm<br>Prokofiev: *Four Portraits and Dénouement*, op. 49 (Symphonic Suite from *The Gambler*)<br>Myaskovsky: Symphony no. 7 in B minor, op. 24<br>Shostakovich: Suite from *The Nose* |
| **23 February 1934**<br>John Duncan (baritone)<br>Cyril Scott (piano)<br>Frank Almgill (flute)<br>Eugene Cruft (double bass)<br>Wireless Chorus<br>Choirboys of St Mark's, North Audley Street<br>Leslie Woodgate (conductor) | concert start: 9.00 pm; broadcast time: 9.05–10.25 pm<br>**British Choral Music**<br>Britten: *A Boy was Born*, op. 3<br>Cyril Scott: Piano Sonata no. 2<br>Rubbra: *Planctus (David's Lament for Jonathan)* for baritone and chorus<br>Rubbra: *Ecce, chorus virginum* for flute and chorus<br>Rubbra: *Hymnus ante somnum* for chorus<br>Rubbra: *Novus amor* for chorus<br>Woodgate: motet, *Te decet hymnus* for chorus |
| **23 March 1934**[2]<br>Edwin Benbow (piano)<br>Wireless Male Voice Quartet<br>members of the London Symphony Orchestra<br>Edward Clark (conductor) | concert start: 9.00 pm; broadcast time: 9.00–10.10 pm<br>**American programme**<br>Henry Cowell: *Sinfonietta*<br>Virgil Thomson: *Capital, Capitals* for four men and piano<br>Adolph Weiss: Andante from Chamber Symphony<br>Varèse: *Octandre* |

Table B.9 (*cont.*)

| performers | programme |
| --- | --- |
| **27 April 1934** | concert start: 9.00 pm; broadcast time: 9.00–10.10 pm |
| Oda Slobodskaya (soprano) | **Stravinsky programme** |
| Kate Winter (soprano) | *Mavra* |
| Betty Bannerman and Mary Jarred (contraltos) | *Les noces* |
| Tudor Davies (tenor), Roy Henderson (baritone) | |
| Victor Hely Hutchinson, Berkeley Mason, Ernest Lush, Edwin Benbow (pianos) | |
| Wireless Chorus | |
| BBC Symphony Orchestra | |
| Ernest Ansermet (conductor) | |
| **25 May 1934** | concert start: 9.00 pm; broadcast time: 9.00–10.15 pm |
| Béla Bartók (piano) | **Bartók programme** |
| Trefor Jones (tenor) | *Két portré* ('Two Portraits'), op. 5 for orchestra |
| Frank Phillips (baritone) | Piano Concerto no. 2 |
| Wireless Chorus | *Cantata profana* (1st performance) |
| BBC Symphony Orchestra | Hungarian folk dances (encore) |
| Aylmer Buesst (conductor) | |
| **29 June 1934**[3] | concert start: 9.00 pm; broadcast time: 9.00–10.20 pm |
| Dennis Noble (baritone) | **British programme** |
| Clara Asher-Lucas (piano) | Van Dieren: *Diafonia* for baritone and chamber orchestra |
| section of the London Symphony Orchestra | Leighton Lucas: Partita for piano and orchestra |
| Leighton Lucas (conductor) | Britten: *Sinfonietta*, op. 1 |
| Edward Clark (conductor) | |

[1] For the 24 November programme, it was originally announced that the programme would consist of Schoenberg's Suite, op. 29, and *Pierrot lunaire*, op. 21, and these works were shown in the *Radio Times* programme listing. On 22 November, the BBC circulated a press release announcing that the programme was changed to op. 11 and op. 21. However, the 'Programmes as Broadcast' records indicate that op. 11, op. 19 and op. 21 were actually performed.

[2] At the 23 March concert, the Weiss and the Varèse works were repeated for those who heard the programme in the Concert Hall; the repetitions were not broadcast.

[3] For the 29 June concert, the *Radio Times* listed the order as Britten, Lucas, Van Dieren. However, the 'Programmes as Broadcast' records indicate that the works were actually performed in the order shown above.

Broadcast times shown are to the nearest five-minute increment.

Table B.10 *The ninth season of BBC Concerts of Contemporary Music, 1934–5*

All eight concerts were given before an invited audience. The concerts were transmitted over the National wavelength, with the exception of the first concert, which was broadcast over London Regional.

| *performers* | *programme* |
|---|---|
| **19 October 1934**<br>BBC Symphony Orchestra<br>Serge Prokofiev (conductor) | concert start:  8.45 pm; broadcast time:  8.50–10.05 pm<br>**Prokofiev programme**<br>Symphony no. 3, op. 44<br>Suite from *Chout*, op. 21 |
| **23 November 1934**<br>Marcelle Meyer (piano)<br>BBC Symphony Orchestra<br>Constant Lambert (conductor) | concert start: 10.15 pm; broadcast time: 10.20–11.15 pm<br>Robert de Roos: Five Studies for piano and<br>    chamber orchestra<br>Erik Chisholm: Overture for chamber orchestra<br>Markevich: Partita for piano and chamber<br>    orchestra<br>Milhaud: Suite from *Maximilian* |
| **21 December 1934**<br>Irene Kohler (piano)<br>BBC Orchestra<br>Paul Hindemith (conductor) | concert start: 10.15 pm; broadcast time: 10.15–11.15 pm<br>**Hindemith programme**<br>*Concert Music* for piano, brass and two harps,<br>    op. 49<br>Symphony, *Mathis der Maler* |
| **18 January 1935**[1]<br>Solomon (piano)<br>BBC Symphony Orchestra<br>Arthur Bliss, Clarence Raybould<br>    (conductors) | concert start: 10.20 pm; broadcast time: 10.20–11.40 pm<br>Roger Sessions: Suite from *The Black Maskers*<br>Arthur Bliss: *Mêlée fantasque*, op. 22<br>George Gershwin: Rhapsody no. 2 for piano and<br>    orchestra<br>Aaron Copland: *Dance Symphony* |
| **8 February 1935**[2]<br>Edward Clark (conductor) | concert start: 10.00 pm; broadcast time: 10.00–11.30 pm<br>Kurt Weill: 'The Tuppenny-Ha'penny opera' |
| **15 March 1935**<br>Margaret Godley (soprano)<br>Betty Bannerman (contralto)<br>Bradbridge White (tenor)<br>Henry Cummings (baritone)<br>Stanley Riley (bass)<br>The Wireless Chorus<br>London Symphony Orchestra<br>Leslie Woodgate and Constant<br>    Lambert (conductors) | concert start: 10.00 pm; broadcast time: 10.00–11.10 pm<br>Peter Warlock: Three Carols<br>Elizabeth Maconchy: Two Motets for double<br>    chorus<br>Van Dieren: *Chinese Symphony* for five voices,<br>    chorus and orchestra, op. 11 (1st public<br>    performance) |

Table B.10 (*cont.*)

| performers | programme |
| --- | --- |
| **12 April 1935** | concert start: 10.20 pm; broadcast time: 10.20–11.35 pm |
| Maria Korchinska (harp) | Hanns Eisler: *Little Symphony*, op. 29 |
| Bradbridge White and Martin Boddey (tenors) | Christian Darnton: Concerto for harp and wind instruments (1st performance) |
| Stanley Riley and Samuel Dyson (basses) | Stravinsky: Octet |
| 'An orchestra' | Stravinsky: *Renard* |
| Ernest Ansermet (conductor) | |
| | |
| **28 June 1935** | concert start: 10.15 pm; broadcast time: 10.15–11.05 pm |
| Laelia Finneberg (soprano) | Janáček: *Mša glagolskaya* ('Glagolitic Mass') |
| Doris Owens (contralto) | |
| Walter Widdop (tenor) | |
| Stanley Riley (bass) | |
| BBC Chorus | |
| BBC Symphony Orchestra | |
| Sir Henry Wood (conductor) | |

[1] Clark was originally supposed to conduct the 18 January programme, but programme building pressures necessitated that Raybould take over in his place.
[2] For the 8 February programme, the tongue-in-cheek title referring to Weill's *Dreigroschenoper* was used, because a radio adaptation, in English, was presented, rather than the complete work.

Broadcast times shown are to the nearest five-minute increment.

Table B.11 *The tenth season of BBC Concerts of Contemporary Music, 1935–6*

All eight concerts were given before an invited audience and were transmitted over the National wavelength.

| performers | programme |
| --- | --- |
| **1 November 1935**[1]<br>Hertha Glatz (contralto)<br>Ernst Krenek (piano)<br>BBC Singers<br>Leslie Woodgate (conductor) | concert start: 10.20 pm; broadcast time: 10.25–11.15 pm<br>**Vocal music by Krenek**<br>Voice and piano:<br>  'Räume', 'Rätselspiel' and 'Die frühen Gräber'<br>    from op. 9<br>  'Ein anderes' from op. 53<br>  *Gesänge des späten Jahres*, op. 71<br>Chorus:<br>  *Die Jahreszeiten*, op. 35<br>Voice and piano:<br>  *Reisebuch aus dem österreichischen Alpen*,<br>    op. 62 |
| **29 November 1935**<br>Adolph Hallis (piano)<br>BBC Orchestra<br>George Lloyd (conductor)<br>Warwick Braithwaite (conductor) | concert start: 10.20 pm; broadcast time: 10.20–11.25 pm<br>**British composers**<br>Van Dieren: Overture: *Anjou* \*\*<br>Christian Darnton: Piano Concerto \*\*<br>George Lloyd: Symphony no. 3 in F major \* |
| **20 December 1935**<br>Oda Slobodskaya (soprano)<br>Betty Bannerman (mezzo-soprano)<br>Hugues Cuénod (tenor)<br>BBC Chorus and BBC Orchestra<br>Igor Markevich (conductor) | concert start: 10.20 pm; broadcast time: 10.20–11.20 pm<br>Markevich: oratorio, *Le paradis perdu* \* |
| **17 January 1936**<br>Florence Hooton ('cello)<br>BBC Orchestra<br>Frank Bridge (conductor)<br>Adrian Boult (conductor) | concert start: 10.20 pm; broadcast time: 10.20–11.30 pm<br>Conrad Beck: *Innominata*<br>Frank Bridge: *Oration (Concerto elegiaco)* \* for<br>  'cello and orchestra<br>Aaron Copland: *Music for the Theatre* |
| **21 February 1936**<br>Ina Souez (soprano)<br>Heddle Nash (tenor)<br>Stanley Pope (baritone)<br>BBC Men's Chorus<br>BBC Symphony Orchestra<br>Edward Clark (conductor) | concert start: 10.20 pm; broadcast time: 10.20–11.35 pm<br>**Malipiero programme**<br>Preludes to *Tre commedie goldoniane*<br>*Filomela e l'infatuato* |
| **3 April 1936**<br>BBC Chorus<br>Leslie Woodgate (conductor) | concert start: 10.20 pm; broadcast time: 10.20–11.20 pm<br>Bax: *Mater ora Filium*<br>Rubbra: Five Motets<br>Pizzetti: *Messa di requiem* |

## Table B.11 (*cont.*)

| performers | programme |
| --- | --- |
| **1 May 1936** | concert start: 10.20 pm; broadcast time: 10.30–11.20 pm |
| Louis Krasner (violin) | **Alban Berg Memorial Concert** |
| BBC Orchestra | Two pieces from the *Lyric Suite* for string |
| Anton Webern (conductor) | orchestra |
| | Violin Concerto ** |
| | |
| **19 June 1936** | concert start: 10.20 pm; broadcast time: 10.25–11.30 pm |
| Joan Cross (soprano) | Lennox Berkeley: Oratorio, *Jonah* * |
| Jan van der Gucht (tenor) | |
| William Parsons (baritone) | |
| BBC Chorus | |
| BBC Orchestra | |
| Clarence Raybould (conductor) | |

  * first performance
** first English performance

[1] For the 1 November concert, Krenek's *Gesänge des späten Jahres*, op. 71, was not included in the *Radio Times* listing of the event; however, the work was included in the official programme listing (found in BBC WAC, R79/2/4), and the 'Programmes as Broadcast' records confirm that it was performed and broadcast.

Broadcast times shown are to the nearest five-minute increment.

# Appendix C  Biographical summaries

This appendix provides brief career summaries of 32 British men who were actively involved with the events described in this book. These people were either BBC employees, significant members of the BBC's music advisory committees, or eminent British critics who gave broadcast talks and who wrote about music broadcasts of the period. In the summaries, emphasis has been given to their associations with the BBC between 1922 and 1936. Birth and death information has been included to the extent that such information was available.

Biographies are included for the following:

Allen, Hugh (Percy)
Beadle, Gerald (Clayton)
Bliss, Arthur (Drummond)
Boult, Adrian (Cedric)
Buesst, Aylmer
Burrows, Arthur R.
Carpendale, C(harles) D(ouglas)
Clark, (Thomas) Edward
Davies, (Henry) Walford
Dawnay, Colonel Alan (Geoffrey Charles)
Dent, Edward J(oseph)
Eckersley, P(eter) P(endleton)
Eckersley, Roger H(uxley)
Evans, Edwin
Graves, Cecil George
Hely Hutchinson, (Christian) Victor

Herbage, Julian (Livingston)
Howgill, Richard (John Frederick)
Jefferies, L(eonard) Stanton
Lewis, C(ecil) A(rthur)
Maine, Basil (Stephen)
Mase, (Anthony) Owen
Millar Craig, David
Newman, Ernest
Nicolls, Basil E(dward)
Pitt, Percy (George)
Reith, John C(harles) W(alsham)
Scholes, Percy A(lfred)
Wellington, (Reginald Everard) Lindsay
Wood, Henry J(oseph)
Wright, Kenneth A(nthony)
Young, Filson

**Allen, Sir Hugh (Percy)** (*b* Reading, 23 Dec. 1869; *d* Oxford, 20 Feb. 1946). After establishing a distinguished reputation as an organist, choral conductor and music pedagogue, in 1918 he accepted simultaneous appointments as Director of the Royal College of Music and Professor of Music at Oxford University. Although he retired from his post at the RCM in 1937, he held his position at Oxford until his death. Allen joined the Music Advisory Committee of the BBC at the invitation of Reith when it was formed in 1925. He served as Chairman from its foundation until August 1942, when the committee was temporarily dissolved due to the war.

**Beadle, Sir Gerald (Clayton)** (*b* 17 April 1899; *d* 6 Nov. 1976). He began his BBC career on 25 September 1923 as an Announcer at the Head Office in London. In February 1924, he became an assistant to Cecil Lewis, the Organiser of Programmes, but left the BBC the following October. Beadle was re-engaged two years later and was appointed Station Director in Belfast on 25 October 1926, a position he held until 1 September 1932. Beadle returned to London to become the Assistant Director of Programmes when Graves was transferred to the Empire Service. During the reorganization of October 1933, Beadle's title became Entertainment Executive. In the restructuring of the upper administration in October 1935, he became Director of Programme Administration. A year later, he was appointed Director of Staff Training, and a year after that, he transferred to Bristol as the West of England Regional Director. In October 1940, Beadle returned to London, where he served as Acting Controller (Administration). However, in April 1943, he went back to his Bristol position as West Regional Director. His title was changed to Controller, West Region, in February 1948. In July 1956, Beadle became Director of Television Broadcasting. He held that position until he retired on 23 July 1961.

**Bliss, Sir Arthur (Drummond)** (*b* London, 2 Aug. 1891; *d* London, 27 March 1975). He received his education at Rugby and at Pembroke College, Cambridge. He studied for a short while at the RCM, but with the beginning of the World War I, joined the Royal Fusiliers, later transferring to the Grenadier Guards. After the war, he pursued a musical career, composing serious and theatrical works and conducting for the Portsmouth Philharmonic Society. He wrote several important pieces during this period, including *A Colour Symphony* (1922), and was recognized as a young British composer of importance. In 1923, he moved to California, where he married before returning to England in 1925. He continued to focus on composing during the years until the war, producing film scores and a ballet, as well as concert works.

In 1933, when the BBC was seeking candidates to assist Boult with creative work in the Music Department, the Music Director strongly recommended Bliss for the job. However, Bliss felt that a full-time post would disrupt his creative work. He offered to serve in a part-time capacity, but was appointed instead to the newly formed Music Programme Advisory Panel in April 1934. Bliss was the central figure on the panel until March 1940. In autumn 1935, when the BBC considered dividing Boult's position and appointing a new administrative head of the Music Department, Boult again nominated Bliss as the most suitable candidate. However, the Music Advisory Committee opposed this choice, and Bliss continued as an external advisor on the panel.

When World War II began, Bliss was living in California, where he remained until he returned to England in 1941. In March of that year, he finally took a full-time position at the BBC, at first serving as Assistant Director for Overseas Music under Kenneth Wright. In April 1942, Bliss became Director of Music, a post he held until 31 March 1944 when he resigned from the BBC.

After the war, Bliss again turned his attention to composing on a full-time basis. In 1950, he was knighted, and in 1953 he was appointed Master of the Queen's Music.

**Boult, Sir Adrian (Cedric)** (*b* Chester, 8 April 1889; *d* Farnham, 22 Feb. 1983). He received his education at Westminster School and at Christ Church, Oxford, where he studied with Sir Hugh Allen. He continued his musical education in Leipzig in 1912–13, particularly studying Nikisch's conducting technique, and in 1914 returned to London, where he joined the staff at Covent Garden. After the war, he began to make his name as a conductor in Britain, directing performances for such organizations as the Royal Philharmonic Society, the Ballets Russes and the British National Opera Company. In 1919, he began to teach at the RCM and in 1924, became conductor of the City of Birmingham Orchestra; he retained both positions until 1930.

In 1928, Boult was appointed to the BBC Music Advisory Committee following Tovey's resignation. Two years later, on 15 May 1930, he joined the permanent staff of the BBC, succeeding Percy Pitt as Music Director and thus taking charge of the administrative running of the Music Department and of the new BBC Symphony Orchestra. A year later, in May 1931, he also became the orchestra's Chief Conductor, assuming a double role within the BBC. Under his leadership, the orchestra attained a reputation throughout Europe for its high standard of performance and programme interest. Boult was a strong advocate of contemporary British music, and also conducted important performances of recent works by continental composers. Although the strain of the two jobs led him to request that his position be divided in 1935, this decision was reversed when a suitable candidate could not be found to assume administrative responsibility for the Music Department.

Boult remained Music Director and Chief Conductor of the BBC until 1942, when Bliss took over administrative powers as Director of Music.

Boult continued as Chief Conductor of the BBC orchestras until 8 April 1950, when he reached the compulsory age of retirement. He then held the position of Music Director of the London Philharmonic Orchestra until 1957. From that time, he made guest appearances internationally, conducted the Birmingham City Symphony Orchestra (1959–60) and taught at the RCM (1962–6).

**Buesst, Aylmer** (*b* Melbourne, 28 Jan. 1883; *d* St Albans, 25 Jan. 1970). He was educated in Melbourne, Brussels, London and, finally, in Leipzig, where he studied conducting with Nikisch. He worked as an opera conductor on the continent before settling in England. He conducted the Beecham Opera Company (1916–17 and 1919–20) and the British National Opera Company (1922–8), of which he was one of the founders. He also taught at the RCM during the late 1920s. On 1 October 1933, he was appointed Assistant Music Director of the BBC under Boult. However, by February 1935 the department had reached an alarming state of deterioration due to lack of leadership, and he was demoted to a lesser position in the Music Department, responsible for hearing auditions, conducting, reading scores submitted to the Corporation, and attending meetings and rehearsals. He left the Corporation at the end of 1935, and subsequently became conductor of the Scottish Orchestra. From 1926, Buesst was married to the soprano, May Blyth.

**Burrows, Arthur R.** (*b* Oxford, 15 Feb. 1882; *d* London, 1947). He first worked in radio during World War I, after which he joined the Marconi company. He was initially based at the Writtle station and later headed the 2LO station in London. Burrows was largely responsible for improving sound quality and raising the standards of programme content in pre-BBC broadcasting. In 1922, he recommended the appointment of a broadcast music director, which resulted in L. Stanton Jefferies' appointment to that position. Burrows joined the British Broadcasting Company soon after its formation, as the first Director of Programmes. A member of the Control Board from the time of its establishment in January 1924, he also headed the Programme Board after it was formed in May of that year. He was known to the listening audience as Uncle Arthur. He left the BBC in March 1925 to take up an appointment as the first Secretary General of the Union Internationale de Radiophonie in Geneva. He rejoined the BBC in 1940 and remained with the organization throughout the war, before retiring in September 1946.

**Carpendale, Vice-Admiral Sir C(harles) D(ouglas)** (*b* 1874; *d* 21 March 1968). He had a distinguished and highly-decorated military career, from which he retired in 1923. He joined the BBC in July of that year as Reith's assistant, and over the next 15 years was a crucial figure in the development of the organization's structure and policies. Known as the Assistant General Manager before October 1923, and then as Controller, Carpendale headed the Control Board when it was formed in January 1924. During the BBC restructuring of 1933, he was put in charge of the Administration Division of the Corporation, with the title, Controller (Administration). In October 1935, he became Deputy Director-General. He left the BBC in 1938, shortly before Reith's resignation. He was well-known in international radio circles, and served as president of the Union Internationale de Radio-diffusion from 1925 to 1935.

**Clark, (Thomas) Edward** (*b* Newcastle-on-Tyne, 10 May 1888; *d* London, 30 April 1962). The son of a dedicated amateur musician, he grew up in an environment that strongly supported and encouraged music and music-making. After finishing his studies at the Royal Grammar School in Newcastle, he toured the continent, studying for a time in Paris, where he was introduced to Debussy, Ravel and Roussel. In 1909, Clark moved to Berlin and studied with the conductor Oskar Fried while working as a *Musical Times* correspondent. He met Schoenberg and Webern in October 1910. After Schoenberg moved to Berlin in September 1911, Clark helped him to raise funds. He studied with Schoenberg between 1911 and 1914, and was an active participant in the composer's circle, attending concerts, discussions and social events with Webern, Hertzka, Busoni, Steuermann and others who lived in Berlin or visited Schoenberg there. In 1914, Clark began to make plans to remain permanently in Germany, but these were aborted when war was declared. He was interned at the Ruhleben race-course near Berlin until 1917, when he was released through the auspices of the Red Cross.

Clark returned to England and worked as a conductor, assisting Ansermet and Boult with the Ballets Russes London seasons. In spring 1921, he conducted his own series of orchestral concerts in London, exploring new music by British and continental composers; he presented a more popular series in December of that year. These projects were financially unsuccessful, and Clark looked for other means of supporting himself and his young family. In August 1924, he was hired by the BBC, soon becoming Musical Director of the Newcastle Station. His imaginative ideas transformed the region's music broadcasts, though it was noted that he lacked administrative skills.

In January 1927, Percy Pitt requested that Clark be transferred to the London station, where he assisted with music programme building, assessed manuscript scores, translated foreign correspondence, read and indexed foreign publications about music and conducted studio broadcasts. His administrative deficiencies led to a reorganization in spring 1928, in which he became the specialist programme builder, responsible for advising Wright about prominent music programmes. Around that time, he joined the committee responsible for selecting British works to recommend to the ISCM international jury. He also became the Music Director and conductor for the Arts Theatre Club in London. Clark neglected his BBC duties and in January 1929, his position was reviewed once again. The central administrators seriously considered dismissal, but intervention from R. H. Eckersley saved his job. In the following months, Clark was crucial to the development of the ingenious structuring of the new BBC Symphony Orchestra.

During the early months of 1929, Clark was tangentially involved in the BBC scandal involving his wife, Dolly, and the BBC's Chief Engineer, Captain P. P. Eckersley. Although Clark and Dolly had separated in summer 1925, her affair with Eckersley in 1929 led to the Chief Engineer's resignation from his BBC position and the break-up of both their marriages.

After the low ebb of 1929, Clark gradually regained his standing and position within the Music Department. With the BBC restructuring of 1933, he retained responsibility for building contemporary, chamber and light classical concerts. His conducting responsibilities were severely curtailed, but he was encouraged to go to Moscow in January 1934 to conduct two public concerts. With the departmental reorganization in 1935, Clark regained his ranking as third in the department, after Boult and Wright, and was put in charge of the programme building subdivision responsible for orchestral, military band, brass band and choral programmes. He also began to conduct broadcast concerts more frequently. However, in early 1936 Clark's integrity was questioned concerning his use of BBC funds during a business trip to the continent. He, in turn, was infuriated by the department's decision to alter programmes he had devised for the orchestra's European spring tour. Clark formally resigned from the BBC on 16 March 1936, and Boult accepted his resignation shortly thereafter.

Although Clark occasionally worked as a consultant programme builder, gave broadcast talks and conducted for the BBC in subsequent years, he never again worked for the Corporation as a full-time employee. In fact, he never again worked anywhere on a full-time basis. In 1938, he met Elisabeth Lutyens and they married in 1942. He was a free-lance conductor and devoted himself to promoting new music, serving as ISCM Honorary Secretary (1936–47), ISCM President (1947–52), LCMC

Chairman (1947–52), and Music Advisor to the Institute of Contemporary Arts (from its inception in 1948). Clark was responsible for organizing the ISCM Festival when it took place in London in 1946. In 1955, he brought a notorious slander suit against the composer Benjamin Frankel, claiming that Frankel had falsely accused him of embezzling ISCM funds.

**Davies, Sir (Henry) Walford** (*b* Oswestry, Shropshire, 6 Sept. 1869; *d* Wrington, Somerset, 11 March 1941). After studying with Parry and Stanford at the Royal College of Music and completing a Cambridge doctorate, he composed, taught counterpoint at the RCM, was organist at various churches of musical importance, and conducted choirs. During World War I, he became Musical Director to the Royal Air Force. After the war, he was appointed Professor of Music at the University of Wales (1919–26). He was nominated Gresham Professor of Music in 1924, and in 1934, was appointed Master of the King's Music, succeeding Elgar.

In the early years of the BBC, Davies became involved with the educational side of broadcasting. On 4 April 1924, he gave his first broadcast music talk in a programme for school children. In July 1925, he was invited to join the first BBC Music Advisory Committee, and he remained an advisor to the BBC until 1939. In September 1925, the Programme Board decided that he should give a half-hour music talk each Tuesday evening, and on 5 January 1926, he gave the first in his extremely popular series, 'Music and the Ordinary Listener'. In these talks, he explained basic musical concepts to listeners with little or no musical knowledge. Davies later published a number of talks from this series and from others that he broadcast over the years.

**Dawnay, Colonel Alan** (Geoffrey Charles) (*b* 1888; *d* 28 Sept. 1938). He was educated at Eton and at Magdalen College, Oxford. He joined the Coldstream Guards in 1909, and served throughout World War I. He was commander of the First Battalion (1928–30) before working in the War Office (1930–33). In conjunction with the BBC restructuring of 1933, he was appointed Controller (Programmes) on 4 September of that year. He only held this position until 1 October 1935, when he left the BBC for health reasons, and his position was taken over by C. G. Graves. Dawnay returned to military work briefly before his death.

**Dent, Edward J(oseph)** (*b* Ribston, Yorkshire, 16 July 1876; *d* 22 Aug. 1957). After studying at Eton and Cambridge, in 1902 he became a Fellow of King's College, Cambridge, where he taught various music subjects. In 1918, he moved to London to work as a music critic, but returned to

Cambridge in 1926 as Professor of Music. After retiring in 1941, he returned to live in London. In his primary role as a highly respected and renowned musicologist, he specialized in seventeenth and eighteenth-century opera. He prepared performance editions and translations of many operatic works, enabling a number of productions of previously unknown operas to be staged in England and in English. He also wrote articles and books about Italian Baroque opera and about Mozart's operas.

However, Dent's professional activities encompassed another important area of interest: in the interwar period, he was a leader in the promotion and dissemination of contemporary music. After World War I, he became involved with the effort to rejuvenate musical connections within the contemporary music world. In this capacity, in August 1922, he attended the first of what would become the annual ISCM festivals, chairing the meeting that formed the international organization at the end of the series of concerts. He and Edwin Evans drew up the society's constitution, and he served as the first president until Evans succeeded him in 1938.

**Eckersley, Captain P(eter) P(endleton)** (*b* La Puebla, Mexico, 1892; *d* 18 March 1963). After studying at Manchester University, he was apprenticed to a motor company. He served in World War I as a wireless equipment officer with the Royal Flying Corps, until he was wounded and left the service. In 1919, he joined the Marconi Wireless Telegraph Company as head engineer of the experimental section and was largely responsible for the technical development of the Writtle station near Chelmsford. Moreover, he was the chief entertainer on many of the broadcasts transmitted from that station in 1922, becoming a popular and well-known personality with the listening audience. When the BBC was formed in autumn 1922, Eckersley, as Chief Engineer, was one of the four original staff members. He continued to develop the technical side of the organization, achieving a world-wide reputation for designing and building the long-wave transmitter at Daventry (5XX), inaugurated in July 1925, and for his development of the transmission of alternative wave-lengths and the consequent regional scheme in 1929. His public popularity continued to grow, due to his many articles and talks about technical aspects of radio transmission and reception. However, he was forced to resign from the BBC in September 1929, after Reith discovered that he was planning to divorce his wife. In 1930, he married Dorothy Clark, Edward Clark's first wife.

**Eckersley, Roger H(uxley)** (*b* Campamento, Gibraltar, Spain, 28 Nov. 1885; *d* 19 Nov. 1955). The older brother of P. P. Eckersley, he had a varied career before he joined the BBC, ranging from law and managing golf clubs to working in the Foreign Office and poultry farming. He began to work for the British Broadcasting Company on 11 February 1924 as an assistant to Cecil Lewis. For a short time in 1925, he was in charge of outside broadcasts, but in September of that year he succeeded Lewis as Organiser of Programmes. He chaired the Programme Board from May 1926, when Lewis resigned from the BBC, until the reorganization of 1933. After the reorganization of 1927, his title became Assistant Controller (Programmes), although he was often referred to as Director of Programmes. When the BBC was restructured in October 1933, Eckersley became Director of Entertainment. In October 1935, the top administrative levels were reorganized again, and he and Gladstone Murray became the Assistant Controllers (Programmes) under C. G. Graves. This arrangement only lasted a year. In October 1936, Eckersley was transferred out of the Programme Division, and until the war he served as the liaison between the Head Office and regional stations.

In October 1939, Eckersley worked briefly for the Foreign Office, before he returned to the BBC to serve as liaison officer with the American broadcasting companies. In June 1941 he became the Chief Censor of the BBC Censorship Unit. He retired from the BBC in November 1945.

In his capacity as programming director in the late 1920s and early 30s, Eckersley was a vital support to the music programme building section. Not only did he back the individuals in the section – particularly Clark – when their activities were criticized, but he often endorsed unusual and expensive proposals for programmes involving contemporary music.

**Evans, Edwin** (*b* London, 1 Sept. 1874; *d* London, 3 March 1945). The son of an organist and writer on music, Evans also devoted himself to writing about music, with a special interest in promoting contemporary repertory. From the age of nine to fifteen, he studied in France and Luxembourg, establishing an early interest in continental matters. He initially pursued a business career, only transferring his professional interests to music in 1901, when he began to write about contemporary French composers. He is first noted for a series of articles, 'Modern British Composers', which appeared in the *Musical Standard* in 1903–4, and he co-founded the Society of British Composers in 1905. From 1918, he advised Diaghilev about the Ballets Russes seasons in London, becoming an advocate for Russian composers associated with that company, particularly Stravinsky. In 1919–20, he prepared another series of articles about British composers of the day, this time published in *The Musical Times*.

In January 1921, Evans became chairman of the London Contemporary

Music Centre, when it was founded as a subsection of the British Music Society. In August 1922, he attended the first of what would become the annual ISCM festivals; when the organization was officially formed at the end of the concert series, Evans offered the use of the British Music Society as a central office for the organization. He and Dent wrote the ISCM constitution, establishing that the LCMC would serve as the British section of the international organization. In January 1923, he was guest of honour at a dinner celebrating his efforts in support of contemporary music. In 1938, Evans succeeded Dent as ISCM president.

Evans was well known during the interwar years for his writings about music. He wrote for *The Pall Mall Gazette* (1912–23) and later for *The Daily Mail* (1933–45); he also contributed articles to the *Liverpool Post* and *Time and Tide*, and was editor of the *Musical News and Herald* and *The Dominant*. He wrote articles on contemporary British and French composers for several editions of the *Grove Dictionary of Music and Musicians*, as well as for other notable music reference books. He was well known as a programme note annotator for London concerts. Evans was the author of several books about music, including *Tchaikovsky* (London: J.M. Dent; New York: E.P. Dutton, 1935), *Stravinsky: Firebird and Petrushka* (London: Oxford University Press, 1933) and a book of essays, *The Margin of Music* (London: Oxford University Press, Humphrey Milford, 1924). His library of books on music and scores became a core part of the Central Music Library collection in London, which was founded in 1948.

**Graves, Cecil George** (*b* 4 March 1892; *d* 12 Jan. 1957). He was educated at the Royal Military College, Sandhurst. At the beginning of World War I, he was sent to France with the Royal Scots regiment and was taken prisoner on 26 August 1914. After the war, he served on the general staff at the War Office (Intelligence Branch). He retired from the military in 1925 and worked for a short time with the Metropolitan-Vickers Company. He joined the BBC in July 1926 as assistant to R. H. Eckersley, the Organiser of Programmes, and was known as the Programme Executive. In 1930, his title changed to Assistant Director of Programmes. In May of that year, the press announced that he was going to take over as Director of Programmes from R. H. Eckersley, but the rumours were immediately denied. In September 1932, Graves founded and became the director of the BBC's Empire and Foreign Services (now the World Service). In October 1935, he returned to domestic programmes as Controller (Programmes), following Dawnay's resignation from the BBC. In May 1938, following Carpendale's retirement, he became Deputy Director-General. In 1942–3, he served as joint Director-General.

**Hely Hutchinson, (Christian) Victor** (*b* Cape Town, South Africa, 26 Dec. 1901; *d* London, 11 March 1947). After studying at Oxford and the Royal College of Music, he became a lecturer in music at Cape Town University in 1922. He joined the BBC Music Department in February 1926 as a staff pianist and composer, and over the following years was acclaimed in the press as the young BBC phenomenon. In 1927, he became an assistant to Clark in the music programme building section. After the reorganization of April 1928, his responsibilities included planning the daily 'Foundations of Music' recitals featuring standard and lesser-known repertory. Over the following five years, he planned and produced this series, assisted with the building of other music transmissions, composed background music for radio features, and performed as conductor and accompanist on broadcasts.

In autumn 1933 Hely Hutchinson left the Corporation to take up an appointment as Professor of Music at the University of Birmingham, a position he held for 10 years. On 1 September 1944 he became the BBC Director of Music, succeeding Arthur Bliss, and held that position until his early death.

**Herbage, Julian (Livingston)** (*b* Woking, Surrey, 10 Sept. 1904; *d* London, 15 Jan. 1976). He studied at the Royal Naval College of Osborne and Dartmouth (1918–21) and at St John's College, Cambridge. In his first job, in 1923, he arranged and conducted light opera at the Everyman Theatre in London. In 1924, he worked as conductor and composer at the Savoy Theatre, and the next year held a similar position at the Liverpool Repertory Theatre. He joined the BBC in June 1927 as an assistant at the London Station; in November of that year, he became Clark's assistant in the Music Department. After the reorganization of April 1928, he became the chief administrative assistant in the music programme building section, second to Wright. In 1930, he was promoted to the position of Programme Organiser, responsible for co-ordinating all music programme building. After the reorganization of 1933, he was responsible for planning and co-ordinating orchestral broadcasts. In spring 1935, he returned to the number three position in the programme building section, after Wright and Clark. At this time, he took over the planning of chamber music programmes, solo recitals and the 'Foundations of Music' series; he was also responsible for the research and development of programmes involving little-known seventeenth- and eighteenth-century works.

By February 1938, with Wright serving as Assistant Music Director and Clark having left the BBC, Herbage had achieved a primary position in the

programme building section, in charge of co-ordinating all music programmes originating from Head Office and serving as the chief musicologist in the department. In January 1939, he became Music Organiser,
heading a new section formed to centralize the production of art music
broadcasts. In December 1940, Wright was transferred out of the Music
Department, and Herbage took over as Assistant Director of Music. He
relinquished this position in September 1944 and became a specialist programme builder in the Music Department, having founded the programme 'Music Magazine' with Anna Instone, whom he married that year.
Although he resigned from the full-time BBC staff on 30 November 1946,
he continued to produce this programme on a free-lance basis with his
wife until 1973.

As a specialist in English music of the seventeenthth and eighteenth centuries, Herbage was responsible for introducing little-known early works
into the music broadcasts. He prepared editions of works by Thomas Arne
and wrote a number of scholarly articles on Arne and Handel.

**Howgill, Richard (John Frederick)** (*b* 21 April 1895; *d* 24 May 1975). He
served in France and Mesopotamia during World War I, after which he
worked on the Mesopotamian Railways (1919–21). Following his return to
England, he was with the Performing Right Society for a year, and pursued
his interests as an amateur composer. In 1923, he joined the BBC as an
assistant in the copyright section. By the late 1920s, he worked closely with
the Music Department, negotiating with publishers about copyright issues
involving music broadcasts and BBC commissioning projects. By
November 1931, he was a member of the BBC New Music Subcommittee
with Clark and Hely Hutchinson. His experience and advice on musical
matters were so valued that in October 1932, the Assistant Music Director
formally requested that Howgill be available on a regular basis for consultation to the Music Department, which was approved.

During the overall restructuring of 1933, Howgill became the
Programme Services Executive. In early 1935, when conditions within the
Music Department deteriorated due to lack of leadership, Howgill was
briefly considered as a possible candidate to replace Buesst as Assistant
Music Director, though Wright was appointed to that position instead.
Later that year, Howgill became Assistant Director of Programme
Administration, and in 1936, he was promoted to Director of Programme
Administration. In 1939, he became Assistant Controller
(Administration), and in 1942 moved back to the programming branch as
Assistant Controller (Programmes). In 1948, Howgill became Controller
(Entertainment), a position he held for four years. Finally, in 1952, he

became the head of BBC music activities, with the title Controller (Music). He remained in this position until 1959, when he retired.

**Jefferies, L(eonard) Stanton** (*b* Weston-Super-Mare, 4 Sept. 1896; *d* 22 Oct. 1961). After studying organ and piano at the Royal College of Music, he was involved in radio from its early days, working initially in the business section of the Marconi company at the Writtle station near Chelmsford. After Arthur Burrows recognized the need for a music director at the 2LO station, Jefferies was appointed in summer 1922. The British Broadcasting Company was founded shortly thereafter, and he became its first Director of Music. During the early days, he was known to listeners as Uncle Jeff. When Percy Pitt was appointed Musical Advisor in May 1923, Jefferies assisted Pitt, seeing to the details of music programming for London and the provincial stations. His many duties included conducting orchestral programmes, arranging for visiting artists' contracts and tours, and supervising the music directors at the other BBC stations; he was also responsible for starting the collection of music which became the foundation of the BBC's extensive music library.

In 1926, Jefferies moved to the technical side of the department, in charge of the balance and control arrangements for music programmes. He remained in that position until he resigned on 30 June 1935. After the war, he returned to the BBC to produce programmes in the Light Music Department. He retired from his permanent position in September 1956 and left the BBC altogether in January 1957.

**Lewis, C(ecil) A(rthur)** (*b* Birkenhead, 19 March 1898; *d* London, 27 Jan. 1997). During his early career, he served in the Royal Flying Corps (from 1915), worked in civil aviation in England (1919) and helped pioneer the development of aviation in China (1920–21). He first worked in radio as part of the Marconi company team at the Writtle station near Chelmsford. He joined the BBC soon after its formation, as deputy to Burrows, the Director of Programmes. He was Organiser of Programmes for a short time, until R. H. Eckersley took over the position in September 1925. In May 1926 he left the permanent staff of the BBC, although he was associated with the organization until May 1929. In the early years, he was responsible for developing the dramatic and literary side of the programmes, producing studio plays, poetry readings and critical talks, and was known to the listening audience as Uncle Caractacus. During the late 1920s, Lewis devoted himself to writing and adapting radio plays. After he left the BBC, Lewis's career included writing for the stage, film, television and newspapers, working in commercial television, and sheep farming.

**Maine, Basil (Stephen)** (*b* Norwich, 4 March 1894; *d* Sheringham, 13 Oct. 1972). He was educated at Queens' College, Cambridge, where he studied with Edward Dent, among others. He taught music and mathematics (1917) and was assistant organist at Durham Cathedral. Between 1925 and 1937, he was music critic for a number of British newspapers, including *The Daily Telegraph* and *The Spectator*. In October 1926, he was invited to give weekly talks for the BBC, entitled 'Next Week's Broadcast Music', in which he introduced the music programmes to be aired during the following week; he continued to give this series until the end of the 1920s. Maine wrote a number of books on musical subjects, including *Behold these Daniels* (1928) about his fellow music critics, *The BBC and its Audience* (1939), *New Paths in Music* (1940) and *Twang with our Music* (1957). In 1939, he was ordained an Anglican priest and held livings in East Anglia from that time.

**Mase, (Anthony) Owen** (*b* Norfolk, 13 Jan. 1892; *d* not known). He joined the Music Department as a staff accompanist on 21 November 1927. In June the following year, he was transferred into the music programme building section as an administrative assistant to Wright. In April 1930, he was promoted to the position of Music Executive, but under strict conditions that revealed that he did not get on well with his colleagues and was not trusted to make musical decisions. Nevertheless, a year later, he was promoted to the important position of Assistant Music Director, to the detriment of his former supervisor, Wright. Continuing problems in the department led the central administrators to demote him to his former position of Music Executive during summer 1933, appointing Aylmer Buesst to the post of Assistant Music Director. Mase remained Music Executive until 30 June 1938, when his contract was terminated by the BBC. He was Director of Opera at Sadler's Wells Theatre until he joined the Royal Air Force in 1940.

**Millar Craig, David** (*b* Edinburgh, 1878; *d* 1965). He studied at Edinburgh University and at the Leipzig Conservatorium. He began to work for the BBC in February 1924 as the first director of the Scottish stations at Glasgow and Aberdeen. Two years later, in April 1926, he became an assistant in the Music Department in London, a position he held until October 1928. He was then appointed *Radio Times* Music Editor; although in March 1929 the Control Board was concerned that his approach was too scholarly for this publication and considered transferring him back to the Music Department, he retained the position. In February 1932, he became an assistant on *World Radio*, a BBC publication which encouraged listeners to tune into foreign programmes. He later became Music and

Programme Editor for that publication, a post he retained until he retired on 5 October 1938. Millar Craig was responsible for translating several contemporary vocal works with German texts which were performed in English by the BBC, including Schoenberg's *Gurrelieder* (performed 27 January 1928) and Hauer's *Wandlungen* (performed 3 December 1928).

**Newman, Ernest** [Roberts, William] (*b* Everton, Lancs., 30 Nov. 1868; *d* Tadworth, Surrey, 7 July 1959). He was educated at Liverpool College and Liverpool University, receiving no formal training in music. He began his career as a bank clerk in Liverpool, teaching himself about music in his spare time. In 1889, he began contributing articles about philosophy and the arts to British publications under the pseudonym Ernest Newman. During the 1890s, he also produced several books on composers, notably *Gluck and the Opera* (1895) and *A Study of Wagner* (1899). In 1904, he gave up his job as a bank clerk, teaching music in Birmingham, and he became music critic for the *Manchester Guardian* a year later. Soon after, he became critic of the *Birmingham Daily Post* (1906–18), and continued to publish books about composers, including Elgar (1906), Wolf (1907), Strauss (1908) and Wagner (1914). In 1919, Newman moved to London, working for a short time as critic of *The Observer*. In 1920, he became music critic for *The Sunday Times*, a position he held until he retired in 1958. His reviews were renowned for their analytical bases and sophisticated insights, as well as for their intrinsic accessibility. He continued to publish books about musical subjects throughout his career, including a four volume work, *The Life of Richard Wagner* (1933–47).

In September 1928, when Percy Scholes left the BBC, Newman replaced him as the BBC Music Critic. He gave bi-weekly broadcast talks reviewing recent musical events of note. The BBC's choice of Newman as Scholes's successor reflected the growth of sophistication of British listening audiences: whereas, the BBC were initially anxious to introduce listeners to the basic concepts and repertory of art music through Scholes's talks, by the end of the 1920s, the Corporation recognized that listeners were ready for more advanced fare and turned to Newman. Newman gave these talks until the beginning of the 1932–3 season, when the BBC suspended them. Nevertheless, the critic continued to contribute to broadcasts, frequently giving introductory talks to important BBC concerts until the war.

**Nicolls, Sir Basil E(dward)** (*b* 29 Aug. 1893; *d* 3 Aug. 1965). He ran a farm in Ontario (1912–14), before returning to Europe to serve in the North Staffordshire Regiment during World War I. After the war, he studied at Christ Church, Oxford (1920–1), and worked on a steel project in Calcutta

(1921–2). He began working for the BBC as the Station Director at Manchester in April 1924, but moved to London in December 1925 to become the 2LO Station Director. In January 1928, he was appointed General Editor of Publications, including the *Radio Times*.

During the reorganization of 1933, Nicolls became the Director of Internal Administration. In October 1935, when the upper administration was reorganized due to the departure of Dawnay, he took over the position of Controller (Administration) from Carpendale, who became the Deputy Director-General. When Graves became the Deputy Director-General upon Carpendale's resignation in 1938, Nicolls took over the post of Controller (Programmes). In October 1944, he became Senior Controller and in January 1948, Director of Home Broadcasting. He became Acting Director-General on 1 August 1952, before retiring from the BBC on 29 August 1953.

From the time that Nicolls took over as Director of Internal Administration in 1933, his influence on the Music Department was increasingly evident, as he imposed severe restrictions on requests to increase department staff and denied funds for projects and ideas originating from the music programme builders. Although long-time supporters of the Music Department and its programme policies, such as R. H. Eckersley, were initially able to override these restrictions, Nicolls's economic approach to BBC programming predominated by the end of the decade.

**Pitt, Percy [Percival] (George)** (*b* London, 4 Jan. 1869; *d* London, 23 Nov. 1932). At the age of twelve, he was sent to France to study; three years later he moved to Germany, where he became known as a pianist, organist and composer and also became acquainted with continental musicians and current European compositional trends. In 1893 he returned to England and initially worked as a choral conductor, organist and accompanist. He became musical advisor at Covent Garden in 1902 and was appointed Musical Director to the Grand Opera Syndicate there in 1907. During World War I, he assisted Beecham as conductor of the Beecham Opera Company, and in 1920 he became Artistic Director of the newly founded British National Opera Company; he held that position until 1924.

On 8 January 1923, Pitt participated in the first BBC outside broadcast, conducting an act of Mozart's *Die Zauberflöte* from Covent Garden. On 1 May 1923 he became Music Advisor to the BBC, a part-time position. By May 1924 he was Music Controller, responsible for the musical side of every concert broadcast from all the Company's stations. On 25 November 1924, Pitt was appointed full-time Director of Music, a post he retained until he was forced to retire on 31 December 1929, having exceeded the BBC's compulsory retirement age of 60.

As Nicholas Kenyon has summarized:

> Pitt was never a well-known public figure, nor even an outstanding conductor; but whether through knowledge or instinct Reith chose someone who was innovative, unrestricted in his outlook, who helped to shape the BBC's musical direction and turn its eyes and ears towards the Continent. He was in touch with important musicians abroad (he used to irritate his BBC superiors by corresponding with these foreigners in their own language, without keeping file copies of his letters) and the fruits of his contacts can clearly be seen in the BBC's concert and broadcast programmes of the 1920s.[1]

The appointment of this unusual musician to head the Music Department during the BBC's infancy – with his cosmopolitan outlook, his extensive knowledge of operatic and orchestral repertoire and his broad experience as a conductor and composer – had a profound influence both on the formation of the department's programming policy and on the choice of personnel to effect it. Nevertheless, the BBC was unwilling to recognize his achievements through a memorial after his death,[2] and historically he has received less recognition than is due for his part in establishing the BBC's innovative music policies during its formative years.

**Reith, John C(harles) W(alsham)**; Lord Reith (*b* 1889; *d* 16 June 1971). After completing his engineering apprenticeship in Glasgow, he worked as an engineer with a London firm (1913). At the beginning of the war, he was on active service until he was wounded. He was then put in charge of munitions contracts between the USA and Britain (1916–17) and worked in the Admiralty (1918). After the war, he worked for the Ministry of Munitions (1919), before managing a private firm (1920). In 1922, he became the General Manager of the newly established British Broadcasting Company, taking the title Managing Director the next year. In 1927, with the formation of the British Broadcasting Corporation, he became the Director-General. He retained that position and title until he resigned from the BBC in 1938. Reith chaired airline companies until he returned to governmental positions during World War II. After the war, he was involved in telecommunications.

During the initial years of the BBC, Reith had the vision to demand that

---

[1] Kenyon, *BBC Symphony Orchestra*, 5.
[2] BBC WAC, 910: Percy Pitt Memorial File (November 1932–September 1933), March–September 1933 [letters between Margaret Pitt and Roger Eckersley, and internal memos concerning the establishment of a Pitt memorial].

the organization develop a broad programming foundation, exploring the educational and cultural possibilities of radio, as well as the popular and entertaining potential of the medium. As a result of his idealistic policies and goals, and perhaps also because of his authoritarian management approach, the BBC had grown into a national institution by the end of the interwar period. Moreover, the Corporation had become the largest and most influential disseminator of art music in Britain and one of the few advocates of contemporary art music in Europe.

**Scholes, Percy A(lfred)** (*b* Leeds, 24 July 1877; *d* Vevey, Switzerland, 31 July 1958). In 1908, after taking the BMus at Oxford, he founded the journal that became *The Music Teacher* and remained its editor until 1921. He became a London music critic, first with the *Evening Standard* (from 1913) and later with *The Observer* (1920–5). In July 1923, he was appointed the first BBC Music Critic. He gave broadcast talks, at first weekly and later bi-weekly, which critically discussed significant musical events that had taken place in London. Often the talks also included basic instruction about music history, harmony, terminology and other general music subjects, aiming to educate the 'ordinary listener', who was being introduced to art music through broadcasts. Scholes became a frequent contributor of articles to the *Radio Times*, and in 1926 was appointed its Music Editor. In that capacity, he introduced explanatory notes into the daily programme listings. During his tenure with the BBC, he wrote a number of books, including *Listener's History of Music* (1923) and *Everybody's Guide to Broadcast Music* (1925), other means by which he made music more accessible and popular for the ordinary listener. In September 1928, Scholes left his BBC positions and moved to Vevey, Switzerland, in order to devote himself to his writing. Later publications of note include the *Oxford Companion to Music* (1938), *The Great Dr Burney* (1948), *The Concise Oxford Dictionary of Music* (1952) and *The Life and Activities of Sir John Hawkins* (1953).

**Wellington, Sir (Reginald Everard) Lindsay** (*b* 19 Aug. 1901; *d* 9 Jan. 1985). After studying at Queen's College, Oxford, he joined the BBC in October 1924 as Presentation Assistant at the London Station. In the 1933 restructuring, he became the Presentation Director. When the upper administration was reorganized again in October 1935, he was appointed Director of Programme Planning. A year later, he became Assistant Controller (Programmes), a position he held until the war. In February 1940, Wellington became Director of Radio Relations in the Ministry of Information. In 1941, he went to New York as North American Director of the BBC, a post he held until 1944. In September of that year, he became

Controller (Programmes) at the Head Office in London. After the war, he headed the Home Service. In 1952, he became Director of Home Sound Broadcasting and retained that position until he resigned from the BBC on 31 August 1963.

**Wood, Sir Henry J(oseph)** (*b* London, 3 March 1869; *d* Hitchin, 19 Aug. 1944). After studying at the Royal Academy of Music, he conducted opera with several London-based companies. His opportunity to become an orchestral conductor came in 1895, when he was asked by the manager of the recently built Queen's Hall to select what was to be a permanent orchestra for the hall and to conduct a ten-week season of concerts. The popular Promenade Concerts, which have been held annually ever since, established Wood as a leading English conductor. Throughout his career, he strove to improve the performance quality of English orchestras, to enlarge the performed orchestral repertory, including in his concerts many first performances of works by contemporary British and continental composers, and to bring orchestral music to a wider English audience.

During the mid-1920s, William Boosey, the managing director of Chappell and Co., then the lessee of the Queen's Hall, believed that the growth of broadcasting would adversely affect the sale of published music and the attendance of live performances. Boosey prohibited broadcasts to be given from the hall, and Wood and the Queen's Hall Orchestra did not take part in any early broadcasts. However, in 1927 financial difficulties forced Chappell's to change its attitude toward broadcasting. At that time, Wood chose to abandon his previous arrangement with Boosey and became a BBC conductor, initially with a three-year contract. The Promenade Concerts were taken over by the BBC from that year, and Wood remained the principal conductor of the series until his death. This highly popular figure also regularly conducted in other broadcast concert series for the BBC, as well as performances for other British music organizations.

**Wright, Kenneth A(nthony)** (*b* East Tuddenham, Norfolk, 5 June 1899; *d* Maida Vale, London, 15 Jan. 1975). Although he always had a profound interest in music and was a composer, he trained as an electrical and mechanical engineer, finishing a Master's degree from Sheffield University in 1921. He first worked for the Metropolitan-Vickers Company, one of the Big Six companies, participating in early radio telephony experiments at Trafford Park near Manchester. He became the first director of the BBC Manchester station (2ZY) in 1922 and was known to early listeners as Uncle Humpty Dumpty. On 1 February 1923, he became Assistant Director at the London station (2LO), where he worked with the station's director, Rex Palmer. On 23 August 1926 he joined the Music Department at the Head Office, where he soon became a central figure as Pitt's assistant, substituting for Pitt when the director was unable to attend administrative meetings, supervising other members of the department and heading the team of music programme builders. By 1927, Wright was Music Executive, second only to Pitt and supervisor of all details of programme building and of the department's administrative workings. After the Music Department reorganization in April 1928, which he designed, he took on additional responsibilities of handling the administrative side of the programme building section, assisted by Herbage, Clark and Hely Hutchinson.

In 1930, Boult took over as Music Director, and the department was restructured. Mase took on Wright's former title of Music Executive, while Wright became Boult's Principal Assistant. He held that position for a year, assisting Boult with the administrative running of the department and working less directly with programme planning, which was reassigned to Herbage. In May 1931, when Boult assumed the dual role of Music Director and Chief Conductor of the BBC Symphony Orchestra, the organization of the Music Department was reviewed once again. At that time, Mase was promoted over Wright into the position of Assistant Music Director, and Wright returned to being the chief programme builder. He retained this position while other changes were effected: Mase was demoted to Music Executive in summer 1933, and Buesst joined the department as Assistant Music Director in October of that year. In February 1935, when Buesst was also demoted, Wright was finally promoted to the position of Assistant Music Director. He retained that title and position, although R. S. Thatcher took over as second-in-command in the department in January 1937, as Deputy Director of Music.

In October 1940, Wright left the Music Department for a time, promoted to the position of Overseas Music Director. In March 1941, Bliss became his assistant in that department. However, in May 1943, Wright returned as Assistant Director of Music, now serving under Bliss, who had been appointed Director of Music in April 1942. In April 1944, following the resignation of Thatcher (in December 1943) and of Bliss (on 31 March 1944), Wright became Deputy Director of Music, eventually assisting Victor Hely Hutchinson, the new director and his old colleague (appointed in September 1944). Upon Hely Hutchinson's early death in 1947, Wright served as Acting Director of Music until a suitable replacement could be found to head the department. In 1948 Steuart Wilson was appointed to that position, and Wright became Artists Manager, a position he held for three years. In July 1951, he transferred to the BBC's television division and remained there until he retired from the Corporation on 1 October 1959. He was also involved with making films during the 1950s.

A composer of light music whose works were frequently aired by the BBC in the 1920s and 30s, Wright's personal interest in new music is apparent from his memos supporting contemporary music programming, from his reports on festivals of contemporary music that he attended, and from his correspondence with composers and contemporary music performers, who were initially business contacts but who frequently became Wright's personal friends.

**Young, Filson** (*b* Ballyeaston, Ireland, 1876; *d* 1937). He began his career as a journalist, writing for the *Manchester Guardian* before becoming literary editor of *The Daily Mail* (1903–4) and editor of *The Outlook* (1904). After serving in World War I, he worked as a war correspondent for several papers (1916–19). After the war, he became the editor of *The Saturday Review* (1921–4). In August 1926, he became a programme advisor to the BBC, a post he held until his death. In this capacity, he was involved with the establishment of 'The Foundations of Music' and with the Bach cantata series. In addition, he wrote and presented many broadcast talks, wrote a significant number of radio dramas, produced several programmes, and contributed a weekly column to the *Radio Times* entitled 'The World We Listen In'.

Young's eclectic interests and experiences resulted in an unusual literary output: his experiences in the Boer War and in World War I are recorded in several books; as a criminologist, he wrote about a number of famous trials; as a motoring enthusiast, he wrote on that subject; he also wrote books about opera and about Ireland.

# Notes

### Introduction

1 Pirie, *The English Musical Renaissance*, 197.
2 Searle and Layton, *Britain, Scandinavia and the Netherlands*, 84.
3 Lutyens, *A Goldfish Bowl*, 167–8.
4 Harries, *A Pilgrim Soul*, 90.
5 A list of the relevant WAC materials that were consulted is included in the bibliography.
6 Kavanagh, 'BBC Archives at Caversham', 341–2.
7 Ibid., 342.
8 BBC Written Archives Centre (WAC), R3/3/2: Control Board/Minutes (1926), 23 June 1926.
9 *BBC Programme Records*, vols. i–vii: *1922–36*. (Further volumes exist, but are not relevant to this study.)
10 Stuart, ed., *The Reith Diaries*.
11 Reith, *Broadcast over Britain*. C. A. Lewis, *Broadcasting from Within*. Burrows, *The Story of Broadcasting*.
12 Roger Eckersley, *The B.B.C. and All That*. P. P. Eckersley, *The Power Behind the Microphone*. Gorham, *Sound and Fury*.
13 Briggs, vol. i: *The Birth of Broadcasting*, and vol. ii: *The Golden Age*. Scannell and Cardiff, vol. i: *Serving the Nation*. LeMahieu, *A Culture for Democracy*. Kenyon, *The BBC Symphony Orchestra*.

### 1 The British music industry and the BBC between the wars

1 For an overview of the BBC's dissemination of art music during its first 75 years, see Doctor, 'BBC History', iv–viii. For a detailed study of post-war BBC practices with respect to fine arts broadcasting, see Carpenter, *The Envy of the World*.
2 For discussions of this phenomenon, see Ehrlich, 'The Marketplace', 39–53; Ehrlich, *The Music Profession*, 186–232.
3 Ehrlich, 'The Marketplace', 40.
4 Ibid., 39.
5 Ibid., 46–7.
6 Ibid.
7 LeMahieu, *A Culture for Democracy*, 235.
8 For an overview of the social and economic conditions for musicians in Germany in the 1930s, see Kater, *The Twisted Muse*, 7–14.

9 The power struggles precipitated by the technology revolution in the first half of the century may be compared to a pattern that is currently emerging due to radical innovations in computerization and communication systems. The music dissemination potentials of the internet, still in a fledgling state, are beginning to threaten the economic structure of today's music industry, with new means of marketing and distribution that potentially ignore current standards of direct item sales, copyright and other procedures of income collection.

10 For information about the development of these organizations, see Ehrlich, *Harmonious Alliance*, and Ehrlich, *The Music Profession*.

11 For discussion of earlier meanings of 'professional' with respect to British musicians, see Ehrlich, *The Music Profession*, 121–3, 129–30.

12 For detailed discussion of early BBC development, see Briggs, vol. i: *The Birth of Broadcasting*.

13 As Briggs has described, 'the multiplicity of radio stations and the scarcity of wavelengths led to interference and overlapping, "a jumble of signals" and a "blasting and blanketing of rival programmes"' (Briggs, vol. i: *The Birth of Broadcasting*, 64).

14 Briggs, vol. i: *The Birth of Broadcasting*, 200.

15 Briggs, vol. ii: *The Golden Age*, 6.

16 It is important to mention that broadcasts originating from some foreign radio stations could be received within Britain. One of these, Radio Luxembourg, became a major competitor to the BBC during the 1930s (see Scannell and Cardiff, vol. i: *Serving the Nation*, 230–2). However, programmes transmitted from Ireland and the continent will not be considered in this study.

## 2  BBC personnel, policies and programmes in the 1920s

1 BBC WAC, Scripts, Reel 458: Percy Scholes, 'Broadcasting Symphonies', 4 Oct. 1923.

2 Briggs, vol. i: *The Birth of Broadcasting*, 125–7.

3 For detailed information about Reith's background, see also McIntyre, *The Expense of Glory*; Briggs, vol. i: *The Birth of Broadcasting*, 136–8; LeMahieu, *A Culture for Democracy*, 142–5.

4 LeMahieu, *A Culture for Democracy*, 183. See also Briggs, vol. i: *The Birth of Broadcasting*, 198–9.

5 LeMahieu, *A Culture for Democracy*, 183.

6 The strong emphasis on lengthy, written communications and the survival of those papers in the BBC filing systems have made a detailed study such as this one possible.

7 Lewis, *Broadcasting from Within*, 57–8.

8 BBC WAC, R34/609: Policy/Programme Planning (1923–37), 7 Aug. 1924.

9 In March 1925 Burrows left the BBC and changes were made to the central committee structure: each week, the Control and Programme boards met

together, chaired by Reith, after which the Programme Board met on its own, chaired by Lewis (note in BBC WAC, R3/3/1: Control Board/Minutes (1925)).

There were further changes in September 1925, when Roger H. Eckersley, P. P. Eckersley's brother, replaced Lewis as the Organiser of Programmes. In an autobiography written in 1946, Eckersley claimed that he did not move into this position until spring 1926 (R. H. Eckersley, *The B.B.C. and All That*, 65), but the Programme Board minutes indicate that he was active in the Programme Department from 1925, and in a position of authority there from September of that year. At that time, separate meetings of the Control and Programme boards resumed, with Lewis chairing the Programme Board until he left the BBC permanent staff in May 1926, at which time R. H. Eckersley took over (BBC WAC, R34/600/3: Policy/Programme Board Minutes (1926), 20 April and 7 May 1926).

For a brief but detailed history of the Programme Board, see 'Programme Board', BBC WAC R34/599: Policy/Programme Board (1925–45), [undated].

10 The early history of the *Radio Times* is described in Briggs, vol. i: *The Birth of Broadcasting*, 297–308.

11 No trace of the Musical Committee minutes has been found at the BBC WAC, and there is a note in the first Control Board minutes file (R3/3/1, 6 Jan. 1925) stating, 'No trace as yet of Musical Committee minutes'. The suspension of the committee is noted in March 1925 (BBC WAC, R34/600/2: Policy/Programme Board Minutes (1925), 31 March 1925).

12 R34/609, 13 May 1924. From August 1923, telephone wires linked the different stations so that SBs could be transmitted across the country.

13 BBC WAC, R3/3/1, 10 Sept. 1925; BBC WAC, R34/600/2, 15 Sept. 1925. For details about how programme correspondence was handled, see BBC WAC, R34/609, 13 May 1924.

From May 1925 the BBC paid two listeners, the 'hired critics', to prepare weekly reports on broadcasts they heard; in February 1926 the number of hired critics doubled. The following October, the Programme Board decided the system was 'valueless', and it was discontinued. In August 1927, the Control Board considered hiring a qualified music critic to report on music broadcasts, but decided against it because of the previous, unsuccessful experience. In 1929, another experiment with external critics was launched, but it was pronounced a failure in December and discontinued. For details, see BBC WAC, R34/600/2, 22 Dec. 1925; R34/600/3, 12 Jan., 2 Feb., 21 Oct. 1926; R3/3/3, 30 Aug. 1927; R3/3/5, 31 Dec. 1929.

14 Briggs, vol. ii: *The Golden Age*, 424.

15 For more information about the early Governors and their relationships with Reith, see Briggs, vol. ii: *The Golden Age*, 424–35.

16 Ibid., 441–2.

17 The organizational system described here was set up in 1927 with the nomenclature 'department', 'section', etc.; in January 1928 the central administrators introduced a new set of terms to refer to the same structure:

'department' became 'branch', 'section' became 'department', etc. (see Briggs, vol. ii: *The Golden Age*, 440). In this discussion, the later designations are used.

18 *BBC Handbook 1928*, 51–2.

19 Ibid.

20 'Seven Gods of the B.B.C.: Choosing Programmes Seven Weeks Ahead', *Evening News*, 26 Jan. 1927; in BBC WAC, P565: Press Cuttings/Personal Publicity (1924–7). Details about the Programme Board during 1927 have been taken from this outside source, since no Programme Board minutes survive for that year (or for 1928).

21 The process as described in the *BBC Handbook* covering 1927 is much the same as it was in 1924 ('Programme Building', *BBC Handbook 1928*, 74–5).

22 Little documentation survives about how music policy and programming decisions were made during the early years. Minutes of the Musical Committee meetings do not survive; music policy files only date back to 1930 (R27/245/1); and files of minutes for the Music Department weekly meetings do not begin until 1933 (R27/221/1). Surviving records of early Music Department activities and decisions consist of: papers in individual contributor files (of which few survive from before 1930); programme-related discussions from Programme Board and Control Board meetings – however, the Programme Board minutes for the 1920s (R34/600/1–4) are incomplete and the Control Board minutes (R3/3/1–5) are not very detailed; reports in the BBC yearbooks, from their first publication in 1928; relevant *Radio Times* articles; and the records of broadcasts, as announced in the *Radio Times* and recorded in the 'Programmes as Broadcast' records (accurate programme details as noted at the time of broadcast).

23 J. C. W. Reith, 'What is Our Policy?', *RT*, 2 (14 March 1924): 442.

24 Reith, *Broadcast over Britain*, 15–16.

25 Ibid., 17–18.

26 LeMahieu interprets this as follows: 'The BBC enhanced its own respectability and that of the medium it monopolized . . . by making the Corporation a privileged enclave of middle-class officials and social values. More important, it self-consciously invented an idealized version of a fragile, never fully realized, middle-class cultural tradition which it then proclaimed to be the natural and authentic culture of the nation' (p. 182). This fascinating social reading of BBC policies is fully presented in LeMahieu, *A Culture for Democracy*, 145–52, 180–4.

27 J. C. W. Reith, 'Wireless and Music', *RT*, 2 (29 Feb. 1924): 361–2.

28 Reith, *Broadcast over Britain*, 34.

29 'A Great Enterprise Develops: Official Statement of Facts and Policy', *RT*, 6 (13 March 1925): 529.

30 J. C. Squire, 'Problems of Programmes', *RT*, 6 (20 March 1925): 578.

31 Ibid. Programme options were available to a small number of listeners as early as 1925: the regional stations aired different programmes from London and some contrast was available from the high-powered transmitter (5XX) at

Chelmsford after it was opened on 21 July 1924. However, crystal sets, the most common receivers at that time, were unable to pick up distant signals; in fact, the Chelmsford transmitter, which usually broadcast the same programme as the London station (2LO), could be received by less than half the country's listeners.

32  For details of events that led to the directors' interest, see Briggs, vol. i: *The Birth of Broadcasting*, 385–7.

33  Letter from W. Witt Burnham to J. C. W. Reith, 7 Dec. 1925, in BBC WAC, CO62/6: British Broadcasting Company/Major Basil Binyon's Papers/File 3a (Sept.–Dec. 1925).

34  BBC WAC, S60/5/2: Reith Diaries, ii/1, p. 92 (7 Dec. 1925).

35  BBC WAC, CO7/3: British Broadcasting Company/Board of Directors/Minutes (1925), 10 Dec. 1925.

36  BBC WAC, R34/600/2, 22 Dec. 1925, and R34/600/3, 5 Jan. 1926.

37  Letter from Binyon to Reith, 11 Jan. 1926, in BBC WAC, CO62/7: British Broadcasting Company/Major Basil Binyon's Papers/File 3b (Jan.–May 1926). The committee's report is not in the file, nor is there any further record of the committee, its findings or Binyon's meeting with Reith about the report in this file, in the file of Board of Directors' meeting minutes or in Reith's diaries. Although at one time the administrators' response to the report could 'be found in the Binyon Papers' (Briggs, vol. i: *The Birth of Broadcasting*, 387, footnote), the memorandum is no longer among that collection of papers at the BBC WAC.

38  Briggs, vol. i: *The Birth of Broadcasting*, 388. Briggs's quotation is from the original administrators' reply to the directors.

39  'The Dawn of a New Era for Listeners: the B.B.C. Announces the First "Alternative Programme"', *RT*, 16 (12 Aug. 1927): 241. See also Briggs, vol. ii: *The Golden Age*, 26–7.

40  For a brief explanation of the technical difficulties, see 'The Dawn of a New Era', 241–2.

41  BBC WAC, R3/3/2: Control Board/Minutes (1926), 17 Nov. 1926.

42  BBC WAC, R3/3/3: Control Board/Minutes (1927), 13 Sept. 1927.

43  See BBC WAC, R34/600/4: Policy/Programme Board Minutes (1927), 25 Jan. and 4 Oct. 1929.

44  A. R. Burrows, 'Broadcast from 2LO', in BBC WAC, CO57: British Broadcasting Company/Request for Listeners' Response (1923), 24 and 25 June 1923.

45  Ibid.

46  'The B.B.C.'s Programme Letter-Bag', *The BBC Handbook 1929*, 274.

47  BBC WAC, R3/3/5: Control Board/Minutes (1929), 9 Dec. 1929.

48  'Ariel', 'Wireless Notes', *MT*, 67 (Jan. 1926): 37. Although 'Ariel' apparently quotes the BBC in this excerpt, he does not identify his original source.

49  A few surveys were done in the early 1930s, but as Maurice Gorham, *Radio Times* editor from 1933 to 1941, later recalled: 'Throughout that time nobody

knew what listeners liked, or even which programmes they listened to . . . It was all based on what the BBC officials themselves thought, plus various odd impressions gathered from correspondence (which is a notoriously unreliable guide), Press comment that nobody in the BBC was supposed to read or at least to take seriously, and occasional *obiter dicta* from friends, charwomen, and people met in the train' (Gorham, *Sound and Fury*, 59). Only in 1936 did the administrators reluctantly agree that more scientific methods should be used to investigate the sociological effects of broadcasting; initial findings resulted in the formation of the BBC Listener Research Department in 1938, headed by R. J. E. Silvey.

50 For details of how programme correspondence was handled, see BBC WAC, R34/609, 13 May 1924.

51 BBC WAC, R34/600/2, 15 Sept. 1925.

52 'Listeners' Criticisms', *BBC Handbook 1928*, 79.

53 Ibid., 80. Although the BBC paid considerable attention to views expressed in correspondence, it ignored those of the mass audience who never put pen to paper.

54 BBC WAC, R3/3/6: Control Board/Minutes (1930), 22 Jan. 1930.

55 'Which Shall We Listen to Tonight?: a Note on the New Art of Listening to the Broadcast Programmes', *RT*, 16 (2 Sept. 1927): 365. It is significant that the BBC provides examples of middle-class entertainments ('a Bernard Shaw play or a Revue'), rather than popular mass-entertainments, such as cinema or music hall.

56 P. P. Eckersley, 'The Art of Listening', *Eve, the Lady's Pictorial*, 7 Dec. 1927; in BBC WAC, P565.

57 Filson Young, 'The Art of Listening', *BBC Handbook 1928*, 349.

58 'Good Listening', *The BBC Yearbook 1930*, 61.

59 Filson Young, 'The World We Listen in: the Art of Listening', *RT*, 29 (10 Oct. 1930): 88.

60 The handbook became available for purchase during the first week of November 1927; see J. C. Squire, 'The BBC Handbook', *RT*, 17 (4 Nov. 1927): 238.

61 'Programme Policy', *BBC Handbook 1928*, 71–3.

62 'London and Daventry News and Notes', *RT*, 14 (14 Jan. 1927): 99.

63 'Programme Building', *BBC Handbook 1928*, 74–8.

64 During times of day when 2LO and 5XX were both operating, they usually transmitted the same programmes; however, 5XX transmitted at times when 2LO did not, and contrasting material was planned a few times a week when both transmitters were operating.

65 *BBC Programme Records, 1922–1926*.

66 Programme details are drawn from listings for the week 5–11 December 1926, in *RT*, 13 (3 Dec. 1926): 564–86.

67 For further details, see 'Programme Building', *BBC Handbook 1928*, 74–8.

## 3  The foundations of music programming, 1922–1926

1  Briggs, vol. ii: *The Golden Age*, 10.
2  Burrows, *The Story of Broadcasting*, 138. Pitt's responsibilities are also outlined in BBC WAC, R34/609: Policy/Programme Planning (1923–37), 13 May 1924.
3  No trace of the Musical Committee minutes has been found at the BBC WAC.
4  BBC WAC, R34/600/2: Policy/Programme Board Minutes (1925), 31 March 1925.
5  Burrows, *Story of Broadcasting*, 138–9.
6  Lewis, *Broadcasting from Within*, 59–60; Burrows, *Story of Broadcasting*, 135; BBC WAC, R34/609, 13 May 1924.
7  BBC WAC, R34/609, 13 May 1924.
8  BBC WAC, R3/3/1: Control Board/Minutes (1925), 14 July 1925.
9  'Official News and Views: Gossip about Broadcasting: Musical Advisory Committee', *RT*, 8 (17 July 1925): 148.
10  Kenyon, *The BBC Symphony Orchestra*, 11. Since virtually no documentation relating to the committee's activities in the 1920s survives at the BBC WAC, it is difficult to trace the extent of the committee's involvement in Music Department decision-making or the specific issues that contributed to such tensions.
11  BBC WAC, R3/3/1, 26 Nov. 1925.
12  Boosey, 'Broadcasting', *Daily Telegraph* (19 May 1923): 11(D).
13  As a popular magazine, aiming to attract audiences of wide-ranging interests and backgrounds, the *Radio Times* frequently changed format during the 1920s. This brief overview of the music-related articles only refers to a few of the longer-running columns.
14  See Table 2.1.
15  BBC WAC, R34/600/2, 29 Sept. 1925.
16  Ibid., 12 May 1925.
17  Irving, 'Schoenberg in the News', 52–70. David Lambourn, 'Henry Wood and Schoenberg', *MT*, 128 (Aug. 1987): 422–7. Arnold Whittall, 'Schoenberg and the English: Notes for a Documentary', *Journal of the Arnold Schoenberg Institute*, 4/1 (1980): 24–33.
18  'Music in Vienna', *MT*, 46 (March 1905): 189.
19  For a detailed examination of British attitudes towards German music and musicians during World War I and the period following, see Kildea, *World War I and the British Music Industry*.
20  'Occasional Notes: Henry Wood on German Music, etc.', *MT*, 59 (Oct. 1918): 446.
21  Alfred Kalisch, 'London Concerts', *MT*, 61 (Feb. 1920): 101–3.
22  This performance is documented in a letter from Moulton to Wellesz, quoted in Benser, *Egon Wellesz*, 59.

23  Paul Bechert, 'Musical Notes from Abroad: Vienna', *MT*, 63 (Feb. 1922): 133.

24  Paul Bechert, 'Musical Notes from Abroad: Vienna', *MT*, 65 (June 1924): 558.

25  Paul Bechert, 'Musical Notes from Abroad: Vienna: Schönberg's Newest Work', *MT*, 65 (Dec. 1924): 1132–3.

26  Adolf Weissmann, 'Musical Notes from Abroad: Germany', *MT*, 65 (Nov. 1924): 1035–6.

27  Cecil Gray, 'Arnold Schönberg – A Critical Study', *Music and Letters*, 3 (Jan. 1922): 73–89.

28  'Schönberg', *Musical Standard* (12 Sept. 1912): 176–8.

29  Statement of purpose on contents page, *The Sackbut*, 1/1 (May 1920).

30  Paul A. Pisk, 'Post-war Tendencies in Austria', *The Sackbut*, 6/1 (Aug. 1925): 3–7.

31  Egon Wellesz, 'Present Tendencies in Austria', *The Sackbut*, 6/2 (Sept. 1925): 42–6.

32  For examples, see: Paul Rosenfeld, 'Schoenberg', chapter in *Musical Portraits: Interpretations of Twenty Modern Composers* (London: Kegan Paul, Trench, Trübner and Co., 1922), 233–43. Rollo H. Myers, 'Harmonic Innovations', chapter in *Modern Music: its Aims and Tendencies* (London: Kegan Paul, Trench, Trübner and Co., 1923), 26–38. George Dyson, 'Texture: Chromaticism', chapter in *The New Music* (London: Oxford University Press; Humphrey Milford, 1924), 90–116. A. Eaglefield-Hull, *A Dictionary of Modern Music and Musicians* (London: J. M. Dent and Sons; New York: E. P. Dutton, 1924). Cecil Gray, 'Arnold Schönberg', chapter in *A Survey of Contemporary Music* (London: Oxford University Press, 1924), 162–83. Adolf Weissman, 'Expressionism and Arnold Schönberg' and 'General Characteristics: Germany and Austria', chapters in *The Problems of Modern Music*, with an Introduction by Edward J. Dent (London: J. M. Dent and Sons; NY: E. P. Dutton, 1925), 175–83 and 208–17. Ralph Dunstan, *A Cyclopædic Dictionary of Music*, 4th edn, enlarged and rev. (London: J. Curwen and Sons; Kegan Paul, Trench, Trübner, [1925]).

33  The talks were given between July 1923 and September 1928; although a number of the scripts survive on microfilm (BBC WAC, Scripts, Reels 458–9), the collection is not complete.

34  Egon Wellesz, 'E. J. Dent and the International Society for Contemporary Music', *Music Review*, 7 (Aug./Nov. 1946): 205.

35  For further details about the 1922 contemporary music festival and the meeting which established the formation of the ISCM, see Edwin Evans, 'The Salzburg Festival: International Chamber Concerts', *MT*, 63 (Sept. 1922): 628–30. The history of the ISCM's foundation is also described in a broadcast talk given by Evans on 18 July 1931.

    The LCMC was founded in January 1921 as an offshoot of the British Music Society; the two organizations were linked until 1931, when the LCMC became independent. In April 1953, the LCMC merged with the Music Section of the Institute of Contemporary Arts (ICA). For more information about the origins of these organizations, see A. Eaglefield Hull, 'A Few Words

About the British Music Society', *MT*, 60 (Feb. 1919): 71; 'Miscellaneous', *MT*, 62 (Jan. 1921): 61; 'London Contemporary Music Centre', *Hinrichsen Year Book* (1944): 187.

36  Edward J. Dent, 'Looking Backward', *Music Today: Journal of the International Society for Contemporary Music*, 1 (1949): 10–11.

37  Edwin Evans, 'Donaueschingen and Salzburg Festivals', *MT*, 64 (Sept. 1923), 631–5.

38  BBC WAC, Scripts, Reel 458: Percy Scholes, 'Weekly Musical Criticism, no. 10', 16 Aug. 1923.

39  For a collection of the British reviews, see *Dossier de presse: Press-book de Pierrot lunaire d'Arnold Schönberg*, 163–74.

40  BBC WAC, Scripts, Reel 458: Percy Scholes, 'Weekly Musical Criticism, [no. 23]', 15 Nov. 1923. In his announcement, Scholes erroneously credited the Music Society with the first British performance; in fact, the first performance was sponsored by the Kensington New Music Club and the second by the Music Society.

41  Ibid.: Percy Scholes, 'Weekly Musical Criticism, no. 24', 22 Nov. 1923.

42  Ernest Newman, 'The Schönberg Case', *Sunday Times*, 25 Nov. 1923; in *Press-book de Pierrot lunaire*, 166.

43  C. [H. C. Colles], 'London Concerts: Pierrot Lunaire', *MT*, 64 (Dec. 1923): 865.

44  Dorothy Moulton was a strong advocate of contemporary music. After World War I, she took recently composed songs by British composers to the continent – including performing most of the British works represented at the Salzburg contemporary music festival in 1922, which her husband, Sir Robert Mayer, had backed financially – and performed German and Austrian contemporary works in Britain.

45  BBC WAC, Scripts, Reel 458: Percy Scholes, 'Weekly Musical Criticism, no. 36', 21 Feb. 1924.

46  E. E. [Edwin Evans], 'London Concerts: Goossens Concerts', *MT*, 65 (April 1924): 357–8.

47  Ernest Newman, 'The World of Music: Broadcasting Music: Some Reflections and a Suggestion: Wireless as Pioneer', *The Sunday Times*, 13 Jan. 1924, 5(B–C).

48  Nationalistic programming was evident also in the British concert halls during the 1920s, continuing the surge of interest in British composers and their works that arose during World War I when music by German composers was avoided. For more details about the growth of interest in British music during the 1910s and 20s, see Kildea, *World War I and the British Music Industry*.

49  'British Composers' Programmes', *RT*, 2 (22 Feb. 1924): 334.

50  McEwen was the principal of the Royal Academy of Music and a member of the BBC Music Advisory Committee.

51  'Chamber Music in Broadcasting', *BBC Handbook 1928*, 98.

52  In February 1925, the BBC considered transmitting a concert featuring first performances of new British works from Wigmore Hall, in a joint venture with Oxford University Press; in the end, the programme was not aired. See BBC WAC, R34/600/2, 9 Feb. 1925.

## 4  The music programmes take shape, 1926–1927

1  'Wireless Notes and Programmes: B.B.C.'s Musical Staff', *Manchester Guardian*, 16 June 1927; in BBC WAC, P565: Press Cuttings/Personal Publicity (1924–7).

2  Edward Clark undoubtedly arranged for Fried, his former teacher, to make this visit to England.

3  The *Radio Times* issue for that week was devoted to Beethoven (*RT*, 14,18 March 1927). This specially titled 'Beethoven Number' presented articles on various aspects of the composer's life and works, including 'The Lesson of the Centenary' by Arnold Bennett, 'Beethoven Broadcast' by George Bernard Shaw, 'The Soul of Beethoven' by Romain Rolland, and a seven-page, illustrated biography, 'The Story of Beethoven', by Percy Scholes.

4  BBC WAC, R34/600/3: Policy/Programme Board Minutes (1926), 28 May 1926.

5  For an example, see 'The 9.45 Recitals: Attractive Programmes for the Winter', *RT*, 12 (10 Sept. 1926): 466.

6  Filson Young, 'The Foundations of Music: the Scheme of a New Series of Broadcast Recitals', *RT*, 14 (31 Dec. 1926): 6.

7  BBC WAC, R34/600/3, 16 July 1926.

8  Ibid., 28 Oct. 1926.

9  'Broadcasting and Music', *BBC Handbook 1928*, 85.

10  For details of planning discussions for the first series of National Concerts, see BBC WAC, R34/600/3, 9, 16, 29 July, 3, 10 Sept. 1926.

11  'British Broadcasting Co.: National Concerts', *National Concert*, Royal Albert Hall, London, 25 Nov. 1926 [programme notes]; in BBC WAC, Symphony Concert Programmes (1927–May 1930).

12  For an example, see 'The B.B.C.'s National Concerts: Preliminary Announcement of an Important New Series', *RT*, 12 (10 Sept. 1926): 470.

13  BBC WAC, R34/600/3, 10 Sept. 1926.

14  Ibid., 16 July 1926.

15  Kenyon, *The BBC Symphony Orchestra*, 12. The attribution to Clark of the details of programming this first series of National Concerts must be considered carefully, since most of the series was planned before Clark was transferred to the London station. Although he may have advised the Music Department while he was still working in Newcastle, providing programme ideas and contacts, no Music Department documents survive to verify this, nor do papers pertaining to the artists involved. Elisabeth Lutyens's biography of Clark suggests that he offered to assist Wright with contemporary music programming during 1926 (in Lutyens's autobiography, *A Goldfish Bowl*,

123–4), although Lutyens is not a reliable source of information on Clark's early years.

16  'The B.B.C.'s National Concerts: Preliminary Announcement of an Important New Series', *RT*, 12 (10 Sept. 1926): 470.

17  'London and Daventry News and Notes', *RT*, 14 (14 Jan. 1927): 99.

18  Ibid.

19  'National Concert Programme: Programme Notes: Verklärte Nacht' [3 Feb. 1927, 2LO, 8.00 pm], *RT*, 14 (28 Jan. 1927): 219.

20  As Appendix A demonstrates, two of the performances were given in 1914, one privately and one publicly; in December 1919, *Verklärte Nacht* was the first Schoenberg work to be performed in Britain after the war; another performance was given in January 1922.

21  For representative reviews, see: F. T. [Francis Toye], 'B.B.C. Concert: Brilliant Music at the Albert Hall', *Morning Post*, 4 Feb. 1927; 'B.B.C. Concert', *The Times*, 4 Feb. 1927; F. B. [Ferruccio Bonavia], 'London Concerts: the B.B.C. at the Albert Hall', *MT*, 68 (March 1927): 263; all in BBC WAC, P478: Press Cuttings/Symphony Concerts (1926–7).

22  BBC WAC, R34/600/3, 5 and 12 Jan. 1926.

23  For details about the autumn festival and the composition competition, see BBC WAC, R34/600/3, 5, 12 Jan., 26 Feb. 1926; R3/3/2: Control Board/Minutes (1926), 5 March, 7 Dec. 1926; R3/3/3: Control Board/Minutes (1927), 14 June, 27 Oct. 1927. In particular, guidelines for the composition competition were determined at a Programme Board meeting on 26 February 1926 (R34/600/3, 26 Feb. 1926).

24  Ibid.

25  'An Opportunity for British Composers: The B.B.C. Offers £1,000 in Prizes for Original Musical Compositions', *RT*, 10 (19 March 1926): 587. 'A Challenge to Young Composers', *RT*, 11 (26 March 1926): 9. 'Our Festival Competition', *RT*, 11 (9 April 1926): 105.

26  It is difficult to reconstruct the exact course of events by which the projected festival was transformed into the National Concerts, since none of the papers documenting the planning of these events survives.

27  'The B.B.C.'s National Concerts: Preliminary Announcement of an Important New Series', *RT*, 12 (10 Sept. 1926), 470.

28  'The Musical Festival Competition: the Judges' Report', *RT*, 13 (24 Dec. 1926): 746.

29  BBC WAC, R3/3/2, 7 Dec. 1926.

30  BBC WAC, R3/3/3, 14 June and 27 Oct. 1927.

31  In fact, no new works by Vaughan Williams or Moeran were presented in those programmes. However, the première of Holst's commissioned work, *The Morning of the Year*, was given at the tenth concert, on 17 March 1927, conducted by the composer. This was the first BBC commission to be completed and broadcast.

32  BBC WAC, R34/600/3, 23 March 1926.

33  Ibid., 6 April and 2 July 1926. German had previously set Kipling's verse with great success, as in the song, 'Rolling Down to Rio'.

34  No more references to the opera project appear in the Programme Board minutes. Work-lists of German's operas verify that his last completed opera was dated 1909. (Work-lists included in: Brian Rees, *A Musical Peacemaker: the Life and Work of Sir Edward German* (Bourne End, Buckinghamshire: Kensal Press, 1986); David Russell Hulme, 'German, Sir Edward', in *The New Grove Dictionary of Opera*, edited by Stanley Sadie (London: Macmillan, 1992), ii, 384–5).

35  BBC WAC, R34/600/3, 12 Jan. 1926, and R3/3/2, 17 Feb. 1926. No BBC documents about the planning and organization of this series survive. Elisabeth Lutyens's biography of Clark suggests that Wright, assisted by Hubert Foss of Oxford University Press, planned the series of Chenil Gallery concerts before Clark's programming ideas began to influence the London programme builders (Lutyens, *A Goldfish Bowl*, 123–4).

36  'B.B.C. Spring Concerts: Chamber Music at Chelsea', *RT*, 11 (26 March 1926): 4.

37  Details of the chamber concert programmes are given in Table B.1 in Appendix B. Neither concert programmes nor any other listing of performed works survive for this series at the BBC WAC. The programmes have been reconstructed from the BBC WAC 'Programmes as Broadcast' records for the transmitted works, and from press reviews for the works that were not transmitted.

38  M. , 'London Concerts: B.B.C. Chamber Concerts', *MT*, 67 (Aug. 1926): 737.

39  BBC WAC, R3/3/2, 17 Feb. 1926.

40  BBC WAC, R34/600/3, 9 July 1926.

41  *Six International Chamber Concerts of New Music*, Grotrian Hall, London, Oct. 1926–March 1927 [series prospectus]; in BBC WAC, P446: Press Cuttings/Outside Broadcasts (1923–6).

42  Details about the concert programmes are listed in Table B. 2 in Appendix B.

43  Basil Maine, 'Music: the Enterprise of the B.B.C.', *The Spectator*, 9 Oct. 1926; in ibid.

44  BBC WAC, R34/600/3, 7 Oct. 1926.

45  *Evening News*, 6 Oct. 1926; in BBC WAC, P446.


## 5  The first wave of Second Viennese School broadcasts, 1927–1928

1  Details about the spring 1928 reorganization, discussed throughout this section, are derived from BBC WAC, R13/242/1: Departmental/Music Department (1928–32), March–June 1928, and L1/88/1: Left staff/Edward Thomas Clark (1924–36).

2  BBC WAC, R13/242/1, 21 March 1928.

3  BBC WAC, L1/88/1, 25 Jan. 1928.

4  Ibid. Wright refers to Sir Hamilton Harty, conductor of the Hallé Orchestra, and Ernest Ansermet, a Swiss conductor of international reputation.

5 Ibid., 2 Feb. 1928.

6 BBC WAC, R13/242/1, 7, 9, 21, 24 March and 3 April 1928.

7 Ibid., 9 March 1928.

8 Ibid., 25 May 1928.

9 Ibid., 21 March 1928.

10 Ibid., 30 April 1928.

11 Ibid., 24 March 1928.

12 Ibid., 4 June 1928. Clark's salary had been frozen while his position was under review; see BBC WAC, L1/88/1, 5 June 1928.

13 Cox, *The Henry Wood Proms*, 30.

14 For details about the BBC's take-over of the Promenade Concerts, see Briggs, vol. ii: *The Golden Age*, 172–3; Cox, *The Henry Wood Proms*, 82–9; Ehrlich, *First Philharmonic*, 204.

15 BBC WAC, R3/3/3: Control Board/Minutes (1927), 12 April and 24 May 1927. Wood had expressed his interest in broadcasting to Reith as early as July 1924 (BBC WAC, S60/5/2: Reith Diaries, ii/1, p. 46 (1 July 1924)), but was unable to pursue this interest actively until the restrictions were lifted in 1927.

16 *The BBC Handbook 1929*, 141, 143.

17 For a list of new works performed at the Proms during the 1920s and 30s, see 'Appendix A: "Novelties" at the Proms 1895–1979', in Cox, *The Henry Wood Proms*, 270–6.

18 The Proms were held in the Queen's Hall through 1940. After the hall was destroyed in a bombing raid in May 1941, the series was transferred to the Royal Albert Hall, where the concerts still take place.

19 Kenyon, *The BBC Symphony Orchestra*, 13. During summer 1927, the BBC entered into a financial dispute with the Royal Albert Hall over one of the concerts in the first National Concert series; on 23 August, the Control Board agreed that 'we should endeavour to put the Albert Hall on the black list, and, if it were practicable, to have no more dealings with them whilst under present management' (BBC WAC, R3/3/3). Hence, it was timely that the Queen's Hall became available for BBC use when it did, or the Corporation would have had difficulty presenting its public concert series.

20 'National Symphony Concerts', *National Symphony Concerts*, People's Palace, London, 18 Nov. 1927, 7–17 [programme notes]; in BBC WAC, Symphony Concert Programmes (1927–May 1930).

21 BBC WAC, R27/431: Music General/Promenade and Symphony Concerts Committee [Minutes] (1927–33), 12 Sept. and 7 Nov. 1927.

22 Elisabeth Lutyens's overview of the 1927–8 National Concert season, in which she reported that Oskar Fried, Scherchen, Stravinsky and Webern participated as conductors, is completely incorrect (Lutyens, *A Goldfish Bowl*, 125).

23 'National Symphony Concerts' [programme article].

24 The six articles by C. Whitaker-Wilson in the 'The Man Behind the Music' series are in *RT*, 17 (Oct.–Dec. 1927): 'October 10, 1813 – Giuseppe Verdi', (7 Oct.): 4; 'October 17, 1849 – Frederic Chopin', (14 Oct.): 60; 'Franz Liszt –

Born October 22, 1811', (21 Oct.): 122; 'Peter Tchaikovsky – Died November 6, 1893', (4 Nov.): 238; 'Christopher von Gluck – Died November 15, 1787', (11 Nov.): 296; 'Wolfgang Amadeus Mozart, Died December 5, 1791', (2 Dec.): 472.

25  The five articles are in *RT*, 18 (March 1928): Richard Capell, 'What do You Listen For?' (2 March): 437–8; Herman Klein, 'When is a Voice Not a Voice?' (9 March): 487, 490; F. Bonavia, 'The Magic of the Violin', (16 March): 543, 567; W. R. Anderson, 'Listening to the Piano', (23 March): 597, 633; W. McNaught, 'The Big Battalions', (30 March): 642, 647.

26  Scholes's seven articles appeared in *RT*, 19 (April–May 1928): 'A Miniature History of Music', (6 April): 11, 10; 'Music as Woven Tone', (13 April): 59, 58; 'Sonatas and Symphonies', (20 April): 103, 106; 'Music as Romance', (27 April): 152–3; 'Music as Drama', (4 May): 191–2; 'Impressionism in Music', (11 May): 241, 243; 'The Music of Today', (18 May): 285–6.

27  'A Miniature Dictionary of Musical Terms', *RT*, 25 (22 Nov. 1929): 567–74.

28  BBC WAC, R3/3/3, 26 July 1927, and R3/3/4: Control Board/Minutes (1928), 3 July 1928.

29  For further information about Bartók's performances, and public and press reaction to them, see Gillies, *Bartók in Britain*, 66–74.

30  Table B.3 in Appendix B shows the Bartók, Stravinsky and Prokofiev works which were also included in the BBC Concerts of Contemporary Music.

31  Bax concerts were broadcast on 20 October 1927, on 22 May 1928 and on 25 June 1928; the third concert was part of the 'New Friends in Music' series.

32  'The Concert Season: Arnold Bax', *Musical Opinion*, 52 (Dec. 1927): 267.

33  'New Friends in Music: John Ireland' [programme notes, 7 March 1928, 5GB, 8.00 pm], *RT*, 18 (2 March 1928): 459.

34  Graham Eltham, 'Debussy – Musical Impressionist', *RT*, 18 (17 Feb. 1928): 325, 324.

35  'Ariel,' 'Wireless Notes', *MT*, 69 (March 1928): 239.

36  Little information survives at the BBC WAC concerning the planning of concerts that included Second Viennese School repertory during the 1920s. Relevant papers include internal BBC papers about the concerts and correspondence between the BBC and composers, publishers, performers and performance venue managers.

   Internal BBC papers: only a few Music Department papers relating specifically to the BBC Concerts of Contemporary Music survive, dating from between 1929 and 1936 (R27/67); concert programmes for the second, third and fourth series are also extant (R79/2/2).

   Composer papers: many relevant BBC composer and artist files survive, but the papers in them often do not date back to the 1920s. Specifically, the following files hold papers only from the dates shown, despite earlier associations with the BBC: Schoenberg composer file (from 1943); Webern composer file (from 1929); no artist files survive for Schoenberg and Webern, although both conducted for the BBC; Berg composer file (from 1933);

Krenek artist file (from 1935) and composer file (from 1947); Wellesz composer file (from 1933) and talks and copyright files (from 1941); Gerhard artist file (from 1932) and composer file (from 1941). There are no files for Eisler, Pisk, Spinner or Hauer. Some of the missing BBC correspondence between Clark and Schoenberg, Berg, Webern and Gerhard survives at the British Library (*GB-Lbl* Add.ms.52256–7) and in the Edward Clark papers at Northwestern University.

Performer papers: of the performers associated with interwar Second Viennese School broadcasts, Steuermann's file dates back to December 1927; however papers in other relevant artist files are later: Hermann Scherchen (from 1934); Ružena Herlinger (from 1930); Marya Freund (from 1937); May Blyth (from 1946; the first file was destroyed); Else C. Kraus (from 1950); Edward Clark (from 1930); Louis Krasner (from 1929). The Kolisch papers were destroyed in 1952, and only two papers relating directly to Erwin Stein survive, both dating from the 1950s.

Publisher papers: the copyright file for Dr Alfred Kalmus (Universal Edition) dates back to 1927; his publisher file to 1929. There are also relevant papers in the Universal Music Agencies publisher file (from 1933) and copyright file (from 1934).

Venue correspondence: papers relating to the 1929–30 series of contemporary chamber concerts survive in the outside broadcasts file for the Arts Theatre Club (R30/44).

37  Details about the concert programmes are listed in Table B.3 in Appendix B.

38  'Chamber Music in Broadcasting', *BBC Handbook 1928*, 98.

39  E. B. [Eric Blom], 'London Concerts: B.B.C. Studio Chamber Concert', *MT*, 69 (Nov. 1927): 1030.

40  BBC WAC, R34/600/2: Policy/Programme Board Minutes (1925), 14 April 1925.

41  E. B. [Eric Blom], 'London Concerts: B.B.C. Studio Chamber Concert', *MT*, 68 (Nov. 1927), 1030–31. For another review, see 'The Concert Season: Vienna String Quartet', *Musical Opinion*, 51 (Nov. 1927): 155.

42  'Both Sides of the Microphone: Modern Music', *RT*, 17 (21 Oct. 1927): 124.

43  'Recital of Contempory Chamber Music – IV: Chamber Symphony, Schönberg' [programme notes, 9 Jan. 1928, 5GB, 8.30 pm], *RT*,18 (6 Jan. 1928): 12.

44  The first British performance of Schoenberg's Chamber Symphony no. 1 was given on 6 May 1921 at the Æolian Hall in London, conducted by Edward Clark. Of course, other Schoenberg works written after the Chamber Symphony had received concert performances in Britain prior to 1927, although they had not yet been broadcast.

45  This attitude may also have reflected concurrent press debates concerning broadcasts of Bartók's and Stravinsky's music.

46  'Ariel', 'Wireless Notes', *MT*, 69 (Feb. 1928): 144.

47  BBC WAC, RCONT1: Edward Steuermann, Artists (1927–62), 31 Dec. 1927.

48 In the 31 December memo, Hely Hutchinson requested that Clark make the arrangements for Steuermann's recitals. Clark and the pianist exchanged a number of telegrams concerning these programmes and a concerto performance Steuermann was to give on 3 February (in BBC WAC, RCONT1: Edward Steuermann, Artists (1927–62), Jan. 1928); however, it is likely that these arrangements were not completed in time for the *Radio Times* deadline and that Mrs Norman O'Neill's programmes were submitted for the listings as a back-up measure.

49 BBC WAC, RCONT1: Edward Steuermann, Artists (1927–62), 26 Jan. 1928.

50 Ibid., 30 Jan. 1928. The date of performance is confirmed by the BBC WAC 'Programmes as Broadcast' records.

51 'Both Sides of the Microphone: The Composer of "Wozzek" [*sic*]', *RT*, 18 (3 Feb. 1928): 213.

52 The BBC WAC 'Programmes as Broadcast' records confirm that the Berg was not broadcast. Moreover, the *Radio Times* programme listing, published only a week after the pre-concert announcement, includes only the songs and the Schoenberg quartet, indicating that the programme change was made prior to the *Radio Times* deadline. The *Lyric Suite* was finally broadcast in a Vienna String Quartet programme given almost exactly a year later, on 12 February 1929.

53 'The Concert Season: Contemporary Chamber Concert', *Musical Opinion*, 51 (March 1928): 594.

54 Ernest Newman, 'Music of the Day', *Glasgow Herald*, 16 Feb. 1928; in BBC WAC, P479: Press cuttings/Symphony concerts (1927–8).

55 The 7 May concert was not included in the *BBC Handbook 1928* announcement of the series, which specified that 'the concerts will be broadcast the first Monday of every month from October to April inclusive' (p. 99); furthermore, no programme for this concert survives in the BBC WAC file (R79/2/2) holding programmes for the seven other concerts. Apparently a late addition, the *Radio Times* and 'Programmes as Broadcast' records indicate that it was 'The Last Concert of the Contemporary Composer Series'.

56 BBC WAC, RCONT1: Edward Steuermann, Artists (1927–62), 29 March and 20 April 1928.

57 The 'Programmes as Broadcast' records list: 'Six Little Piano Pieces', op. 19.

58 'The Concert Season: Contemporary Chamber Music', *Musical Opinion*, 51 (June 1928): 894.

59 Carbon copy of letter from Clark to Schoenberg, 24 June 1927, in Writings Folder, Edward Clark papers, Northwestern University Music Library. The correspondence about the Newcastle performance exchanged by Clark and Schoenberg prior to Clark's move to London apparently does not survive.

60 Carbon copy of letter from Clark to Schoenberg, 6 Feb. 1927, in ibid.

61 Letter from Schoenberg to Clark, 11 Feb. 1927, in Edward Clark Letters, *GB-Lbl* Add.ms.52257, fol. 55.

62 Letter from Schoenberg to Clark, 24 Feb. 1927, ibid., fol. 49–50. At the end of the letter, Schoenberg added, 'My best compliments to Percy Pitt. I look forward to his news and thank him for his friendly telegram', indicating that he was also in direct communication with the Music Director.

63 BBC WAC, RCONT1: Alfred A. Kalmus, Copyright, file 1 (1927–50), 23 Feb. and 14 March 1927.

64 BBC WAC, R3/3/3, 5 April 1927.

65 Carbon copy of letter from Clark to Schoenberg, 24 June 1927, in Writings Folder, Edward Clark papers, Northwestern University Music Library.

66 Telegram from Schoenberg to Clark, 22 July 1927, in Edward Clark Letters, *GB-Lbl* Add.ms.52257, fol. 51. Letter from Schoenberg to Clark, undated (received by BBC registry on 23 July 1927), in ibid., fol. 52.

67 Letter from Schoenberg to the BBC, 17 Oct. 1927, in ibid., fol. 53.

68 Letter from Schoenberg to Clark, undated (received by BBC registry on 20 Oct. 1927), in ibid., fol. 54.

69 Letter from Schoenberg to Clark, 23 Dec. 1927, in ibid., fol. 56.

70 Letter from Schoenberg to the BBC, 8 Jan. 1928, in ibid., fol. 57.

71 BBC WAC, L1/88/1, 25 Jan. 1928.

72 'Both Sides of the Microphone: an Outstanding Musical Event', *RT*, 17 (30 Dec. 1927): 712.

73 Percy A. Scholes, '140 Players and "Some Big Iron Chains!"', *RT*, 18 (13 Jan. 1928): 49–50.

74 'The Songs of Gurra: Gurrelieder', *RT*, 18 (20 Jan. 1928): 103.

75 BBC WAC, Scripts, Reel 319: Basil Maine, 'Next Week's Broadcast Music', 21 Jan. 1928.

76 Ibid. Information in curly brackets { } is crossed out in the transcript.

77 Arnold Schönberg, 'This "Rebel" Music', *Evening News*, 27 Jan. 1928; in BBC WAC, P479.

78 'A Talk with Schönberg', *The Observer*, 29 Jan. 1928; in BBC WAC, P479.

79 E. B. [Eric Blom], 'Schonberg's "Gurrelieder": Composers London Success', *Manchester Guardian*, 28 Jan. 1928; in BBC WAC, P479.

80 For an example, see 'Arnold Schönberg: "Gurrelieder" at Queen's Hall', *The Times*, 28 Jan. 1928; in BBC WAC, P479.

81 'Schonberg and the B.B.C.', *Evening Standard*, 28 Jan. 1928; in BBC WAC, P479.

82 H. G., 'London Concerts: Schönberg's "Gurrelieder"', *MT*, 69 (March 1928): 256.

83 Ernest Newman, 'Music of the Day', *Glasgow Herald*, 2 Feb. 1928; in BBC WAC, P479.

84 Letter from Schoenberg to Clark, 8 Feb. 1928, in Edward Clark Letters, *GB-Lbl* Add.ms.52257, fol. 58.

85 'The National Concerts, 1927–8', *The BBC Handbook 1929*, 132–4.

86 BBC WAC, Scripts, Reel 458: Percy Scholes, 'Weekly Musical Criticism', 7 Aug. 1924.

87   H. J. B. , 'Listener's Letters: Too Much Modern Music?', *RT*, 6 (27 Feb. 1925): 439.

88   Scannell and Cardiff, vol.i: *Serving the Nation*, 220–1.

89   'Chamber Music in Broadcasting', *BBC Handbook 1928*, 97–9.

90   The article erroneously gave the year as 1925.

91   F. J. Hargreaves, 'Listeners' Letters: Chamber Music', *RT*, 34 (4 March 1932): 578.

92   Sacheverell Sitwell, 'Igor Stravinsky', *RT*, 16 (8 July 1927): 54. Clark had previously conducted a staged performance of the work at the Newcastle People's Theatre in autumn 1926, and the first broadcast had been given on 27 January 1927 from Glasgow.

93   Percy Scholes, 'The Danger of Infallibility: Two Questions and a Moral', *RT*, 16 (22 July 1927): 125.

94   Percy Scholes, 'Is Bartok Mad – or are We?', *RT*, 17 (9 Dec. 1927): 525–6.

95   For these and other examples of letters written by listeners in response to Scholes's article, see 'The Madness of Bartok and Other Matters: Discussed in Letters to the Editor from Listeners', *RT*, 18 (6 Jan. 1928): 3.

96   Percy A. Scholes, 'The Music of Today', *RT*, 19 (18 May 1928): 285–6.

## 6   Refining the music programmes, 1928–1929

1   Prior to his resignation, Lewis wrote and adapted radio plays.

2   See, for example, 'The Shy B.B.C.', Daily News, 7 June 1929; in BBC WAC, P566: Press cuttings/Personal publicity (1928–9).

3   'Wireless Notes: Resignation of Captain Eckersley', *Manchester Guardian*, 6 June 1929; in BBC WAC, P566.

4   P. P. Eckersley, *The Power Behind the Microphone*, 152.

5   'Decree Nisi Against Former Chief Engineer to B.B.C.', *The Times*, 4 March 1930; in BBC WAC, P567: Press cuttings/Personal publicity (1930).

6   James Clark, interview by the author, 9 June 1992, London.

7   Interestingly, in Roger Milner's account of this event (in *Reith: the B.B.C. Years*, 175), Eckersley is portrayed as being hopelessly in love with a blond, referred to throughout as 'Miss Clark'. No mention is made of the blond's marriage to Edward Clark. Miles Eckersley, P. P. Eckersley's son, has researched this topic thoroughly and will present the details in his forthcoming biography of his father.

8   BBC WAC, L1/88/1: Left staff/Edward Thomas Clark (1924–1936), 31 Dec. 1928.

9   For details, see Wright's letter to Clark in BBC WAC, RCONT1: Edward Steuermann, Artists (1927–62), 14 Dec. 1928.

10   Ibid., 17 Jan. 1929.

11   Ibid., 31 Jan. 1929.

12   Ibid., 2 April 1929.

13   Ibid., 5 March 1929.

14  Ibid., 12 March 1929.

15  Ibid., 2 April 1929.

16  Ibid., 3 April 1929.

17  Ibid., 23 April 1929.

18  BBC WAC, R3/3/2: Control Board/Minutes (1926), 16 Nov. 1926.

19  Although plans for a permanent BBC orchestra began to be discussed during this season, the body of musicians brought together for these symphony concerts was not the same as the permanent BBC Symphony Orchestra formed in 1930. For more information about the musicians who performed in these concerts and the establishment of the permanent orchestra, see Kenyon, *The BBC Symphony Orchestra*, 1–48.

20  'Both Sides of the Microphone: People's Palace Concerts', *RT*, 25 (25 Oct. 1929): 237.

21  Filson Young, 'A New Sunday Feature', *RT*, 19 (11 May 1928), 233–4.

22  Francis Toye, 'How to Listen to Opera', *RT*, 20 (14 Sept. 1928): 469–70.

23  Edwin Evans, 'Points of View: Is Modern Music Inferior?', *RT*, 20 (31 Aug. 1928): 370.

24  H. A. Scott, 'This Modern Music!: Product of an Age of "Stunts"', *RT*, 20 (28 Sept. 1928): 642.

25  'What the Other Listener Thinks', *RT*, 21 (2 Nov. 1928): 301.

26  BBC WAC, Scripts, Reel 362: Ernest Newman, 'Next Week's Broadcast Music, no. 6', 3 Nov. 1928. In his weekly critical talks in October and November 1928, Newman played an important role in the BBC campaign to explain and defend contemporary music broadcasts.

27  See 'What the Other Listener Thinks' columns in *RT*, 22: (1 Feb. 1929): 299; (15 Feb.): 427.

28  Edwin Evans, 'What the New Composer is Driving At', *RT*, 22 (1 Feb. 1929), 255–6.

29  See 'What the Other Listener Thinks' columns in *RT*, 22: (1 March 1929): 547; (8 March 1929): 609; (22 March 1929): 735.

30  The complete programme for the 4 March Bartók concert is listed in Table B.4.

31  Although the author of the letter identified the described work as 'the last item, a Sonata', the 'Programmes as Broadcast' records reveal that the last item broadcast was the Rumanian Folk Dances, arranged for violin and piano.

32  Details about the concert programmes are listed in Table B.4 in Appendix B.

33  BBC WAC, R3/3/3: Control Board/Minutes (1927), 15 Feb. 1927.

34  Undated BBC memo from Clark to the Assistant Music Director, Kenneth Wright: autobiography written *c.* 1930, in Memorial Folder, Edward Clark papers, Northwestern University Music Library. Clark requested permission to conduct at the Arts Theatre Club occasionally in a memo dated 1 March 1928; see BBC WAC, L1/88/1, 1 March 1928.

35  'Both Sides of the Microphone: a New Home of Chamber Music', *RT*, 19 (18 May 1928): 291.

36  K. A. W. [Kenneth A. Wright], 'The New Series of B.B.C. Chamber Concerts', *RT*, 20 (31 Aug. 1928): 381.

37  BBC WAC, Scripts, Reel 362: Ernest Newman, 'Next Week's Broadcast Music, no. 3', 13 Oct. 1928.

38  Ibid., Ernest Newman, 'Next Week's Broadcast Music, no. 4', 20 Oct. 1928.

39  'Wild Career of the B.B.C.', *Star*, 13 Oct. 1928; in BBC WAC, P447: Press cuttings/Outside broadcasts (1927–9).

40  Announcements of the Webern String Trio broadcast were included in: 'Forward: Musical Events', *Talks and Lectures: Broadcast September to December 1928* [*c.* Aug. 1928]: 9; K. A. W. , 'The New Series of B.B.C. Chamber Concerts', *RT*, 20 (31 Aug. 1928): 381; 'Both Sides of the Microphone: Contemporary Chamber Music – II', *RT*, 21 (5 Oct. 1928): 5.

41  BBC WAC, Scripts, Reel 362: Ernest Newman, 'Next Week's Broadcast Music, no. 3', 13 Oct. 1928.

42  Ibid., Ernest Newman, 'Next Week's Broadcast Music, no. 4', 20 Oct. 1928.

43  Ernest Newman, 'The World of Music: the Week's Music', *Sunday Times*, 21 Oct. 1928; in BBC WAC, P447.

44  C. G. [Cecil Gray], 'Contemporary Chamber Music', *Daily Telegraph*, 16 Oct. 1928; in BBC WAC, P447.

45  'B.B.C. Chamber Concert', *The Observer*, 21 Oct. 1928; in BBC WAC, P447.

46  Ibid.

47  Ernest Newman, 'The World of Music: the Week's Music', *Sunday Times*, 21 Oct. 1928; in BBC WAC, P447.

48  BBC WAC, Scripts, Reel 362: Ernest Newman, 'Next Week's Broadcast Music, no. 6', 3 Nov. 1928.

49  Eugene Goossens, quoted in BBC WAC, Scripts, Reel 132: Edwin Evans, 'Musical Criticism', 7 Dec. 1928.

50  See BBC WAC, R3/3/4: Control Board/Minutes (1928), 3 July 1928.

51  'Both Sides of the Microphone: Composer's Chinese Model', *RT*, 21 (23 Nov. 1928): 509.

52  For correspondence and other papers relating to the translation, see BBC WAC, RCONT1: Alfred A. Kalmus, Copyright, file 1 (1927–50), 3 Oct.–26 Nov. 1928.

53  Ibid., 12 Oct. 1928.

54  Ibid.

55  Ibid., 15 Oct. 1928. The translation from the original German was prepared by the BBC on receipt of the letter.

56  'Both Sides of the Microphone: Composer's Chinese Model', *RT*, 21 (23 Nov. 1928): 509.

57  BBC WAC, Scripts, Reel 362: Ernest Newman, 'Next Week's Broadcast Music, no. 10', 1 Dec. 1928.

58  Ernest Newman, 'The World of Music: the Week's Music', *Sunday Times*, 9 Dec. 1928; in BBC WAC, P447.

59  'Modern Continental Chamber Music: B.B.C. Concert', *Manchester Guardian*, 4 Dec. 1928; in BBC WAC, P447.

60  For Evans's view, see BBC WAC, Scripts, Reel 132: Edwin Evans, 'Musical Criticism', 7 Dec. 1928.

61  BBC WAC, RCONT1: Edward Steuermann, Artists (1927–62), 31 Aug. 1928. Further detailed correspondence relating to this broadcast may also be found in this file (31 Aug.–21 Dec. 1928).

62  Ibid., 3 Sept. 1928.

63  BBC WAC, RCONT1: Edward Steuermann, Artists (1927–62), 3 Nov. 1928.

64  Ibid., 14 Dec. 1928. Clark informed the Viennese agent, Paul Bechert, that the department intended to engage the conductor Malko, when, according to Wright: 'Pitt has not at all agreed to him and the matter has only gone so far as my memo to him which followed on your requesting me to write.' When Wright tried to discover what was planned for the Amar Quartet's April broadcast, not only was he unable to find Clark's programme outline – 'I assume that you have it written in your pocket book' – but the entire Amar file was missing. Concerning another contemporary concert, featuring Stravinsky's *Les noces* conducted by Ansermet, Wright wrote despairingly, 'I want to be getting on with this concert, and I cannot find the date. All I know is that a certain sum had been agreed for the translation of 'Les Noces'. Does it involve an orchestra? If so how large? How many rehearsals? How many are there in the chorus? I have written to Ansermet for details and he must think our organisation pretty rotten'.

65  'Both Sides of the Microphone: Contemporary Music', *RT*, 21 (28 Dec. 1928): 856.

66  The International String Quartet consisted of André Mangeot, Doris Pecker, Frank Howard and Herbert Withers. The quartet was joined by violist Raymond Jeremy for the Vaughan Williams quintet.

67  BBC WAC, R30/44: Outside broadcasts – Sound/Arts Theatre (1929–1930), 5 Jan. 1929.

68  Ibid., 7 Jan. 1929.

69  Ibid.

70  E. B. [Eric Blom], 'BBC Chamber Music: a Vaughan Williams Quintet', *Manchester Guardian*, 8 Jan. 1929; in BBC WAC, P447.

71  C. G. [Cecil Gray], 'Chamber Music: Van Dieren's String Quartet', *Daily Telegraph*, 8 Jan. 1929; in BBC WAC, P447.

72  Ernest Newman, 'The World of Music: Broadcasting Music: Some Reflections and a Suggestion: B.B.C. Concert', *Sunday Times*, 13 Jan. 1929, 5(B).

73  E. B. [Eric Blom], 'London Concerts: B.B.C. Modern Chamber Concert', *MT*, 70 (Feb. 1929): 158.

74  BBC WAC, Scripts, Reel 362: Ernest Newman, 'Next Week's Broadcast Music, no. 4', 20 Oct. 1928.

75  Paul Bechert negotiated on behalf of the Viennese musicians whom Clark wanted for the performance, including Rudolf Kolisch and Benar Heifetz of the Vienna String Quartet.

76  BBC WAC, RCONT1: Edward Steuermann, Artists (1927–62), 14 Dec. 1928.

77  See BBC WAC, R30/44: Outside Broadcasts – Sound/Arts Theatre
    (1929–1930), 1 Jan. 1929, and RCONT1: Edward Steuermann, Artists
    (1927–62), undated [*c.* Jan. 1929].
78  'Chamber Music: The Vienna String Quartet' [programme listing, 12 Feb.
    1929, 5GB, 10.15 pm], *RT*, 22 (8 Feb. 1929): 335.
79  BBC WAC, Scripts, Reel 363: Ernest Newman, 'Music Criticism, no. 3', 15 Feb.
    1929.

## 7  Pitt's final season, 1929–1930

1  See 'B.B.C. Musical Talks', *The Times*, 14 Nov. 1929; 'Musical Talks of Sir
   Walford Davies: New Arrangement with B.B.C.', *Daily News*, 14 Nov. 1929;
   'Sir Walford Davies', *Evening Standard*, 15 Nov. 1929; all in BBC WAC, P566:
   Press Cuttings/Personal Publicity (1928–9).
2  'Change at the B.B.C.: Mr. Percy Pitt Likely to Give up his Post as Music
   Director', *Evening Standard*, 7 March 1929; in BBC WAC, P566.
3  'Mr. Percy Pitt and B.B.C.', *Daily Telegraph*, 8 March 1929; in BBC WAC, P566.
4  'Age Limit for B.B.C. Officials: Mr Percy Pitt's Successor', *Morning Post*, 2
   May 1929; in BBC WAC, P566.
5  'Mr. Percy Pitt's Successor', *Popular Wireless*, 4 May 1929; in BBC WAC,
   P566.
6  'New Post for Dr. Adrian Boult', *Manchester Guardian*, 8 June 1929; in BBC
   WAC, P566.
7  'Mr. Adrian Boult: Policy as New B.B.C. Music Director', *Daily Telegraph*, 16
   July 1929; 'B.B.C. Music Director', *Sunday Times*, 8 Dec. 1929; both in BBC
   WAC, P566. For further details about Boult's accession to his position in the
   BBC, see Kenyon, *The BBC Symphony Orchestra*, 38–40.
8  BBC WAC, R3/3/5: Control Board/Minutes (1929), 22 Oct. 1929. This
   minute was cancelled during the next meeting.
9  Notice in *Daily Telegraph*, 3 Jan. 1930; 'Mr. Percy Pitt', *Daily Telegraph*, 4 Jan.
   1930; both in BBC WAC, P566.
10 Kenyon, *The BBC Symphony Orchestra*, 38.
11 In the series prospectus published prior to the season, the BBC announced
   that Beecham would conduct no fewer than ten of the concerts, reflecting
   ties that had developed as Beecham and the Music Department negotiated to
   establish a permanent orchestra under his direction. By autumn 1929, the
   negotiations had soured into legal wrangles, and they were abandoned by the
   new year. In the end, Beecham only conducted five of these concerts. For
   more information about the BBC's negotiations with Beecham, see Kenyon,
   *The BBC Symphony Orchestra*, 15–34.
12 The Ansermet programme was broadcast on 31 Jan. 1930 and the Spanish
   programme on 28 March 1930.
13 'Both Sides of the Microphone: the Bach Cantatas', *RT*, 25 (25 Oct. 1929): 236.
14 Scott Goddard, 'The Coming Season of Broadcast Opera', *RT*, 24 (6 Sept.
   1929): 469, 504.

15  BBC WAC, R27/55/1: Music General/Commissioned Works (1929–37), undated.

16  Minutes of the weekly Music Meetings before 1933 do not survive, but Wright reproduced details about the commissioning decision in a memo to Clark; see BBC WAC, R27/55/1, 16 May 1929.

17  Walton and Lambert were to receive 50 guineas each. Since Hely Hutchinson's composition came within the terms of his BBC staff contract, he requested special leave to compose his work. Walton was to make his own fee arrangements with Sitwell, while the BBC would pay Cecil Lewis 20 guineas for *The Town*.

18  BBC WAC, R27/55/1, 21 Aug. 1929, 12 Jan. and 13 March 1930.

19  Ibid., 1 April 1930.

20  Ibid., 27 March 1930.

21  Ibid.

22  Ibid., 1 April 1930.

23  Ibid., 8 and 11 April 1930.

24  'Both Sides of the Microphone: Music Specially Written for Radio', *RT*, 27 (25 April 1930): 189.

25  BBC WAC, R27/55/1, 30 May 1930.

26  Ibid., 6 June 1930.

27  Walton, quoted in a letter from Foss to Howgill, in BBC WAC, R27/55/1, 25 June 1930.

28  Ibid., 26 June 1930.

29  Ibid.

30  Ibid., 14 July 1930.

31  Walton, quoted in a letter from Foss to Howgill, in BBC WAC, R27/55/1, 12 Aug. 1930.

32  Ibid., 13 Aug. 1930.

33  The first performance of *Belshazzar's Feast* was given by the London Symphony Orchestra, conducted by Sargent, at the Leeds Triennial Festival on 8 October 1931. The BBC Symphony Orchestra, conducted by Boult, gave the first London performance of the work on 25 November at the Queen's Hall.

34  BBC WAC, R27/55/1, 6 Aug. 1930.

35  Ibid., 5 Nov. 1930.

36  Ibid., 11 Nov. 1930. Discussions concerning Lambert's commission continued for some months; see BBC WAC, R27/55/1, 10 and 22 Dec. 1930, 27 Aug. and 1 Sept. 1931.

37  Ibid., 19 Sept. and 17 Oct. 1930.

38  Ibid., 12 Nov. 1930.

39  Victor Hely Hutchinson, *Settings of Lyrics by G. K. Chesterton* (London: Elkin, 1933).

40  'What the Other Listener Thinks', *RT*, 25 (25 Oct. 1929): 244.

41  'What the Other Listener Thinks', *RT*, 27 (4 April 1930): 12.

42  BBC WAC, Scripts, Reel 363: Ernest Newman, 'Music Criticism, no. 18', 27 Sept. 1929.

43  BBC WAC, Scripts, Reel 363: Ernest Newman, 'Music Criticism, no. 22', 22 Nov. 1929. Newman gave similar arguments in previous talks; see Scripts, Reel 362: Ernest Newman, 'Next Week's Broadcast Music, no. 3', 13 Oct. 1928, and 'Next Week's Broadcast Music, no. 4', 20 Oct. 1928.

44  BBC WAC, Scripts, Reel 277/8: Peter Latham, 'Is Modern Music Bad?', 17 Jan. 1930, and *The Listener*, 3 (22 Jan. 1930): 161–2.

45  BBC WAC, R29/157: Orchestra General/Contemporary Concerts (1929–39), 29 April 1929. This memo was written in response to a critical memo written by the Presentation Assistant, Wellington, which has not been traced.

46  Programme details are listed in Table B.5 in Appendix B.

47  BBC WAC, R30/44: Outside Broadcasts – Sound/Arts Theatre (1929–1930), 6 May 1929.

48  BBC WAC, R34/600/4: Policy/Programme Board Minutes (1929), 17 May, and R30/44,18 June and 22 Aug. 1929.

49  BBC WAC, R30/44, 23 Aug. 1929.

50  BBC WAC, R27/67: Music General/Contemporary Concerts (1929–36), 5 Sept. 1929.

51  Ibid., 9 Sept. 1929.

52  BBC WAC, R34/600/4, 15 Nov. 1929.

53  It has not been possible to discover why the larger hall was used, since papers concerning outside broadcasts from these venues do not survive for this time. At the BBC WAC, the earliest paper in the file for Kingsway Hall (R30: Outside Broadcasts – Kingsway Hall General (1931–46)) dates from 26 November 1930; in the file for Central Hall, Westminster (R30/278/1: Outside Broadcasts – Sound/Central Hall Westminster (1928–46)), no papers dating between May 1929 and November 1937 survive.

54  For example, see 'Both Sides of the Microphone: Free Tickets for B.B.C. Concerts', *RT*, 26 (17 Jan. 1930): 129.

55  'Uses of a Full Audience', *Evening News*, 18 Jan. 1930; in BBC WAC, P449: Press Cuttings/Outside Broadcasts: Concerts (1930–31).

56  'Both Sides of the Microphone: Contemporary Music', *RT*, 25 (11 Oct. 1929): 85.

57  Isaacs refused the BBC permission to use the club on that date; see BBC WAC, R30/44, 22 Aug. 1929.

58  Letter from Clark to Steuermann, in BBC WAC, RCONT1: Edward Steuermann, Artists (1927–62), 13 April 1929. Clark was apparently referring to the piano version, op. 3a, of Ullmann's *Variationen und Doppelfuge über ein Thema von Arnold Schönberg*.

59  Letter from Clark to Steuermann, in ibid., 29 Aug. 1929.

60  'Both Sides of the Microphone: the Composer of the "Gurrelieder"', *RT*, 25 (25 Oct. 1929): 236.

61  BBC WAC, Scripts, Reel 319: Basil Maine, 'Next Week's Broadcast Music', 26 Oct. 1929.

62  'Concerts of Contemporary Music' [programme notes, 4 Nov. 1929, 5GB, 8.00 pm], *RT*, 25 (1 Nov. 1929): 331.

63  C. G. [Cecil Gray], 'Contemporary Music', *Daily Telegraph*, 5 Nov. 1929; in BBC WAC, P447: Press Cuttings/Outside Broadcasts (1927–9).

64  J. A. W. [Jack Westrup], 'Monotony of Schonberg: Viennese Music at B.B.C. Concert', *Daily Mail*, 5 Nov. 1929; in BBC WAC, P447.

65  Ernest Newman, 'The World of Music: the Week's Music: Contemporary Chamber Music', *Sunday Times*, 10 Nov. 1929; in BBC WAC, P447.

66  For a summary of Webern's conducting career with the BBC, see Foreman, 'Webern, the BBC and the Berg Violin Concerto', 2–10.

67  The telephone conversation is mentioned in a letter Webern wrote to Clark on 8 July 1929, in Edward Clark Letters, *GB-Lbl* Add.ms.52257, fol. 149 verso.

68  Carbon copy of letter from Clark to Webern, 1 July 1929, in Writings Folder, Edward Clark Papers, Northwestern University Music Library.

69  Letter from Webern to Clark, 8 July 1929, in Edward Clark Letters, *GB-Lbl* Add.ms.52257, fol. 149 verso.

70  Berg's *Der Wein* was performed by Ružena Herlinger at a studio orchestra concert on 10 February 1934.

71  The second July letter from Webern to Clark, referred to in Webern's letter of 18 August, is not in any of the three collections in which the rest of the correspondence has been found.

72  Letter from Webern to Clark, 18 Aug. 1929, in Edward Clark Letters, *GB-Lbl* Add.ms.52257, fol. 158.

73  BBC WAC, 910: Anton Webern, file 1 (1929–33), 2 and 3 Oct. 1929.

74  Letter from Webern to Clark, 6 Nov. 1929, in Edward Clark Letters, *GB-Lbl* Add.ms.52257, fol. 159.

75  Letters from Webern to Clark, 12 and 18 Nov. 1929, in ibid., fols. 160–1.

76  BBC WAC, 910: Anton Webern, file 1 (1929–33), 19 Nov. 1929.

77  Letter from Webern to Clark, 19 Nov. 1929, in Edward Clark Letters, *GB-Lbl* Add.ms.52257, fol. 162.

78  BBC WAC, 910: Anton Webern, file 1 (1929–33), 21, 24 and 26 Nov. 1929.

79  Webern's diary entry, his letter to Schoenberg, dated 3 December 1929, and Moldenhauer's assessment are found in Moldenhauer, *Webern*, edition in *Schubert/Webern Series: Programme Book*, 338.

80  'Both Sides of the Microphone: "The Shadow of a Tune"', *RT*, 25 (22 Nov. 1929): 541.

81  'Concerts of Contemporary Music' [programme listing, 2 Dec. 1929, 5GB, 7.45 pm], *RT*, 25 (29 Nov. 1929): 637.

82  'A B.B.C. Concert of Contemporary Music', *RT*, 25 (29 Nov. 1929): 641.

83  The repetition of the Webern was reported in the press reviews; for example, see B. M. [Basil Maine], 'B.B.C. concert: Some Fleeting Fragments of Music', *Morning Post*, 3 Dec. 1929; in BBC WAC, P447.

84  Ernest Newman, 'The World of Music: the Week's Music: Chamber Music', *Sunday Times*, 8 Dec. 1929; in BBC WAC, P447.

85  BBC WAC, Scripts, Reel 363: Ernest Newman, 'Music Criticism, no. 23', 6 Dec. 1929.

86 Webern diaries, quoted in Moldenhauer, *Webern*, 339.

87 Clark's addendum to a letter from Webern to Schoenberg, *c.* 2 December 1929, quoted in Moldenhauer, *Webern*, 339.

88 Letter from Clark to Steuermann, in BBC WAC, RCONT1: Edward Steuermann, Artists (1927–62), 29 Aug. 1929.

89 A reference in BBC WAC, RCONT1: Edward Steuermann, Artists (1927–62) indicates that relevant papers were held in a file called 'Pierrot Lunaire Ensemble', which has not been traced.

90 'A Music Diary for Listeners', *The Listener*, 3 (29 Jan. 1930), 216.

91 BBC WAC, RCONT1: Edward Steuermann, Artists (1927–62), 8 Feb. 1930.

92 Telegrams between Clark and Steuermann in ibid., 7–8, 14–17 March 1930. Letter from Steuermann to Clark in ibid., 19 March 1930.

93 Formerly referred to as the Vienna String Quartet by the BBC.

94 'Both Sides of the Microphone: For the Sake of Pierrot', *RT*, 26 (28 March 1930), 757.

95 'Both Sides of the Microphone: Concert of Schonberg's Music', *RT*, 26 (28 March 1930): 757.

96 'For the Musical Listener: Notes on the Week's Programmes: the Ardent Disciples of Schönberg', *RT*, 27 (4 April 1930): 14.

97 Erwin Stein, 'The Moon-Struck Pierrot Comes to London', *RT*, 27 (4 April 1930): 9.

98 R. C. [Richard Capell], 'Last Night's Wireless Infliction', *Daily Mail*, 8 April 1930; in BBC WAC, P449.

99 E. B. [Eric Blom], 'Modern Music Broadcast: a Schonberg Programme', *Manchester Guardian*, 8 April 1930; in BBC WAC, P449.

100 Ernest Newman, 'The World of Music: the Week's Music: Schönberg and Bartok', *Sunday Times*, 13 April 1930; in BBC WAC, P449.

101 M. D. Calvocoressi, 'A Schönberg Concert', *The Listener*, 3 (9 April 1930): 648.

102 For examples, see: 'What the Other Listener Thinks: In Praise of Modern Music – And in Dispraise', *RT*, 27 (25 April 1930): 194; 'What the Other Listener Thinks: Pierrot Lunaire', *RT*, 27 (2 May 1930): 258.

103 'Both Sides of the Microphone: This Modern Stuff!', *RT*, 27 (25 April 1930): 188.

104 W. J. Turner, 'Modernist Music, or "Devastating the Home"', *RT*, 27 (16 May 1930): 363.

## 8  Boult's initial seasons, 1930–1931, 1931–1932

1 For a detailed description of Broadcasting House and the effects of the move on the organization, see Briggs, vol. ii, *The Golden Age*, 458–66.

2 Gorham, *Sound and Fury*, 45.

3 Surviving documentation of music programming policies from 1930 to 1936 has been derived from many sources. Relevant files at the BBC WAC include: papers directly related to music programme policy, 1930–6 (R27/245/1,

R27/326/1–2 and R34/609); minutes for the Music Department weekly
meetings, 1933–6 (R27/221/1–2); meeting minutes and other papers relating
to the Music Advisory Committee, 1933–6 (R6/46, R6/47/1, R6/48/1 and
R6/50); meeting minutes and other papers relating to the Music Programme
Advisory Panel, 1933–6 (R27/249/1–2 and R27/250/1); papers concerning
public concert policy, 1933–5 (R27/432); papers concerning the Five-Year
Plan, 1934–5 (R27/100); and relevant papers relating to the Ullswater
Report, 1935–6 (R4/7/12, R4/7/8/1–7 and R27/219). Additional information
has been derived from: the Reith Diaries (S60/5); surviving minutes of Board
of Governors, Programme Board, Control Board and D.G.'s meetings; the
BBC yearbooks; and articles in the *Radio Times*, *The Listener* and
contemporary newspapers.

4 For further details, see 'The First Week of Alternative Programmes', *RT*, 26 (7
March 1930): 557, 566. See also Briggs, vol. ii: *The Golden Age*, 27–31.

5 'Ten Years of Broadcasting: Music', *The BBC Yearbook 1933*, 19.

6 Paper 16 in BBC WAC, R4/7/8/1: Ullswater Committee 1935/Other Written
Evidence/Papers 1–30.

7 For details about the negotiations and political maneouverings that were
involved in Boult's appointment and the building of the orchestra during
spring 1930, see Kenyon, *The BBC Symphony Orchestra*, 38–48. Boult also
provided a brief history of the formation of the orchestra in his evidence to
the Ullswater Committee; see BBC WAC, R27/219: Music General/Music and
Music Department 1931–43), [July] 1935 ('Memorandum by Dr Adrian
Boult, Director of Music, Submitted to The Broadcasting Committee,
1935').

8 BBC WAC, R13/242/1: Departmental/Music Department (1928–32),
4 March 1930.

9 Ibid., 4 March 1930.

10 Ibid., 14 March 1930.

11 Ibid., 24 March, 4, 10 and 29 April 1930.

12 Kenyon, *The BBC Symphony Orchestra*, 64.

13 BBC WAC, R13/242/1, 21 April 1931.

14 Ibid., 8 May 1931.

15 Ibid, 21 April 1931.

16 Ibid., 9 May 1931.

17 Ibid., 8 May 1931.

18 Ibid., 15 May 1931.

19 BBC WAC, R27/219, 22 May 1931.

20 'Musicians on the B.B.C. Staff', *The BBC Yearbook 1932*, 139–40.

21 For details, see Harvey Grace, 'Weekly Notes on Music: the B.B.C. Symphony
Concerts', *The Listener*, 4 (8 Oct. 1930): 570; W. J. Turner, 'The Winter
Season of Symphony Concerts', *RT*, 29 (17 Oct. 1930): 157.

22 'Music of the Week: Attractive Concerts for Sunday Evenings', *RT*, 29 (24
Oct. 1930): 238.

23 'Broadcasting: the Programme and the Listener', *The Observer*, 28 Sept. 1930, 2(B).

24 Editorial, *RT*, 29 (3 Oct. 1930): 12.

25 'Broadcasting: the Programme and the Listener', *The Observer*, 5 Oct. 1930, 5(B).

26 Percy A. Scholes, 'B.B.C. and "Difficult" Music', *The Observer*, 12 Oct. 1930; in BBC WAC, P131: Press Cuttings/Programme Matters (1930).

27 Editorial, *RT*, 29 (24 Oct. 1930): 232.

28 Transcripts of the talks in this series are found in BBC WAC, Scripts, Reel 204: Victor Hely Hutchinson, 11 April–4 July 1932.

29 'Music, New and Old – I' [programme listing, 11 April 1932, Daventry National, 7.30 pm], *RT*, 35 (8 April 1932): 88.

30 BBC WAC, Scripts, Reel 204: Victor Hely Hutchinson, 2 May 1932.

31 BBC WAC, RCONT1: Ernest Newman, Talks, file 1 (1931–6), 13 July 1932. The BBC announced this new policy in September; see 'Both Sides of the Microphone: Before the Concert', *RT*, 36 (2 Sept. 1932): 537.

32 'Both Sides of the Microphone: Is he the Greatest Composer of Today?', *RT*, 29 (28 Nov. 1930): 582.

33 Robin H. Legge, 'Schonberg at his Dullest: "Pelléas" at the Queen's Hall', *Daily Telegraph*, 11 Dec. 1930; in BBC WAC, P483: Press Cuttings/Symphony Concerts (Oct. 1930–Jan. 1931).

34 BBC WAC, R27/67: Music General/Contemporary Concerts (1929–36), undated.

35 Ibid., 21 Nov. 1930.

36 Ibid., 22 Dec. 1930.

37 Programme details are listed in Table B.6 in Appendix B.

38 Carbon copy of letter from Clark to Schoenberg, 9 Sept. 1929, in Writings Folder, Edward Clark Papers, Northwestern University Music Library.

39 Schoenberg told Clark about his new opera in a letter of 14 Aug. 1929, in Edward Clark Letters, *GB-Lbl* Add.ms.52257, fol. 61.

40 Letter from Clark to Schoenberg, 9 Sept. 1929.

41 Only the Schoenberg side of the correspondence is extant. See letters from Gertrud Schoenberg to Clark, 22 Sept. and 14 Oct. 1929, and letter from Schoenberg to Clark, 15 Oct. 1929, in Edward Clark Letters, *GB-Lbl* Add.ms.52257, fol. 62, 64 and 65.

42 Postcard from Schoenberg to Tillett, 25 July 1930, in Edward Clark Letters, *GB-Lbl* Add.ms.52257, fol. 66.

43 Note added to the bottom of Schoenberg's postcard, ibid.

44 Only the letter of invitation to Hinnenberg-Lefèbre survives; see BBC WAC, RCONT1: Margot Hinnenberg-Lefèbre, Artists (1930–62), 16 Aug. 1930.

45 BBC WAC, R27/67, 21 Nov. 1930.

46 Ibid., 10 Dec. 1930.

47 For details of these negotiations, see BBC WAC, RCONT1: Margot

Hinnenberg-Lefèbre, Artists (1930–62), 24 Aug., 28 Nov., 6 Dec., 10 Dec. and 11 Dec. 1930.

48  BBC WAC, R27/67, 10 Dec. 1930.

49  Ibid., 21 Nov. 1930.

50  'Both Sides of the Microphone: Schonberg', *RT*, 29 (26 Dec. 1930): 865. The 'Music of the Week' column in the same issue also promoted this concert (p. 872).

51  'What the Other Listener Thinks', *RT*, 30 (2 Jan. 1931): 8.

52  'Schönberg to Conduct his Own Music this Week', *RT*, 30 (2 Jan. 1931): 10. Despite the amount of discussion that surrounded the decision to place the concert on Friday, the caption under the drawing misleadingly read: 'Arnold Schönberg, whose music fills the programme of Monday's Contemporary Music Concert'.

53  Ibid., 12.

54  'The New Music', *Evening News*, 10 Jan. 1931; in BBC WAC, P132: Press Cuttings/Programmes (1931).

55  H. H. [Herbert Hughes], 'Schonberg on the Wireless: Musical Melodrama', *Daily Telegraph*, 10 Jan. 1931; in BBC WAC, P132.

56  E. N. [Ernest Newman], 'The Week's Music: Schönberg's Grand Guignol', *Sunday Times*, 12 Jan. 1931; in BBC WAC, P132.

57  Constant Lambert, 'London Concerts: Schönberg's "Erwartung"', *MT*, 72 (Feb. 1931): 167.

58  Letter from Schoenberg to Clark, 20 Jan 1931, in Edward Clark Letters, *GB-Lbl* Add.ms.52257, fol. 68.

59  Berg's personal description of his trip is documented in the daily letters that he wrote to his wife; see *Alban Berg: Letters*, 373–9. For a historical account of this visit, see Chadwick, 'Berg and the BBC', 46–8.

60  Letter from Berg to Clark, 20 Dec. 1930, in Edward Clark Letters, *GB-Lbl* Add.ms.52256, fol. 43 (transcription and translation in Chadwick, 'Berg and the BBC', 47). Letter from Julius Schloss, a Berg pupil, to Clark, 2 Jan. 1931, in ibid., fol. 44. Letter from Berg to his wife, 15 Jan. 1931, in *Alban Berg: Letters*, 378.

61  Letter from Webern to Clark, 4 Feb. 1931, in Edward Clark Letters, *GB-Lbl* Add.ms.52257, fol. 163.

62  BBC WAC, 910: Anton Webern, file 1 (1929–33), 18 Feb. 1931.

63  Carbon copy of letter from Clark to Webern, in ibid., 19 Feb. 1931.

64  Letter from Webern to Clark, 2 March 1931, in Edward Clark Letters, *GB-Lbl* Add.ms.52257, fols. 164–6.

65  Letter from Webern to Clark, 6 April 1931, in ibid., fols.167–8.

66  BBC WAC, 910: Anton Webern, file 1 (1929–33), 10 April 1931.

67  Letter from Webern to Clark, 15 April 1931, in Edward Clark Letters, *GB-Lbl* Add.ms.52257, fol. 169.

68  BBC WAC, 910: Anton Webern, file 1 (1929–33), 17 April 1931.

69  Letter from Webern to Clark, 21 April 1931, in Edward Clark Letters, *GB-Lbl* Add.ms.52257, fol. 170.

70  BBC WAC, 910: Anton Webern, file 1 (1929–33), 21 and 24 April 1931.

71  Letter from Webern to Clark, 28 April 1931, in Edward Clark Letters, *GB-Lbl* Add.ms.52257, fol. 172.

72  BBC WAC, 910: Anton Webern, file 1 (1929–33), 1 and 4 May 1931. Telegram from Webern to Clark, 4 May 1931, in Edward Clark Letters, *GB-Lbl* Add.ms.52257, fol. 173.

From the 4 May letter, Lewis Foreman inferred that Boult himself was involved with the piano rehearsal: 'Sir Adrian Boult, ever courteous in these matters, arranged to greet the distinguished visiting musician personally: the piano rehearsal is arranged "at Mr Boult's room", and the soprano soloist, Enid Cruickshank is bidden attend at 11.45 am' ('Webern, the BBC and the Berg Violin Concerto', 5). Foreman may have been misled by the closing, 'For Director of Programmes (Music Department)', which appeared under the space for the signature on the carbon copy of the letter that survives in the BBC WAC Webern file. In fact this conclusion, which was usually used on Music Department correspondence at this time, did not imply that Boult wrote or even saw the letter, but merely that it came from his department. The carbon is clearly initialled by Herbage and marked at the top 'PM/JH', leaving no doubt that Herbage, not Boult, was the author of the letter. Although Boult must have courteously given permission for his room to be used for the piano rehearsal, there is no evidence that he was at his room on the morning of the 8th to greet Webern.

73  'Both Sides of the Microphone: Jekyll-and-Hyde Webern', *RT*, 31 (24 April 1931): 191.

74  'Concerts of Contemporary Music – V' [programme listing, 8 May 1931, London Regional, 9.00 pm], *RT*, 31 (1 May 1931): 292.

75  'Music of the Week: Schönberg and Webern', ibid., 262.

76  No Newman scripts dating between 20 December 1929 and 27 March 1931 survive at the BBC WAC; however, Newman described the talk and public response to it in the letter in which he made his recommendations; see BBC WAC, RCONT1: Ernest Newman, Talks, file 1 (1931–6), 5 Feb. 1931.

77  BBC WAC, RCONT1: Ernest Newman, Talks, file 1 (1931–6), 11 Feb. 1931.

78  Ibid., 17 Feb. 1931.

79  Ibid., 12 May 1931.

80  Ibid., 13 May 1931.

81  Ibid., 14 and 15 May 1931.

82  Ibid., 18 May 1931.

83  Edwin Evans, 'New Music from the World's Four Corners', *RT*, 32 (17 July 1931): 117.

84  R. L. Henderson, 'Edward Clark – A Memoir', typescript proposal for biography (never realized), dated 1963, in Clark Folder, Edward Clark Papers, Northwestern University Music Library.

85  Wright informed Graves, the Assistant Director of Programmes, that he and Clark would attend the 1930 ISCM Festival; see BBC WAC, R27/326/1: Music General/Opera/General Memos, file 1 (1929–34), 28 July 1930.

86  Specific details of how the BBC became involved with the choral and orchestral concerts are no longer extant. The earliest papers in the BBC files devoted to the ISCM (R27/157/1–2) date from 1939, but a few papers relating to the 1931 festival have been traced: in RCONT1: Prof. Edward J. Dent, Talks (1931–56), papers dating from May and June 1931 provide information about the BBC's attitude toward the festival; those in BBC WAC, R30: Outside Broadcasts – Queen's Hall/International Festival 1931 provide information about conductors of the orchestral programmes and who received free tickets to festival events.

87  BBC WAC, RCONT1: Prof. Edward J. Dent, Talks (1931–56), 1 May 1931.

88  Ibid.

89  Ibid., 28 May 1931.

90  Ibid., 2 June 1931.

91  Ibid., 9 June 1931. Dent regularly refused to give broadcast talks until 1936, when a former student of his, George Barnes, helped him to overcome his fear of speaking before the microphone. From that time, he spoke fairly frequently on music-related subjects.

92  BBC WAC, Scripts, Reel 132: Edwin Evans, 'The Contemporary Music Festival', 18 July 1931.

93  Editorial, *RT*, 32 (3 July 1931): 6.

94  Edwin Evans, 'New Music from the World's Four Corners', *RT*, 32 (17 July 1931): 117.

95  Edwin Evans, 'Musicians of Many Countries', *The Listener*, 6 (22 July 1931): 143.

96  'Both Sides of the Microphone: Festival at Oxford', *RT*, 32 (10 July 1931): 60. 'Music of the Week: Oxford, Salzburg, and Canterbury', *RT*, 32 (17 July 1931): 124, 126, 142. 'Music of the Week: Gershwin Looks at an American in Paris', *RT*, 32 (24 July 1931): 176, 178, 211.

97  Robin Hey, 'Music that Expresses Contemporary Life', *RT*, 32 (10 July 1931): 59.

98  W. R. Anderson, 'Modern Music Battle: Anderson *v.* Hey', *RT*, 32 (24 July 1931): 167, 190.

99  The Polish composer, Koffler, had been a Schoenberg pupil (1920–4), and Jokl was a pupil of Berg. According to Benser's biography, Wellesz attended the entire festival (*Egon Wellesz*, 72); this fact is confirmed by the 'Supplementary List of Free Tickets for Festival', which includes Wellesz's name (BBC WAC, R30: Outside Broadcasts – Queen's Hall/International Festival 1931, undated).

Since Webern had just visited London in May, he was not present to hear his Symphony. Clark invited him to conduct a broadcast of popular music on 20 July to help finance the journey, but the composer declined the offer (BBC

WAC, 910: Anton Webern, file 1 (1929–33), 1 May 1931, 15 June–23 July
1931). Moldenhauer attributed this decision not only to financial
considerations, but also to fear of critical rejection:

> The composer was apprehensive since recent press reaction, beginning
> with the all-Webern concert in Vienna, had been so totally negative . . .
> On 10 April the Symphony, Op. 21, had been performed in Berlin under
> Otto Klemperer. The newspaper comments were devastating . . . Small
> wonder that Webern shied away from such notoriety. (Moldenhauer,
> *Webern*, 363.)

100  The logistics behind this broadcast were explained in BBC publicity; see
'Oxford, Salzburg, and Canterbury', 126.

101  For examples, see: C. G. [Cecil Gray], 'Modern Music at Oxford', *Daily
Telegraph*, 24 July; 'Modern Music at Oxford', *The Times*, 24 July; H. F.
[Harry Farjeon] 'The Week's Music: The Oxford Festival', *Sunday Times*, 26
July; 'A Concert of the Moderns', *Daily Telegraph*, 28 July; 'B.B.C. Orchestral
Concert', *The Times*, 28 July; E. B. [Eric Blom], 'The International Music
Festival', *Manchester Guardian*, 28 July; H. F. [Harry Farjeon] 'The Week's
Music: I.S.C.M. Festival', *Sunday Times*, 2 Aug.; all in BBC WAC, P449: Press
Cuttings/Outside Broadcasts: Concerts (1930–1). See also: Edwin Evans,
'The Oxford Festival', *MT*, 72 (Sept. 1931): 803–6; Henry Boys, 'The Oxford
Festival', *Monthly Musical Record*, 61 (Sept. 1931): 266–7; Ralph Hill,
'Contemporary Music Festival', *Musical Mirror and Fanfare* (Sept. 1931):
245–7.

102  Editorial, *RT*, 32 (7 Aug. 1931): 274.

103  Eric Blom, 'The Listener's Music: Music of the Month', *The Listener*, 6 (12
Aug. 1931): 251.

104  'Motor Horns in an Orchestra: a Plain Amateur Endures his Jazziest Night:
Musical Shockers', *The Star*, 28 July 1931; in BBC WAC, P449: Press
Cuttings/Outside Broadcasts: Concerts (1930–1).

105  Second Viennese School works were performed at the Proms on two
previous occasions, but were not broadcast: the première of Schoenberg's
Five Pieces for Orchestra, op. 16, on 3 September 1912 and Krenek's
*Potpourri* for orchestra, op. 54, on 26 August 1930. In addition, Schoenberg's
arrangments of two Bach Chorale Preludes were presented on 20 September
1928, but were not broadcast.

106  'Music of the Week', *RT*, 32 (14 Aug. 1931): 356, 360.

107  Eric Blom, 'The Listener's Music: Music of the Month', *The Listener*, 6 (9
Sept. 1931): 412.

108  For correspondence about these negotiations, see BBC WAC, RCONT1:
Margot Hinnenberg-Lefèbre, Artists (1930–62), 12, 15, 24, 28 June and *c.* 3
July 1931.

109  Ibid., 24 June 1931.

110  Ibid., 20 Aug. 1931.

111  Ibid., 1 Sept. 1931.

112  Ibid., 2 and 3 Sept. 1931.

113  'Promenade Concert' [programme notes, 15 Sept. 1931, Daventry National, 8.00 pm], *RT*, 32 (11 Sept. 1931): 576.

114  Eric Blom, 'The Listener's Music: Music of the Month', *The Listener*, 6 (14 Oct. 1931): 631.

115  'Letters to the Editor: Alban Berg', *MT*, 72 (Oct. 1931): 936.

116  'Letters to the Editor: Alban Berg is Not Alarming', *MT*, 72 (Nov. 1931): 1026. For subsequent letters, see: 'Letters to the Editor: Alban Berg', *MT*, 72 (Dec. 1931): 1125–6; 'Letters to the Editor: Alban Berg', *MT*, 73 (Jan. 1932): 62.

117  Wright's original request is not longer extant, but he explained the chronology in a subsequent memo; see BBC WAC, R27/67, 17 Sept. 1931.

118  BBC WAC, R27/245/1: Music General/Music Policy (1930–43), undated.

119  BBC WAC, R27/67, 16 Sept. 1931.

120  For further discussion of these criticisms, see Kenyon, *The BBC Symphony Orchestra*, 68–9.

121  Wright made his proposal in two memos, both dated 17 September 1931; see BBC WAC, R27/67.

122  Programme details are listed in Table B.7 in Appendix B.

123  BBC WAC, R27/67, 16 Sept. 1931.

124  Stuckenschmidt, *Arnold Schoenberg*, 344–8.

125  'Both Sides of the Microphone', *RT*, 33 (30 Oct. 1931): 336.

126  'In the Air: Programmes at a Glance', *RT*, 33 (6 Nov. 1931): 427.

127  The daily programme listing specified only the titles and performers; see 'Concerts of Contemporary Music – I' [programme listing, 13 Nov. 1931, London Regional, 8.00 pm], *RT*, 33 (6 Nov. 1931): 477.

128  Since none of Ernest Newman's talks scripts survive at the BBC WAC for the period between 17 July 1931 and 1 January 1932, it is not possible to check this.

129  Edwin Evans, 'Schönberg and the B.B.C.', *Time and Tide*, 21 Nov. 1931; in BBC WAC, P485: Press Cuttings/Symphony Concerts (Sept.–Dec. 1931).

130  F. B. [Ferruccio Bonavia], 'Schonberg's Music: the Old Style and the New: a B.B.C. Broadcast', *Daily Telegraph*, 14 Nov. 1931; in BBC WAC, P132.

131  E. N. [Ernest Newman], 'The Week's Music: Schönberg', *Sunday Times*, 15 Nov. 1931; in BBC WAC, P132.

132  'New Work of Schonberg: B.B.C. Contemporary Music Concert', *Manchester Guardian*, 14 Nov. 1931; in BBC WAC, P132. This important review was not signed.

133  This Schoenberg essay, written in May 1923, appears as 'Twelve-Tone Composition' in *Style and Idea*, ed. Leonard Stein, trans. Leo Black (London: Faber and Faber, 1975), 207–8.

134 'Both Sides of the Microphone', *RT*, 33 (6 Nov. 1931): 418–19.

135 Edwin Evans, 'Schönberg: Dreamer and Mathematician', *RT*, 33 (13 Nov. 1931): 509, 569.

136 'The Fifth of the B.B.C. Symphony Concerts' [programme notes, 18 Nov. 1931, Daventry National, 8.00 pm], *RT*, 33 (13 Nov. 1931): 540.

137 E. N. [Ernest Newman], 'The Week's Music: Schönberg', *Sunday Times*, 22 Nov. 1931; in BBC WAC, P485.

138 Eric Blom, 'The Listener's Music: Music of the Month', *The Listener*, 6 (9 Dec. 1931): 1004.

139 'B.B.C. Symphony Concert', *Manchester Guardian*, 19 Nov. 1931; in BBC WAC, P485.

140 'What the Other Listener Thinks', *RT*, 33 (11 Dec. 1931): 840.

141 Press release in BBC WAC, R79/2/3: Contemporary Concerts, file 3 (1931–4), 4 May 1932. See also 'Both Sides of the Microphone: Contemporary Concert', *RT*, 35 (6 May 1932): 332.

142 Although the Committee (later Society) for the Promotion of New Music was not founded for this purpose until 1943, the London Contemporary Music Centre had sponsored London performances of contemporary music since 1921. In addition, the Active Society for the Propagation of Contemporary Music, founded and organized by Erik Chisholm, presented concerts in Glasgow during the 1930s.

143 R. K. Silver, 'Those "Contemporary" Concerts', *RT*, 35 (6 May 1932): 336, 373. The BBC also published responses to this article; see 'What the Other Listener Thinks': *RT*, 35 (27 May 1932): 537 and (10 June 1932): 665.

144 'Both Sides of the Microphone: Contemporary Concert', *RT*, 35 (6 May 1932): 332.

145 'Concerts of Contemporary Music – VII' [programme listing, 13 May 1932, London Regional, 8.35 pm], *RT*, 35 (6 May 1932): 378.

146 BBC WAC, R27/67, 10 May 1932.

147 C. L. [Constant Lambert], 'B.B.C. Contemporary Music', *Sunday Referee*, 15 May 1932; in BBC WAC, P132.

148 C. D. G. , 'Three Moderns: a Broadcast Concert', *Daily Telegraph*, 14 May 1932; in BBC WAC, P132.

149 Benser, *Wellesz*, 97.

## 9  Transition to the new régime, 1932–1933, 1933–1934

1 BBC WAC, R13/242/1: Departmental/Music Department (1928–32), 26 Oct. 1932.

2 A scribbled note written by Clark is the only indication of this sub-committee's existence; see BBC WAC, RCONT1: Alfred A. Kalmus, Music Publisher, file 1 (1929–31), 23 Nov. 1931.

3 BBC WAC, R13/242/1, 31 Oct. 1932.

4 Ibid., 10 Nov. 1932.

5 Ibid., 14 Nov. 1932. Beadle replaced Graves as Assistant Director of Programmes in September 1932, when the latter founded and became the head of the BBC Empire Service.

6 A copy of Beadle's memo includes handwritten annotations to this effect, made in November 1933 by Nicolls (then Director of Internal Administration), when the programme builder's work-loads were again under scrutiny.

7 BBC WAC, R13/242/1, 19 Nov. 1932. In order to avoid confusion between Hubert Foster Clark and Edward Clark, the former was usually referred to as Foster Clark. That convention will be followed here.

8 BBC WAC, R13/242/2: Departmental/Music Department (1933–4), 10 April 1933.

9 Ibid., 12 April 1933.

10 As listed in *The BBC Yearbook 1932*, 454.

11 BBC WAC, S60/5/3: Reith Diaries, iii/2, p. 209 [26 Jan. 1933].

12 BBC WAC, R6/46: Advisory Committees/Music Advisory Committee/General (1933–5), 11 Feb. 1933.

13 BBC WAC, R27/249/1: Music General/Music Programme Advisory Panel (1933–5), 24 Feb. 1933.

14 Ibid.

15 BBC WAC, R6/46, 15 March 1933.

16 BBC WAC, R27/249/1, 23 Feb. 1933.

17 Ibid.

18 The articles appeared in Ronald's weekly column, 'Mainly About Music': 'Putting Britain on the Musical Map', *News Chronicle*, 1 April 1933, 15(C–E); 'Do the Public Want Concerts?', *News Chronicle*, 29 April 1933, 9(C–E); 'A Few Words about the London Musical Festival', *News Chronicle*, 6 May 1933, 15(C–E).

19 BBC WAC, R6/46, 12 May 1933.

20 BBC WAC, R27/432: Music General/Public Concert Policy (1933–5), 13 May 1933.

21 BBC WAC, S60/5/3: Reith Diaries, iii/2, p. 234 [22 May 1933] and p. 236 [29 May 1933].

22 BBC WAC, R6/46, 1 June 1933.

23 Ibid., 26 May 1933.

24 BBC WAC, R13/242/2, 1 June 1933.

25 Ibid., 1 June 1933.

26 Ibid., 5 June 1933.

27 BBC WAC, R6/46, 26 May 1933.

28 BBC WAC, R13/242/2, 13 June 1933.

29 Ibid., 13 June 1933.

30 Ibid.

31 Ibid., 15 June 1933. Nicolls specified candidates in a separate memo; see ibid., 22 June 1933.

32  BBC WAC, S60/5/3: Reith Diaries, iii/2, p. 238 [13 June 1933].

33  BBC WAC, R13/242/2, 2 July 1933. Boult had previously expressed doubts about the viability of the panel, but eventually agreed to it; see ibid., 13 June 1933.

34  Minute of the Music Advisory Committee meeting of 29 June 1933, as recorded in a memo written by R. E. L. Wellington, BBC WAC, R27/249/2: Music General/Music Programme Advisory Panel (1936–40), 16 April 1937.

35  BBC WAC, R6/46, 20 June 1933.

36  BBC WAC, R27/249/1, 31 July 1933. Buesst was soon appointed as Assistant Music Director.

37  Ibid., 15 Aug. 1933.

38  Ibid., 17 Aug. 1933.

39  For details of the discussions, see ibid., 11 [i.e., 6 or 7], 15, 18 Sept., 20, 23 Nov. 1933.

40  Ibid., 7 Sept. 1933.

41  Ibid., 22 and 23 March 1934. The selection process was delayed while it was decided whether compositions by panel members could be broadcast. The question was finally resolved in March 1934, and letters of invitation sent to the candidates; see ibid., Dec. 1933–March 1934. Boult's serious apprehensions concerning Dale were given credence when the latter, misreading Reith's rather well-known name on the letter of invitation, addressed his letter of acceptance to 'W. W. Neill, Esq'.

42  Ibid., 18 April 1934.

43  Entries in the Reith diaries from 6 January 1933 reveal that he was contemplating the reorganization. On 8 March, he discussed his ideas with Carpendale and Goldsmith, and on 22 March he presented the plan to the Board of Governors. BBC WAC, S60/5/3: Reith Diaries, iii/2, Jan.–March 1933.

44  Briggs, ii: *The Golden Age*, 443. For further details, see Briggs, ii: 442–7.

45  Minute 1, Minutes of 26 Sept. 1933, in BBC WAC R3/11/1: D.G.'s Meeting/Minutes (1933–4). This basic structure remained intact for two years. In January 1935, Dawnay resigned for health reasons (Minute 14, Minutes of 30 Jan. 1935, BBC WAC, R1/1/4: Board of Governors/Minutes (1935)), though he didn't leave the BBC until October. At that time, Carpendale became Deputy Director-General, Nicolls took over as Controller (Administration) and Graves took Dawnay's place as Controller (Programmes), assisted by Eckersley and Gladstone Murray. The D.G. Meetings were discontinued, and the Control Board meetings reinstated.

46  Gorham, *Sound and Fury*, 53–4.

47  BBC WAC, R13/242/2, Sept. 1933.

48  Hely Hutchinson left the Corporation at the end of summer 1933 to become Professor of Music at the University of Birmingham.

49  BBC WAC, R13/242/2, 19 Oct. 1933.

50  Ibid., 31 Oct. 1933.

51  Ibid., 2 Nov. 1933.

52  Ibid., 8 Nov. 1933.

53  Ibid., 16, 17, 20, 21 and 22 Nov. 1933.

54  Ibid., 29 Nov. 1933.

55  Ibid., 14 Dec. 1933.

56  Ibid., 1 and 25 Jan. 1934.

57  Hubert J. Foss, 'Fair Treatment, Please, for Modern Music', *RT*, 36 (26 Aug. 1932): 479.

58  BBC WAC, R27/67: Music General/Contemporary Concerts (1929–36), 28 Oct. 1932.

59  Bernard van Dieren had been born in the Netherlands in 1884, but lived in London from 1909 until his death in 1936.

60  Programme details are listed in Table B.8 in Appendix B.

61  'A Page of Short Articles for the Music-Minded: the Rest of the Week', *RT*, 37 (16 Dec. 1932): 822. See also the press release in BBC WAC, R79/2/3: Contemporary Concerts, file 3 (1931–4), 14 Dec. 1932.

62  'B.B.C. Concerts of Contemporary Music – II' [programme listing, 23 Dec. 1932, London Regional, 9.0 pm], *RT*, 37 (16 Dec. 1932): 867.

63  S. G. [Scott Goddard], 'The B.B.C. Concert: Skilful Piano Playing', *Morning Post*, 24 Dec. 1932; in BBC WAC, P134: Press Cuttings/Programmes (1932).

64  'Modern Music: Schonberg the Obscure', *Glasgow Herald*, 24 Dec. 1932; in BBC WAC, P134.

65  No correspondence with the composer relating to the planning of this performance has been traced.

66  'B.B.C. Symphony Concert – XII' [programme listing, 8 Feb. 1933, Daventry National, 8.15 pm], *RT*, 38 (3 Feb. 1933): 278.

67  Constant Lambert, 'At This Week's Symphony Concert: a Constructive Anarchist', *RT*, 38 (3 Feb. 1933): 248.

68  Gordon Beckles, 'Arnold Schonberg's Musical "Strafe" To-night: How 100 British Bandsmen will Rend the Air', *Daily Herald*, 8 Feb. 1933; in BBC WAC, P488: Press Cuttings/Symphony Concerts (Jan.–March 1933). For other examples, see 'The Mystery Man of Music', *Glasgow Herald*, 6 Feb. 1933, and 'Thunder in Berlin', *Evening News*, 8 Feb. 1933; both in BBC WAC P488.

69  *BBC Symphony Concerts*, Queen's Hall, London, 8 Feb. 1933 [programme notes]; in BBC WAC, P488.

70  BBC WAC, RCONT1: Ernest Newman, Talks, file 1 (1931–6), 5 Jan. 1933.

71  H. S. , 'Did You Listen to Schonberg's Op. 31?', *Daily Herald*, 9 Feb. 1933; in BBC WAC, P488. The transcript does not survive at the BBC WAC.

72  Edwin Evans, 'Schonberg as Conductor: Complexities of his "Variations"', *Daily Mail*, 9 Feb. 1933; in BBC WAC, P488.

73  Richard Capell, 'Schonberg at Queen's Hall: Conducts his Own "Variations": Music in Torture Chamber', *Daily Telegraph*, 9 Feb. 1933; in BBC WAC, P488.

74  G. A. H. , 'Schonberg's New Work at the Queen's Hall', *Manchester Guardian*, 9 Feb. 1933; in BBC WAC, P488.

75 For more examples, see 'B.B.C. Symphony Concert: Herr Schonberg's Visit', *The Times*, 9 Feb. 1933, and E. N. [Ernest Newman], 'Schonberg's Variations', *The Sunday Times* 12 Feb. 1933; both in BBC WAC P488.

76 'Arnold Schönberg: Repercussions from a Recent Broadcast', *Music Teacher*, March 1933; in BBC WAC, P488.

77 BBC WAC, S60/5/3: Reith Diaries, iii/2, p. 211 (9 Feb. 1933).

78 C. L. [Constant Lambert], review in the *Sunday Referee*, 19 Feb. 1933; in BBC WAC, P425: Press Cuttings/Programmes: Music (1933).

79 G. A. H. , 'Alban Berg Suite', *Manchester Guardian*, 14 Feb. 1933; in BBC WAC, P425.

80 Eric Blom, 'Notable Music of the Week: the Tragedy of a Soldier', *RT*, 38 (3 March 1933): 517.

81 M. D. Calvocoressi, 'The Listener's Music: Alban Berg's "Wozzeck"', *The Listener*, 9 (8 March 1933): 376.

82 *BBC Symphony Concerts*, Queen's Hall, London, 8 March 1933 [programme notes]; in BBC WAC, P488.

83 BBC WAC, Scripts, Reel 132: Edwin Evans, 'Prefatory Talk to Symphony Concert', 8 March 1933.

84 Constant Lambert, review in the *Sunday Referee*, 12 March 1933; in BBC WAC, P488.

85 P. P. , '"Wozzeck" Fragments', *Evening Standard*, 9 March 1933; in BBC WAC, P488.

86 E. N. [Ernest Newman], 'The Week's Music: Sceneless Fragments of "Wozzeck"', *Sunday Times*, 12 March 1933; in BBC WAC, P488.

87 BBC WAC, 910: Anton Webern, file 1 (1929–33), 23 Sept. 1932.

88 Ibid., 27 Sept. and 7 Oct. 1932.

89 BBC WAC, R27/67, 28 Oct. 1932.

90 Webern had previously conducted the Krenek song cycle at the 1932 ISCM Festival in Vienna. Lewis Foreman suggests that Hedda Kux was unavailable and was replaced by Elsie Suddaby ('Webern, the BBC and the Berg Violin Concerto', 5). In fact, the 'Programmes as Broadcast' records confirm that Elsie Suddaby sang in the Mahler Symphony no. 4 performance on 23 April, and Hedda Kux sang the Krenek songs on 21 April as planned.

91 Programme details were given in a letter to Webern; see BBC WAC, 910: Anton Webern, file 1 (1929–33), 2 Dec. 1932.

92 BBC WAC, RCONT1: Edward Steuermann, Artists (1927–62), 2 March 1933. The pianist had been invited to participate in the 21 April concert the previous autumn; see ibid., 22 and 26 Nov., and 2 Dec. 1932. He was offered a fee of 60 guineas for the two concerts. Kolisch received 50 guineas; see BBC WAC R27/221/1: Music General/Music Department Meetings (Weekly)/Minutes (Jan. 1933–Jan. 1936), 9 March 1933.

93 BBC WAC, 910: Anton Webern, file 1 (1929–33), 2 March 1933. Contracts had been sent the previous December; see ibid., 2 and 14 Dec 1932.

94 Ibid., 10 and 14 March 1933.

95 Ibid., 3 April 1933.

96   Ibid., 7 and 11 April 1933.

97   Letter from Webern to Clark, 11 April 1933, in Edward Clark Letters, *GB-Lbl* Add.ms.52257, fol. 174. This letter is the first in which Webern used the familiar form of address in extant correspondence to Clark.

98   Press release in BBC WAC, R79/2/3: Contemporary Concerts, file 3 (1931–4), 16 Feb. 1933.

99   'B.B.C. Concerts of Contemporary Music – VI' [programme notes, 21 April 1933, London Regional, 9.00 pm], *RT*, 39 (14 April 1933): 116.

100  'Sunday Orchestral Concert – 23' [programme notes, 23 April 1933, London Regional, 9.05 pm], *RT*, 39 (21 April 1933): 146.

101  Edwin Evans, ' "Advanced" Music: Alban Berg's Concerto Broadcast', *Daily Mail*, 22 April 1933; in BBC WAC, P425.

102  E. N. [Ernest Newman], 'B.B.C. Contemporary Music', *Sunday Times*, 23 April 1933; in BBC WAC, P425.

103  W. McN. [William McNaught], 'Why, Oh Why? Composers of High Culture Who Write Distorted Stuff', *Evening News*, 22 April 1933; in BBC WAC, P425.

104  Letter from Webern to Schoenberg, 3 May 1933, quoted in Moldenhauer, *Webern*, 396–7.

105  Letter from Berg to Clark, 13 May 1933, as translated in Chadwick, 'Berg and the BBC', *British Library Journal*, 11 (1985): 49. The original letter survives in Edward Clark Letters, *GB-Lbl* Add.ms.52256, fol. 45; for a transcription of the original, see Chadwick, 48.

106  C. Whitaker-Wilson, 'Symphony *Versus* Cacophony', *RT*, 39 (21 April 1933): 138.

107  C. Henry Warren, 'And Still the Battle Goes On!', *RT*, 39 (28 April 1933): 198.

108  For correspondence relating to the 15 January 1933 concert, see BBC WAC, RCONT1: Roberto Gerhard, Artists (1932–52), 14 Dec.–5 Jan. 1933. Although the Gerhard songs were included in the *Radio Times* daily programme listing (*RT*, 38 (6 Jan. 1933): 41), the 'Programmes as Broadcast' records confirm that they were not performed.

109  BBC WAC, RCONT1: Egon Wellesz, Composer (1933–51), 1 March 1933. Other correspondence relating to the submitted scores is dated 6 and 14 March 1933.

110  BBC WAC, R29/157: Orchestra General/Contemporary Concerts (1929–39), 16 Aug. 1933.

111  Programme details are listed in Table B.9 in Appendix B.

112  The attention given to Britten in both the 1932–3 and 1933–4 BBC Concerts of Contemporary Music was remarkable, considering that he was only beginning to establish his professional reputation. After the *Sinfonietta* performance on 29 June 1934, the composer wrote to Clark: 'It was very good of you to take such trouble over my "Sinfonietta" the other night. It was by far the best performance it has ever had, and it has done me a[lot] of good in many ways!' (Letter from Britten to Clark, 12 July 1934, in Edward Clark Letters, *GB-Lbl* Add.ms.52256, fol. 81. The quotation from Britten's letter is © copyright the Trustees of the Britten–Pears Foundation, and may not be

further reproduced without their written permission.)

113 The Wellesz works were identified only by the titles shown here. The 'Tanzstück' may refer to one of the pieces by that name in his op. 42. The 'Pastorale' may be one of the *Idyllen*, op. 21.

114 'BBC Chamber Concert – IV' [programme notes, 1 Dec. 1933, London Regional, 9.00 pm], *RT*, 41 (24 Nov. 1933): 611. Ernst Schoen, 'Notable Music of the Week: Music from Austria', *RT*, 41 (24 Nov. 1933): 560.

115 See 'B.B.C. Chamber Concert', *The Observer*, 3 Dec. 1933, and 'Viennese Quartet, *Daily Mail*, 2 Dec. 1933; both in BBC WAC, P425.

116 Postcard from Schoenberg to Clark, 30 May 1933, in Edward Clark Letters, *GB-Lbl* Add.ms.52257, fol. 71. For details about Schoenberg's emigration from Germany in May 1933 and his subsequent renewal of interest in Jewish issues, see Stuckenschmidt, *Schoenberg*, 366–70.

117 No further correspondence with Schoenberg concerning the November 1933 broadcasts survives.

118 BBC WAC, R29/157, 16 Aug. 1933.

119 'The Symphonies Begin', *RT*, 41 (6 Oct. 1933): 11.

120 BBC WAC, RCONT1: Edward Steuermann, Artists (1927–62), 13 Oct. 1933.

121 In a memo entitled 'Foreign Artists' Engagements' (BBC WAC, RCONT1: Edward Steuermann, Artists (1927–62), 3 Oct. 1933), Wright requested that Boult approve plans to invite continental artists, including Steuermann, to participate in music broadcasts. This addition to programme planning procedure was apparently instigated to limit the number of foreign artists broadcasting in the months following the Music Advisory Committee disputes.

122 'Both Sides of the Microphone: Eccentric Pierrot', *RT*, 41 (10 Nov. 1933): 396. Cecil Gray, 'Notable Music of the Week: Schönberg's 'Pierrot Lunaire'", *RT*, 41 (17 Nov. 1933): 481.

123 Press release in BBC WAC, R79/2/3, 15 Nov. 1933.

124 Notice in the *Manchester Guardian*, 1 Nov. 1933; in BBC WAC, P489: Press Cuttings/Symphony Concerts (1933).

125 Press release in BBC WAC, R79/2/3, 22 Nov. 1933. Steuermann also played Schoenberg's Piano Pieces, op. 19. The programme planned for 29 November was also altered: Schoenberg's arrangement of the Handel *Concerto grosso* was omitted from the concert altogether; instead, a Mendelssohn overture, Beethoven's Piano Concerto no. 1, with Cortot, and Bruckner's Symphony no. 9 were presented.

126 Stuckenschmidt, *Schoenberg*, 372.

127 BBC WAC, RCONT1: Edward Steuermann, Artists (1927–62), 9 Nov. 1933.

128 '"Contemporary" Music: a B.B.C. Concert', *The Times*, 25 Nov. 1933; in BBC WAC, P425.

129 Edwin Evans, 'Elusive Music: Schonberg Programme at B.B.C. Concert', *Daily Mail*, 25 Nov. 1933; in BBC WAC, P425.

130 R. C. [Richard Capell], 'Esotericism for the Million: the Generosity of the B.B.C.', *Daily Telegraph*, 25 Nov. 1933; in BBC WAC, P425.

131 A performance of *Pelleas und Melisande*, op. 5, was planned for the BBC Symphony Concert on 22 January 1936, but the performance was postponed due to the death of George V, and was rescheduled as a studio broadcast. Although Schoenberg works were not presented at BBC Symphony Orchestra concerts given in London between 1933 and 1939, they were included in programmes the orchestra presented on tour. During the European tour of spring 1936, the orchestra, under Boult, gave the Viennese première of Schoenberg's Variations for Orchestra, op. 31, on 23 April.

132 In a list of 'First Performances by the BBC Symphony Orchestra, 22 October 1930–22 October 1980', Kenyon incorrectly gives the date of this concert as 10 March 1934 and the conductor as Scherchen (Kenyon, *The BBC Symphony Orchestra*, 452). The 'Programmes as Broadcast' records confirm 10 February and Heger as conductor.

133 BBC WAC, RCONT1: Ružena Herlingerova, Artists, file 1 (1930–49), 20 Oct. 1933.

134 Ibid., 28 Dec. 1933.

135 Ibid., 10 and 12 April 1934.

136 BBC WAC R27/221/1, 28 June 1934.

137 BBC WAC, 910: Anton Webern, file 1 (1929–33), 27 Aug. 1933.

138 Ibid., 11 Sept. 1933.

139 Ibid., 4 Oct. 1933.

140 Ibid., 11 Oct. 1933.

141 Ibid., 9, 12, 15 and 27 Jan., 8 and 28 Feb. and 2 March 1934.

142 Ibid., 27 March 1934. For details about Webern's financial difficulties in spring 1934, see Moldenhauer, *Webern*, 407–16.

143 BBC WAC, 910: Anton Webern, file 2 (1934–9), 10 April 1934.

144 Postcard from Webern to Clark, 17 April 1934, in Edward Clark Letters, *GB-Lbl* Add.ms.52257, fols. 175–6.

145 BBC WAC, R27/326/1: Music General/Opera/General Memos, file 1 (1929–34), 28 July 1930.

146 Ibid., 3 May 1932.

147 The first British broadcast performance of Berg's Three Fragments from *Wozzeck* was given on 13 May 1932, and the first British public performance, also broadcast, was presented on 8 March 1933.

148 BBC WAC, R27/326/1, 2 Jan. 1933.

149 BBC WAC, RCONT1: Alban Berg, Composer (1933–62), 9 Aug. 1933. BBC WAC, RCONT1: Universal Music Agencies/Music Publishers, file 1 (1933–62), 11 Aug. 1933.

150 BBC WAC, RCONT1: Alban Berg, Composer (1933–62), 24 Aug. 1933. Reich sent the pamphlet on 1 September 1933. Over the following weeks, Berg and Wright corresponded about the translation and the casting of the leading roles; see ibid., 31 Aug. and 19 Sept. 1933.

151 Ibid., 25 Oct. 1933.

152 Ibid.

153 Ibid., 12, 16 Aug., undated and 17 Aug. 1933.

154  BBC WAC, R13/242/2, 19 Oct. 1933.

155  BBC WAC, RCONT1: Alban Berg, Composer (1933–62), 12 Dec. 1933.

156  BBC WAC, R27/405/1: Music General/Opera Wozzeck, file 1 (1934–5), 22 Dec. 1933.

157  Ibid., 28 Dec. 1933.

158  Surviving documentation concerning the engagement of the artists and understudies and the rehearsal arrangements are in BBC WAC, R27/405/1.

159  The 14 March 1934 performance of *Wozzeck* was recorded. Parts of this recording survive and may be accessed at the National Sound Archive in the British Library, London.

160  'Both Sides of the Microphone', *RT*, 42 (2 March 1934): 617.

161  The original production actually took place in Berlin.

162  Edwin Evans, '"Wozzeck", the Under-Dog', *RT*, 42 (9 March 1934): 712–13.

163  M. D. Calvocoressi, 'Alban Berg's "Wozzeck"', *The Listener*, 11 (14 March 1934): 440–2.

164  The transcript of Heward's talk has not been traced.

165  BBC WAC, R34/600/5: Policy/Programme Board/Minutes, file 5 (1933), 8 March 1934.

166  'B.B.C. Performance of "Wozzeck": Alban Berg's Opera', *Daily Telegraph*, 1 March 1934; in BBC WAC, P490: Press Cuttings/Symphony Concerts (1934).

167  S. R. Nelson, 'Prepare to Hear "Wozzeck"', *Era*, 7 March 1934; in BBC WAC, P490.

168  See BBC WAC, P490.

169  J. A. Forsyth, '"Wozzeck" is Certainly a Sensation', *The Star*, 15 March 1934; in BBC WAC, P490.

170  Richard Capell, 'Alban Berg's "Wozzeck": First Performance in England: a Modernist Orgy', *Daily Telegraph*, 15 March 1934; in BBC WAC, P490.

171  Edwin Evans, ''Alban Berg's "Wozzeck": Last Night's Performance: Audience Thrilled', *Daily Mail*, 15 March 1934; in BBC WAC, P490.

172  E. B. [Eric Blom], '"Wozzeck" Produced by the B.B.C.: Alban Berg's Great Modern Opera: Features of an Impressive Concert Version', *Birmingham Post*, 15 March 1934; in BBC WAC, P490.

173  Constant Lambert, 'Matters Musical: "Wozzeck" at Last!', *Sunday Referee*, 18 March 1934; in BBC WAC, P490.

174  'The Case of "Wozzeck"', *Daily Telegraph*, 17 March 1934; in BBC WAC, P490.

175  Constant Lambert, 'Matters Musical: "Wozzeck" at Last!', *Sunday Referee*, 18 March 1934; in BBC WAC, P490.

176  BBC WAC R27/221/1, 15 March 1934.

177  BBC WAC, R27/405/1, 16 and 27 March 1934.

178  Ibid., 16 March 1934.

179  Letter from Berg to Boult, 15 March 1934, quoted in translation in Moore, ed., *Music and Friends*, 113–14. A BBC translation of this letter was circulated to staff who were involved with the concert (BBC WAC, RCONT1: Alban Berg, Composer (1933–62), 15 and 23 March 1934).

180  Letter from Boult to Berg, 26 March 1934, in BBC WAC, RCONT1: Alban

Berg, Composer (1933–62); for a full transcription, see Chadwick, 'Berg and the BBC', 50–1.

181  BBC WAC, RCONT1: Universal Music Agencies/Music Publishers, file 1 (1933–62), 5 April 1934.

182  Letter from Berg to Clark, 22 March 1934, as translated in Chadwick, 'Berg and the BBC', 50. The original letter survives in BBC WAC, RCONT1: Alban Berg, Composer (1933–62); a transcription of the original text may be found in Chadwick, 50.

183  BBC WAC, R27/405/1, 13 April 1934.

184  Ibid., 18 April 1934.

185  'The B.B.C. Drops a Bomb: Storm over an Opera', *Sunday Chronicle*, 1 April 1934; in BBC WAC, P490.

186  BBC WAC, R27/405/1, 18 April 1934.

187  BBC WAC, RCONT1: Alban Berg, Composer (1933–62), 14 June 1934.

188  Ibid., 4 July 1934.

189  BBC WAC, R27/405/1, 26 June 1934.

190  BBC WAC, RCONT1: Universal Music Agencies/Copyright, file 1 (1933–62), 5 July 1934.

191  BBC WAC, R27/405/1, 14 Aug. 1934.

192  BBC WAC, RCONT1: Alban Berg, Composer (1933–62), 23 Aug. 1934.

193  Letter from Berg to Wright, 28 Aug. 1934, as translated in Chadwick, 'Berg and the BBC', 52. The original letter survives in BBC WAC, RCONT1: Alban Berg, Composer (1933–62); a transcription of the original text may be found in Chadwick, 51–2.

194  Surviving papers may be found in BBC WAC, R27/405/1.

195  Ibid., 20 Dec. 1934.

196  Ibid., 1 Feb. 1935.

197  BBC WAC, RCONT1: Alfred A. Kalmus, Music Publishers, file 2 (1932–9), 31 Jan. 1935.

198  BBC WAC, R27/250/1: Music General/Music Programme Advisory Panel/Minutes (Oct. 1934–June 1936), 12 Feb. 1935.

199  The letter to Kalmus survives in BBC WAC, R27/405/1, 14 Feb. 1935.

200  Letter from Berg to Boult, 19 Feb. 1935, as translated in Chadwick, 'Berg and the BBC', 53–4. The original letter survives in BBC WAC, RCONT1: Alban Berg, Composer (1933–62); a transcription of the original may be found in Chadwick, 52–3.

201  BBC WAC, RCONT1: Alban Berg, Composer (1933–62), 27 Feb. 1935; for a full transcription of this letter, see Chadwick, 'Berg and the BBC', 54–5.

202  Surviving memos about other possibilities are in BBC WAC, R27/405/1. See also Chadwick, 'Berg and the BBC', 55–8.

## 10  Policies and politics, 1934–1935, 1935–1936

1  The only change occurred in September 1934, when Foster Clark was appointed Music Director of the Birmingham station. It is not clear when his

successor, St George Phillips, joined the staff, although he was working as a music programme builder by spring 1935. No Left Staff file or personnel card survives at the BBC WAC, and he was not mentioned in the Staff Entries minutes of the D.G.'s meetings, where appointments were generally noted.

2  BBC WAC, R13/242/3: Departmental/Music Department (1935–9), 7 Feb. 1935.

3  Ibid., 11 Feb. 1935.

4  Ibid., undated ('Suggested Organisation and Allocation of Duties of Music Department Creative Side').

5  Ibid., 8 March 1935.

6  Ibid., 21 March 1935.

7  Ibid., 22 March 1935. A chart showing the proposed structure was also prepared, probably by Wright; see ibid., undated.

8  Ibid., 12 April 1935.

9  Ibid., 21, 23 May, 17, 26 June 1935. Much discussion centred on whether Clark's request for an assistant was justified, which involved detailed scrutiny of his responsibilities and duties.

10  Ibid., 26 June 1935.

11  Ibid., undated and 4 July 1935.

12  BBC WAC, R13/242/2: Departmental/Music Department (1933–4), 15 June 1933.

13  BBC WAC, R13/242/3, 14 March 1935.

14  Ibid., 26 Aug. 1935.

15  Ibid., 2 Sept. 1935.

16  Ibid., 3 Sept. 1935.

17  Ibid., 5 Sept. 1935. In view of his approaching departure from the BBC, Dawnay relegated the matter to Graves, his successor as Controller (Programmes).

18  Ibid., 10 Sept. 1935; also BBC WAC, R3/11/2: D.G.'s Meeting/Minutes (1935), 10 Sept. 1935.

19  BBC WAC, R1/1/4: Board of Governors/Minutes (1935), 25 Sept. 1935.

20  BBC WAC, R6/47/1: Advisory Committees/Music Advisory Committee/ Minutes and Agendas (1933–7), 10 Oct. 1935.

21  BBC WAC, R1/1/4, 13 Nov. 1935. The minutes did not specify why the committee objected to Bliss's candidacy.

22  BBC WAC, R6/47/1, 13 Feb. 1936.

23  BBC WAC, S60/5/4: Reith Diaries, iv/3, p. 193B ([24] Feb. 1936).

24  Ibid., p. 196A ([3] March 1936).

25  Ibid., p. 196B ([4] March 1936).

26  BBC WAC, R1/1/5: Board of Governors/Minutes (1936–7), 11 March 1936.

27  BBC WAC, S60/5/4: Reith Diaries, iv/3, p. 199A, ([12] March 1936).

28  BBC WAC, R1/1/5, 25 March 1936.

29  Ibid., 29 April 1936.

30  Although Kenyon states that Thatcher took up his appointment on

1 October 1936 (*The BBC Symphony Orchestra*, 130), Thatcher's personnel file at the BBC WAC (L1/415) indicates that he did not officially begin until 11 January 1937; he did, however, attend some Music Department meetings during the preceding autumn. He retained his position until December 1943.

31  Boult, *My Own Trumpet*, 100.

32  See minutes dating from October 1934 to June 1936, in BBC WAC, R27/250/1: Music General/Music Programme Advisory Panel Minutes (1934–6).

33  The Blattnerphone system was used by the BBC from 1931 for recording rehearsals and broadcasts. This early recording method stored sound as electric currents on steel tape; see 'Recording Apparatus', *The BBC Yearbook 1932*, 367–71.

34  BBC WAC, R27/249/1: Music General/Music Programme Advisory Panel (1933–5), 11 July 1934.

35  The rating system was implemented during summer 1933; see minute 7, Minutes of 29 June 1933, in BBC WAC R27/221/1: Music General/Music Department Meetings (Weekly)/Minutes (Jan. 1933–Jan. 1936).

36  BBC WAC, R27/250/1, 16 Oct. and 13 Nov. 1934.

37  See ibid., 23 July and 22 Oct. 1935.

38  The earliest surviving minutes of the Music Programme Advisory Panel date from 9 October 1934, but Mase prepared a report of the first meeting; see BBC WAC, R27/249/1, 25 April 1934.

39  Ibid., 16 Aug. 1934.

40  Ibid., 17 Aug. and 5 Sept. 1934.

41  Ibid., 5 Sept. 1934.

42  Ibid., 10 Sept. 1934.

43  Ibid., 13 Sept. 1934. For Dawnay's reply, see ibid., 14 Sept. 1934.

44  Ibid., 10 April 1935.

45  BBC WAC, R27/249/2: Music General/Music Programme Advisory Panel (1936–40), 1 April 1937.

46  Ibid., 16 April 1937.

47  BBC WAC, R6/47/1, 7 June 1934. Few papers relating to the Concerts Committee's activities survive. One extant page from the 24 May 1934 minutes lists the committee members: Beadle (Entertainment Executive and committee Chairman), Boult (Music Director), Mase (Music Executive), Thompson (Concerts Manager), P. E. Cruttwell (Programme Finance), Miss L. E. Lord (Assistant, Supplementary Publications) and G. H. Dunbar (Business Manager, Publications Department) (BBC WAC, R29/157: Orchestra General/Contemporary Concerts (1929–39)).

48  The Concerts Committee's report is no longer extant. Both the committee's recommendations and the Music Advisory Committee's responses to them are included in the latter committee's minutes; see BBC WAC, R6/47/1, 7 June 1934, Minute 4.

49  Ibid.

50  BBC WAC, R6/47/1, 4 Oct. 1934.

51  BBC WAC, R27/432: Music General/Public Concert Policy (1933–5), 10 Oct. 1934.

52  Ibid., [20 Nov. 1934].

53  The minutes of the 14 December 1934 meeting of the Music Advisory Committee do not survive, but Eckersley reported on it in a detailed memo to Reith; see BBC WAC, R27/432, 18 Dec. 1934.

54  Boult's initial draft statements concerning the foreign artists and box office issues survive in BBC WAC, R27/432, 14 and 16 Dec. 1934.

55  BBC WAC, R6/47/1, 14 Feb. 1935. The final version of the foreign artists statement survives in BBC WAC, R6/48/1: Advisory Committees/Music Advisory Committee/Papers (1935–40), [14 Feb. 1935].

56  BBC WAC R6/47/1, 6 June 1935, Minute 5. Interestingly, the Board of Governors had found the statement unobjectionable; see BBC WAC, R1/1/4, 16 Jan. 1935, Minute 4.

57  BBC WAC, R27/432, 31 Jan. 1935.

58  Ibid., 7 Feb. 1935.

59  Ibid., 27 Feb. 1935.

60  Ibid., 19 Feb. 1935.

61  BBC WAC, R6/47/1, 6 June 1935.

62  BBC WAC, S60/5/4: Reith Diaries, iv/2, p. 123 [6 June 1935].

63  BBC WAC, R6/47/1, 7 June 1934, Minute 4.

64  BBC WAC, R27/100: Music General/Five-Year Plan (1934–5), 18 Oct. 1934. At a Programme Board meeting, the Controller (Programmes), Dawnay, asked Eckersley to prepare a report on this with Boult and Beadle; see BBC WAC, R34/600/6: Policy/Programme Board Minutes (1934), 4 Oct. 1934.

65  The number of BBC Symphony Concerts was reduced to twelve in 1934–5 as a result of poor attendance during the previous season. The drop in audience size was attributed to the declining economic climate. The BBC briefly negotiated with Beecham and the Royal Philharmonic Society during spring 1934 about reducing both organizations' public performances and arranging for Beecham and Boult to conduct in both series. The conducting arrangements fell through. For further details, see BBC WAC, R3/11/1: D.G.'s Meeting/Minutes (1933–4), 14 Nov. 1933–27 March 1934.

66  BBC WAC, R27/100, 15 Nov. 1934.

67  Ibid., 5 Nov. 1934.

68  Beadle's preliminary version of the report does not survive. Eckersley's first draft was prepared in early December; see BBC WAC, R27/100, 10 Dec. 1934. Both Boult's and Wellington's comments on it also survive; see ibid., 21, 24 and 28 Dec. 1934. Eckersley's second draft was prepared later in the month; see ibid., 31 Dec. 1934.

69  Ibid., 3 Jan. 1935. Dawnay became seriously ill around this time, and Murray took over his work, using the title Acting Controller (Programmes), in

addition to continuing his own responsibilities as Director of Information and Publications.

70 BBC WAC, R1/1/4, 16 Jan. 1935.

71 BBC WAC, R27/100, 17 Jan. 1935.

72 BBC WAC, R6/48/1, [14 Feb. 1935].

73 BBC WAC, R6/47/1, 14 Feb. 1935.

74 The first public examination took place in 1925 by the Crawford Committee.

75 Paragraph 1, 'Report of the Broadcasting Committee, 1935', Cmd. 5091 (Feb. 1936), in BBC WAC, R4/7/12: Ullswater Committee 1935/Report (Oct. 1935–March 1936).

76 Paragraph 2, ibid.

77 For detailed discussion about the Ullswater Committee, its review and its report, see Briggs, ii: *The Golden Age*, 476ff.

78 Paper 16 in BBC WAC, R4/7/8/1: Ullswater Committee 1935/Other Written Evidence/Papers 1–30.

79 In 1935, Clement Attlee was the leader of the Labour Party in the House of Commons; a decade later, he became Prime Minister (1945–51).

80 BBC WAC, S60/5/4: Reith Diaries, iv/2, p. 126 [19 June 1935].

81 Ibid., p. 127 [20 June 1935].

82 Paper 83 in BBC WAC, R4/7/8/5: Ullswater Committee 1935/Other Written Evidence/Papers 71–90.

83 For an example, see Paper 105, 'Memorandum Submitted by Sir Hamilton Harty 10th July 1935', in BBC WAC, R4/7/8/6: Ullswater Committee 1935/Other Written Evidence/Papers 91–110.

84 Paper 90 in BBC WAC, R4/7/8/5: Ullswater Committee 1935/Other Written Evidence/Papers 71–90.

85 BBC WAC, S60/5/4: Reith Diaries, iv/2, p. 131 (3 and 4 July 1935).

86 BBC WAC, R27/219: Music General/Music and Music Department (1931–43), [July] 1935.

87 When disagreement between the BBC and its external music advisors turned into a public rift during the Ullswater proceedings, the central administrators were tempted to disband the committee altogether; however, Reith considered such a move to be inadvisable while the Ullswater Committee was preparing its recommendations. A larger, more diversified Music Advisory Committee was convened after the Ullswater Report was published. For further details, see: Minute 31 from the Minutes of the Board of Governors meeting on 26 February 1936, in BBC WAC R1/1/5; and Minute 1 of the Minutes of the Music Advisory Committee meeting on 21 May 1936, in BBC WAC, R6/47/1.

88 Paragraph 8, 'Report of the Broadcasting Committee, 1935', Cmd. 5091 (Feb. 1936), in BBC WAC, R4/7/12: Ullswater Committee 1935/Report (Oct. 1935–March 1936).

89 Paragraph 7, ibid.

90 Paragraph 96, ibid.

 91  Paragraph 97, ibid.

 92  BBC WAC, R29/157, 25 May 1934.

 93  This refers to the annual ISCM Festival.

 94  BBC WAC, R29/157, 21 July 1934.

 95  Ibid., 5 June 1934. The new BBC studio at Maida Vale, London, came into use for orchestral studio broadcasts in autumn 1934.

 96  Ibid., 25 July 1934.

 97  Ibid., 18 Sept. 1934.

 98  Ibid.

 99  Ibid., 22 Sept. 1934.

100  Programme details are listed in Table B.10 in Appendix B.

101  BBC WAC, R79/2/4: Contemporary Concerts, file 4 (1935–7), 10 April 1935.

102  Plans for this concert were made in July, when Herlinger asked to broadcast on her next visit to London. The BBC negotiated dates and fees, and the contract was finalized on 21 September (BBC WAC, RCONT1: Ružena Herlingerova, Artists, file 1 (1930–49), 12 July and 21 Sept. 1934).

103  Edwin Evans, 'Notable Music of the Week: the Songs of Gurra', *RT*, 46 (8 March 1935): 12.

104  L. S. Peppercorn, 'Notable Music of the Week: Modern Music from Vienna, Venice, and London: Revolutionary Music', *RT*, 46 (15 March 1935): 14–15.

105  BBC WAC, RCONT1: Alban Berg, Composer (1933–62), 11 Sept. 1934. The letter was written originally in English, and a German translation was sent to the composer. The Concerts Manager wrote to Berg to confirm this news; see ibid., 17 Sept. 1934.

106  BBC WAC, RCONT1: Alban Berg, Composer (1933–62), 13 Nov. 1934. Wright sought guidance since the work had not yet been performed; the first performance was given in Berlin on 30 November 1934, conducted by Erich Kleiber.

107  Ibid., 20 Nov. 1934. The original text of the quotation: 'hoher, beweglicher Sopran'.

108  Letter from Berg to Boult, 19 Feb. 1935, in BBC WAC, RCONT1: Alban Berg, Composer (1933–62); for a transcription and translation of this letter, see Chadwick, 'Berg and the BBC', 52–4.

109  BBC WAC, RCONT1: Alban Berg, Composer (1933–62), 27 Feb. 1935; for a full transcription of this letter, see Chadwick, 'Berg and the BBC', 54–5.

110  Letter from Berg to Boult, 5 March 1935, in Edward Clark Letters, *GB-Lbl* Add.ms.52256, fols. 47–8; for a transcription and translation of this letter, see Chadwick, 'Berg and the BBC', 55–7.

111  'Another Season of Broadcast Music: a First Glance at the Plans for 1934–5', *RT*, 45 (12 Oct. 1934): 90–91.

112  'Both Sides of the Microphone: Novelty Night', *RT*, 46 (8 March 1935): 4.

113  Scott Goddard, 'Notable Music of the Week: Modern Music from Vienna, Venice, and London: an Erotic Opera', *RT*, 46 (15 March 1935): 14.

114  M. D. Calvocoressi, 'The Listener's Music: Alban Berg and the Opera', *The Listener*, 13 (20 March 1935): 474.

115 Edwin Evans, 'New Opera Music by B.B.C. Orchestra: Heifetz's Fine Playing', *Daily Mail*, 21 March 1935; in BBC WAC, P492: Press Cuttings/Symphony Concerts (1935).

116 'The B.B.C. Orchestra: Malipiero and Berg', *The Times*, 21 March 1935; in BBC WAC, P492.

117 BBC WAC, RCONT1: Alban Berg, Composer (1933–62), 3 April 1935.

118 Letter from Berg to Boult, 15 April 1935, as translated in Chadwick, 'Berg and the BBC', 58. The original letter survives in BBC WAC, RCONT1: Alban Berg, Composer (1933–62); a transcription of the original may be found in Chadwick, 57–8.

119 BBC WAC, RCONT1: Alban Berg, Composer (1933–62), 17 April 1935.

120 The idea of Clark settling Webern's taxes is ironic, to say the least, since Clark had a history of problems relating to his own taxes.

121 Letter from Webern to Clark, 28 Feb. 1935, in Edward Clark Letters, *GB-Lbl* Add.ms.52257, fols. 177–8.

122 BBC WAC, 910: Anton Webern, file 2 (1934–9), 9 March 1935. Webern also wrote to Clark on 16 March, asking that he intercede in this matter; ibid., 16 March 1935.

123 Ibid., 20 March 1935. In fact, the BBC had already issued a new contract for 45 guineas (£47.50.–) on 15 March; ibid., 15 March 1935.

124 Ibid., 22 March 1935.

125 Ibid., 26 March 1935.

126 Ibid., 10 April 1935.

127 Webern conducted two movements of this version at a contemporary concert in April 1933, but that performance was not open to the public.

128 Ralph Hill, 'B.B.C. Symphony Concerts', *RT*, 49 (18 Oct. 1935): 13.

129 'Notes on the Week's Programmes: From the "Lyric Suite" of Alban Berg', *The Listener*, 14 (16 Oct. 1935): 687.

130 BBC WAC, Scripts, Reel 363: Ernest Newman, 'Symp Concrt [*sic*]', 23 Oct. 1935. The surviving transcript is written in a personal shorthand devised by the author.

131 E. N. [Ernest Newman], 'The Week's Music: The B.B.C. Concert', *Sunday Times*, 27 Oct. 1935; in BBC WAC, P493: Press Cuttings/Symphony Concerts (1935–6).

132 'B.B.C. Symphony Concert: Bach, Berg, and Brahms', *The Times*, 24 Oct. 1935; in BBC WAC, P493.

133 Programme details are listed in Table B.11 in Appendix B. No significant evidence about the planning of this series has been traced.

134 BBC WAC, RCONT1: Ernst Krenek, Artist (1935–62), 16 May 1935.

135 Ibid., 15 Sept. 1935.

136 Ibid., 27 Sept. 1935.

137 Ibid., 28 Sept. 1935. Krenek and Glatz had given the first performance of Adorno's op. 3 songs in Vienna.

138 Ibid., 5 Oct. 1935. On 16 October, the BBC sent Krenek a contract, at a fee of 35 guineas.

139 'The BBC Concerts of Contemporary Music – I' [programme notes, 1 Nov. 1935, National, 10.20 pm], *RT*, 49 (25 Oct. 1935): 72.

140 BBC WAC, RCONT1: Ernst Krenek, Artist (1935–62), 7 Dec. 1935. The original text of the quoted phrase was 'in unserem Kreis'.

141 'Notes on the Week's Programmes: Ernst Krenek', *The Listener*, 14 (23 Oct. 1935): 735–6.

142 W. McN. [William McNaught], 'Music Too Glum to be Entertaining: Relieved by a Gracious Singer', *Evening News*, 2 Nov. 1935; in BBC WAC, P139: Press Cuttings/Programmes (1935).

143 J. A. W. [J. A. Westrup], 'Ernst Krenek in London: B.B.C. Contemporary Music Concert', *Daily Telegraph*, 2 Nov. 1935; in BBC WAC, P139.

144 E. N. [Ernest Newman], 'The Week's Music: Krenek', *Sunday Times*, 3 Nov. 1935; in BBC WAC, P139.

145 Krenek himself returned to the BBC to present the first British performance of his Piano Concerto no. 2 on 8 April 1938.

146 The pianist was not named in the programme listing or in the 'Programmes as Broadcast' records.

147 Koffler, a Polish composer, had studied with Schoenberg between 1920 and 1924. His String Trio (1929) was given in Oxford during the 1931 ISCM Festival, but the performance was not broadcast.

148 Edwin Evans, 'Giant Symphonic Poem', *RT*, 50 (17 Jan. 1936): 13.

149 'The Boyd Neel String Orchestra' [programme notes, 1 Feb. 1936, Regional, 8.30 pm], *RT*, 50 (24 Jan. 1936): 43.

150 Benser, *Wellesz*, 100.

151 BBC WAC, RCONT1: Egon Wellesz, Composer, file 1a (1933–51), 25 Oct. 1935.

152 Ibid., 4 April 1934.

153 Ibid., 2 May 1934.

154 Ibid., 8 June 1934.

155 Extracts of Wellesz's letter to Mrs Hamilton, dated 1 June 1934, survive in ibid.

156 Ibid., 4 June 1934.

157 BBC WAC, R27/635: Music General/Music Reports (1928–54), Egon Wellesz, 14 Sept. 1932.

158 BBC WAC, RCONT1: Egon Wellesz, Composer, file 1a (1933–51), 17 Aug. 1934.

159 Ibid., 12 Sept. 1934.

160 Ibid.

161 Ibid., 7 Nov. 1934.

162 Ibid., 13 Nov. 1934.

163 'The B.B.C. Orchestra' [programme notes, 25 May 1936, National, 10.15 pm], *RT*, 51 (22 May 1936): 26.

164 M. D. C. [M. D. Calvocoressi], 'Notes on the Week's Programmes: the Wellesz Piano Concerto', *The Listener*, 15 (20 May 1936): 989–90.

165  A surviving recording of this performance is commercially available: *Webern Conducts Berg Violin Concerto*, compact disc SBT 1004, Continuum Records, 1991.

166  Correspondence between Webern and the BBC and other papers concerning the May 1936 concerts survive in BBC WAC, 910: Anton Webern, file 2 (1934–9), Oct. 1935–May 1936. The letters have been transcribed, translated and discussed in Chadwick, 'The Berg Violin Concerto in London', 330–45. The performances are also discussed in Foreman, 'Webern, the BBC and the Berg Violin Concerto', 7–9. The notes accompanying the commercial recording include another Foreman essay, 'Webern Conducts for the BBC 1929–1936', as well as an essay by Louis Krasner, 'About Webern as Conductor', in which the violinist describes his memories of the Barcelona première and the BBC performance (liner notes, compact disc SBT 1004, Continuum Records, 1991).

167  Letter from Webern to Clark, 6 Dec. 1935, as translated in Chadwick, 'The Berg Violin Concerto in London', 332. The original letter survives in BBC WAC, 910: Anton Webern, file 2 (1934–9); a transcription of excerpts from the original may be found in Chadwick, 332.

168  BBC WAC, RCONT1: Alban Berg, Composer (1933–62), 24 Dec. 1935.

169  BBC WAC, 910: Anton Webern, file 2 (1934–9), 31 Dec. 1935.

170  Krasner, 'About Webern as Conductor', 5. Webern was supposed to conduct the Barcelona performance, but overcome by the emotional stress at the last minute, he withdrew and Scherchen took over. See Moldenhauer, *Webern*, 454–8.

171  Letter from Webern to Wright, 11 Jan. 1936. The original letter survives in Edward Clark Letters, *GB-Lbl* Add.ms.52257, fols. 179–80; a full transcription of the original and its translation may be found in Chadwick, 'The Berg Violin Concerto in London', 334–8.

172  BBC WAC, RCONT1: Louis Krasner, Artist (1929–62), 31 Jan. 1936.

173  Ibid., 18 Jan. 1936.

174  Ibid., 20 and 31 Jan. 1936.

175  Ibid., 31 Jan. 1936.

176  Letter from Webern to Clark, 12 March 1936, as translated in Chadwick, 'The Berg Violin Concerto in London', 339–40. The original letter survives in BBC WAC, 910: Anton Webern, file 2 (1934–9); a full transcription and translation of the original may be found in Chadwick, 'The Berg Violin Concerto in London', 338–9.

177  BBC WAC, 910: Anton Webern, file 2 (1934–9), 2 April 1936.

178  BBC WAC, R29/157, 23 April 1936.

179  Ibid.

180  BBC WAC, RCONT1: Ernest Newman, Talks, file 1 (1931–6), 24 April 1936.

181  The script of the 'Keyboard Talks' programme, given by Leslie Heward and Victor Hely Hutchinson, has not been traced at the BBC WAC.

182  BBC WAC, RCONT1: Ernest Newman, Talks, file 1 (1931–6), 24 April 1936.

183 BBC WAC, Scripts, Reel 363: Ernest Newman, 'Introductory Talk Alban Berg', 1 May 1936.

184 W. McN. [William McNaught], 'Alban Berg's "Requiem": his Violin Concerto One of the Finest Modern Works', *Evening News*, 2 May 1936; in BBC WAC, P141: Press Cuttings/Programmes (1936).

185 R. C. [Richard Capell], 'In Memory of Alban Berg: the New Violin Concerto', *Daily Telegraph*, 2 May 1936; in BBC WAC, P141.

186 BBC WAC, RCONT1: Louis Krasner, Artist (1929–62), 11 May 1936.

187 Capell, 'In Memory of Alban Berg'.

188 BBC WAC, 910: Anton Webern, file 2 (1934–9), 5 May 1936.

189 Ibid., 6 May 1936. No record has been traced of Arthur Bliss's views on Webern's rehearsal technique.

190 BBC WAC, R27/250/2: Music General/Music Programme Advisory Panel/Minutes (July 1936–Dec. 1937), 23 March 1937.

## 11 Clark's legacy

1 BBC WAC, L1/88/2: Left Staff/Edward Thomas Clark (1924–1936), 6 Feb. 1936.

2 Ibid., 11 Feb. 1936.

3 Ibid., 18 Feb. 1936.

4 Clark, quoted in Linden Laing, '"Why I Resigned from the B.B.C.": Music Arranger and "Drastic" Changes', unidentified newpaper article, *c.* 28 March 1936, in Edward Clark clippings file in private collection of James Clark.

5 BBC WAC, L1/88/2, undated.

6 Ibid., 23 March 1936.

7 Ibid., 23 March 1936.

8 Ibid., 24 March 1936.

9 'B.B.C. Resignation: Music Expert Explains his Decision', *News Chronicle*, 28 March 1936, 1(B).

10 BBC WAC, L1/88/2, 15 June 1936.

11 Ibid., 24 June 1936.

12 See also Table 7.1 for a summary of Second Viennese School works broadcast between 1927 and spring 1930, while Pitt was Music Director.

# Selected bibliography

The list of sources that were consulted during the course of this study is organized as follows:

Unpublished sources
    Sources held at the BBC Written Archives Centre, Caversham
        British Broadcasting Company files
        Radio files
        Radio contributor files, staff files and Reith's diaries
        Talks transcripts
    Other unpublished sources

Published sources
    Concert programmes and flyers
    Primary source articles
        Primary source articles that appeared in BBC journals
        Primary source articles that appeared in newspapers and music journals
    Other books and articles

## Unpublished sources

### Sources held at the BBC Written Archives Centre, Caversham

*British Broadcasting Company files*

CO7/3: British Broadcasting Company/Board of Directors/Minutes (1925).
CO57: British Broadcasting Company/Request for Listeners' Response (1923).
CO62/5–7: British Broadcasting Company/Major Basil Binyon's Papers/File 3a–b (January 1925–May 1926).

*Radio files*

R1/1/4–5: Board of Governors/Minutes (1935–7).
R1/3/22: Board of Governors/D.G.'s Reports & Papers, file 2 (April–May 1936)
R3/3/1–7: Control Board/Minutes (1925–31).
R3/11/1–2: D.G.'s Meeting/Minutes (1933–5).
R4/7/8/1–6: Ullswater Committee 1935/Other Written Evidence/Papers 1–110.
R4/7/12: Ullswater Committee 1935/Report (October 1935–March 1936).
R6/46: Advisory Committees/Music Advisory Committee/ General (1933–5).
R6/47/1: Advisory Committees/Music Advisory Committee/Minutes and Agendas (1933–7).

R6/48/1: Advisory Committees/Music Advisory Committee/Papers (1935–40).

R6/50: Advisory Committees/Music Advisory Committees (1936).

R13/242/1–3: Departmental/Music Department (1928–39).

R27/55/1: Music General/Commissioned Works (1929–37).

R27/67: Music General/Contemporary Concerts (1929–36).

R27/100: Music General/Five-Year Plan (1934–5).

R27/157/1–2: Music General/ International Society for Contemporary Music (1939–54).

R27/219: Music General/Music and Music Department (1931–43).

R27/221/1–2: Music General/Music Department Meetings (Weekly)/Minutes (1933–8).

R27/245/1: Music General/Music Policy (1930–43).

R27/249/1–2: Music General/Music Programme Advisory Panel (1933–40).

R27/250/1–2: Music General/Music Programme Advisory Panel Minutes (1934–7).

R27/272: Music General/New Musical Compositions (1935–40).

R27/326/1–2: Music General/Opera/General Memos, file 1 (1929–39).

R27/405/1: Music General/Opera Wozzeck, file 1 (1934–5).

R27/417: Music General/Oxford University Press (1933–9).

R27/431: Music General/Promenade and Symphony Concerts Committee [minutes] (1927–33).

R27/432: Music General/Public Concert Policy (1933–5).

R27/635: Music General/Music Reports (1928–54).

R27/653: Music General/Opera 'Lulu' (1935).

R29/157: Orchestra General/Contemporary Concerts (1929–39).

R30/44: Outside Broadcasts – Sound/Arts Theatre (1929–1930).

R30/278/1: Outside Broadcasts – Sound/Central Hall Westminster (1928–46).

R30: Outside Broadcasts – Kingsway Hall General (1931–46).

R30: Outside Broadcasts – Queen's Hall/International Festival 1931.

R34/599: Policy/Programme Board (1925–45).

R34/600/1–6: Policy/Programme Board Minutes (1924–6, 1929, 1933–4).

R34/609: Policy/Programme Planning (1923–37).

R41/114/1: Programmes Correspondence Section/Musical Classical (1929–42).

R43/140/2–3: Publications/Radio Times, files 2–3 (1926–34).

R79/2/2–4: Contemporary Concerts, file 3 (1925–37).


*Radio contributor files, staff files and Reith's diaries*
(arranged in alphabetical order by subject's name)

RCONT1: Alban Berg, Composer (1933–62).

S236/21: Special Collections/Arthur Burrows.

L1/88/1–2: Left Staff/Edward Thomas Clark (1924–1936).

RCONT1: Edward Clark, Artists (1930–62)

RCONT1: Prof. Edward J. Dent, Talks (1931–56).

RCONT1: Marya Freund, Artists, file 1 (1937–49).
RCONT1: Roberto Gerhard, Artists (1932–52).
RCONT1: Ružena Herlingerova, Artists, file 1 (1930–49).
RCONT1: Margot Hinnenberg-Lefèbre, Artists (1930–62).
RCONT1: Alfred A. Kalmus, Copyright, file 1 (1927–50).
RCONT1: Alfred A. Kalmus, Music Publishers, file 1–2 (1929–39).
RCONT1: Louis Krasner, Artist (1929–62).
RCONT1: Ernst Krenek, Artist (1935–62).
RCONT1: Ernest Newman, Talks, file 1 (1931–6).
910: Percy Pitt Memorial File (November 1932–September 1933).
S60/5/2–4: Reith Diaries, vols. ii–iv (May 1923–May 1936).
RCONT1: Hermann Scherchen, Artists (1934–51).
RCONT1: Arnold Schoenberg, Composer (1943–62).
RCONT1: Edward Steuermann, Artists (1927–62).
RCONT1: Universal Music Agencies/Copyright, files 1–2 (1932–62).
RCONT1: Universal Music Agencies/Music Publishers (1933–62).
910: Anton Webern, file 1–2 (1929–39).
RCONT1: Egon Wellesz, Composer (1933–51).

*Talks transcripts*
(in order of microfilm reel number)

Reel 48: Adrian Boult
    'Queen's Hall Symphony Concerts 1936–7', 16 October 1936.
    'Music of the Week', 2 January 1938.
    'Music of the Week', 27 February 1938.
    'Music of the Week', 8 March 1938.
    'Music of the Week', 2 October 1938.
    'Music of the Week', 26 March 1939.
Reel 132: Edwin Evans
    'Musical Criticism', 7 December 1928.
    'The Contemporary Music Festival', 18 July 1931.
    'Prefatory Talk to Symphony Concert', 8 March 1933.
Reel 204: Victor Hely Hutchinson
    'Music Old and New', 11 April – 4 July 1932.
Reel 277/278: Peter Latham
    'Is Modern Music Bad?', 17 January 1930.
Reel 319: Basil Maine
    'Next Week's Broadcast Music', 21 January 1928.
    'Next Week's Broadcast Music', 26 October 1929.
Reel 362: Ernest Newman
    'Next Week's Broadcast Music, no. 3', 13 October 1928.
    'Next Week's Broadcast Music, no. 4', 20 October 1928.
    'Next Week's Broadcast Music, no. 6', 3 November 1928.

'Next Week's Broadcast Music, no. 10', 1 December 1928.
Reel 363: Ernest Newman
    'Music Criticism, no. 3', 15 February 1929.
    'Music Criticism, no. 18', 27 September 1929.
    'Music Criticism, no. 22', 22 November 1929.
    'Music Criticism, no. 23', 6 December 1929.
    'Symp Concrt [*sic*]', 23 October 1935.
    'Introductory Talk Alban Berg', 1 May 1936.
Reel 418: Alan Pryce-Jones.
    'Schoenberg and Vienna', 5 January 1952. Including an insert written and read
        by Edward Clark, 'Arnold Schönberg in Berlin'.
Reel 458: Percy Scholes
    'Broadcasting Symphonies', 4 October 1923.
    'Weekly Musical Criticism, no. 10', 16 August 1923.
    'Weekly Musical Criticism, [no. 23]', 15 November 1923.
    'Weekly Musical Criticism, no. 24', 22 November 1923.
    'Weekly Musical Criticism, no. 36', 21 February 1924.
    'Weekly Musical Criticism', 7 August 1924.

## Other unpublished sources

Edward Clark Letters. British Library, Add.ms.52256–7.
Edward Clark Papers. James Clark, personal collection.
Edward Clark Papers. Northwestern University Music Library. Including:
    Letters. In Writings Folder.
    Autobiography, undated, but written *c.* 1930. [BBC memo from Clark to the
        Assistant Music Director, Wright.] In Memorial Folder.
    Autobiography, undated, but written *c.*1950. In Moldenhauer Folder.
    Biography (possibly autobiography) of Edward Clark, written *c.*1952 with later
        annotations. In Memorial Folder.
    Adrian C. Boult. Tribute to Edward Clark, written in 1963. In Letters Folder.
    R. L. Henderson. 'Edward Clark – A Memoir', dated 1963. [Typescript proposal
        for biography (never realized).] In Clark Folder.
James Bowness Clark, Will. Somerset House, London. (Died, 20 June 1934.
    Probate, Newcastle-upon-Tyne, 20 September 1934.)
James Clark. Interview by author, 9 June 1992, London.

## Published Sources

### Concert programmes and flyers
### (arranged chronologically)

*Four Orchestral Concerts: Edward Clark, Conductor.* Queen's Hall and Æolian Hall,
    London, 8 and 20 April, 6 and 20 May 1921 [series flyer]. In Moldenhauer
    Folder, Edward Clark Papers, Northwestern University Music Library.

*Third of Four Orchestral Concerts Conducted by Edward Clark.* Æolian Hall, London, 6 May 1921 [concert programme]. In Moldenhauer Folder, Edward Clark Papers, Northwestern University Music Library.

*Six International Chamber Concerts of New Music.* Grotrian Hall, London, October 1926–March 1927 [series prospectus]. In BBC WAC, P446: Press Cuttings/Outside Broadcasts (1923–6).

*National Concert.* Royal Albert Hall, London, 25 November 1926. In BBC WAC, Symphony Concert Programmes (1927–May 1930).

*National Symphony Concerts.* People's Palace, London, 18 November 1927. In BBC WAC, Symphony Concert Programmes (1927–May 1930).

*BBC Symphony Concerts.* Queen's Hall, London, 8 February 1933. In BBC WAC, P488: Press Cuttings/Symphony Concerts (January–March 1933).

*BBC Symphony Concerts.* Queen's Hall, London, 8 March 1933. In BBC WAC, P488: Press Cuttings/Symphony Concerts (January–March 1933).

*Percy Pitt Memorial Concert,* Concert Hall, Broadcasting House, London, 10 March 1933. In BBC WAC, 910: Percy Pitt Memorial File.

## Primary source articles

### *Primary source articles that appeared in BBC journals* (arranged chronologically)

'Official News and Views: Gossip about the B.B.C.: New Scottish Controller'. *RT,* 2 (22 February 1924): 323. [article about David Millar Craig]

'British Composers' Programmes'. *RT,* 2 (22 February 1924): 334.

J. C. W. Reith. 'Wireless and Music'. *RT,* 2 (29 February 1924): 361–2.

J. C. W. Reith. 'What is our Policy?' *RT,* 2 (14 March 1924): 441–2.

H. J. B. 'Listeners' Letters: Too Much Modern Music?' *RT,* 6 (27 February 1925): 439.

'A Great Enterprise Develops: Official Statement of Facts and Policy'. *RT,* 6 (13 March 1925): 529–30.

J. C. Squire. 'Problems of Programmes'. *RT,* 6 (20 March 1925): 577–8.

'Official News and Views: Gossip about Broadcasting: Musical Advisory Committee'. *RT,* 8 (17 July 1925): 148.

'An Opportunity for British Composers: The BBC Offers £1,000 in Prizes for Original Musical Compositions'. *RT,* 10 (19 March 1926): 587.

'B.B.C. Spring Concerts: Chamber Music at Chelsea'. *RT,* 11 (26 March 1926): 4.

'A Challenge to Young Composers'. *RT,* 11 (26 March 1926): 9.

'Our Festival Competition'. *RT,* 11 (9 April 1926): 105.

'The 9.45 Recitals: Attractive Programmes for the Winter'. *RT,* 12 (10 September 1926): 466.

'The B.B.C.'s National Concerts: Preliminary Announcement of an Important New Series'. *RT,* 12 (10 September 1926): 470.

'The Musical Festival Competition: the Judges' Report'. *RT,* 13 (24 December 1926): 746.

Filson Young. 'The Foundations of Music: the Scheme of a New Series of
    Broadcast Recitals'. *RT*, 14 (31 December 1926): 6.
'London and Daventry News and Notes'. *RT*, 14 (14 January 1927): 99.
'National Concert Programme: Programme Notes: Verklärte Nacht'. [3 February
    1927, 2LO, 8.00 pm] *RT*, 14 (28 January 1927): 219.
Sacheverell Sitwell. 'Igor Stravinsky'. *RT*, 16 (8 July 1927): 54.
'The Headquarters of British Broadcasting'. *RT*, 16 (15 July 1927): 84. [drawing of
    Savoy Hill premises]
Percy Scholes. 'The Danger of Infallibility: Two Questions and a Moral'. *RT*, 16
    (22 July 1927): 125.
'The Dawn of a New Era for Listeners: the B.B.C. Announces the First "Alternative
    Programme"'. *RT*, 16 (12 August 1927): 241–2.
'Which shall we Listen to Tonight?: a Note on the New Art of Listening to the
    Broadcast Programmes'. *RT*, 16 (2 September 1927): 365.
C. Whitaker-Wilson. 'The Man Behind the Music'.
    'October 10, 1813 – Giuseppe Verdi'. *RT*, 17 (7 October 1927): 4.
    'October 17, 1849 – Frederic Chopin'. *RT*, 17 (14 October 1927): 60.
    'Franz Liszt – Born October 22, 1811'. *RT*, 17 (21 October 1927): 122.
    'Peter Tchaikovsky – Died November 6, 1893'. *RT*, 17 (4 November 1927): 238.
    'Christopher von Gluck – Died November 15, 1787'. *RT*, 17 (11 November
        1927): 296.
    'Wolfgang Amadeus Mozart, Died December 5, 1791'. *RT*, 17 (2 December):
        472.
'Both Sides of the Microphone: Modern Music'. *RT*, 17 (21 October 1927): 124.
J. C. Squire. 'The B.B.C. Handbook'. *RT*, 17 (4 November 1927): 238.
Percy Scholes. 'Is Bartok Mad – or are We?' *RT*, 17 (9 December 1927): 525–6.
'Both Sides of the Microphone: an Outstanding Musical Event'. *RT*, 17 (30
    December 1927): 712.
'The Madness of Bartok and Other Matters: Discussed in Letters to the Editor
    from Listeners'. *RT*, 18 (6 January 1928): 3.
'Recital of Contempory Chamber Music – IV: Chamber Symphony, Schönberg'.
    [Programme notes, 9 January 1928, 5GB, 8.30 pm] *RT*, 18 (6 January 1928):
    12.
Percy A. Scholes. '140 Players and "Some Big Iron Chains!"' *RT*, 18 (13 January
    1928): 49–50.
'The Songs of Gurra: Gurrelieder'. *RT*, 18 (20 January 1928): 103.
'Both Sides of the Microphone: the Composer of "Wozzek"'. *RT*, 18 (3 February
    1928): 213.
Graham Eltham. 'Debussy – Musical Impressionist'. *RT*, 18 (17 February 1928):
    325, 324.
Richard Capell. 'What do You Listen for?' *RT*, 18 (2 March 1928): 437–8.
'New Friends in Music: John Ireland'. [Programme notes, 7 March 1928, 5GB,
    8.00 pm] *RT*, 18 (2 March 1928): 459.
Herman Klein. 'When is a Voice Not a Voice?' *RT*, 18 (9 March 1928): 487, 490.
F. Bonavia. 'The Magic of the Violin'. *RT*, 18 (16 March 1928): 543, 567.

W. R. Anderson. 'Listening to the Piano'. *RT*, 18 (23 March 1928): 597, 633.

W. McNaught. 'The Big Battalions'. *RT*, 18 (30 March 1928): 642, 647.

'Both Sides of the Microphone: Composers, Please Note'. *RT*, 19 (6 April 1928): 3.

Percy A. Scholes. Series of articles:

   'A Miniature History of Music'. *RT*, 19 (6 April 1928): 11, 10.

   'Music as Woven Tone'. *RT*, 19 (13 April 1928): 59, 58.

   'Sonatas and Symphonies'. *RT*, 19 (20 April 1928): 103, 106.

   'Music as Romance'. *RT*, 19 (27 April 1928): 152–3.

   'Music as Drama'. *RT*, 19 (4 May 1928): 191–2.

   'Impressionism in Music'. *RT*,19 (11 May 1928): 241, 243.

   'The Music of Today'. *RT*, 19 (18 May 1928): 285–6.

Filson Young. 'A New Sunday Feature'. *RT*, 19 (11 May 1928), 233–4.

'Both Sides of the Microphone: a New Home of Chamber Music'. *RT*, 19 (18 May 1928): 291.

'What the Other Listener Thinks'. *RT*, 20 (13 July 1928): 59.

Edwin Evans. 'Points of View: Is Modern Music Inferior?'. *RT*, 20 (31 August 1928): 370.

K. A. W. [Kenneth A. Wright]. 'The New Series of B.B.C. Chamber Concerts'. *RT*, 20 (31 August 1928): 381.

'Forward: Musical Events', *Talks and Lectures: Broadcast September to December 1928* [*c*. August 1928]: 9.

Francis Toye. 'How to Listen to Opera'. *RT*, 20 (14 September 1928): 469–70.

'Both Sides of the Microphone: Mr. Percy Scholes'. *RT*, 20 (28 September 1928): 609.

H. A. Scott. 'This Modern Music!: Product of an Age of "Stunts"'. *RT*, 20 (28 September 1928): 642.

'Both Sides of the Microphone: Contemporary Chamber Music – II'. *RT*, 21 (5 October 1928): 5.

'What the Other Listener Thinks'. *RT*, 21 (2 November 1928): 301.

'Both Sides of the Microphone: Composer's Chinese Model'. *RT*, 21 (23 November 1928): 509.

'Both Sides of the Microphone: Chamber Music'. *RT*, 21 (7 December 1928): 648.

'Both Sides of the Microphone: Contemporary Music'. *RT*, 21 (28 December 1928): 856.

Edwin Evans. 'What the New Composer is Driving at'. *RT*, 22 (1 February 1929), 255–6.

'What the Other Listener Thinks'. *RT*, 22 (1 February 1929): 299.

'Chamber Music: The Vienna String Quartet'. [Programme listing, 12 February 1929, 5GB, 10.15 pm] *RT*, 22 (8 February 1929): 335.

'What the Other Listener Thinks'. *RT*, 22 (15 February 1929): 427.

'What the Other Listener Thinks'. *RT*, 22 (1 March 1929): 547.

'What the Other Listener Thinks'. *RT*, 22 (8 March 1929): 609.

'What the Other Listener Thinks'. *RT*, 22 (22 March 1929): 735.

Scott Goddard. 'The Coming Season of Broadcast Opera'. *RT*, 24 (6 September 1929): 469, 504.

'Both Sides of the Microphone: Contemporary Music'. *RT*, 25 (11 October 1929): 85.

'Both Sides of the Microphone'. *RT*, 25 (25 October 1929): 236–7.

'What the Other Listener Thinks'. *RT*, 25 (25 October 1929): 244.

'Concerts of Contemporary Music'. [Programme notes, 4 November 1929, 5GB, 8.00 pm] *RT*, 25 (1 November 1929): 331.

'Both Sides of the Microphone: "The Shadow of a Tune"'. *RT*, 25 (22 November 1929): 541.

'A Miniature Dictionary of Musical Terms'. *RT*, 25 (22 November 1929): 567–74.

'Concerts of Contemporary Music'. [Programme listing, 2 December 1929, 5GB, 7.45 pm] *RT*, 25 (29 November 1929): 637.

'A B.B.C. Concert of Contemporary Music'. *RT*, 25 (29 November 1929): 641.

'Both Sides of the Microphone: Free Tickets for B.B.C. Concerts'. *RT*, 26 (17 January 1930): 129.

Peter Latham. 'Is Modern Music Bad?' *The Listener*, 3 (22 January 1930): 161–2.

'A Music Diary for Listeners'. *The Listener*, 3 (29 January 1930): 216.

'Both Sides of the Microphone'. *RT*, 26 (28 March 1930): 757.

Erwin Stein. 'The Moon-Struck Pierrot Comes to London'. *RT* (4 April 1930): 9.

'What the Other Listener Thinks'. *RT*, 27 (4 April 1930): 12.

'For the Musical Listener: Notes on the Week's Programmes: The Ardent Disciples of Schönberg'. *RT*, 27 (4 April 1930): 14.

M. D. Calvocoressi. 'A Schönberg Concert'. *The Listener*, 3 (9 April 1930): 648.

'Both Sides of the Microphone'. *RT*, 27 (25 April 1930): 188–9.

'What the Other Listener Thinks'. *RT*, 27 (25 April 1930): 194.

'What the Other Listener Thinks'. *RT*, 27 (2 May 1930): 258.

W. J. Turner, 'Modernist Music, or "Devastating the Home"'. *RT*, 27 (16 May 1930): 363.

'Both Sides of the Microphone: Composers, Please Note!'. *RT*, 28 (19 September 1930): 598.

Editorial. *RT*, 29 (3 October 1930): 12.

Filson Young. 'The World We Listen In: the Art of Listening'. *RT*, 29 (10 October 1930): 88.

Editorial. *RT*, 29 (24 October 1930): 232.

'Both Sides of the Microphone: Is he the Greatest Composer of Today?' *RT*, 29 (28 November 1930): 582.

'Both Sides of the Microphone: Schonberg'. *RT*, 29 (26 December 1930): 865.

'Music of the Week'. *RT*, 29 (26 December 1930): 872.

'What the Other Listener Thinks'. *RT*, 30 (2 January 1931): 8.

'Schönberg to Conduct his Own Music this Week'. *RT*, 30 (2 January 1931): 10.

'Both Sides of the Microphone: Jekyll-and-Hyde Webern'. *RT*, 31 (24 April 1931): 191.

'Music of the Week: Schönberg and Webern'. *RT*, 31 (1 May 1931): 262.

'Concerts of Contemporary Music – V'. [Programme listing, 8 May 1931, London Regional, 9.00 pm] *RT*, 31 (1 May 1931): 292.

Editorial. *RT*, 32 (3 July 1931): 6.

Robin Hey. 'Music that Expresses Contemporary Life'. *RT*, 32 (10 July 1931): 59.

'Both Sides of the Microphone: Festival at Oxford'. *RT*, 32 (10 July 1931): 60.

Edwin Evans. 'New Music from the World's Four Corners'. *RT*, 32 (17 July 1931): 117.

'Music of the Week: Oxford, Salzburg, and Canterbury'. *RT*, 32 (17 July 1931): 124, 126, 142

Edwin Evans. 'Musicians of Many Countries'. *The Listener*, 6 (22 July 1931): 143.

W. R. Anderson. 'Modern Music Battle: Anderson *v*. Hey'. *RT*, 32 (24 July 1931): 167, 190.

'Football for America, Othello for England'. *RT*, 32 (24 July 1931): 175. [article about Percy Scholes]

'Music of the Week: Gershwin Looks at an American in Paris'. *RT*, 32 (24 July 1931): 176, 178, 211.

Editorial. *RT*, 32 (7 August 1931): 274.

Eric Blom. 'The Listener's Music: Music of the Month'. *The Listener*, 6 (12 August 1931): 251–2.

'Music of the Week'. *RT*, 32 (14 August 1931): 356, 360.

Eric Blom. 'The Listener's Music: Music of the Month'. *The Listener*, 6 (9 September 1931): 412.

'First Commentator Still Scared of Mike: Young Filson'. *RT*, 32 (11 September 1931): 553.

'Promenade Concert'. [Programme notes, 15 September 1931, Daventry National, 8.00 pm] *RT*, 32 (11 September 1931): 576.

Eric Blom. 'The Listener's Music: Music of the Month'. *The Listener*, 6 (14 October 1931): 631.

'Both Sides of the Microphone'. *RT*, 33 (30 October 1931): 336.

'Both Sides of the Microphone'. *RT*, 33 (6 November 1931): 418–9.

'In the Air: Programmes at a Glance'. *RT*, 33 (6 November 1931): 427.

'Concerts of Contemporary Music – I'. [Programme listing, 13 November 1931, London Regional, 8.00 pm] *RT*, 33 (6 November 1931): 477.

Edwin Evans. 'Schönberg: Dreamer and Mathematician'. *RT*, 33 (13 November 1931): 509, 569.

'The Fifth of the B.B.C. Symphony Concerts'. [Programme notes, 18 November 1931, Daventry National, 8.00 pm] *RT*, 33 (13 November 1931): 540.

Eric Blom. 'The Listener's Music: Music of the Month'. *The Listener*, 6 (9 December 1931): 1004.

'What the Other Listener Thinks'. *RT*, 33 (11 December 1931): 840.

F. J. Hargreaves. 'Listeners' Letters: Chamber Music'. *RT*, 34 (4 March 1932): 578.

'Music, New and Old – I'. [Programme listing, 11 April 1932, Daventry National, 7.30 pm] *RT*, 35 (8 April 1932): 88.

'Both Sides of the Microphone: Contemporary Concert'. *RT*, 35 (6 May 1932): 332.

R. K. Silver. 'Those "Contemporary" Concerts'. *RT*, 35 (6 May 1932): 336, 373.

'Concerts of Contemporary Music – VII'. [Programme listing, 13 May 1932, London Regional, 8.35 pm] *RT*, 35 (6 May 1932): 378.

'What the Other Listener Thinks'. *RT*, 35 (27 May 1932): 537.

'What the Other Listener Thinks'. *RT*, 35 (10 June 1932): 665.

Hubert J. Foss. 'Fair Treatment, Please, for Modern Music'. *RT*, 36 (26 August 1932): 479.

'Both Sides of the Microphone: Before the Concert'. *RT*, 36 (2 September 1932): 537.

'Both Sides of the Microphone: Recorded Programmes'. *RT*, 37 (28 October 1932): 255.

Hubert J. Foss. 'English Composers and the World at Large'. *RT*, 37 (4 November 1932): 344.

'Then and Now: a Page of Contrasts'. *RT*, 37 (11 November 1932): 418.

Adrian C. Boult and Henry J. Wood. 'Percy Pitt, November 23, 1932'. *RT*, 37 (2 December 1932): 673.

Robin H. Legge. 'Percy Pitt'. *World-Radio*, 15 (2 December 1932): 1213.

Filson Young. 'The World We Listen In: In Memoriam'. *RT*, 37 (9 December 1932): 748. [Obituary of Percy Pitt]

'A Page of Short Articles for the Music-Minded: the Rest of the Week'. *RT*, 37 (16 December 1932): 822.

'B.B.C. Concerts of Contemporary Music – II'. [Programme listing, 23 December 1932, London Regional, 9.0 pm] *RT*, 37 (16 December 1932): 867.

Constant Lambert. 'At this Week's Symphony Concert: a Constructive Anarchist'. *RT*, 38 (3 February 1933): 248.

'B.B.C. Symphony Concert – XII'. [Programme listing, 8 February 1933, Daventry National, 8.15 pm] *RT*, 38 (3 February 1933): 278.

Eric Blom. 'Notable Music of the Week: the Tragedy of a Soldier'. *RT*, 38 (3 March 1933): 517.

M. D. Calvocoressi. 'The Listener's Music: Alban Berg's "Wozzeck"'. *The Listener*, 9 (8 March 1933): 376.

'B.B.C. Concerts of Contemporary Music – VI'. [Programme notes, 21 April 1933, London Regional, 9.00 pm] *RT*, 39 (14 April 1933): 116.

'Both Sides of the Microphone: Primavera'. *RT*, 39 (21 April 1933): 133. [reminiscences of Savoy Hill]

C. Whitaker-Wilson. 'Symphony *versus* Cacophony'. *RT*, 39 (21 April 1933): 138.

'Sunday Orchestral Concert – 23'. [Programme notes, 23 April 1933, London Regional, 9.05 pm] *RT*, 39 (21 April 1933): 146.

C. Henry Warren. 'And Still the Battle Goes On!' *RT*, 39 (28 April 1933): 198.

'The Radio Times: Tenth Anniversary'. *RT*, 60 (29 September 1933): 721–30. [Includes articles: Percy A. Scholes: 'The Musical Journal with Far-and-Away the Largest Circulation in the World'; 'How the Programmes come to "The Radio Times"'; 'How "The Radio Times" comes to its Readers'; 'Our Contributors']

'The Symphonies Begin'. *RT*, 61 (6 October 1933): 11.

'Both Sides of the Microphone: Eccentric Pierrot'. *RT*, 41 (10 November 1933): 396.

Cecil Gray. 'Notable Music of the Week: Schönberg's "Pierrot Lunaire"'. *RT*, 41 (17 November 1933): 481.

Ernst Schoen. 'Notable Music of the Week: Music from Austria'. *RT*, 41 (24 November 1933): 560.

'B.B.C. Chamber Concert – IV'. [Programme notes, 1 December 1933, London Regional, 9.00 pm] *RT*, 41 (24 November 1933): 611.

'Both Sides of the Microphone'. *RT*, 42 (2 March 1934): 617.

Edwin Evans. '"Wozzeck", the Under-Dog'. *RT*, 42 (9 March 1934): 712–13.

M. D. Calvocoressi. 'Alban Berg's "Wozzeck"'. *The Listener*, 11 (14 March 1934): 440–2.

'Another Season of Broadcast Music: a First Glance at the Plans for 1934–5'. *RT*, 45 (12 October 1934): 90–1.

'Both Sides of the Microphone: Novelty Night'. *RT*, 46 (8 March 1935): 4.

Edwin Evans. 'Notable Music of the Week: the Songs of Gurra'. *RT*, 46 (8 March 1935): 12.

Scott Goddard. 'Notable Music of the Week: Modern Music from Vienna, Venice, and London: an Erotic Opera'. *RT*, 46 (15 March 1935): 14.

L. S. Peppercorn. 'Notable Music of the Week: Modern Music from Vienna, Venice, and London: Revolutionary Music'. *RT*, 46 (15 March 1935): 14–15.

M. D. Calvocoressi. 'The Listener's Music: Alban Berg and the Opera'. *The Listener*, 13 (20 March 1935): 474.

'Notes on the Week's Programmes: From the 'Lyric Suite' of Alban Berg'. *The Listener*, 14 (16 October 1935): 687.

Ralph Hill. 'B.B.C. Symphony Concerts'. *RT*, 49 (18 October 1935): 13.

'Notes on the Week's Programmes: Ernst Krenek'. *The Listener*, 14 (23 October 1935): 735–6.

'The B.B.C. Concerts of Contemporary Music – I'. [Programme notes, 1 November 1935, National, 10.20 pm] *RT*, 49 (25 October 1935): 72.

Edwin Evans. 'Giant Symphonic Poem'. *RT*, 1 (17 January 1936): 13.

'The Boyd Neel String Orchestra'. [Programme notes, 1 February 1936, Regional, 8.30 pm] *RT*, 1 (24 January 1936): 43.

M. D. C. [M. D. Calvocoressi]. 'Notes on the Week's Programmes: the Wellesz Piano Concerto'. *The Listener*, 15 (20 May 1936): 989–90.

'The B.B.C. Orchestra'. [Programme notes, 25 May 1936, National, 10.15 pm] *RT*, 51 (22 May 1936): 26.

*Primary source articles that appeared in newspapers and music journals* (arranged chronologically)

In this section, items that were accessed in the BBC press cuttings files are identified with a BBC WAC catalogue number in parentheses following the entry. The catalogue numbers refer to the boxes of press cuttings at the archives, as listed below:

P131: Press Cuttings/Programme Matters (1930)
P132: Press Cuttings/Programmes (1931)
P134: Press Cuttings/Programmes (1932)
P139: Press Cuttings/Programmes (1935)
P141: Press Cuttings/Programmes (1936)
P425: Press Cuttings/Programmes: Music (1933)
P446: Press Cuttings/Outside Broadcasts (1923–6)
P447: Press Cuttings/Outside Broadcasts (1927–9)
P449: Press Cuttings/Outside Broadcasts: Concerts (1930–31)
P478: Press Cuttings/Symphony Concerts (1926–7)
P479: Press Cuttings/Symphony Concerts (1927–8)
P483: Press Cuttings/Symphony Concerts (October 1930–January 1931)
P485: Press Cuttings/Symphony Concerts (September–December 1931)
P488: Press Cuttings/Symphony Concerts (January–March 1933)
P489: Press Cuttings/Symphony Concerts (1933)
P490: Press Cuttings/Symphony Concerts (1934)
P492: Press Cuttings/Symphony Concerts (1935)
P493: Press Cuttings/Symphony Concerts (1935–6)
P565: Press Cuttings/Personal Publicity (1924–7)
P566: Press Cuttings/Personal Publicity (1928–9)
P567: Press Cuttings/Personal Publicity (1930)

'Music in Vienna'. *MT*, 46 (March 1905): 189.
'Schönberg'. *The Musical Standard* (12 September 1912): 176–8.
'Occasional Notes: Henry Wood on German Music, etc'. *MT*, 59 (October 1918): 446.
A. Eaglefield Hull. 'A Few Words about the British Music Society'. *MT*, 60 (February 1919): 71.
Edgar L. Bainton. 'Music in Ruhleben Camp'. *MT*, 60 (February 1919), 72–3.
Edwin Evans. 'The Russian Ballet at the Empire'. *MT*, 60 (December 1919): 695.
Statement of Purpose on contents page. *The Sackbut*, 1/1 (May 1920).
Alfred Kalisch. 'London Concerts'. *MT*, 61 (February 1920): 101–3.
'Miscellaneous'. *MT*, 62 (January 1921): 61. [about the formation of the London Contemporary Music Centre]
Cecil Gray. 'Arnold Schönberg – A Critical Study'. *Music and Letters*, 3 (January 1922): 73–89.
W. McN. [William McNaught]. 'London Concerts: Other Orchestral Music'. *MT*, 63 (January 1922): 41.

Paul Bechert. 'Musical Notes from Abroad: Vienna'. *MT*, 63 (February 1922): 133.

Edwin Evans. 'The Salzburg Festival: International Chamber Concerts'. *MT*, 63 (September 1922): 628–30.

P. A. S. [P. A. Scholes]. 'London Concerts: London Contemporary Music'. *MT*, 63 (November 1922): 794.

C. 'In the Concert Room'. *Monthly Musical Record*, 52 (November 1922): 282.

'Dinner and Presentation to Edwin Evans'. *MT*, 64 (February 1923): 127.

William Boosey. 'Broadcasting'. *The Daily Telegraph*, 19 May 1923, 11(D).

Edwin Evans. 'Donaueschingen and Salzburg Festivals'. *MT*, 64 (September 1923): 631–5.

C. [H. C. Colles]. 'London Concerts: Pierrot Lunaire'. *MT*, 64 (December 1923): 865.

Ernest Newman. 'The World of Music: Broadcasting Music: Some Reflections and a Suggestion: Wireless as Pioneer'. *The Sunday Times*, 13 January 1924, 5(B–C).

E. E. [Edwin Evans]. 'London Concerts: Goossens Concerts'. *MT*, 65 (April 1924): 357–8.

Paul Bechert. 'Musical Notes from Abroad: Vienna'. *MT*, 65 (June 1924): 558.

Adolf Weissmann. 'Musical Notes from Abroad: Germany'. *MT*, 65 (November 1924): 1035–6.

Paul Bechert. 'Musical Notes from Abroad: Vienna: Schönberg's Newest Work'. *MT*, 65 (December 1924): 1132–3.

Greville, Ursula. 'Broadcasting: Some Second Thoughts'. *The Sackbut*, 5 (January 1925): 153–5.

Paul A. Pisk. 'Post-War Tendencies in Austria'. *The Sackbut*, 6/1 (August 1925): 3–7.

Egon Wellesz. 'Present Tendencies in Austria'. *The Sackbut*, 6/2 (September 1925): 42–6.

'Ariel'. 'Wireless Notes'. *MT*, 67 (January 1926): 37.

M. 'London Concerts: B.B.C. Chamber Concerts'. *MT*, 67 (August 1926): 737.

'B.B.C. Chamber Concerts: International Series'. *The Daily Telegraph*, 27 September 1926. (P446)

'75 Minutes of Chamber Music and No Alternative'. *Evening News*, 6 October 1926. (P446)

Basil Maine. 'Music: the Enterprise of the B.B.C.' *The Spectator*, 9 October 1926. (P446)

'At 2LO'. *The Star*, 15 January 1927. (P565)

'Seven Gods of the B.B.C.: Choosing Programmes Seven Weeks Ahead'. *Evening News*, 26 January 1927. (P565)

F. T. [Francis Toye]. 'B.B.C. Concert: Brilliant Music at the Albert Hall'. *Morning Post*, 4 February 1927. (P478)

'B.B.C. Concert'. *The Times*, 4 February 1927. (P478)

F. B. [Ferruccio Bonavia]. 'London Concerts: the B.B.C. at the Albert Hall'. *MT*, 68 (March 1927): 263.

'Wireless Notes and Programmes: B.B.C.'s Musical Staff'. *Manchester Guardian*, 16 June 1927. (P565)

'The Concert Season: Vienna String Quartet'. *Musical Opinion*, 51 (November 1927): 155.

E. B. [Eric Blom]. 'London Concerts: B.B.C. Studio Chamber Concert'. *MT*, 68 (November 1927): 1030–31.

P. P. Eckersley. 'The Art of Listening'. *Eve, the Lady's Pictorial*, 7 December 1927. (P565)

'The Concert Season: Arnold Bax'. *Musical Opinion*, 51 (December 1927): 267.

Arnold Schönberg. 'This "Rebel" Music'. *Evening News*, 27 January 1928. (P479)

'Schonberg and the B.B.C.'. *Evening Standard*, 28 January 1928. (P479)

E. B. [Eric Blom]. 'Schonberg's "Gurrelieder": Composer's London Success'. *Manchester Guardian*, 28 January 1928. (P479)

'Arnold Schönberg: "Gurrelieder" at Queen's Hall'. *The Times*, 28 January 1928. (P479)

'A Talk with Schönberg'. *The Observer*, 29 January 1928. (P479)

Ernest Newman. 'Music of the Day'. *Glasgow Herald*, 2 February 1928. (P479)

Ernest Newman. 'Music of the Day'. *Glasgow Herald*, 16 February 1928. (P479)

'Ariel'. 'Wireless Notes'. *MT*, 69 (February 1928): 144.

Article on P. P. Eckersley. *Evening Telegraph and Post* [Dundee], 14 March 1928. (P566)

'Personal and Otherwise: Percy Pitt'. *Musical Opinion*, 51 (March 1928): 582–3.

'The Concert Season: Contemporary Chamber Concert'. *Musical Opinion*, 51 (March 1928): 594.

'Ariel'. 'Wireless Notes'. *MT*, 69 (March 1928): 239.

H. G. 'London Concerts: Schönberg's "Gurrelieder"'. *MT*, 69 (March 1928): 256.

'The Concert Season: Contemporary Chamber Music'. Musical Opinion, 51 (June 1928): 894.

'Wild Career of the B.B.C.'. *Star*, 13 October 1928. (P447)

C. G. [Cecil Gray]. 'Contemporary Chamber Music'. *The Daily Telegraph*, 16 October 1928. (P447)

'B.B.C. Chamber Concert'. *The Observer*, 21 October 1928. (P447)

Ernest Newman. 'The World of Music: The Week's Music'. *The Sunday Times*, 21 October 1928. (P447)

'Modern Continental Chamber Music: B.B.C. Concert', *Manchester Guardian*, 4 December 1928. (P447)

Ernest Newman. 'The World of Music: The Week's Music'. *The Sunday Times*, 9 December 1928. (P447)

C. G. [Cecil Gray]. 'Chamber Music: Van Dieren's String Quartet'. *The Daily Telegraph*, 8 January 1929. (P447)

E. B. [Eric Blom]. 'B.B.C. Chamber Music: A Vaughan Williams Quintet'. *Manchester Guardian*, 8 January 1929. (P447)

Ernest Newman. 'The World of Music: Broadcasting Music: Some Reflections and a Suggestion: B.B.C. Concert'. *The Sunday Times*, 13 January 1929, 5(B).

E. B. [Eric Blom]. 'London Concerts: B.B.C. Modern Chamber Concert'. *MT*, 70 (February 1929): 158–9.

'Change at the B.B.C.: Mr. Percy Pitt Likely to Give Up his Post as Music Director'.
     *Evening Standard*, 7 March 1929. (P566)

'Mr. Percy Pitt and B.B.C.'. *The Daily Telegraph*, 8 March 1929. (P566)

'Age Limit for B.B.C. Officials: Mr Percy Pitt's Successor'. *Morning Post*, 2 May
     1929. (P566)

'Mr. Percy Pitt's Successor'. *Popular Wireless*, 4 May 1929. (P566)

'Wireless Notes: Resignation of Captain Eckersley'. *Manchester Guardian*, 6 June
     1929. (P566)

'New Post for Dr. Adrian Boult'. *Manchester Guardian*, 8 June 1929. (P566)

'Mr. Adrian Boult: Policy as New B.B.C. Music Director'. *The Daily Telegraph*, 16
     July 1929. (P566)

J. A. W. [Jack Westrup]. 'Monotony of Schonberg: Viennese Music at B.B.C.
     Concert'. *The Daily Mail*, 5 November 1929. (P447)

C. G. [Cecil Gray]. 'Contemporary Music'. *The Daily Telegraph*, 5 November 1929.
     (P447)

Ernest Newman. 'The World of Music: The Week's Music: Contemporary
     Chamber Music'. *The Sunday Times*, 10 November 1929. (P447)

'Music Talks of Sir Walford Davies: New Arrangement with B.B.C.'. *The Daily
     News*, 14 November 1929. (P566)

'B.B.C. Musical Talks'. *The Times*, 14 November 1929. (P566)

'Sir Walford Davies'. *Evening Standard*, 15 November 1929. (P566)

B. M. [Basil Maine]. 'B.B.C. Concert: Some Fleeting Fragments of Music'.
     *Morning Post*, 3 December 1929. (P447)

Ernest Newman. 'The World of Music: The Week's Music: Chamber Music'. *The
     Sunday Times*, 8 December 1929. (P447)

'B.B.C. Music Director'. *The Sunday Times*, 8 December 1929. (P566)

Notice about Pitt's resignation in *The Daily Telegraph*, 3 January 1930. (P566)

'Mr. Percy Pitt'. *The Daily Telegraph*, 4 January 1930. (P566)

'Uses of a Full Audience'. *Evening News*, 18 January 1930. (P449)

'Decree Nisi against Former Chief Engineer to B.B.C.'. *The Times*, 4 March 1930.
     (P567)

R. C. [Richard Capell]. 'Last Night's Wireless Infliction'. *The Daily Mail*, 8 April
     1930. (P449)

E. B. [Eric Blom]. 'Modern Music Broadcast: a Schonberg Programme'.
     *Manchester Guardian*, 8 April 1930. (P449)

Ernest Newman. 'The World of Music: The Week's Music: Schönberg and Bartok'.
     *The Sunday Times*, 13 April 1930. (P449)

'Broadcasting: the Programme and the Listener'. *The Observer*, 28 September
     1930, 2(B).

'Broadcasting: the Programme and the Listener'. *The Observer*, 5 October 1930,
     5(B).

Percy A. Scholes. 'B.B.C. and "Difficult" Music'. *The Observer*, 12 October 1930.
     (P131)

Robin H. Legge. 'Schonberg at his Dullest: "Pelléas" at the Queen's Hall'. *The Daily
     Telegraph*, 11 December 1930. (P483)

H. H. [Herbert Hughes]. 'Schonberg on the Wireless: Musical Melodrama'. *The Daily Telegraph*, 10 January 1931. (P132)

'The New Music'. *Evening News*, 10 January 1931. (P132)

E. N. [Ernest Newman]. 'The Week's Music: Schönberg's Grand Guignol'. *The Sunday Times*, 12 January 1931. (P132)

Constant Lambert. 'London Concerts: Schönberg's "Erwartung"'. *MT*, 72 (February 1931): 167.

C. G. [Cecil Gray]. 'Modern Music at Oxford'. *The Daily Telegraph*, 24 July 1931. (P449)

'Modern Music at Oxford'. *The Times*, 24 July 1931. (P449)

H. F. [Harry Farjeon]. 'The Week's Music: The Oxford Festival'. *The Sunday Times*, 26 July 1931. (P449)

'A Concert of the Moderns'. *The Daily Telegraph*, 28 July 1931. (P449)

E. B. [Eric Blom]. 'The International Music Festival'. *Manchester Guardian*, 28 July 1931. (P449)

'Motor Horns in an Orchestra: a Plain Amateur Endures his Jazziest Night: Musical Shockers'. *The Star*, 28 July 1931. (P449)

'B.B.C. Orchestral Concert'. *The Times*, 28 July 1931. (P449)

H. F. [Harry Farjeon]. 'The Week's Music: I.S.C.M. Festival'. *The Sunday Times*, 2 August 1931. (P449)

Henry Boys. 'The Oxford Festival'. *Monthly Musical Record*, 61 (September 1931): 266–7.

Ralph Hill. 'Contemporary Music Festival'. *Musical Mirror and Fanfare* (September 1931): 245–7.

Edwin Evans. 'The Oxford Festival'. *MT*, 72 (September 1931): 803–6.

'Letters to the Editor: Alban Berg'. *MT*, 72 (October 1931): 936.

F. B. [Ferruccio Bonavia]. 'Schonberg's Music: the Old Style and the New: a B.B.C. Broadcast'. *The Daily Telegraph*, 14 November 1931. (P132)

'New Work of Schonberg: B.B.C. Contemporary Music Concert'. *Manchester Guardian*, 14 November 1931. (P132)

E. N. [Ernest Newman]. 'The Week's Music: Schönberg'. *The Sunday Times*, 15 November 1931. (P132)

'B.B.C. Symphony Concert'. *Manchester Guardian*, 19 November 1931. (P485)

Edwin Evans. 'Schönberg and the B.B.C.'. *Time and Tide*, 21 November 1931. (P485)

E. N. [Ernest Newman]. 'The Week's Music: Schönberg'. *The Sunday Times*, 22 November 1931. (P485)

M.-D. Calvocoressi. 'Music in the Foreign Press: Schönberg on Himself'. *MT*, 72 (November 1931): 993.

'Letters to the Editor: Alban Berg is Not Alarming'. *MT*, 72 (November 1931): 1026.

'Letters to the Editor: Alban Berg'. *MT*, 72 (December 1931): 1125–6.

'Letters to the Editor: Alban Berg'. *MT*, 73 (January 1932): 62.

C. D. G. 'Three Moderns: a Broadcast Concert'. *The Daily Telegraph*, 14 May 1932. (P132)

C. L. [Constant Lambert]. 'B.B.C. Contemporary Music'. *Sunday Referee*, 15 May
        1932. (P132)

'Modern Music: Schonberg the Obscure'. *Glasgow Herald*, 24 December 1932.
        (P134)

S. G. [Scott Goddard]. 'The B.B.C. Concert: Skilful Piano Playing'. *Morning Post*,
        24 December 1932. (P134)

Obituary of Percy Pitt. *MT*, 74 (January 1933): 79.

'The Mystery Man of Music'. *Glasgow Herald*, 6 February 1933. (P488)

Gordon Beckles. 'Arnold Schonberg's Musical "Strafe" To-night: How 100 British
        Bandsmen will Rend the Air'. *Daily Herald*, 8 February 1933. (P488)

'Thunder in Berlin'. *Evening News*, 8 February 1933. (P488)

H. S. 'Did You Listen to Schonberg's Op. 31?' *Daily Herald*, 9 February 1933.
        (P488)

Edwin Evans. 'Schonberg as Conductor: Complexities of his "Variations"'. *The
        Daily Mail*, 9 February 1933. (P488)

Richard Capell. 'Schonberg at Queen's Hall: Conducts his own "Variations":
        Music in Torture Chamber'. *The Daily Telegraph*, 9 February 1933. (P488)

G. A. H. 'Schonberg's New Work at the Queen's Hall'. *Manchester Guardian*,
        9 February 1933. (P488)

'B.B.C. Symphony Concert: Herr Schonberg's Visit: Bad Stage Management'. *The
        Times*, 9 February 1933. (P488)

E. N. [Ernest Newman]. 'The Week's Music: Schonberg's Variations'. *The Sunday
        Times*, 12 February 1933. (P488)

G. A. H. 'Alban Berg Suite'. *Manchester Guardian*, 14 February 1933. (P425)

C. L. [Constant Lambert]. Review in the *Sunday Referee*, 19 February 1933.
        (P425)

P. P. '"Wozzeck" Fragments'. *Evening Standard*, 9 March 1933. (P488)

Constant Lambert. Review in the *Sunday Referee*, 12 March 1933. (P488)

E. N. [Ernest Newman]. 'The Week's Music: Sceneless Fragments of "Wozzeck"'.
        *The Sunday Times*, 12 March 1933. (P488)

'Arnold Schönberg: Repercussions from a Recent Broadcast'. *The Music Teacher*
        (March 1933). (P488)

Landon Ronald. 'Mainly about Music: Putting Britain on the Musical Map'. *News
        Chronicle*, 1 April 1933, 15(C–E).

Edwin Evans. '"Advanced" Music: Alban Berg's Concerto Broadcast'. *The Daily
        Mail*, 22 April 1933. (P425)

W. McN. [William McNaught]. 'Why, oh Why? Composers of High Culture who
        Write Distorted Stuff'. *Evening News*, 22 April 1933. (P425)

E. N. [Ernest Newman]. 'B.B.C. Contemporary Music'. *The Sunday Times*, 23
        April 1933. (P425)

Landon Ronald. 'Mainly about Music: Do the Public Want Concerts?' *News
        Chronicle*, 29 April 1933, 9(C–E).

Landon Ronald. 'Mainly about Music: a Few Words about the London Musical
        Festival'. *News Chronicle*, 6 May 1933, 15(C–E).

Notice about Schoenberg in the *Manchester Guardian*, 1 November 1933. (P489)

Edwin Evans. 'Elusive Music: Schonberg Programme at B.B.C. Concert'. *The Daily Mail*, 25 November 1933. (P425)

R. C. [Richard Capell]. 'Esotericism for the Million: the Generosity of the B.B.C.' *The Daily Telegraph*, 25 November 1933. (P425)

'"Contemporary" Music: a B.B.C. Concert'. *The Times*, 25 November 1933. (P425)

'Viennese Quartet'. *The Daily Mail*, 2 December 1933. (P425)

'B.B.C. Chamber Concert'. *The Observer*, 3 December 1933. (P425)

'B.B.C. Performance of "Wozzeck": Alban Berg's Opera'. *The Daily Telegraph*, 1 March 1934. (P490)

S. R. Nelson. 'Prepare to Hear "Wozzeck"'. *Era*, 7 March 1934. (P490)

E. B. [Eric Blom]. '"Wozzeck" Produced by the B.B.C.: Alban Berg's Great Modern Opera: Features of an Impressive Concert Version'. *Birmingham Post*, 15 March 1934. (P490)

Edwin Evans. 'Alban Berg's "Wozzeck": Last Night's Performance: Audience Thrilled'. *The Daily Mail*, 15 March 1934. (P490)

Richard Capell. 'Alban Berg's "Wozzeck": First Performance in England: a Modernist Orgy'. *The Daily Telegraph*, 15 March 1934. (P490)

J. A. Forsyth. '"Wozzeck" is Certainly a Sensation'. *The Star*, 15 March 1934. (P490)

'The Case of "Wozzeck"'. *The Daily Telegraph*, 17 March 1934. (P490)

Constant Lambert. 'Matters Musical: "Wozzeck" at Last!' *Sunday Referee*, 18 March 1934. (P490)

'The B.B.C. Drops a Bomb: Storm over an Opera'. *Sunday Chronicle*, 1 April 1934. (P490)

Edwin Evans. 'New Opera Music by B.B.C. Orchestra: Heifetz's Fine Playing'. *The Daily Mail*, 21 March 1935. (P492)

'The B.B.C. Orchestra: Malipiero and Berg'. *The Times*, 21 March 1935. (P492)

'B.B.C. Symphony Concert: Bach, Berg, and Brahms'. *The Times*, 24 October 1935. (P493)

E. N. [Ernest Newman]. 'The Week's Music: the B.B.C. Concert'. *The Sunday Times*, 27 October 1935. (P493)

J. A. W. [J. A. Westrup]. 'Ernst Krenek in London: B.B.C. Contemporary Music Concert'. *The Daily Telegraph*, 2 November 1935. (P139)

W. McN. [William McNaught]. 'Music Too Glum to be Entertaining: Relieved by a Gracious Singer'. *Evening News*, 2 November 1935. (P139)

E. N. [Ernest Newman]. 'The Week's Music: Krenek'. *The Sunday Times*, 3 November 1935. (P139)

'B.B.C. Resignation: Music Expert Explains his Decision'. *News Chronicle*, 28 March 1936, 1(B).

Linden Laing. '"Why I Resigned from the B.B.C.": Music Arranger and "Drastic" Changes'. Unidentified newspaper article, *c.* 28 March 1936. In Edward Clark clippings file in private collection of James Clark.

R. C. [Richard Capell]. 'In Memory of Alban Berg: the New Violin Concerto'. *The Daily Telegraph*, 2 May 1936. (P141)

W. McN. [William McNaught]. 'Alban Berg's "Requiem": his Violin Concerto one of the Finest Modern Works'. *Evening News*, 2 May 1936. (P141)

## Other books and articles

*BBC Programme Records.* Vol. i–vii: 1922–36. London: BBC, [n.d.].
BBC yearbooks
  *BBC Handbook 1928.* London: BBC, 1928.
  *The BBC Handbook 1929.* London: BBC, 1929.
  *The BBC Year-book 1930.* London: BBC, 1930.
  *The BBC Year-book 1931.* London: BBC, 1931.
  *The BBC Year-book 1932.* London: BBC, 1932.
  *The BBC Year-book 1933.* London: BBC, 1933.
  *The BBC Year-book 1934.* London: BBC, 1934.
  *BBC Annual 1935.* London: BBC, 1935.
  *BBC Annual 1936.* London: BBC, 1936.
  *BBC Annual 1937.* London: BBC, 1937.
  *BBC Handbook 1938.* London: BBC, 1938.
  *BBC Handbook 1939.* London: BBC, 1939.
Beaumont, Cyril W. *The Diaghilev Ballet in London: a Personal Record.* London:
  Putnam, 1940.
Benser, Caroline Cepin. *Egon Wellesz (1885–1974): Chronicle of Twentieth-
  Century Musician.* American University Studies, vol. ix, no. 8. New York:
  Peter Lang, 1985.
[Berg, Alban.] *Alban Berg: Letters to his Wife.* Edited, translated and annotated by
  Bernard Grun. London: Faber and Faber, 1971.
Boult, Adrian Cedric. *My Own Trumpet.* London: Hamish Hamilton, 1973.
Bowles, Garrett H. *Ernst Krenek: a Bio-Bibliography.* Bio-Bibliographies in Music,
  no. 22. New York: Greenwood Press, 1989.
Breuer, János. 'Kodály in England – a Documentary Study'.
  Part i: '1913–28'. *Tempo,* no. 143 (December 1982): 2–9.
  Part ii: '1928–45'. *Tempo,* no. 144 (March 1983): 15–20.
Briggs, Asa. *The History of Broadcasting in the United Kingdom.*
  Vol. i: *The Birth of Broadcasting.* London: Oxford University Press, 1961.
  Vol. ii: *The Golden Age of Wireless.* London: Oxford University Press, 1965.
*British Broadcasting: a Bibliography.* London: The British Broadcasting
  Corporation, 1958.
*British Broadcasting, 1922–1972: a Select Bibliography.* Jubilee Edition. London:
  British Broadcasting Corporation, 1972.
Brittain, Sir Harry. *The ABC of the B.B.C.* London: C. Arthur Pearson, [1932].
Burrows, A. R. *The Story of Broadcasting.* London: Cassell, 1924.
Cain, John. *The BBC: 70 Years of Broadcasting.* London: BBC, 1992.
Carner, Mosco. *Alban Berg: the Man and the Work.* London: Gerald Duckworth,
  1975.
Carpenter, Humphrey, with research by Jennifer Doctor. *The Envy of the World:
  Fifty Years of the BBC Third Programme and Radio 3.* London: Weidenfeld,
  1996.
Chadwick, Nicholas. 'Alban Berg and the BBC'. *British Library Journal,* 11 (1985):
  46–59.

'The Berg Violin Concerto in London: Webern's Correspondence with the BBC, 1935–6'. In *Sundry Sorts of Music Books: Essays on the British Library Collections Presented to O. W. Neighbour on his 70th Birthday*, ed. Chris Banks, Arthur Searle and Malcolm Turner, 330–45. London: The British Library, 1993.

Chamier, J. Daniel. *Percy Pitt of Covent Garden and the B.B.C.* London: Edward Arnold, 1938.

Clark, T. E. *Paper on a Modern French Composer: Claude Debussy.* [Newcastle, 1908.] In James Clark, private collection.

Colles, H. C. *Walford Davies: a Biography.* London: Oxford University Press, 1942.

Copley, I. A. *The Music of Peter Warlock: a Critical Survey.* London: Dennis Dobson, 1979.

Cox, David. *The Henry Wood Proms.* London: British Broadcasting Corporation, 1980.

Davies, Walford. *The Pursuit of Music.* London: Thomas Nelson and Sons [1935].

Dent, Edward J. *Terpander, or Music and the Future.* To-day and To-morrow Series. London: Kegan Paul, Trench, Trubner; J. Curwen and Sons [1926].

'Looking Backward'. *Music Today: Journal of the International Society for Contemporary Music,* i (1949): 6–22.

Doctor, Jennifer. *The BBC and the Ultra-Modern Problem: a Documentary Study of the British Broadcasting Corporation's Dissemination of Second Viennese School Repertory, 1922–36.* PhD dissertation, Northwestern University, 1993.

'BBC History' and 'BBC Making Music', in supplement: 'Sound on Vision: Celebrating 75 Years of BBC Music'. *BBC Music Magazine* (November 1997), iv–viii, xii–xiii.

*Dossier de presse: Press-book de Pierrot lunaire d'Arnold Schönberg.* Anthologie de la critique musicale: Dossiers de presse, edited by François Lesure, vol. ii. Geneva: Editions Minkoff, 1985.

Dunstan, Ralph. *A Cyclopædic Dictionary of Music.* 4th edn, enlarged and rev. London: J. Curwen and Sons; Kegan Paul, Trench, Trübner [1925].

Dyson, George. *The New Music.* London: Oxford University Press; Humphrey Milford, 1924.

Eaglefield-Hull, A. *A Dictionary of Modern Music and Musicians.* London: J. M. Dent and Sons; New York: E. P. Dutton, 1924.

Eckersley, P. P. *The Power Behind the Microphone.* London: Jonathan Cape, 1941.

Eckersley, Roger. *The B.B.C. and All That.* London: Sampson Low, Marston and Co. [1946].

Ehrlich, Cyril. *First Philharmonic: a History of The Royal Philharmonic Society.* Oxford: Clarendon Press, 1995.

*Harmonious Alliance: a History of the Performing Right Society.* Oxford: Oxford University Press, 1989.

'The Marketplace'. *Blackwell History of Music in Britain,* vol. vi: *The Twentieth Century,* ed. Stephen Banfield. Oxford: Blackwell, 1995. pp. 39–53.

*The Music Profession in Britain Since the Eighteenth Century: a Social History.* Oxford: Clarendon Press, 1985.

'Taste, Function and Technology: Some Conjectures'. *Proceedings of the Second British-Swedish Conference on Musicology*, ed. Anne Buckley et al, Musikmuseets skrifter, xxi. Göterborgs Universitet, 1991.

Foreman, Lewis. *From Parry to Britten: British Music in Letters 1900–1945*. London: B. T. Batsford, 1987.

'Webern, the BBC and the Berg Violin Concerto'. *Tempo*, no. 178 (September 1991): 2–10.

'Webern Conducts for the BBC 1929–1936'. *Webern Conducts Berg Violin Concerto*. Compact disc SBT 1004. Continuum Records, 1991. [Liner notes]

Gillies, Malcolm. *Bartók in Britain: a Guided Tour*. Oxford: Clarendon Press, 1989.

Glock, William. *Notes in Advance: an Autobiography in Music*. Oxford: Oxford University Press, 1991.

Gorham, Maurice. *Sound and Fury: Twenty-One Years in the B.B.C.* London: Percival Marshall, 1948.

Gray, Cecil. *A Survey of Contemporary Music*. London: Oxford University Press, 1924.

*Peter Warlock: a Memoir of Philip Heseltine*. London: Jonathan Cape, 1934.

*Predicaments; or Music and the Future: an Essay in Constructive Criticism*. London: Oxford University Press; Humphrey Milford, 1936.

*Grove's Dictionary of Music and Musicians*. 4th edn, edited by H. C. Colles. London: Macmillan, 1940.

'Davies, Sir Henry Walford', by H. C. Colles. Vol. ii, 21–3, and supplementary volume, 151–2.

*Grove's Dictionary of Music and Musicians*. 5th edn, edited by Eric Blom. London: Macmillan, 1954.

'Evans, Edwin (ii)', by H. C. Colles. Vol. ii, 980–81.

'Hely-Hutchinson, (Christian) Victor', by H. C. Colles. Vol. iv, 236.

'Scholes, Percy A. (Alfred)', by H. C. Colles. Vol. vii, 524.

Harries, Meirion and Susie Harries. *A Pilgrim Soul*. London: Michael Joseph, 1989.

Hibberd, Stuart. *This – is London*. London: Macdonald and Evans, 1950.

Hill, Ralph. 'English Poetry and Song: Edwin Evans'. *RT*, 79 (26 March 1943): 4.

*Hinrichsen's Year Book*. London: Hinrichsen, 1944.

'London Contemporary Music Centre', 187–8.

'Who's Who Among the Contributors', 293–4. [article on Edwin Evans]

Irving, John. 'Schönberg in the News: the London Performances of 1912–1914'. *Music Review*, 48 (February 1988): 52–70.

Kater, Michael H. *The Twisted Muse: Musicians and their Music in the Third Reich*. New York: Oxford University Press, 1997.

Kavanagh, Jacquie. 'BBC Archives at Caversham'. *Contemporary Record*, 6 (Autumn 1992): 341–9.

Kennedy, Michael. *Adrian Boult*. London: Hamish Hamilton, 1987.

Kenyon, Nicholas. *The BBC Symphony Orchestra: the First Fifty Years 1930–1980*. London, British Broadcasting Corporation, 1981.

Kildea, Paul F. M. *World War I and the British Music Industry*. MM thesis, University of Melbourne, 1991.

Krasner, Louis. 'About Webern as conductor'. *Webern Conducts Berg Violin Concerto*. Compact disc SBT 1004. Continuum Records, 1991. [Liner notes]

Lambert, Constant. *Music Ho!* London: Faber, 1934.

Lambourn, David. 'Henry Wood and Schoenberg'. *MT*, 128 (August 1987): 422–7.
    *Modernism in British Music 1900–1922*. Draft of MM thesis, Cambridge University.

LeMahieu, D. L. *A Culture for Democracy*. Oxford: Oxford University Press, 1988.

Lewis, C. A. *Broadcasting from Within*. London: George Newnes [1924].

Lutyens, Elisabeth. *A Goldfish Bowl*. London: Cassell, 1972.

McIntyre, Ian. *The Expense of Glory: a Life of Lord Reith*. HarperCollins, 1993.

McKibbin, Ross. *Classes and Cultures: England 1918–1951*. Oxford: Oxford University Press, 1998.

McNaught, W[illiam]. *A Short Account of Modern Music and Musicians*. London: Novello, [1937].

Maine, Basil. *The B.B.C. and its Audience*. Discussion Books, no. 56. London: Thomas Nelson and Sons, 1939.
    *New Paths in Music*. Discussion Books, no. 75. London: Thomas Nelson and Sons: 1940.
    *Reflected Music and other Essays*. London: Methuen, 1930.

Mason, Colin. 'Edwin Evans'. *The Listener*, 33 (8 March 1945): 277.

Mehta, Ved. 'Onward and Upward with the Arts: The Third'. *New Yorker* (19 May 1963).

Milner, Roger. *Reith: The BBC Years*. Edinburgh: Mainstream Publishing, 1983.

Moldenhauer, Hans, in collaboration with Rosaleen Moldenhauer. *Anton von Webern: a Chronicle of his Life and Work*. London: Victor Gollancz, 1978; edition in *Schubert/Webern Series: . . . Programme Book*, London: Sinfonietta Productions, 1978.

Moore, Jerrold Northrop, ed. *Music and Friends: Seven Decades of Letters to Adrian Boult from Elgar, Vaughan Williams, Holst, Bruno Walter, Yehudi Menuhin and Other Friends*. London: Hamish Hamilton, 1979.

Myers, Rollo H. *Modern Music: its Aims and Tendencies*. London: Kegan Paul, Trench, Trübner and Co., 1923.

Neighbour, Oliver, Paul Griffiths and George Perle. *The New Grove Second Viennese School*. London: Macmillan, 1980.

*The New Grove Dictionary of Music and Musicians*. 6th edn, edited by Stanley Sadie. London: Macmillan, 1980.
    'Allen, Sir Hugh (Percy)', by H. C. Colles and Malcolm Turner. Vol. i, 281.
    'Bliss, Sir Arthur (Drummond)', by Hugo Cole. Vol. ii, 791–4.
    'Boult, Sir Adrian (Cedric)', by Ronald Crichton. Vol. iii, 108–9.
    'Davies, Sir (Henry) Walford', by Hugh Ottaway. Vol. v, 280.
    'Dent, Edward J(oseph)', by Anthony Lewis and Nigel Fortune. Vol. v, 376.
    'Herbage, Julian (Livingston-)', by Noël Goodwin. Vol. viii, 497.

'Maine, Basil (Stephen)', by H. C. Colles/Peter Platt. Vol. xi, 538.

'Newman, Ernest', by William S. Mann. Vol. xiii, 163–4.

'Wood, Sir Henry J(oseph)', by Ronald Crichton. Vol. xx, 516–18.

*The New Grove Dictionary of Opera.* Edited by Stanley Sadie. London: Macmillan, 1992.

'Buesst, Aylmer', by Harold Rosenthal. Vol. i, 635.

'German, Sir Edward', by David Russell Hulme. Vol. ii, 384–5.

'Pitt, Percy (George)', by Arthur Jacobs. Vol. iii, 1023.

Newman, Ernest. *Essays from The World of Music: Essays from The Sunday Times.* Selected by Felix Aprahamian. London: John Calder, 1976.

*A Musical Critic's Holiday.* London: Cassell and Company, 1925.

Paulu, Burton. *Television and Radio in the United Kingdom.* London: Macmillan, 1981.

Pegg, Mark. *Broadcasting and Society, 1918–1939.* London and Canberra: Croom Helm, 1983.

Pirie, Peter J. *The English Musical Renaissance.* London: Victor Gollanz, 1979.

*Radio and Television Who's Who.* 3rd edn. London: George Young, 1954.

*Radio Who's Who.* Compiled and edited by Cyrus Andrews. London: Pendulum Publications, 1947.

Rees, Brian. *A Musical Peacemaker: the Life and Work of Sir Edward German.* Bourne End, Buckinghamshire: Kensal Press, 1986.

Reith, J. C. W. *Broadcast over Britain.* London: Hodder and Stoughton, [1924].

Rosenfeld, Paul. *Musical Portraits: Interpretations of Twenty Modern Composers.* London: Kegan Paul, Trench, Trübner and Co., 1922.

Scannell, Paddy, and David Cardiff. *A Social History of British Broadcasting.* Vol. i: *Serving the Nation, 1922–1939.* Oxford: Basil Blackwell, 1991.

Schoenberg, Arnold. *Style and Idea.* Edited by Leonard Stein and translated by Leo Black. London: Faber and Faber, 1975.

Scholes, Percy A. *Everybody's Guide to Broadcast Music.* With a foreword by J. C. W. Reith. London: Humphrey Milford, Oxford University Press, 1925.

*The Listener's Guide to Music: With a Concert-Goer's Glossary.* 10th edn. London: Oxford University Press, 1942.

*The Radio Times Music Handbook: Being a Complete Book of Reference Giving Both Meaning and Pronunciation of the Technical Words found in Programmes.* 3rd edn. London: Oxford University Press for the BBC, 1936.

Schuller, Gunther. 'A Conversation with Steuermann'. *Perspectives of New Music*, 3 (Fall–Winter 1964): 22–35.

Searle, Humphrey, and Robert Layton. *Britain, Scandinavia and the Netherlands.* New York: Holt, Rinehart and Winston, 1972.

Shead, Richard. *Constant Lambert.* [Revised and corrected edn.] London: Thames Publishing, [1986].

Slonimsky, Nicolas. *Music Since 1900.* 4th edn. New York: C. Scribner's Sons, 1971.

Smith, Anthony. *British Broadcasting.* Newton Abbot: David and Charles, 1974.

Smith, Joan Allen. *Schoenberg and his Circle: a Viennese Portrait*. New York: Schirmer; London: Collier Macmillan, 1986.

Stewart, John L. *Ernst Krenek: the Man and his Music*. Berkeley: University of California Press, 1991.

Stuart, Charles, ed. *The Reith Diaries*. London: Collins, 1975.

Stuckenschmidt, H. H. *Arnold Schoenberg: his Life, World and Work*. Translated by Humphrey Searle. London: John Calder, 1977.

Tenant-Flowers, Sarah Jane. *A Study of Style and Techniques in the Music of Elisabeth Lutyens*. PhD dissertation, University of Durham, 1991.

*Webern Conducts Berg Violin Concerto*. Compact disc SBT 1004. Continuum Records, 1991.

Weissman, Adolf. *The Problems of Modern Music*. With an Introduction by Edward J. Dent. London: J. M. Dent and Sons; NY: E. P. Dutton, 1925.

Wellesz, Egon. 'E. J. Dent and the International Society for Contemporary Music'. *Music Review*, 7 (August/November 1946): 205–8.

Whitehead, Kate. *The Third Programme: a Literary History*. Oxford: Clarendon Press, 1989.

Whittall, Arnold. 'Schoenberg and the English: Notes for a Documentary'. *Journal of the Arnold Schoenberg Institute*, 4/1 (1980): 24–33.

*Who's Who 1989*. London: A and C Black, 1989.

*Who's Who in Music*. Edited by Landon Ronald. London: Shaw, 1937.

*Who's Who in Music*. Edited by L. G. Pine. London: Shaw, 1949–1950.

*Who's Who in Music and Musicians' International Directory*. 4th edn, edited by Peter Townend and David Simmons. London: Burke's Peerage, 1962.

*Who's Who in Music and Musicians' International Directory*. 5th edn. London: Burke's Peerage, 1969.

*Who was Who.*

Vol. iii: *1929–1940*. London: Adam and Charles Black, 1941.

Vol. iv: *1941–1950*. London: Adam and Charles Black, 1952.

Vol. v: *1951–1960*. London: Adam and Charles Black, 1961.

Vol. vi: *1961–1970*. London: Adam and Charles Black, 1972.

Vol. vii: *1971–1980*. London: Adam and Charles Black, 1981.

Vol. viii: *1981–1990*. London: A and C Black, 1991.

Wright, Kenneth A. 'Friends of British Music'. *Tempo*, no. 3 (May 1939): 5–6.

Undated autobiography, written after 1959. In Elisabeth Lutyens: *A Goldfish Bowl*, 122–3. London: Cassell, 1972.

# Index